THEATRE LIBRARY ASSOCIATION

Founded in 1937, Theatre Library Association supports librarians and archivists affiliated with theatre, dance, performance studies, popular entertainment, motion picture and broadcasting collections. TLA promotes professional best practices in acquisition, organization, access and preservation of performing arts resources in libraries, archives, museums, private collections, and the digital environment. By producing publications, conferences, panels, and public events, TLA fosters creative and ethical use of performing arts materials to enhance research, live performance, and scholarly communication.

Theatre Library Association meets annually to conduct its business in the fall of each year. It presents a plenary and related programming during the annual meeting of the American Society for Theatre Research, and frequently cooperates with other professional and scholarly organizations in the sponsorship of symposia, events, and publications.

Theatre Library Association publishes *BROADSIDE*, an online newsletter, and *Performing Arts Resources*, a monograph series, as well as conference compendia.

It is governed by a constitution which provides for officers and an executive board of directors elected by the membership.

OFFICERS AND BOARD MEMBERS, 2011

THE THEATRE LIBRARY ASSOCIATION BOOK AWARDS

Two awards are presented annually for books of unusual merit and distinction in the fields served by the Association.

The George Freedley Award, established in 1968, honors work in the field of theatre published in the United States. Only books with subjects related to live performance will be considered. They may be biography, history, or criticism.

The Richard Wall Award, established in 1973, honors work published in the United States in the field of recorded performance, which includes motion pictures, radio, and television. Formerly known as the Theatre Library Association Award, the prize was renamed in 2010 to honor the memory of the late Richard Wall, longtime TLA member and Book Awards Chair.

Works ineligible for both awards are: textbooks; anthologies; collections of essays previously published in other sources; reprints; works on dance, ballet, and opera; plays and similar dramatic works. Translations of significant works, other than play texts, will be considered. Entries will be judged on the basis of scholarship, readability, and general contribution of knowledge to the field. No galley sheets or proofs will be accepted. Books nominated for awards must be published in the calendar year prior to the presentation of the awards.

Authors, publishers, and members of Theatre Library Association are invited to submit nominations for these awards. For more information, visit: http://www.tla-online.org/awards/bookawards.html

Performing Arts Resources, the monograph series of Theatre Library Association, is designed to gather and disseminate scholarly articles dealing with the location of resource materials related to theatre, film, television, radio, and popular entertainments; descriptions, listings or evaluations of such collections, whether public or private; and monographs of previously unpublished original material. Volumes have focused on historical periods, performance genres, and professional issues in archives and libraries.

Performing Arts Resources is managed by the Publications Committee of the Theatre Library Association. Guest editors share the responsibility for single subject volumes and monographs. We invite all readers to submit proposals for issues or for individual articles. Calls for proposals and the subjects of future single volumes of *Performing Arts Resources* will be announced on the TLA web site: http://www.tla-online.org/

PERFORMING ARTS RESOURCES
VOLUME TWENTY-EIGHT

A Tyranny of Documents:
The Performing Arts Historian as Film Noir Detective

Essays Dedicated to
Brooks McNamara

Edited by
Stephen Johnson

Published by the Theatre Library Association

Published by Theatre Library Association

Headquarters: c/o The New York Public Library for the Performing Arts,
40 Lincoln Center Plaza, New York, New York 10023

Website: http://www.tla-online.org/

Membership dues: $30 personal; $20 students/non-salaried; $40 institutional

The Library of Congress catalogued this serial as follows:
Performing Arts Resources
Vols. for 1974—issued by the Theatre Library Association
ISSN 03603814
1. Performing arts—Library resources—United States—Periodicals
I. Theatre Library Association
Z6935.P46 016.7902'08 75–646287
ISBN 978-0-932610-24-9.

Front cover image: For credit information on the collage imagery, see the full illustrations in this volume on pp 16, 33, 102, 111, 129, 187, 196, 210, 218, 254

Cover and page design: Sans Serif, Saline, Michigan
Printed by McNaughton and Gunn, Saline Michigan
Manufactured in the United States of America

This serial is printed on acid-free paper.

CONTENTS

A Queer Memory: Guilt, Disappearance, and the Youtube "Archive"

By Andrew Brown 329

The Document: A Youtube tirade against *Darling! The Pieter-Dirk Uys Story* (2007), about the Afrikaaner drag performer's touring solo HIV/AIDS awareness cabaret.

Afterword—Scarred Texts: Etudes on Absence

Odai Johnson 336

A general essay. Documents include: *Minutes of the Kirk, St. Cuthberts,* Scotland, 1743–1745, National Archives of Scotland; the letters of Josiah Wedgewood, 1767/9; St. Catherine's Parish Minute Books, Baptisms, Marriages, Burials, Spanish Town, Jamaica, 1779–1791.

Contributors 345

INTRODUCTION AND ACKNOWLEDGEMENTS

STEPHEN JOHNSON

It makes sense that I would edit a volume dedicated to Brooks McNamara devoted to essays exploring personal encounters with archival documents. I first met Brooks when I was a prospective doctoral student, and interviewed for an internship at the Shubert Archive, then under his Directorship. I can't imagine how I managed to get the job; I had just left the bus station after an all-night ride from Toronto, and the very-early-morning Times Square clientele were avoiding *me* on my way to the interview. And yet hired I was, and my own personal, life-long encounter with archival documents began. I spent a year at that extraordinary collection re-cataloguing orchestral parts for touring musical theatre, a seemingly endless stream of telegrams reporting on touring productions, typescripts of plays that may or may not have been produced, and comic review sketches. I learned to tie a library knot (very useful), and breathed the air of eighty years of storage (not so useful). I became sensitive to the personal, physical investment in the creation of documents by individuals: the beauty of a costume design that was after all meant as a disposable model for a work of art, not a work of art in itself; and, in contrast, the plea telegraphed to head office by a troubled road manager, desperately requesting that it send a farce (he was touring Ibsen in 1910s Oregon, and it wasn't going well). I learned to appreciate the fragility of the content, the meaning of which seemed so easily lost—revue sketches that were no longer funny, lyric references to long-forgotten once-important events. I also learned to appreciate the physical qualities of archival work, something incomprehensible to the uninitiated, but palpable to all the contributors to this volume—the texture of the paper, the smell of dust and disintegrating film stock, and most particularly the aura of a material object that is as physically precarious as the event to which it bore witness was ephemeral. Of course Brooks McNamara, as a Professor of Performance Studies at New York University, did much more for me. He was teacher, thesis supervisor, mentor—he and his wife Nan even loaned me the only furniture I had, during my first year of study, that wasn't scrounged from the streets. But the job at the archive had the greatest effect.

The "call" sent out for this volume provides its name. It is an old conceit that historians are detectives in the archives, following the "clues" to solve a "case." If polled, I have no doubt historians would provide a greater-than-average percentage of detective fiction enthusiasts. But that being the case, few "cases" are resolved neatly—and sometimes (often?) the historian is less Hercule Poirot than Mike Hammer in, for example, the late baroque film noir *Kiss Me, Deadly* (1955; dir. Robert Aldrich). Poor Mike, in that narrative, doesn't really understand the case, or why he's on it, but he can't stop following the clues because he's obsessed with the idea that there is something very important out there to find—"the Great Whatsit." He encounters wealthy playboys, opera lovers, foreign powers, corrupt coroners caring for corrupt bodies, atomic power, and Emily Dickinson—and he's ill prepared for any of it. The clues, the case, the victims and the "perps" all tyrannize him. But he is obsessed, so he blunders through, fists flying. This, sometimes, is what our research is like.

I understand this engagement in terms of that area of historiography called microhistory, which calls for a close re-examination of individual documents and events, questioning the preconceptions with which we approach them, looking among them for what has been called the "opaque document" or the "exceptional normal," the document or piece of information that clearly exists as a clue to the meaning of the event we are trying to understand, but just as clearly flies in the face of the easy answer.[1] It is history, as Thomas Postlewait (a contributor to this volume) usefully notes, "in the Chekhovian mode"—referring to:

> "that microhistorical moment in Chekhov's *The Cherry Orchard* when that mysterious string breaks, sounding over the landscape. A ripple in time? A rupture? Something happened, but what? After a pause, the events of the play continue as if nothing had occurred, and yet, when viewing the play, we cannot but wonder about that mysterious sound. And we must speculate on its meanings, despite lack of evidence."[2]

Postlewait elaborates on this "mode" in his indispensable *Introduction to Theatre Historiography*, calling to our attention its pitfalls as well as its advantages, and the importance of negotiating always between the close examination of particular documents and the variety of contexts within which they must be understood. Both the evocation of how we engage with documents, and the caution with which we should temper this engagement, describe the tenor of the essays in this volume.[3]

The direction given to contributors was this: to focus on a personal experience with a "tyrannical" document from the archive, a document that would not allow for an otherwise apparent conclusion, that flew in the face of the evidence, or that carried embedded in it some aspect of the event that was incomprehensible, no matter how much additional research was brought to bear on it. Contributors were asked to reflect on the difficult balance sought among and between the historian's respect for documentary evidence, the need to generate significance from it, and the natural-but-dangerous tendency to smooth out the rough edges of evidence. For the historian and archivist of the performing arts those problems are intensified. It is one thing to examine the documents pertaining to a battle, an epidemic, or a famine; the effects of the event were palpable, measurable in some sense. It is quite another thing to try to read a document representing the detritus of a performance, the effects of which are far more difficult to measure. An audience is moved, and minds are changed forever.

In this volume you will find engagements with documents from late medieval Russia to the present-day digital cloud, referencing a broad range of performances, from commedia dell'arte to burlesque revival, from 18th century opera to South African drag, from *Mazeppa* to the desperate, life-or-death miming of a lost arctic explorer. You will find a range of writing styles here as well, including some engaged explicitly with the idea of the detective in manner and tone—cold cases, femme fatales, deep mysteries, trick endings and red herrings—and some more personal, more elegiac, lamenting the loss of certainty, the passage of time, the disintegration of any links to the ephemeral event. There is a good deal of hard-boiled detective work in this volume, invoking and interrogating the most recent scholarship in the field; and there is also poetry.

This volume draws together scholars and archivists specializing in theatre, film, dance, music, and popular and cultural performance, representing a cross-section of the academy from graduate students to some of our most recognized scholars and archivists emeritus. This is all as it should be in a volume dedicated to Brooks, who dealt as easily—and democratically—with those at the beginning of their careers as with seasoned "pros," with any and all attitudes toward the serious study of performance, with any and all potential audiences, and with the broadest possible definition of the discipline. For Brooks—to borrow, as he would have, a phrase from popular advertising—"there is no box."

The first person singular is the voice of choice in these essays, representing personal relationships with documents that, certainly in my reading of them, resonate with one another. You will find here discussions of:

- documents that should exist but do not (Frick), and that should not exist, at least not where they have been found—and yet there they are (Schweitzer, White)
- documents that—intentionally and unintentionally, through polemic, parody, or caricature—obscure their own capacity to provide tangible evidence about performances and performers (Hill, Scott, Smith, Fern)
- documents that are more than usually tempting to accept at face value, because if we do so the event is easier to understand, and more narratively satisfying (Sperdakos, Riley, Bryan)
- documents with information so inconsequential as to seem unworthy of attention, but that might—just might—in fact carry evidence of a relationship that will all but "close the case" (Hughes, Solomon, Harris)
- documents created by individuals whose relationship with the events in question seem unusually troubled—or unusually accepting (Curley, May, Venning)

Here are researchers:

- who discover uncharacteristic documents in unusual places, and consider the resulting effect on their understanding of events (Donohue, Blum)
- who re-evaluate the manipulations of documents by those who control their creation and dissemination, including the effects of "editing" on the writing of later history (Bovet, Colleary, Postlewait)
- who confront the limitations of extant documents to allow access to the original power of an event (Ghartey-Tagoe Kootin, Davis-Fisch)
- who discover that the most significant aspect of a document, after all, may rest in where it's travelled, and who has touched it (Couch, Bringardner)
- for whom new evidence comes to light that challenges and complicates what the authors thought they already knew (Ryder, Cook)
- who negotiate relationships with the creators and the "caregivers" of archives, in turn altering the way they interpret the documents (Vogt, Turner)
- who return to the evidence after some time, re-examining their own earlier work in the archive (Muse, Cohen-Stratyner), or the work of others (Fitzgerald, Crane), concluding that "cases" are never really "closed"
- who meditate on the physical act of being in the archive, of confronting and manipulating a document, of watching it disappear (Boyle, Harries, Brown)
- who go that extra distance to understand the way a performance was created, by re-creating the performance, only to discover that the stick won't slap the way it should, or that it simply isn't possible to "ride like Mazeppa" (Stoesser, Mayer)

Of course, even as I attempt to group these essays, I realize that all of them might be mentioned under several categories, and I risk stern emails from contributors; it is at this point that I long for the multiple keyword searches of an on-line publication. Even for the *Table of Contents*, there was no obvious choice. Organizing chronologically by the date of the document gives a sense of the passage of time; but they might just as productively been listed by region, type of document, the attitude of the researcher, or the kind of relationship with the document.

These essays are book-ended. At the outset, Don Wilmeth articulates just why, in fact, we should honor Brooks McNamara in a volume of *Performing Arts Resources*. If you have not been introduced to Brooks, this is your chance; afterwards, you can visit the library and continue the relationship. Odai Johnson provides the *coda*, reflecting eloquently on a number of issues that evoke the subject of this volume, both the tyranny of documents, and the deep sense of love and loss found in the archive. We live with the consequences of people making documents: people who commit deliberate acts of remembering, and of erasure, with a particular agenda in mind; as well as those who commit haphazard, careless and incompetent acts which can mean that we will never know what happened. We can suffer from amnesia; but we can also commit the act with deliberation.

I am indebted to the Publications Committee of the Theatre Library Association for its support and advice during this process, in particular its Chair, Rob Melton. I have also appreciated the support of my colleagues on the Board of the Theatre Library Association, in particular its ever-attentive (and quick-witted) Secretary, David Nochimson. The University of Toronto provided an important financial intervention, all the more appreciated because unusual in these difficult times. Susie Kenyon and Barb Gunia at Sans Serif Press have been thorough, attentive, helpful, patient and completely professional; I recommend their services. My special thanks goes to Emma W. Johnson for her diligence as Illustrations Coordinator, taking care of the permissions work for contributors and ensuring that the best quality illustrations were obtained, a formidable task for this volume. Most particularly, I thank the contributors for their good will, and attention to detail and to time. Quite honestly, I have never had a better editorial experience, and with so many contributors this is no small statement. Finally, I thank Wendy Warnken for her support in all things. I met her when she was Associate Curator of the Theatre Collection at the Museum of the City of New York, and I was a down-at-the-heels researcher. So really—the tyranny of documents notwithstanding—the archives have been very good to me.

ENDNOTES

[1] "Exceptional normal" is used by Edoardo Grendi, quoted in Giovanni Levi, "On Microhistory," from the now old *New Perspectives on Historical Writing*, edited by Peter Burke (Cambridge: Polity Press, 1991) pp 93-113; reference p109. "Opaque document" is from Robert Darnton, *The Great Cat Massacre* (NY: Random House, 1984) p5. Carlo Ginzburg uses the word "dissonance," in *The Cheese and the Worms* (NY: Penguin, 1982) pxix. See also Ginzburg's "Microhistory: Two or Three Things that I Know About It" (*Critical Inquiry* 20:1 Autumn 93), 10-35.

[2] From "Writing History Today" (*Theatre Survey* Nov 2000) pp83-106, reference p104: "If only we could write history in the Chekhovian mode, then, perhaps, we could see that documentary study and cultural speculation are two aspects of a complex yet united understanding." At the end of this article, we are admonished: "So, back to work, as Chekhov also urged in full ironic understanding of what it will deliver." (105) The mention of irony in the context of writing this kind of history is entirely appropriate, as many of the essays in this volume will illustrate.

[3] Any reader of this volume will want to read two works released during its preparation, both involving Thomas Postlewait. The first is *The Cambridge Introduction to Theatre Historiography* (Cambridge, CUP 2009). I recommend in particular his "Introduction," pp8-20, in which he discusses the relationship between "event" and "context," and warns against the extreme stances of the "isolationist" and "universalist." Readers will also want to examine *Representing the Past: Essays in Performance Historiography*, edited by Charlotte M. Canning and Thomas Postlewait (Iowa City: University of Iowa Press, 2010).

Foreword—Brooks McNamara: Master of the Archive, or What Really Matters

DON B. WILMETH

What a pleasure—and a stimulating experience—it is to revisit the written work of Brooks McNamara. For those few who have not read his large body of books (13 written or edited) and essays by the dozens, let me urge you to do so. His contributions to our knowledge of American performance are enormous; as a stylist he was a master of economy and yet at the same time comprehensive in his ability to pull together in a direct and incisive manner a large number of ideas and facts; his prose was noted for its clarity and accessibility. As a director of over 100 dissertations at New York University, he insisted that his students follow his example and the result has been a surprisingly large number of theses revised (often with minimum effort) into publishable books and essays, too numerous to list here. Brooks was truly a history detective, drawn to the archive, and fascinated by theatrical/performance artifacts that stimulated his scholarship to explore theatrical and entertainment forms that had previously been virtually ignored—or at best, had been given only cursory, anecdotal attention. In the next few pages I'd like to review a number of these key efforts and demonstrate briefly how Brooks circled the wagons and honed in on his targets.

In January 2010 PBS broadcast "Benjamin Latrobe: America's First Architect," the first documentary to survey the roller coaster career of this fascinating yet frequently jinxed architect (1764–1820) who, despite enormous contributions to U.S. architecture (the central portion of the U.S. Capitol building; the splendid Baltimore Basilica; the White House portico; and the no longer standing Bank of Philadelphia) and an even greater influence, had project after project go awry. Thanks to Brooks McNamara, one of Latrobe's important visionary ideas, never even begun beyond drawings, is given full analysis and place of honor in Brooks's first book, *The American Playhouse in the Eighteenth Century* (1969)—forty years before PBS reclaimed Latrobe as a national treasure. Those who may only know Brooks's later work on various forms of popular entertainments might be surprised at his expertise on architecture, but Brooks was originally trained as a scenic designer, and early in his career he designed environmental spaces in collaboration with his colleagues Richard Schechner and Jerry Rojo (he worked on The Performance Group's *Dionysus in '69* and *Makbeth*).

The American Playhouse established a research philosophy, a career-long dependence on archives (and critical selectivity in the use of archival material), an ability to cut through scholarly jargon and unnecessary excess in historical description, and an ongoing interest in theatrical/performance spaces (one reason, as explained below, for his interest in popular entertainments). As this brief essay will illustrate, the principles indicated above will be revisited in almost all of his books, essays, exhibit articles, and even his prefaces and introductions to the work of others. In the case of *The American Playhouse,* a landmark study and still as fresh and important as it was in 1969 (there was nothing like it then); only a few studies since have dealt with early American theatre architect (Odai Johnson's 1969 *Absence and Memory in Colonial American Theatre* comes to mind; Odai Johnson has an essay in this volume). Brooks set out, as he stated, to make "no attempt to create exhaustive annals of the American playhouse, but" [to concentrate] "on delineating and interpreting the major patterns of expansion and change that characterized the work of the theater-builder in the eighteenth-century." Not an easy task given the lack of existing theatre structures from the Colonial period. But he succeeds masterfully. Furthermore, in a closing chapter he taps into one of our richest archives, the Library of Congress, where he finds the surviving drawings for an advanced and, typical of Latrobe, imaginative playhouse designed for Richmond, Virginia. It provides a tantalizing notion of what could have been but, like so many of Latrobe's projects, it never happened (in 1969 there was a belief that something like Latrobe's design would be constructed in Richmond; alas, it was not to be).

A group of McNamara's projects following *The American Playhouse* would be as influential and important as this first one, but on the surface quite different. The first was an essay in the March 1974 issue of *The Drama Review* (while serving as a contributing editor) titled "The Scenography of Popular Entertainment." This was his first major statement on an area of inquiry that would dominate much of his scholarship, thinking, and writing until his death. He would constantly refine the basic seven organizational/architectural/design schemes that he outlines here, "scenography based on the ways in which space and design are employed by the showman": "booths and other arrangements of space by itinerant street performers; improvised theatres; the scenography of variety entertainments; the scenography of popular theatre; performance spaces devoted to spectacle or special effects; processional forms; and entertainment environments such as the traveling carnival and the amusement park, where the spectator himself organizes the event." Once more, McNamara's intense interest in the performance space and its impact on various forms of entertainment is a major theme. Many of us over the years have found this and his similar organizational taxonomies most useful methods for analyzing the complex forms of popular entertainments that have existed.

1974 was a significant preparatory year for Brooks's subsequent major work. The *Emerson Society Quarterly* published one of the first full-statements by Brooks focusing on the significance of popular theatre "that ought to be studied on its own terms" and in an introductory page he sets out all the salient arguments for doing so. The stated purpose of the essay is to offer what is essentially the first serious history of the American Dime Museum ("'A Congress of Wonders': The Rise and Fall of the Dime Museum"). And until his student Andrea Stulman Dennett published in 1997 her book *Weird and Wonderful: The Dime Museum in America* (one of those projects inspired by Brooks) it remained the sole overview available. Also in 1974 Brooks published in *Theatre Quarterly* his second essay on the American medicine show (the first, "The Indian Medicine Show" appeared in *Educational Theatre Journal* in 1971), "Medicine Shows: American Vaudeville in the Marketplace," a unique and innovative piece that establishes another of McNamara's interests in his treatment of popular forms, that is, the illustrative use of performative material in attempting to describe a typical performance, in this case using the "bits" of the medicine show, and the first-person memories of professional performers. Subsequent comments will reiterate these methods.

A second mid-1970s landmark book publication was *Theatres, Spaces, Environments: Eighteen Projects* written by McNamara, Rojo, and Schechner (largely through round-table conversation), which returned to Brooks's analysis of performance space. Published in 1975, this study remains the most comprehensive statement of what became known as "environmental theatre." The three pioneer authors discuss three basic types of construction for performance: an existing space transformed by the creation of a fixed performance environment; temporary environments built in the same space; and projects built in four different environments. Although the projects are based on what was then very contemporary, one can see the kinship of this analysis of space with Brooks's work on popular entertainment. Incidentally, this same year Brooks published in *Education Theatre Journal* an interview (done in November 1974) with Percy Press, to some the greatest of the modern Punch and Judy showmen (he began performing on the street in 1918). The interview, "An Interview with PERCY PRESS and A Portfolio of Buskers," combines Brooks's interests in performance spaces and itinerant street performers. Unfortunately, a projected full-length study of buskers was never completed.

But it was his third book, published in 1976, *Step Right Up: An Illustrated History of the American Medicine Show,* that cemented his efforts to date and established his reputation as a leading scholar in the study of popular entertainments. Like his earlier essay in *Theatre Quarterly,* his full-length history of the uniquely American brand of medicine shows is a winner in all respects: its lively reconstruction of the material of the show; its historically-accurate background and context; its wise analysis and explanation of significance; its ability to never lose sight of the humor underlying medicine shows (intended or not); and its magnificent illustrations (including a portfolio, in color, of trade cards, given as free souvenirs by med men, which, sadly, were excluded when the book was reissued by the University of Mississippi in 1995, but with a useful new final chapter; see Chase Bringardner's essay in this volume inspired by Brooks's original publication). *Step Right Up,* thoroughly researched and documented, especially makes great use of archives, from the trade cards to patent medicine almanacs, show songsters, first-hand show accounts, and various versions of comic bits (several included in appendices). Not surprisingly, given Brooks' frequent use of performance in his books and essays, his study served as a catalyst for *The Vi-Ton-Ka Medicine Show,* a reconstructed old-time med show performed at New York's American Place Theatre in 1983, and featuring most of the few remaining medicine show performers and hawkers.

In 1976 another reiterated McNamara topic emerged, the interchange between popular entertainment and commercial film, a subject he evocatively explored in "'Scavengers of the Amusement World': Popular Entertainment and the Birth of the Movies," an essay that appeared in a catalogue (dated 1976) to an exhibit on *American Pastimes* at the Brockton (Massachusetts) Art Center in early 1977. In this piece he focuses on the showbill (another archival gem) for the public showing of Edison's first motion picture at Koster and Bial's New Music Hall on April 23, 1896 (as turn number eight). Brooks would return to the stage/film theme on several occasions after 1976, most notably in *Before Hollywood: Turn of the Century Film from American Archives* (prepared as an accompanying publication to a film exhibition, another of his archival projects), published a decade later by The American Federation of Arts. "Scene Design and the Early Films" also returns Brooks to his early training in scenic design, performance spaces, and, in this case, early film's use of (and frequent borrowing) of stock interior stage sets combined with realistic exteriors, common practice until c. 1910. McNamara's knowledge of early films in this essay is quite stunning.

Sometime early in the 1980s, during a theatre conference, Brooks and I sat in an outdoor café in San Francisco in rapt attention as that great teller of jokes, the late Ralph G. Allen, burlesque authority and creator of the musical/burlesque recreation *Sugar Babies,* regaled us with hilarious one-liners. Brooks likely saw another great archival idea as we laughed non-stop for several hours (no doubt skipping out on several scholarly papers). A few years later (1983) Brooks, as only he could, gathered from numerous rare sources (many in his own collection) material that had often informed his popular entertainment scholarship. Titled *American Popular Entertainments* (and I note that Ralph Allen is acknowledged by Brooks) it is organized like a typical gagbook (with a superb essay on the kind of material included—jokes, monologues, lectures, sketches, dialogues, a rich selection of the kind of comic material common during the late 19th and early 20th centuries). For those of us who taught courses on popular entertainment, this was a god-send, all too soon allowed to go out of print.

In the early 1990s McNamara demonstrated his long-standing theatre historian's love for his city, Manhattan (he lived for decades on the edge of Washington Square), in two essays, both impressive overviews of areas/spaces in New York City devoted in major ways to entertainment. The impressive collection *Inventing Times Square* (1991) includes Brooks's "The Entertainment District at the End of the 1930s" and the equally comprehensive collection *Greenwich Village: Culture and Counterculture* (1993) included a piece close to Brooks's heart, "'Something Glorious': Greenwich Village and the

Theater." A number of Brooks' students (John Frick—a contributor to this volume—and Mary C. Henderson come mind) were inspired by Brooks to write important studies of New York playhouses and areas of the City of theatrical importance.

Space here remains for brief comment on only three remaining titles from Brooks's body of work, but together they represent a kind of capstone to his life's scholarship and his always evolving research interest.

In 1976, with Brooks as director, the Shubert Foundation founded the Shubert Archive to deal with some six million items relating to the American theatre (roughly 1900 to 1940, the heyday of the Shubert dynasty). Brooks was in his element—a gigantic archive that required someone just like him (or probably, just him!) to locate relevant items in various venues, identify them, bring them together, begin a catalogue, and devise storage for this vast collection. Brooks gloried in this challenge and continued to lead the effort—along with others key in this process (Curators Brigitte Kueppers and Mary Ann Chach in particular)—until he retired in 1999. For those who might not have known Brooks personally, the Shubert Centennial Edition of the Archive's newsletter *The Passing Show* (2002) includes a series of wonderful statements about him from friends, colleagues, students, and mentors. Few could garner such admiration. One of the major products of Brooks's effort with the Archive was his telling of the lives and times of the three Shubert brothers (Sam, Lee, and J.J.) in the wonderful *The Shuberts of Broadway* (1990), a history of Broadway drawn almost exclusively from the Archive, illustrated with 200 rare illustrations and written in Brooks's inimitable style with his usual clarity and selectivity.

In 1997 Brooks broke new ground with his thorough research in another great archive, The Museum of the City of New York. Drawing upon first-hand accounts, great illustrations, and his own historical perspective (and ability to make theatrical connections in unlikely places), *Day of Jubilee: The Great Age of Public Celebrations in New York, 1788–1909* explores in wonderful descriptions how urban Americans created civic performances and commemorations in order to honor prominent individuals, mark significant events and issues of importance (mourning to joyous celebration) to New York City. Once more Brooks taught us how to mine a rich archive and how to frame applicable questions to show relevance and meaning to today's culture.

The final scholarly effort of Brooks McNamara (2002) was written early during his illness with a degenerative nerve disorder and, though it was not easy for Brooks to complete this effort, he was determined to do so and worked on it as diligently as any of his previous publishing ventures. I know this because *The New York Concert Saloon: The Devil's Own Nights* was in a book series that I edited for Cambridge University Press. This pioneer effort garnered some good reviews and was honored with a book award from the Victorian Society.

Most significantly for this volume, Brooks's investigation, a real detective story, enlightens us all about a form of American variety entertainment little known, other than by name, until his research and the recording of his findings in this modest book. His love for New York and its history and for the unearthing of details about American popular entertainment forms receives the McNamara touch for one last time. And for a book dedicated to the use of archives and the role of theatre scholars as history detectives, this book serves as a fitting conclusion. Brooks selected two key sources in relation to the New York concert saloon for his research and studied them in detail: the "sporting and theatrical" paper *The Clipper* and the papers of The Society for the Reformation of Juvenile Delinquents. From the former he focused on a series of fourteen articles (from 1864) that go a long way toward providing background and descriptions of these unique venues. But as Brooks noted, this was not enough for a book; but Brooks also owned a collection of reports on concert saloons and their shows created by the Society for the Reformation of Juvenile Delinquents. Armed with these two primary sources, Brooks began his detective work; the result is his book.

This essay was not meant to be a survey of all of Brooks McNamara's published work, but a dipping into some of the more influential and significant books and articles. However, for the record I'd like to mention in quick succession a few not discussed above. In 1980 I published *American and English Popular Entertainment: A Guide to Information Sources* (Gale Research), and, with some trepidation, approached Brooks to write a preface to this modest effort. I considered him a true friend, colleague, and also an inspiration and mentor; I also stood in awe of his accomplishments. I should not have been hesitant to approach him: he enthusiastically agreed to tackle this task and penned what I think was the single best statement then available on the status of this "new field of theatre research." His pioneer efforts for *The Drama Review* culminated in his role as co-editor of *The Drama Review: Thirty Years of Commentary on the Avant-Garde* (1986). He often agreed to take on similar assignments. When one of his graduate students, David Payne-Carter, passed away before the publication (in 1999) of his book on Gower Champion, Brooks stepped in and put all in order (credited as co-editor with Steve Nelson). For Signet Classics he edited volumes of contemporary plays, and in 1992 wrote and published a children's book on a down-at-the heels traveling vaudeville troupe, *The Merry Muldoons and the Bright Eyes Affair,* which also was adapted for an off-Broadway musical. For a number of years Brooks was active at The Players and in particularly with its Hampden-Booth Theatre Collection, for which in 1989 he helped organize and write a catalogue for "Edwin Booth's Legacy." With his colleague James V. Hatch and his then graduate student Annemarie Bean, Brooks edited *Inside the Minstrel Mask* (1996), a still in demand collection of key readings on nineteenth-century blackface minstrelsy. And, finally (not really; this summary could go on) when he retired to Doylestown, Pennsylvania, he helped in 2000 to write a history of his new hometown.

In Arnold Aronson's sensitive and very complete obituary written for the American Society for Theatre Research's website, another *TDR* essay ("Broadway: A Theatre Historian's Perspective") written by Brooks in 2001 is singled out for a statement that Arnold identifies as McNamara's credo. I agree with this assessment and conclude with the key quote in that essay: "The theatre in any time is not exclusively made up of high art, but of a complex of related forms: popular and amateur entertainment, and in the 20th century, to a great extent, radio and television, motion pictures, and the internet. Until recently, most of these have been ignored by historians of theatre and drama, though they are important influences on the theatre and are influenced by it." Thanks to Brooks and a few like him, the last decade has seen the acceptance of his notion of what should be defined as theatre, and its serious study is now readily accepted and almost commonplace.

SOURCES BY BROOKS MCNAMARA CITED
(Listed as They Appear in the Essay)

1969. *The American Playhouse in the Eighteenth Century.* Cambridge, MA: Harvard UP.

1974. "The Scenography of Popular Entertainment." *TDR* (T-61, March): 16–24.

1974. "'A Congress of Wonders': The Rise and Fall of the Dime Museum." *ESQ* (Vol. 30,3rd Quarter): 216–32.

1974. "Medicine Shows: American Vaudeville in the Marketplace." *Theatre Quarterly* Vol. 4 (May-July): 19–30.

1971. "The Indian Medicine Show." *Educational Theatre Journal* Vol. 23 (December): 431–45.

1975. *Theatres, Spaces, Environments: Eighteen Projects.* With Jerry Rojo and Richard Schechner. New York: Drama Book Specialists (Publishers).

1975. "An Interview with Percy Press and a Portfolio of Buskers." *Educational Theatre Journal* Vol. 27, no. 3 (October): 313–22.

1976. *Step Right Up: An Illustrated History of the American Medicine Show.* Garden City, New York: Doubleday; 1995. Rev. ed. Jackson: U. Press of Mississippi.

1976. "'Scavengers of the Amusement World': Popular Entertainment and the Birth of the Movies." In *American Pastimes.* Brockton, MA: Brockton Art Center-Fuller Memorial. Catalogue to exhibit, Jan. 27–April 17, 1977. Pp. 17–19.

1986. "Scene Design and the Early Film." In *Before Hollywood: Turn-of-the-Century Film from American Archives.* New York: The American Federation of Arts. Pp. 51–56.

1983. *American Popular Entertainments: A Collection of Jokes, Monologues, & Comedy Routines.* NY: Performing Arts Journal Publications.

1989. *Edwin Booth's Legacy: Treasures from the Hampden-Booth Theatre Collection at The Players.* With Raymond Wemmlinger. [New York]: Hampden-Booth Library.

1991. "The Entertainment District at the End of the 1930s." In *Inventing Times Square: Commerce and Culture at the Crossroads of the World.* Ed. William R. Taylor. New York: Russell Sage Foundation. Pp. 178–190.

1993. "'Something Glorious': Greenwich Village and the Theater." In *Greenwich Village: Culture and Counterculture.* Eds. Rick Beard and Leslie Cohen Berlowitz. New Brunswick, NJ: Rutgers UP for The Museum of the City of New York. Pp. 308–19.

1990. *The Shuberts of Broadway: A History Drawn from the Collections off the Shubert Archive.* New York: Oxford UP.

1997. *Day of Jubilee: The Great Age of Public Celebrations in New York, 1788–1909,* New Brunswick, NJ: Rutgers UP.

2002. *The New York Concert Saloon: The Devil's Own Nights.* New York and Cambridge: Cambridge UP.

1980. Foreword. In *American and English Popular Entertainment: A Guide to Information Sources.* By Don B. Wilmeth. Detroit: Gale Research Co.

1986. *The Drama Review: Thirty Years of Commentary on the Avant-Garde.* Ed. with Jill Dolan and Oscar Brockett. Ann Arbor: UMI Research Press.

1999. *Gower Champion: Dance and American Musical Theatre.* With David Payne-Carter and Stephen Nelson. Westport, CT: Greenwood Press.

1992. *Plays from the Contemporary British Theatre.* New York: Signet.

2002. *Plays from the Contemporary American Theatre.* New York: Signet.

1992. *The Merry Muldoons and the Brighteyes Affair.* New York: Orchard Books.

1996. *Inside the Minstrel Mask: Readings in Nineteenth-Century Blackface Minstrelsy.* Ed. with Annemarie Bean and James V. Hatch. Hanover, NH: University Press of New England for Wesleyan UP.

2000. *Doylestown.* Charleston, SC: Arcadia Publishing.

2001. "Broadway: A Theatre Historian's Perspective." *TDR* Vol. 45, no. 4 (T-172, Winter): 125–28.

"Bands of Up to a Hundred *Skomorokhi*": Rethinking *Stoglav* 41:19

JOHN WESLEY HILL

Open any book, article, or encyclopedia entry that treats on popular performance in Old Russia and the term *skomorokh* will appear. The source will define skomorokh as an ancient Russian class or social group (often described in Russian accounts as a *soslovie*: estate, order, community) of professional performers—actors, singers, acrobats, storytellers, musicians, etc.—either coeval with or predating the official establishment of Christianity in Rus'[1]. This notion of a professional caste of entertainers interacting with other "estates" throughout the pre-Petrine period but remaining always distinct is one of a number of theses that exist like weeds in the garden of scholarship on Old Russian performance, reproducing and spreading avidly and choking out informed speculation on possible alternatives to this narrative. In the following essay, I will examine a single historical document from among the primary sources on skomorokhi in order to challenge established conclusions and suggest an alternate model for popular performance in Old Russia.

The document, a mid 16th century source, contains the following passage:

> And jongleurs [skomorokhi] wander through faraway lands, gathered together in large bands of up to sixty and seventy and a hundred men, and eat and drink much in the villages at the peasants' expense, and steal their goods from the larders, and rob men on the roads. . . .[2]

"Faraway lands" accurately conveys the strange and perplexing (to modern ears at least) phrase: *da po dal'nim stranam*. These "lands," however, are not foreign countries, but the outer reaches of Muscovy, the far-flung provinces. A logical assumption is that this sort of lawlessness did not take place closer to the center. But the real problem with this passage is the number of skomorokhi given: sixty, seventy, even a hundred.[3] Could this be possible; on the outer reaches of a sparsely populated 16th century Russia could such large groups be viable? Even if the local authorities in these "faraway lands" had no power to curtail the actions of such bands of marauders, could there possibly have been enough chickens and pigs to steal, enough travelers to mug, and enough locals to visit uninvited for dinner to sustain groups of sixty or more "wanderers?" This seems unlikely. Something else must have been going on. There must be some "back story" here.

The excerpt, from the report of the decisions of a council of the Russian Orthodox Church in 1551 called *Stoglav,* has been a crucial source for the history of Russian performance ever since these "jongleurs" caught the attention of scholars in the mid 1800s.[4] The passage, though, is confusing. This and other historical documents referring to skomorokhi have been used to support the unexamined assumptions and lack of critical rectitude that have plagued the consideration of performançe in Old Russia.

The word skomorokh was most likely used in the earliest texts of Slavonic literacy not to describe native Slavic performance, but as a term to translate an entire spectrum of phenomenon related to the Byzantine hippodrome.[5] Ecclesiastic writers and thinkers of the first Christian millennium, such as John Chrysostom and Basil the Great, condemned the skomorokh-ish behavior of the laity in the urban centers of the Eastern Empire (Constantinople, Antioch). At first, the use of "skomorokh" in Slavonic language documents appeared in citations and retellings of Greek originals. Only centuries later did "skomorokh" come to be used by Slavic literati to describe native Slavic performance. This is a strong indication that the term initially was *not* used to describe native performance among the Slavs. In fact, the earliest accounts of specifically Slavic performance use words other than skomorokh like piper and player.[6] When the term skomorokh finally made the semantic leap from Hippodrome spectator and faction member to Slavic popular performer, it brought all its baggage with it, including the anti-performance prejudice of early Christian ideology, as well as the pagan classical bias against actors, dancers, and mimes. Religious thinkers of the Eastern Church perpetuated these ideas and added their own twists, specifically notions advanced by Chrysostom and others that performers and their audiences were controlled by demons, that the uncanny skills of professional entertainers were not attainable without diabolical intervention, and that spectators at these shows were also subject to supernatural influence.[7] Our specific passage does not *directly* show the influence of this line of thought—the skomorokhi referred to in *Stoglav* 41:19 are earthly marauders—but other questions in the chapter show the equation of performance with devils in Orthodox thinking.[8]

Stoglav 41:19 does not equate skomorokhi with the supernatural. Rather, it is an example of another technique used by medieval Russian Orthodox literati to discredit "the skomorokhi" and turn secular authorities against them. The skomorokhi in our passage are portrayed not as the creatures of demons, but as ordinary outlaws. The way that medieval Russian ecclesiastics turned popular performers into outlaws was by first making them outsiders—drifters and vagrants—with no durable connection to the local communities they entertained. I believe that the standard historical interpretation of skomorokhi as a caste of itinerant professional performers is highly exaggerated: in most cases, skomorokh performance was the work of members of local communities during holiday celebrations such as Yuletide and Shrovetide, where Bakhtin-esque carnival license was the rule of the day.

Portraying amateur performers and enthusiastic holiday celebrants as beyond the pale of pious existence began when Slavic religious writers concerned about the laity's impious behavior recycled classical and Byzantine

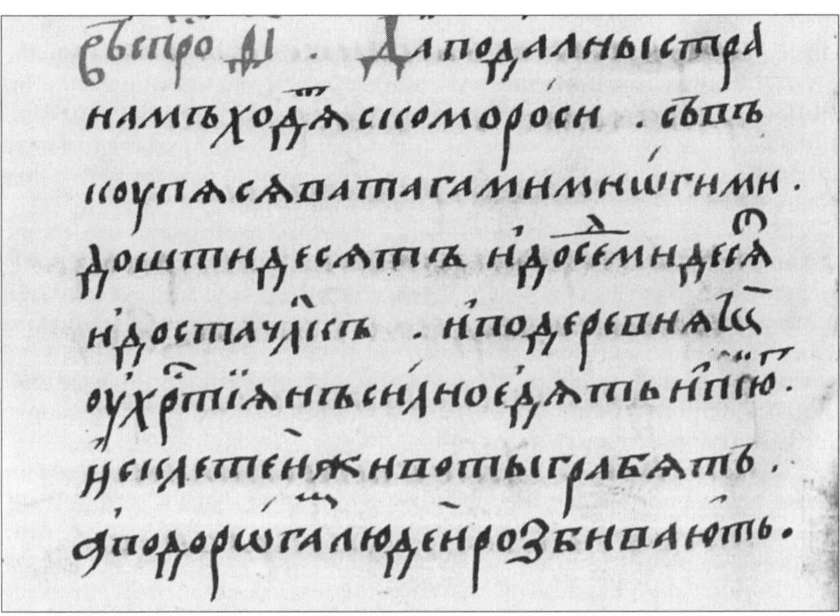

From *Stoglav* (Resolutions of the Moscow Council of 1551), chapter 41, question 19. Archive of the Holy Trinity-St. Sergius Lavra, MS No. 215, section of folio 127 verso.

exhortations to the faithful to avoid participating in expressions of non-canonical, popular belief.[9] When combined with motifs of supernatural influence, the eventual result was the reification of holiday celebrants into members of a class permanently outside of the proper Orthodox lifestyle. Thus celebrants were turned into skomorokhi, who in turn were classified as outlaws. In reality, ritual celebrants went back to their everyday lives as pious members of traditional communities at the close of the holiday period. Accounts of "skomorokhi" in medieval and early modern documents laid the groundwork for the notion of "skmorokhi" as a class of itinerant, professional entertainers found in modern scholarly accounts of Old Russian performance by creating an enemy, or at least a rhetorical target, whose existence in reality fell far short of what was achieved on the page.

A milestone in the reclassification of festive participants in local communities into outsiders and eventually criminals began at the end of the 15th century and gathered steam as the 1500s progressed. I refer to a class of historical document called administrative charters, where skomorokhi are often mentioned in the context of *Namestnichestvo*, a form of regional administration whereby an official is appointed by the Tsar or local Prince. The charters represent attempts to regulate systemic abuses by the local viceroy and members of his retinue through the granting of privileges and exceptions to specific local entities. The documents concerning skomorokhi are responses to complaints by peasants or their immediate superiors that the viceroy's men enriched themselves at the expense of local peasants.

A typical passage about skomorokhi from an administrative charter reads like this: "skomorokhi are not to play [perform]."[10] The word *sil'no*, forcefully, occurs in many of the charters, whereby skomorokhi "are not to play by force."[11] Many scholarly accounts of the skomorokhi give some variation on the following interpretation: The *namestnik* (viceroy) kept bands of skomorokhi for his own entertainment. Rather than pay them a salary, the story goes, he let skomorokhi loose on the local population to play forcefully, that is, force commoners to watch their shows, and demand payment from them.[12]

There are clues in the charters that cast doubt on this established interpretation. First are curious variations in the highly standardized language and format of the charters that mention skomorokhi. There are two categories of charters referring to them: prohibitive and permissive.[13] Both were granted by a secular authority (local Prince or Tsar). The first category prohibited skomorokh "play" in specific locations. The second type "sanctions" (*ne oslobozhdaet*) skomorokh play. Prohibitive charters concerned what happened in villages and settlements under the jurisdiction of monasteries and were addressed to an "abbot and brothers." Permissive charters were granted to population centers *not* under the control of ecclesiastic landowners. Prohibitive charters were granted by a civil authority in response to the petition of an abbot to prohibit skomorokh activity in areas under monastic jurisdiction. The early modern Russian ecclesiastics who requested such charters—the spiritual children of the medieval Slavic literati who passed on the Byzantine theory of performance as an un-Christian, even demonic, activity—were only being true to their doctrinal roots. In population centers not included in the holdings of an ecclesiastic entity (monastery), there was no thought of issuing a blanket prohibition on secular performance. Hence permissive charters typically contain wording that allows all skomorokh activity or allows it under certain conditions. "Skomorokhi are not prohibited from playing."[14] Another charter made the voluntary admission of skomorokhi into a home legal, but "forcible play" was not.[15] Both the 15th century clerical petitioners and the 19th and 20th century scholars of Russian history and popular performance were swayed in their interpretation by Byzantine rhetoric like Chrysostom's advice to his contemporaries not to admit mimes into one's home.[16] Standard historical accounts of skomorokhi depend on the assumption that professional entertainers, both individuals and "bands," were a common occurrence in Old Russia.

In medieval and early modern Russia, however, rather than professional performers and entertainers, which *were* a common occurrence in the late classical Mediterranean basin with its long, well-documented history of various highly-developed performance genres and sophisticated audiences, it is more likely that the "entertainers" that villagers let into their homes were their neighbors making holiday visits, i.e., engaging in ambulatory ritual practices that manifest variously across many times and places as such things as mumming, caroling, and trick-or-treating. Such practices have been well documented in Russia ever since recording such phenomena in a scholarly, systematic fashion began in the mid 19th century. Another bit of evidence to support this conclusion is the wider context of the references to "skomorokhi" in the administrative charters. The documents address issues that concern the behavior of outsiders—the namestnik's people, such as sheriffs, tax collectors, foresters and game wardens—*vis-a-vis* local communities, specifically, whether or not these visitors had the right to a dinner, a place to sleep, feed for horses, and so on, at the expense of the peasants.[17] There is language in many of the charters concerning the presence of outsiders at the holiday feasts held by members of local communities. These dinners of pooled resources (*v skladchinu*) were off limits even to members of the local administration's "upper management" such as the regional chief and his deputies.[18]

When read in the context of peasants fed up with having their parties crashed by local officials out "slumming it," the measures to curtail "playing forcefully" begin to make sense. Ethnographic descriptions from the 19th and 20th centuries of holiday practices among traditional Russian communities provide a possible modern equivalent for the "forceful players" of the 16th century. Participants in ambulatory rituals, primarily mummers (*riazhenye*) but also sometimes carolers (*koliadniki*) were not guaranteed entrance at each house where they knocked. If admitted, they would enter, do their bit—sing, dance, do a skit, scare the children if they were masked, or wish the householders well—and get their reward: money or food. Sometimes they would be invited to sit down at table with their hosts. Not all householders, though, were inclined to admit such groups. A group of children carrying a star and singing about the Savior would have been one thing, but a "band" of rowdy, teen-aged equivalents to contemporary trick-or-treaters would have been something else entirely. Even carolers were not always admitted; texts of carols almost invariably contain sections in which householders are praised and promised good things if they open their doors and bad things if they refuse. Thus local monastic leaders of the 16th century petitioned for, and received, the total prohibition of ambulatory rituals (which they understood only as the work of "professional" outsiders controlled by demonic forces) in villages under their control. Leaders of villages that were not part of the holdings of monasteries did not seek to have ambulatory ritual practice banned entirely, for this was an integral part of their practice of folk Christianity, but merely their right to deny entrance to groups of (masked?) outsiders as they saw fit.[19]

One final aspect of holiday ritual behavior in traditional communities will provide a fascinating possibility for the reinterpretation of *Stoglav* 41:19 and its meaning for the history and meaning of performance in Old Russia. This is the practice known as ritual hooliganism. In the last two centuries, the majority of attestations of this behavior indicate that it was most common at Yuletide. It can most succinctly be characterized for the American reader as the "trick" in "trick-or-treat." The actions of ritual hooliganism were typically the work of young, unmarried men, and involved vandalism and other anti-social deeds committed in the dark of night such as blocking neighbors' doors and chimneys, dragging large tools and conveyances far from their owners homes, and even ramming a dwelling with a log forcefully enough to knock the icons off the wall.[20]

Could the situation described in *Stoglav* 41:19 be the combination of an epidemic of well-heeled party crashers and the excesses of rowdy teenagers on holiday sprees? I believe this possibility is worth considering. Since its first use in native Slavic literary production, "skomorokh" was a receptacle for anti-performance rhetoric, exaggerations, and sheer fabrications about performers and audiences in Old Russia. I think it reasonable to approach *Stoglav* 41:19 with a great deal of skepticism without rejecting its accusations entirely. Recalling who was likely to have written this section of *Stoglav* will be useful. Chapter 41 of *Stoglav* was the work of regional church authorities.[21] In the case of 41:19, which treats happenings in "faraway lands," it is fair to assume that clerics from remote areas brought this issue to the table. The laconic nature of the answer, "let no such violence and outrage exist anywhere and at any time," suggests that the council was ready to concede that such disorderly conduct was undesirable, but not worth extended consideration. It is possible that the regional ecclesiastic authorities who posed question 41:19 at the Council may have exaggerated crimes and misrepresented the perpetrators. Indeed, talk of "skomorokhi" may well have been a ploy to obscure the real issue, which was that there may well have been itinerant groups afoot in the far provinces scrounging for food. The reason for such desperation may have had more to do with abuses associated with large monasteries acting as major regional landowners than with the practices of wandering "entertainers."[22]

In 1854, Ivan Dmitrievich Beliaev published "On Skomorokhi," the first monograph on the subject, which set the tone for the interpretation of the *Stoglav* passage and for the overall tenor of skomorokh studies.[23] Beliaev was also one of the first modern scholars to consider *Stoglav*.[24] Beliaev writes that since *skomoroshestvo* [skomorokh performance] was based on pre-Christian beliefs and practices employing music and comic play, "the people," who were reluctant to part with their old habits, kept inviting skomorokhi to their "weddings, funerals, and banquets" giving food, drink, and even money to the performers. He goes on to propose that this popular demand for professional entertainers "made the class of skomorokhi increase. But, as it increased, the inclination towards a free, homeless lifestyle grew, on the one hand, while the possibility of earning a living from skomoroshestvo became more difficult." Thus, according to Beliaev, "the people became victims of their own passion for skomorokh performance." *Stoglav* 41:19, then, fits seamlessly into this conception of skomrokhi in Old Russia. "By the mid 16th century," Beliaev concludes, "skomorokhi started not just to play forcefully [. . .] they started forming marauding bands of 60, 70 and up to 100 men, [thus preying on commoners] in areas farthest from the center."[25]

Beliaev thus took *Stoglav* at its word, putting no critical distance whatsoever between the way that 16th century Russian life was presented in the contemporary document and his own, mid 19th century, interpretation. This pattern was followed for over a century. Russell Zguta, whose *Russian Minstrels* was the first (and only) book length monograph in English on skomorokhi, challenged the numbers but not the basic scenario: "Allowing for the possibility that the figures [. . .] are exaggerations for shock value," Zguta reasons that skomorokhi, "apparently traveled in large groups, and they had a reputation for lawlessness."[26] Aleksandr Morozov also took a skeptical view of the passage. How could there have been bands of 60–100 high-level professional entertainers, he wondered, suggesting that perhaps the bands, if they were that large, consisted of all manner of itinerants, from wool carders to blind beggars.[27]

These cracks in the dike of a literal reading of *Stoglav* 41:19 have so far not led to a breach. Indeed, the general histories and textbook chapters of Russian performance that follow in the wake of monographs and original research have remained resolutely in the camp of tendentious readings of not just *Stoglav,* but all period accounts of skomorokhi in Old Russia, especially those penned by ecclesiastics.

I propose that notions of skomorokhi's apartness and professionalism have been highly exaggerated. Rather, skomorokh performance in Old Russia, which even contemporary ecclesiastics concede was centered on expressions of traditional agricultural- and life-cycle calendar-based festive behavior, was both produced and consumed by members of local communities. Representatives of the Orthodox hierarchy, especially its literate members with access to the anti-performance legacy of the classical Mediterranean world and the pre-classical near-East, saw the laity's festive expressions of performativity through this tendentious prism, which colored their descriptions and responses.

It is hard to know anything for certain about the skomorokhi: the testimony of their enemies is clearly compromised, and the voices of the skomorokhi themselves in the medieval and early modern period cannot be recovered. Rather than merely recycle the old prejudices and present them as a balanced, complete picture of Old Russian performance, notions of skomorokhi as itinerant, separate, and often predatory must be accompanied by a robust critique of the sources that support these conclusions. The opposing possibility, that "skomorokhi" were members of traditional communities celebrating various seasonal festivals, while not in any way provable definitively, should be offered as a possibility that cannot be altogether disproven.

ENDNOTES

[1] This occurred in 988. Rus' was the first significant polity to emerge among the eastern Slavs. Its capital was Kiev.

[2] Web Resource: "Council of A Hundred Chapters" https://tspace.library.utoronto.ca/citd/RussianHeritage/3.CS/3.L/3.L.18.html accessed 1 October 2010.

[3] The language is reminiscent of St. Mark's Gospel at 4:8, quoted here in the King James version, "And other fell on good ground, and did yield fruit that sprang up and increased; and brought forth, some thirty, and some sixty, and some an hundred." The verbal constructions in *Stoglav* and the Slavonic Bible are not identical. Still, the monks and priests who composed the passage would have known the verse because Mark 4:8 is read every year on the 13th Friday after Pentecost. "Sixty, seventy, and even a hundred," may perhaps be a rhetorical device rather than reflect actual numbers.

[4] The name *Stoglav* comes from its formatting into a hundred chapters or *sto glav*. Chapter 41 of *Stoglav,* which is where our passage is found, contains many questions concerning the moral conduct of the laity. Issues raised in Chapter 41 include false prophets, magicians, heretical books, impious holiday behavior, and performance.

[5] Sergei A. Ivanov, "Slavic Jesters and the Byzantine Hippodrome," *Dumbarton Oaks Papers* (Vol. 46, Homo Byzantinus: Papers in Honor of Alexander Kazhdan, 1992) 129–132, 131.

[6] Sergei Ivanov observes that, "[o]riginal Slavic works [in this early period] use many words of similar meaning (*igrec* [player], *glumec* [mocker], *sopelnik* [piper], etc.), but never *skomrah*." Ibid., 129.

[7] See Ruth Webb, *Demons and Dancers: Performance in Late Antiquity* (Cambridge: Harvard University Press, 2008) 220 and passim.

[8] For example, musical expressions of popular faith (songs) observed on St. John's Day (midsummer), Christmas, and Epiphany are described in question 24 as "demonic."

[9] That is, from the very first use of "skomorokh" in documents composed in the Slavonic language.

[10] *"skomorokhi u nikh v tekh selekh ne igraiut." Skomorokhi v pamiatnikakh pismenosti [SPP]*, (St. Petersburg: Nestor-Istoriia, 2007) 13.

[11] *"i skomorokhom u nikh siloiu ne igrat'."* SPP, 23

[12] This interpretation is most thoroughly developed by A.A. Belkin in the chapter "Skomorokhi v russkom obshchestve" [Skomorokhi in Russian Society] of his *Russkie skomorokhi* (Moscow: Nauka, 1975) 53–109.

[13] *SPP*, 5

[14] *"A skomorokhi u nikh v volosti igrati ne oslobozhdaet."* SPP, 18.

[15] *"Kto [skomorokhov] pustit na dvor dobrovol'no, i oni tut igraiut; a uchnut u nikh skomorokhi po derevniam igrati sil'no, i oni ikh iz volosti vyshliut von bezpenno." SPP*, 19

[16] Allardyce Nicoll, *Masks, Mimes, and Miracles: Studies in Popular Theater* (London: George G. Harrap & Co. Ltd, 1931), 108. Ruth Webb explains that this "criticism of those who invite mimes and dancers into their houses for parties" is found in "an account of the benefits to be derived from the Psalms," *Demons and Dancers*, 175. This notion may well have originated in Christ's admonition to the Apostles from Luke 10:7 not to go "house to house." The initial intention was likely to discourage aggressive proselytizing, and instead to have people come to a teacher and get Christ's message if they wanted it. Perhaps the rhetorical device of "going house to house" came to be understood in later centuries as something sinful in itself.

[17] Such as the decree whereby a constable could not demand dinner and a place to sleep from the same household: *"a gde dovodchik obedaet, tut emu ne nochevati, a gde nochuet, tut emu ne obedati." SPP*, 19

[18] *SPP*, 6

[19] From this perspective, there emerges an interesting possibility. What if the abuses described in the administrative charters were cases where the viceroy's men used the occasion of holiday visits to neighbors to eat and drink at villagers' expense by exploiting folk practices such as mumming and other forms of ambulatory ritual behavior? Accounts of near-contemporary folk performance practices (19th and early 20th centuries) often contain descriptions of young lads from neighboring villages "crashing" a Yuletide party arranged by local youths by storming in unannounced and uninvited in disguise (dressed as mummers). One textbook example is in N.S. Preobrazhenskii's 1864 article about a Yuletide party in the rural Vologda region, "Bania, igrishche, slushan'e i shestoe ianvaria: Etnograficheskie ocherki Kadnikovskogo uezda" [Bathhouse, Merrymaking, Prognostication, and January 6th: Ethnographic Sketches from Kadnikovskii District] *Sovremennik*. T. CIV. 1864. Igor' Morozov and Irina Sleptsova discuss the socio-cultural dynamics of the interactions of "ours" and "theirs" during the ritualized play of Yuletide parties in Vologda province during the 19th and early 20th centuries. I.A Morozov and I.S. Sleptsova, *Krug igry: prazdnik i igra v zhizni severnorusskogo krest'ianina (XIX-XX vv.)* [The Circle of Play: Holiday and Play in the Life of the Northern Russian Peasant, 19th and 20th Centuries] (Moscow: Indrik, 2004) 534–538, and elsewhere.

[20] See Sergei Maksimov's description of ritual hooliganism at Yuletide (*Sviatki*) in *Nechistaia, nevedomaia, i krestnaia sila* [Unclean, Unknown, and Holy Powers] (St. Petersburg, 1903, and many reissues). For an account of practices observed at the end of the 20th century identical to the customs described by Maksimov, see V.L. Kliaus, "Dvizhenie

liudei/dvizhenie predmetov v zabaikal'skom sviatochnom obriade zavalivanie vorot" [The Movement of People/the Movement of Objects in the Yuletide Ritual of Blocking Entrances in the Trans-Baikal] *Kontsept dvizheniia v iazyke i kul'ture* [The Concept of Movement in Language and Culture] (Moscow: Indrik, 1996) 271–283.

[21] Chapter 41, according to Dmitrii Stefanovich, was, with a couple of exceptions (questions 31 and 32), "the work of the eparchial clergy, of both senior and junior levels, who came to the Council from various corners of the Russia land." *Stoglav: Ego proiskhozhdenie, redaktsii i sostav* (St. Petersburg, 1909) 71.

[22] The landowning practices of monasteries were a key issue raised at the Stoglav Council.

[23] "O skomorokhakh" *Vremennik obshchestva istorii i drevnosti rossiiskikh* [Journal of the Society of Russian History and Antiquities] (Moscow, 1854), 69–92,

[24] Beliaev's initial studies were based on the examination of manuscript copies, since the document was not published in Russia until 1862.

[25] Beliaev, "O skomorokhakh" 88.

[26] Russell Zguta, *Russian Minstrels* (Oxford: Clarendon Press, 1978), 47.

[27] A.A. Morozov, "K voprosu ob istoricheskoi roli i znachenii skomorokhov" [On the Question of the Historical Role and Significance of the Skomorokhi], *Russkii fol'klor XVI, Istoricheskaia zhizn' narodnoi poezii* [Russian Folklore 16, The Historical Life of Folk Poetry] (Leningrad: Nauka, 1976) 35–67, at 46.

Who Was Robert Triplupart L'Andouiller? Or, an Actors' Quarrel in Late Sixteenth-Century Paris

VIRGINIA SCOTT

So little is known about the Paris theatre of the late sixteenth century that any information about it is potentially important, although certain kinds of information can be difficult to use. In 1585 a series of pamphlets was published that mark a quarrel between an Italian Arlequin and a French actor referred to as Robert Triplupart l'Andouiller. Italian scholars have demonstrated convincingly that the Arlequin in this instance was the celebrated Tristano Martinelli,[1] but the identity of his adversary is still in question. My purpose has been to try to identify the French actor both from evidence internal to the pamphlets and through comparison of that evidence to several visual documents.

The first of the pamphlets is a *Histoire plaisante des faicts et gestes de Harlequin commedien italien.* [*Comic History of the actions and movements of Harlequin italian actor*].[2] It was bound with *La Sallade de Harlequin a luy envoiee par le Capitaine le Roche, appotiquaire Luquoys, pour la guarison de sa maladie Neapolitaine* [*The Salad of Harlequin sent to him by Captain le Roche, apothecary of Lucca, for the cure of his Neapolitan malady*]. The *Histoire* narrates a parodistic version of Orpheus and Eurydice; in this instance Harlequin travels to the underworld to retrieve Mère Cardine, an infamous bordello keeper. In the *Sallade,* far more salacious and scatological than its predecessor, Harlequin is accused of sodomy and prescribed a thoroughly disgusting cure for his Neapolitan disease, i.e., syphilis.

The second pamphlet is entitled *Response di gestes de Arlequin au poete fils de Madame Cardine, en Langue Arlequine, en façon de prologue, par luy mesme; de sa Descente aux Enfers et du retour d'iceluy* [*Response to the actions of Arlequin to the poet son of Madame Cardine, in the Arlequinian Tongue, in the fashion of a prologue, by himself; of his descent into Hell and of his return*].[3] It is accompanied by a brief *Excuse faite au seigneur Arlequin par le poetrillon morfondu* [*Excuse made to Seigneur Arlequin by the sniveling poetrillon*].[4] Both are attacks on the "poet" who dared to make fun of the great Italian comic actor.

The final pamphlet includes three distinct pieces: *La Duplique* [*Dupique*] *faite pour le Seigneur Arlequin, en forme de contrepeterie au nez de Robert Triplu-plart* [*Triplupart*] *l'Andouiller, urinal des Poëtes, & Colonnel des Gadoues de la Bastille de Proserpine* [*The Second Response of the defendent made for Seigneur Arle-*

LA

DVPLIQVE

FAITE POVR LE SEIgneur Arlequin, en forme de contrepeterie au nez de Robert Tripluplart l'Andouiller, vrinal des Poëtes, & Colonnel des Gadoues de la Baſtille de Proſerpine

Auec vn Recipe de Haulte-fuſtaye pour desembrener ceſte grand' piece poltroneſque.

A PARIS.

1585.

Title page for "La Duplique faite pour le seigneur Arlequin" (1585), Bibliothèque Nationale de France.

quin, in the form of contrepeterie *to the nose of Robert Triplupart l'Andouiller, chamberpot of Poets & Colonel of the Honeymen of Proserpine's Fortress*][5]; a brief *Recipé pour guerir les Tranchees Sainct Mathurin de Robert l'Andouiller de l'Autruche, urinal des poëtes morfondus* [*A Recipe to cure the fits of madness of Robert l'Andouiller of the Ostrich, chamberpot of sniveling poets*][6]; and, finally, a *Festin* addressed *A ce Lifrelofrier de l'Hostel de Bourgogne, qui en ces vers poltrons ofe attaquer le Seigner Arlequin* [*To this Swagbelly of the Hôtel de Bourgogne, who in these cowardly verses dares attack Seigneur Arlequin*].[7]

This is difficult material for various reasons. The pamphlets are all badly written in ungrammatical verse and filled with scurrilous and scatalogical language. Even more challenging, however, *La Duplique*—which potentially yields the largest amount of information about the two participants in the quarrel—is "in the form of a *contrepèterie*," in English a "spoonerism."[8] On the title page the word "duplique" appears, meaning "a rejoinder; or, the second answer of a defendant."[9] It also suggests duplication, duplicity, and double meanings. On the first page of text, however, the word in the title is "dupique," a *contrepet* for *pudique*, meaning "chaste," or "modest." Although "dupique" is not a word, "dupe" or "duppe" is, and while it means, of course, as it does in English, someone who has been tricked, it also means, according to Cotgrave, "a bird that loves ordure so well, that she even nestles in it."[10] This single *chassée-croisée* of sound and meaning suggests just how difficult it is to unravel the *equivoques* and riddles in *La Duplique* which might reveal the true name of the "poëte morfondu" who slandered Arlequin. I confess to failure so far. I have not teased out any fully convincing evidence of the poet's identity, although I think that I have advanced the search.

There appear to be three possibilities. The Italian scholars seem convinced that Robert l'Andouiller was the French actor-farceur Robert Guérin. The evidence? First, of course, his name was Robert. Second, he performed farce as Gros-Guillaume whose image from the 1630's is familiar: a fat man whose figure is divided into three parts by belts worn above and below his vast belly and thus "Robert Triplupart." Third, Guérin also performed as La Fleur, and a verse in *La Duplique* might refer to that:

> Je fermeray mon nez pour ta fleur ne sentir
>
> Bellefleur, qui voudroit le Los appuantir
>
> Du Heros Arlequin . . .
>
> [I will shut my nose so as not to smell your flower Bellefleur, who would like to besmirch the praises of the hero Arlequin . . .][11]

Finally, a number of references in the various pamphlets indicate that "Robert" was a fat, lazy glutton, which could well apply to Guérin's character Gros-Guillaume if not to the actor himself.

While this argument has a certain force, it also presents certain problems. Guérin is first mentioned in any extant document as a member of the troupe of Benoist Petit in 1598 and 1599, years after the pamphlet war.[12] According to Sauval, he was nearly 80 when he died in 1634,[13] but no hard evidence attests to that, and while he may have been old enough and important enough to be worth attacking in 1585, legal documents from the seventeenth century call that into question. In 1626, for instance, when the marriage contract for his third marriage was drawn up, he was the father of three minor sons, still to be sent to *petites écoles* and apprenticed to professions, rather young to be the sons of a man born in 1554.[14] He was also not a writer, so far as is known, unlike his colleagues Bruscambille and Gautier-Garguille. His name certainly appears in the titles of a number of fugitive *facéties*, but with no evidence that he wrote any of them. Finally, while Robert Triplupart could refer to Gros-Guillaume's appearance, a more probable reading is *tripe plupart,* that is, "mostly tripe." This connects directly to l'Andouiller, the maker of tripe sausages. Andouille sausages, in the sixteenth century, were not made of cow stomach but of intestines stuffed with intestines, hence l'Andouiller is a metaphor for a poet whose verses are shit.

If Robert Guérin was not Robert l'Andouiller, then who was? Another possibility is a farceur named Agnan Sarat, first named in a contract in 1578, seven comfortable years before the pamphlet war, when he agreed that his troupe would perform for the Confrérie de la Passion at the Hôtel de Bourgogne.[15] He is also featured in at least eight woodcuts, several engravings, a drawing and a painting which have been studied with some care by art historians, although not by theatre historians.[16] Agnan is mentioned twice *La Duplique,* but unfortunately not unambiguously.

The first mention of Agnan is at the very beginning. The author addresses Robert:

> Fi vilain gadouard, où laisse tu le train
> De tes fouillemardons? dis, coquin à gros grain,
> Pendant qu'avec Agnan ton Roux serpent se jouë,
> Qui cure de Platon la breneuse gadouë.
>
> [Fie, you vile honeyman, where do you empty your shitholes? Tell us, you rascally hayseed, who cleans the shit out of Pluto's cesspit, while with Agnan your Red serpent performs?]

"Se jouë" could mean "performs" as in a play or "performs" as in the sexual act or perhaps both. In Rabelais (*Fourth Book of Pantagruel,* Chapter 38), the andouille sausage stands for the penis, as does the serpent, which would suggest that Robert's "red serpent" "performs" with Agnan. In any case, here Agnan is not the "vile honeyman" but someone connected with him.

The second mention of Agnan comes some forty lines later:

> Or dis moy Fressurier, Gadouard venerable,
> Puis que tu luy as faict une amande honorable,
> Qui t'a degarroté de ton enfer puant?
> Est-ce pas le credit de ton Thesée Aignan?
> Ha! je voy bien que c'est, il t'arracha par force,
> Mais pour gaige a resté ton bout de bras d'entorce.
>
> [But tell me, Seller of offal, venerable Honeyman, since you have made an *amende honorable* to him(Arlequin), who dragged you from your

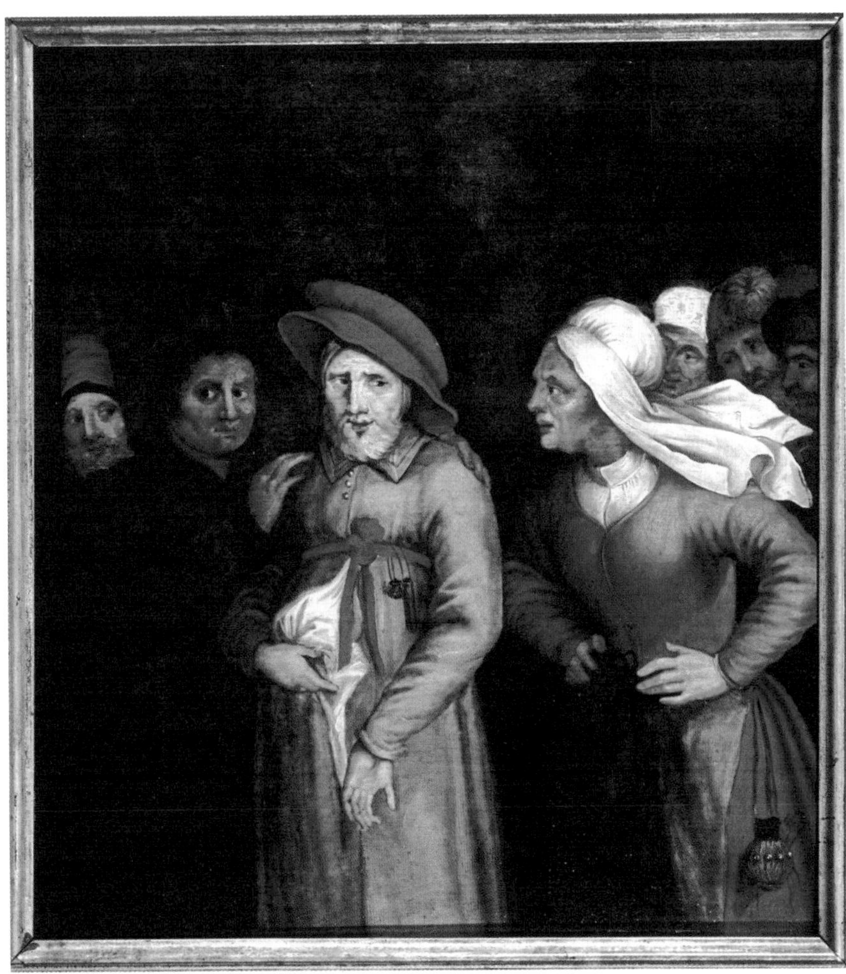

"Agnan à la laide trogne et sa troupe" with the permission of Collections de la Comédie-Française. Photo. Patrick Lorette.

> stinking hell? Is it not to the credit of your Theseus Aignan? Ha! I see perfectly that's it, he snatched you by force, but the twisted end of your arm remained as a pledge.]

Again, there are several possible ways to read this, but one of them is that Arlequin/Theseus dragged Agnan/Pirathous from hell—there is not space enough to explain what they were doing there—and in the process Agnan's hand was twisted. This reading can be clarified by a comma, something writers in the sixteenth century could be careless with: "Is it not to the credit of your Theseus, Aignan?"

The twisted hand is very interesting. In the Archives of the Comédie-Française is a painting that has been entitled *Agnan à la laide trogne et sa troupe*.

It is anonymous and its provenance is unclear.[17] So far as I know, this painting has never been published, although it is part of a group of images that includes a drawing, at least two engravings, and a woodcut. I suggest, largely because of the specific and naturalistic details of the faces of Agnan and his two companions, that the painting is the source of the other images.[18] It shows Agnan with a curiously twisted hand that is, moreover, a focal point of the painting. The twisted hand appears in the drawing and the various prints as well. It does not appear in the six woodcuts featuring Agnan that are part of the Recueil Fossard,[19] suggesting the possibility of a recent injury.

Attention is drawn to Robert's deformity at other points in the various pamphlets as well. He is "malautru," deformed, "de bras desherité," of arm deprived, and the possessor of a "bras court," short arm. He is also called a pedant, which might refer to Agnan's usual role as a village schoolmaster. He is accused of writing verses in a barbarous language used by the most ignorant villagers, with neither rule nor measure, and of speaking an unintelligible Breton *patois*. All of this could apply to Agnan, none of it seems to apply to Guérin, but is it convincing enough to overcome the opening verses that distinguish Robert from Agnan?

A third possibility is that Robert was another member of Agnan Sarat's troupe, perhaps the actor performing Arlequin in the two woodcuts from the Receuil Fossard that appear to represent an interlude with Agnan as a shepherd and Arlequin stealing a tool from him (and a phallic tool, at that).[20] Many scholars have assumed that the Arlequin here is Martinelli himself and that the images represent a collaboration between the Italian troupe and Agnan's troupe. I propose, however, on the basis of evidence in the pamphlets, that the Arlequin is a member of Agnan's troupe imitating Martinelli. The woodcut both shows Arlequin to be a thief, and represents the theft of the character by Agnan's troupe. The woodcut may, then, participate in the discourse of the quarrel.

In the *Response di gestes de Arlequin au poete* Arlequin dreams that he goes to Hades to rescue not Madame Cardine but her son, Cardinon, that is, the poet who dared to attack Arlequin in the first pamphlet. He tells Cardinon: "De ce pays jamais ne sortiras / Si tu ne rens cela que tu robas . . . [From this country you will never depart / If you do not return what you have stolen.] He also brags that he will find ways to torture the poet back on earth, including the following:

> Et ne faire plus le sot:
> Faisant ici le poëte au vers crevé.
> Mais tu iras vuider le bas privé,
> Encore bon j'ay trouvé,
> Quand tu viendras voir les comedians
> Tu paieras à beaus deniers contans,
> Et ne passe plus francs.
>
> [And no longer perform the fool: playing here the poet who makes broken verses. But you will go empty the privy, I've found another good

idea, When you go to see the actors you will pay in ready cash and not get in free.]

Whatever Robert did, in Arlequin's view he deserved to be banished from the theatre, presumably the Hôtel de Bourgogne, where he had been playing farce.

The author of the *Duplique* continues in the same vein, but makes Robert's sin clearer: "quand chez lui tu entrois, / Pour desrober ses tours, un sol tu ne payois" [when you entered his house / To steal his tricks, you did not pay a sou]. Or even more clearly, he notes that Arlequin is "brave en commedie" and "non . . . comme toy vieil yvrogne / Qui refrippe ses jeux, en l'Hostel de Bourgogne [not like you, you old drunk, / Who reuses his routines at the Hôtel de Bourgogne].

A final connection with Agnan and his troupe is the conclusion of the last pamphlet, bound with the *Duplique* and entitled *A ce Lifrelofrier de l'Hostel de Bourgogne, qui en ces vers poltrons ose attaque le Seigneur Arlequin: Festin.* The feast ends with the prediction that the poet will pass eternity in Hades for having spoken ill of Arlequin:

> En ses membres entier, alaigre, sain dispoz
> Mieux composé que toy de l'Esprit & des oz,
> Pour faire vivre encor de Rome & de la grece
> Dessus nostre Eschafault la moralle sagesse,
> Pour nous representer ce que (sot) tu ne scez,
> De vice & de vertu les diferens succez,
> Certain enseignemens, vivre plus profitables,
> Que tes vers ne sont sots, mal faicts, & detestables.
>
> [Whole in his members, agile, soundly formed, better composed than you in Mind and in bone, in order to bring the Moral Wisdom of Rome and greece to life again on our stage, to represent for us the different results of vice and virtue, which you (fool) do not know, certain teachings, perhaps as profitable as your verses are foolish, badly made, detestable.]

Agnan, or someone in his camp, may have answered this final attack. Two of the images based—probably—on the painting at the Comédie-Française include a caption of eight lines of verse defending the moral value of farce:[21]

> La farce des Grecx descendue,
> Hommes sur tous ingenieux,
> C'est pour nostre France rendue,
> Pour remonstrer jeusnes et vieulx.
> Elle taxe les vicieux,
> Les dévoiex elle radresse,
> Et rend petit les glorieulx,
> Chantant du monde la finesse.
>
> [Farce descended from the Greeks, men ingenious above all others, is

> restored for our France, to teach anew the young and the old. It censures the vicious, those who have strayed it puts right, and renders the great ones small, celebrating what is most fine in the world.]

We might doubt that either Arlequin or Agnan actually specialized in the teaching of morality, although satire that "renders the great ones small" was almost certainly a feature of both their performances.

At this point I am wondering if the counterattack on behalf of Martinelli might have fused Agnan, the head of the troupe and its likely "poet," and the actor who actually performed the Arlequin counterfeit. I believe that the pamphlets in this late sixteenth-century actors quarrel have more information to yield, although mining them will be both exceptionally difficult, especially when so much is hidden in *contrepèteries* and other word play, and exceptionally distasteful. Still, Agnan Sarat is worth a certain amount of scholarly distress, having been according to Tallemant des Réaux the first actor "who had a reputation in Paris." Unfortunately, as is often the case when evidence is fragmentary and ambiguous, my conclusion so far can only be "nothing proven."

ENDNOTES

[1] See Ileana Florescu, "Parigi 1585: la querelle degli acteurs-bouffons," in *Viaggi teatrali dall'Italia a Parigi fra cinque e seicento* (Genoa: Costa & Nolan, 1989), pp. 109–127 and an earlier article, "Harlequin, nom de comédien,"; *Biblioteca teatrale* 4 (1986), pp. 21–59; Delia Gambelli, *Arlecchino a Parigi: dall'inferno alla corte del re sole*, Vol. I (Rome: Bulzoni Editore, 1993), pp. 149–174; Siro Ferrone, *"Arlecchino: Vita e avventure de Tristano Martinelli attore* (np; Editore Laterza, 2006). Although Gambelli has included transcriptions of the various pamphlets, I have used the originals where available.

[2] Paris: Didier Millot, 1585. For the full title and publication information see the catalogue of the Bibliothèque Nationale de France.

[3] Paris: Pour Monsieur Arlequin, 1585. The original has not survived. The *Response* and the *Excuse* are reproduced in a collection entitled *Les Joyeusetez facecies et folastres imaginacions de Caresme Prenant, Gauthier garguille, Guillot Gorju, Roger Bontemps, Turlupin, Tabarin, Arlequin, Moulinet, etc.* (Paris: Techener, 1834). Individually paginated.

[4] "Poetrillon" appears to be another invention. A "rillon" is a pork crackling, leftover after pork fat is rendered, so a poet who produces poems out of the very last product of the pig?

[5] Brackets indicate where the first page of the text differs from the title page.

[6] More wordplay. "Tranchées" also means "severe attacks of intestinal colic." "De l'Autruche" has been interpreted as referring to an inn where Robert was living, but could also suggest that he had the stomach of an ostrich, that is, a stomach capable of eating and digesting everything.

[7] (A Paris: 1585). The original is in the Réserve collection of the BNF and is available online at Gallica. This would appear to be the only extant copy.

[8] "Spoonerism" refers to the Reverend William Spooner, Warden of New College, Oxford, whose most famous spoonerism was "kinkering congs" for "conquering kings." Spoonerisms or *contrepèteries* very often invert sounds to create something indecent out of something innocent. In the sixteenth century, according to Randle Cotgrave's *Dictionairie of the French and English Tongues* (London: Adam Islip, 1611; facsimile ed. Columbia, S.C.: University of South Carolina Press, 1968), *contrepèterie* could also mean something counterfeit, a "duperie."

[9] See Cotgrave.

[10] Ibid.

[11] All translations are my own.

[12] S.W. Deierkauf-Holsboer, *Vie d'Alexandre Hardy, Poète du Roi*, in *Proceedings of the American Philisophical Society* 91:4 (1947), pp. 385–6.

[13] Henri Sauval, *Histoire et recherches des antiquités de la ville de Paris*, vol. 3 (Paris: Charles Moette & Jacques Chardon, 1724), p. 38. Sauval is the source of most of the various eighteenth-century biographical entries on Guérin, but Sauval was 10 when Guérin died, so his knowledge is not personal, and his ms, which was published long after his death, was amplified by the editor.

[14]Alan Howe, *Le Théâtre professionnel à Paris 1600–1649* (Paris: Centre historique des Archives Nationales, 2000), pp. 372–3. The "biographies" of Gros-Guillaume and his colleagues Gaultier-Garguille and Turlupin are so deeply contaminated by anecdotes and wishful thinking as to be almost totally worthless. The subject deserves a study of its own; for the moment, let me note that Guérin was born not in Normandy (as is often claimed) but in Paris. Hugues Quéru (Gaultier-Garguille) *was* born in Normandy but in Sées not in Caen and in 1582 not 1573. He was 51 when he died and not 60 as Sauval claims. Sauval also tells us that Guérin left an only daughter in such poverty that she was obliged to become an actress, but we know from his 1623 will that his daughter Catherine was married to a tanner in Gisors. For the facts, see Howe, pp. 366, 370, 371.

[15] Eudore Soulié, *Recherches sur Molière et sur sa famille* (Paris: Hachette, 1863), pp. 152–3).

[16] See Jean Adhémar, "Deux Scènes de comédie gravées d'après François Clouet," *Die Graphischen Künste* 2 (1937), 136–9; Adhémar, "French Sixteenth Century Genre Paintings," *Journal of the Warburg and Courtauld Institutes* 8 (1945), 191–5; Agne Beijer, "Quelques Documents sur les farceurs français et italiens," *Revue d'Histoire du Théâtre* 9 (1957), 54–60; Anthony Blunt, "Georges de la Tour at the Orangerie, " *The Burlington Magazine* 114 (1972), 516–525; A. E. Popham, "A Drawing by François Clouet?" *Die Graphischen Künste* N.S. 3 (1938), 3–4; Martha Kellogg Smith, "Georges de La Tour's 'Old Man' and 'Old Woman' in San Francisco," *The Burlington Magazine* 121 (1979), 288–194). Most of these articles are concerned with the possible relationship of one or more of the Agnan images to the important French artist François Clouet.

[17] The inventory no. is I 307. Former archiviste George Monval wondered if the painting were by François Clouet (*Les Collections de la Comédie-Française: Catalogue historique et raisonné* [Paris: Société de Propagation des Livres d'Art, 1897]), but a later curator concluded, on the basis of a consultation with Agne Beijer, that it is not (Comédie-Française, dossier).

[18] For a view of the other images and information about them, see n. 16 above.

[19] These images are available in a number of places, but probably the most generally accessible source is Pierre Louis Duchartre, *The Italian Comedy* (New York: Dover, 1966), p. 125, pp. 316–18.

[20] Duchartre, p. 125.

[21] See the engraving by Le Blon in Adhemar (1937) and the woodcut by Jean II de Gourmont in Cesare Molinari, *La Commedia dell'Arte* (Milan: Mondadori, 1985), p. 115.

Pursuing Hollar's Sketch of the Second Globe Playhouse

TIM FITZPATRICK

This story begins in Los Angeles, cinematic home of some original gumshoes. It is 1996, and I have flown fifteen hours non-stop across the Pacific to the World Shakespeare Conference. One evening I leave the conference and make my way to LAX. I'm catching the red-eye to the east coast, because there's a sketch there that I need to see. I've contacted the Yale Center for British Art, so they're expecting me. I can get a Greyhound from JFK up to New Haven, look at the sketch and arrange to have it photographed, and be back at JFK in time to catch an evening flight back to the conference—all in 24 hours. When you've spent fifteen hours in the air just getting to LA, anywhere else in the US is 'in the neighbourhood', so you feel you should seize the opportunity.

Why such devotion to the academic cause? The sketch in question is one of a number made by the Czech panoramist Wenzel Hollar in preparation for his 1647 engraving, the *Long View of London*. Sometime in the 1630s he climbed to the top of the tower of Southwark Cathedral, and did four sketches of the city that stretched out below him. One looked down river towards Greenwich, two covered the main part of the city across the Thames, and the other looked up river towards Westminster. The sketches were done in pencil, and subsequently (and probably not on site) partly inked-over. And in the sketch that looked up river, Hollar captured the second Globe playhouse in the middle distance, some 400 metres away.

The first Globe—the playhouse where most of Shakespeare's plays were performed and (it is believed by many) for which they were written—burnt down in 1613 during a performance of *King Henry VIII*, and the King's Men immediately began planning a replacement. The second Globe opened in 1614, and was eventually dismantled in the 1640s after the Puritans had closed the theatres. We would have been more fortunate had Hollar been in London twenty years earlier, but despite the fact that his window of opportunity opened onto the second rather than first Globe, the playhouse he captured is of enormous significance because it was built on the same site, and indeed on the same foundations as the first Globe—so conclusions about its size and configuration might provide invaluable evidence for the first Globe too.[1] I'd seen the sketch reproduced in lots of books—but badly, I suspected:

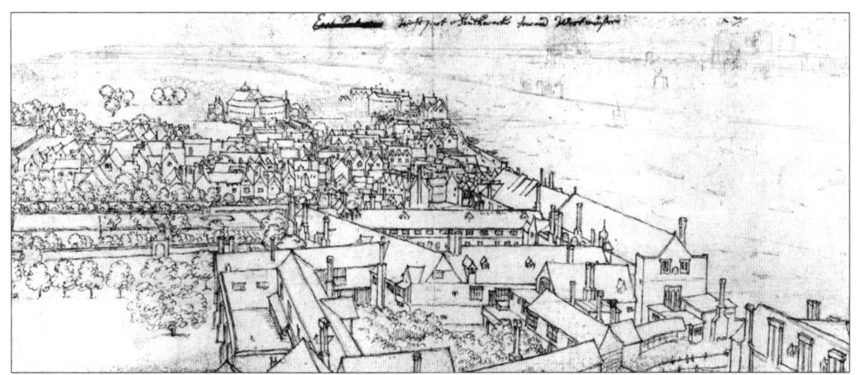

Wenceslaus Hollar, "A View from St Mary's, Southwark, Looking towards Westminster" c. 1638. Yale Center for British Art, Paul Mellon Collection.

the reproductions showed differing degrees of detail. So the original at Yale was reason enough in itself to cross the continental USA in the dead of night. However I had more compelling reasons.

The sketch had been a key piece of evidence used in the reconstruction of Shakespeare's Globe in London, at that time nearing completion. I had been there the previous year to participate in the International Workshop Season in the as-yet unfinished playhouse; and I didn't like what I saw. I thought it was too big, and the configuration of the stage was unsympathetic. So I started re-examining the research that had fed into it. The key input had come from prominent British scholar John Orrell. His 1983 book, *The Quest for Shakespeare's Globe*,[2] had involved a monumental investigation of Hollar's sketch. Amongst other things he claimed it was not a sketch at all, but a punctilious topographic drawing. Trigonometrical calculations of the angles of the various landmarks in the sketch, and comparisons with ordnance survey maps led him to the conclusion that the drawing was so accurate that Hollar must have taken a topographic glass with him up the stairs of the tower. A topographic glass is a gridded glass pane set in a frame, with an adjustable sight in front of it. It is set up so the artist can see the scene he wishes to draw through the glass, and sight various points (high points of landmarks, junction points of buildings etc.) over the gun sight. From there, one can proceed in a number of ways. The sighted points can be registered directly on the glass, and these marks that make up the panorama on the glass transferred by tracing onto a sheet of tissue paper, and thence to the drawing paper by pin-pricking.[3] Or the sightings can be registered immediately on the drawing paper if it has been ruled up with a grid that matches that on the glass.[4] Such was the trigonometrical accuracy of the positions of key landmarks in the views that Orrell became convinced they could only have been achieved by use of some such draughting technique rather than by means of freehand sketching:

> This image of Southwark towards Greenwich is a table of indexical signs, each line caused by a line in reality, each proportion answering to

> the proportions of the real scene as if it were indeed projected onto a screen by some undistorting lens. In this preparatory drawing, then, we have an image that has—so far as it may be checked—the authority of a photograph.[5]

It was this trigonometrical accuracy of the main landmarks in the views that led Orrell to argue for a mechanical 'topographic' technique, and this also meant that the result of 'joining the dots' was a drawing so accurate that it could be used to calculate the diameter of the original playhouse. His calculation came out at around 100',[6] and this then became the preferred size of the London Globe—which had seemed to me too large.

Such a mechanical draughting process as Orrell describes would be laborious and time-consuming, so one might wonder whether it would have been suitable for Hollar's situation; and it was principally this reservation about Orrell's view of Hollar's view that led me to visit the original and re-assess it—part of the continuing process whereby we and our documents tyrannise each other. If Orrell was right, Hollar would have had to set up his equipment four times, once for each of the views; then it must have taken hours to sight the myriad junction points relevant to the hundreds of houses and other buildings that lay before him. And if he were inking directly onto the glass he would then have to trace onto tissue paper (again a time-consuming process), and erase the marks on the glass before moving to his next viewpoint. Having built and used an analogous mechanism known as a 'Cigoli Frame' (after its Renaissance inventor Ludovico Cigoli), I can attest that the simple mechanical technique described by Orrell, though very laborious, can result in extremely accurate drawings—but so too would a hybrid technique that merely took sightings to locate the principal features, and then saved time by sketching in the detail.

Despite his arguments for the stunning accuracy of the sketch and its underlying technique, some of Orrell's comments on Hollar's other sketches seem to suggest that he felt Hollar was using just such a hybrid technique. Discussing Hollar's 'London and Old St Paul's from the Thames', he comments:

> We must notice that there are limits to its accuracy. For one thing, the skyline seems too neatly arranged as a set of towers and spires, many of which appear to out-scale their surroundings. For another, the lantern on Middle Temple Hall seems over-large, leaving doubts about other details in the view. What the artist has got abundantly right are the intervals between the major landmarks; these are presented with all the accuracy of a topographical survey, while the details of the view are subject to the artist's interpretive vision.[7]

The accurate location but inaccurate scale which Orrell sees in these sketches might suggest that Hollar was indeed using a hybrid technique that would involve a limited number of 'marker' sightings and then freehand sketching. This would disqualify them as the basis for calculating the size of buildings, but Orrell proceeded to make just such calculations to arrive at a figure of 100' for the Globe's diameter.

However it struck me that even the suggestion of such a hybrid shortcut underestimates the draughting power of trained artists sketching in freehand. Watching a landscape artist at work is to watch a multi-phased process of draughtsmanship ('blocking out') and then filling in detail.

An extreme case in point is the celebrated autistic artist Stephen Wiltshire, who has attracted widespread attention for his detailed panoramas of large modern cities.[8] Most of the commentary on his work focuses on his extraordinary 'photographic' memory: as he does a preliminary viewing of the city from one or more viewpoints (often from a moving helicopter) he builds up and 'records' a mental archive of detailed visual images which he then integrates to produce a panorama from one particular point of view. But what is equally surprising is his capacity to draught the positions of and relationships between buildings in the panorama from that particular viewpoint. He first 'blocks out' on his drawing paper the main shapes, and then fills in the detail with extraordinary accuracy. Unlike Hollar he does this directly in pen, but Hollar's sketches of London show a not dissimilar staged process: in the one in question on the far side of the Thames we can see rough and summary pencil 'blocking out' of the main landmarks such as the pre-fire St Paul's; at other points detailed pencil sketching has been done; and then some of these pencil lines have been inked over, not always accurately. Such consideration of common non-mechanical drawing techniques provides a different perspective on Hollar's sketch. Could the image at Yale provide indications that Orrell's interpretation of its underlying techniques was questionable?

My curiosity to see the original was further piqued by a particular claim that Orrell made. He was in possession of a 1:1 photograph of the sketch that had been taken in the 1930s which he claimed contained details that must since have faded from the original,[9] so that he could see pencil lines that other scholars hadn't. Had the original faded in the last 80 years? Which lines had faded, and why? At the Yale Center for British Art, on time and on schedule, I was provided with the sketch. It's not a large object, and the detail I was interested in was less than two centimetres across. But focussing in on it with a powerful magnifying glass in the slanting rays of the early spring sun was a revelation.

All of the lines Orrell claimed to see in his photograph were still clearly visible in the original: he may have seen lines in his photograph that hadn't been properly reproduced in photographs or published images used by other scholars, but they were all there. Well, nearly all of them: one particular pencil line which Orrell suggested might have marked one of the vertical timbers of the polygon turned out to be merely a crease in the paper, its shadow in his photograph making it indistinguishable from other pencil lines.

But there was more in the sketch (because it was already telling me that it was a sketch, not a drawing): there were other lines that even Orrell hadn't noticed in his photograph. For instance, there were three base lines, which Hollar had marked tentatively to indicate where he thought the building met the ground behind a row of bushes. Three lines cannot be the result of three sightings, two of which are unaccountably wrong: they must be three tentative sketch lines. Neither did multiple pencil lines elsewhere fit with Orrell's theory of punctilious sightings. Some had not been drawn as one would expect if they were the result of sightings: if you are sighting,

Wenceslaus Hollar, The second Globe playhouse, detail from "A View from St Mary's, Southwark, Looking towards Westminster" c. 1638. Yale Center for British Art, Paul Mellon Collection.

you establish first a particular junction point, for example the point on a building where roof ridge meets gable. You mark that, and then when you come to draw the ridge and gable lines you draw them *from* that point. Instead these lines had been drawn *to* the junction and indeed past it, overshooting the point of intersection. This was a rapid sketching technique, not laborious and time-consuming sightings of junction points and then drawing from those points. In fact there were no signs at all that the junction points had been sighted and the paper grid-marked or pin-pricked accordingly, as Hollar would have done had he been following one or other of Orrell's supposed topographic drawing processes. As well, it was clear that the inking had not always been done as 'meticulously' as Orrell argued.[10] Some of the inking, probably done later off-site, was inaccurate; sometimes it seemed to 'average out' multiple pencil lines, at other times it disregarded the pencil and struck out on its own.

As I returned to LA I knew that the effort I'd taken to come into close physical contact with the original meant I now had the beginnings of a completely new theory about the sketch. And that this piece of evidence would be just the beginning: the image would dominate and even tyrannise (in the nicest possible way) my academic career for some time to come.

But I have not been a solitary victim of tyranny; the academic gumshoe was able to develop a close working relationship with an offsider in the person of the Technical Director of Performance Studies at Sydney University, Russell Emerson—who happens to have a set of investigative and technical skills that complement my obsessive curiosity. Dealing with visual material rather than texts is at or beyond the limits of my disciplinary training, and the research has unfolded as a complex to-and-fro of ideas, hypotheses and suggestions that materialise in the space between us. In this work of detection I hesitate to invoke the names Holmes and Watson, simply because I'm not at all sure who is which. The work has evolved as a series of 'what if?' questions to each other. What if Hollar had given us an accurate sketch of the building? What if we assumed that this sketch, even though it was no use in calculating the size of the playhouse, at least gave an accurate account of its component parts and their relationship to each other? What if we tried to build it, tried to intuit the structure that underlay what Hollar showed us—the skeleton beneath Hollar's skin? Could we say meaningful and useful things about its inside, about the size, shape and other characteristics of its stage?

That is what we have done over more than a decade. First we designed and built a computer-aided design (CAD) model that captured an underlying structure that would give rise to a building that looked like Hollar's. This involved learning about Elizabethan timber-frame building techniques, and working out a geometrical and structural logic that would enable the rational integration of the building's four components: how and where would you attach a large rectangular stage cover and two rectangular external stair turrets to the drum of the main polygonal structure? What would such a theoretical object look like from Hollar's point of view? This involved collaboration with archaeologists at the Museum of London, who provided us with the relative distance, angle and elevation of Hollar's point of view from the foundations of the Globes uncovered in 1989. This enabled us to 'sit' our CAD object on the archaeology and view it from Hollar's point of view, and the result was sufficiently promising to warrant the construction of a 1:50 scale model, which again we were able to photograph from Hollar's point of view. The correspondence between our object and Hollar's sketch is striking, and the few discrepancies are simply explained and throw further light on Hollar's sketching and inking process. More importantly, work on the underlying structure enables us to infer internal characteristics that Hollar's sketch does not show. The stage and the wall behind it must be of a shape and configuration quite different from that at the London Globe, and the stageposts that we know from other sources supported the cover over the stage must be positioned, for structural reasons, further upstage and closer together, providing the actors with a more sympathetic downstage acting space. These issues are discussed in an article in *Early Modern Literary Studies*.[11] In summary, we claim that if our building had been there on the Bankside when Hollar climbed the tower of Southwark Cathedral, it would have resulted in a sketch very like the one he has left us. It is possible that another sort of integrated structure might be even more similar to the sketch, but that is a challenge for other scholars: the work of interpreting documents is never done, and the more scholars involved in this tyrannical to-and-fro the better.

Our most recent work is to build this structure in a detailed way in CAD as part of an international initiative to build an accurate reconstruction of the second Globe, possibly in Staunton, Virginia. The work will involve discussion with structural engineers (to tell us if our building would stand up), and with Peter McCurdy, the master builder who built the London Globe and who knows all there is to know about Elizabethan timber framing. He will tell us whether the Elizabethans would in fact have even thought of constructing such a building. We are also talking with art historians, to shed even more light on the techniques and purposes of such preparatory sketching exercises in the period, and investigating the possibility of using near infra-red spectrography on the sketch (should the Yale Center for British Art approve such an intervention).

In addition to the interdisciplinarity that such a document calls for, it complicates the task of communicating research findings to other academics. If they, like me, come from a textual analysis background, they are not necessarily well equipped to follow an argument based on visual analysis: an article with lots of words and some attached diagrams will quite possibly fail to communicate. I therefore resolved to employ another medium, and started to work with PowerPoint. It is well-known that this software in the hands of the inexperienced can lead to disastrous presentations (a colleague of mine says "Power corrupts, PowerPoint corrupts absolutely"), but I was interested in its potential to privilege the image and to put words into a secondary role. It has served our purposes well: my PowerPoint presentation to the American Shakespeare Center Conference in Staunton in October 2009 finally broke through and enabled our academic colleagues to 'get' what we had achieved.[12]

The title of John Orrell's book, *The Quest for Shakespeare's Globe*, implies a researcher in a knight errant role. While there is and must be an obsessive streak in most of us, we need to guard against the danger of letting it dominate our considerations and cause us to end up tilting at windmills. The work we have done on this project is less heroic: it is systematic, humdrum, thorough—the sort of work needed in the humble enterprise of detection.

ENDNOTES

[1] The sharing of foundations by the two playhouses has only recently been confirmed by the archaeologists' final report on the excavations of the Globe done in 1989: Julian Bowsher and Pat Miller, *The Rose and the Globe: Playhouses of Tudor Bankside, Southwark: Excavations 1988–91*. London, MOLAS, 2009, p. 127.

[2] John Orrell, *The Quest for Shakespeare's Globe*, Cambridge, Cambridge University Press, 1983.

[3] Orrell, *Quest*, p. 83.

[4] Orrell, *Quest*, p. 26.

[5] Orrell, *Quest*, p. 75.

[6] Orrell, *Quest*, pp. 84ff.

[7] Orrell, *Quest*, p. 19.

[8] His website contains a range of impressive panoramas of cities from specific points of view or from a point of view 'aggregated' from multiple sightings from a helicopter flight over the city: www.stephenwiltshire.co.uk.

[9] Orrell, "The Accuracy of Hollar's Sketch of the Globe", *Shakespeare Bulletin*, 11.2 (Spring 1993): 5–9; p. 8.

[10] Orrell, *Quest*, p. 76.

[11] Tim Fitzpatrick, "Reconstructing Shakespeare's Second Globe using CAD design tools", *Early Modern Literature Studies* March 2004 (online journal http://extra.shu.ac.uk/emls/si-13/si-13toc.htm).

[12] An earlier version of this PowerPoint designed to be 'read' as an article rather than experienced as a lecture can be downloaded (filename: Fitzpatrick TF + RE Reconstructing Hollar's Globe.ppt) from http://ses.library.usyd.edu.au/handle/2123/3567.

Pointless Clues? Reviving Declamation through the Punctuation of Jean Racine's *Phèdre et Hippolyte* (Paris: Barbin, 1677)

JEANNE BOVET

The Stakes

Over the past 15 years, 17th-Century stage declamation has become an interesting if controversial field of research for French theater historians. Drawing on rhetorical as well as dramatic treatises of the period, scholars such as Sabine Chaouche, Georges Forestier, Julia Gros de Gasquet and myself have attempted to define the theoretical principles of declamation in order to reconstitute as far as possible the "authentic," original performance conditions of Molière, Corneille and Racine's plays.[1] Among these principles, the widely asserted orality of punctuation is particularly seductive. It implies that by using punctuation marks as indications of pausing and breathing, 17th-Century playwrights could literally inscribe, and thus *ascribe* the rhythm of the actor's declamation beforehand, within the dramatic text itself. Similar in that respect to a musical score, the dramatic text therefore stands out as key evidence for the reconstitution of historical performance practice.

Racine's famous 1677 tragedy *Phèdre et Hippolyte* seems to eloquently prove the point, as it features many significant uses of punctuation, particularly regarding the tormented breathing of the oppressed, dying Phèdre—adding therefore a poignant performative dimension to her tragic fate. However, as obvious as these textual marks of declamation may seem, several historical facts weigh heavily against them: the absence of any manuscript of the play; the very limited control the 17th-Century playwright had on the editing and printing of his work; as well as the fact that (as was usual at the time) the play was published months after the first series of performances, making it more than doubtful that the printed punctuation is actually faithful to Racine's intentions or, for that matter, to the original stage performance. In the face of such daunting uncertainties, how can one grant any performative authority or "authenticity" to the "original" text that we do have, the 1677 first edition of *Phèdre et Hippolyte*? And yet, considering its undeniable performative use of punctuation, how can one discard as pointless such a meaningful, telling piece of evidence? Tracing it back, step by step and comma by comma, this essay will discuss the terms, and the possible resolutions of this methodological dilemma.

The Lead

In 1707, Jean-Léonor Le Gallois de Grimarest (1659–1713) published in Paris the first edition of his *Traité du récitatif dans la lecture, dans l'action publique, dans la déclamation, et dans le chant. Avec un traité des accens, de la quantité, et de la ponctuation.*[2] A man of many trades, who taught French grammar as well as mathematics, Grimarest was also a theater *aficionado*, the author of a few "comédies de salon," and was closely acquainted with Molière's daughter Esprit-Madeleine Poquelin. Encouraged by the supportive reaction of the Parisian press to his 1706 *Addition à la vie de Mr. de Moliére*,[3] Grimarest claims that it prompted him to pursue even further, that is, to provide his readers with the detailed principles of theatrical action, i.e. stage declamation—hence this new book (1707, I–III).

In the end, the scope of Grimarest's *Traité du récitatif* turned out to be much broader than stage declamation. As the subtitle indicates, he does not limit his work to the theater, but extends his attention to all forms of public speech—reading, pleading, preaching, declaiming, and singing, all of which he includes under the general term of "récitatif". In his introduction, he clearly stresses his ambitious goal—to preserve the principles inherited from the Golden Age of the 17th-Century, as the mastery of the art of "récitatif" is, according to him, already starting to decline.[4] The work begins with his effort to submit public speech to the grammatical categories of accentuation, quantity, and punctuation, and there is a hint of the grammarian boasting as he insists on the importance of these categories, which account for the first 70 pages of the book.[5] But he also provides a more relevant, artistic argument, since according to him these grammatical rules were perfectly understood and followed by the great actors of the years 1660–1690, whose skillful declamation he is endeavouring to preserve (Grimarest 1707, 190–191).

Chapter III, devoted to punctuation, is the longest (30 pages), and the most interesting regarding the art of both the playwright and the actor. Whereas nowadays French punctuation holds a mainly syntactic function, at the turn of the 17th to 18th-Century its function was still essentially oral. As reading aloud remained the most common way of communicating a text, punctuation marks were meant as the author's indications as to where the reader can, or even must, pause and take a breath, in order not only to be able to read comfortably, but also to convey properly the text's meaning to the audience.[6] Inherited from the great tradition of oratory art, the hierarchy of punctuation follows a simple, gradual logic—the comma marks the smallest pause, the semicolon asks for a longer one, the colon's is longer still, whereas the period requires not only a full stop, but also a breath intake. These principles are steadily reasserted by 17th and 18th-Century rhetorical treatises such as Michel Le Faucheur's,[7] which Grimarest acknowledges in his preface. Grimarest clearly stresses that he has no intention of challenging these well-established principles,[8] then just as clearly reasserts the rules.[9] His personal contribution is to be found in his choice of examples—instead of turning to oratory models, almost all the illustrative excerpts he quotes are drawn from famous 17th-Century tragedies by Pierre Corneille and Jean Racine.

As Grimarest comments on the merits and faults of each example, it becomes clear that the declamatory art of pausing and breathing is as much the playwright's as the actor's responsibility. For it is initially the playwright who inscribes the punctuation marks within the dramatic text, thus ascribing the rhythm of the actor's declamation beforehand, just as a composer would do for a singer in a musical score. In paying attention to the original punctuation of 17th-Century plays, theater historians could thus rediscover a precious key, not only to the reconstitution of historical performance practice, but also to a better understanding of the oral-aural poetics of French classical playwriting. This is particularly true of Racine's theater, so much so that Georges Forestier, editor of the most recent "Bibliothèque de la Pléiade" authoritative edition of Racine's complete works, has systematically restored the original punctuation, and detailed his reasons for doing so in a substantial explanatory note (Forestier 1999a).

The Evidence

Racine's last profane tragedy appears to perfectly prove the point. Drawing from Euripides and Seneca, *Phèdre et Hippolyte* stages the infamous, unrequited love of Phèdre, daughter of Minos and Pasiphaé and wife of Thésée, for her stepson Hippolyte. The tragedy starts to unfold in Scene 3 of Act I, where Phèdre makes her first, pitiful entrance—tormented by her silent passion, she is wasting away, having not slept nor eaten for three days (lines 187–194). After much reluctance, she finally gives in to her nurse Oenone's insistence and reveals her shameful secret. In the scene's final, famous tirade, she recalls how her passion for Hippolyte began in Athens, and how she dutifully tried to escape it, until she managed to persuade Thésée to send his son away: "Je pressay son exil, & mes cris éternels/ L'arracherent du sein, & des bras paternels." (Lines 293–296.)

The next passage opens with a short, significant sentence expressing Phèdre's relief at having banished Hippolyte: "Je respirais, Oenone."—I breathed again, Oenone (line 297). The phrase is to be taken literally, for the choice of words is doubled by the choice of punctuation, as the statement is framed by two periods, each of them commanding a full stop and a breath intake, thus making Phèdre's sigh of relief not only conceivable, but also audible. These indicators of declamation make the hemistich (half line of verse) stand out against the rest of the text, drawing attention to the central motif of breath, which will actually develop in all that follows.

Indeed, Phèdre's second wind soon proves to be rather short of breath, as her longest sentences consist of no more than a couplet, and suddenly come to a halt when she evokes the fatal moment where Hippolyte re-appeared before her eyes. From then on, the flow of Phèdre's narration is definitely broken. Each of the following lines—in which she evokes the overwhelming strength and horror of her passion—ends with a period, forming a succession of five very short sentences. For the actress playing Phèdre, this means that she must stop for breath after having uttered each line, even though she obviously doesn't have the physiological need to do so. Enhanced by the frequency and intensity of these mandatory pauses and breath intakes, the fractured rhythm of this crucial passage efficiently conveys the sense of oppression of Phèdre's overwhelming, unspeakable feelings.

By contrast, the impact of the final five lines of the tirade becomes all the more potent, since they contain only four commas, and therefore ask to be declaimed with four very slight pauses in one single breath. This means that after having needlessly but, as has just been shown, meaningfully gathered her breath in the previous five, short sentences, the actress will now have to let it all out in one long sentence, at the end of which she will find herself literally out of breath on the final word "s'exhaler"—to be exhaled. Now this is precisely what Phèdre is asking Oenone: to allow her to draw her last breath. There again, the use of punctuation proves to be closely connected to

& HIPPOLYTE. 15

Voyage infortuné ! Rivage malheureux,
Falloit-il approcher de tes bords dangereux ?

PHEDRE.

Mon mal vient de plus loin. A peine au Fils d'Egée,
Sous les loix de l'Hymen je m'eſtois engagée,
Mon repos, mon bon heur ſembloit eſtre affermi,
Athenes me montra mon ſuperbe Ennemi.
Je le vis, je rougis, je palis à ſa veuë.
Un trouble s'éleva dans mon ame eſperduë.
Mes yeux ne voyoient plus, je ne pouvois parler,
Je ſentis tout mon corps & tranſir, & brûler.
Je reconnus Venus, & ſes feux redoutables,
D'un ſang qu'elle pourſuit tourmens inévitables.
Par des vœux aſſidus je crus les détourner,
Je luy bâtis un Temple, & pris ſoin de l'orner.
De victimes moy meſme à toute heure entourée,
Je cherchois dans leurs flancs ma raiſon égarée.
D'un incurable amour remedes impuiſſans !
En vain ſur les Autels ma main brûloit l'encens.
Quand ma bouche imploroit le nom de la Déeſſe,
J'adorois Hippolyte, & le voyant ſans ceſſe,
Meſme au pié des Autels que je faiſois fumer,
J'offrois tout à ce Dieu, que je n'oſois nommer.
Je l'évitois partout. O comble de miſere !
Mes yeux le retrouvoient dans les traits de ſon Pere.
Contre moy-meſme enfin j'oſay me revolter.
J'excitay mon courage à le perſecuter.
Pour bannir l'Ennemy dont j'eſtois idolatre,
J'affectay les chagrins d'une injuſte Maraſtre,
Je preſſay ſon exil, & mes cris éternels
L'arracherent du ſein, & des bras paternels.
Je reſpirois, Oenone. Et depuis ſon abſence
Mes jours moins agitez couloient dans l'innocence.

B ij

16 PHEDRE

Soûmiſe à mon Epoux, & cachant mes ennuis,
De ſon fatal hymen je cultivois les fruits.
Vaines précautions ! Cruelle Deſtinée !
Par mon Epoux lui meſme à Trézene amenée
J'ay reveû l'Ennemi que j'avois éloigné.
Ma bleſſure trop vive auſſi-toſt a ſaigné.
Ce n'eſt plus une ardeur dans mes veines cachée,
C'eſt Venus toute entiere à ſa proye attachée.
J'ay conceu pour mon crime une juſte terreur.
J'ay pris la vie en haine, & ma flâme en horreur.
Je voulois en mourant prendre ſoin de ma gloire,
Et dérober au jour une flâme ſi noire.
Je n'ay pû ſoûtenir tes larmes, tes combats.
Je t'ay tout avoüé, je ne m'en repens pas,
Pourveu que de ma mort reſpectant les approches
Tu ne m'affliges plus par d'injuſtes reproches,
Et que tes vains ſecours ceſſent de rappeller
Un reſte de chaleur, tout preſt à s'exhaler.

SCENE IV.

PHEDRE, OENONE, PANOPE.

PANOPE.

JE voudrois vous cacher une triſte nouvelle,
Madame. Mais il faut que je vous la revele.
La mort vous a ravi voſtre invincible Epoux,
Et ce malheur n'eſt plus ignoré que de vous.

Phèdre's first confession, Act I, Scene 3. Jean Racine, *Phèdre et Hippolyte* (Paris: Barbin, 1677) p. 15–16. Courtesy Bibliothèque nationale de France.

the tragic content of Racine's text. Through its sonorous *signifiant,* it gives Phèdre's tirade a *signifié* which not only matches, but also reinforces and considerably enriches its literal meaning. Between the sound of her initial and final breath, from her revival in "Je respirais" to her death in "s'exhaler," Phèdre's entire fate is already sealed by Racine in the punctuation of her first tirade.

The Pitfall

Too good to be true? In 2007, French scholar Alain Riffaud proceeded to challenge the very assumption of the orality of punctuation in French 17th-Century drama.[10] His demonstration is far from being flawless, as he tries to turn everything to account, resulting in a lack of discrimination that unfortunately matches that of Sabine Chaouche, which he had precisely set himself the task of denouncing.[11] However, Riffaud's main argument against the supposed orality of 17th-Century plays' punctuation remains entirely relevant. It focuses on the complex relation between the world of the theater and the world of print. Only a handful of 17th-Century French theater manuscripts have come down to us, as it was customary to discard them after publication. We have no manuscripts of Racine's plays; they have come down to us only in print, punctuation and all. As Riffaud emphasizes, to posit that the 17th-Century printer's punctuation was faithful to the playwright's would be too much of an extrapolation. The stage and the printing house are two separate, different spaces, with distinct practices, traditions, and knowledge. One cannot presuppose their permeability or systematic correspondence, but rather must take their problematic relation into account.[12]

The problem begins with the nature of the manuscript itself. 17th-Century plays go through several different manuscript states, depending on their particular destination. In the context of the first staging of a play, the playwright gives the original, full manuscript to the troupe copyist, who then makes a copy of each separate role for the actors, and perhaps a prompt-book as well. Except in the case of pirated editions, it is likely that neither of these initial manuscripts (the playwright's or the copyist's) was provided to the printer, but rather a new manuscript prepared by the playwright especially for publication. The authorized manuscript might thus differ in several respects, not only from the play's original manuscript version, but also from its original stage performance. There are many known instances in which the playwright has rewritten passages to make them more suitable for publication, notably regarding the moral criterion of *bienséance,* i.e. decorum. The same may be said for the more technical item of punctuation. Hence, nothing allows us to infer Racine's original staging intentions nor to reconstitute the effective first stage performance from the breathing and pausing indications printed in the 1677 edition of *Phèdre et Hippolyte.*

Nor can we be sure that these printed indications are even faithful to the text of Racine's authorized manuscript, for that manuscript is lost, making the comparison impossible, and the text has gone through many stages in the publishing process. The manuscript is prepared for composition by a copy editor, the "corrector," who is responsible for standardizing the spelling and adding capitals, accents and punctuation marks. The compositor who sets the pages might also alter the punctuation, depending on his habits, preferences, and understanding of the text. It is then the proofreader's task to identify and correct any possible mistake made by the compositor—due to time and travel constraints, the proof was rarely sent to the playwright for verification. Thus, the punctuation of the text may have changed significantly from the author's copy to the final print, the ultimate responsibility falling to the printer.

One last argument in favor of the printer's responsibility for punctuation is the frequent mention of the carelessness of 17th and 18th-Century authors towards what they seem to regard as a trivial matter, unworthy of their concern. Grimarest himself deplores the fact and its consequences, as he blames the ignorance of the author and corrector alike.[13] Some authors, however, seem to pay more attention. Roger Chartier[14] gives the convincing example of La Bruyère—in the last edition of *Les Caractères* revised by the author and published in 1696, punctuation appears as an indicator of various reading *tempi,* each *Remarque* being treated "as a sole musical phrase unbroken by periods, alternating agitated sequences, the rhythm of which is given by a succession of commas, with longer sequences without punctuation." (Chartier 1999, 19) Could the same be said of Racine and the 1677 edition of *Phèdre et Hippolyte?* Or can there be another explanation for the meaningful punctuation of Phèdre's tirade?

The (Re)Solution?

Phèdre et Hippolyte premiered on January 1, 1677, at the prestigious Hôtel de Bourgogne theater, starring la Champmeslé as Phèdre. The *privilège* for print was granted in February, and the original edition came out in March, divided between two editors, the bookseller Claude Barbin and the bookseller and printer Jean Ribou. A mere 10 days after the first 78–page print run, a second print run was published, this time set on 74 pages. The text of the play remains the same in both runs. The discrepancies concern misprints, spelling, grammar . . . and punctuation.

Although some of the changes in punctuation appear to be an improvement, the systematic replacement of exclamation points by question marks seems to indicate that the second run was more hastily composed, since only one of these replacements is actually appropriate.[15] But this is not enough to conclude that Racine's manuscript was more closely followed, or that Racine himself might have had his say, in preparing the first rather than the second print run. The interesting thing is, however, that the second run shows absolutely no difference in punctuation in the passage we are interested in, Phèdre's Act I Scene 3 final speech.[16] This could simply be a matter of chance, but it could also be a sign that, in both runs, special care was taken to set that particular punctuation correctly.

According to Georges Forestier's notes,[17] the punctuation of this passage stayed the same even in the 1687 and 1697 editions (Forestier 1999b, 1647). Due to their authoritative, complete works status, it is an acknowledged fact that these later editions were revised by Racine, at a time when he was no longer writing for the stage. Forestier claims that the 1697 edition, in particular, tends towards a more syntactic use of punctuation (1999b, 1640). Of course, the unanswerable question remains: even if he had approved of it, was this syntactic shift the work of Racine or the printer's staff? Yet the fact also remains that the punctuation of Phèdre's speech has been identically set from the original 1677 to the authoritative 1697 edition, thus suggesting that its initial function stayed relevant throughout the years.

Keeping this in mind, it is now worth turning from the production process to the destination of the printed text. It is clear that Barbin or Ribou's edition of *Phèdre et Hippolyte* was destined for the use of readers, not actors. Yet as the text passed from the stage to the *salon* or the study, its fundamental oral-aural purpose remained. Indeed, contrary to our 21th-Century habits, reading aloud was the 17th-Century norm, even for scholars who also practiced silent reading.[18] The oral-aural appropriation of the printed text is all the more obvious when the genre calls for it, as is the case for drama, where the habit of reading aloud is reinforced by the typographical setting of the dialogue, as well as by the reader's prior knowledge that the lines were written for the stage, and, possibly, by his memory of having heard them performed—a familiarity which, one might safely presume, was also shared by printer and publisher.

Which brings us back to declamation. Even if the 17th-Century stage and printing house are two separate spaces, they coexist within the same horizon of expectation: the general, rhetorical culture of the spoken word. Reading, pleading, preaching, declaiming, singing—from the wider-spread skill to the more specialized ones, these various modes of public speech are situated along the same, cultural continuum. They follow the same basic, rhetorical principles, including the rules of pausing and breathing according to textual punctuation. Due to the genre's oral-aural destination, these principles apply to the dramatic text regardless of its material support. The playwright's manuscript is destined for stage declamation, the printed play is destined for reading aloud—in both cases, the orality of punctuation stays paramount. One might even argue that the oral-aural code of punctuation may have been more carefully applied in print than in manuscript, considering that, in rehearsal, the playwright's possible carelessness for written punctuation could be compensated for by his verbal indications or by the actor's art and experience, whereas the ordinary reader, facing the silent pages of a book, would have to rely more closely on the rhythmic guidance[19] of printed punctuation. Thus, printed editions may turn out to be the best material for understanding the role of punctuation as an indicator of declamation.

There is no way to reconstitute the original stage performance of *Phèdre et Hippolyte* from the original 1677 edition. The printed punctuation of Act I Scene 3 may or may not be faithful to Racine's. It may or may not be the reproduction of la Champmeslé's pausing and breathing. But as it clearly contributes to what Roger Chartier calls "the collective production of the text" (Chartier 1999, 45), it is as "authentic" and valuable an access to the rhythm of 17th-Century declamation as could be Racine's lost manuscript or a contemporary description of the art of la Champmeslé. Because it can significantly emphasize, enhance, or even add to the performative effects of the dramatic text, printed punctuation plays a key part in the formation of the oral-aural poetics of 17th-Century French drama. As such, it remains a rich and relevant piece of evidence for theater historians and period performers alike.[20]

ENDNOTES

[1] Chaouche, Sabine. 2001. *L'Art du comédien: déclamation et jeu scénique en France à l'âge classique (1629–1680).* Paris: Champion, Lumière classique; Forestier, Georges. 1999a. "Lire Racine". In Jean Racine, *Théâtre, poésie.* Paris: Gallimard, Bibliothèque de la Pléiade, pp. 1611–1660; Gros de Gasquet, Julia. 2006. *En disant l'alexandrin: l'acteur tragique et son art (XVIIe-XXe siècle).* Paris, Champion, Lumière classique; Bovet, Jeanne. 1998. "L'art de la déclamation classique". In *L'Annuaire théâtral,* 24, pp. 141–154. (To be published in 2011: *Écrire la voix au XVIIe siècle: rhétorique et poétique de la déclamation dans la dramaturgie classique.*)

[2] Grimarest, Jean-Léonor Le Gallois de. 1707. *Traité du récitatif dans la lecture, dans l'action publique, dans la déclamation , et dans le chant. Avec un traité des accens, de la quantité, et de la ponctuation.* Paris: Le Febvre et Ribou; Grimarest, Jean-Léonor Le Gallois de. 1760. *Traité du récitatif dans la lecture, dans l'action publique, dans la déclamation , et dans le chant. Avec un traité des accens, de la quantité, et de la ponctuation. Nouvelle édition corrigée et augmentée de plusieurs remarques necessaires.* The Hague: Pierre Gosse Jr.

[3] Gimarest, Jean-Léonor Le Gallois de. 1706. *Addition à la vie de Mr. de Molière, contenant une Réponse à la Critique que l'on en a faite.* Paris: Le Febvre et Ribou.

[4] "[. . .] il est tems de fixer le goût, & l'usage, s'il est possible, & de commencer à donner des regles pour les conserver." (Grimarest 1707, 2)

[5] "C'étoit une nécessité, qu'avant d'entrer dans le sujet qui m'a déterminé à écrire, je préparasse mon Lecteur sur les trois connoissances dont il a indispensablement besoin pour reciter, déclamer, & chanter : c'est à dire sur les Accens, qui déterminent le son, & la longueur d'une bonne partie de nos silabes; sur la Quantité, qui est la mesure de la prononciation de ces silabes; sur la Ponctuation, qui regle les silences nécessaires pour détacher les expressions, qui forment un discours [. . .]." (Grimarest 1707, 71–72)

[6] " [. . .] de maniere que l'Auditeur puisse plus aisement entendre le sens qu'elles [les expressions] rendent : & pour donner à celui qui prononce le tems de reprendre son haleine à des endroits où le sens de l'Auteur ne soit point interrompu." (Grimarest 1707, 72) For a broader, historical perspective on Western punctuation, cf. Parkes, Malcolm B. 1993. *Pause and Effect: An Introduction to the History of Punctuation in the West.* Berkeley and Los Angeles: University of California Press.

[7] Le Faucheur, Michel. 1657. *Traité de l'action de l'orateur ou De la prononciation et du geste.* Paris: Augustin Courbé. For instance: "[. . .] vous devez prendre garde à vous arrester en des endroits commodes & convenables, c'est à dire aprés deux points, ou pour le moins après une virgule" (Le Faucheur 1657, 169).

[8] "Je ne suis pas d'un assez grand poids pour innover dans cette rencontre [. . .]. Je m'en tiens donc à ce qui est fait : bienheureux encore, si je puis parvenir à faire connoître l'usage que l'on doit faire de la Ponctuation qui est établie." (Grimarest 1707, 48)

[9] "Je répete donc à mon Lecteur, que quand il est obligé de lire, ou de reciter un ouvrage, il doit scrupuleusement s'assujettir à la Ponctuation; en établissant pour principes, que le Point marque la plus longue pause : que les deux Points demandent un moindre repos : que le Point avec la Virgule veut plus de silence que la Virgule, dont la pause est presque imperceptible. Si un Lecteur s'arrête aux endroits où il n'y a aucunes de ces marques, à moins que ce ne soit une transition, il ne se fait point entendre ; & ne peut donner à l'ouvrage d'un Auteur l'esprit, ou l'action qu'il y a voulu mettre." (Grimarest 1707, 69–70)

[10] Riffaud, Alain. 2007. *La Ponctuation du théâtre imprimé au XVIIe siècle.* Genève: Droz, Travaux du Grand Siècle.

[11] For instance, Riffaud has obviously misread Le Faucheur and Grimarest when he claims that in 17th and 18th-Century treatises, the word "punctuation" bears no relation to the textual marks, but only to the art of speech delivery, and should therefore be understood solely as "pausing" or "phrasing" (Riffaud 2007, 43). Since he so profusely quotes the 1707 *Traité du récitatif,* one also wonders why Riffaud limits his case studies to plays published between 1630 and 1660, as if the half-century time gap were irrelevant—not to mention Racine, who is ruled out altogether.

[12] "Il existe malgré tout une séparation entre deux lieux différents (la scène et l'atelier d'imprimerie), avec des pratiques, des traditions et des savoirs distincts. On ne peut pas présupposer aussi rapidement la perméabilité et la correspondance systématique entre ces deux espaces, et faire comme si leur relation n'était pas problématique" (Riffaud 2007, 47).

[13] "Chaque Auteur a sa maniere de ponctuer; & quelque irreguliere qu'elle soit bien souvent, il croit cependant entendre parfaitement la ponctuation. D'ailleurs il en abandonne souvent le soin à des Correcteurs, qui ponctuent presque tous sans reflexion, ou sans connaissance." (Grimarest 1707, 68–69)

[14] Chartier, Roger. 1999. *Publishing Drama in Early Modern Europe.* London: The British Library, The Panizzi Lectures 1998.

[15] Indeed, it is the only replacement question mark that Georges Forestier has retained in his Bibliothèque de la Pléiade edition. For a complete list of discrepancies, as well as the printing history of the original edition, c.f. Barko, Ivan. 1966. "Du nouveau sur l'édition originale de *Phèdre", Australian Journal of French Studies,* 3, pp. 282–311.

[16] Whereas there are quite a few in her opening dialogue with Oenone, which was set by the same compositor as Phèdre's speech (Barko 1966, 309–310).

[17] Forestier, Georges. 1999b. "*Phèdre et Hippolyte:* notice, notes et variantes". In Jean Racine, *Théâtre, poésie.*Paris: Gallimard, Bibliothèque de la Pléiade, pp. 1611–1660.

[18] For further consideration on the private and social functions of reading aloud in the 17th-Century, c.f. Chartier, Roger. 1990. "Loisir et sociabilité: lire à haute voix dans l'Europe moderne". In *Littératures classiques,* 12, pp. 127–147. Cf. also Chartier, Roger. 1996. *Culture écrite et société: l'ordre des livres (XIVe-XVIIIe siècle).* Paris: Albin Michel; as well as the founding work of Martin, Henri-Jean. 1969. *Livre, pouvoirs et société à Paris au XVIIe siècle (1598–1701).* Genève, Droz, 2 vol.

[19] Hawcroft, Michael. 2006. "Points de suspension chez Racine: enjeux dramatiques, enjeux éditoriaux". In *Revue d'histoire littéraire de la France,* 106, 2, pp. 307–335; "[. . .] la ponctuation servait d'aide au lecteur qui pouvait, par ce moyen, imaginer ou recréer une représentation orale du texte dramatique" (333).

[20] Special thanks to Nathaniel Watson for keeping a watchful eye on my sometimes not so idiomatic written English.

Choreography and Cholera: The Extended Life of Dance Notation

NENA COUCH

While working at the Harvard Theatre Collection, I became intrigued by a volume of eighteenth-century dance notations bound together. My initial interest, as a dance historian, was in the notations themselves. They are dances by Anthony L'Abbé composed between 1715 and 1731 and notated and published by Edmund Pemberton. L'Abbé, royal dancing master following George I's accession, created dances celebrating royal birthdays and honoring members of the royal family, and most of the dances in this volume follow the pattern.[1] The dance notations, bound in reverse chronological order, include "The Prince of Wales's Saraband (1731), "Queen Caroline" (1728), "The Prince of Wales" (1727), "Prince Frederick" (1725), "The Canary" (1724), "The New Rigodon" (1723), "Prince William" (1721), "The Princess Ann's Chacone" (1719), "The Princess Amelia" (1718), "The Royal George" (1717), "The Princess Anna" (1716), and "The Princess Royale" (1715).[2] They are, in fact, all of L'Abbé's dances published individually by Pemberton with the exception of "The Prince of Orange" (1733).[3] My first response to this work was to wonder why "The Prince of Orange" was not included. It would, I thought, be interesting to know if the owner was also acquiring other dance works notated and published by Pemberton during this period, including *An essay for the further Improvement of Dancing* (1711) and a number of individual dances by Mr. Isaac. Is there another volume somewhere of Isaac's dances?

But those proved to be questions for another day. As I looked more closely at the volume, I became fascinated by the unusual marginalia in the book, which included copying of text and signature, and medical lore. What, I wondered, did all these markings mean? How and why were they made at all, and why in this book? How, indeed, did a book of such a specialized, technical nature make its way to Columbus? Who had handled this book, and how had they treated it? I found myself looking closely at everything in the text but the text; and in order to understand this marginalia, I wanted to know its provenance.

Two pages from a volume of bound notations of the dances of Anthony L'Abbé, published by Edmund Pemberton between 1715 and 1731, with 18th/19th century marginalia. Harvard Theatre Collection, Houghton Library

The Provenance

My true fascination with this volume began with the inscription on the inside cover: "From Joseph Sullivant. Columbus Ohio through William M. Awl June 26, 1838." Sullivant had given the volume to the American Antiquarian Society where it was recorded in the donation book as "ancient music book."[4] In 1976, the volume was purchased from the American Antiquarian Society by the Harvard Theatre Collection. I was excited because the names of Sullivant and Awl are very important in the history of Columbus. William M. Awl was a highly respected physician and surgeon who came to Columbus in 1833, became the physician of the penitentiary, was appointed superintendent of the Ohio Lunatic Asylum, was named physician for the Ohio Institution for the Education for the Blind, and was an original member of the American Medical Association, among other accomplishments.[5] One of his early achievements was to be the first surgeon west of the Allegheny Mountains to ligate the carotid artery, apparently only the fourth time the procedure had been done in the United States.[6]

Joseph Sullivant was the youngest of the three sons of Lucas Sullivant, founder of Franklinton, the beginnings of Columbus. Lucas Sullivant was a surveyor who was part of the early group who "penetrated the unbroken wilderness which then covered the present State of Ohio."[7] This group encountered numerous challenges including attacks by native Americans, scarcity of provisions, and dangerous wildlife. Lucas settled in Ohio on the west bank of the Scioto River opposite the mouth of the Olentangy, founding Franklinton in 1797.[8] After establishing himself at Franklinton, Sullivant went back to Kentucky where he had previously resided, and married Sarah Starling, the daughter of William and Susanna Lyne Starling. Joseph Sullivant's maternal grandfather was William Starling who came from Virginia where he was raised by a guardian, Colonel William Lyne. He married Lyne's sister Susanna, to the displeasure of her family, and the couple moved to Kentucky, where they settled in Mercer County. Starling was known as an educated, well-read man, and wife Susanna came from an old English family that also valued books and reading.[9] According to Joseph Sullivant's genealogical work based on family tradition, the earliest Starling he identifies is William Starling, Lord Mayor of London in 1670. There appear to be some difficulties with this identification: the Lord Mayor in 1669 was Samuel Starling,[10] not William; however, Samuel was from "the Luton hamlet of Stopsley" in Bedfordshire[11] where Sullivant locates William Starling. Another issue raised by genealogists has to do with Samuel Pepys's statement that "Alderman Starling" had no children[12]; nevertheless, this entry was in 1666, prior to Starling's term as lord mayor and certainly prior to his death, so children were still a possibility.

In any event, on both sides, Sullivant's family had a history of valuing books and reading, and was of sufficient social standing to conceivably participate in dances such as those included in the L'Abbé volume. The eldest Sullivant son, William, became an eminent bryologist whose collection on his death was given to Harvard College.[13] Joseph (1809–1882) was very well-read, interested in sciences, arts, and education.[14] He was instrumental in the founding and development of The Ohio State University (then the Agricultural and Mechanical College), and designed a seal for the infant college that embodied his vision for it—a pyramid with a base of agriculture, above which he placed arts, then science, and finally letters, all of which were topped with the lamp of knowledge.[15]

Joseph started his own quest for knowledge early, attending the first two classical schools in Columbus, a boarding school in Worthington, Ohio, and Ohio University. When Joseph was fifteen years old, in winter 1825 he left Columbus to travel to Center College in Danville, Kentucky. Once he crossed the Ohio River, the trip became very difficult—roads were bad; food, inns, and stage horses were expensive (due to the various kinds of currency in circulation, he discovered toward the end of the trip that he had been cheated on the value of his U. S. bills); and the weather was terrible. Somehow he managed to get to Center College only to find that the roof had burned off the building the night before. Discouraged and now feeling ill, he decided to press on to his grandfather's home in Springfield. A woman who turned out to be his aunt took a look, said she knew he was kin, but which one, and he was welcomed to his grandfather's home.[16] While Joseph does not give details on his relatives' libraries, he does note certain items that caught his attention: pre-Revolutionary war almanacs including one of Benjamin Franklin's *Poor Richard's Almanacs* at his grandfather's[17] and "old British drama" at his uncle Edmund Lyne Starling's.[18] My hope in working on the provenance of this volume was to prove that it was part of a family library brought from England by Sullivant's Starling ancestors. That line of inquiry has not yet been fruitful. However, there are several notations that include "Mercer County" in the volume of dance notations, so it seems very likely that, whether the volume came from family or another source, Sullivant acquired it on a visit to Kentucky.[19]

The Marginalia

Beyond the inscription, there were a number of interesting annotations in the volume, none of which were related to the dances. It is clear from dates written in, that at least some of these annotations were made in the 1830s. At a certain point in time, the dances in the volume were no longer danced, and the notation no longer read. The value of the white space around the notations became greater on the frontier than the notations themselves. Somewhere and sometime between the collection of the L'Abbé dances and when the volume came into Joseph Sullivant's hands, it began to be used as a combination copybook and commonplace book. The blank space on the pages of notation and the versos provided opportunities to practice penmanship and to write down a variety of items of importance. That combination of uses is demonstrated with the first notation in the volume, "The Prince of Wales's Saraband." The first couplet (page of notation) was converted primarily to a practice page for capital letters with flourishes. Under the title is written "he is a Saraband Prince" with at least the word Prince appearing to be an effort to copy the printed Prince of the title. On the verso of the title page, the title page information for the second edition of *Patterson's Church Music* published in Cincinnati in 1815 is copied.

The second couplet serves more the copybook function again, with several signatures including R. S. Sutherland and John A. Meeks. At the bottom of the page is a Southern saying, "I am as mad as an old wet hen," followed by "and have been all day," possibly in a different hand. The verso of that couplet and recto and verso of the third couplet are entirely covered with a long Biblical passage, John 12:1–20, from the King James Version. However, there are a few differences such as "Bethlehem" for "Bethany" and "merical" for "miracle" that would lead one to think that the writer copied from another miscopied version or perhaps wrote while someone else read. On the last page of the tract, and not in relation to it, is written "1828." The hand for this Biblical passage is different from the hands of our copybook writers, and, while difficult to date, appears to have been written with a quill and has characteristics of a later eighteenth-, early nineteenth-century American hand.[20]

And finally, the verso of couplet four was again used to practice penmanship, several of the six names with multiple efforts—John A. Meeks (4), I. C. Reall (3), and R. S. or Robert S. Sutherland (3). Meeks and Sutherland provided valuable information by also including "Mercer County" which makes a direct link to Sullivant's maternal family home.

One of the most tantalizing annotations is on the first couplet for "Prince William"—"Prince William is a scoundrel." Prince William was the second son of George II, born in 1721 when the dance was composed; he died in 1765. He had a number of titles including Duke of Cumberland, but history has given him another name. Cumberland received a military commission at an early age. His reputation was set when, victorious in a bloody battle at Culloden against Charles Edward Stuart's Jacobite forces in 1746, he ordered the hunting down and execution of survivors, and very quickly became known as "the Butcher."[21] How tempting it is to wish that the annotation was written after Culloden and before William's death—that it was a contemporary indictment.

There are other interesting phrases and passages, but I found two particularly fascinating: "Indian Remedy for Cholera," and "Crertain [sic] Cure for a Snake Bite." The snake bite treatment was contributed to the volume by another Sutherland—James—on 8 July 1832. In combination with the Mercer County annotations, the snake bite cure securely places the volume in Kentucky with the use of bark from the blue ash tree. According to the cure, the blue ash bark can be used both topically on the sore and drunk as a tea. In *The North American Sylva* (1819), F. Andrew Michaux describes the tree as found only in Tennessee, Kentucky, and southern Ohio. In listing its uses—carriage frames, house flooring, exterior covering, and sometimes roof shingles—he also provides some evidence for a variation of Sutherland's cure using leaves instead of bark: "Milk in which the leaves have been boiled is said to be an unfailing remedy for the bite of the rattle-snake;" but wisely goes on to caution, "we may be allowed however to doubt its efficacy till it is attested by enlightened physicians."[22] A certain cure for snake bite would have been of great interest to Joseph Sullivant. In his *Genealogy,* he relates several rattlesnake stories. Lucas told him a story of being on the Scioto River in canoes and "encounter[ing] a most peculiar and sickening odor. . . ." which was revealed to be a "prodigious number of snakes, principally rattle snakes, which, just awakened from their winter torpor, were basking in the spring sunshine."[23] In that same place which came to be known as the Marble Cliff quarries, the snakes continued to hold sway during Joseph's boyhood and he tells several stories of attempts to burn them out, blow them up, and feed them to hogs.[24]

In beginning the exploration into the "Indian Remedy for Cholera" it seemed likely, since the volume had been in Kentucky and there was another treatment clearly fixed in Kentucky, that "Indian" in this context was native American. However, that was not the case. Cholera in the nineteenth century was a very deadly and pervasive disease, and a number of works were published in the century on cholera. One which seems particularly apt to this discussion because it was published in Cincinnati in 1832 is *A Practical Treatise on the History, Prevention, and Treatment of Epidemic Cholera, Designed Both For the Profession and the People* by Daniel Drake, a well-respected and active doctor.[25] In *A Practical Treatise,* Drake gives a brief history of the current epidemic, placing its beginning at the delta of the Ganges River in 1817. Unlike other occurrences, the cholera did not wane, rather it continued for twelve years in India before crossing into Russia in 1829, generally regarded as the first occurrence in Europe, although Drake notes that the disease appeared but did not continue six years earlier near the Caspian Sea. Yet by summer 1830, cholera was on the move north and westward, in England in 1831, devastating Ireland, and violently attacking Paris.[26]

Drake then looks at cholera in the New World, beginning with June 1832, barely six weeks before the date in the preface of his book. Working with gazettes, he examines the ravages of the disease in Quebec and Montreal, and asks whether it is possible that this is a localized occurrence of the disease, one that will not travel south.[27] Nevertheless, he feels that it must be considered as epidemic until proven otherwise, and calls attention to cases of diarrhea and "mild endemic cholera" in Cincinnati, conditions which appeared to be precursors to the virulent epidemic cholera that struck England.[28] And he writes, prophetically for Columbus, "The pestilence may not, however, overspread the United States during the present summer, for it has often lingered a year on the confines of a country without entering, and then made a sudden and mortal irruption."[29]

In India the disease continued, taking a terrible toll. Doctors struggled to find treatments, and when one seemed to work, they hurried to share it. One such treatment was published in the *Bengal Hurkaru,* 10 November [1831] with a 29 October item from Nusseerabad on cholera at Ajmeer in which 233 were taken ill. 174 took the remedy given in the article, and of these, 165 recovered. 68 died—all those who did not take this medicine and six others. The full remedy was given in the article which was republished on 27 June 1832 in *The United States Weekly Telegraph.*[30] On 8 July 1832, it was copied into the Sullivant volume by W. W. T. While there are some minor differences (Salamonia instead of the printed Sal ammonia, unslack instead of unslacked, stoped instead of stopped, etc.), the timing of *The United States Weekly Telegraph* article and the copy make their relationship likely.

In any event, the remedy was timely. If the volume was in Sullivant's possession by 1832, the remedy would have proved useful in 1833 when cholera struck Columbus, running a course from 14 July to the death of the last victim on 29 September.[31] Dr. William Awl, the person who delivered the volume of notations to the American Antiquarian Society on behalf of Joseph Sullivant, had just settled in Columbus in the spring of 1833, and almost immediately was thrown into fighting the cholera epidemic, not only among the public at large but also in the penitentiary. According to a memoir written of him, while Awl primarily used calomel as a treatment, and once saline venous injections, these were "among other things."[32] Could those other things have included the Indian remedy?

So the end result of my provenance search for this volume is that I have not been able to trace its path definitively. There are some possibilities—"Mercer County" written in the volume places it where Joseph Sullivant's Starling relatives settled in Kentucky, a family whose members were known to be well-read and educated, a family which came from English relatives who were well-to-do and might have had dance notation in their libraries.

On the other hand, as an avid reader, Sullivant might well have acquired the volume, either by purchase or gift. The remedy for cholera and the snake bite cure would surely have excited his civic, medical, and botanical interests. In the end, what matters is that this volume clearly had a fascinating extended life over two centuries, documenting not only dances composed by a major eighteenth-century dancing master, but also revealing elements of pioneer life in America and reminding us of the worldwide devastation of epidemic. For me, it serves as a reminder that nothing we do stands alone—that a book, an object, an idea, can be significant, even indispensible, to people in different times for many different reasons.

ENDNOTES

[1] See Moira Goff, "Edmund Pemberton, Dancing-Master and Publisher." *Dance Research: The Journal of the Society for Dance Research* 11.1 (Spring, 1993): 52–81.

[2] There are very few extant copies of these dances. See Meredith Ellis Little and Carol G. Marsh, *La Danse Noble: An Inventory of Dances and Sources* (Williamstown: Broude Brothers Limited, 1992). Little and Marsh have treated the notations in this volume individually.

[3] Pemberton included a Passacaille by Mr. L'Abbé in An essay for the further improvement of dancing. . . . To which is added, three single dances, . . . 1711. For discussion and analysis of L'Abbé, Pemberton and the birthday dances, in addition to Goff's "Edmund Pemberton, Dancing-Master and Publisher" see also Moira Goff and Jennifer Thorp, "Dance Notations Published in England c. 1700–1740 and Related Manuscript Material." *Dance Research: The Journal of the Society for Dance Research*. 9.2 (Autumn, 1991)32–50); Jennifer Thorp and Ken Pierce, "Taste and Ingenuity: Three English Chaconnes of the Early Eighteenth Century." *Historical Dance* 3.3 (1994): 3–16.

[4] Email and pdf of relevant page from AAS 1830s donation book from Tracey Kry, Assistant Curator of Manuscripts & Assistant Reference Librarian, American Antiquarian Society, 7 July 2010.

[5] J. H. Pooley, M.D., *Memoir of William Maclay Awl, M.D., of Columbus, Ohio* (s.l.: s.n., 1876?), 11–13.

[6] Pooley, 9.

[7] Joseph Sullivant, *A Genealogy and Family Memorial* (Columbus: Ohio State Journal Book and Job Rooms, 1874), 104.

[8] Charles C. Cole, Jr., *A Fragile Capital: Identity and the Early Years of Columbus Ohio* (Columbus: Ohio State University Press, 2001), 2; Opha Moore, *History of Franklin County, Ohio* (Topeka: Historical Publishing Co., 1930), 101.

[9] Sullivant, 10–16.

[10] Valerie Hope, *My Lord Mayor: Eight Hundred Years of London's Mayoralty* (London: Weidenfeld and Nicolson, 1989), 186.

[11] Joyce Godber, *History of Bedfordshire* (Bedford: Bedfordshire County Council, 1969), 271.

[12] Samuel Pepys, *Diary of Samuel Pepys*, Vol. II, (London: J. M. Dent & Co., 1906), 98. Entry for Saturday, 8 September 1666.

[13] See William S. Sullivant, *The Musci and Hepaticae of the United States East of the Mississippi River: Contributed to the Second Edition of Gray's Manual of Botany* (New York: George P. Putnam, 1856).

[14] Correspondence to Joseph Sullivant in the Joseph Sullivant Papers deals primarily with scientific and educational topics, including minerals, microscopes, insects, water works, and the foundation of what became The Ohio State University. There is an interesting letter from John J. Audubon as well as correspondence from botanist Asa Gray. Joseph Sullivant Papers, MSS220AV, Ohio Historical Society.

[15] William A. Kinnison, *Building Sullivant's Pyramid: An Administrative History of the Ohio State University, 1870–1907* (Columbus: Ohio State University Press, 1970), 73.

[16] Sullivant, 16–22.

[17] Sullivant, 23.

[18] Sullivant, 68.

[19] Two of Sullivant's notebooks of lists of books are included in the Joseph Sullivant Papers, one of which is only scientific titles, and the other of which has multiple categories; however, it seems likely that the lists must have been started after the volume of dance notations was given to the American Antiquarian Society. The first listing in the categorized notebook under Medical (the first page in the notebook) is *Effects of Hydropathy*, Ed. Johnson, 1846. Joseph Sullivant Papers, MSS220AV, Ohio Historical Society.

[20] I am grateful to Ann Alaia Woods for her consultation on the handwriting in the volume.

[21] W. A. Speck, "William Augustus, Prince, duke of Cumberland (1721–1765)," *Oxford Dictionary of National Biography* (Oxford University Press, 2004), http://www.oxforddnb.com.proxy.lib.ohio-state.edu /view/printable/29455 (accessed 12 June 2010).

[22] F. Andrew Michaux, *The North American Sylva, Or A Description of the Forest Trees, of the United States, Canada and Nova Scotia*. Vol. III. (Philadelphia: Thomas Dobson, 1819), 73–74, http://books.google.com/books?id=2ecnAAAAYAAJ&printsec=frontcover&dq=north+american+sylva&source=bl&ots=hEYjUj4PKq&sig=ah-cSYe-GtpFOQeVCcDoxAia64U&hl=en&ei=UcqWTMeKEc2jnQeQjJGWBw&sa=X&oi=book_result&ct=result&resnum=2&ved=0CBYQ6AEwAQ#v=onepage&q&f=false (accessed 12 June 2010).

[23] Sullivant, 112–113.

[24] Sullivant, 113–114.

[25] Robert G. Paterson, "The Decline of Epidemics in Ohio," *The Ohio State Archaeological and Historical Quarterly* 55.4 (October-December 1946), 311–337, http://publications.ohiohistory.org/ohstemplate.cfm?action=detail&Page=0055311.html&StartPage=310&EndPage=337&volume=55&newtitle=Volume%2055%20Page%20310 (accessed 15 September 2010).

[26] Daniel Drake, A *Practical Treatise on the History, Prevention, and Treatment of Epidemic Cholera, Designed Both for the Profession and the People* (Cincinnati: Corey and Fairbank, 1832), 7–20.

[27] Drake, 23.

[28] Drake, 24–25.

[29] Drake, 25.

[30] "Indian Remedy for Cholera," in "The Cholera Morbus" *United States Weekly Telegraph* 6.15 (27 June 1832), 472–73. http://books.google.com/books?id=waZYAAAAMAAJ&pg=PA472&dq=%22indian+remedy+for+cholera%22&hl=en&ei=HdGWTLLhNp7enQe53Ln_Bg&sa=X&oi=book_result&ct=result&resnum=1&ved=0CC8Q6AEwAA#v=onepage&q=%22indian%20remedy%20for%20cholera%22&f=false (accessed 12 June 2010).

[31] Cole, 24.

[32] Pooley, 11.

Le Bordel and *L'Art De F*****:* Confounding Clues on Title Pages

DANIEL SMITH

This is a tale of two brothels: one seedy, the other sumptuous. It is also a tale of two title pages, title pages that could make a theatre historian salivate over the prospect of piecing together prurient private performances of the past. These are title pages like any other, except for their casually negligent relationship with telling the truth. Smiling lasciviously, one of them offers archaic sexual slang instead of useful information, while the other lists the names and dates and places. It gets specific—maybe too specific. Never trust a title page, especially one from the eighteenth century.

It all started at the Arsenal Library in Paris . . .

The Bibliothèque de l'Arsenal holds a five-volume *recueil factice* that includes the play *Le Bordel* [*The Brothel*] and the ballet parody *L'Art de foutre,* represented on its title page as *L'Art de F****** [i.e., *The Art of F**king*].[1] Each piece has a title page, and *Le Bordel*'s title page identifies a ballet that is attached (i.e., *L'Art de foutre*). The information provided by the title pages playfully suggests that these plays were not performed, but circulated in print to a community of readers in the know. *Le Bordel* and *L'Art de foutre* have been characterized as belonging to the category of clandestine, erotic, or libertine theatre in eighteenth-century France. Scholarly literature on this topic has generally focused on the performance of such plays in private venues for wealthy participants.[2] Yet the title page of *Le Bordel,* along with other paratextual evidence, suggests that the play was not meant to be performed. Paradoxically, the title page of *L'Art de foutre,* along with evidence from the text, also seems to preclude the possibility of performance via over-saturated references to an imaginary performance. The evidence provided by these title pages calls for a revision in our understanding of these plays. First, it may be necessary to distinguish among more nuanced types of obscene plays, rather than employing one category for all erotic drama in eighteenth-century France.[3] Second, the lack of production history suggested by these title pages requires a consideration of other avenues of consumption. Rather than full productions in brothels or private theatres, *Le Bordel* and *L'Art de foutre* were probably read, whether by solitary readers imagining performances or groups of readers for the purpose of laughter and titillation.[4] Viewing these title pages through the lens of book history thus affords a potential recuperation of play-reading in theatre history.

The title page of *Le Bordel* as it appears in this *recueil factice* employs broad humor in identifying the title and genre of the play, a fictive place of publication, an imaginary bookseller, and ridiculous coordinates for a place of purchase, while offering no details about where the play might have been performed. The document reads as follows:

> Le Bordel ou le Jean-Foutre Puni,
>
> Comédie,
>
> À laquelle est joint un BALET en trois scènes
>
> A Ancone
>
> Chez Jean Chouard, à l'Enseigne du Morpion Couronné
>
> MDCC XLVII[5]
>
> [The Brothel, or the Fuck-John punished,
>
> Comedy
>
> To which is joined a BALLET in three scenes
>
> At Ancone
>
> Jean Chouard, at the Sign of the Crowned Crab-louse
>
> 1747]

This page establishes the contents of both part three and part four of the *recueil factice*, stating the title of *Le Bordel* and mentioning the "Ballet in three scenes" that is joined to it, *L'Art de Foutre*. The listed place of publication, Ancone, is a false imprint.[6] While there are towns with the name Ancone in France and in Italy, the name was probably chosen because of its punning similarity to the present tense of the vulgar verb "enconner" (lit. "to enter the vagina"). The fictitious publisher and bookseller's shop is located "at the sign of the crowned crab louse." Given the variety and the quest for notoriety in Parisian sign-making in the eighteenth century, such a sign is not entirely outside the realm of possibility, though it does seem unlikely.[7] A bookseller specializing in clandestine titles would probably not want to draw that kind of attention. Nor would such a bookseller want to be named Jean Chouard, which is a slang term for "penis."[8] As an effort to circumvent state censorship, the creation of fictive places of publication, publishers, and booksellers is not an unusual strategy for obscene texts of eighteenth-century France.[9]

Although no author is listed on the title page, *Le Bordel* is attributed to the Comte de Caylus, a wealthy patron of the arts and connoisseur of the Ancient world who took up engraving as a hobby and apparently became quite skilled at it. Caylus maintained a libertine circle of friends known as the Société du Bout du Banc. Their primary activities appear to have been drinking heavily and sharing Anacreontic poetry with each other. It is probable that *Le Bordel* was read aloud at one of their gatherings, though there is no evidence of this. The testimony of bibliophile Paulmy d'Argenson suggests that *Le Bordel* was not intended to be performed. In his catalogue entry, d'Argenson dates *Le Bordel* "around 1732" and characterizes the play as "pour n'être point représentée" [not to be performed].[10] D'Argenson also paints Caylus as a sort of ethnographer of the Parisian underworld, offering the linguistic

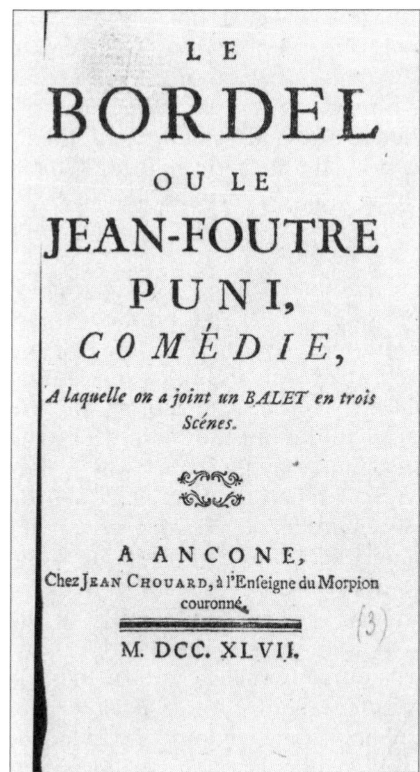

LE

BORDEL

OU LE

JEAN-FOUTRE

PUNI,

COMÉDIE,

A laquelle on a joint un BALET en trois Scénes.

A ANCONE,

Chez JEAN CHOUARD, à l'Enſeigne du Morpion couronné.

M. DCC. XLVII.

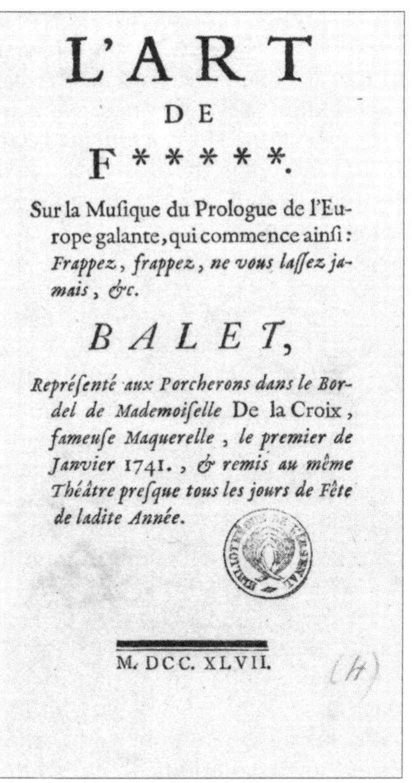

L'ART

DE

F*****.

Sur la Muſique du Prologue de l'Europe galante, qui commence ainſi : *Frappez, frappez, ne vous laſſez jamais, &c.*

BALET,

Repréſenté aux Porcherons dans le Bordel de Mademoiſelle De la Croix, *fameuſe Maquerelle, le premier de Janvier* 1741., *& remis au même Théâtre preſque tous les jours de Fête de ladite Année.*

M. DCC. XLVII.

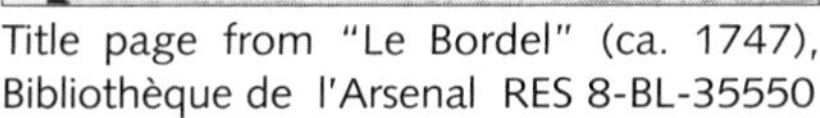

Title page from "Le Bordel" (ca. 1747), Bibliothèque de l'Arsenal RES 8-BL-35550

Title page from "L'Art de F*****" (ca. 1747), Bibliothèque de l'Arsenal RES 8-BL-35550

"saltiness" of the play as a testament to Caylus's intimate knowledge of brothels.[11] Indeed, *Le Bordel* is quite invested in prostitution as a social problem, presenting economic details, raising concerns about venereal disease, and challenging the arbitrary nature of police surveillance and punishment of individual sex workers. But all we get from the title page in the Arsenal's *recueil factice* are dirty jokes.

The title page for *Le Bordel* mentions a ballet in three scenes that is attached, but does not give the title of the ballet in question. The title page of the latter text claims that it was performed in the brothel of Mademoiselle De la Croix on New Year's Eve, 1741, and reprised on all feast days of that year. This seductive documentation has led scholars to classify *L'Art de foutre* as part of a tradition of clandestine erotic performance in eighteenth-century France.[12] But this document's flirtations with history are frustrating; nearly every clue to performance history is counterbalanced by ironic excess. The printer's advertisement that copies can be purchased "at the sign of the crowned crab louse" employs a typical tactic of clandestine publishing, here taken to a ridiculous extreme. The lush and lascivious stage directions flout the bounds of possibility, but it is possible to read these as taking poetic license. A cast list on the second page has been annotated to list the famous prostitutes who ostensibly starred in the performance, but the date of this annotation is unclear. Baculard d'Arnaud, the author listed on other (non-extant) print versions, spent some time in the Bastille for having written such smut. The documents related to his arrest focus entirely on the illicit printing of the obscene text and not on the performance. After a tortuous search for corroborating evidence, I have concluded that *L'Art de foutre* was probably not in fact performed, at least not under the conditions suggested on its title page.

While *Le Bordel* purportedly presents a fictional brothel, *L'Art de foutre* is ostensibly an entertainment created for an actual Parisian brothel. A parody of the prologue of *L'Europe galante*, an opera by André Campra with a libretto by Houdar de la Motte, *L'Art de foutre* revels in luxury, presenting sensationalist spectacle after sensationalist spectacle. After noting the title as "L'Art de F****" and indicating the place in the musical score where the parody should begin, the title page proclaims that the ballet was in fact performed at a brothel: "Représenté aux Porcherons dans le Bordel de Mademoiselle De la Croix, fameuse Maquerelle, le premier de janvier 1741., & remis au même théâtre presque tous les jours de Fête de ladite Année."[13] ["Represented at Porcherons, in the brothel of Mademoiselle De la Croix, famous bawd, the first of January 1741, and remounted at the same theatre almost every Feast Day of that year."] The asterisks now strike me as odd, given that the word "foutre" is spelled out on the title page of *Le Bordel*. Scholars who have written about *L'Art de foutre* tend to take this statement at its word, mining police records not only for evidence of author Baculard d'Arnaud's stay in the Bastille, but also for discussions of Mademoiselle De la Croix's post-performance fate. Robert Dawson speculates that she wound up in Bicêtre hospital or the Mississippi colony.[14] This latter piece of information is, alas, not to be found there.

The librarian at the Arsenal pegged me right away. She had seen my type before. "You want the Archives of the Bastille, don't you?" Dawson had told me where to look.[15] *He had also mentioned that the documents would mostly tell me about Baculard's friend Harnoncourt, who funded the printing. I thought I heard a hint about Mademoiselle de la Croix. But no dice. Then I started figuring about her name, and it came to me. What do the French call it when you sign your name with an "X"? "Marquer d'une croix." So Mademoiselle de la Croix might just be Madam X.*

Maintaining the pretense of an actual performance in a brothel, the cast of characters is listed, with names disguised by asterisks, followed by "whore," "second whore," "third whore," etc. The full names of prostitutes have been hand written in faded ink above the asterisks:

> Mademoiselle de la C**** [Croix], Maquerelle
>
> Mademoiselle P**** [Petit] la jeune, Putain
>
> Mademoiselle Le S**** [Le Sueur], autre putain
>
> Mademoiselle DuP****** [DuPlessis], troisieme putain
>
> Mademoiselle R******* [Rouselle], quatrieme putain
>
> Mademoiselle M***** [not listed], cinquieme putain

Mademoiselle L'E******* [L'Empereur], sixieme putain

Mesdemoiselles A********[Antonia], R****, & J****[Joly], garces

This style is reminiscent of the roman à clef. Literally "a novel with a key," a *roman à clef* is a novel whose characters are based on actual historical people.[16] Here, the names remain unlisted to create an aura of scandal. The owner has ostensibly filled in the names of infamous prostitutes of the day. But which owner? And what day? Is the annotator the first owner of the book from 1747? Was the annotator looking back on 1741? Did he or she fill in the names of famous sex workers from 1741, 1747, or some later date?

The remainder of the dramatis personae introduces a level of vulgar humor that begins to approach the level of absurdity of the title page of *Le Bordel*:

Monsieur d'A****, Commissaire

Choeur des Garces, Maquerelles, Maquereaux, & Piliers de Bordel, tirés des Comédies Françoise et Italienne & de l'Opera.

Mousquetaires. [Musketeers]

Fouteurs, au nombre de six. [Fuckers, numbering six.]

Archers, qu'on ne voit pas, mais qu'on entend. [Policemen, who are not seen, but heard.]

Suite des Garces à cul et des Laveuses de vit. [Entourage of Ass-sluts and Dick-washers.]

The most intriguing of these entries for a theatre historian is "Chorus of Sluts, Madams, Pimps, and Regulars of the Brothel, drawn from the Comédie-Française, the Comédie-Italienne, and the Opera." Calling on the authority of the three major theatre troupes would appear to be an effort to raise the status of this text, or to tear down the status of the official theatres. It seems unlikely, however, that members of these troupes would be available for a performance in a brothel several times throughout the year. Rather, casting such actors and actresses in this ballet draws on stereotypes about actors' and actresses' libertinism and the sexual availability of actresses.[17] This bit of casting, taken in tandem with the shift to obscene language, arguably subverts the verisimilitude of *L'Art de F*****'s* title page.

If the cast list challenges the title page's authority, the stage directions weaken it further. The opening stage directions call for the addition of thirty-six prostitutes not specified in the dramatis personae (but probably drawn from the ranks of the official theatres) to present the Postures of Aretino in the background, while the six main prostitutes are downstage, *"toutes dans des postures différentes, et prêtes à être foutuës"*[18] [*"All in different positions, and ready to be fucked"*]. As the "six elected fuckers" prepare for the sexual encounter, the Madam begins to sing. The six prostitutes repeat a variant of her verse, and then the Chorus joins in. Further stage directions specify:

Les six Putains avancent et les six Fouteurs; cela forme une scene muette. Deux des Fouteurs ne bandent point; deux putains leur mettent la main au vit, et tâchent de rappeller chez eux la nature. Des autres fouteurs qui bandent, l'un

veut foutre en charette brisée, l'autre en levrette, ainsi du reste; le tout est accompagné de lassis et de cadences charmantes.[19]

[*The six Prostitutes advance, and so do the six Fuckers; this forms a dumb-show. Two of the Fuckers do not get erections; two prostitutes take their cocks in hand and work to bring nature back to them. Of the other fuckers who are hard, one wants to fuck in the style of the broken chariot (?), another doggie-style, and so on for the rest; all this is accompanied by charming lazzi and cadences.*]

The stage directions call for a specific number of men to have erections and to not have erections at this point (four and two, respectively). While it is possible that the text attempts a metaphorical recording of an event that took place in Mademoiselle de la Croix's brothel on one occasion, it strikes me as unlikely that this event could be repeated on each feast day with this precise proportion of erectile functionality. It would be possible to use fake phalli to stage this scene.

After the departure of the Commissioner, the musketeers pair off with the 36 prostitutes in the background, which makes for a total of 72 supernumeraries. As Robert Dawson points out, "There would seem to have been precious little room for spectators."[20] The stage directions at the end of the ballet combine the sublime and the ridiculous: "*On fout; il se fait là une décharge générale de foutre, qui forme le plus beau coup du Théâtre du monde.*" ["*Everyone fucks. There is a general discharge of semen, which makes the most beautiful coup de théâtre in the world.*"][21] After a brief song by a female soloist, the action is repeated: "*On fout encore, à peu près, dans la même situation que la première fois; toute la différence qui s'y trouve, c'est que la décharge dure plus long-tems, & que les culetis sont plus répétés: un silence profond accompagne l'action.*" ["*Everyone fucks again, basically in the same situation as the first time; the only difference is that the orgasm lasts longer, and the thrusting is more frequent: a profound silence accompanies the action.*"][22] Again, these stage directions bask in sensual luxury and the preposterous. The absurdity of these stage directions undermines the factual value of the title page.

In analyzing these two plays' potential for production, the data remain frustratingly unclear. Paratextual evidence related to *Le Bordel* is inconclusive, though there are some indications that the play was not produced. The preface to *Le Bordel* indicates that it had not been performed at the time it was published, though not rejecting the possibility of production. However, Paulmy d'Argenson characterizes it as not being intended for performance. The ridiculous stage directions of *L'Art de foutre* seem to contradict the assertion on the title page that it was presented at Mademoiselle de la Croix's brothel on New Year's and all feast days in 1741. Evidence related to the possibility of productions of *Le Bordel* and *L'Art de foutre* exhibits opposite approaches to the question of theatrical performance, with the Preface to *Le Bordel* stating that it was not performed and the title page of *L'Art de foutre* claiming that it was played in a brothel. Both title pages are tricky. While the texts present visions of a Parisian underworld that would tantalize any film noir detective, the title pages create a nearly impenetrable mystery for theatre historians. That mystery, I contend, is best solved by appealing to the idea of play readers rather than performers and spectators.

ENDNOTES

[1] Bibliothèque de l'Arsenal, RES 8–BL-35550.

[2] A starting point for most research in this area is G. Capon and R. Yve-Plessis, *Paris galant au XVIIIe siècle: Les Théâtres clandestins* (Paris: Plessis, 1905). Karl Toepfer, *Theatre, Aristocracy, and Pornocracy: The Orgy Calculus.* (New York: PAJ Publications, 1993) insists on the play texts' potential for inciting orgy. A focus on visual display is developed by Céline Santini, "Théâtralité et exhibition dans le théâtre pornographique du XVIIIe siècle" *Cahiers d'histoire culturelle* 5 (1999): 39–48. Other scholars have analyzed political aspects of erotic theatre, notably Michèle Bokobza Kahan, "Entre licence et conformisme: Etude sur les théâtres érotiques de société au XVIIIe siècle." *Studi Francesi* 47.1 (March-April 2003): 90–98. Most recently, Laurence Senelick has argued that these plays anticipate Diderot's dramatic theory by allowing for improvisation. See Senelick, "The Word Made Flesh: Staging Pornography in Eighteenth-Century Paris." *Theatre Research International* (Summer 2008): 192–203.

[3] Marie-Emanuelle Plagnol-Diéval offers a distinction between "erotico-scatological" plays and "pretext-for-sexual-exhibition" plays. See Plagnol-Diéval, *Le Théâtre de société: un autre théâtre?* (Paris: Champion, 2003).

[4] Thomas Wynn theorizes a solitary reader mentally staging erotic plays "in a private and imaginary theatre." See Wynn, *Sade's Theatre: Pleasure, Vision, Masochism* (Oxford: Voltaire Society, 2007), 195.

[5]Bibliothèque de l'Arsenal RES 8–BL-35550, vol. 3.

[6] On false imprints in the eighteenth century, see Jim Mitchell, "Investigating False Imprints," Eds. M. Crump and M. Harris, *Searching the Eighteenth Century*, (London: British Library Board, 1983) 43–58; and Treadwell, Michael. "On False and Misleading Imprints in the London Booktrade, 1660–1750," Robin Myers and Michael Harris, eds. *Fakes and Frauds: Varieties of Deception in Print and Manuscript* (New Castle, DE: Oak Knoll Press, 1989) 29–46.

[7] Indeed, a character in *Le Bordel* makes a joke about a certain locksmith named Ledru, which is similar to the name of the proprietress of the eponymous brothel. Ledru's sign-maker had apparently created a sign that said "Ledru pose des sonnettes dans le cul-de-sac" ["Ledru makes bells in the cul-de-sac] but arranged the "de-sac" portion such that viewers at first glance saw "Ledru pose des sonnettes dans le cul" ["Ledru puts belles in his ass."] According to Louis-Sébastien Mercier, this sign made Ledru's fortune, as the double entendre made his shop fashionable. See Mercier, "L'orthographe public" in *Tableau de Paris*, ed. Jean-Claude Bonnet, vol. 1 (Paris: Mercure de France, 1994) 100–103.

[8] See Walter Kelly's note on Mahérault's successful French translation of Catullus in *Erotica: The Poems of Catullus and Tibullus*, ed. and trans. Walter K. Kelly (London: G. Bell, 1880), 94.

[9] See Patrick Wald Lasowski, "Les Enfants de la messe de minuit," Eds. Marie-Françoise Quignard and Raymond-Josué Seckel, *L'Enfer de la bibliothèque: Eros au secret* (Paris: Bibliothèque Nationale de France, 2007), 39. Lasowski cites an earlier version of *Le Bordel* also ostensibly published at Ancone, but sold "Chez La Veuve Grosse-Motte" [The Widow Large-Muff].

[10] René Louis de Voyer de Paulmy, marquis d'Argenson, *Notices sur les ??uvres de Théâtre*, ed. H. Lagrave. *Studies on Voltaire and the Eighteenth Century* XLII (Genève: Insitut et Musée Voltaire Les Delices, 1966) 397.

[11] This aspect of *Le Bordel* is discussed in Manuel Herrman, *Count de Caylus: A Remarkable 18th Century Polygraph* (PhD Diss. Case Western Reserve University, 1972) 494.

[12] See, most recently, Laurence Senelick, "The Word Made Flesh: Staging Pornography in Eighteenth-Century Paris." *Theatre Research International* (Summer 2008): 192–203. A performance history based almost entirely on the evidence of the title page and the text is

found in G. Capon and R. Yve-Plessis, *Paris galant au XVIIIe siècle: Les Théâtres clandestins* (Paris: Plessis, 1905).

[13] Recueil factice, BA RES 8–BL-35550, 120.

[14] See Robert Dawson, *Baculard d'Arnaud: Life and Prose Fiction* (Oxford: Voltaire Foundation, 1976), 55–59.

[15] Archives de la Bastille, Ms. 11480, ff. 125–239.

[16] The name derives from keys that circulated, purporting to match the characters with the persons they represented. There are few general introductions to *roman à clef* as a concept. Most studies indicate particular novels as belonging to the *roman à clef* genre. An interesting comparative perspective on European *roman à clef* and "historical referentiality" in Chinese fiction is found in Jue Chen, "Poetics of Historical Referentiality: Roman à Clef and Beyond." (PhD Diss., Princeton University, 1997).

[17] See Lenard Berlanstein, *Daughters of Eve: A History of Theater Women from the Old Regime to the Fin-de-Siecle* (Cambridge: Harvard University Press, 2001).

[18] RES 8–BL-35550, 123.

[19] Ibid., 129.

[20] Dawson 57.

[21] RES 8-BL-35550, 130.

[22] Ibid., 130.

Determining Whether the Český Krumlov Slapstick is "Just the Thing" or "Just a Thing"

PAUL J. STOESSER

In September 2001 the Gardiner Museum of Ceramic Art in Toronto presented an exhibition, *Harlequin Unmasked,* in conjunction with which the author was engaged to design *The World of Harlequin: Then and Now,* a commedia dell'arte-style performance. Among the many outstanding international pieces curator Meredith Chilton had gathered for the exhibition was a slapstick, one of the pre-eminent commedia dell'arte artifacts from the collection of Castle Český Krumlov in the Czech Republic. Since the production[1] required a functioning slapstick for a variety of scenes involving Arlecchino and, as neither detailed dimensions nor descriptions of the mechanism of this device were readily available in the commedia dell'arte literature,[2] I obtained permission to examine and to measure, but not to operate, this unique specimen dating from the mid-eighteenth century.

This paper details the results of that examination. Like many good detective stories and much archival work, this examination involves doubling back. In this instance, the doubling back necessitated a review of assumptions that seem to be automatically attached to artifacts which by their mere presence, their very being, are often imbued with misconstrued values that more often than not mislead the theatre historian. The present investigation utilizes this extraordinary commedia dell' arte theatre property, like a backward-looking telescope, to peer from this side of the "scrim of modernity"[3] through the (literal) dust into practical performance conditions surrounding the evolving use of Arlecchino's slapstick or *batocio.*

According to many of my native Italian *amici,* including a professionally trained Arlecchino from the Lombard town of Brescia,[4] *batocio* is a mercurial Italian term which derives from the verb *battere* meaning to beat.[5] The batocio, known by many names and in several guises, becomes in English "a flexible, divided lath"[6] or as Chilton refers to it, a "flapstick" and more commonly a slapstick. It has also been referred to in Italian as a "dagger of lath."[7] In France it is generally known as *la batte* and in some instances as *un couteau de bois* or wooden knife[8] while in the southern part of the country it is also known as *coustelo*[9] where it shares an affinity with the *échanvroir* which is a simple wooden bat-like utensil employed for separating retted hemp fibres.[10] This association connects the "classical" Arlecchino character with the regional character of Petassou, himself a derivative of the *uomo selvaggio* tradition, and a character that in engravings, paintings, and stonework is invariably depicted with some form of a wooden club.[11] Furthermore, there is a credible genealogy linking the batocio as a typical property used by early Roman comedians as well as in earlier Etruscan and Greek dramas.

Other than one extreme application, tenuously supported by a probable late seventeenth century Parisian production by Evaristo Gheraldi called "*Arlequin Mercure Galant,*" in which the batocio is connected to the magical powers of the mythological Mercury's caduceus,[12] the commedia dell'arte employed the batocio as a realistic object for natural purposes only. In this regard the expansive and authoritative *Enciclopedia dello spettacolo* introduces an altogether different term in describing Arlecchino's *spatola* thus: "Also the paddle serves clownishly as a most antique scepter, translates farcically into the club of Hercules, as well as becomes the necessary spatula required to stir the copper pot of the traditional food of the Bergamo peasant, polenta."[13] Goldoni introduces him thus: "I am Arlechin Batocio/ Blind in one ear and deaf in one eye."[14] Whether used as a club in the manner of Hercules, as a scepter or spoon, or as a vulgar extension of his virility, the batocio or slapstick as underscored in these passages is undoubtedly the most multi-functional and important as well as the most iconically definitive stage property of the Arlecchino mask.

My immediate difficulties in reproducing this property seemed to have been surmounted since the exhibition batocio was "just the thing." With the data derived by inspection and my expertise as designer, technical director, and craftsman, the task of reproducing the Český Krumlov batocio appeared to be relatively uncomplicated. The following review of the physical characteristics of this unique specimen provides a more complete understanding of its construction and operation.

The most salient physical attributes of the Český Krumlov artifact are that it appears to be constructed from a single piece of wood, 457.2 millimeters in length overall, 45.0 mm wide, and 31.8 mm thick, and significantly with four, not two, battens or slats. The handle portion, including the end boss or pommel is 193.7 mm in length which creates a ratio of approximately 1:3 with the blade. The blade, consisting of twice as many battens or slats as usually associated with this device, has been formed to the hilt of the handle by three relatively parallel rip cuts through the edge of the wood. In the photographic image these cuts are more readily discernible under magnification. An extremely thin saw created these cuts since the resulting kerfs, or spaces, are only 2.0 mm wide at the end. These battens are slightly tapered in thickness along their length, which may be deliberate, or the result of inaccurate cutting. The grain below the heavily patinated surface is very smooth, consistently fine and partly flecked, and is characteristic of a hardwood like maple (*Acer campestre*) found throughout northern Europe. This species of wood, often used for the necks and neck supports in stringed instruments such as violins and guitars, is valued by musical instrument makers for its stability, strength, and sonorous qualities. The anomalous presence of two wooden

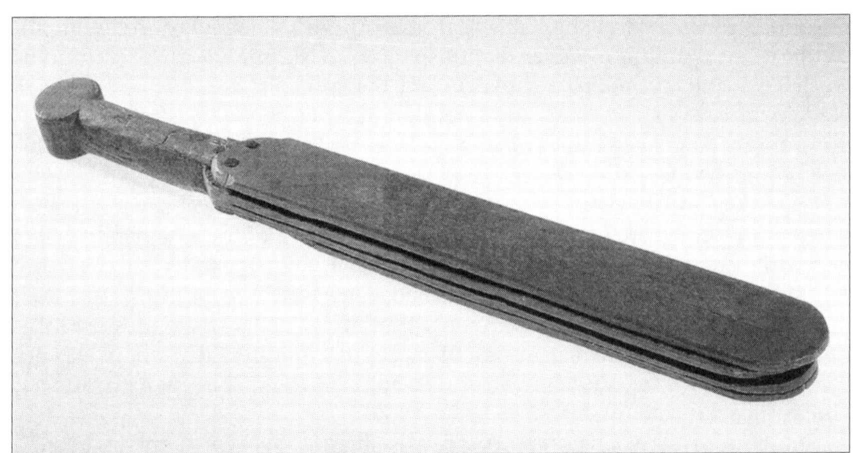

Commedia dell'Arte Batocio, mid-18th Century. Castle Český Krumlov, Czech Republic.

pins in the surface at the juncture of the handle and the blades is the result of a repair to the top batten which at some time had been broken from the main body. Close inspection revealed that the top batten in fact is a replacement piece and not part of the original batocio. Thus the presence of the pins leads us to see them as necessary for the restoration of the piece but not necessarily for its normal functioning as a theatrical property.[15]

Based on the derived information a modern version of this specimen was constructed and then, with great anticipation, operated. Replicating the Český Krumlov data did not, however, result in a functioning batocio that performed according to our expectation. At best this reproduction generated a modest clap but nothing remotely like the anticipated loud crack, or slap, that we have come to associate with such devices. The urgent return to the drawing board was confounded by the dearth of literature. The paucity of descriptive documentation regarding commedia artifacts yielded neither an account of its size nor a description of its simple mechanics. In the absence of available written accounts there were numerous illustrations of Arlecchino in a range of media and more importantly these depictions cover almost the entirety of the history of this mask.[16]

In the Musée Municipal de Bayeux France a painting believed to date from 1572 by the Bruges artist Francis Porbus[17] is the earliest known illustration of Arlecchino.[18] He is somewhat obscured by the grouping which foregrounds Charles IX performing with members of his court in costume and consequently Arlecchino cannot be determined to have any batocio-like property with him.[19] We do want to believe that he does.

Among the earliest commedia illustrations, Arlecchino is well represented in the remarkable forty-two engraved plates of the *Receuil Fossard* (1577)[20] where, no less than fifteen times, he is depicted in a somewhat ragged white costume randomly covered with irregular and variously shaded patches. He wears his leather bag or purse known as a *scarsela*,[21] his felt cap often trimmed with a feather,[22] as well as his dark half mask, and, in these illustrations a short, sword-shaped object is an unmistakable accoutrement. All of these are defining physical features of the mask known as Arlecchino as we have come to understand them.[23] In Fossard's illustrations Arlecchino's batocio is always short, sharp, and pointed. Its impression is definitely that of a weapon-like dagger rather than a club or even the slapstick that we typically equate with the character.

Less than thirty years later in Tristano Martinelli's *Compositions de Rhétorique* (1601), Arlecchino is still represented with all of these same attributes but with some noticeable changes.[24] Although still dressed in motley, the two-piece suit has finished and trimmed edges and the patches are much more regular in their mostly geometrical patterning. Most significant to this investigation is that the dagger-like property from earlier illustrations has become more rounded and less harmful in appearance. If it is not a slapstick, it at least has bat-like qualities.

Subsequent early seventeenth century illustrations represent the batocio as very plain and about as long as the actor's forearm, rounded at the end, and tapering gently towards the handle. In only a few instances is the split between the battens apparent.[25] By the end of the century depictions of Arlecchino regularly represent fine and fitted tailoring of the suit constructed of exact geometrical triangle or diamond shapes separated by raised piping. Consistent with this appearance the slapsticks too have more refined features as indicated by the increasing ornamentation of the handles.[26] These refinements have the effect of enhancing an element of swagger perhaps because they have become significantly longer—often as long as the actor's arm.[27] Sticks of this size suggest that they were even used to lean on or employed as walking sticks.[28] Supporting this last idea is the asymmetrical pommel, which is more characteristic of the handle of a gentleman's walking stick.[29] On the basis of this synopsis of the illustrated history of Arlecchino, three physical attributes including the batocio, the costume, and the facial half-mask are unquestionable critical visual components of the characterizations. Nevertheless, these mute considerations do not provide any evidence of when the batocio created, if ever, the loud crack that we have come to associate with it. The following comparative attribution is helpful in understanding some of the dramaturgical processes at work:

> In Martinelli's *Compositions de Rhetorique* one illustration [shows] Arlecchino no longer in his more old-fashioned white costume, threadbare and full of patches. Kneeling, with his head uncovered, his cap between his joined hands he begs in a pose in which it is possible to note his stereotypical character, as it is evident by comparing it with the known image from previous years included in the *Recueil Fossard*.[30]

The changing representation of the mask underscores the suppliant yet more devious characterization in *Compositions de Rhetorique* with the naïve simplicity of the Arecchino representation in the *Recueil Fossard*.[31]

This foreshortened history demonstrates in my view of the evidence, a consistency in the characteristics of the mask[32] but at the same time a profusion of batocio styles—all of which complicated our production's immediate practical concerns. Archival dust made way for the sawdust of the woodshop lab as various experimental models were replicated, tested, and refined. In all, five other prototypes, including one with as many as five battens but most with only two, were constructed based on the derived data. All test models were similar in both width and thickness to the original while their lengths varied from 444.5 mm to 558.8 mm. For reasons of economy these prototypes were produced primarily in those softwoods such as pine, spruce, and cedar usually associated with theatre scene shops. Had any one of them functioned reasonably close to expectation, it would have then been reproduced in maple like the one from Castle Český Krumlov. The most successful early results were obtained with a long, double batten that was hinged with leather between the blade and the handle.[33] In addition to the prototypes, at least as many more provisional attempts made it only as far as the scrap bin.

Differences in the species of wood, the relative elasticity of the material, and the overall length are the primary structural and technical considerations in all of these attempted reproductions but the central concern is the critical action of the lever. In its simplest form, the batocio is a hinged mechanism that is a kind of a lever operated by rapidly snapping the wrist. This action causes the battens to open on the backstroke and close on the forestroke. Practically speaking, the quicker and more forceful the snap of the wrist, the more explosive the sonic "crack" created by the instantaneous snapping together of the battens, not unlike hands clapping, or in Italian, *battere le mani*. The disappointment in the Český Krumlov reproduction's inability to generate this sonic crack caused a reconsideration of my predicament on two levels. Certainly the most pressing was to solve the immediate need—an impending opening night does spur one towards practical and timely solutions—but I was intrigued by the larger issue of how much I had believed that this reproduction would work. After all, the data had been obtained from "just the thing"—an actual batocio.

Practical solutions required revisiting the physics of the device by specifically examining the lever action. As one of the six simple machines that make work easier to accomplish, levers do so by moving a load around a pivot using a force. In the Český Krumlov batocio the hinge in front of the handle at the juncture of the battens acts as the fulcrum, or the pivot, of a class I lever as in the see-saw or teeter-totter and this type of lever is defined by the placement of the fulcrum at any point between the effort and the load. With the slapstick hinged at the end, that is to say behind the hand instead of in front of it, the resulting action is that of a class III lever. Examples of this class include tongs and tweezers and the class is defined by the application of the effort anywhere between the fulcrum and the load.[34]

For the production a hybrid but suitably explosive batocio of two battens was ultimately developed by mounting a 2.4 mm. thick piece of Brazilian rosewood (*Dalbergia nigra*), an equatorial rainforest hardwood, to an 8.0 mm. thick piece of white pine (*Pinus strobus*), a northern hemisphere softwood. These two 558.8 mm. long pieces were positively connected by affixing them at the extreme end as in a class III lever configuration with two flush-mounted 4.8 mm. diameter threaded machine bolts. Notwithstanding

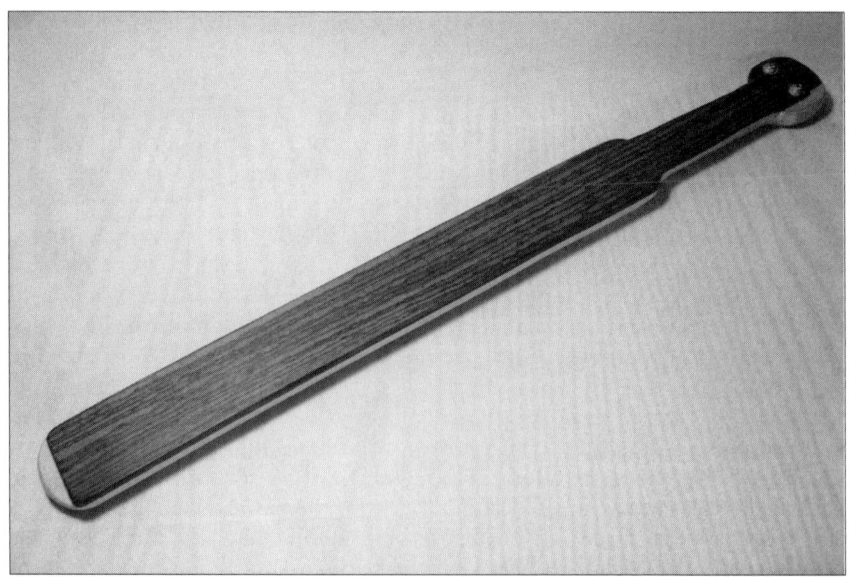

Commedia dell'Arte Batocio, 21st Century. Paul J. Stoesser, Toronto.

obvious dissimilarities with the carefully measured artifact, it nevertheless performed to our expectation.

The success of this solution is largely due to the significant difference in the coefficients of elasticity between the two different wood species. The relative rigidity of the pine base and the extreme flexibility and durability of the rosewood batten combined to provide the performer with both the sonic and operational qualities required for performance. With the hinge at the end of the slapstick, the performer had ultimate control over the entire slapstick and therefore could rapidly slide it into his belt without the anxiety of it inadvertently opening or being misdirected. In performance this style of connection proved optimum, especially in comparison with those other models tested with the hinge in front of the handle. Our Arlecchino took to the stage with his batocio in his belt just as the early Arlecchino wore "in his belt a stocky wooden sword, the harmless stage prop which later transformed into the classic 'slapstick.'"[35]

This investigation into the practical operation of the slapstick indicates that the mask of Arlecchino changes over time. If we postulate three stages (obviously and without question such transformations are infinitely more subtle) through the changing dress and habit, we can perceive similar changes in the use of the batocio. These changes represent a gradual but significant modification in performance styles from rough buffoonery to impish knavery and ultimately to a point of refined gentility. In this last developmental phase the underlying historical character traits would have been recognized, understood, and accepted by the audience. Several protagonist characterizations of this kind are found in the works of Goldoni, Gozzi, and Moliere as well as in the earliest Commedia scenarios of Flaminio Scala.

In addition to functioning as one of the principal visual identifiers for the mask, the batocio was utilized dramaturgically for provoking or changing actions onstage such as in the following examples of "prototypal scenarios" where it factors directly into

> an extremely effective exit technique, since it is usual for the characters to exit fighting [. . .]
>
> *Arlecchino to revenge Pedrolino's slap; he sees him and beats him up; everyone draws a weapon, and they go off up the street fighting.*
>
> Alternatively, the fight has begun offstage, and the combatants are separated by a third party.[36]

Based on this admittedly contracted history we can ascribe to Arlecchino in his buffoon phase a defensive weapon as represented in the engravings of the *Receuil Fossard* and not necessarily a batocio; in the knavish phase, a batocio as we have come to think of it; and in the later stages of the character, a property that can still be described as a batocio but one used for more refined purposes, and not for the roguery of early Arlecchinos. Consequently, since the eighteenth century Český Krumlov specimen belongs to this later phase, the slapstick was conceivably modified to produce a polite clap rather than the conjectured explosive snap of its earlier forms.

The "tyranny" then to which we are most susceptible in this historical investigation is not the document, but rather our dramaturgical compression of over two hundred years of this character's practical on-stage development with the short-hand ascription of iconic merit to the thing. That it was not "the" thing for our needs, and that some other solution suited our expectations better, only underscores the over-riding need to question the document or artifact in context and not in isolation. An early point of reference for this investigation insists that the rules of evidence are as critical to the theatre historian as they are to the jurist. It encourages the historian to ensure that evidence is obtainable, fully represented, accurately represented,[37] and then subjected to rigorous cross-examination, always cautioning against the privileging of documents isolated from their original performance context with present day assumptions whether scholarly or practical. That is to say that evidence fully represented and examined in context is the most effective way to minimize conclusions founded simply on the existence of a document or an artifact. The tyranny for me was my belief of how the Český Krumlov batocio should have sounded. Had it produced the expected loud crack, it would have been "just the thing."

> Le coq a chanté Cric, crac, mon conte est achevé!
>
> —Arlequin

ENDNOTES

Translations by the author.

[1] The production company, Heartfeltricks, operates from Toronto, Canada. This production of *The World of Harlequin: Then and Now* was subsequently remounted and toured in 2004.

[2] Katritzky's promising study of the visual records of the Commedia dell'arte became available five years after the production and exhibition which form the subject of this paper. Unfortunately the visual record here is comprised almost exclusively of paintings and similar representations and does not treat any physical objects from the theatre. See M. A. Katritzky, *The Art of Commedia: a Study in the Commedia dell'Arte 1560–1620 with Special Reference to the Visual Records, Internationale Forschungen zur allgemeinen und vergleichenden Literaturwissenschaft.* (Amsterdam: Rodopi, 2006).

[3] This evocative and wholly appropriate theatrical image represents the duality of considerations that the existence of an artifact brings into play. See Carl E. Schorske. *Thinking with History: Explorations in the Passage to Modernism* (68), quoted in Thomas Postlewait, "Writing History Today" *Theatre Survey* 41:2 (Nov 2000), p86.

[4] Gian Giacomo Colli, performer, director, and Commedia dell'arte specialist, trained with Carlo Boso, Orazio Costa and Vittorio Gassman.

[5] This object admits to many variant spellings such as *battocio, batocchio, batocco,* even in some instances *battuta* as well as in various commedia transcriptions derivatives such as *batticulo* and *batticore*. See Faust Nicolini, *Vita di Arlecchino* (Milano: R. Ricciardi, 1958) pp181, 245. These terms are dependant entirely on regional dialect. The Arlecchino mask originated in Lombardy where typically consonants are rarely doubled in the local dialect and therefore on this authority *batocio* is spelled with single consonants throughout this paper. Nicolini adopts this spelling for twelve separate citations (p436).

[6] See "Slapstick," in Phyllis Hartnoll, ed. *The Oxford Companion to the Theatre* (Fourth ed. London: Oxford UP, 1985).

[7] In Italian, *daga di legno* (Nicolini 135).

[8] See (Nicolini 115).

[9] This term is a variant of *coutelas* 'a large kitchen knife' and *coustille* 'a soldier's short, straight cutlass.' The latter term is common in heraldic descriptions.

[10] Consider also its domestic etymology as *le battoir,* a peasant implement *'un objet bien ordinaire'* used for laundering. Flaubert refers to this particular usage in his short story "Un Coeur simple". See *Three Tales. Translated with an introd. by Robert Baldick, Penguin Classics.* ([Harmondsworth, Middlesex]: Penguin Books, 1961) p37, where the term is anglicized as "battledore" likely to convey the impression of the object's paddle-like shape.

[11] See the excellent and varied illustrated examples in Ambrogio Artoni, *Il Teatro degli zanni: rapsodie dell'arte e dintorni, Studi di storia del teatro e dello spettacolo.* (Genova: Costa & Nolan, 1999) pp70–7.

[12] A 1685 frontispiece illustration of this play depicts the *deus ex machina* descent of Arlecchino as Mercury on Jove's eagle. Held high is a caduceus entwined around his batocio. See Napoléon-Maurice Bernardin, *La Comédie italienne en France et les théâtres de la foire et du boulevard, 1570–1791.* (Paris: Revue bleue, 1902). See also the transformation description *il "batocio" ha assunto la forma del caduceo* 'the batocio has assumed the form of the caduceus' (Nicolini 180).

[13] See the entry *"Arlecchino"* which includes this passage: *"Anche la spatola era l'antichissimo scettro giullaresco nonché la traduzione comica della clava d'Ercole; ma poteva servire, occonrrendo, per rimestare nel paiolo il tradizionale cibo dei villani bergamschi, la polenta"* (*Enciclopedia dello spettacolo Vol 1,* 906).

[14] *" . . . mi son Arlechin Batocio/Orbo de na recia e sordo da un occhio . . . "*

[15] See Meredith Chilton, *Harlequin Unmasked: the Commedia dell'arte and Porcelain Sculpture* (New Haven: YaleUP; George R. Gardiner Museum of Ceramic Art, 2001) pp43, 45. A significant question arises from the disparity between the photographic image of the slapstick and the accompanying textual description which, unresolved, leads to the intriguing speculation that there may be a second *batocio* at the Czech museum.

[16] While concerned mainly with the commedia dell'arte's far-reaching influence as a multilingual social force, Jaffe-Berg is nevertheless quick to acknowledge the importance of the numerous commedia illustrations and artifacts and the resulting wealth of icono-

graphic detail deriving from them. See Erith Jaffe-Berg, *The Multilingual Art of Commedia dell'arte* (Ottawa: Legas, 2009) p13n4.

[17] Also known as Pourbus, Franz (the Elder), he lived from1540–1582. Both his father and his son were also Flemish painters, active in this area.

[18] This claim was made by Duchartre in the original 1928 publication of *La Comédie italienne*. See Pierre-Louis Duchartre, *The Italian Comedy: the Improvisation, Scenarios, Lives, Attributes, Portraits, and Masks of the Illustrious Characters of the Commedia dell'arte*. Translated by R. T. Weaver (NY: Dover Publications. Original edition, 1928/9; 1966) p86.

[19] See the colour plate reproduction in which Duchartre also identifies Arlecchino *qui est, sans doute, Alberto Ganassa* 'who is, without doubt, Alberto Ganassa' in Pierre-Louis Duchartre, *La Commedia dell'arte et ses enfants* (Paris: Éditions d'art et industrie, 1955) facing p16, plate II. See also Katritzky's commentary about "The Bayeux Painting" (140–2).

[20] See the Publisher's Note regarding these unique sixteenth century engravings in Duchartre's 'Comedy' p314.

[21] As described in Giacomo Oreglia, *The Commedia dell'arte* (New York: Hill and Wang, 1968) p58.

[22] In later practice the feather was sometimes replaced with a small piece of fur. See, for example, the anonymous mid-eighteenth century engraving of Carlin Bertinazzi as Harlequin (Chilton 39, Pl 37).

[23] Nicolini enumerates these features in a list that also includes the description *ora dal lato destro, ora da quello sinister, il famoso "batocio"* 'now on the right side, now on the left, the famous "batocio"' (9).

[24] Several examples of these illustrations are included in the Pictorial Supplement of Duchartre's ('Comedy' 340–8).

[25] A fine example is shown in N. Bonnarte Vers' 1675 engraving reproduced in Duchartre's 'Commedia' 131, Fig. 91.

[26] See for example the handle detail in Kenneth and Laura Richards, *The Commedia dell'arte: a Documentary History* (Oxford: B. Blackwell for The Shakespeare Head Press, 1990) p232, pl 43.

[27] Several fine examples are illustrated in Cesare Molinari, *La commedia dell'arte*. (1a ed. Milano: Mondadori, 1985) pp184, 188, 220, 222, 228; and Allardyce Nicoll, *The World of Harlequin: a Critical Study of the Commedia dell'arte* (Cambridge: UP, 1963) p7f.

[28] Consider later English characterizations by David Garrick and John Rich and especially depictions of Harlequin by Cezanne, Degas and others. The exaggerated lengths of their slapsticks are not fanciful flourishes by the artists but rather represent extreme developments in the changing physical features of this stage property.

[29] An excellent example of asymmetric handle styling is shown in a porcelain figurine in (Chilton 240, Pl 378).

[30] *Un'illustrazione ci mostra l'Arlecchino teatrale nel suo costume più "arcaico", bianco, sdrucito, e pieno di toppe. È in ginocchio, a capo scoperto, il cappello tra le mani giunte a mo' di supplica, in una posa di cui è possibile rimarcare il carattere stereotipato, come risulta evidente da un confronto con una nota immagine di qualche anno precedente, compresa nel Recueil Fossard* (Artoni 31).

[31] From the images found in Duchartre's 'Comedy' compare Martinelli's illustration (343) for the similarity of Arlecchino's pose (320) as well as for the difference of demeanour (123).

[32] "The Theatre," an essay which accompanied the exhibition, contains a succinct historical rendering including considerations of some of the economic imperatives faced by the early commedia companies. See especially the comments regarding the evolution of commedia materials and conventions in Domenico Pietropaolo, "The Theatre" in Chilton, pp27f.

[33] The details of this particular design including the placement of the leather hinge were variations on a suggestion by Domenico Pietropaolo.

[34] An excellent representation of this style of batocio is featured in Jacques Callot's engraving *Franca Trippa e Fritellino* (1622) reproduced in (Molinari 143).

[35] *Alla cintura porta una tozza spada di legno, innocuo oggetto di scena che successivamente si trasformerà nel classico batocio* (Artoni 31).

[36] See Tim Fitzpatrick, Tim, "Flaminio Scala's Prototypal Scenarios: Segmenting the Text/Performance" in The Science of Baffoonery: Theory and History of the Commedia dell'arte, edited by D. Pietropaolo (Ottawa: Dovehouse Editions, 1989) p187.

A *Femme Fatale* of Eighteenth-Century American Theatre Research: Reading William Bradford's *Cato* Letter

MARK EVANS BRYAN

At the Valley Forge cantonment of George Washington's Continental Army, William Bradford attended a production of Joseph Addison's *Cato*, an heroic tragedy that even then, in the spring of 1778, was associated with his general-in-chief. The letter in which Bradford described the performance has subsequently played a remarkable role in intellectual and cultural histories of the North American eighteenth century.[1] The barest trace that a play—a favorite of Washington himself, a treatise on honorable conduct in revolution and resistance to tyranny, a text central to what Bernard Bailyn called the "'Catonic' image" in revolutionary American political culture—might have been performed by soldiers at the conclusion of the Valley Forge winter so neatly satisfies a particularly attractive narrative for intellectual and theatre historians that a scholarly tradition has developed fueled by the tools of literary analysis, a deteriorating chain of secondary references, and desire.[2] And from the *doxa* of earlier historians, scholars have invented a narrative of performance and power, rebellion and nation-building. Indeed this narrative has become, for twentieth- and twenty-first century theatre and performance detectives, a *femme fatale* of astonishing allure. For generations this historiographical hearsay beguiled scholars and prompted us to a particularly seductive conclusion, that Washington or his aides arranged or ordered the staging, that the drama's producers were likely aware of its rhetorical and symbolic value, and that, as a consequence, the play was staged for the large community of revolutionaries tempered in the crucible of Valley Forge. The traditional narrative elevates this particular performance, played for these men and women, and at this already mythologized moment, to something more than an entertainment (and much more than an opportunity for ambitious subaltern officers to seek attention from and display aristocratic potential for the elite of Washington's commanders, as I argued in the January 2010 issue of *William and Mary Quarterly*).[3] In my own work, it was only by asking the basic investigative questions of *film noir*'s hardboiled detective that the complexity of the case came into focus, challenging several generations of inquiry. Who are the suspects (among the performers and in the audience)? What is the context of the act (a performance by and for members of Washington's army well after the eighth article of the Continental Congress's 1774 non-consumption accord had "discountenance[d]" the "extravagance and dissipation" of the theatre)?[4] Where could it have been performed at Valley Forge? And why did this witness—a theatre enthusiast and amateur dramatist himself, but also a strong adherent to the philosophy of non-consumption—write his account at all?

The key piece of evidence offers few details.[5] In a letter to his young sister, Rachel, "on a visit" to their father, Bradford imagines the "entertainment" she would find if she "extend[ed] her Jaunt" to Valley Forge. "The manouvering of the Army," he writes, "is in itself a sight that would charm," but "Besides these, the Theatre is opened." Several days before, "Cato was performed before a very numerous and splendid audience," which included George and Martha Washington (whom Bradford refers to as "His Excellency and Lady," common honorifics for the Washingtons); General William Alexander (whom he calls "Lord Stirling," Alexander's preferred sobriquet and the way the supposed aristocrat is addressed in Washington's correspondence), Mrs. Alexander, and their daughter; and Catherine Greene, a popular hostess at camp and the wife of General Nathanael Greene. Bradford reported only that the "Scenery was in Taste," "the performance admirable," and that "Col George" had done "his part to admiration—he made an excellent *die* (as they say) . . . " If the army were to remain in its winter quarters, he writes, "our Theatrical amusements will continue," with plans apparently for productions of *The Fair Penitent* by Nicholas Rowe, *The Padlock* by Isaac Bickerstaffe, and George Farquhar's *The Recruiting Officer*, a comedy especially popular with military audiences in the eighteenth century. A subsequent letter to Rachel, however, announced that soldiers' organized amusements had been canceled as the army prepared to move.[6] Bradford's letter is the only extant witness testimony that the production of *Cato* took place at Valley Forge.

Ironically, perhaps the first historian to be seduced by the suspicion of a highly symbolic *Cato* and the prospect of Washington's authorial involvement in the production endeavored in the same treatise to debunk an earlier legend in the mythology of the general-in-chief at Valley Forge. The eminent narrative historian Samuel Eliot Morison's 1932 oration, "The Young Man Washington," began by accusing "older biographers" of "conspir[ing] to create the legend" of the first U.S. president and pronounced the Parson Weems' tale of an iconic Washington, alone in prayer among the trees at Valley Forge, a "pure fable."[7] Published several times, this address to Harvard students was largely not an historical account, but an inspirational homily on Washingtonian self-discipline. Morison located the source of young Washington's resolve in the Stoicism of the Cato of Plutarch and Addison. And at Valley Forge, Morison embroidered, "when the morale of the army needed a stimulus, Washington caused *Cato* to be performed, and attended the performance."[8] Morison's transposition of passive attendance with active direction, and his connection between the *Cato* Bradford describes and the rising spirit of a revolutionary army, infected generations of historical scholarship, with versions of this story appearing in major works of U.S. history,

My dear Rachel   May 14th 1778

I find by a Letter from my father that you are on a visit at Trenton. I should be happy could you extend your Jaunt as far as full View – The Camp could now afford you some entertainment. The manoeuvring of the Army is in itself a sight that would Charm you. – Besides these, the Theatre is opened – Last Monday Cato was performed before a very numerous & splendid audience. His Excellency & Lady, Lord Sterling, the Countess & Lady Kitty, & Mrs Green were part of the Assembly. The Scenery was in Taste – & the performance admirable – Col George did his part to admiration – he made an excellent <u>die</u> (as they say) – Pray heaven he dont die in earnest – for yesterday he was siezed with the pleurisy & lies extremely ill – If the Enemy does not retire from Philada soon, our Theatrical amusements will continue – The fair Penitent with the Padlock will soon be acted. The "recruiting Officer" is also on foot. –

I hope however we shall be disappointed in all these by the more agreeable Entertainment of taking possession of Philada – There are strong rumors that the English are meditating a retreat – Heaven send it – for I fear we shall not be able to force them to go these two months –

I scrawl these few lines to accompany a letter which I send to my Father – Love to sister Betsy & all Friends –

Adieu ma chere soeur, je suis votre WB

Courtesy of the Historical Society of Pennsylvania. William Bradford, Jr., "To Rachel Bradford," May 14, 1778, John William Wallace Papers, Bradford papers, vol. 1, p. 58.

such as David Hackett Fischer's *Albion's Seed: Four British Folkways in America* and Forrest McDonald's *Novus Ordo Seclorum: The Intellectual Origins of the Constitution;* academic and popular biographies of Washington and Alexander Hamilton; and works of theatre history by exceptional scholars, including references in books by Marvin Carlson, Heather S. Nathans, and Jeffrey H. Richards.[9]

Scholars have consequently and perhaps unsurprisingly read the performance of *Cato* itself as "self-consciously and performatively enacted" nation-building (Randall Fuller); a demonstration of Washington's self-conscious construction of his image and a gesture of solidarity with his army, a "collective stripping of the sleeve to display wounds already endured in their new nation's service and a . . . willingness to shed further blood" (Jason Shaffer); and an ideologically complex performance with Washington's imprimatur, for which the Valley Forge audience "was specially prepared . . . [to] see through its artifice" and look on their general-in-chief as "all that Cato had been—as unbending in his virtue and as heroic in his stature among Americans" (Albert Furtwangler).[10] Whether these studies attribute the performance to Washington's active direction or passive approval—all three of the articles I've cited cast doubt in varying degrees on the Morison thesis that Washington himself arranged for the production—their seductive conclusions rest also on assumptions for which there is no evidence.[11] Fuller asserts that the production was "presented on an open-air stage near the banks of the Schuylkill River" for "the ragged soldiers in Washington's camp," an audience "that included foot soldiers" as well as "those who imagined themselves a modified version of European aristocracy," whom Bradford "breathlessly described" in a manner that recalled Samuel Pepys. "More importantly," Fuller writes, this *Cato* was "aimed" at the British army in occupied Philadelphia, part of the "bombastic salvos" of literary and theatrical exchange between Whig and Tory in revolutionary America.[12] Shaffer argues that the performance, "designat[ed]" part of the camp's "celebration of the French alliance," offered Washington the opportunity to "publicly" renew "the vows of loyalty between [himself] and the Continental Army," and, like Fuller, Shaffer contends that *Cato* was a "counterperformance," "doubtless aimed" at the nearby British (he also claims that the letter passed between Valley Forge and Philadelphia, rather than Trenton, which alters the context of the account appreciably).[13] Finally, Furtwangler's conclusions about the meanings of the performance rest with the assumption, perhaps the same one that Morison made, that "it was for Washington to approve the staging of any play" at the encampment.[14]

These elements (Washington's somewhat more than tacit approval; the performance of the play in public, in the open air, for a large audience of soldiers and possible observation by British agents; the connection of the production with the *feu de joie* and banquet on May 6 which had commemorated the Treaty of Alliance) are essential to the symbolic readings of the Valley Forge *Cato*. And the possibility that any of these ultimately critical details might be true is indeed tantalizing; I had imagined some of them too when I first encountered the Bradford letter while preparing a conference paper some years ago. But with the exception of Fuller's inclusion of the army's quasi-aristocracy in the play's audience, none of these presumptions is corroborated by historical detective work.

If the production of *Cato* had been a public event, part of the camp-wide tribute to Franco-American cooperation, which did, in fact, take place during the week prior to the performance, then Furtwangler's assumption, "that it was for Washington to approve the staging of a play" is reasonable; the planning for the *feu de joie*, for instance, is carefully outlined in Washington's general orders.[15] But apart from Bradford's letter, the relatively generous archive of journals and correspondence that chronicled the encampment is silent on the production or describes the conspicuous quiet of the camp after May 6. The diary of Samuel Armstrong, for instance, excitedly recalls the "fue-de-Joy" and his invitation to dinner after the spectacle ("when I came to my Hutt was informed that Genl. Washington gave all officers an Invitation to dine with him, which I accepted!!!"); but for Thursday, May 7, through Friday, May 14, as far as Armstrong was concerned, "Nothing Remarkable" occurred.[16] Except for its proximity in time to the celebration of the alliance, there is no reason to assume that the production of *Cato* was related to the camp-wide festivity. On the contrary, Bradford's letter seems to suggest the *Cato* performance was part of a schedule of amusements. And there is no evidence that it was "for Washington to approve" camp amusements or any of the variety of leisure activities that took place at Valley Forge, from organized games of "bandy wicket" to the dancing lessons in James Thacher's camp hospital.[17]

That the play was produced for a large assembly of both officers and enlisted soldiers, and consequently outdoors to accommodate such a number (and to counter the spectacles of the British), is central to the myth of the Valley Forge *Cato*. There is no evidence that points to this; it is simply the way scholars have concluded it would need to have happened in order to satisfy the traditional narrative. But the primary accounts of the encampment describe no suitable structure or outdoor playing space. And though the performance could have taken place in the open air, as Fuller suggests, this would have made the Valley Forge *Cato* even more exceptional: it was the custom of British military theatre to produce in large rooms, in preexisting playhouses or convertible spaces, and the production of a formal drama outdoors would be unprecedented in records of performance in British North America.[18] What evidence there is of performance at Valley Forge points instead to production behind closed doors and for an elite, and relatively small, audience.

Bradford's letter is the only record of the performance of *Cato* on May 11, 1778. But there is evidence of theatre production at Valley Forge earlier in the spring. On April 15, Ensign George Ewing recorded in his journal that he "receivd a ticket for the Play to be acted this evening at the Bakehouse." When he arrived, in a group with four other officers, "the house was so full [they] could not get in."[19] And though the "Bakehouse" is no longer extant and has never been identified in archeological surveys, it is the most likely venue for the production of *Cato* almost three weeks later. The "Bakehouse" appears to have had open space under its roof—it was also the site of the Court Martial on several occasions—but was likely not a particularly large structure.[20] The performance Ewing describes required tickets and the producers appear to have over-sold the limited room in their makeshift playhouse. This unnamed April production, at least, was not a large-scale public performance.

Bradford describes the audience for *Cato* as "very numerous & splendid." "Numerous" is a relative term; "splendid" is, however, somewhat more definable and provides a clue to the demographics of the audiences for the two performances.[21] Bradford, a lieutenant colonel, watched an actor with the same rank "make an excellent die," in an audience with the general-in-chief and his wife, another general and his wife and daughter, and the wife of a third general. (The connections among the named spectators and the one identified participant in the two performances do not, incidentally, end with their commissions: Ewing and Major Joseph Bloomfield, one of his companions on April 15, shared common mustering duties with Bradford and *Cato* actor George Noarth, and Ewing and Lieutenant Colonel Noarth had both joined the fraternity of the artillery park prior to the plays' productions.[22]) Nowhere in the historical archive are there references to a mixed class audience for either of these plays and descriptions of formal social interaction between high-ranking officers and "ragged soldiers" in army encampments like Valley Forge are quite rare.[23] Charles Royster has argued that the new petty aristocracy of the Continental Army hierarchy began, at Valley Forge, "to claim vested rights to a status that, according to the ideals of 1775, ought not even to exist in a free country"; Augustan drama was associated with English gentility and its production among the officers is not surprising.[24] The "Col George" of *Cato* was a striver, appointed to his rank by the Continental Congress but marooned in an administrative position and desirous of a transfer to the staff of a field commander, where, presumably, he might establish himself and claim the status Royster describes.[25] Though we do not know who arranged for the production of *Cato*, Noarth is a very plausible suspect. The democratic audience of plebeian revolutionaries communing with their Catonic leader is a seductive image, but not one that is reflected in the records of the performances, or in the behavior of officers in 1778.

With the exception of Furtwangler, who accurately identifies Bradford and bases his analysis, in part, on Bradford's extant correspondence, no account of the production has investigated the witness who provided its only description (Kenneth Silverman, in *A Cultural History of the American Revolution*, even mistakenly divides Bradford into two separate, unnamed spectators).[26] Fuller's characterization of Bradford "breathlessly drop[ping] names" in the style of Pepys' "descriptions of court spectacles" advances most forcefully a presumption Fuller shares with other accounts: that Bradford endorsed the production of a recognizably republican drama at Valley Forge.[27] And though Bradford had been an amateur dramatist and was, throughout his pre-1774 and post-war lifetime, an avid consumer of popular theatre, the Philadelphia Bradfords were fierce advocates of the philosophy of non-consumption (William Sr., in fact, had been among the leaders of the Sons of Liberty when they denied Philadelphia anchorage to the tea-laden *Polly* in December of 1773 and served on a Committee of Inspection and Observation after the non-consumption accord). The younger Bradford's letters during his military service criticized the luxuries of his fellow officers and lamented the inefficiencies of the Continental Army. At Valley Forge, his communications to family condemned the wasteful practice of paying bounties for new recruits (a draft, he argued to his brother-in-law, would obviate the "extravagant" sums paid to new soldiers); lamented the camp's "Disorder" (and the lack of gunpowder, writing to Rachel, "they say the Devil is in Camp [but] I can find no Brimstone . . . & I believe it would require a Shower of it, like that on Sodom" to "eradicate" the chaos); and inveighed against his delinquent colleague in the mustering service, George Noarth (Bradford complained that the actor who appears to have played "Cato" or "Sempronius"—"he made an excellent *die*"—avoided his duties, was "confounded lazy," and did "little else than breathe").[28]

The *Cato* letter itself begins ironically. Shuffled between their sister's home and their father's navy posting in New Jersey, Rachel Bradford was well into her sixth month of exile from their home in occupied Philadelphia when her older brother described to her the performance of *Cato*. Bradford's invitation to his fourteen-year-old sister to "extend [her] Jaunt" to Valley Forge ought to be a clear signal that this note, enclosed with a lost letter to their father, cannot be read as straightforward reportage. Indeed, given Bradford's radical politics, his frustration with the army's failure to dispossess the British of his native Philadelphia, and the ongoing dispute between his father and General Washington over the defense of Pennsylvanians along the Delaware River, the note to Rachel takes on a very different cast.[29] "It may be," I've argued, "that the very making of a record of the performance was [Bradford, Jr.'s] criticism: a communication to his father at Trenton, informing him of the performance, at a time when the leadership of the Continental army was under debate and the consumption of English drama remained a contested marker of revolutionary self-image."[30]

The mythology of the *Cato* performance, at the conclusion of the already heavily mythologized Valley Forge encampment, is supported by none of the available evidence that touches on Bradford's brief testimony. Moreover, it runs counter to current historical scholarship on non-consumption and the theatre during the revolutionary period in British North America. But it is an extraordinary, and fatally seductive, narrative. All it took was Morison to distort what seemed a very minor detail in his discourse on Washington's character, and the heads of generations of literary and historical detectives were turned. The interpretations of the event as an intersection between performance and revolution, or a locus of performance as revolution, or even as a telling episode in the creation of Washingtonian hagiography, are seductive and persuasive in many ways, but based more in scholarly desire than evidence and, in the end, too good to be true.

ENDNOTES

[1] William Bradford, Jr. (1755–1795), was a lieutentant colonel in the mustering department of the Continental Army at the time of the Valley Forge encampment. A native of Philadelphia and the son of patriot newspaper publisher, William Bradford, Sr., Bradford was educated at the College of New-Jersey at Princeton, where he was a student of John Witherspoon and a clubmate and friend of Hugh Henry Brackenridge, Philip Freneau, and

James Madison. After his military service, Bradford resumed his legal career in Philadelphia and was appointed first to the Pennsylvania Supreme Court and then to Washington's cabinet as the second Attorney General of the United States (1794–1795). A poet and dramatist in college, Bradford remained an astute consumer of drama throughout his lifetime and the author of several published poems, including "The Lament of Washington," which became the lyrics of the popular song "Lafayette" ("La Fayette—A Song," *New-York Magazine; or Miscellaneous Repository* 2.68 [October 19, 1796], 127).

[2] Bernard Bailyn, *The Ideological Origins of the American Revolution* (Cambridge: Belknap/Harvard UP, 1992), 44.

[3] Mark Evans Bryan, "'Slideing into Monarchical extravagance': *Cato* at Valley Forge and the Testimony of William Bradford, Jr.," *William and Mary Quarterly*, 3rd Series, 57.1 (January 2010), 123–144.

[4] "October 20, 1774," *Journals of the Continental Congress, 1774–1789, Vol. 1: 1774* (Washington: Government Printing Office, 1904), 75–80, http://memory.loc.gov/ammem/amlaw/lwjc.html.

[5] William Bradford, Jr., to Rachel Bradford, May 14, 1778, in Bradford Papers, John William Wallace Collection, 1725–1854, vol. 1, 58, Collection 686, Historical Society of Pennsylvania, Philadelphia. The letter was published in full in 1899 and again in 1916 (in Paul Leicester Ford, *Washington and The Theatre* [New York: Dunlap Society, 1899; rpt. New York: Burt Franklin, 1970, 25–26] and in "Selections from the Wallace Papers," *Pennsylvania Magazine of History and Biography* 40.3 [July 1916], 342–43).

[6] William Bradford, Jr., to Rachel Bradford, May 20, 1778, *ibid.*, vol. 1, 59.

[7] Samuel Eliot Morison, *The Young Man Washington: An Address Delivered at Sanders Theatre, Cambridge, February 22, 1932* (Cambridge: Harvard UP, 1932; rpt. in *The Great Parade*, ed. H.J. Duteil [New York: Doubleday, Doran & Co., 1935], 118–40). Quotations from *The Great Parade*, 118 and 121. Morison's reference appears to be the first from the mainstream historical profession. An additional source of the problematic narrative tradition may be the 1928 performance of *Cato* outdoors at the then Valley Forge State Park, produced by the Valley Forge Park Commission (see Bryan, "'Slideing into Monarchical extravagance,'" 128 n. 11).

[8] *The Great Parade*, 127–28.

[9] David Hackett Fischer, *Albion's Seed: Four British Folkways in America* (New York: Oxford UP, 1989), 317; Forrest McDonald, *Novus Ordo Seclorum: The Intellectual Origins of the Constitution* (Lawrence: UP of Kansas, 1985), 195. There are many examples of this in biographies of the "founders": see, for instance, Ron Chernow, *Alexander Hamilton* (New York: Penguin, 1994), 107; Edward G. Lengel, *General George Washington: A Military Life* (New York: Random House, 2005), 11; Jeffrey H. Morrison, *The Political Philosophy of George Washington* (Baltimore: Johns Hopkins UP, 2009), 91; Michael Novak and Jana Novak, *Washington's God* (New York: Basic Books, 2006), 13; Willard Sterne Randall, *George Washington: A Life* (New York: Henry Holt, 1997), 43; Richard Norton Smith, *Patriarch: George Washington and the New American Nation* (Boston: Houghton Mifflin, 1993), 263; and many others. In *Voltaire and the Theatre of the Eighteenth Century*, Marvin Carlson remarked on the enduring eighteenth-century popularity of Addison's tragedy, noting that "George Washington arranged for the play to be presented before his troops at Valley Forge in 1777 as an inspiration in their fight against tyranny" ([Westport, CT: Greenwood P, 1998], 27); Heather S. Nathans writes, in *Early American Theatre from the Revolution to Thomas Jefferson: Into the Hands of the People*, that Washington "staged productions of his favorite pieces, such as *Cato*, to raise the sagging spirits of his army during the hard winter at Valley Forge" ([Cambridge: Cambridge UP, 2003], 37); Jeffrey H. Richards records that "Washington staged *Cato* at Valley Forge in spring 1778 no doubt to inspire morale" (*Theater Enough: American Culture and the Metaphor of the World Stage, 1607–1789* [Durham: Duke UP, 1991], 248). Chernow's new *Washington: A Life* (New York: Penguin, 2010), which includes my *WMQ* article in its bibliography, recasts

the assumptions of his 1994 biography of Hamilton on the Valley Forge *Cato*, noting only that Washington "allowed junior officers to stage" the play (331).

[10] Randall Fuller, "Theaters of the American Revolution: The Valley Forge 'Cato' and the Meschianza in Their Transcultural Contexts," *Early American Literature* 34.2 (September 1999), 126–46 (quotation, 129); Jason Shaffer, "'Great Cato's Descendants': A Geneaology of Colonial Performance," *Theatre Survey* 44.1 (May 2003), 5–28 (quotation, 19); Albert Furtwangler, "Cato at Valley Forge," *Modern Language Quarterly* 41.1 (March 1980), 38–53 (quotation, 52). See also Shaffer, *Performing Patriotism: National Identity in the Colonial and Revolutionary American Theater* (Philadelphia: U of Penn P, 2007) and "'Making an Excellent Die': Death, Mourning, and Patriotism in the Propaganda Plays of the American Revolution," *Early American Literature* 41.1 (Spring 2006), 1–27; Furtwangler, *American Silhouettes: Rhetorical Identities of the Founders* (New Haven: Yale UP, 1987); and Frederic M. Litto, "Addison's *Cato* in the Colonies," *William and Mary Quarterly*, 3rd Series, 23.3 (July 1966), 431–49.

[11] Though Fuller initially notes that the production was "staged at the behest" of Washington ("Theaters of the American Revolution,"128), he later admits that there is no evidence of Washington "actually requesting" the performance (132). Shaffer concludes that Washington displayed his "approval" by attending ("Great Cato's Descendants," 19). And though Furtwangler assumes Washington recognized the ideological possibilities of a camp production of *Cato*, he also declares that he has "not been able to discover who had the idea of staging the play and for what motives" ("Cato at Valley Forge," 49–50).

[12] Fuller, "Theaters of the American Revolution," 128 and 130. He also calls the production "hastily rehearsed" (128) though there is no record of the rehearsal process.

[13] Shaffer, "Great Cato's Descendants," 19 and 20.

[14] Furtwangler, "Cato and Valley Forge," 51.

[15] George Washington, "General Orders," May 5, 1778, George Washington Papers at the Library of Congress, http://memory.loc.gov/ammem/gwhtml/gwhome.html.

[16] Joseph Lee Boyle, ed., "From Saratoga to Valley Forge: The Diary of Lt. Samuel Armstrong," *Pennsylvania Magazine of History and Biography* 121.3 (July 1997), 237–270 (quotation, 268).

[17] James Thacher, *A Military Journal during the Revolutionary War from 1775 to 1783*, 2nd ed. (Boston: Cottons and Barnard, 1827), 121.

[18] Bryan, "'Slideing into Monarchical extravagance,'" 127–28.

[19] George Ewing, *George Ewing, Gentleman: a Soldier of Valley Forge* (Yonkers, New York: Thomas Ewing, 1928), 38.

[20] For a discussion of the elusive "Bakehouse," see Bryan, "'Slideing into Monarchical extravagance,'" 127–29.

[21] The more generally positive contemporary connotation for "splendid" was not shared by late eighteenth-century writers. John Walker's *Critical Pronouncing Dictionary and Expositor of the English Language*, first published in London in 1791 and published in one of its many editions by William Bradford's brother and nephew in Philadelphia in 1818, defines "splendid" as "Showy, magnificent, sumptuous" (quotation, 3rd American ed. [New York: Stansbury and others, 1808], 796.)

[22] See Bryan, "'Slideing into Monarchical extravagance,'" 130 and 130 n. 18 for the identification of "Col George" as Noarth and discussion of Bloomfield's connections with Bradford. Noarth began spending much of his time at the artillery park in December 1777 (Bradford to Rachel Bradford, December 17, 1777, John William Wallace Collection, Bradford papers, vol. 1, 53) and Ewing began frequenting the "Aty Park" (*George Ewing, Gentleman*, 36–37, 41) in April, resigning his commission on April 28 and volunteering two days later with a "Compy of Arty" (43) with whom he spent the rest of the encampment.

[23] Ewing, in fact, is responsible for a famous exception: on May 4, 1778, he writes that "His Excellency [Washington] dined with G Nox [General Henry Knox, commander of

Washington's artillery] and after dinner did us the honor to play at Wicket with us" (*George Ewing, Gentleman*, 47).

[24] Charles Royster, *A Revolutionary People at War: The Continental Army and American Character, 1775–1783* (New York: W.W. Norton, 1981), 198. Royster's chapter on Valley Forge is an exceptional study of the aristocratic ventures of officers in an army at rest (190–254).

[25] Bryan, "'Slideing into Monarchical extravagance,'" 139–40.

[26] Kenneth Silverman, *A Cultural History of the American Revolution* (New York: Columbia UP, 1987), 350. Silverman, who is a major source for subsequent references to the Valley Forge *Cato* in non-specialized studies, relies on several secondary accounts, including John Joseph Stoudt's poorly-cited *Ordeal at Valley Forge* (Philadelphia: U of Penn P, 1963).

[27] Fuller, "Theaters of the American Revolution," 130.

[28] Bradford to Joshua Wallace, January 27, 1778, John William Wallace Collection, Bradford papers, vol. 1, 54; Bradford to Rachel Bradford," December 17, 1777, *ibid.*, vol. 1, 53.

[29] Washington had ordered that a fleet of galleys be burned in order that they not fall into enemy hands; Bradford, Sr., refused, arguing that the boats protected American landowners along the river. See Bryan, "'Slideing into Monarchical extravagance,'" 141 n. 53.

[30] Bryan, "'Slideing into Monarchical extravagance,'" 141.

Clues in the Caricature: The Case of "The Prospect Before Us"

ANNETTE FERN

On June 17, 1789 the King's Theatre in the Haymarket, London's venue for the performance of Italian opera, burned to the ground. Arson was suspected but no charges were brought, and William Taylor, the controversial long-time manager of the theatre, immediately prepared to rebuild it. However, the King's Theatre had no Royal patent; it had been operating under an annual license, and the destruction of the building presented an opportunity for a consortium of nobles, among them Lord Salisbury, to propose an alternative opera house with a different style of management, and do away with the Haymarket company entirely. Since Salisbury was Lord Chamberlain, and was therefore the person responsible for the licensing of theatres, his involvement and particularly his financial investment in the new company created a conflict of interest, and to conceal this a dummy board of trustees was set up, with Robert Bray O'Reilly, an attorney and amateur architect, as the nominal manager of the organization. O'Reilly commissioned plans for a new building in Leicester Square, but difficulties in acquiring the land, together with the rapid construction of Taylor's new building in the Haymarket, caused him to abandon that scheme, and instead he acquired the lease of the Pantheon, a concert and party room in Oxford Street, and engaged its original architect to remodel it for use as a theatre. Both Taylor and O'Reilly hired complete opera companies, ballet companies, orchestras, and support staff for their respective theatres, and by Fall 1790 it appeared that the nobility and gentry would be able to choose between two full-scale Italian opera companies performing in London—a situation which clearly would be of benefit to no one. At the end of December 1790 a Committee of Arbitration met at the Prince of Wales's residence at Carlton House to determine whether a compromise could be reached; by mid-January 1791, after four lengthy meetings, the Committee had decided that there was no hope of compromise, a license had been granted to O'Reilly to present opera at the Pantheon, and Taylor was pressing on with his building, unable to believe that the Lord Chamberlain and the King would continue to refuse him permission to perform.[1]

That is how matters stood on January 13, 1791 when the publisher S. W. Fores issued two caricatures by Thomas Rowlandson depicting a likely outcome of the situation. Both are titled "The Prospect Before Us." One of them, with the caption, "Humanely inscribed to all those Professors of Music and

Thomas Rowlandson, "The Prospect Before Us" (1791). From the Harvard Theatre Collection, Houghton Library.

Dancing whom the cap may fit," shows a ragged crew of singers, dancers and orchestra musicians from the Haymarket company begging in the street for funds to complete their building. Many of the figures are thought to be caricatures of the actual performers hired for the season; the central figure has been identified as Madame Hilligsberg, the Haymarket's prima ballerina. The second of Rowlandson's pair shows two euphoric dancers on the stage of the Pantheon; the house is packed, and the King is in attendance. Below is the caption, "Respetfully [sic] dedicated to those Singers, Dancers & Musical Professors, who are fortunately engaged with the Proprietor of the King's Theatre, at the Pantheon."

The prints are satires: Rowlandson has created two imaginary events to lampoon a real-life social and political issue, and his point, apparently, is that the Pantheon is going to make it and the Haymarket is not. What is not so clear is which elements of the images can be associated with actual events and persons, and which are imaginary or allusive. The event in the Haymarket print is certainly imaginary, although it is populated with real people and many of the background details allude to current events.[2] The Pantheon print is also supposed to include portraits, and to be at least in part documentary evidence. This caricature is much better known than the Haymarket image, and taken by itself it loses much of its satiric impact and can almost be read as an illustration. In this context, the figures in it have been identified as Charles Didelot and Madame Théodore and the performance as Dauberval's *Amphion and Thalia,* the ballet performed on opening night at the Pantheon;[3] the scene as a rendering of that opening night, despite the publication date on the print, more than a month before the opening date of February 17;[4] and the costumes and poses as evidence of the state of rehearsals for the ballet on the date that the print was issued.[5] Since the rivalry of the two Italian opera companies was covered extensively in London newspapers of the period it is not difficult to get a general idea of the circumstances which provoked the satire. Confirming or disproving which of Rowlandson's details are documentary and which are imaginary is not so easy. Where can we discover who the dancers are, and whether a specific ballet is being depicted? What are the arguments for or against this being a depiction of the Pantheon's opening night? Could this be a rehearsal, and what would we need to know before we decide that it is? Neither Rowlandson nor any of his contemporaries appears to have left any commentary about the prints, but clues exist in many contemporary sources. This paper is an attempt to follow out some of those clues to discover whether the Pantheon "Prospect Before Us" is really documentary evidence, and if so, of what.

Until recently many details of the history of the opera house at the Pantheon have been shrouded in mystery, but in 1985 scholars discovered a substantial collection of administrative documents among the papers of the Duke of Bedford. These have formed the basis for a thorough reinvestigation of the London opera scene in the last quarter of the eighteenth century. But even with the help of the Bedford Opera Papers, some features of these images remain obscure, possibly because Rowlandson himself is a little mysterious. He created an enormous body of work, but he left no diaries and apparently very few letters, and although he figures in a variety of contemporary reminiscences, the details of his day-to-day life seem to have been very hard to pin down.[6] Though he is considered one of the greatest graphic satirists of his period and has a pervasive presence in any general work about eighteenth century English caricature, there is no full-scale modern work about his prints. Nineteenth century critics were embarrassed by the caricatures, and when he was rediscovered in the twentieth century it was as a watercolorist. Therefore there is a considerable and very helpful body of modern scholarship about Rowlandson's drawings, in which the prints are present as a sort of by-product, but the only book devoted entirely to the caricatures was written by Joseph Grego in 1880.[7]

In the absence of eighteenth-century comments about these prints, most modern writers seeking to identify the performers depicted in them have relied on the authoritative catalog of the political and social satires in the British Museum compiled by F. G. Stephens and M. Dorothy George. George's source for the names is an article by Grego published as an appendix to a history of dance in 1898.[8] Grego was unaware of the existence of two rival companies, and in this article he does not cite his authority for the names of the dancers. Nevertheless, Didelot and Madame Théodore were widely publicized as the stars of the Pantheon ballet company, and presumably Grego drew his inference from newspaper advertisements, some of which he had quoted in his earlier book. Art historians have claimed that Rowlandson's caricatures generally depict types rather than actual people, and yet he was able to produce a recognizable portrait when he chose to do so; in the light of other iconographic and written evidence the identification of Madame Théodore is plausible, though not absolutely certain. She was renowned for her lightness of foot, unimpaired, say the newspapers, by the fact that she seemed to have gained a little weight since her last London appearance.[9] Her features and hair are not unlike those in other portraits of her, though they are also much like those of any fashionable beauty of the period. In addition, her costume resembles the one described for her character in *Amphion and Thalia* in the wardrobe book for the ballet preserved in the Bedford Opera Papers.[10] However, according to the ballet libretto the tambourine on the stage is a prop which belongs to another dancer, and an extant drawing by Rowlandson shows this same dancer, in this same costume, actually dancing with the tambourine in her hand.[11] If the tambourine in the print is significant, it could mean either that the dancer is Madame Théodore in another ballet from an earlier season, or that the ballet is *Amphion and Thalia,* and the character is not Thalia (Théodore's role) but the nymph who danced with the tambourine.

The identification of the second dancer as Didelot is still less convincing. He is shown from the rear, in a conventional pose for a "demi-caractère" dancer, which he was, but his costume, according to the Bedford Opera Papers wardrobe book, belongs to somebody else in the cast.[12] There is nothing about these costumes that makes them unique to this production—they could have been used for any number of pastoral ballets—so Rowlandson could have been drawing imaginary dancers, and the fact that the costume colors and props match so well with those described for the ballet in the Bedford Papers could be a happy coincidence. On the other hand, if Rowlandson really was drawing Didelot, he could have decided that for the purposes of the engraving he looked better in stripes than in plain white, and artistic license could account for the presence of props from other scenes as well. In either case, the fact remains that the earliest source for the identification of the dancers and the ballet is Joseph Grego—an unreliable historian writing almost a hundred years after the event.

If the print really shows a rehearsal, it would be important to know how and where Rowlandson could have seen it. Might he have simply wandered into the theatre while it was under construction? Did someone connected with the company provide him with access? Were rehearsals held outside the Pantheon, in some more public venue? Part of the answer to these questions might be found if it were possible to determine who commissioned the prints. Rowlandson was a professional artist and he would not have created these as speculations, but no one has mentioned any evidence of his having had direct connections with O'Reilly or any of the other major figures at the Pantheon. His friend Henry Wigstead might have provided a link. Wigstead was a house painter with a very high-end clientele, and in 1788, while decorating Carlton House, he had engaged Rowlandson to engrave several political satires on behalf of the Prince of Wales. In 1791 Wigstead and Rowlandson had been friends and traveling companions for about ten years; Rowlandson had engraved some of Wigstead's drawings and had used ideas of his in caricatures.[13] Wigstead is known to have ghost-written pamphlets and articles for O'Reilly, and was employed in the remodeling of the Pantheon. It is possible, therefore, that it could have been Wigstead who brought in Rowlandson to give a graphic boost to O'Reilly's opera house prospects.

Though there is no actual evidence that he did so, Rowlandson could possibly have gained access to the Pantheon before the opening on February 17 or even before the open rehearsals for subscribers on February 10 and 11, but it is difficult to figure out precisely what he might have seen once he got there. The Bedford Opera Papers include some clues about when the theatre might have been in use for rehearsals, but there are none for this first season. Newspapers give reports of how things are going, but it is hard to know how much is publicity and how much is actual reporting.[14] The London *Times* reported on January 4 that the theatre was nearly ready, that dresses were made, and that the dancers had been practicing for the last three weeks, which suggests that if Rowlandson had access to the theatre he ought to have been able to see a rehearsal of something well before the January 13 publication date on his print. But there were other ballets in rehearsal—originally a second ballet was planned for opening night, and there were dances in the opera itself—so those rehearsals may or may not have been for *Amphion and Thalia.* When a public rehearsal of the opening-night opera, *Armida,* finally took place on February 10, the *Times* reported that there were no costumes for the principals and, significantly, that there was no rehearsal of the intended dances. This may have been a problem of time; on opening night a week later the performance ran until well after midnight, necessitating severe cuts in *Amphion and Thalia* and the elimination of the second ballet altogether. Nevertheless, the author of a report of the separate public ballet rehearsal on February 11, the night after the opera rehearsal, complained that the dancers were nearly naked—

peculiar, for a production which sounded like it was in such good shape six weeks earlier.[15] Reports of other rehearsals, mostly of the music, had appeared sporadically in the weeks between January 4 and February 10, but the ballet of *Amphion and Thalia* is never named in pre-opening ads. When on January 27 the opera of *Armida* is finally announced as the opening production, the advertisement in the *Times* says only that it will be accompanied by "two grand ballets," and that further information will be forthcoming. As far as I can tell, the first mention of *Amphion and Thalia* in *Times* advertisements came on February 16, in the actual notice of opening night.

We cannot know what a stroller passing S. W. Fores's shop window in mid-January 1791 would have seen in these prints, but we can make some educated guesses. He would know that they referred to the opera company dispute, because Rowlandson told him so in the captions. If he was a ballet fan, he might have recognized Madame Théodore, a London favorite, and he would certainly have appreciated the contrast of the plump and cheerful Théodore with the scrawny, raffish Hilligsberg in the other print—a piece of real-life casting which must have struck Rowlandson as a gift from the gods—whether or not he knew who they were meant to be. He might or might not have been able to put a name to the male dancer, and he most probably would not have had a name for the ballet.

What additional information, then, do we have that we can read with confidence? It seems likely that the female dancer is meant to be Madame Théodore, and it is not impossible that her partner is Didelot. It is harder to prove that the ballet is actually meant to be *Amphion and Thalia.* There is little in the costumes or props to differentiate it from any other pastoral ballet of the period, or to suggest that Rowlandson must have seen it in order to draw it. He could have simply depicted his dancers in generic costumes which happened to resemble those for *Amphion and Thalia,* and subsequent dance and print historians, knowing what the ballet ought to have looked like, have appropriated the image as authentic. On the other hand, if Rowlandson had seen *Amphion and Thalia,* he could have made alterations for esthetic reasons which could account for the discrepancies in costume and props between those in the print and those described in the libretto and wardrobe book. The suggestion that the drawings of the Pantheon print represent the actual scene at opening night is certainly not correct, first of all because the print appears to have been published several weeks before the event, and additionally because both the drawings and the print include the King in his box, and the King did not attend a performance at the Pantheon until February 22, a week after the opening. If the scene documents a rehearsal, it would still be necessary to determine how and where Rowlandson could have witnessed it. Several imaginative scenarios are possible, but there is as yet no actual evidence to support any of them.

One alternative view is that the date on the prints is completely wrong. If it could be proven that the caricatures were actually issued after the command performance on February 22, but before the opening of the Haymarket on March 26 (and there is a certain amount of evidence for this in the Haymarket print) that would make the identification of the performers and the ballet more plausible and account for the presence of the King at the performance;

the print might then be evidence of an event, perhaps even an eyewitness account, especially since *Amphion and Thalia* was the ballet performed on that evening. The image then becomes useless as evidence of the state of rehearsals on January 13, and the meaning of the title is slightly altered to suggest that Rowlandson meant that Taylor had little hope of ever catching up, but this explanation makes it unnecessary to imagine how Rowlandson could have had pre-opening access to the theatre, and is not contradicted by anything internal to either of the prints.[16] But this is still merely speculation. Until we learn more about the dating of eighteenth-century prints, or until more information about rehearsals at the Pantheon in December 1790 and January 1791 becomes available, or until a modern scholar writing about Rowlandson caricatures unearths new evidence from Rowlandson or contemporary commentary about the prints, it seems that we cannot safely assume that the Pantheon "Prospect Before Us" is actually documentary evidence of anything.

The King's Theatre Pantheon opened on February 17, 1791 with the serious opera of *Armida* and two grand ballets, and continued with a full opera and ballet schedule until the end of the season, though to very poor business. The King's Theatre Haymarket did not secure a license to perform opera. After two open rehearsals of the serious opera of *Pirro,* unstaged, it finally opened for business on March 26 with "entertainments of music and dancing"—concerts of opera arias and fully-staged ballets. Both companies continued in ruinous competition until the end of the season. The King's Theatre Haymarket was unable to reopen for the following season, but the King's Theatre Pantheon did, only to burn to the ground after its fourth performance, on January 14, 1792. Arson was suspected, but no charges were brought. Henry Wigstead made a drawing of the ruins, which was published by his friend Rowlandson. In the season of 1793, Italian opera returned to the new opera house in the Haymarket.

ENDNOTES

1 See Curtis Price, "Italian Opera and Arson in Late Eighteenth-Century London," Journal of the American Musicological Society, Vol. 42, no. 1 (Spring 1898), 55–107, for a fuller account of these circumstances. The complete story, brought up to date by recent manuscript discoveries, can be found in Curtis Price, Judith Milhous, and Robert D. Hume, *Italian Opera in Late Eighteenth-Century London, Volume I: The King's Theatre, Haymarket 1778–1791* (Oxford: Clarendon Press, 1995), and Judith Milhous, Gabriella Dideriksen, and Robert D. Hume, *Italian Opera in Late Eighteenth-Century London, Volume II: The Pantheon Opera and its Aftermath 1789–1795* (Oxford; Clarendon Press, 2001).

2 An early version of this study was presented at the conference "The Stage Represented: Images and Iconography of the Theatre," University of Toronto Graduate Centre for Study of Drama, October 21–23, 2004. My paper there dealt with both of the "Prospect Before Us" caricatures.

3 See, for example, Mary Grace Swift, *A Loftier Flight: the Life and Accomplishments of Charles-Louis Didelot, Balletmaster* (Middletown, CT: Wesleyan University Press, 1974), 41. Highfill, Burnim, and Langhans, in their biographical dictionary of eighteenth-century actors and stage personnel in London, use it as a portrait of Didelot.

4 Raymond Mander and Joe Mitchenson, *The Lost Theatres of London* (London: Rupert Hart-Davis, 1968), pl. 60; Bernard Falk, *Thomas Rowlandson: his Life and Art* (London and New York: [1949]), facing p. 108; *The Georgian Playhouse: Actors, Artists, Audiences and Architecture*

1730–1830 (London: Arts Council of Great Britain, 1975), no. 266a. It is important to note that all of these sources reproduce undated drawings, not the published print.

[5] *Italian Opera in Late Eighteenth-Century London,* Vo. II, 557. The ballet of *Amphion and Thalia* and Rowlandson's depiction of it are discussed at length on p. 555–557.

[6] Bernard Falk's biography, *Thomas Rowlandson: his Life and Art* (London and New York: Hutchinson & Co., 1949) is subtitled " A Documentary Record," and although Falk spends a good deal of time correcting the errors of his predecessors, the documents he uses are generally from the public record. He admits that documents from the hand of Rowlandson himself are almost non-existent; in 1949 he knew of only one letter. I believe that the total now stands at five.

[7] Joseph Grego, *Rowlandson the Caricaturist.* 2 v. (London: Chatto and Windus, 1880, repr. New York: Collectors Editions, c1978). Grego's discussion of the 1791 "Prospect Before Us" prints appears in Vol. I, 283–287.

[8] Mary Dorothy George, *Catalogue of Political and Personal Satires Preserved in the Department of Prints and Drawings in the British Museum,* Vol. VI, 1784–1792 (London: British Museum, 1938), 863, no. 8008. George cites "Grego in Vuillot, Hist. of Dancing, 1898, ii. 401" for the names of the dancers, but she has mistaken the author's name; "Vuillot" should be "Vuillier."

[9] Unsourced and undated (possibly 17 February 1791) newspaper clipping in a scrapbook in the Harvard Theatre Collection, *Pantheon and Princess Theatre* (TS 326.1).

[10] *Italian Opera in Late Eighteenth-Century London,* Vol. II, 702–728.

[11] John Riely, *Rowlandson Drawings from the Paul Mellon Collection* (New Haven:Yale Center for British Art, 1977), 29, no. 39. The drawing can be seen online at http://www .bridgemanart.com/image/Rowlandson-Thomas-1756–1827/Female-Dancer-with-a-Tambourine-1790–95–w-c-with-pen-inks-and-graphite-on-paper/39b8ca7e88a5434694c408 ade78248b6?key=&artistid=7746a258–61f5–414c-94a0–93c7b5f813ad&thumb=x150& num=15&page=12

[12] *Italian Opera in Late Eighteenth-Century London,* Vol. II, 798. Eighteenth century caricatures are hand-colored, and there is often variation from one example to another. Copies of this print at the British Museum, Harvard, Yale, and the Metropolitan Museum of Art all show the male dancer in a jacket striped in pink and white, which suggests to me that they were colored by the publisher and reflect Rowlandson's intentions. The Bedford Papers wardrobe book specifies a white suit for Amphion (Didelot's character), and gives the pink-and-white stripes to Monsr. Duquesney, performing as a "Berger de Phocide."

[13] M. T. W. Payne and J. E. Payne, "Henry Wigstead, Rowlandson's Fellow-Traveller." *British Art Journal,* Vol. IV, No. 3 (Autumn 2003): 27–38.

[14] Many of the newspaper items cited here were first examined in scrapbooks of clippings in the Harvard Theatre Collection and elsewhere, where they are frequently dated in manuscript, sometimes erroneously. All citations to the London Times have been verified in *The Times Digital Archive 1785–1985,* published by Gale.

[15] Newspaper article from a scrapbook in the Mander and Mitchenson collection, dated in MS 14 Feb. 1791, cited in *Italian Opera in Late Eighteenth-Century London,* Vol. II, p. 399. The suggestion here is that the dancers were in rehearsal clothes or some such; there is no indication in the wardrobe book or the reviews that the costumes themselves were particularly scanty.

[16] The question of reliability of publication dates on eighteenth-century British prints is a very interesting one, and one which does not seem to have received much attention from art historians. The date is there to establish copyright, and so far I have found no literature on how publishers chose the dates, or how well they corresponded with the actual date that a print appeared in the shops in the normal course of business. Print scholars that I've asked about the issue are of the opinion that these dates might be no more reliable than the publication dates on modern books, and didn't seem to be particularly distressed about it (e-mail from Marjorie B. Cohn and Antony Griffiths).

Portrait of a Lady Hamlet

AMY MUSE

The setting of this mystery is the Folger Shakespeare Library, a repository of many secrets. It begins as I sit in the dark grandeur of its reading room, a large, leather-bound portfolio on the table before me. Embossed on its hide is "George Henry Harlow, *Original Drawings of Contemporary Theatrical Characters,* Originally Belonging to Lady Hamilton, 1802–1806." Opening it, I discover a scrapbook filled with hundreds of tiny pasted-in watercolor and pen-and-ink sketches, primarily of actors in character from various London productions. Underneath some are handwritten notes identifying the specific play, actors, theatre, and/or date. I need turn no further than the very first page, however, as it is there I find what I have come seeking.

It is an arresting watercolor sketch of two actors in the "Closet Scene" from *Hamlet.* Handwritten along the bottom of the sketch is a line from that scene, "Here is your husband," as well as "Mrs. Ansell & Mrs. Powell 1802" and the initials "D.L."

This is it: a portrait of Jane Powell, the first woman to play Hamlet in London, the first who, as Jane Moody has put it, "challenged the metropolitan ownership of Hamlet by men."[1] In my years spent in archives around Britain, hot on the trail of the first female Hamlets, I have never spied its equal. I must be looking at the first illustration of a female Hamlet in performance.

What am I seeing? In many ways, a conventional Romantic-era stage scene of *Hamlet.* This postcard-sized sketch, irregularly cut as though it came from a larger piece of paper and the scrapbooker didn't have effective scissoring skills, is a close-up of two actors sitting side by side on chairs with the sketchiest of stage sets in the background (gray-washed indications of two columns and of the bottom corners of two framed paintings).[2] The Queen is on the viewer's left, Hamlet on our right, thrusting a miniature portrait under his mother's face (which, covered with her arm, offers no counter gaze, no interaction) to show her "Here is your husband." (The other portrait, of his father, Hamlet holds in his left hand.) Hamlet's expression is fervent, eyes boring into his mother's face, penetrating the Queen's conscience. His dark hair is short, tousled and curly, and the appearance of a small mustache adds to a rather sinister appearance, suited to this scene, perhaps the most verbally violent in the play, in which the Queen expresses fear that Hamlet will kill her. The costume—black, of course—consists of a tunic with white cuffs and a white ruffled collar, a pendant (a medallion, or perhaps the

[Thomas Baxter], Watercolor sketch "Mrs. Powell and Mrs. Ansell, 'Here is your husband'" (1802) By permission of the Folger Shakespeare Library.

holding place for the kings' portraits) hanging around his neck on a wide pale-blue ribbon, and knickers, below which one stocking is falling down to indicate, apropos of Ophelia's description, Hamlet's disheveled appearance, and exposing a well-muscled calf. Long before Freud and Ernest Jones will point it out and Olivier will stage it, the latent eroticism is everywhere manifesting in this scene.[3] Hamlet's right thigh presses against his mother's left knee, and he thrusts his right arm under the Queen's left one to force the picture under her breast, calling attention to her ample bosom. The Queen's draped white dress is clingy, revealing a sensually curvy figure and rounded thighs; her left arm is outstretched as if to ward Hamlet off, but the gesture is so weak it looks as though she is gently brushing arms with him instead. While her legs are slanted toward Hamlet, her feet hardly touching the ground, giving the impression that she could easily be blown away, Hamlet embodies aggression in his firmly-footed, wide-legged stance.

It is a blistering Hamlet, apotheosizing his transformation into a tempestuous, moody rebel from Garrick's loyal son and, long before that, his birth as a Renaissance revenger. Edmund Kean has always been given credit for having created this stage version: the Romantic Hamlet, electrifying audiences with his "Romantic fire."[4] In this sketch Hamlet is wild, tousled, sexy, aggressive, intense—all adjectives that could describe Kean in performance—and the costume is strikingly reminiscent of his own for Hamlet at Drury Lane; the face, with its intensity of expression, recalls George Clint's watercolor of Kean as Sir Giles Overreach in *A New Way to Pay Old Debts*. But the date of this sketch, 1802, places it a good twelve years before Kean arrives in London in 1814. And this passionate Hamlet is a woman. Or so its handwritten caption says.

Is Jane Powell pioneering the Romantic Hamlet? That could go a long way toward explaining why her reviews are so outrageously mixed. Thomas Gilliland gushes in *Dramatic Synopsis* (1804), "perhaps the vigour of her genius was never so thoroughly shewn as in her performance of Hamlet," remarking that as Hamlet

> she had ample room for the display of her uncommon powers . . . her pathos appeared so natural, and her manner appeared so easy and unaffected, that an auditor might have supposed she had simply learned the words of the part by rote, and relied upon the feelings of the moment to prompt her to deliver them with truth and propriety.[5]

But Leigh Hunt sharply dissents in *Critical Essays on the Performers of the London Theatres* (1807), where he snaps, "What honest critic . . . could refrain from giving Mrs. Powell some advice on her frequent whim of assuming the character of Hamlet?" and proceeds to ridicule her as mad for even thinking she could conceivably take on the role.

> I have heard indeed of females, whom the vapours have induced to imagine themselves tea-pots; others have bewailed their transformation into pincushions, shuddering whenever they saw a needle or a bodkin; and there was a lady in Mr. Pope's time who insisted she was a goose-pye and was ready to fall into fits at the sight of a bishop or an alderman: but we never before knew an instance of a female, who imagined herself so thoroughly a man in habits and in experience, as to be able to represent the most difficult picture of man on the stage.[6]

Reading reviews so sharply divergent, even incommensurable, I like to think that I am witnessing Jane Powell most in harmony with herself, following Oscar Wilde's logic in the Preface to *The Picture of Dorian Gray* that when critics disagree the artist is in accord with himself. Perhaps this is the detractors' fear, that in an era filled with men proclaiming "I have a smack of Hamlet myself" (Coleridge in 1798) and "we are Hamlet" (Hazlitt in 1817), that she also considers herself Hamlet.

I bask in my Schliemann moment, beholding my own version of the mask of Agamemnon. It seems that this portrait is unknown even to most specialists. Neither of Powell's entries in the *Oxford Dictionary of National Biography* or in the *Biographical Dictionary of Actors, Actresses. . . 1660–1800* lists it among the known illustrations of her.[7] At the Folger it is obscurely catalogued; my searches under key terms of "Jane Powell" or "Mrs. Powell" or "Hamlet performance," terms that have unearthed materials in other archives, have been for naught. So grateful I am, then, that I have come to this visit at the Folger bearing a call number: Art Vol. d47 (2a), shared graciously (especially because he had not yet viewed the sketch himself and might have wanted to retain the digging rights) by Alan Young. Delighted with my discovery, I include the image in my doctoral dissertation, brandish it in two conference presentations, and publish it in a subsequent article.

Several years pass. Professor Young's book *Hamlet and the Visual Arts, 1709–1900* is published, and I read it, eager to see what he thought of the portrait. However, I note, to my surprise and growing dismay, that although many *Hamlet* illustrations from the Folger's collection are included, this particular portrait of Jane Powell—the very one to which he directed my attention—is not. I contact him to inquire. He hesitated to publish it in the book, he replies (it is included in his database of *Hamlet* images), because when he saw it, he wasn't convinced it was Powell.

Oh.

Who is in this Hamlet portrait?

I return to the scene.

Back at the Folger, I order up the portfolio, noting under "Provenance" in their catalogue that "the bookseller attributed the forming and mounting of the collection to Emma, Lady Hamilton and the title page and binding note Lady Hamilton as the former owner. The binding bears the stamp of Sangorski and Sutcliffe, a London firm established in 1901. The volume was purchased by the Folgers from Gabriel Wells March 4, 1919 (Cs. 818)."

When it arrives, I comb through the entire portfolio, examining it for evidence. A slip of paper has been inserted between two later pages. Typed on creamy paper, it reads:

> From Lady Hamilton's Collection. An exceedingly interesting collection of more than 300 Theatrical Portraits, all being original drawings in watercolour or pen and ink by G. H. Harlow. Each drawing has a contemporary inscription giving in most cases the name of personage, the play, and further the theatre and date. This collection was formed by Emma, Lady Hamilton, who was an enthusiastic theatre-goer. The drawings were mounted on coarse paper by Lady Hamilton, and these original sheets are preserved in sunk mounts, bound in a large 4to volume, full crushed levant morocco extra, gilt edges, by Sangorski & Sutcliffe. The Drawings include: Mrs. Ansell and Mrs. Powell, "Here is your Husband." (Mrs. Powell as a girl had been fellow servant with Lady Hamilton in the service of Dr. Budd.)

In the advertisement, then, the portrait of Jane Powell is a selling point, and whoever created and sold the portfolio wants to remind us of the connection between Lady Emma Hamilton and first-female-Hamlet-in-London actress Jane Powell. It leads us to believe that Lady Hamilton clipped and mounted the sketches herself (although there is no indication as to whether she wrote the identifying information beneath the sketches or even compiled and organized this volume, placing the image of Powell as Hamlet on the first page). Throughout the volume, pictures of Mrs. Powell are highlighted with notes made in a different handwriting from that which created the captions for the sketches. Reinforcing the connection, someone—post-sale, I'm assuming, a Folger librarian rather than the bookseller—has scribbled in next to the *Hamlet* sketch on the first page a comment, "Mrs."—and then a caret pointing upward to where the name "Jane" has been inserted—"Powell had as a girl been in the same service with Lady Hamilton (Dr. Budd's)."

It's quite a tale. These two dames of humble origin met while employed as servants in the kitchen at Chatham Place, Blackfriars: young Jane Powell an ardent spouter of dramatic lines, desiring more than anything a life on the stage, and Amy Lyon (as she was then known) also keenly seeking a way out of servitude by banking on her beauty and charm. Many years later the two reunited in a Green Room gossip writer's fantasy: at Drury Lane, with Jane Powell onstage and the now Emma Hamilton watching from the box of her lover Lord Nelson.[8]

It makes perfect sense that Lady Hamilton would collect images of her old friend. Scholarly suspicion has been cast on this portfolio, but in so doing, it only reinforces the connection and may authenticate Powell as Hamlet. In the late 1970s it was discovered by art historian Geoffrey Ashton that in all probability these sketches are not the work of George Henry Harlow after all, but of a less exalted painter, Thomas Baxter (1782–1821). They had been "attributed by bookseller and binding to Harlow," as the Folger's art catalogue reads; inquirers of the Harlow portfolio are directed to an entry that now reads: "Baxter, Thomas. *Sketches of London Stage Productions, 1802–06.*" The descriptive catalogue of the Original Works on Paper of the Folger collection states: "All of the items bear the initials of a London theater and most are dated with a year. Some of the sketches note the actor depicted and the title of the play being performed. None are signed. . . . It is assumed that these sketches were taken from actual performances viewed by Baxter." A note to readers about Ashton's find—"The volume was formerly catalogued under Harlow but has been reattributed here due to the research of Geoffrey Ashton who has convincingly linked Baxter to the Folger volume"—also advises us to see Ashton's *British Theatrical Painting c. 1800–1820: with a special reference to George Henry Harlow and Thomas Baxter*, his Ph.D. thesis from the Courtauld Institute in 1983. (Held only at the Courtauld and the British Library.) And—more tantalizing—there is a reference for a "forthcoming" study by Ashton, *Thomas Baxter's Drawings of the London Stage, 1802–6*, which, it appears, remained unpublished at the time of his unfortunate early death.

Now, Thomas Baxter, it turns out, was a friend of Emma Hamilton's,[9] and it is tempting to imagine, heedless of all warnings from performance historians but in line with the bookseller's and Folger catalogue's premise, that this portrait captures a moment from an actual production, one that he saw, perhaps that they both saw, but that she at least delighted in seeing a representation of and clipped to save and remember. In John Genest's account, on June 4, 1802, Jane Powell played Hamlet for her benefit, with Mrs. Ansell as the Queen and Ophelia by Mrs. Jordan.[10] This is the evening I imagine when I look at the sketch, treating it as a photograph, believing I can communicate with the dead. But Shearer West cautions us against assuming that theatrical portraits "convey the specific nature of performances"; instead, they were "coded responses to the performances which had as much to do with prevailing tendencies in art as with the minutiae of theatrical presentation."[11] Therefore it is likely that the sketch says more about Baxter and Romantic-era attitudes toward the stage, theatrical portraiture, and the emerging Hamlet than it does about this particular female Hamlet.

When looking with cold, dispassionate eyes at the sketches in this portfolio I am forced to admit that what I initially took for the distinctive intensity of Powell's Hamlet now looks like a conventional "actor expression" when it appears on the faces of nearly all the figures. Put differently, most of the figures' faces are indistinguishable. (A striking exception: Sarah Siddons is unmistakably herself, recognizable instantly by her noble bearing and triangular Roman nose.) Confusion really sets in with sketches of Powell as the Queen in *Hamlet*, a role she played more often than the Prince. In a couple of black and white drawings she is identified alongside "Cooper as Hamlet," and thus we know she is Gertrude. But in one sketch, the scene is of three people: on the left, a Hamlet who looks like Powell, with a markedly feminine face and exactly the same costume as in the watercolor sketch; and then a pair of figures, a Gertrude who also looks like Powell, and a more clearly male Hamlet, who is in the same costume as Powell's Hamlet. This one has no caption on it, but it appears to be a comparison of Hamlets, Jane Powell on the left, Cooper on the right (with Jane Powell again in the middle as the Queen)—and another indication, perhaps, that the artist is sketching imaginatively, working around with the figure of Hamlet, rather than journalistically recording actual performances.

What is more, the portrait ostensibly of Powell doesn't actually bear much resemblance to other extant and authenticated portraits of the actress. You might think that alone would close the case. Yet I've proceeded undeterred because the very disparity has propped up my presumption (in both senses) that Hamlet was a revelatory role for Jane Powell. The Baxter watercolor of Hamlet reveals a being strikingly different from the Powell depicted in portraits of other characters.

To take a Romantic turn, it appears in the Baxter portrait that Jane Powell *is* Hamlet, unleashing an intensity and passion in this role that brings to mind Bert States' observation that when a performance is realistic "one might even suspect that the actor's performance was an open display of a hidden, or at least possible, self . . . doesn't the playing of Hamlet, after all, require a dredging up of a Hamlet from somewhere within?"[12] The hypothesis illuminates odd comments made by observers of her, such as F. G. Waldron's that Powell "should never attempt any thing in the tender or pathetic. Her action possesses too much nerve and energy for a female performer, and her deportment is deficient of ease," a portrait of the Romantic Hamlet if there ever was one.[13] Absorption into Hamlet might be implied in actor-manager F. C. Wemyss' remark that "her acting spoke more to the heart than that of any lady I ever saw before or since, identifying herself with the character she was performing until you forgot the woman in the actress."[14]

I must confess: I have become entangled in this case and cannot be trusted to see objectively. This is the story as I want to see it—a story inspired by this portrait that I have taken as genuine, a relic of the actual onstage performance, a piece of evidence to be privileged above contradictory comments by critics who were after all eyewitnesses to the scene. When I look at this sketch I see Jane Powell forging a new Hamlet, the modern Hamlet, the Hamlet who transcends his position as a mere literary character and who becomes, for men and women alike, a cultural icon.[15]

ENDNOTES

I would like to express my gratitude to the NEH for the support of a Summer Stipend, which allowed me time to research this situation. Any views, findings, conclusions, or recommendations expressed in this essay do not necessarily reflect those of the National Endowment for the Humanities. Thanks also to Alan Young for leading me to this fascinating sketch and to entertaining my lingering questions about it, and to Georgianna Ziegler, Head of Reference, and Erin Blake, Curator of Art, at the Folger Shakespeare Library.

[1] Jane Moody, "Dictating to the Empire: Performance and Theatrical Geography in Eighteenth-Century Britain," in *The Cambridge Companion to British Theatre, 1730–1830*, eds. Moody and Daniel O'Quinn (Cambridge University Press, 2007), 21–42. See page 27.

[2] Alan Young notes that in the earliest productions Hamlet would have directed his mother's attention to two portraits hanging on the back wall. After about 1730, stage Hamlets began carrying miniatures of the two kings, and the composition of this scene is reminiscent of the staging for the late eighteenth century actor John Henderson's portrayal of Hamlet, illustrated by Robert Dunkerton in 1777 showing Henderson seated in a chair with his "head is turned to the left, his eyes raised as if staring intently at something/one (presumably Gertrude). His right hand crosses his body and his left hand is raised to shoulder height. In each hand he holds a miniature. That in his left hand has a small ribbon attached to it." See Alan R. Young, *Hamlet and the Visual Arts, 1709–1900* (Newark: University of Delaware Press, 2002), 217–218.

[3] Bernice Kliman has argued that such a sexual subtext was present as early as a 1714 engraving of the scene by Louis du Guernier, which includes a bed in the Closet Scene; see Young, *Hamlet and the Visual Arts, 1709–1900*, 221.

[4] Anne Russell discusses this, claiming it was Kean who brought the "Romantic passion" to Hamlet; "*after* Kean," she says, "romantic acting styles which privileged passion came to dominate the English stage" (emphasis added). See "Tragedy, Gender, Performance: Women as Tragic Heroes on the Nineteenth-Century Stage," *Comparative Drama* 30.2 (Summer 1996): 140. "Romantic fire" comes from Anthony B. Dawson, *Hamlet* (Manchester and New York: Manchester University Press, 1995), 44.

[5]. Thomas Gilliland, *A Dramatic Synopsis, containing an Essay on the Political and Moral Use of a Theatre; involving Remarks on the Dramatic Writers of the Present Day, and Strictures on the Performers of the Two Theatres* (London, 1804), 103.

[6]. [Leigh Hunt],*Critical Essays on the Performers of the London Theatres by the author of the Theatrical Criticisms in the weekly paper called the News* (London: John Hunt, 1807), 44–46.

[7] It does get mentioned, though neither described nor reproduced, in Frank Nicholas Clary, "Pictures in the Closet: Properties and Stage Business in *Hamlet* 3.4," *Stage Directions in Hamlet*, ed. Hardin L. Aasand (Cranbury, NJ and London: Associated University Presses, 2003), 170–188. See page 179.

[8] An undated clipping by W. Macqueen Pope in Jane Powell's biographical file at the Theatre Museum, London states that the play was *The Grecian Daughter* (poetically rounding out a story that she recited from that very play when the two were maids together), but a more recent study gives evidence for Sheridan's *Pizarro*. See Kate Williams, *England's Mistress: The Infamous Life of Emma Hamilton* (New York: Ballantine Books, 2006), 35–37 and 258–259.

[9] Kate Williams notes that Baxter, as party guest, was recruited to perform in her piece "The Favourite Sultana," and that his illustrated book of ancient costumes "owed much to her." See *England's Mistress*, 287, 357.

[10] John Genest, *Some Account of the English Stage: from the Restoration in 1660 to 1830*, vol. 7 (Bath: H. E. Carrington, 1832), 538–539.

[11] Shearer West, *The Image of the Actor: Verbal and Visual Representation in the Age of Garrick and Kemble* (London: Palgrave Macmillan, 1991), 26.

[12]. Bert O. States, *Great Reckonings in Little Rooms: on the Phenomenology of Theatre* (Berkeley: University of California Press, 1985), 199.

[13] F. G. Waldron, *Candid and Impartial Strictures on the Performers* (London, 1795). Qtd. in Powell's entry in Philip H. Highfill, Jr., Kalman A. Burmin, and Edward A. Langhans. *A Biographical Dictionary of Actors, Actresses, Musicians, Dancers, Managers, and Other Stage Personnel in London, 1660–1800.* 16 vols. (Carbondale and Edwardsville: Southern Illinois University Press, 1973–93), 145.

[14] Francis Courtney Wemyss, *Theatrical Biography: Or, the Life of an Actor and Manager* (Glasgow: R. Griffin and Company, 1848), 38. Wemyss worked with her later in her life, on the Harrogate and Kendal circuit in 1816–1817, when she was acting as Mrs. Renaud—and still playing Hamlet.

[15] See Amy Muse, "Actresses and the Making of the Modern Hamlet," *Text & Presentation, 2007:* 137–148.

John B. Gough's Afternoon at the Theatre; Or, the Tyranny of an Account Book

AMY E. HUGHES

Although rarely remembered now, John B. Gough (1817–1886) was one of the most celebrated Americans of the nineteenth century, internationally renowned for his entertaining temperance lectures.[1] I became interested in Gough while researching *The Drunkard; or, The Fallen Saved,* the famous temperance melodrama written by actor and former alcoholic W. H. Smith, along with an anonymous collaborator.[2] First produced by Moses Kimball at the Boston Museum in 1844, the drama eventually became so popular that it ran one hundred performances without interruption at P. T. Barnum's American Museum in New York—an extremely rare occurrence at the time.

But my investigation centered not so much on *The Drunkard* as the *drunkard*: the stereotypical male inebriate who, in many ways, constitutes a spectacle in himself. As a way to understand this cultural construction, I began researching Gough's meteoric rise to fame, which occurred in the Boston region immediately prior to and alongside of *The Drunkard.* A unique ability to conjure images while he spoke was one of Gough's most lauded talents. He performed, in essence, one-man melodramatic sensation scenes: virtual tableaux that amused, saddened, and horrified his spectators. The ways in which he personified reformation—presenting his body, once gripped by ardent spirits, as spectacular proof of the potential for redemption—fascinated audiences. I had a hunch that Gough's enactments of the *delirium tremens,* which he frequently incorporated in his orations, may have inspired Smith to include a DTs scene in Act IV of his play (which became, arguably, its most well-known feature). Many commentators argued that Gough's personal struggle with drink contributed to his effectiveness as a speaker. Smith, too, was a recovered drunkard, and his personal history probably ghosted his portrayal of Edward Middleton, the protagonist in *The Drunkard.*

I suspected that multiple dimensions of the Gough phenomenon—the anecdotal and the actual, the public and the private—might illuminate why the DTs played such a prominent role in Boston performance culture during the 1840s. However, most of my evidence connecting the lecturer's notoriety to the play's popularity was circumstantial. Did points of overlap exist between

1844		John B. Gough	Dr	
March	2	To amount brought over	$474	08
		To 1 years Subscription to the Olive branch	2	00
	3	To cash given at Collection	1	00
		To Sundries $1.50 Omnibus Tickets .50	2	00
	5	To Expenses to Danvers $1.25. Books. 50.	1	75
		Lent Richardson	5	00
	6	Expenses to & from Tremont Temple	1	00
		Cash pd Mrs Fuller for Lukes Board	2	00
	7	Expenses to Framingham	2	00
	8	Cash given for Missionary Operations	10	00
	11	To Omnibus Tickets	1	00
	12	To Books &c	3	00
		Expenses to Boston		50
		Cash pd for Board	5	00
		Cash pd for Washing	3	00
	15	Expenses to Marblehead	1	25
		Table Cloth $1.50 Jujube Paste &c $1.00	2	50
	16	Cash pd for Board	5	00
		Tickets to Museum .50 Candy .50 Omnibus Tickets 1.00	2	00
		Cash lent Samuel Parks	50	00
	18	Cash pd for Wood &c	6	00
	19	Expenses to Rockport	1	50
	20	Expenses from Gloucester	1	00
	22	Expenses to & from Dover	5	00
		Phrenological Chart $1.00. Sundries 75c	1	75
	23	Expenses to Boston $1.00, Given away $1.50	2	50
		Cash paid Mrs Fuller for Board & sawing wood	2	87½
	25	Cash pd for Shawl $20.00 Gloves $1.00	21	00
	26	Expenses to Westboro	2	00
	27	Cash given to wife	5	00
		Mr Walkers Bill	23	75
		Hutchinson & Crosbys Bill	16	25
			662	70

An entry in John B. Gough's personal account book, indicating he purchased "tickets to museum" on March 16, 1844. Did the temperance lecturer see W. H. Smith's *The Drunkard* at the Boston Museum? John B. Gough, Account Book (Roxbury, MA) 1843–1844. Courtesy of American Antiquarian Society oratorical and theatrical circles at that time? And if so, how could I document them?

While examining one of Gough's personal account books at the American Antiquarian Society (AAS), I came across an intriguing entry for "museum tickets" in March 1844. Could this notation indicate that he and his wife attended *The Drunkard*, which by then was one month into its run? I scoured newspapers, city directories, and other documents in Gough's personal papers in order to ascertain whether the lecturer could have been in the audience that day. Ultimately, an unequivocal answer to my question remained elusive; moreover, I realized that the solution to this mystery was not altogether relevant to the argument I was constructing. My experience with this tyrannical document underscored for me the strong attractions and pleasurable distractions of the tangential research problem.

The Mystery

Gough's early success as a speaker was inspired and supported by a community of working-class temperance advocates that came to be known as the Washingtonians. Established by a small group of Maryland artisans in May 1840, the Washington Temperance Society of Baltimore quickly caught the imagination of the nation. According to Ian R. Tyrrell, "The older evangelicals had lacked personal experience of drink and sought converts chiefly among the already sober; the new group of reformers focused the attention of the temperance movement on the drinkers themselves." In addition, the Washingtonians popularized the notion of total abstinence to a greater degree than any other temperance society had been able or willing to do. Although at first not all reformers embraced this ethic, it gradually gained traction across the board.[3] Most Washingtonian chapters disbanded or transformed into fraternal lodges within a decade, but they had an indelible impact on the antebellum temperance movement.[4] Gough, who became sober as a result of an encounter with a Washingtonian, was only twenty-five years old when he began telling his story in public (in the form of "experience speeches," as they came to be known) in 1842.

Unlike other temperance advocates who traveled and spoke throughout New England, Gough was a different kind of spectacle—an oddity, an anomaly, a freak. He seems to have been the kind of "abnormally interesting" person that Joseph Roach describes in *It*, embodying the paradoxical qualities of "strength *and* vulnerability, innocence *and* experience, and singularity *and* typicality" in myriad ways.[5] Even as a relatively inexperienced lecturer in his mid twenties, he had a powerful voice and an uncanny ability to imitate characters—strengths that contrasted with his youthful vulnerability. Furthermore, middle-class audiences viewed Gough as somewhat innocent, due to his lack of polish and education (he never finished school, coming from an impoverished family). And yet, he also had a wealth of "experience" as a reformed drunkard, which not only inspired his lectures, but also made him an authority on the subject. Finally, Gough was both singular and typical because he differed markedly from most of the men—clerics and physicians—who frequented the lecture circuit.

Such contradictions can be detected in the plethora of newspaper clippings that Gough collected in his personal scrapbooks, now housed by the AAS.[6] Spectators struggled to pinpoint what made Gough so compelling. A writer in the *Flushing Journal* once lamented, "It needs a more competent hand than mine to give anything like a sketch of the speaker's fire and power . . . One must be *present,* as in a battle or a ship-wreck, to be able to form a just idea and estimation of such things."[7] But the clippings reveal that his admirers considered his spectacles to be not only *e*ffective but also *a*ffective. Gough's appeal as a performer seemed to center on two talents: his power of imitation, and his ability to generate breathless moments of emotional collectivity in his audiences.

Interestingly, critics often compared Gough to famous actors. His pleasing voice, his elaborate gestures and postures, and, above all, his mutability of character were frequently discussed. A *Gloucester Telegraph* reporter asserts, "The stage actor's varied accomplishments were never nearer the pulpit: and never were their evident comedial [*sic*] attractions exhibited or exerted in a better cause." A writer for the *Commercial Advertiser* went even further in likening Gough's oratory to theatrical performance: "I have listened to [some] of the greatest tragic actors of the time when theatres were in fashion; but none of them in the highest wrought scenes of Shakspeare [*sic*] could ever move my feelings as they were moved by that son of Nature in his simple lectures in favor of temperance."[8] Whether intentionally or not, such comparisons alluded to a somewhat embarrassing biographical detail in the orator's past: before taking the pledge of sobriety, he worked for a time as a professional actor, including short stints at the Franklin Theatre in New York City and the Lion Theatre in Boston. Gough occasionally mentioned this in his writings or lectures in order to illustrate the depths to which he had sunk as a drunkard.[9] For example, in his 1848 autobiography, when telling the story of how he (unsuccessfully) sought a position at Thomas S. Hamblin's Bowery Theatre, Gough exclaims, "so low had I fallen and so desperately had I backslidden, that at the very door of that same theatre, which I had, five years before, wished destroyed, as a temple of sin, I stood applying for a situation as an actor and comic singer!"[10]

I often wondered (and still do) whether such disavowals were genuine or strategic. In the unpublished manuscript of an oration he wrote late in life, Gough enthusiastically discusses his youthful love affair with the theatre, admitting that as a playgoer, "I cried and *laughed,* I was thrilled by the tragedy, and *convulsed* by the farce. It was a new world."[11] Could it be that Gough was ambivalent, perhaps even conflicted, about performance and performing? But an even larger question was at stake, relating to Gough's authenticity and honesty. Public suspicions about whether or not Gough was truly reformed dogged him throughout his life. Did his critiques of the theatre represent his true feelings, or were they deliberate attempts to buttress his persona as a respectable and trustworthy man?

Similar questions percolated around most Washingtonian speakers, who collectively constituted a new breed of lecturer. Unlike most lecturers on the temperance circuit, these grassroots reformers were working-class men, sometimes uneducated and often unrefined—unconventional in multiple senses. Simultaneously attracted and repulsed, audiences wondered if the drunkard before them was genuinely rehabilitated. A public testimonial or "experience speech" presented curious spectators with an opportunity to read the truth upon their bodies. The ambiguity inherent in Gough's personage and presentation was a key reason for his popularity, and that of all Washingtonians. Fans and foes alike speculated, in private and in print, whether Gough was truly sober. Were his declarations and anecdotes true? Could we trust him? Could we, in short, believe in him? It was in this spirit that I came across the mysterious entry in Gough's account book.

The Document

Between September 1843 and the premiere of Smith's play in February 1844, Gough gave more than 40 lectures in Boston, including engagements at Faneuil Hall, Boston Tabernacle, the Odeon, the Melodeon, and Tremont Temple, among other venues. During the original run of *The Drunkard*, Gough continued to speak regularly there.[12] Among his personal papers at the AAS is an account book he kept during this period, and I decided to examine it for clues as to his whereabouts and activities. As I read it, I paused at an entry dated March 16, 1844: "Tickets to Museum 50¢ Candy 50¢ Omnibus Tickets 1.00."[13]

Did this entry document expenses related to seeing *The Drunkard*, which at that point had been one month on the boards at the Boston Museum?

I searched several Boston newspapers to see how Kimball was advertising the play. An ad in the *Evening Transcript* on March 16 indicates that Kimball offered a special matinee of *The Drunkard* "for the convenience of families and strangers, commencing at 3 o'clock." The ad further boasts that it "will be played as perfect and with the same effect as in the evening." Admission was twenty-five cents. This seems to have been the first of what would be many matinees at the museum catering to women, families, and other individuals for whom an evening performance was either inconvenient or morally problematic. According to McConachie, matinees of this type became a staple of not only Kimball's museum in Boston, but also P. T. Barnum's in New York. If this entry in Gough's account book was, indeed, for two tickets to the Boston Museum on that day, it would suggest he was aware of Kimball's great hit and wanted to see it for himself—especially when given the opportunity to attend a special matinee performance.[14]

I felt as though I had stumbled upon a smoking gun. To me, Gough's feelings about the theatre had always represented a fascinating paradox. Gough had carefully publicized, whether strategically or genuinely, his dislike of the theatre; and here, innocuously sandwiched between "Cash pd for Board" and "Cash lent Samuel Parks," seemed to be evidence to the contrary. Stirring inside me, too, was excitement. Had I found the answer to my question in something as banal as an account book? Could an account book disclose the truth about Gough's theatre-habits? The familiar, ardent hope of the archival researcher welled up: maybe I had discovered something new, or made a novel connection between two related questions, using data hidden in plain sight.

For most historians who labor in archives, this perpetual hope is one of the work's key attractions. It is the carrot that taunts us in our pursuit of the overlooked document, the source that will facilitate a discovery (or rediscovery, or reinterpretation) of some vital aspect of our project. Simultaneously, I was conscious that my judgment could be clouded by my hunch (hope?) that Gough appreciated the theatre more than he ever let on. Was I, like his audiences, dazzled by the theatricality of his lectures—the quality that conservative commentators most fervently criticized? Like a nineteenth-century visitor to Barnum's museum, I wanted to see through Gough's humbugging; I wanted to find him out. Using one of his most intimate records—a personal book of accounts, never meant for other eyes—I sought to learn something about the private man who worked so carefully to protect his public image.

Trying to remain objective, I interrogated the entry phrase-by-phrase. Could "Tickets to Museum" conceivably refer to an institution other than Kimball's? I searched city directories for the year 1844 to see if there were any others operating at the time, and found none. I looked at issues of the *National Aegis* and the *Massachusetts Spy*, both based in nearby Worcester, Massachusetts, and neither advertised amusements in March 1844, other than a few musical concerts at Town Hall (incidentally, the same venue where Gough lectured). I consulted a scrapbook in another manuscript collection at the AAS and found a clipping from 1851 announcing the opening of the Worcester Museum—ruling out the possibility that Gough visited a museum there in 1844, because it did not yet exist.[15]

I considered "Omnibus Tickets 1.00." Could I determine the feasibility of a trip to Boston? I consulted another manuscript in Gough's papers: a journal in which he recorded the dates and venues of his speaking engagements, as well as the miles traveled, the number of temperance pledges collected, and the monetary compensation received on each date.[16] He noted the distance to Boston as four miles—a reasonable number to travel by omnibus. But in many ways, the journal only served to complicate the mystery. It indicated that he "Spoke at a Concert" in Boston on March 15, but on the date he bought museum tickets (March 16), Gough noted that he "went on business" to Worcester—a much greater distance of forty-five miles. Each manuscript seemed to contradict the other. As much as I wanted to prove Gough's afternoon at the theatre, I could not resolve how he could be in two places at once. Perhaps I had confronted an eccentricity in Gough's record-keeping; perhaps he had made a mistake somewhere. But the evidence remained circumstantial at best.

The Dénouement

How does this story of documentary tyranny and film-noir mystery end? Despite the substantial time I invested in pursuit of this question, my research into Gough's possible visit to the Boston Museum ended up comprising only one paragraph in my study. In the wider context of my research on the DTs, melodrama, and reform culture, it was not altogether relevant whether Gough had seen America's most famous temperance play. In truth, the account book entry constituted an intriguing but inconsequential tangent in my research. It did not necessarily matter whether Gough had seen *The Drunkard* or not, because my investigation of him was, at the heart, an investigation of his world: an inquiry about the cultural factors influencing spectators and theater-makers at a pivotal moment in the teetotalism movement. If I do discover incontrovertible evidence that Mr. and Mrs. Gough enjoyed an afternoon at the theatre, its significance will be that of a minor footnote in comparison to the larger, more significant story I am attempting to tell.

The simultaneous advent of these two public phenomena, John B. Gough and *The Drunkard*, continues to haunt me. It seems possible—even likely—that the Washingtonian orator's enactment of the DTs, which became one of his most popular routines, inspired Smith to include such a scene for himself in his play. Newspaper accounts frequently mention that one of Gough's most effective bits was "his vivid portraiture of the horrors of the delirium tremens," which the *Princeton Whig* declared to be "the masterpiece of the whole performance." Another testimony regarding Gough's performance of the DTs emphasizes the sensational, bodily nature of the spectators' response: "He made the flesh to creep with horror, as he described, with startling distinctness, the horrible terror, the dreadful, the terrible inflictions, of that intensely terrifying disease, the *delirium tremens*—the last stage of the drunkard's terrible career."[17] During these moments, perhaps the lecturer created a scene that had something in common with the *delirium tremens* sequence in Smith's drama. But because Gough tended to speak extemporaneously, it is impossible to identify textual ties between the orator's version of the DTs and that of Smith.[18]

Perpetually plaguing the historian is the humbling knowledge that, for better or worse, our (hi)stories are based on educated guesses, conditional connections, and fragile links. In archival detective work, smoking guns are few and far between. So historians are trained to be suspicious of their own excitement—always to be aware that we, too, are storytellers, spinning tales about a handful of traces that have somehow survived to the present. In my case, an entry in an account book sent me down an interminable rabbit hole. In the exhilaration of the hunt, it is sometimes difficult to remember which rabbits we are really after.

ENDNOTES

My initial exploration of the John B. Gough Papers was supported by a grant from the Martin S. Tackel American Theatre Research Fund at the CUNY Graduate Center. Subsequently, I was able to do additional work funded by a Jay T. and Deborah Last Fellowship from the American Antiquarian Society. I am deeply thankful for this support. I also thank Thomas Augst for our provocative and productive conversations about Gough—the most famous American nobody knows.

[1] As John W. Crowley has noted, the few extant biographies of Gough (all written before 1930) were intended for a popular audience and "are, in effect, hagiographies" ("Slaves to the Bottle: Gough's Autobiography and Douglass's Narrative," in *The Serpent in the Cup: Temperance in American Literature*, ed. David S. Reynolds and Debra J. Rosenthal [Amherst: University of Massachusetts Press, 1997], 135 n. 38). To remedy this, Thomas Augst is developing a cultural biography of Gough (in progress). His published scholarship on Gough includes "Temperance, Mass Culture, and the Romance of Experience," *American*

Literary History 19, no. 2 (Summer 2007): 297–323; and "A Drunkard's Story," *Common-Place* 10, no. 3 (April 2010), http://www.common-place.org. See also Graham Warder's unpublished dissertation, "Selling Sobriety: How Temperance Reshaped Culture in Antebellum America" (PhD diss., University of Massachusetts-Amherst, 2000), 108–220.

[2] For more on Rev. John Pierpont's possible involvement in authoring *The Drunkard,* see John W. Frick, *Theatre, Culture and Temperance Reform in Nineteenth-Century America* (Cambridge: Cambridge University Press, 2003), 116–18; and Amy E. Hughes, "Answering the Amusement Question: Antebellum Temperance Drama and the Christian Endorsement of Leisure," *New England Theatre Journal* 15 (2004): 1–19.

[3] Ian R. Tyrrell, *Sobering Up: From Temperance to Prohibition in Antebellum America, 1800–1860* (Westport, CT: Greenwood Press, 1979), 135–58.

[4] Ibid., 159, 60, and 73. For more on the Washingtonians and their decline, see Mark Edward Lender and James Kirby Martin, *Drinking in America: A History* (New York: Free Press, 1982), 75–79; Jack S. Blocker, Jr., *American Temperance Movements: Cycles of Reform* (Boston: Twayne Publishers, 1989), 39–51; and Thomas R. Pegram, *Battling Demon Rum: The Struggle for a Dry America, 1800–1933* (Chicago: Ivan R. Dee, 1998), 24–31. The Washingtonians viewed Gough with contempt once he achieved notoriety, yet Lyman Abbott, in his introduction to an 1886 anthology of Gough's stories and lectures, states, "If the Washingtonian movement had done the world no other service, the world would owe it a large debt for giving us John B. Gough." John B. Gough, *Platform Echoes: Or, Living Truths for Head and Heart,* with an introduction by Rev. Lyman Abbott (Hartford, CT: A. D. Worthington, 1886), 35.

[5] Joseph Roach, *It* (Ann Arbor: University of Michigan Press, 2007), 1 and 8.

[6] John B. Gough, John B. Gough Papers (hereafter *JBGP*), folio vols. 1–19, American Antiquarian Society (AAS), Worcester, MA. The AAS groups the materials by size as well as content; Gough's scrapbooks are classified as "folio volumes" and the smaller bound manuscripts, such as his journals, are catalogued as "volumes." Given the limited scope of my project, I consulted the first three folios of the scrapbook collection, spanning the years 1842–1845, 1845–1848, and 1849–1850. Unfortunately, the press clippings are inconsistently identified. Because Gough seems to have placed the clippings in chronological order, I offer approximate dates by taking into account their context in the scrapbook as well as information about Gough's whereabouts in his lecture journal (JBG Journal, 1843–1858, *JBGP,* octavo vol. 6), in which he tracked the date, location, expenses incurred, compensation received, and number of pledge signatures collected at each engagement.

[7] *Flushing Journal* (NY), n.d. (ca. April 1845), *JBGP,* folio vol. 1, n.p. (original emphasis).

[8] "John B. Gough," *Gloucester Telegraph* (MA), n.d. (ca. March 1844) and "Temperance," *Commercial Advertiser* (NY), n.d. (ca. late 1844), in *JBGP,* folio vol. 1, n.p.

[9] This paradox is evident in T. Allston Brown, *A History of the New York Stage* (New York: Dodd, Mead, 1903), 1:255–56. Brown interrupts his narrative of theatrical facts and anecdotes with a paragraph about Gough: "During the season of 1835–36, John B. Gough appeared here [National Theatre] under the name of Gilbert. His stage career was a brief one, for he soon afterwards returned to his first trade of book-binding. He reappeared in 1837 as a low comedian at Providence, R. I., and he afterwards acted at the Old Lion Theatre, Boston. He traveled with a diorama and sang comic songs, and ultimately became famous as a temperance lecturer. He died at Frankford, Pa., Feb. 15, 1887 [*sic*]." The inclusion of Gough in Brown's narrative reveals that this famous solo performer was difficult to classify. Interestingly, Brown does not use a modifier such as "lecturer" or "orator," implying that as late as 1903, Gough was still a familiar name.

[10] John B. Gough, *An Autobiography* (Boston: J. B. Gough, Gould, Kendall & Lincoln, 1848), 28–29.

[11] John B. Gough, "I Have Often Been Asked Why I Did Not Adopt the Theatrical Profession," Lectures, *JBGP,* octavo vol. 3, n.p. (his emphasis).

[12] John B. Gough, JBG Journal, *JBGP,* 6–14.

[13] John B. Gough, Account Book (Roxbury, MA) 1843–1844, *JBGP*, octavo vol. 9, n.p.

[14] Advertisement for *The Drunkard*, by W. H. Smith, Boston Museum, *Evening Transcript*, 16 March 1844, 3; Gough, Account Book, n.p.; Bruce A. McConachie, *Melodramatic Formations: American Theatre and Society, 1820–1870* (Iowa City: University of Iowa Press, 1992), 164. An advertisement in the Boston *Transcript* the previous day indicates that Kimball was offering *The Drunkard* matinee "at the request of numerous families."

[15] "Museum," *Palladium* (MA), 17 September 1851, n.p.; in Benjamin Thomas Hill Papers, The Early Drama in Worcester 1787–1854 (oversize vol. 1), American Antiquarian Society, Worcester, MA.

[16] Gough, JBG Journal, 16.

[17] "Mr. Gough—His Style of Speaking," *Princeton Whig*, n.d. (ca. April 1845) and unidentified clipping (probably *National Intelligencer*), n.d. (ca. March 1845), *JBGP*, folio vol. 1, n.p.

[18] Spectators' fascination with Gough derived, in part, from his talent for speaking without a script.

Lost! Or, What To Do When Your Principal Primary Document is Missing

JOHN W. FRICK

Every researcher has approached the document delivery window, only to hear those dreaded words, "I'm sorry, but that document has been lost;" or its variant, "that text is no longer extant," delivered by a page or a reference librarian. Years ago, while conducting research for a book on temperance melodrama that I was writing (*Theatre, Culture and Temperance Reform in Nineteenth-Century America*, Cambridge University Press, 2003), I had that unfortunate experience—at repository after repository.

During my preliminary research on temperance melodrama, I had repeatedly encountered a play variously titled *Little Katy, or the Hot Corn Girl* or *Hot Corn; or, the Story of Little Katy*. Initially, I believed that this was a "minor" play, hardly comparable to the two temperance classics: *The Drunkard* and *Ten Nights in a Bar-room*. Subsequent research, however, proved this assumption wrong, for not only was *Hot Corn* arguably the third most important temperance drama ever written; but on stage in the 1850s it was second in popularity only to the all-time theatrical popularity leader, *Uncle Tom's Cabin*. When I learned that, like *Uncle Tom's Cabin*, there were multiple versions of *Hot Corn* on Broadway simultaneously, that some of the same theatres that had mounted *Uncle Tom's Cabin* (i.e., Barnum's American Museum and Purdy's National Theatre) had produced *Little Katy*, and that the same actress, Cordelia Howard, had played both Little Eva in *Uncle Tom's Cabin* and Little Katy in *Hot Corn* at the National, performing a death and ascension scene in both, I was convinced that I had inadvertently stumbled upon a significant temperance play.

Reviews of the plays as well as George Odell's records both show that the source of the theatrical *Hot Corns* was a series of articles in a New York newspaper. Originating in 1853 as a serialized exposé of New York slum life in Horace Greeley's *New York Tribune* and published as a novel the following year by Solon Robinson, author of the original *Tribune* articles and a temperance activist, *Hot Corn* told the story of a "poor and miserable" corn seller on the Bowery who fell asleep on the street; was robbed while she slept; upon her return home, was severely beaten by her drunkard mother for not having sold all of her corn; and subsequently died from the injuries inflicted by her mother. While the social issues of poverty, alcoholism and child abuse were pushed to the foreground by the play's "documentary" style, Little Katy herself served as the archetypal temperance child who, despite her own suffering, endeavored through personal purity and force of character to redeem an alcoholic parent. Faced with imminent death, Katy forgave her mother for her cruelty and issued a final plea for her redemption, imploring: "Mother – don't – drink – anymore – mother – good b___."[1] The narration that followed stated simply that before Katy finished her good-bye, another angel had been added to the heavenly host. As testimony to both the power of Robinson's story and of the temperance message it contained, during the 1853–1854 season, three separate versions of the play (by H. J. Conway for Barnum's American Museum, C. W. Taylor's adaptation at Purdy's National Theatre and a third version by an unnamed author at the Bowery) were mounted in New York, where they rivaled in popularity both the George Aiken version of *Uncle Tom's Cabin* at Purdy's National Theatre and the Conway version of the Stowe classic story at Barnum's, and the death scene of the National Theatre production of *Hot Corn,* with Cordelia Howard in the title role, was as gut-wrenching as its counterpart in the George Aiken stage adaptation of the Harriet Beecher Stowe classic.

Overjoyed at my discovery of an "important" play, I went immediately to the ancient and idiosyncratic card catalogue at the Billy Rose Theatre Collection, New York Public Library at Lincoln Center and there I promptly slammed into a scholastic brick wall:

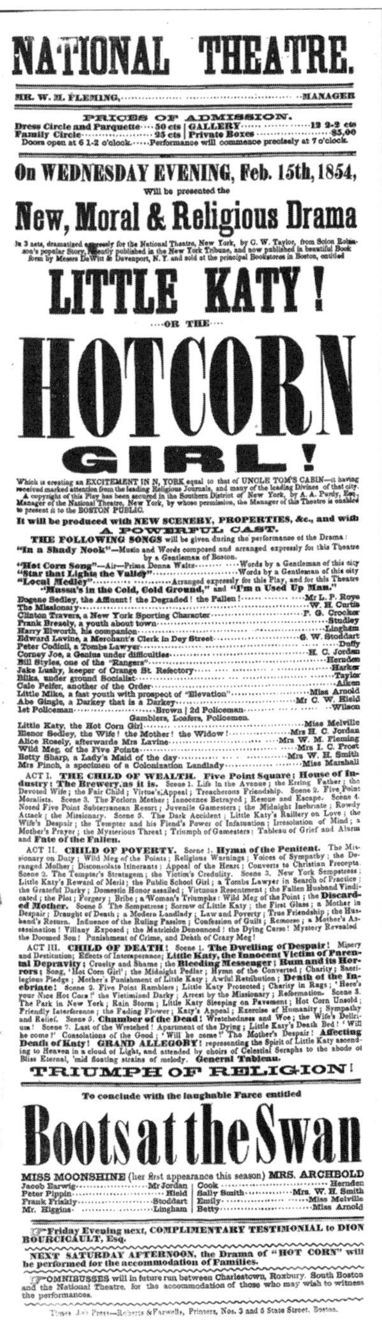

NATIONAL THEATRE.

MR. W. M. FLEMING, ... MANAGER

PRICES OF ADMISSION.

Dress Circle and Parquette .... 50 cts | GALLERY .... 12 2-2 cts
Family Circle .... 25 cts | Private Boxes $5,00
Doors open at 6 1-2 o'clock......Performance will commence precisely at 7 o'clock.

On WEDNESDAY EVENING, Feb. 15th, 1854,

Will be presented the

New, Moral & Religious Drama

In 3 acts, dramatized expressly for the National Theatre, New York, by C. W. Taylor, from Solon Robinson's popular Story, recently published in the New York Tribune, and now published in beautiful Book form by Messrs DeWitt & Davenport, N. Y. and sold at the principal Bookstores in Boston, entitled

LITTLE KATY!

....OR THE....

HOTCORN

GIRL!

Which is creating an EXCITEMENT IN N. YORK equal to that of UNCLE TOM'S CABIN—it having received marked attention from the leading Religious Journals, and many of the leading Divines of that city. A copyright of this Play has been secured in the Southern District of New York, by A. A. Purdy, Esq., Manager of the National Theatre, New York, by whose permission, the Manager of this Theatre is enabled to present it to the BOSTON PUBLIC.

It will be produced with NEW SCENERY, PROPERTIES, &c., and with

A POWERFUL CAST.

THE FOLLOWING SONGS will be given during the performance of the Drama:

"In a Shady Nook"—Music and Words composed and arranged expressly for this Theatre by a Gentleman of Boston.
"Hot Corn Song"—Air—Prima Donna Waltz........ Words by a Gentleman of this city
"Star that Lights the Valley"........ Words by a Gentleman of this city
"Local Medley"........ Arranged expressly for this Play, and for this Theatre
"Massa's in the Cold, Cold Ground," and "I'm a Used Up Man."

Eugene Sedley, the Affluent! the Degraded! the Fallen! .... Mr L. P. Roys
The Missionary .... W. H. Curtis
Clinton Travers, a New York Sporting Character .... F. G. Crocker
Frank Brezely, a youth about town .... Studley
Harry Elworth, his companion .... Lingham
Edward Lavine, a Merchant's Clerk in Dey Street .... G. W. Stoddart
Peter Codicil, a Tombs Lawyer .... Duffy
Corney Joe, a Genius under difficulties .... H. C. Jordan
Bill Styles, one of the "Rangers" .... Hernden
Jake Lushy, keeper of Orange St. Refectory .... Harker
Bilks, under ground Socialist .... Taylor
Cale Peifer, another of the Order .... Aiken
Little Mike, a fast youth with prospect of "Elevation" .... Miss Arnold
Abe Gingle, a Darkey that is a Darkey .... Mr C. W. Hield
1st Policeman .... Brown | 2d Policeman .... Wilson
Gamblers, Loafers, Policemen.
Little Katy, the Hot Corn Girl .... Miss Melville
Elenor Sedley, the Wife! the Mother! the Widow! .... Mrs H. C. Jordan
Alice Rosely, afterwards Mrs Lavine .... Mrs W. M. Fleming
Wild Meg, of the Five Points .... Mrs I. C. Frost
Betty Sharp, a Lady's Maid of the day .... Mrs W. H. Smith
Mrs Pinch, a specimen of a Colonization Landlady .... Miss Marshall

ACT I. **THE CHILD OF WEALTH. Five Point Square; House of Industry: The Brewery, as it is.** Scene 1. Life in the Avenue; the Erring Father; the Devoted Wife; the Fair Child; Virtue's Appeal; Treacherous Friendship. Scene 2. Five Point Moralists. Scene 3. The Forlorn Mother; Innocence Betrayed; Rescue and Escape. Scene 4. Noted Five Point Subterranean Resort; Juvenile Gamesters; the Midnight Inebriate; Rowdy Attack; the Missionary. Scene 5. The Dark Accident; Little Katy's Raillery on Love; the Wife's Despair; the Tempter and his Fiend's Power of Infatuation; Irresolution of Mind; a Mother's Prayer; the Mysterious Threat; Triumph of Gamesters; Tableau of Grief and Alarm and **Fate of the Fallen.**

ACT II. **CHILD OF POVERTY.** Scene 1. **Hymn of the Penitent.** The Missionary on Duty; Wild Meg of the Points; Religious Warnings; Voices of Sympathy; the Deranged Mother; Disconsolate Itinerants; Appeal of the Heart; Converts to Christian Precepts. Scene 2. The Tempter's Stratagem; the Victim's Credulity. Scene 3. New York Sempstress; Little Katy's Reward of Merit; the Public School Girl; a Tombs Lawyer in Search of Practice; the Grateful Darky; Domestic Honor assailed; Virtuous Resentment; the Fallen Husband Vindicated; the Plot; Forgery; Bribe; a Woman's Triumphs: Wild Meg of the Point; the **Discarded Mother.** Scene 5. The Sempstress; Sorrow of Little Katy; the First Glass; a Mother in Despair; Draught of Death; a Modern Landlady; Law and Poverty; True Friendship; the Husband's Return. Influence of the Ruling Passion; Confession of Guilt; Remorse; a Mother's Assassination! Villany Exposed; the Matricide Denounced! the Dying Curse! Mystery Revealed the Doomed Son! Punishment of Crime, and Death of Crazy Meg!

ACT III. **CHILD OF DEATH!** Scene 1. **The Dwelling of Despair!** Misery and Destitution; Effects of Intemperance; **Little Katy, the Innocent Victim of Parental Depravity:** Cruelty and Shame; the **Bleeding Messenger; Rum and its Horrors;** Song, 'Hot Corn Girl'; the Midnight Pedlar; Hymn of the Converted; Charity; Sacrilegious Pledge; Mother's Punishment of Little Katy; Awful Retribution; **Death of the Inebriate!** Scene 2. Five Point Ramblers; Little Katy Protected; Charity in Rags; 'Here's your Nice Hot Corn!' the Victimized Darky; Arrest by the Missionary; Reformation. Scene 3. The Park in New York; Rain Storm; Little Katy Sleeping on Pavement; Hot Corn Unsold; Friendly Interference; the Fading Flower; Katy's Appeal; Exercise of Humanity; Sympathy and Relief. Scene 5. **Chamber of the Dead!** Wretchedness and Woe; the Wife's Delirium! Scene 7. Last of the Wretched! Apartment of the Dying; Little Katy's Death Bed! 'Will he come?' Consolations of the Good; 'Will he come?' The Mother's Despair! **Affecting Death of Katy! GRAND ALLEGORY!** representing the Spirit of Little Katy ascending to Heaven in a cloud of Light, and attended by choirs of Celestial Seraphs to the abode of Bliss Eternal, 'mid floating strains of melody. **General Tableau.**

TRIUMPH OF RELIGION!

To conclude with the laughable Farce entitled

Boots at the Swan

MISS MOONSHINE (her first appearance this season) MRS. ARCHBOLD

Jacob Earwig .... Mr Jordan | Cook .... Hernden
Peter Pippin .... Hield | Sally Smith .... Mrs. W. H. Smith
Frank Friskly .... Stoddart | Emily .... Miss Melville
Mr. Higgins .... Lingham | Betty .... Miss Arnold

☞ Friday Evening next, COMPLIMENTARY TESTIMONIAL to DION BOURCICAULT, Esq.

NEXT SATURDAY AFTERNOON, the Drama of "HOT CORN" will be performed for the accommodation of Families.

☞ OMNIBUSSES will in future run between Charlestown, Roxbury, South Boston and the National Theatre, for the accommodation of those who may wish to witness the performances.

Roberts & Farwells, Printers, Nos. 3 and 5 State Street, Boston.

Broadside for Hot Corn, National Theatre, New York, 1854. Harvard Theatre Collection, Houghton Library.

there was no record whatsoever that the Theatre collection had ever owned a copy of a *Hot Corn* script. In fact, there was not even a record of a script of the play ever having been published. Undaunted by my initial failure, however, I pushed on and expanded my search for the elusive play text to include the Theatre Collection at the Museum of the City of New York; the Harvard Theatre Collection; the Library of Congress; and the Library at the Players. Still *Nothing*!

Frustrated, I enlisted colleagues in the United States, Canada and England in my search for the elusive play script and was fortunate that Annette Fern at the Harvard Theatre Collection and Kathryn Johnson, Head of the Manuscript Division of the British Library in London volunteered to assist me in my quest. However, even with their expertise and generous expenditure of time, a script of *Hot Corn* remained missing and a consensus was developing among the seasoned reference librarians I had consulted that the play might well be lost forever. This raised a conundrum. Do I merely mention the play—that it once existed and was important in its own time—or should I attempt to recreate enough of the performance to allow even a cursory analysis?

In the end, it was really a Hobson's Choice, for not only was *Hot Corn* one of the most popular play of its time; it was also one of the most significant moral reform dramas in American theatrical history. To theatre historians, the moral reform drama was the ideal vehicle for disseminating progressive ideology during the middle years of the nineteenth century.[2] Predicated upon the Enlightenment belief that Man was divine, that mankind was perfectible, and consequently no social problem could be considered intractable, nineteenth-century reform was designed to promote and encourage human improvement. This overriding conviction—the belief in man's perfectibility—led naturally and inexorably to a sentimentalized view of the world, a sentimentalized world view shared by the antebellum melodrama.

Although characterized as melodrama and lumped with the other variations of the form in conventional theatre histories, moral reform dramas differed markedly from the other types, not only in their ultimate nature, but in their intent. During the nineteenth century, literary historian Jane Tomkins asserts, most drama was, by definition, a form of discourse that had *no* designs upon influencing the course of events.[3] It made no attempt to change things, but merely elected to represent them, and its value lay in its representational nature. In contrast to these purely representational works—which constituted the majority of theatrical offerings—were those dramas whose claim to value lay in their stated intention to influence, often significantly, the course of history; to propose solutions to the problems that shaped a particular historical moment. Frequently these dramas were as ideologically radical as the reforms they espoused: slaves escaped from their masters or denounced the institution of slavery (e.g., *Uncle Tom's Cabin, Dred, Neighbor Jackwood, Osawattomie Brown*); laborers went on strike against their employers or smashed the machinery in their factories (e.g., *The Rent Day; The Factory Girl; The Factory Lad; Distraining for Rent);* prohibition was aggressively advocated nearly seventy years before the passage of the 18th Amendment (e.g., *The Drunkard; Ten Nights in a Bar-room; Fifteen Years of a Drunkard's Life; One Cup More, or the Doom of the Drunkard*) and gambling was denounced (e.g., *The Gambler; Six Degrees of Crime, of Wine Women, Gambling, Theft, and the Scaffold*). These then were the plays that have been conveniently clustered under the rubric Moral Reform Drama.

In order to recreate enough of the moral reform drama, *Hot Corn,* to study, I turned to one of the most basic techniques available to the theatre historian: the reconstruction of performance. Performance reconstruction is a process that virtually every theatre historian has, by necessity, been forced to utilize in order to do her/his work, while at the same time knowing and acknowledging that any reconstruction will be incomplete. As defined by theorist Patrice Pavis, the reconstruction of performance (or what he labels *Analysis as Reconstruction*) is the restoration of a lost performance, always done *"post festum,"* which is accomplished by collecting "pieces of evidence, relics, or documents pertaining to performance, as well as artists' statements of their intentions . . . and mechanical recordings" in a variety of forms (audiotapes, video tapes, etc.) [4] Analysis as reconstruction, Pavis continues, is designed to afford the historian an understanding of a performance's contexts and characteristics with the hope that a sense of the actors' on-stage behavior and the overall mise-en-scene is restored to such a degree that she/he may imagine what it was like to be an audience member. [5] This, of course, is an ideal; no performance can be re-captured in its entirety, nor can analysis as reconstruction be a substitute for what Pavis calls *Analysis as Reportage*—the documentation of a performance as it takes place. Despite the belief of Pavis and others that *reconstruction of performance* is arguably a dated historical approach, it was nonetheless a logical choice given my predicament—in fact, it was my *only* choice.

The "testing" and validating of a document using other documents to corroborate information, then, is one of the most common historical techniques. In the "standard" performance reconstruction, conventionally the historian will utilize the text of the performed play as a primary document, comparing descriptions of the staged production contained in reviews, eyewitness accounts, prompt books, etc. to the script in order to assess how faithfully the production reproduced the play text. Unfortunately, in the case of *Hot Corn*, the document to be validated is missing; thus, by default the primary document became the novel upon which the plays were based and my task was to determine how faithful the plays were to Robinson's original narrative and where playwrights took liberties with the story. It would be this factor—the necessity of recreating not only a performance, but reconstructing to some degree or another, a base text—that would distinguish this historical reconstruction from the others I had done previously.

The few reviews of *Hot Corn,* which simply mentioned that the scenery evoked a sense of the Bowery, but mentioned nothing of the nature of the text nor the action on stage, were of little use; nor were those clippings in various archives that merely repeated publicity announcements in the "Amusements" section of New York newspapers useful. Even George Odell's usually informative chronicles were disappointing, offering only the *Dramatis Personae* for the National Theatre production. While his account allowed me to see which of Robinson's characters playwright Taylor retained and which he jettisoned, as well as what new characters he added, it said nothing of which scenes from the novel were kept or deleted. Intriguingly, the most useful documents in assessing the scenic composition of the shows were the handful of broadsides that were stored in the Harvard Theatre Collection.

What, then, can be learned through the study of the extant broadsides? Paired with Odell's cast list, the broadsides for the National Theatre production of *Hot Corn* corroborated the *Dramatis Personae* of the show; while the broadsides for Barnum's American Museum likewise furnished the cast for his *Hot Corn*. Like Odell's listing of the National Theatre cast and the broadsides for the National, Barnum's broadsides indicate which of Robinson's characters Conway kept; while a clipping in the Billy Rose Theatre Collection testifies that several characters (Little Katy, her mother, Wild Meg) were translated directly from the novel to the stage. From these documents, I was also able to ascertain that while Conway and Taylor retained Robinson's original focus upon intemperance as a female problem (not just a male one), they significantly downplayed the prevalence of alcoholism among the Irish. In his original narrative, Robinson had repeatedly foregrounded the problem of intemperance in the Irish populace of New York; but when transferred to the stage, many of the characters in his novel were anglicized, presumably to appeal to an audience that included a large number of non-Irish. In the process, the problem of intemperance was universalized and the concentration upon a purely Irish problem was significantly minimized.

While the broadsides yielded much valuable information about the characters of both the Conway and the Taylor *Hot Corns*, they were also important in determining the scenic flow of the plays and the dramas' conformity (or lack of conformity) to the Ur-text: Robinson's novel. Broadsides for both theatres generously listed at their bottom the nature and location of the scenes of the plays. Not surprisingly, such legendary urban locations like the notorious Five Points slum, the Bowery and the infamous Brewery (the multi-story tenement on Paradise Square) were included; but beyond their near-obligatory inclusion, the playwrights, for the most part, freely selected from the myriad lurid scenes in the New York landscape. However, despite the playwrights' seemingly ignoring Robinson's scenic placement, and while there was seldom a one-to-one correlation between the scenes in the novel and those in the plays, Conway and Taylor nevertheless remained faithful to Robinson's larger purpose of exposing the horrors of urban decay, crime and human degradation.

While documents dealing *directly* with *Hot Corn*—both the plays and the novel—were used in the reconstruction of both performance and texts, there exists an additional tool of the reconstructer—one that Pavis considers one of the most basic in analysis as reconstruction: i.e., the context in which a play is created. In this case, that context consisted of the antebellum conventions that governed adapting a novel to the stage. According to an unidentified clipping in the Billy Rose Theatre Collection, in transferring *Hot Corn* from page to stage, characters and scenes were not the only dramatic elements appropriated. In their "conversion" of the novel to play texts, Conway and Taylor lifted entire passages of dialogue from Robinson's original text and then simply interpolated them into their scripts. While today copying and using entire passages of a written text verbatim would be both unethical and illegal, such was not the case in antebellum times. In the pre-copyright era, such practices were not only legal but common, as evidenced by both Aiken's and Conway's appropriating verbatim large passages of dialogue from Mrs. Stowe's novel and incorporating them wholesale into their play texts. In the cases of both *Uncle Tom's Cabin* and *Hot Corn*, with no copywright laws to restrict them, antebellum dramatists were free to appropriate as much of another author's text as she/he wished. Therefore, with the Conway and the Aiken *Uncle Tom's Cabin*s as examples of typical authorial practices, it is reasonable to assume that the unidentified Lincoln Center clipping is accurate and that, in crafting their scripts for *Hot Corn*, Conway and Taylor would have likewise lifted dialogue from Robinson's narrative.

Admittedly, the resultant reconstructions of both texts and performances were incomplete and lacking in details; yet, even these minimal reconstructions yielded valuable insights. Even with new characters added, original ones omitted, and scenic venues changed, the plays nevertheless retained the exposé nature of Robinson's original narrative. In the process, they showed audiences many of the dangerous, forbidden areas of the urban landscape; they graphically illustrated the myriad horrors of poverty; and they vividly depicted the nightmare that was intemperance.

Unfortunately, all that I have written above does little to answer the underlying question inherent in my unfulfilled quest for play texts: Why, given the documented popularity of *Hot Corn* on stage in the mid-1850s, are there no extant scripts? This question is even more vexing and frustrating because there were several different scripts that were mounted on New York stages. In the final analysis, faced with the absence of play texts, we are left to speculate. Were these scripts ever published?[6] Were they published and then lost? Do they exist somewhere I haven't looked? Someday, hopefully, these questions will be answered and future researchers will either be able to scrutinize one or more of these historically significant scripts and utilize them to reveal more about theatre and temperance reform in the nineteenth century, or at least resolve themselves to the fact that a vital part of our theatre history is lost forever.

ENDNOTES

1 Solon Robinson, *Hot Corn: Life Scenes in New York Illustrated* (New York: DeWitt & Davenport Publishers, 1853), p. 113.

2 See John W. Frick, "Not From the Drowsy Pulpit: The Moral Reform Melodrama on the Nineteenth Century Stage, " *Theatre Symposium* 15 (2007): 41–51.

3 Jane P. Tomkins, *Sensational Designs: The Cultural Work of American Fiction, 1790–1860.* (New York: Oxford UP, 1985), p. 125.

4 Patrice Pavis, *Analyzing Performance: Theater, Dance and Film* (Ann Arbor: U of Michigan P, 2003)

5 Pavis, p. 11.

6 Although pioneer play publisher Samuel French started his publishing business in 1854, he didn't fully specialize in dramas until 1859 when he met London dramatic publisher Thomas Hailes Lacy. Therefore, conceivably no one was readily available in 1853 to print the scripts of *Hot Corn*.

Barnum's Last Laugh? General Tom Thumb's Wedding Cake in the Library of Congress[1]

MARLIS SCHWEITZER

In most if not all archives, food is strictly prohibited. This is certainly the case at the Library of Congress, where researchers entering the Manuscript Reading Room are required to place all personal belongings in specially designated lockers and present all pencils, papers, computers, and cameras to a guard before gaining admittance to the room. You can imagine my surprise, then, when one of the archivists turned to me after delivering my first boxes from the Minnie Maddern Fiske Papers and said, in a conspiratorial tone, "Before you finish with the collection, ask to see Tom Thumb's wedding cake." I laughed and said I would be sure to request the cake, but I was puzzled. What was cake, *anyone's* cake, doing in the Library of Congress? And *how* had wedding cake from one of P.T. Barnum's greatest nineteenth-century stars found its way into the collection of an actress celebrated for introducing American audiences to Ibsen in the early-twentieth?[2]

Here was a real mystery.

Although my interest was piqued, I held off on requesting Tom Thumb's cake. I was hot on the trail of another mystery involving Harrison Grey Fiske, Minnie Maddern Fiske's husband, and didn't want to waste my time with a frivolous—or so I thought—diversion. But as I worked through the Fiskes' correspondence, I came upon a letter and calling card from the Countess M. Lavinia Magri, the former "Mrs. General Tom Thumb," addressed to Harrison Grey Fiske as President of *The Dramatic Mirror* Co. In the letter, dated February 16, 1905, the Countess writes:

> Allow me to present you with a piece of my Wedding Cake which was made when I was married to Charles S. Stratton known as the only original General Tom Thumb—Feb. 10th 1863 at Grace Church New York City. My anniversary was the 10th of Feb. 1905. The Cake is now Forty two years old.[3]

The Countess's letter answered my question about how the wedding cake had found its way into the collection, but new questions arose. What had compelled the former Mrs. General Tom Thumb to write to Fiske? The formality of the letter seemed to indicate that she did not know Fiske personally. Was she perhaps hoping for a notice in the *Dramatic Mirror,* one of the most widely read and influential theatrical newspapers of the period? Or did she simply want someone of Fiske's caliber and influence to know that she was still alive and still devoted to the memory of her former husband? And what about Fiske? Why had he included the cake with the rest of the material he submitted to the Library of Congress? What was so special about this cake anyway?

I decided that before my time at the Library was over, I would see the cake for myself. There was something so deliciously perverse, so utterly Barnumesque about requesting a box of cake from the Library of Congress. Still, the prospect of looking at a piece of century-old cake was far from appetizing. Would there be anything left to see? Would it be moldy or magotty? Just a bunch of crumbs?

The cake arrived in a thin cardboard container like the ones used by the Manuscript Division for all of its collections. There was nothing to signal the rather unusual object inside. After lifting the flap of the container, I carefully withdrew another box covered with a thick beige fabric. It looked like a scrapbook or book of photographs—nothing out of the ordinary—with a label on the side that simply read "Minnie Maddern Fiske 147." I lifted the lid of the box and . . . there was the cake, encased behind glass in a small, presumably airtight, space, wrapped in what appeared to be parchment paper (Fig. 1). The cake was dark brown and lumpy, almost brownie-like but with some questionable yellow spots. I've never seen 137–year old cake before so was surprised that it had held together this well, all things considered. Beneath the cake was a soiled box with a label reading "E.F. Tinkham, Watchmaker, Jeweler, and Optician, Middleboro, Mass."

I will confess: I was disappointed. I'm not sure what I'd expected to see—some monumental slab of fruit cake slathered in royal icing, perhaps?—but the sight of this sad-looking lump beside a grease-stained box didn't jibe with the elaborate spectacles I associate with Barnum and General Tom Thumb. Why would someone like the Countess Magri want to give *this* cake to an acquaintance like Fiske forty-two years after her wedding day? I realized that I knew very little about nineteenth century weddings and wedding cakes and even less about Tom Thumb's 1863 wedding to Miss Lavinia Warren. I endeavored to find out.

The Wedding of the Century

The February 1863 wedding of Charles S. Stratton (otherwise known as General Tom Thumb) to Mercy Lavinia Warren Bump (better known as Lavinia Warren) was one of the most spectacular and eagerly-discussed performance events of the mid-nineteenth century. According to one source, over 15,000 people clamored for an invitation to the "Lilliputian" union of Stratton, one of Barnum's most celebrated performers, and the lovely and diminutive Warren, who appeared daily at Barnum's American Museum as the "Queen of Beauty."[4] Photographs of the wedding party taken by renowned photographer Mathew Brady were so popular that "miserable engravings" and "spurious impositions" flooded the market.[5]

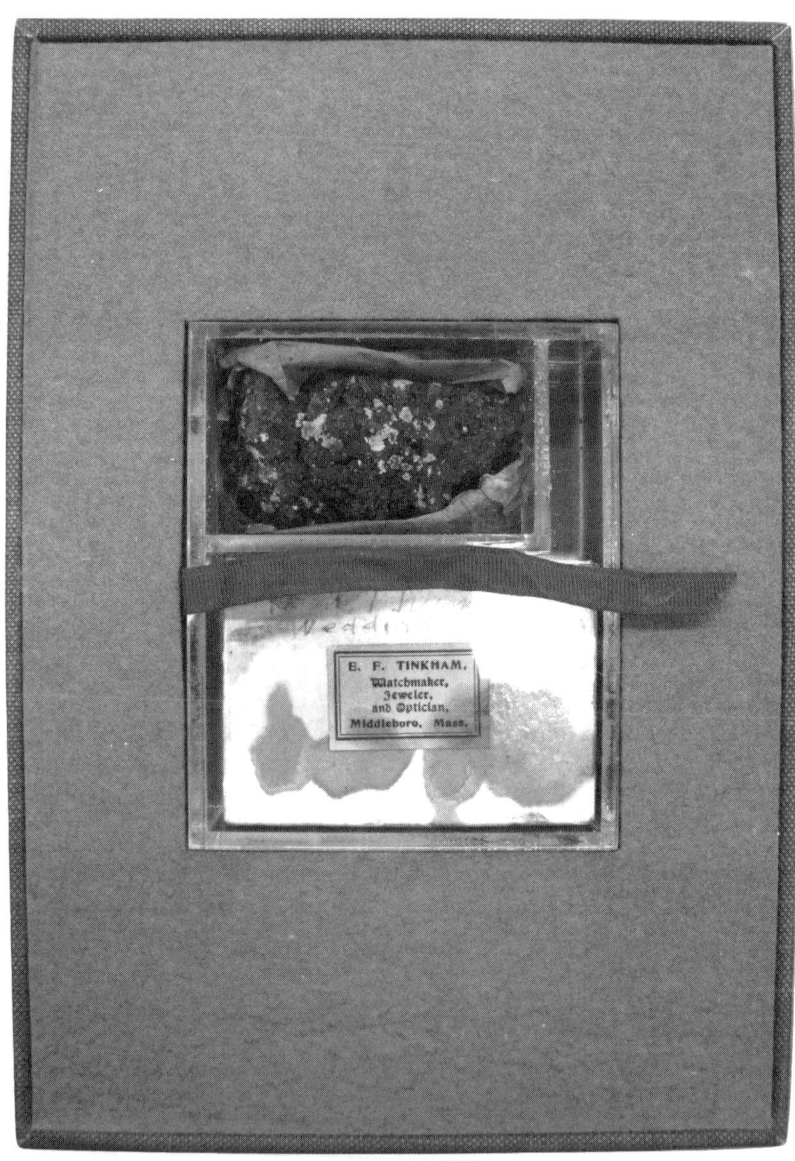

A piece of wedding cake from the marriage of Charles Stratton and Lavinia Warren is preserved in the Minnie Maddern Fiske Papers at the Library of Congress. Photo by author.

Like Stratton, Warren was a midget[6] with well-proportioned features, a charming singing voice, and an air of sophistication. Born to one of New England's oldest and most respected families, she had been taught to value "integrity, morality, and charity."[7] This education did not, however, prevent her from desiring a career on the stage and she had been drawn into show business as a teenager. After performing on a Mississippi show boat for several years, she met Barnum (always on the lookout for new talent), and willingly accepted his offer of employment. Under Barnum's management, Warren held formal afternoon receptions or levees at the American Museum, during which she entertained Civil War Generals and members of New York's social elite. "She has a full, round, dimpled face, and her fine black eyes fairly sparkle when she becomes interested in conversation," a reporter for the *New York Tribune* enthused in December 1862. "She moves about the drawing room with the grace and dignity of a queen, and yet she is devoid of affectation, is modest and lady-like in her deportment."[8]

In the early winter of 1863, New York papers began publishing detailed accounts of General Tom Thumb's initial meeting with and subsequent wooing of Lavinia Warren.[9] Although skeptics argued that the courtship was simply another of Barnum's schemes to boost business, both Barnum and Warren insisted that the marriage was a love match.[10] In the 1873 edition of *Struggles and Triumphs; Or Forty Years' Recollections of P.T. Barnum,* Barnum describes the first meeting between Warren and General Tom Thumb and the General's declaration to Barnum that he "must marry that young lady."[11] Although Commodore Nutt (George Washington Morrison Nutt), a midget from New Hampshire whom Barnum had recently introduced to Museum audiences, had likewise declared his devotion to Warren, Gen. Tom Thumb was determined to win her for his bride. On January 8, 1863 he reportedly wrote to Warren's parents in Middleboro, Mass. requesting their daughter's hand in marriage (a copy of the letter found its way to the *New York Times,* likely with Barnum's assistance). A week later, the *Times* reported that "[t]he envoy of Gen. Thumb has returned with the joyful information that Miss Warren's kind parents have consented to grant their daughter's wish."[12]

Critics had good cause to suspect Barnum's hand in the marriage negotiations, as do present-day historians. After the formal announcement of the couple's engagement and the subsequent report that Warren would retire from show business after the wedding, crowds of 20,000 or more visited Barnum's Museum daily hoping to catch a glimpse of the delightful Queen before she withdrew from public life.[13] Many of these visitors also purchased *cartes de visite* of the young performer, who apparently sold them herself (often with her famous fiancé's assistance).[14] By Barnum's account, "daily receipts at the Museum were frequently over three thousand dollars" during this period.[15] Although invitations to the wedding ceremony could not be purchased—some apparently tried, offering upwards of $60 for a single invitation[16]—tickets *were* available for the reception at the Metropolitan Hotel where the couple's wedding gifts and cake would be displayed.[17] While Barnum later admitted that he "did not hesitate to seek continued advantage from the notoriety of the prospective marriage," he stopped short of moving

P.T. Barnum stands between Lavinia Warren and Charles Stratton (to his right). Best man Commodore Nutt is far left. Photo by Matthew Brady. Courtesy of the Library of Congress.

the event to the Academy of Music, even though it would have meant $25,000 in profits. "I had promised to give the couple a genteel and graceful wedding," he writes, "and I kept my word."[18]

On February 10, 1863, Gen. Tom Thumb and Lavinia Warren were married at Manhattan's fashionable Grace Church before "a highly select audience of ladies and gentlemen," including "governors of several States," General Ambrose Burnside, Mrs. John Jacob Astor, and Mrs. William H. Vanderbilt.[19] (Fig. 2) Warren's fifteen-year old sister Minnie, also a midget and described as "the dearest little duck of a creature on the face of the globe," was maid of honor while Commodore Nutt, who had apparently come to terms with his romantic defeat, stood as the General's best man. Outside the church, thousands of well-wishers representing "all classes of society" gathered to watch the bridal party arrive and waited expectantly throughout the ceremony for their reemergence as Mr. and Mrs. Tom Thumb.[20]

After greeting the couple with cheers, shouts, and whistles, the crowd moved swiftly up Broadway to the Metropolitan Hotel for the reception. There, a cosmopolitan group of well-wishers, "comingled in charming confusion, out-Barnuming Barnum in their unsurpassed conglomeration of all specimens of humanity."[21] Those fortunate enough to possess tickets to the reception ascended to a large second floor drawing room, where the wedding party stood waiting on a "carpeted platform" to welcome their guests. From the drawing room, guests moved through three "parlors beyond" to view the impressive collection of bridal presents. These ranged from jewelry, silver spoons, and an easy chair to a billiard table and miniature silver horse and chariot created by Tiffany and Co. Several "stout policeman" stood guard in each room to keep watch over the gifts, the smallest and most expensive of which were carefully arranged behind a large glass case in a manner reminiscent of one of Barnum's museum exhibits.[22]

In addition to the lavish and expensive gifts, one of the "main attractions" at the reception was the "munificent bridal cake with its delightful four cupids."[23] This brief description suggests that the Stratton/Warren cake was in keeping with recent trends in bridal cakes. According to historian Emily Allen, the vogue for towering, elaborately decorated bridal cakes began in England during the 1850s as bakers attempted to replicate the artistry and technical wizardry of the newly erected Crystal Palace.[24] A series of royal weddings in the 1850s and 1860s (as Victoria's children reached maturity) further fueled the craze for spectacular cakes. For example, the cake for the 1858 nuptials of Queen Victoria's eldest daughter, Victoria Adelaide Mary Louise, to Prince Frederick William of Prussia, was a monumental three-tiered creation over six feet in height, complete with royal arms, classical statuary, charming cupids, and an imperial crown.[25] Given Barnum and Gen. Tom Thumb's earlier successes at Victoria's court, Barnum's attempts to capitalize on American fascination with royalty, and the showman's taste for the spectacular, it is certainly possible that he ordered a cake to rival Princess Victoria's.[26]

There is little evidence to confirm whether Gen. Tom Thumb and his bride cut the bridal cake during the reception or if it remained on display, like the bride and groom, for the pleasure and delight of their guests. However, considering that there were "several thousand persons" in attendance, it is doubtful that the "munificent bridal cake" was ever intended for consumption, at least by the general public.[27] Newspaper accounts nevertheless note that each lady received "an elegant little box of cake as she passed out of the door,"[28] which suggests that multiple cakes were prepared for the reception: one for show, the others for sharing. It is to the latter category that the Library of Congress cake belongs.

But what did these little boxes of cake mean to the women who took them home? Did they see them as tokens of remembrance, as objects infused with the auras of the celebrated couple, or as something else altogether?

Eating Cake, Celebrating Unity

In her 2003 article on Victorian wedding cakes, Emily Allen offers a helpful framework for thinking about the cultural significance of Tom Thumb's wedding cake. As Allen explains, "the distribution of the [wedding] cake is always an apportioning of responsibility, an act of inclusion via gustatory performance."[29] By accepting and eventually eating the bridal cake, wedding guests publicly declare their support for the marriage. Their bodily act of consumption thus promotes and anticipates the bodily act of *consummation* that will symbolize the couple's physical and spiritual union. In other words, eating cake celebrates marriage and anticipates sex in the name of unity.

The equation of cake with sex may have been particularly appropriate in the case of the Tom Thumb and Lavinia Warren. In her examination of "mini-marriages" between animals, midgets, children, and other "cute" beings, Rachel Poquilin argues that "always lurking behind [the] vision of fairy perfection is a degree of titillation."[30] The erotic appeal of the mini-marriage was not lost on Barnum, who was accused of encouraging public speculation about the couple's sexual relationship.[31] The marriage of two child-like yet sexually mature adults—*Harper's Bazar* took note of Lavinia Warren's "full bust" while the *New York Times* described her as "externally all that the most fastidious of the lords of creation could desire"[32]—raised provocative questions about the couple's sexual relationship (*did* they do it and if so *how?*). Though Neil Harris argues that Barnum "did nothing to nourish the idle gossip," the showman seems to have done nothing to stop it either.[33] Read in this light, the gift of the cake-in-a-box can be seen as a sexualized prop in an elaborate sexual drama, the object of a highly eroticized exchange between the crowds of curious onlookers and the child-like newlyweds.[34]

But while Tom Thumb's wedding cake may have aroused a certain *frisson* of sexual excitement in some guests, it may also have held a much more complicated meaning for others. Staged against the backdrop of Civil War, *General* Tom Thumb's nuptials inevitably provoked questions about Barnum's intentions and the symbolic importance of the marriage itself. Was the couple's union in the midst of war—several months after the Union defeat at the Battle of Fredericksburg, five weeks after Lincoln's "Emancipation Proclamation," and weeks before the First Conscription Act—designed as a welcome distraction for demoralized Northern audiences? Barnum's critics certainly thought so. In a seven-page pamphlet entitled *The Pigmies and the Priests,* published shortly after the wedding, a poet named "Cymon" accused Barnum of conspiring with Lincoln to create a spectacle that would turn the public eye away from the horrors of the battlefield. In the following passage, Cymon imagines "the great Bamboozleem" (Barnum) comforting the downtrodden "Foo Foo" (Lincoln):

> You fret because you haven't got one mighty man to show,
> What matter for the giants, then when pigmies are the go;
> There's but one great *Invisible,* we always have been told,
> And now it's fully proved the great invisible is—Gold.[35]

Although it's doubtful that the Stratton/ Warren wedding was a *deliberate* diversion orchestrated by Barnum on Lincoln's behalf, it is worth noting that the newlyweds did little to disguise their sympathies for the Union cause. Both had close ties to the Union Army. As noted above, Lavinia Warren had entertained Union Generals and other high-ranking officers during her levees at Barnum's museum and several of these men, most notably Major General Ambrose Burnside, had been honored guests at the couple's wedding.[36] Stratton's brother, stationed in a Union camp in Washington, DC, had been unable to attend the wedding, so the newlyweds promptly traveled to Washington to visit him, with their media circus in tow. While in the capital city, the couple attended a special honeymoon party at the White House hosted by the Lincolns. During the festivities, Mrs. Tom Thumb reportedly told the President that she strongly supported the Union cause and would allow the General to volunteer should he be called upon.[37]

To return to the cake then, if consuming wedding cake is a performative act that unites guests in a collective endorsement of marital union—an act that celebrates unity *through* unification—the distribution of over 1,000 pieces of wedding cake to those attending the Stratton/Warren reception can be seen as a symbolic declaration of support for the Union as well as faith in the concept of national unity.[38] As the outbreak of war dissolved national and familial bonds, the marriage of one of the nation's most beloved performers to his "Queen of Beauty" represented not only a promise between a man and a woman but also a promise that national unity would someday be restored. By consuming Tom Thumb's wedding cake, thousands of Northerners shared in this dream of reunification.

But what of the wedding cake at the Library of Congress? What emotions did Countess Magri hope to elicit when she sent Harrison Grey Fiske a box containing a forty-three-year old piece of wedding cake, two decades after the General's death and four decades after the end of the Civil War? Did she want to inspire him? Shame him? Entice him? Was she in the habit of giving out gifts of wedding cake to influential acquaintances or was the gesture one of genuine admiration? The publication of the Countess's autobiography the following year (September 1906) in the *New York Tribune Sunday Magazine* offers some compelling, if circumstantial, evidence to suggest that she was keen to publish her life story and in search of an interested editor/publisher.[39] In her letter to Fiske she expressed concern that the general public assumed that she was dead and so may have wanted to rectify the situation with his help.

I have found no evidence that Fiske ever responded to Countess Magri, though he may well have. Certainly the cake's presence in the Minnie Maddern Fiske Papers suggests that he was honored by her gift and considered it a personal and professional treasure. As the editor of one of the country' most influential theatre newspapers, Fiske had extensive knowledge of the profession and its history and may have viewed the cake in a talismanic light—as a material object that connected him physically and emotionally to Barnum, Gen. Tom Thumb, Lavinia Warren, and the thousands of men and women who had attended the "Lilliputian" wedding of the century.

Beyond this kind of guesswork, however, the cake's existence at the Library of Congress remains a delightful mystery, a fanciful diversion, a delicious morsel for the archive-bound historian to nibble upon.

ENDNOTES

[1] I owe a huge debt of gratitude to the amazing archivists and staff in the Library of Congress Manuscropt Room for sharing this treasure with me and for assisting me with my other research. I would also like to acknowledge the financial support of the John W. Kluge Center at the Library of Congress and the Social Sciences and Humanities Research Council of Canada.

[2] On Minnie Maddern Fiske, see Alexander Woolcott, *Mrs. Fiske: Her views on actors, acting, and the problems of production* (New York: Century Co., 1917).

[3] Letter from Countess M.L. Magri to Harrison Grey Fiske, 16 February 1905. Container 12 (Ma-My), Minnie Maddern Fiske Papers, Library of Congress.

[4] "Local Intelligence," *New York Times* 9 Feb. 1863, 2.

[5] "Classified Ad 8—No Title," *New York Times* 31 May 1863, 7. For those unable to attend the wedding, purchasing *cartes de visite* was one way to participate in the much-hyped event. Today Brady is best known for his photographs of Civil War soldiers and battle sites. See for example, Roy Meredith, *Mr. Lincoln's Camera Man: Mathew B. Brady* 2nd ed. (Dover Publications, 1974); Alan Trachtenberg, *Reading American Photographs: Images as History; Mathew Brady to Walker Evans* (Hill and Wang, 1990); Mary Panzer, *Mathew Brady and the Image of History* (Washington, DC: Smithsonian Books, 2004); George Sullivan, *In the Wake of Battle: The Civil War Images of Mathew Brady* (Prestel Publishing, 2004).

[6] I use the term "midget" purposefully here, as this is the word that has historically been used to refer to "perfectly shaped and proportioned 'little people'" Lori Merish, "Cuteness and Commodity Aesthetics: Tom Thumb and Shirley Temple,"in *Freakery: Cultural Spectacles of the Extraordinary Body,* ed. Rosemarie Garland Thomson, pp. 185–203 (New York and London: NYU Press, 1996), 190. I nevertheless acknowledge the problematic etymology of the word (from "midge" referring to an insect) as well as the way it has been used as a derogatory term. In 2009, a joke about "midget tossing" on Donald Trump's *Celebrity Apprentice* prompted an outraged response from the Little People of America. See Lynn Harris, "Who you calling a 'midget'?" *Salon.com* 16 July 2009, http://www.salon.com/life/feature/2009/07/16/m_word/index.html, Accessed 28 January 2011.

[7] Countess M. Lavinia Magri, "Mrs. Tom Thumb's Autobiography," *New York Tribune Sunday Magazine* 16 September 1906. http://www.disabilitymuseum.org/lib/docs/1130.htm?page=2. Accessed 2 September 2010. On P.T. Barnum see Neil Harris, *Humbug: The Art of P.T. Barnum* (Boston, Toronto: Little, Brown and Company, 1973); Philip B. Kunhardt, Jr., et. al, *P.T. Barnum: America's Greatest Showman* (New York: Alfred A. Knopf, 1995); Bluford Adams, *E Pluribus Barnum: The Great Showman & the Making of U.S. Popular Culture* (Minneapolis, London: University of Minnesota Press, 1997); James W. Cook, *The Arts of Deception: Playing with Fraud in the Age of Barnum* (Cambridge, Mass. and London, Eng.: Harvard University Press, 2001)

[8] Quoted in "Mrs. Tom Thumb's Autobiography."

[9] See, for example, "Local Intelligence: Loves of the Lilliputians," *New York Times* 10 Jan. 1863; "Tom Thumb's Courtship," *New York Times* 14 Jan. 1863, 2.

[10] On Cymon's critical pamphlet, see Harris, *Humbug*, 164.

[11] P.T. Barnum, *Struggles and Triumphs; Or Forty Years' Recollections of P.T. Barnum* (1873), 586.

[12] "Tom Thumb's Courtship," 2.

[13] "Local Intelligence: Warren-Thumbiana," *New York Times* 9 Feb. 1863, 2.

[14] The sale of Lavinia Warren's photographs alone brought in an average of $300 each day. Barnum, *Struggles and Triumph*, 601.

[15] Barnum, *Struggles and Triumphs*, 601.

[16] "Local Intelligence: Warren-Thumbiana," 2. See also Barnum, *Struggles and Triumphs*, 603.

[17] I've read numerous accounts of the wedding ceremony and reception, but only the *New York Times* report mentions the wedding cake.

[18] Barnum, *Struggles and Triumphs*, 603.

[19] Barnum, *Struggles and Triumphs*, 603; Harris, *Humbug*, 163.

[20] "The Loving Lilliputians," *New York Times* 11 Feb. 1863, 8.

[21] "The Loving Lilliputians," 8.

[22] "Miscellany: The Wedding of Tom Thumb," *Lewiston Daily Evening Journal* 7 Feb. 1863. Web. 2 Sept. 2010; "The Loving Lilliputians," 8.

[23] "The Loving Lilliputians," 8. See also "Tom Thumb and His Wife," *Harper's Weekly* 21 February 1863, 114; "General Tom Thumb's Wedding," *Daily Southern Cross* xix,1829, 28 May 1863, 4.

[24] Emily Allen, "Culinary Exhibition: Victorian Wedding Cakes and Royal Spectacle," *Victorian Studies* 45.3 (Spring 2003): 457.

[25] Carol Wilson, "Wedding Cake: A Slice of History," *The Journal of Food and Culture* 5.2 (Spring 2005): 69–72.

[26] In the summer of 1844, while in England with General Tom Thumb, Barnum had purchased a state robe reportedly worn by Queen Victoria. Sending the garment home to his business partner Moses Kimball, he enthused that if properly exhibited, it could make twenty-thousand dollars in three years. In later years, Barnum oversaw the installation of a wax figure made in the likeness of Queen Victoria, which stood beside figures of Napoleon and other celebrated historical figures in a special hall of the museum. Harris, *Humbug*, 95, 165.

[27] The newlyweds had originally intended to embark upon a European tour shortly after the wedding but public interest in the couple at home was so strong that they ultimately decided to postpone their travels abroad and hold a series of receptions at various locations throughout the country. Within days of the wedding, 2,500 invited guests attended a Bridal Reception at the home of Gen. Tom Thumb's mother in Bridgeport, Connecticut. Those left off the invitation list contented themselves by swarming the couple wherever they appeared, going so far as to invade their living establishment. "[N]othing short of a double lock and a pair of patent bolds has proved sufficiently powerful to preserve the sanctity of their bed-chamber!" the *Bridgeport Evening Standard* salaciously revealed. "Misfortune of being too Celebrated," reprinted in *New York Times* 24 Feb. 1863, 8. By April, the couple had reversed their earlier decision to retire from show business and held a series of public receptions (levees) at New York's Irving Hall for which Mrs. Tom Thumb appeared dressed in her "costly bridal robe." There is no indication whether cake was also served at these later receptions though it may well have been. "The Reception of Gen. Tom Thumb and Wife," *New York Times* 5 Apr. 1863, 6.

[28] "Miscellany: The Wedding of Tom Thumb." The reference to the "elegant little box" helps to explain the presence of the small, stained box with the label for "E.F. Tinkham, Watchmaker, Jeweler, and Optician" in the Minnie Maddern Fiske Collection. As a resident of Middleborough, Massachusetts, Tinkham presumably knew the Warren family and wanted to participate in the wedding in some way. Though it is doubtful that he made the cake that went into the boxes, it seems likely that he provided the *boxes* in exchange for the promotional opportunity. According to the *New York Times*, numerous tradesmen and artisans from New York viewed the wedding as an excellent chance to "obtain a little gratuitous advertising" and prepared lavish gifts to present to the couple with their names and/or craftsmanship prominently displayed. "The Loving Lilliputians," 8.

[29] Emily Allen, "Culinary Exhibition," 457. Earlier wedding traditions in England held that "guests must eat a small piece [of cake] to ensure that the happy couple are blessed with children." Wilson, "Wedding Cake," 69.

[30] Poliquin, "The Visual Erotics of Mini-Marriages," 4.

[31] Harris, *Humbug*, 163; Rachel Poliquin, "The Visual Erotics of Mini-Marriages," *The Believer* (November/ December 2007), 1 http://www.believermag.com/issues/200711/?read=article_poliquin. Accessed 1 September 2010.

[32] *Harper's Bazar*, quoted in Poliquin, "The Visual Erotics of Mini-Marriages," 1; "The Loving Lilliputians," 8. See also Merish, "Cuteness and Commodity Aesthetics: Tom Thumb and Shirley Temple," esp. 192–194.

[33] Harris, *Humbug*, 163. In later years, when the couple's desire for a child went unrealized, Barnum apparently acquired infants from a local orphanage to stand-in for the couple's child. Poliquin, "The Visual Erotics of Mini-Marriages," 2.

[34] In the twentieth-century, church and community groups throughout the United States often held special "Tom Thumb" weddings, fictional events where a pre-teen couple would go through the marriage ritual in order to develop a greater appreciation for the institution of marriage. Michelle V. Agins, "Tom Thumb Weddings: Only for the Very Young," *New York Times* 16 June 1991. http://query.nytimes.com/gst/fullpage.html?res=9D0CE4DE1230F935A25755C0A967958260. Accessed 6 December 2010. Tom Thumb weddings are still held today as a recent *eHow* article providing tips on "How to Plan a Tom Thumb Wedding" suggests. http://www.ehow.com/how_6459422_plan-tom-thumb-wedding-fundraiser.html. Accessed 6 December 2010.

[35] Quoted in Harris, *Humbug*, 164. In his autobiography, Barnum describes a bizarre encounter with a lady claiming to have written the accusatory pamphlet. Handing the showman a copy, she invited him to buy the "copyright and the entire edition," warning that it said "some frightful things" about him. Barnum refused to take the bait, "fairly roar[ing] at this exceedingly feeble attempt at black-mail," and told the woman that she was free to publish as many editions of the pamphlet as she chose as long as she mentioned him by name. Barnum, *Forty Years*, 608.

[36] "The Loving Lilliputians."

[37] Stanley Kimmel, *Mr. Lincoln's Washington*, 113–114, as cited on http://www.mrlincolnswhitehouse.org/inside.asp?ID=210&subjectID=3

[38] As Emily Allen argues in her analysis of the cakes created for of Queen Victoria and her children, "Looking at cakes, especially those regal confections that celebrated a dream wedding between matter and ideology, became not only an act of visual consumption but also an act of national participation." Allen, Culinary Exibition," 459.

[39] Countless Magri, "Mrs. Tom Thumb's Autobiography."

Adaptation, Copyright, and the Case of Dion Boucicaults *The Poor of* ____

JUSTIN A. BLUM

It was the pursuit of another lead that brought me to the Manuscripts Reading Room of the British Library, face to face with the bust of George Bernard Shaw that sits atop what must surely be the last working card catalogue on Earth. I was hot on the trail of *London Day By Day*, an 1889 Adelphi melodrama that had been giving me the slip for nearly a year. Because the script is unpublished all I had to go on were conflicting reviews would neither entirely confirm nor deny my hunch that this was the first drama to appear on the legitimate London stage with a villain consciously intended by its producers to evoke the uncaptured perpetrator of five (or more, or less) murders in and around Whitechapel in the Autumn of 1888, alias Jack the Ripper. The disorderly text of the handwritten MS held in the Lord Chamberlain's collection didn't exactly settle the question, but in reading it under the watchful eye of G.B.S. I had come to the realization that the play was part of a long line of works descended from the dramatic adaptation of one episode of an 1842 serial novel by Eugène Sue called *Les Mystères de Paris*. This story, dramatized first in France as *Les Bohémians de Paris* and then independently translated and staged simultaneously at both the Surrey and Adelphi in November of 1843, had its setting transferred to London the following year.[1] It washed back and forth across the Channel for the next five decades, with Parisian playwrights adapting London plays based on a French original that were then re-appropriated by Londoners in a vertiginous flow of dramatic free trade. But the story I mean to tell now, though adaptation and exchange are leading players alongside false leads, theft, and multiple identities, is a different one involving fleeting glimpses into the economic and cultural mysteries of the second half of the nineteenth century and the man who was its most commercially successful playwright.

Dion Bouciault had already appeared on the edges of my vision as the author of one variation of one of these "bohemians" dramas, the 1867 *After Dark: A Tale of London Life*.[2] My research into the Adelphi had also showed that it hosted an 1883 revival of his 1864 blockbuster sensation play *The Streets of London*, which had been adapted from his own 1857 stateside hit *The Poor of New York;* I was interested in this as an important and widely seen dramatization of metropolitan life staged in the same venue and only a few years prior to the play that was at the center of my research. At the same time, since only the New York version of the play seems ever to have been published, I had a personal curiosity about exactly what changes Boucicault had made to adapt his drama to an English setting that I hoped the MS would answer. The text of *London Day By Day* that I found in the Lord Chamberlain's Collection seems to be a rough draft, hand-written on several different sizes and qualities of paper and filled with revisions and rearrangements that seem likely to be the compositional work of its authors Sims and Pettit; in my wildest dreams I imagined that the text of *The Streets of London* might either be a manuscript written in Boucicault's own hand or a printed copy of *The Poor of New York* edited by Boucicault or an assistant to reflect the British setting.[3]

What I did not imagine was that I would have any difficulty actually laying hands on the play. Knowing that it had appeared in 1864 at the Princess's Theatre with the title *The Streets of London,* I gave a nod to Shaw's cast-iron visage as I retrieved one of the "S" drawers and found—nothing in the catalogue of that name. Reflexively I went for a "P" drawer thinking the play might have been examined under the title *The Poor of New York,* but drew another blank. Shaw may have been smirking, just a bit, as my fingers walked back through the cards and found one for *The Poor of London* at the Grecian Theatre, with a date of 1864. This surprised me only for the moment it took me to remember that Boucicault had shown his play at the Grecian in Shoreditch at the same time it was appearing at the Princess's in the West-end[4]; since being passed once made a play legal to perform in all venues covered by the Lord Chamberlain's authority[5] it seemed odd but not unthinkable that this one might have been submitted first in the name of the less prestigious East-end theatre.

What appeared in response to my request slip was not the drama I had expected. Hand-written and announcing itself in the licensing request as "to be produced at the Grecian Theatre on Monday May 9th '64," this play had only three acts instead of Boucicault's five. Its story—of a businessman forced to live in penury until his daughters reclaim his fortune from the heartless banker who stole it—might well have been inspired by Boucicault's play about the family of a sea captain enduring squalor until they can recover his fortune from a similarly recreant banker. The anonymously written play, though, contains some of the most bathetic dialogue that I have ever encountered even as an avid student of nineteenth century melodrama. I cast my eyes over such gems as "Hush! Poor Caroline, you know that the Doctor predicted that this sleep would last an hour, and if by daybreak your mother experience no violent emotion she would be saved."[6] Needless to say a violent emotion *is* soon experienced and mother is not saved; in the moment I could only wonder what Boucicault, who famously referred to *The Poor of New York* as so much "guano" for its perceived lack of literary quality, would have managed as an epithet for this piece.

Shaw's metallic expression seemed to have become just a bit smug as I returned the Grecian manuscript and went back to the card catalogue, fresh in the recollection that the first performance of what became *The Streets of London* had actually been given as *The Poor of Liverpool* at that city's Royal

THE POOR OF

PROLOGUE.

SCENE.—*The private office of a banking-house in Liverpool. The bank is seen through the large glazed partition which forms the flats, in which also there is a glazed door L. H. This bank is furnished with desks, shaded lamps, stools, clerks, &c., and beyond this again is seen the windows which look out on the street, in which the gas lamps are seen. Door R. H. leading to a side street.*

The Poor of ____, p2, c. British Library Board (Add. 53029.O, f.2).

Amphitheater and that, just as importantly, the 1843 reforms that officially abolished the Patent Monopoly had extended the Lord Chamberlain's jurisdiction to include provincial theaters operating on Parliamentary licenses. Sure enough *The Poor of Liverpool* was in the catalogue—I might have found it before *The Poor of London* had I not been flipping backward from an absent *New York*—and I paused for a knowing wink at the mug of the author of *Plays Unpleasant* as I pencilled in and submitted another request slip.[7]

A play by Dion Boucicault did come out in response to this request; but it was a document that deepened rather than alleviating my growing sense of mystery. Nestled into the folio of plays passed by the Lord Chamberlain in January and February of 1864 was neither the commercially printed copy of *The Poor of New York* I had suspected I might find, nor the manuscript in Boucicault's own hand that I had allowed myself to fantasize about. The printed pages beneath the unprinted red cover with the Lord Chamberlain's hand-written approval scrawled on it didn't exactly surprise me: plays were often "printed in slip as MS for use of actors" throughout the century.[8] What took me back was the title on the play's first page: "*The Poor of* _____."[9] Not London. Not Liverpool. Just _____.

Reading through the play, I found it devoid of clues as to the location or identity of the printer. The text itself is a very lightly modified form of *The Poor of New York,* in which the villain's name has been changed from Gideon Bloodgood to Crawley, but the other characters are identical. Elements of the dialogue have been altered to reflect British dialect and pronunciation, a change most noticeable in the speech of the street-level characters like the comic hero Badger and the Puffy family who trade in goods like "'ot pies" and "three ha'porth of milk,"[10] though the better heeled characters have also been given a dash of this treatment. The currency throughout the script has been changed from dollars to pounds, and in the opening scene when he believes his financial malfeasance is about to be discovered Crawley of _____ plots an escape to New York while the American Bloodgood contemplates slipping away "on board the packet for Liverpool."[11] Otherwise the narrative thrust and the order of the scenes appear to be the same between the two plays. While the first stage direction indicates "a banking house in Liverpool,"[12] throughout the rest of the text _____ appear whenever any sort of specific geographical or commercial landmark or enterprise is mentioned. Union Square, Delmonico's, the Bowery, Brooklyn and Broadway are all converted to empty spaces which need only be filled in to reset the play in any British city.

The state of this strange document poses some troublesome questions about precisely what sort of theatrical commodity the British version of the play was meant to be. Boucicault's biographers have typically presented the adaptation of *The Poor of New York* as the act of a financially hard-up playwright who, having squandered a fortune earned from *The Colleen Bawn* in several unsuccessful attempts at theatre management in London, fled to Liverpool and desperately dusted-off an old success. The Lord Chamberlain's document would seem, at least, to bely Townsend Walsh's intimation that it was only after the success of *The Poor of Liverpool* that Boucicualt thought to offer the play to London managers[13]: that he incurred the expense necessary to produce *The Poor of* ____ as a printed document prior to the Liverpool opening suggests that he intended from the first to offer it in other British cities.

The Poor of _____ almost certainly, then, reveals two features of Boucicault's commercial personality: his audacity as a playwright in assuming that the drama would be as successful in Liverpool as it had been in New York and be demanded in other locales, and his foresight as a producer in recognizing that a fill-in-the-blanks document would ease the mounting of the play in subsequent cities. It might, though, be something else as well: evidence of the complex legal and economic environment in which Boucicault worked, and of the shaping power that this environment and his determination to succeed financially in it had on his work as a dramatist. Given the convoluted state of Anglo-American copyright law in the 1860s, when a play's having been published or performed in one country made it fair game for adaptation or wholesale remounting in the other without the playwright giving consent or receiving remuneration, I want to suggest that we can see *The Poor of* _____ as one of many strategies which Dion Boucicault used in his trans-Atlantic business to maximize his own ability to adapt the work *of* others while protecting what he regarded to be his own literary and dramatic property from adaptation *by* others.

In 1861, Boucicault had been financially burned by this state of legal affairs when he was unable to prevent or to profit from performances of *The Colleen Bawn* given throughout the British provinces because the play had already been staged and published in the United States.[14] According to Richard Fawkes, Boucicault's response to this was to begin to make alterations to those of his other plays he wished to produce on the other side of the pond from their first performance, so that the result could at least nominally be considered a "new" work and granted copyright protection in Britain if first performed in the U.S. or vice-versa.[15] Depositing *The Poor of* _____ with the Lord Chamberlain, rather than a copy of the already commercially printed *The Poor of New York*, effectively implied that this was a *different* play over which he could exercise a kind of legal authority not available to him if the two were regarded as equivalent.

At the same time, though, printing a version in which details of geography were left indeterminate suggested that the further adaptations necessary to completely localize the play were already anticipated in the text, and thus part of a stable literary property. This document tries, I think, to have it both ways: to assert that some relatively minor changes to the words of *The Poor of New York* to render it British make it a new property, while other equally minor changes leave *The Poor of Liverpool* equivalent to *The Streets of London* or any version set in a locale where pounds would signify money and a villain looking to put distance between himself and his troubles might plan to abscond for New York. In addition to whatever theatrical utility it had for actors who could literally fill-in-the-blanks, *The Poor of* _____ as printed would have entered into the official juridical protection of the Lord Chamberlain's register an assertion that the play was a unique dramatic entity which already anticipated its own ability to undergo further changes while remaining wholly the property of Dion Boucicault.

What's revealed in this document, if I'm reading it correctly, is one playwright and businessman's attempt to put the brakes on a long-running process of more-or-less free translation, adaptation, and appropriation of dramatic and literary works. This was both ingenious and disingenuous: as we have already discussed and has been well documented elsewhere[16], Boucicault based all of his most successful plays on either novels or foreign dramas, which he combined with spectacular stage effects that were also frequently poached from other sources. Even *The Poor of New York* was based closely on Edouard Brisebarre and Eugène Nus' *Les Pauvres De Paris*, with Boucicault's primary addition being a climactic fire scene and the appearance on-stage of a real fire engine to put out the conflagration.[17] Boucicault the impresario and showman was, then, attempting to create a document in *The Poor of* _____ that would call a temporary halt to a cultural process of adaptation that his own career was built on.

The standards of copyright that govern most of the world today would identify almost all of Boucicault's theatrical output (and, indeed, much of the dramatic work staged in Britain in the nineteenth century) as "derivative work" trespassing on the intellectual property of others. It is, however, of little use to judge his practices according to an anachronistic legal standard or even, as John Russell Stephens has done, to see them in the context of a gradual development of rational legal structures that today allow authors their rightful control over dramatic literature. While he is certainly correct in his description of "the inconsistencies, pitfalls, and dangers for the unwary dramatist which the complexity of [nineteenth century] copyright law harboured,"[18] Stephens characterizes the second half of the century as a period of gradual progress leading to "much needed changes in the operation of British-American copyright."[198] In this version of the story, Boucicault and his fellow playwrights struggled against unscrupulous managers to control their written work and eventually establish the essentially just regime of intellectual property under which we currently live.

Dion Boucicault, though, was both a manager and a dramatist who was sometimes victimized by the state of the law but just as often turned "inconsistencies, pitfalls, and dangers" into opportunities, springboards, and the occasional cash-cow. The nineteenth century theatre was a cultural mechanism in which the freedoms to translate foreign works, adapt non-dramatic literature, and appropriate stage business while claiming the results as one's own were major cogs. Boucicault made full use of this machine to do his own creative work, and he tried various strategies to arrest its motion in order to derive profit from that work. The "combination system," which he famously imported from the United States to Britain, was one such wrench in the gears: by sending touring versions of a play out at the same time it was running in the metropolitan center, regional managers could be prevented from creating adaptations or pirated versions of urban successes.[20] The creation of *The Poor of* _____ is, in my reading, evidence of another such strategy: one that sought to preempt potential competitors by maximizing the legal protections that could be claimed for the literary part of the theatrical property. This gambit seems never to have been tested: while the Grecian's other *The Poor of London* may have been an attempt to capitalize on the success enjoyed there by *The Poor of the London Streets* the former is broadly similar to but not explicitly derivative of the latter, and no other imitations or adaptations seem to have demanded the playwright's legal attention during his lifetime.

The Poor of _____ remains for me a puzzling document. Performances of all versions of Boucicault's play in New York, London, Liverpool and elsewhere ended by exhorting each member of the audience individually that "when you leave this place, as you return to your homes, should you see some poor creatures by the wayside, extend your hands to them, and the blessings that will follow you on your way will be the most grateful tribute you can pay to the POOR OF _____."[21] That this earnest appeal to charity was made at the end of what its author intended as a brazen money-spinner is one major incongruity. The way the blanks in the script as archived by the British Library can be read as a claim to both difference and identity is another. An understanding of how both this performance and its document are riddled with such contradictions may suggest that our own regimes of theatrical business and intellectual property are backed by a tangled history of individuals navigating and shaping a complex and sometimes arbitrary system of laws and conventions; it might indeed awaken us to the possibility that our own legal and intellectual assumptions about creative property are complex, occasionally arbitrary, and susceptible to manipulation. Might an understanding of Boucicault's process ask us to question the iron-clad control over intellectual property currently extended to film-makers who use 3D and other computer generated effects to spin well-worn mythic and melodramatic story-structures into massive science fiction franchises? How might a study of nineteenth century wranglings over the definition and control of literary, dramatic, and scenic properties inform debates about fair use and fan fiction in the YouTube era? Animated by the contradictions of its age, *The Poor of _____* asks us to understand not only the complexities and competing interests that shaped past views of theatrical property, but also to consider how the strategies and solutions deployed by authors, managers, and other historical actors have created the legal and ideological landscape within which we map own definitions of intellectual and dramatic property and propriety.

ENDNOTES

[1] By both T.W. Moncrief (*The Scamps of London* at the Royal Victoria) and Charles Selby (*London By Night* at the Strand).

[2] Boucicault's most famous addition to this particular dramaturgical complex was a scene involving the last-second rescue of its hero from an onrushing train—an effect which he took from the American playwright Augustin Daly's *Under the Gaslight*. Though Daly also seems to have poached the manner of staging the effect from the 1865 British play *The Engineer*, he won an injunction against Boucicault's play in the United States.

[3] Finding what appear to be compositional drafts has been a commonplace in my experience with the 19th century parts of the Lord Chamberlain's Collection. Once a fair copy had been produced for the use of the actors, technicians, and prompter a compositional draft would have little theatrical utility, and probably seemed a good candidate for the archival oblivion of the Lord Chamberlain's office.

[4] For a brief account of this double production see John Russell Stephens, *The Profession of the Playwright: British Theatre 1800–1900*. (Cambridge: Cambridge University Press, 1992), 55–6. At the Grecian the play was apparently billed as *The Poor of the London Streets*, a detail which, had I remembered it, might have mitigated my surprise at the document that appeared when I requested the Grecian's *The Poor of London*.

[5] Which is, of course, why I was searching for an 1864 script while researching an 1883 production in the first place.

[6] Anonymous, *The Poor of London* (Lord Chamberlain's Plays Collection, British Library, ADD MS 53032.A [May-June 1864]), 2.

[7] The Manuscript Room has, I regret to have to add, since switched to the same online item requests as the rest of the British Library. And so with the end of scrawling on carbon slips with stubby, dull pencils another blow is struck against sensuous experience in the scholarly world.

[8] Henry Arthur Jones, *The Shadow of Henry Irving*, quoted in Stephens, *The Profession of the Playwright*, 104.

[9] Dion Boucicault, *The Poor of _____* (Lord Chamberlain's Plays Collection, British Library, ADD MS 53029.O [January-February 1864]), p. 1. Page numbers here, and elsewhere, refer to those printed in the document; additional numbers have been added by hand as part of the collation of the Lord Chamberlain's collection, and because the cover has been numbered as both the first and last pages of the document these are one greater than the printed number throughout.

[10] Boucicault, *The Poor of _____*, 6.

[11] Boucicault, *The Streets of New York*, 4.

[12] Boucicault, *The Poor of _____*, 2.

[13] Townsend Walsh. *The Career of Dion Boucicault* (New York: Benjamin Blom, 1915), 93.

[14] See Stephens, *The Profession of the Playwright*, 104–6.

[15] Richard Fawkes, *Dion Boucicault: A Biography* (London: Quartet Books, 1979), 134.

[16] Beginning, even, in Boucicault's lifetime with "A Little Light Upon After Dark," *The Mask: A Humorous and Fantastic Review of the Month*, 1 no. 8 (September 1868), 237–243. The author of this article criticizes the play not for its use of a borrowed plot or of the brazen

theft of the train effect from Daly's but because he finds it dramatically inferior to Moncrieff's *The Scamps of London.*

[17] Michael R. Booth gives an account of this scene, as well as some of the advances in lighting technology that made it so compelling to audiences, in *Victorian Spectacular Theatre 1850–1910* (London: Routledge & Kegan Paul, 1981), 63–4.

[18] Stephens, *The Profession of the Playwright,* 115.

[19] *Ibid,* p. 109.

[20] For a discussion of Boucicault's innovation in "parcelling out" rights in various geographic locations, as well as a thorough discussion of touring and the economic relationship between foreign countries, the British provinces, and London as the metropolitan "arena of greatest prestige" see Chapter 10 "Theatre as Cultural Capital" of Tracy C. Davis, *The Economics of the British Stage, 1800–1914* (Cambridge: Cambridge University Press, 2000), 334–62.

[21] Boucicault, *The Poor of* _____, 37.

Aglooka's Ghost: Apparitions in the Archive[1]

HEATHER DAVIS-FISCH

When John Franklin's expedition vanished in the central Arctic in the late 1840s, it left few material traces. A lone written record, found in a cairn at Victory Point on King William Island in 1859, reported that Franklin's ships were beset by ice in 1846, that Franklin died in 1847, and that in April 1848, the men who remained alive abandoned their ships to head for Back's Fish River. Personal items and human remains, strewn south along the coastline, testified to an ultimately fatal retreat from the ships. The search parties that discovered these material traces also uncovered, and at times produced, a second set of remains: a series of performances. Precisely because the material remains of the expedition were so scattered, so mute, so inconclusive, performances constituted an alternate way for those involved in the search for the expedition to understand what its disappearance meant. The range of these performances is remarkable, including an original pantomime produced by British officers on a search ship; the attempts of explorers to imitate Inuit behavior by "going native"; Jane Franklin's refusal to wear appropriate mourning clothes to protest the Admiralty's decision to declare her husband dead; and Charles Dickens's performance as a doomed Arctic explorer in the melodrama *The Frozen Deep*. These performances attempted to intervene in the question of what happened by passing on, through embodied performance, experiential knowledge of what the disappearance and loss of the expedition meant.

American explorer Charles Francis Hall went to the Arctic in 1860[2] because he was convinced that Franklin survivors "might yet be found" and "though no *civilized* persons knew the truth . . . Esquimaux were aware of it."[3] Hall was an "unlikely polar explorer" with "no scientific background, no knowledge of navigation, and no training in any related skills,"[4] but despite his lack of qualifications, his abrasive and frequently irrational personality, and his attitude toward Inuit, which often comes across as racist, he was a diligent interviewer and researcher. Although he failed to find survivors, Hall is the key figure responsible for recording Inuit stories of meeting Franklin survivors while the events were within living memory. One of the most widely circulated, well preserved, and compelling of these stories concerns Inuit meeting white men travelling in the King William Island area.

Hall's account of this story demonstrates that, like Europeans, Inuit used performance to transmit knowledge of what happened to Franklin's men and, furthermore, that often *only* through performance were these experiences of contact communicated.

On 18 May 1869, after hearing second-hand accounts of a meeting between four Inuit families and a group of 30 *qallunaat* approximately 20 years earlier,[5] Hall finally met Owwer and Teekeeta, men who were actually present that day. Through Inuit translators and "pantomimed" actions, he learned the details of the encounter.[6] While the story provides a tantalizing glimpse of what the Franklin survivors might have experienced in their final months, as an archival document it is inscrutable: it cannot be "cracked" to reveal exactly what happened. Moreover, both the genealogy of the story's transmission and the inherent difficulties of transcribing gesture into words mean that Hall, despite his best intentions, is an unreliable witness. Yet I do not think the story is a dead-end: it allows one to consider what happens as stories move from oral to written, from repertoire to archive.[7] By resisting the urge to reconstruct the performance and turning instead to the lingering affective power of the story, one can reconsider Hall's account as the narrative of a ghostly performance in which the absent body and unknown experience of a Franklin survivor become temporarily present.

Owwer and Teekeeta told Hall that they were seal hunting with two other men and their families when they saw a group of white men in the distance. Two of those men approached and met them across a crack in the ice. Owwer said that the first man used an "oo-loo" (a knife) to cut the ice "with a peculiar kind of circling motion," then took these ice chips and "put his hand up to his mouth & then lowered it along down his neck & breast as if to say he wanted to get something to eat."[8] In specifying that Owwer demonstrated this motion using the knife on the igloo floor, Hall explicitly acknowledges that he learned the details of the encounter not only through his translators' words but also through watching a re-enactment.

Following the request for food, the white men crossed the crack in the ice, moving closer to the Inuit. Hall records, "On the 2 Kob-lu-nas (white men) getting to them the 1st man who was Ag-loo-ka spoke to them saying Man-nik Too-me at the same time stroking 1st one & then the other down the breast & also shook hands with each repeating Man-nik-too-me several times. The other man with Ag-loo-ka did all the same in shaking hands & speaking Man-nik-too-me!"[9] Hall's account of the greeting tells us that Aglooka and his companion attempted to use the phrase "man-nik-too-me" to indicate their peaceful intentions, then used both an Inuit gesture—the stroking of the breast—and a British one—the handshake—to reinforce the idea of friendship.

The white man called Aglooka then tried to speak to the Inuit, but apparently "of all he then said they could only make out one word which was 'I-wil-ik'", the Inuktitut name for Repulse Bay.[10] According to Hall, Owwer spent "15 to 20 minutes . . . describing in pantomimic way just how Ag-loo-ka appeared & imitating his words. Ag-loo-ka pointed with his hand to the Southward & Eastward & at the same time repeating the word I-wil-ik."[11] Hall concludes: "The Innuits [sic] could not understand

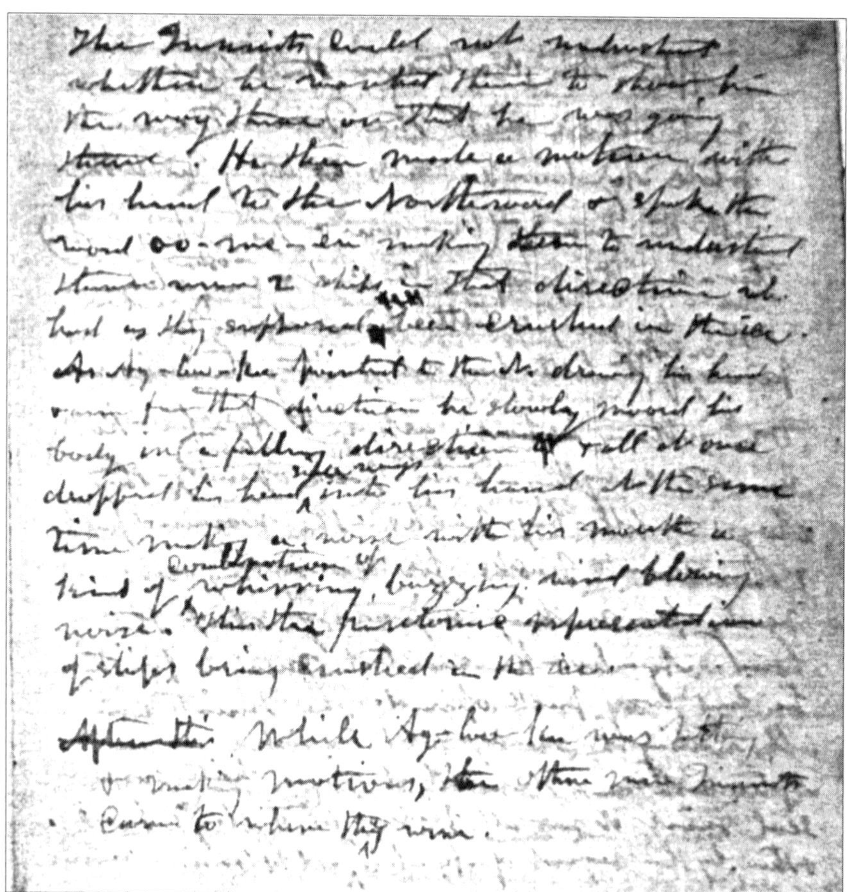

The Innuits could not understand whether he wanted them to show him the way there or that he was going there. He then made a motion with his hand to the Northward & spoke the word oo-me-en making them to understand there were 2 ships in that direction which had as they supposed been crushed in the ice. As Ag-loo-ka pointed to the N. drawing his hand away from that direction he slowly moved his body in a falling direction & all at once dropped his head sideways into his hand, at the same time making a noise with his mouth a kind of combination of whirring, buzzing and blowing noise. This the pantomimic representation of ships being crushed in the ice [illegible]

Afterwards While Ag-loo-ka was talking & making motions, the other two Innuits came to where they were.

"Hall describes Owwer's renactment of Aglooka's ships being crushed," Fieldnotes of Charles Francis Hall's Arctic expedition to find the Franklin Expedition, 18 May 1869 (Book 38 of 62, item 103). National Museum of American History, Behring Centre, Smithsonian Institution.

whether he wanted them to show him the way there or that he was going there."[12] Commmunication failed, suggesting that it was unclear whether Aglooka was asking a question or passing on information about his plans. But since Aglooka's immediate concern was probably with survival, did his intention really matter? He wanted to go to Iwilik. The Inuit could presumably have communicated this to search parties, regardless of whether Aglooka was asking for directions or passing on information. Setting aside the question of intention, what interests me is *how* Hall characterizes Owwer's performance. Hall uses the theatrical term "pantomimic" to describe how Owwer recreated Aglooka's actions, underlining that Hall's account does not simply recount a contact narrative but records a reenactment of a mimed, gestural performance.

The next passage of Hall's account relates that Aglooka:

> [M]ade a motion with his hand to the Northward & spoke the word oo-me-en making them to understand there were 2 ships in that direction which had as they supposed been crushed in the ice. As Ag-loo-ka pointed to the N. drawing his hand & arm from that direction he slowly moved his body in a falling direction & all at once dropped his head sideways into his hand. At the same time making a noise with his mouth a kind of combination of whirring, buzzing, wind blowing noise. This the pantomimic representation of ships being crushed in the ice.[13]

Hall's passage conveys what Aglooka did—but only by erasing Owwer's reenactment: Hall allows his readers to imagine Aglooka's performance only by forgetting that he is actually describing Owwer's actions. The information contained in Aglooka's performance is crucial for historians attempting to determine what happened to the Franklin expedition: knowing how and when the ships were destroyed would shed considerable light on why the expedition failed. But as we will see, it is impossible to reconstruct all the details of this encounter or to recuperate what Aglooka actually did because one cannot even determine precisely what Hall saw in watching Owwer enact his memory of Aglooka's performance: how can one know, almost 150 years later, how Hall translated Owwer's gestures and sounds into written description? Yet recognizing the difficulty of reconstruction does not eliminate my desire to imagine Owwer's—and Aglooka's - performances. In Hall's account, something remains of the event Aglooka's gestures refer to that, although irretrievable, cries out to be known.

One can fill in some details about the encounter with speculations. Although we do not know exactly who Aglooka was,[14] he was likely the travelling party's senior officer, since he came forward to speak to the Inuit. One can imagine, months or years after the ships' abandonment,[15] Aglooka leading his exhausted men south across the tundra. Seeing Inuit hunters must have given him an initial rush of hope that they could save his men from the scurvy and starvation that plagued them—most British explorers believed Inuit were phenomenal hunters—followed by the realization that these four Inuit men could not support their own families and the additional men. After Aglooka attempted to communicate that they needed food, that they were friendly, and that they were going to Iwilik, he told the story of his ships being crushed. Although the story of the ship's destruction might have aroused Inuit sympathy, there is no sign in Owwer's recollection that it was understood as part of Aglooka's request for help: why did Aglooka spend time telling Inuit the story? The ships' destruction would have been terrifying and devastating to the expedition and an immense professional and personal failure for the commanding officer. Considering this, Aglooka's decision to enact the ships' destruction suggests he needed to testify to this terrible experience, this enormous failure, to ensure that the event didn't disappear when he and his men, almost inevitably, died.

Hall's description has a quality of absence, as though words can't quite capture what Owwer did or Owwer's body couldn't quite replicate what Aglooka did. Aglooka gestured to the north and said oo-me-en (Hall's translation of *umiaq*, Inuktitut for boat), "making them to understand there were 2 ships in that direction which had as they supposed been crushed in the ice."[16] It is unclear how the Inuit understood that there were two ships—perhaps Aglooka used his fingers to suggest this—or that the ships had been crushed. Here, Hall erases his editorial process: either he omits a detail of Owwer's performance or he retroactively explains something that was initially unclear. Aglooka then performed what reads as a complex movement: pointing to the north, "drawing his hand & arm from that direction, he slowly moved his body in a falling direction & all at once dropped his head sideways into his hand."[17] Breaking the gesture into individual movements—hand and arm, torso, head and hand—reveals a range of possibilities: Did Aglooka draw his arm across his body or into his body? Did he fall to the ground or did his gesture suggest falling? Was he on the ground or upright when he dropped his head into his hand? Considering what Aglooka's body represented produces more questions: Was Aglooka demonstrating what he felt as his ship was crushed, falling to the ground at the moment of impact? Was Aglooka representing his experience in a symbolic way, with his head in his hand signifying defeat? Was Aglooka using his body to represent the body of the boat, with his arm signifying, perhaps, the mast collapsing? Considering the sounds Aglooka made, the "combination of whirring, buzzing, wind blowing noise"[18], raises still more questions: Was Aglooka representing what he actually heard as the ship was crushed? Was he making sounds to clarify what happened for his Inuit audience? Was he doing both, recreating his experience and reproducing the sounds objectively? Was he simultaneously representing himself, through his bodily gestures, and the outside elements, through his voice? Questions also arise surrounding Aglooka's choice of performance conventions: why not, for instance, use snow to produce props representing ships and ice, like the "food" he used to show hunger? Owwer also told Hall in a later interview that Aglooka had a man with him, called "Dok-took," who his translators were convinced was Dr. McDonald, formerly a surgeon on a whaler, who "could talk so that they [Inuit] could understand him better than they could Aglooka"[19]: This raises the question of why Aglooka performed the event at all instead of simply asking "Dok-took" to translate.

Hall's description of Owwer's performance permits multiple interpretations of what Aglooka did and, if one follows these interpretations in a signifying chain back to the original event of the ship being crushed, this uncertainty also allows one to attribute multiple meanings to that event, both for Aglooka and for historians attempting to determine what happened to Franklin's expedition. At one point while working with this account, I hoped it was possible to produce a coherent, if tentative, interpretation of Aglooka's performance: that the performance was a sign, for example, that the ships' loss constituted an unspeakable trauma. I am now convinced that this story, like other Inuit stories of Franklin survivors, is spacious enough for multiple interpretations to exist simultaneously and that it can be read to mean almost anything one needs or wants it to.

Although the story appears to prohibit a coherent interpretation as performance event, and thus fails to contribute conclusively to an understanding of what happened to the expedition, it possesses remarkable staying power. I keep returning to the story because it also illustrates how a remembered performance can be almost—but not quite—captured and preserved with words. Aglooka's performance communicated something crucial but intangible about the experience of the ships being crushed; this performance then resonated in Owwer's imagination for twenty years before he shared it with Hall; Hall's fieldnotes evoke something about his experience of watching Owwer's reproduction of Aglooka's performance. The performance genealogy allows room to imagine what happened, generating affect for a lost experience that cannot quite be reconstructed: this process of looking harder, of straining to interpret, ultimately engages one in a sustained relationship with Aglooka and his lost men.

Inuit recalled their encounters with Franklin's men using language reminiscent of ghost stories. Cathy Towtongie, for example, remembers her grandmother's stories of seeing Franklin survivors: they were "a raggedy bunch and their clothing was not well made. Their skins were black and the meat above their teeth was gone; their eyes were gaunt. Were they *tuurngait*—spirits—or what?"[20] In Hall's story, Aglooka emerges as a ghostly presence, in both a literal sense—he was dead when the story was told—and metaphorically. To Owwer, as to Towtongie's grandmother, Aglooka and his men must have looked terrifying, even inhuman, suffering from scurvy and starvation. Hall spent the better part of a decade looking for traces of Franklin's men: hearing this story must have had an eerie quality, particularly because Hall's encounter with the story was in a sense what trauma theorists might term a missed encounter, a glimpse of an event whose truth was irretrievable. Alice Rayner's work on theatrical ghosting is helpful for theorizing about the story's lingering power and its productive potential. Rayner writes that ghosts "animate our connections to the dead, producing a visible, material, and affective relationship to the abstract terms of time and repetition . . . absence and presence . . . A ghost, particularly in the theater, ought to startle the audience into attention with a shiver. Doubt rationalizes the shiver, but it also signals an encounter."[21] Hall's account of Owwer's reenactment of Aglooka's performance has this quality of absence/presence: Aglooka is present in Owwer's reenactment, but the reenactment draws attention to his actually missing body. Aglooka's manifestation through Owwer's performance, which Hall's discursive erasure of Owwer underlines, produces the shiver, the sense of a close encounter. Rayner argues that ghosts' mysterious power emerges because "they are fully embodied and material but are unrecognized without a certain mode of attention, a certain line of sight that can perceive the mysterious object that is distinct from, yet embodied by, the theatrical object."[22] This sense of oscillation emerges in Hall's language: Aglooka comes into and out of presence, allowing Hall and the reader to forget, but only for a second, that the story is not about Aglooka's actions but about Owwer's. The performance achieves its staying power not because of its content, which remains ambiguous and ephemeral, but because of its affect, because of the shiver. As we have seen, the attempt to parse the performance, to analyze Hall's account to clarify what Hall or Owwer or Aglooka did, is impossible. According to Rayner, this impossibility is symptomatic of a ghostly presence: a ghost is "not the sort of object that can be dissected, parsed into constituent elements, revealed, or critiqued. Instead a ghost appears only from an oblique perspective and emerges only from the sideways glance at the void of death or the blanks in memory."[23]

So who is the ghost? Hall's account, as it survives in the archive, collapses not only Aglooka and Owwer, but also Hall, erasing him as narrator: in the space created by this triple collapse, the ghost, the no-thing, appears. The identity of this ghost is unstable, its affective power seems to shift for each reader of Hall's account; my own reading leads me to see the ghost not in the figure of Aglooka, but as the unknowable thing that was the catalyst of the disaster that doomed the expedition. This "no-thing" might have been the event of the ships being crushed by ice floes, but it also might have been something less tangible and "event-full": a series of occurences, a failure to create an event, a failure to act. Rayner writes, "ghosts hover where secrets are kept and demand that secrets come out from the crypts of time, they are everywhere . . . Some secrets can wait forever. Some compel their ghosts to appear, and the ghosts are impatient for the living to set them right, do them justice, and release them into time."[24] The thing (the no-thing) that happened to the Franklin expedition, the event or events that historians speculate about and that no one knows about, is what Hall's story, ultimately, refers to. It defies archival scrutiny not only because of banal questions about who was involved, when it occurred, what exactly happened, but precisely because it is the story of a secret. And, in the context of recent Parks Canada searches and the number of literary and scientific works devoted to the question of what happen to Franklin's expedition, it seems that these stories of the ghosts of Franklin and his men continue to signal the location of a secret that waits to be revealed, continue to engage us many years after the physical disappearance of these men.

ENDNOTES

[1] I would like to thank Alan Filewod, Danny O'Quinn, Michelle Elleray, Stephen Johnson, and Jerry Wasserman for their insightful comments on earlier drafts of this article. This paper was written with the support of a Social Sciences and Humanities Research Council postdoctoral fellowship.

[2] Hall conducted two expeditions in search of Franklin's men: first, from 1860–62 and then from 1864–69. He returned to the Arctic in 1871 as captain of the *Polaris* expedition, a short-lived quest for the geographic North Pole. Hall died months into the expedition from arsenic poisoning. See Chauncey Loomis, *Weird and Tragic Shores: The Story of Charles Francis Hall, Explorer* (New York: Knopf, 1971), 297–354 for details of the circumstances surrounding Hall's death.

[3] Charles Francis Hall, *Life with the Esquimaux: A Narrative of Arctic Experience in Search of Survivors of Sir John Franklin's Expedition* (1864. Edmonton: M.G. Hurtig, 1970), 4.

[4] Pierre Berton, *The Arctic Grail: The Quest for the North West Passage and the North Pole, 1818–1911* (Toronto: McClelland and Stewart, 1988), 345.

[5] Hall was not the first to hear stories of this meeting—John Rae and Francis McClintock heard about it in the 1850s. Hall was, however, the first to hear the story from Inuit who were actually present.

[6] The story appears in Hall's fieldnotes; J.E. Nourse, the editor of Hall's notes from his second expedition, did not include it verbatim in the published *Narrative of the Second Arctic Expedition*. I first came across the story in David Woodman's *Unravelling the Franklin Mystery*

(1991), which uses Inuit testimony to attempt to reconstruct what happened after Franklin's men abandoned their ships in 1848.

[7] My use of the terms repertoire and archive are drawn from the first chapter of Diana Taylor's *The Archive and the Repertoire: Performing Cultural Memory in the Americas* (Durham: Duke UP, 2003), in which she uses the term "repertoire" to refer to the corpus of embodied and socially transmitted memory, to the supposedly ephemeral, to performance as practice, and "archive" to refer to textual and material remains, the supposedly permanent artifacts of practices.

[8] Charles Francis Hall, *Fieldnotes from 18 May 1869*. Book 38 of 62. Item 103. National Museum of American History, Behring Centre, Smithsonian Institution. No pagination.

[9] Hall, *Fieldnotes*, book 38. Aglooka probably thought that "Man-nik-too-me" meant "we are friends," which he would have learned from earlier accounts of encounters with Inuit. Inuit "greeted" John Ross with this phrase and by tapping him on the breast in 1830 (See Dorothy Eber, *Encounters on the Passage: Inuit Meet the Explorers* (Toronto; Buffalo: University of Toronto Press, 2008), xiv); Francis McClintock recorded that the phrase meant "We are friends" (Francis Leopold McClintock, *The Voyage of the 'Fox' in the Arctic Seas: A Narrative of the Discovery of the Fate of Sir John Franklin and his Companions* (London: J. Murray, 1869), 261). McClintock (and likely Ross and Aglooka) misunderstood the phrase: it actually means, "do it smoothly, not aggressively" (Eber, *Encounters*, xiv).

[10] Hall, *Fieldnotes*, book 38.

[11] Hall, *Fieldnotes*, book 38.

[12] Hall, *Fieldnotes*, book 38.

[13] Hall, *Fieldnotes*, book 38.

[14] Hall was convinced that Aglooka was Francis Crozier, captain of HMS *Terror* and Franklin's second-in-command. In the 1820s, Crozier went to the Arctic three times; while there, he traded names with an Inuk boy named Aglooka and became known by that name Crozier was one of several white men known as Aglooka, which means "long strides" (Eber, *Encounters*, 42); John Rae and James Clark Ross were both known by the same name and Aglooka "could legitimately be given to any tall purposeful white man" (David Woodman, *Unravelling the Franklin Mystery: Inuit Testimony* (Montreal: McGill-Queen's UP, 1991), 195). David Woodman argues, based on this evidence, that there is no reason to assume that Crozier must have been the Aglooka who met Owwer (Woodman, *Unravelling*, 160).

[15] It is unclear when Aglooka and his men met Owwer. Hall's informants's first attempt to establish the year of the encounter resulted in a date of 1844, the year before Franklin sailed. A second attempt resulted in 1849. Hall ultimately concluded that the encounter occurred in 1848, perhaps in an attempt to be consistent with the Victory Point record (Hall, *Second*, 415). John Rae was told that it took place in 1850 (John Rae, *John Rae's Correspondence with the Hudson's Bay Company on Arctic Exploration, 1844–55*, ed. E.E. Rich (London: The Hudson's Bay Record Society, 1953), 274). Francis McClintock interpolated from Inuit stories that the meeting took place in 1848 (McClintock, *Voyage*, 249). Establishing the year in which Aglooka told Inuit his ship (or ships) were crushed would assist in resolving a number of debates concerning what happened after the Victory Point record was deposited; because the year cannot be firmly determined, the story remains tantalizing and frustrating.

[16] Hall, *Fieldnotes*, book 38.

[17] Hall, *Fieldnotes*, book 38.

[18] Hall, *Fieldnotes*, book 38.

[19] Hall, *Fieldnotes*, qtd. in Woodman, *Unravelling*, 127.

[20] Eber, *Encounters*, xi.

[21] Alice Rayner, *Ghosts: Death's Double and the Phenomena of Theatre* (Minneapolis, University of Minnesota Press, 2006), xiii.

[22] Rayner, *Ghosts*, xvii.

[23] Rayner, *Ghosts*, xxii.

[24] Rayner, *Ghosts*, xxxv.

Riding for a Fall: A Saddle for Mazeppa's Fiery Steed

DAVID MAYER

As far as I know, there are only two theatrical characters who ride horses in the nude. One, the better known, is Lady Godiva. Godiva, protesting her noble husband's excessive taxes on the people of Coventry, rides naked through the medieval streets where she is witnessed only by Peeping Tom, blinded for his prurient gaze.[1] The other nude rider is Mazeppa, whose tale of equestrian fortitude was first narrated in a poem (1819) by Lord Byron. By 1823 Henry M. Milner had turned Byron's poem into a spectacle-melodrama for London's minor—especially equestrian—theatres. *Mazeppa,* the play, enacts the endurance and revenge of a tartar prince apprehended courting Olinska, the Palatine of Poland's daughter, who is already betrothed to a local nobleman. For his presumption, Mazeppa, his spine forced against the back of a spirited wild horse, is stripped of his clothes, bound so that he cannot escape, and, thus humiliated and distressingly mounted, is driven into the Carpathian wilderness to his supposed death, pursued by wolves and hovering vultures determined to devour both the galloping horse and its helpless rider. There the exhausted horse is trapped by a falling tree limb, but, as wolves close in and vultures swoop, Mazeppa is providentially rescued. Revived and restored to his Tartar inheritance, he and his father lead a successful mounted attack on the Polish court. Mazeppa's rival is slain, Mazeppa is betrothed to Olinska, and the two nations, joined by conquest and this marriage, are obliged to make peace.

It wasn't riding naked that attracted me to the idea of a production of Milner's hippodrama. Rather, a sequence of experiences where, along the way, I contracted a virulent case of hubris, overconfident that I could step into the world of equine drama and, with research and patience and only intermediate riding skills, solve its staging problems. In mitigation, I was years younger than now, and there was no thought of the many stringent health and safety regulations that would have stopped me and this project dead in our tracks. I had been fortunate to spend much of my adolescence and non-academic adulthood on Colorado's Western Slope. Saddle horses were always present. In London in 1970, researching a book, I was charged by mounted police when I participated in an anti-Vietnam War protest before the American Embassy in Grosvenor Square. The police horses, while terrifying, I observed, were immaculately trained and obedient. Charging at a controlled canter, they would knock us to the ground but not step on us, leaving us to the sadly finite mercies of the foot police who followed at their heels. Later, attending a football (i.e., soccer) match in Manchester in the early '80s, I again encountered police horses used more benignly for crowd control. Each animal stood its ground or moved the crowd as instructed by its rider. It didn't spook. Also in Manchester, teaching drama in the university, I watched as the university's Grounds and Estate workers bulldozed, levelled, and paved in loose cinders a three-quarter-acre car park immediately outside our theatre building, surrounding the new carpark with a seven-foot high berm of soil and rubble bulldozed from the scraped earth. The carpark awaited cars but remained unused.

Teaching and researching the drama of the long 19th century, I had, of course, read Milner's *Mazeppa*[2] and enthusiastically contested the critical view that this roaring equine drama was degenerate and debased theatre. It was, rather, a significant play that spoke to 19th century horse culture and popular spectacle, first presented at the Coburg, then Astleys, and eventually in almost every British and American community that boasted a hippodrome[3] or travelling circus or even a stage that would accommodate a live horse. Robertson Davies had written of *Mazeppa* that " . . . it was no more than crude story-telling . . . " but he had also acknowledged that the play was

> . . . Byronic in spirit, if crude in dramaturgy. The sense of it being a "grand equestrian spectacle", in which Mazeppa's ride bound on the back of the "fiery, untamed steed" in front of a moving panorama is the great sensation, should not blind us to the fact that this was Byron for the people, and that some of the undoubted Byronic spirit gleams through it.[4]

Coarse acting had contributed to *Mazeppa*'s tawdry reputation. Revised as a full equestrian spectacle by Milner and re-staged by Andrew Ducrow for Astley's Royal Amphitheatre in 1831, the stentorian[5] John Cartlitch performed the role of Mazeppa in excess of 1500 times, eventually taking the drama to America. If 20th century historians stigmatized the bawling Cartlitch performances as excessive, they were even more prepared to attack the Victorian stage on finding that the leading male role was played *en-travestie* from 1861 by the American actress Adah Isaacs Menken.[6] Menken, costumed in flesh-colored tights and flesh-colored silk trunks and jerkin, represented to censorious-but-titillated Victorian audiences the furthest limit of permissible stage nudity. However, Menken's cross-dressed success as Mazeppa instantly removed previous expectations that only male performers would be cast in this role. *Mazeppa*'s almost-unbroken popularity from 1823 into the early decades of the 20th century[7] also identified the Victorian age as the final period of an active equine culture in which horse ownership and horse traffic enabled cities to expand and function, and in consequence of which, equestrian prowess was a much-admired skill. Astley's and the numerous hippodrama-circuses that it spawned were expressions of this horse-based culture, offering their patrons vivid examples of superbly trained horses and adroit and sometimes spectacular riding.[8] As my appreciation of the popular drama of the 19th century stage increased, I viewed *Mazeppa* as a pinnacle of visual melodrama, a play to read and to admire with wistful acceptance that a modern production was probably beyond our means to realize.

It was when the carpark was graded and cinder-coated that the idea of actually staging Milner's drama struck. Every July, after classes and examinations had ended, our Drama Department offered a "summer company" of plays in repertoire in the University Theatre. Why not take advantage of this potential performance space? Why not offer spectator seating in a part of the carpark but keep a wide space for a full equestrian production of *Mazeppa,* ringing the spectacle with flaming torches set into the enclosing berm? I concurrently approached the University's Grounds and Estates Committee and the Greater Manchester Police and proposed a Drama Department production of *Mazeppa* using this space and employing police horses (which we would stable in a tent nearby). The university acquiesced. The police, increasingly under criticism for abusively heavy-handed crowd control in the miners' strikes, saw my proposal as a useful occasion to restore their smudged reputation, and they eagerly agreed.

This initial success left me with two related problems: recruiting student actors who were prepared to ride; and, crucially, learning to ride like Mazeppa—facing backwards, to control a cantering horse with the back of the rider's head on the horse's neck and the feet somehow braced on its rump. I began by looking for actors. English girls sometimes have ponies and are known to spend their pre-pubescent years in pony clubs. English boys are usually hopeless with animals larger than cats. As we were in the month of March with a production projected for July, there was time to train a student for the role of Mazeppa and time, as well, to train others as Tartar and Polish mounted warriors. No volunteers came forth, apart from one girl with considerable riding experience but whose acting ability was negligible. Prospects were beginning to dim.

Nevertheless, I wasn't ready to give up on the idea, so I arranged with a farmer to borrow a pair of horses and to rent us a soggy field near Oldham, north of Manchester. There, in March and April, when it was reasonably soft and safe to fall off, the pair of us set about devising a control harness and a hidden "saddle" which would support a rider lying on his/her back with his/her head along the horse's neck and feet high up on its rump. At the Polish sovereign's command, "Bring forth the fiery untamed steed", the actor playing Mazeppa would have to be lifted, apparently struggling and protesting, onto the horse's back, be secured—an illusion—with rope bindings, then, driven at a canter from the Poles' castle, make several circuits of the playing area before disappearing. Later, still bound, and now pursued by wolves and by a vulture which circled overhead (two more unaddressed staging problems), the rider would make a further circuit, and s/he would appear for a final time, still so uncomfortably mounted, for the scene in which the horse's movement is arrested by a fallen tree branch.

When it came to devising a saddle, I remembered Margie Greenough and other female trick riders on the Colorado rodeo circuit whom I had watched as a boy and, from these memories, gradually recalled how their saddles were constructed (e.g., short pole at the pommel, additional foot-loops on the skirts and cantle, breast collar, and double cinching so that the saddle couldn't slide or lift when the rider's weight was cantilevered over the horse's neck). But a trick-rider's saddle would spoil the illusion of an unfettered horse. So how to create this illusion? Because we had chosen an out-of-door venue, I surmised that we would have to make several circuits of a "ring", relying, like all ring-based equestrian acts, on centrifugal force to assist the rider keeping her/his place.

Pursuing further research to find a safe saddle, I consulted the numerous theatrical illustrations—playbills, prints, cartoons, and Staffordshire pottery—relating to *Mazeppa*. Collectively, the evidence was contradictory. No two Mazeppas and no two fiery steeds were bound back-to-back in a similar fashion. Individually, the images depicted bindings which were, in all likelihood, impractical if not downright dangerous. The dramatic zinc-block image used by numerous provincial circus companies and derived from Théodore Géricault's 1823 painting *Mazeppa*, shows Mazeppa lashed by heavy rope bindings to a rearing horse. Mazeppa's legs dangle on either side of the horse's hindquarters and, hanging thus, might obstruct the horse's movement and simultaneously injure the rider's ankles. The cover and title page to Dick's edition of Milner's script to *Mazeppa* show lighter, less restrictive bonds, but little to suggest a solution. A Staffordshire china sculpture, (ca. 1840) depicts a naked Mazeppa sprawled across the back of Astley's zebra,[9] a sash placed modestly across his crotch and no further indication of either bonds or saddle. Illustrated posters and sheet music covers depicting Menken, posed in post-coital languor, on a rearing black horse—to which she appears lashed by a sash only somewhat larger than the Astley rider's and more modestly covering both her breast and groin—suggest that she must be adhering to the horse's back with Victorian superglue. The only remotely plausible solution appears in a satiric 1851 *Punch* cartoon by John Tenniel.[10] Purporting to depict Mazeppa's ride from behind the scenes at Astley's and published above a line from Byron's poem which ironically refers to the wild horse's relentless gallop, it shows a somnolent pony being tugged across the stage by Widdicome, the ringmaster, who crouches behind a side wing and ground row. The rider (Cartlitch?) sprawled with knees flexed on the pony's back, has tucked his upstage foot beneath a rope harness which runs the length of the animal's body and which also offers a grip for his upstage hand. We tried the harness pictured by *Punch*'s cartoonist, but it didn't work for us: too loose, it slipped off and offered no security; too tight, it scraped the horse's skin or acted as a "flanking cinch", a device to encourage reluctant rodeo horses to buck.

Neither did we solve the problem of controlling the horses' head. We rode with our elbows through the reins of a bridle fitted with a soft snaffle bit. It is highly likely that Astley's and other equestrian drama horses were far better trained than anything we were able to practice on, and would canter at a steady pace around the hippodrome's ring and up ramps onto its stage where they were then led to a treadmill on which the horse galloped before a moving backcloth. I now doubt that Cartlitch or Menken or any other Mazeppa was really tied on. Had his horse bolted, being truly tied to its back

MAZEPPA.

A ROMANTIC DRAMA, IN THREE ACTS.

Dramatized from Lord Byron's Poem, by H. M. MILNER, *and Adapted to the Stage under the direction of* MR. DUCROW.

As Performed at the Royal Ampitheatre, Westminster Bridge, under the management of Messrs. Ducrow and West, on Easter Monday, 1831.

☞ This Drama is printed from the original "Prompt Book." Not to expatiate upon the glaring errors of former Editions, the present attempt to correct mistakes, expunge redundance, and supply omission, will be coupled with such features of utility as it is, perhaps, in the power of the Editor alone to afford. The Equestrian Manager will at once be enabled to appreciate the clearness and fidelity of this version, by a perusal of those points upon which the *Great Andrew Ducrow* with most rigid firmness founded his claim to the success of "Mazeppa."

Dramatis Personæ. [*See page* 9.

POLES.

THE CASTELLAN OF LAURINSKI ...	Mr. Hart.	SENTINEL	Mr. Taylor.
PREMISLAS, COUNT PALANTINE ...	Mr. S. Foster.		
RUDZOLOFF (Chamberlain of the Household)	Mr. Lawrence.	OLINSKA (Daughter of the Castellan)	Mrs. Pope.
DROLINSKO	Mr. Herring.	AGATHA (her Nurse)	Mrs. Bradley.
OFFICER	Mr. J. Smith.	ZEMILA	Mrs. Yates.

Knights, Officers, Guards, Heralds, Domestics, Ladies, &c.

No. 620. Dicks' Standard Plays.

Title page from *Mazeppa* (ca. 1870?). Author's collection.

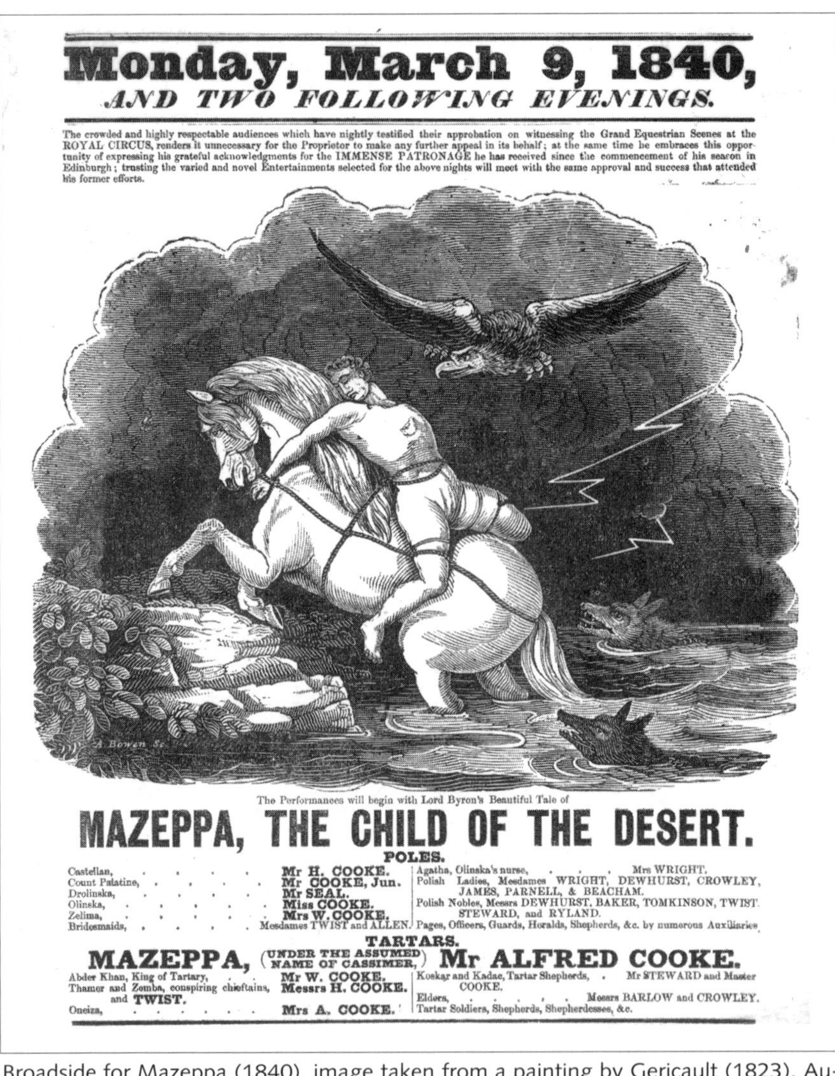

Broadside for Mazeppa (1840), image taken from a painting by Gericault (1823). Author's collection.

would have been dangerous. We preferred to fall off to running the risk of being squashed against scenery.

Still without a saddle, we took turns riding as Mazeppa. She was 5′3″. I am a foot taller. I now know that one reason why Adah Isaacs Menken was a successful equestrienne Mazeppa was that she was short, only a few inches above five feet. In practical equestrian terms that meant that, sprawled on a horse's back, her head leaning on the animal's mane, she was able to brace her feet on the horse's rump. Her legs could extend no further. If the reader views Google images of Menken with various male partners (e.g., Dumas *pere*, or Swinburne), s/he will note that Menken is petite, too short for her

Mazeppa. "Again he urges on his wild career!!!"

Cartoon about Mazeppa from Punch (1851). Author's collection.

feet to do any unintentional mischief. I, in contrast (and possibly like other male Mazeppas before me), was able to begin with my feet placed on the rump, but, sooner or later (usually sooner), my feet, jolted by the cantering horse, were likely to tangle with the horse's tail or slide under the tail. The horses' responses on being goosed by an intrusive foot were identical: they bucked me off onto the sodden turf. Repeatedly. I never completed a full circuit of the field.

We reported our research results to the Drama students. Aware of my bruises and the mud in my hair and ears, they wanted none of it. *Mazeppa* was abandoned. We had devised neither a means of controlling the horse nor riding securely.

Many years later, I became aware of the motion picture *Heller in Pink Tights.* Directed in 1960 by George Cukor, with a script by Dudley Nichols and Walter Bernstein based on a novel by Louis L'Amour and an unacknowledged D.W. Griffith screenplay[11], the film enacts the tribulations of travelling theatrical company barnstorming America's Western Frontier in the 1880s. Arriving in Cheyenne and forbidden to perform Offenbach's scandalous *La Belle Hélene,* the company resorts to a production of *Mazeppa* with Sophia Loren assuming the title role. Loren (or her blonde-wigged double) rides à la Mazeppa around the circumference of the auditorium and onto the obligatory stage treadmill. She keeps her feet far from the horse's back-side. The well-trained horse wears a bridle and bit and a wide leather cinch probably securing some sort of saddle. Because they are watching a voluptuous semi-naked female Mazeppa, not one of the watching cowboys and miners seems to mind that the steed she rides is neither untamed nor in the least fiery.

An equestrian *Mazeppa* can be staged, but apparently not by me. I just didn't manage the trick.

ENDNOTES

[1] Allardyce Nicoll, *A History of English Drama, 1660–1900,* vols. 4 & 5, lists two Godiva dramas—melodramas, hippodramas, comedies, pantomimes—before 1850 and nine between 1851–1900.

[2] Henry M. Milner, *Mazeppa;* or, *The Wild Horse of the Ukraine,* Coburg 3 November, 1823, revised and retitled by Milner as *Mazeppa;* or, *The Wild Horse of Tartary,* Astley's Royal Amphitheatre 4 March, 1831. This revised version was published by Dicks, no. 620 and Cumberland's Minor, vol. v. Milner's 1831 *Mazeppa* is also re-published in a modern edition, James L. Smith (ed.), *Victorian Melodramas: Seven English, French and American Melodramas,* London and Towata NJ (Dent / Rowman & Littlefield), 1976.

[3] British and American hippodromes, the term derived from the Greek compound hippodromos (horse-race/course/road), were theatres devised with the intent of displaying equestrian performance. Most were built with conventional stages and stage houses, but with circular auditoria floors—in other theatres occupied by the "orchestra" or "stall" seats - covered in sand, sawdust, or other soft materials and used for displays of animals. Spectator seating was located around this circle and faced toward the circle and stage.

[4] Robertson Davies, "Playwrights and Plays, 1830–1840", Michael R. Booth, Richard Southern, Frederick & Lise-Lone Marker, Robertson Davies *The Revels History of Drama in English,* Vol. VI, *1750–1880,* London (Methuen & Co., Ltd), 1975, p. 222.

[5] *New York Times,* April 30, 1882.

[6] Bernard Falk, *The Naked lady, A Biography of Adah Isaacs Menken,* London (Hutchinson), revised, 1952.

[7] Nicoll (*op. cit.*) cites only Milner's version before 1850 but lists nine further versions—equestrian plays and burlesques—between 1852 - 1893. *Mazeppa* was also made into films on five occasions by five different directors from five nations between 1908—1919. Of these, Frank Dudley's 1908 British version and Francis Boggs 1910 American version were based on the Milner text. On the limited evidence available, the other films appear to have adhered more closely to Byron's narrative. All films have been lost.

[8] A[rthur} H. Saxon, *The Life and Art of Andrew Ducrow & the romantic age of the English Circus,* Hamden CT (Archon Books), 1978.

[9] All three-dimensional Staffordshire china figurines are known to have been derived from two-dimensional images. No printed image survives. Astley's did exhibit a zebra, but there is no evidence that one was used in a performance of *Mazeppa.* The addition of zebra striping to a horse must have come from the potter's imagination.

[10] *Punch,* 8 November, 1851.

[11] In 1945, three years before his death, Griffith filed a 90–page screenplay with the Screen Writers' Guild entitled *The Twilight Revellers,* a narrative of a strolling theatre company facing the vicissitudes of the American frontier in the 1840s. Griffith's biographer Richard Schickel has observed the similarities between Griffith's screenplay and both the overall structure of—and incidents in—Cukor's film. Griffith, however, did not envision a performance of *Mazeppa.*

The Phantom Dancer, or, the Case of the Mysterious Toe Shoe in the Frontier Prop Closet

ANDREA HARRIS

> *"[O]f Dove Eye and Hazel Eye there is much to be said, but the limitations of space are inexorable; but all who have seen Morlacchi in the mazes of the ballet will be delighted to recognize in her wonderous step the fawnlike bound of the antelope—if the antelope ever bounds on the points of its toes."*[1]

At the age of six, she entered the Imperial Academy of Dancing and Pantomime in Milan, then the world's leader in classical dance. Before long, she was invited to join Her Majesty's Ballet in London. It was while she was in Barcelona, performing by Royal command, that she was engaged by an American producer to come to New York City to star in the ballet-spectacle *The Devil's Auction*. After quickly gaining fame in these extravaganzas, Giuseppina Morlacchi left them to start her own company. Making its home in Boston, the Morlacchi Ballet toured the United States performing Romantic and post-Romantic works.

In her dancing, critics saw the essence of European high culture transported to American stages. "Many of the refined and cultivated people [. . .] whose knowledge of art has been perfected by European experiences have been the first in America to detect the genius of this danseuse," asserted Boston papers.[2] How interesting, then, to find Morlacchi, the embodiment of European classicism, the exemplar of cultured taste, appearing as the American Indian princess Dove Eye alongside "Buffalo Bill" Cody and "Texas Jack" Omohundro in the frontier drama, *The Scouts of the Prairie, And, Red Deviltry As It Is!*

Dove Eye was Morlacchi's first speaking role, but the part remained linked to her star image as the consummate ballerina. "The Italian Danseuse . . . Mlle Morlacchi!" crowed advertisements for *The Scouts of the Prairie*, capitalizing on the fact that, though she'd only been in the U.S. for five years at the time of the play's premiere, she was already a celebrity.[3] Though several reviews of the drama mention Morlacchi's dancing, the excerpt quoted above represents the only source I have found that suggests her dancing in the play was "on the points" of her toes, that is, in the classical ballet idiom in which she was so well trained. Tiny as it is, this archival gem conjures a truly "tyrannical" image—the combination of frontier buckskin and Parisian *pointe* shoes in this first western drama to star Cody, the famous scout, as himself.[4]

Written by Ned Buntline, the dime novel author who christened William F. Cody "Buffalo Bill," *The Scouts of the Prairie* was the start of a fourteen-year theatrical tradition that launched *Buffalo Bill's Wild West*. Scholars have long credited Cody's *Wild West* as "the most important commercial vehicle for the fabrication and transmission of the Myth of the Frontier," the thesis that the road to modernity was necessarily fraught with violent conflicts between "civilized" and "savage" peoples.[5] The lion's share of the scholarship focuses on Cody's better-known large outdoor spectacles, sidelining the theatrical combinations that started his thespian career. More recent studies are expanding our knowledge of Cody's stage plays, but even here, no one has questioned the incongruous casting of a La Scala-trained, Milanese ballerina as an American Indian woman, and the intrusion of European academic dance onto Buffalo Bill's (otherwise) "wild" frontier stage.[6] Most authors mention that the cast of *The Scouts of the Prairie* included a well-known Italian dancer, but stop short of asking what kind of dance she did in the play, why dance might have been included, or what meanings it might have expressed.[7] But by casting such a neutral lens on the dancing Dove Eye, scholars have failed to understand dance *itself* as a meaningful text in the play.

Trying to uncover that meaning, however, poses a host of challenges. In contrast to most melodrama scholarship, textual analysis is impossible. Morlacchi's movement is lost. As no script has survived, the relationship dance might have had to the plot, or even when dancing occurred in the play also cannot be determined. Still further, the extant critical sources are insufficient for understanding the curious combination of ballet in this "queerest compound imaginable."[8]

Little venom was spared in reviewers' appraisal of *The Scouts of the Prairie* or its "unwashed" audience, but Morlacchi was often set apart. "Mlle Morlacchi deserves a word by herself in this wholesale slaughter," declared the Boston critic. "In the opening piece [. . .] she danced exquisitely and with all her accustomed grace and skill."[9] Penned another, "[I]n her opening performance she gave a number of her beautiful dances as gracefully and as equisitely [*sic*] as ever."[10] Yet another noted that the "Indian scalping, buffalo shooting and redskin-whooping drama" appealed to the gallery (where the lower classes sat), while the more cultivated patrons preferred Morlacchi's dancing in the curtain raiser.[11] According to these critics, ballet helped the drama 'up' its artistic 'ante'. But frontier drama criticism is especially indicative of a cultural hierarchy emerging in the latter nineteenth century, as critics positioned themselves as the gatekeepers of taste in a "struggle to establish aesthetic standards, to separate true art from the purely vulgar."[12] For critics, ballet might have been an oasis of decorum in the midst of this "entertainment for the toiling masses."[13] But such criticism cannot demonstrate how the mostly male, working-class audience that cheered *The Scouts of the Prairie* would have read this intrusion of the Eastern metropolis onto the Western frontier, and Morlacchi, the darling of the cosmopolitan elite, into "their" drama.[14]

Also problematic is that critical accounts of Morlacchi's dancing persistently fall back on contemporary aesthetic conventions for describing women dancers—words like "exquisite" and "graceful." This critical practice of idealizing and feminizing dancers, to which I will return in a moment, is frustratingly vague on the subject of the actual dancing. The inadequacy of such criticism for understanding dance in *The Scouts of the Prairie* is further illustrated, as you might have noticed in the above examples, by critics' tendency to pay more attention to Morlacchi's dancing in the curtain raisers, which appear to have been more traditionally styled like the popular ballet-spectacle divertissements, than they did to her part in the drama, where ballet rubbed against Dove Eye's running, fighting, chasing, shooting, and war-whooping.

However, while challenging, these historiographical stumbling blocks—bodily gestures and movement that defied written documentation, the lack of evidence for audience reception—are not unique to my research. Performance historians deal with such problems regularly. Worthy of our attention, though, is the way in which the archives cannot be trusted to tell Morlacchi's story, not just because information is missing, but further, because its absence has a history of its own.

Ballet belonged to the realm of the senses rather than the intellect in nineteenth-century American thought. For its detractors, ballet's sensuality was its greatest offense, but even in less condemnatory cases, the assumption that ballet is all body and no mind limits the methodological usefulness of the critical sources, and handicaps our historical understandings of ballet on the American stage. Images of ballet ranging from the immoral "PUBLIC EXPOSURE OF A NAKED FEMALE,"[15] to a model of feminine grace and refinement, to a "bewildering forest of female legs"[16] can be found in criticism across the 1800s. But the female dancing body is almost always circumscribed within discourses of gender, pleasure, and morality, indicating quite clearly how the representation of women on stage reflected cultural anxieties over the suitable role of women in the public sphere, but telling us very little about the dancing itself or its role in theatrical productions.[17] At best, the ballet-girl was

> "hired to look pretty and to appear in little clothing. The rest of the performance [her dancing and pantomime] is merely a tribute to conventional notions which still require that if a nearly naked woman be brought upon the stage, she shall be given something to do."[18]

For nineteenth-century critics, the purpose of dance was female display. But the movements themselves were not considered important; they were just "something to do." The idea that the dancing body could create its own meaning rarely, if ever, occurs in the ballet criticism of the era. The ballerina could be a sign of virtue or an object of desire, but not an authorial subject.

So if Morlacchi's dancing in *The Scouts of the Prairie* has gone persistently unnoticed, it is not just because dance was not captured in the written or spoken text, or that it eluded written description; but further, the archives are marked by critical blind spots that could not ascribe the notion of discursive subjecthood to the female dancing body, and that lacked a conceptual framework for understanding dance as something that could represent social meanings in the play. Michel-Rolph Trouillot argues that such "silences" are an inherent part of historical production, and more than an incomplete story, they point to operations of power that make some narratives more possible than others.[19] The class and gender biases in the archives have allowed the significance of dance in *The Scouts of the Prairie* (as well as subsequent western dramas in which Morlacchi played a balletic Indian) to pass unseen.[20] I believe that recovering dance can illuminate aspects of frontier melodrama that are obscured by text-based analyses, as well as expand our understanding of the moving body in performance and in history.[21]

In the very few studies that give her more than a passing mention, Dove Eye is seen as a Pocahontas figure who gives up her people and culture for the love of a white man, in this case Cody. Dove Eye is thus interpreted as "the ubiquitous friendly native maiden,"[22] or the fantasy of the "'Indian-grandmother' who can provide European immigrants with a fulfillment of their 'all-consuming goal' of connecting with royalty."[23] A common trope on the nineteenth-century stage, the Pocahontas character presents "a chaste and virtuous Princess whose 'civilized' and 'un-Indian' features are emphasized in contrast to the savage, bloodthirsty Indians."[24] Although no one has yet included dance in this analysis, at first glance it would seem likely that the casting of the famous Italian ballet star, exemplifying European high culture, would reinforce the Pocahontas stereotype: ballet signaled that Dove Eye was more civilized, closer to European culture than her tribesmen, especially in contrast to the *other* Indians' war and scalp dances that were also included in the play. After all, as Joellen Meglin has shown, this was the function of dance in the pre-Romantic productions on Native American themes at the Paris Opéra, where ballet served as "the symbol of French civilization triumphing over savagery."[25] Thus, as a Indian, Dove Eye could be a woman wild enough for the frontier, and for the likes of Cody, while ballet assured viewers she was not all savage, and affirmed the supremacy of white culture.

But here the plot thickens. A reading of Dove Eye as Pocahontas is definitely plausible in text-based analysis, and, given our own cultural understandings of ballet as a "high" art, ballet would seem to reinforce that reading, literally replacing a native dance form with a European one on Dove Eye's body.[26] This interpretation was certainly possible for audience members, given the popularity of the Pocahontas story in western drama. However, unlike on the Opéra stage, to the American public in 1872, neither ballet nor the *pointe* shoe would have served as an uncomplicated or necessarily positive symbol of white civilization.

Throughout the nineteenth century, ballet was considered a "foreign" form, and debates over its presence on U.S. soil were haunted by the question of what America would become. Some hoped that the European art would help America develop its own high culture, but ballet's dissenters saw it as a threat to the moral, social, and political fabric of the country. By the time Morlacchi appeared as Dove Eye, American theatre managers had been importing swarms of Italian ballet dancers for over a decade to satisfy the growing taste for musical extravaganzas, a genre whose popularity reflected the changing tastes of a growing bourgeois class of theatergoer.[27] These ballet-spectacles were perceived as foreign debauchery, especially by clergy who denounced these "imported nudities"[28] for trying "to stir [men's] blood with material agencies as the Maria Bonfantis [. . .] and Morlacchis do."[29] But still others saw the growing popularity of ballet as evidence of an influential new American leisure class, a "shoddy aristocracy" drunk on money and "content with nothing less than [. . .] an ever-changing life of amusements."[30] In George Ellington's *The women of New York*, the "shoddyites" make up a feminized metropolitan under-world, "devoted to pleasure only."[31] Among other places, they can be found flaunting their extravagance at the theatre, "throw[ing] bouquets to the bare-legged dancers."[32] When foreign correspondents wrote columns home about the corruptions of Parisian society, ballet was central to their warnings. The Parisian ballet-girl was a representative of "the loosest class in the world": self-indulgent and reckless with her body, her money, and her health.[33] And Paris promised a proliferation of amusements, to be sure; but behind its cafes, theatres, operas, and ballets lurked the ruins of revolutionary ideals and the renewed supremacy of the French government: "Liberty [here] does not imply freedom of political action and opinion. On the contrary it means to be free from all concerns of government and to have license to do anything they please with themselves and their property."[34] Dime novels and newspaper short stories followed the adventures of good American girls, who, finding themselves in the ballet world (usually because they suffer financial distress, and lack a mother's moral guidance), are forced to navigate its moral and physical dangers.[35] In Ned Buntline's own such novella, published seven years before he gave up urban mysteries for Buffalo Bill tales, the ballet theatre is a locus of underground crime, where wealthy and licentious immigrants prey on poor American girls.[36] In the nineteenth-century American public eye, ballet was a foreign other, a symbol of a decadent and degenerate European culture and political system, and a menace to republican values.

If we take such historical contexts on ballet into account, it becomes difficult to see Dove Eye's role as narrowly as "the link between civilization and savagery in the play," or to interpret her character only through the lens of the Pocahontas stereotype.[37] Morlacchi's dancing Dove Eye was not only about Indians; the character was also in dialogue with anxieties over gender, class and a growing consumer culture.[38] And far from affirming Dove Eye's "civilized" side, Morlacchi's ballet put the notion of "civilization" under glass, pointing beyond the stage to worries about the deleterious effects of too much civilization, too much wealth, too much excess. One might even speculate that, as Buffalo Bill and Dove Eye embrace in front of a backdrop of a speeding locomotive at the end of *The Scouts of the Prairie*, perhaps the European, feminized, elite culture signified by the Italian ballerina was even *more* in need of containment by the masculine, stabilizing Cody than the savagery represented by the Indian Dove Eye. Indeed, it was the former of these—the threat of the European immigrant to the working class, and hence, to the economic, political, and moral health of the nation—on which playwright Buntline almost always had his nativist gaze fixed.[39] If, as Roger Hall writes, frontier drama "represents the victory of the wilderness over the city, of the unlearned over the educated, of the popular masses over the critical establishment, and of the democracy of the 'unwashed' over the aristocracy of the well-dressed," then in *Scouts*, that battle was waged, at least in part, on Morlacchi/Dove Eye's satin/buckskin, foreign/native, elite/savage body.[40]

This, I believe, is the real potential for "tyranny" that the mysterious *pointe* shoe in the frontier prop closet holds: it generates extratextual evidence that challenges text-based histories of this frontier melodrama. The representation of the American Indian as the savage alterity to American white civilization has been well analyzed in Cody's spectacles. But in *The Scouts of the Prairie*, the earliest prototype of the *Wild West* mythology, dances the spectre of a European "other," capable of arousing deep anxieties and prejudices not about savagery, but rather about the social conflicts of the civilizing project.

ENDNOTES

1 "Academy of Music," Indianapolis, Clipping, n.d n.p, William F. Cody Collection, "Buffalo Bill Stage Plays and Notices 1872–1880," Manuscript 6, William F. Cody, roll 1. Buffalo Bill Historical Center. This is a microfilm of the Troop C Ledger, held at Buffalo Bill Historical Society, which contains numerous newspaper clippings cut so as to fit as many as possible on a page. Most of these clippings do not include dates or page numbers, and in some the location has been omitted as well. Hereafter: BBHC. The review in full follows (it could not be reproduced effectively for this publication):

> When the celebrated Waverly Novels burst upon the astonished vision of an admiring world, a new interest was awakened in Scottish and English history, and many things hitherto concealed in the womb of time came forth into the light of day, and mysteries of a previous age became the clearest facts of the present. So when the alchemy of Ned Buntline's imaginative pen puts into the mouth of the tawny but not tawdry Dove Eye the confession that the Grand Duke did make advances to her, and wished to encircle her wrists, ankles and neck with diamonds more numerous than ever salted Arizona's field, which she could not and would not reciprocate, because the noble form of Buffalo Bill was among the retinue of Sheridan's party, we can have at once the mystery of that pensive melancholy which sat on Alexis' cheek after his return from the grand buffalo hunt, and has driven him in a mad chase around the rest of the world, and ended in his writing a book of travels. All this, and much more was revealed as the plot of the "Scouts of the Prairie" was unraveled at the Academy of Music last night to one of the largest and most vociferous audiences we have ever seen there. It's as good as a half dozen plays, and as the heroes of the plains, Buffalo Bill and Texas Jack, come down upon and destroy the last vestige of the Teton Sioux, so that no more annuities are required in that direction, breathing fire from their strident nostrils and discharging six-shooters with each hand, the whoop of despair of the dying Indians is answered back by the yell of triumph of the gods of the gallery, who fairly split their skins by the convulsive beatings of their excited lungs. We regret that the Governor's Message, the Editorial Convention, the coal election, and other matters have such a demand on our columns to-day for abstracts, reports and explanations, that we can not go into the details of the piece as its novelty and merit demands. Suffice it to say that there is but one Buffalo Bill, and although his Nebraskian constituents appeal to him to return to the legislative halls to which they consigned him, he will not disappoint the expectations of the polished society of Indianapolis and elsewhere of seeing the great exemplar of the buffalo jerker, and the bull-whacker, and will continue his association with Texas Jack, who is also *sui generis*, and appear again at the Academy tonight, and tomorrow at the

> matinee. Of Dove Eye and Hazel Eye there is much to be said, but the limitations of space are inexorable; but all who have seen Morlacchi in the mazes of the ballet will be delighted to recognize in her wonderous step the fawnlike bound of the antelope—if the antelope ever bounds on the points of its toes.

There will be a crowded house tonight, and it will be necessary to go early to get seats.

[2] Qtd. in Barbara Barker, *Ballet or Ballyhoo: The American Careers of Marie Bonfanti, Rita Sangalli, and Giuseppina Morlacchi* (New York: Dance Horizons, 1984), 121.

[3] *Philadelphia Sun*, Clipping, n.d n.p, BBHC.

[4] Besides Cody, Omohundro, and Morlacchi, the play also featured playwright Ned Buntline (the pseudonym of E.Z.C. Judson) as trapper Cale Durg and actress Eleo Carfano as Hazel Eye, Durg's ward.

[5] Richard Slotkin, *Gunfighter Nation: The Myth of the Frontier in Twentieth-Century America* (New York: Atheneum, 1992), 87, 86.

[6] Sandra K. Sagala's monograph is the most comprehensive source on these theatrical productions: see *Buffalo Bill on Stage* (Albuquerque: University of New Mexico Press, 2008). See also Roger A. Hall, *Performing the American Frontier, 1870–1906* (Cambridge: Cambridge University Press, 2001), 50–67.

[7] Roger Hall's book on western drama includes a photograph of Morlacchi and Omohundro in which Morlacchi, dressed in full Romantic tutu, index finger lightly pressed to her lip, hovers over a sleeping Texas Jack in fringed buckskin in front of a prairie background: a frontier *sylphide*. Hall uses this photograph as the cover image for his book, presumably because its juxtaposition of rough frontier and refined ballet exemplifies "the paradoxical elements that tumble through the frontier melodrama" on which his study centers (10). He does not, however, explore the historical context of ballet in the image or the plays.

[8] "The Scouts of the Prairie" [Review at Niblo's Garden], n.d n.p, BBHC.

[9] "Music and the Drama: The Scouts of the Prairie," *Boston Daily Advertiser*. 4 March 1873, issue 54, col. G.

[10] Qtd. in Nieuwenhuyse, 50.

[11] Qtd. in Sagala, 64.

[12] Lawrence Levine, *Highbrow/Lowbrow: The Emergence of Cultural Hierarchy in America* (Cabridge: Harvard University Press, 1988), 128. Also see Hall, 12–14, and Sagala, 16, 64.

[13] "Amusements: Nixon's Ampitheatre," *Chicago Daily Tribune*, 19 December 1872, 4.

[14] Although Cody's combinations attracted a mixture of classes, increasingly so over their fourteen-year run, most critical accounts of *The Scouts of the Prairie* document the audience as predominantly male and working-class.

[15] Samuel F.B. Morse on the 1827 New York City appearance of ballet dancer Francisque Hutin, qtd. in Robert C. Allen, *Horrible Prettiness: Burlesque and American Culture* (Chapel Hill: University of North Carolina Press, 1991), 88.

[16] From a *New York Tribune* review of The Black Crook, 22 October 1867. Qtd. in George Freedley, "The Black Crook and the White Fawn," in *Chronicles of the American Dance: From the Shakers to Martha Graham*, ed. Paul Magriel (New York: Da Capo Press, 1978), 77.

[17] On the critical idealizations of women dancers, see Christopher Martin, "Naked Females and Splay-Footed Sprawlers: Ballerinas on the Stage in Jacksonian America," *Theatre Survey* 51, no. 1 (May 2010): 95–114.

[18] "The Social Morality of the Day," *Brooklyn Eagle*, 8 June 1871, sec: front page, 1.

[19] Michel-Rolph Trouillot, *Silencing the Past: Power and the Production of History* (Boston: Beacon Press, 1995), 26.

[20] Morlacchi appeared in *The Scouts of the Prairie* from its 1872 premiere until May 1873, when she was replaced by Bessie Sudlow, who apparently substituted her own opera singing for Morlacchi's ballet dancing. Morlacchi returned to the troupe in October 1873 to play the Indian maiden Pale Dove, who similarly befriends the white scouts, in *The Scouts of the Plains*, which also added Wild Bill Hickok to the cast. She stayed with Cody's company through the 1875 season, when she and Texas Jack, who had married in August 1873, split

from the troupe to produce their own frontier combinations. Morlacchi continued to play American Indian women in these productions: the mute Wanita in *Texas Jack on the Plains,* and a Sioux Maiden in *Life in the Rocky Mountains,* for example. Morlacchi alternated appearances in Western dramas such as these with principal roles in ballets, often her own choreography, including *Ahmed, The French Spy, La Bayadère* and *The Black Crook,* moving continually between frontier melodrama and ballet productions. For Morlacchi's biography, see Barker, 111–167.

21 Though no script survives, scholars have been able to rebuild much of the plot through program scene synopses and newspaper reviews. Early studies that mention the plot include James Monaghan, "The Stage Career of Buffalo Bill," *The Journal of the Illinois State Historical Society* 31, no. 4 (December 1938), 414–416; and William S.E. Coleman, "Buffalo Bill on Stage," *Players* 47, no. 2 (1971), 80–91. Craig Francis Nieuwenhuyse's unpublished dissertation remains the most detailed study of *The Scouts of the Prairie,* and his attempted reconstruction of the plot the most thorough. See Nieuwenhuyse, "Six-Guns on the Stage: Buffalo Bill Cody's First Celebration of the Conquest of the American Frontier" (Ph.D. diss., University of California, Berkeley, 1981), see especially 43–74 for the plot. Sagala also includes a detailed discussion of the narrative (21–23).

22 Hall, 54.

23 Nieuwenhuyse, 154.

24 Maria Lyytinen, "The Pocahontas Myth and Its Deconstruction in Monique Mohica's Play," in *Native American Performance and Representation,* ed. S.E. Wilmer (Tucson: University of Arizona Press, 2009), 80.

25 Joellen Meglin, "'Sauvages,' Sex Role and Semiotics: Representations of Native Americans in the French Ballet 1736–1837, Part Two: The Nineteenth Century," *Dance Chronicle* 23, no. 3 (2000): 291.

26 I am grateful to Renée E. D'Aoust, whose reading of this essay helped make it better, for this insight.

27 The rise of the ballet-spectacle coincided with the remodeling of the theatre into a predominantly middle-class space in the mid-nineteenth century. See Bruce McConaghie, *Melodramatic Formations: American Theatre and Society, 1820–1870* (Iowa City: University of Iowa Press, 1992), 231–257 (especially 242–243 on ballet-spectacles, or "musical extravaganzas"). Such socio-economic changes were reflected in the fact that, although predominately Italian, dancers were typically billed as "French" to cater to the tastes of the *nouveau riche* who saw Paris as the apex of cultural refinement.

28 Qtd. in Allen, 112.

29 Qtd. in Barker 18.

30 George Ellington, *The women of New York : or, the under-world of the great city: illustrating the life of women of fashion, women of pleasure, actresses and ballet girls, etc.* (New York: New York Book Co., 1869), 24.

31 Ellington, 163.

32 Ellington, 117.

33 "The Ballet-Girls of Paris," *Brooklyn Eagle,* 22 February 1870, pg. 6.

34 "Foreign Correspondence," *Brooklyn Eagle,* 9 January 1858, pg. 2.

35 See, for example, "The Ballet Dancer," *Brooklyn Eagle,* 20 August 1853, sec: front page, 1.

36 Ned Buntline, "Rose Seymour, or The Ballet Girl's Revenge, a tale of the New-York Drama" (New York: Hilton, 1865).

37 Nieuwenhuyse, 153.

38 The ballet-girl was a specific manifestation of the "New York woman," a character type vilified in the urban exposé novels that became popular in the 1860s (such as Ellington's book cited in this essay). In these critiques, fears about the post-Civil War rise of consumer culture are projected onto women, who embody the lack of self-control and tendency for excess that threatens to undermine the republic. Ballet and the ballet-girl were central to

this genre, symbols of a pleasure-seeking, European-loving class quickly reshaping the metropolis. I am currently expanding this analysis for a longer research version of this article.

[39] Buntline was a member of several nativist movements in the middle of the nineteenth century, perhaps best known as one of the instigators of the 1849 Astor Place Riot. A longtime advocate of the working classes, Buntline focused much of his work, as an writer and an activist, on the frontlines of class conflict. In Buntline's urban mysteries, the city is a dangerous and unpredictable place, full of dark, secret corners of ethnic crime and vice where foreign-born villains prey on working class heroes and heoines.

[40] Hall, 14.

"A Most Dreadful Position":[1] Amateur Reputations in a Professional World

EILEEN CURLEY

By 1890, Mary Nevins Blaine, the estranged daughter-in-law of United States Secretary of State Blaine, had moved to New York to embark upon a professional acting career, but was sidelined by illness. In February, Daniel Frohman and other theatre community members produced a benefit performance for Blaine, who was financially struggling to support herself and her young son due to rheumatic inflammation. The actors in the final benefit performance included amateurs and professionals, but Frohman dropped the amateur performers, Alice and Rita Lawrence, from the event, claiming a full bill. In response, Alice Lawrence sent a panicked letter not to Frohman, but to Herbert Kelcey, his leading man. In this letter, she claimed innocence (about unclear infractions), disparaged Frohman, and begged Kelcey to save her reputation with others in the Lyceum Company. Her tantalizing letter reveals the proximity of amateurs to the professional stage while implying concerns over the propriety of this connection. The source of her histrionic defensiveness and the potential taint to her reputation remains unclear, however. The sisters hired professional coaches and sometimes actors for their amateur charity theatricals; a mixed performance was not scandalous. And yet, the letter hints at unspoken concerns about a nebulous and potentially damaging interpretation of the sisters' involvement, be it their motives for participating in the benefit, the performance environment, or perhaps the choice of charity.

Alice Lawrence's letter to Herbert Kelcey alludes to events and presents some facts that can be corroborated by other documents in the historical record. On Tuesday, 18 February 1890, a benefit performance was held in the Broadway theatre for Marie Nevins Blaine, a socialite turned performer who was meant to lead a professional company on a tour for Daniel Frohman during the 1889–1890 season.[2] Her decision to go on the stage appears to have led to the estrangement of the couple, although her divorce pleading in 1891 suggested that her husband abandoned her.[3] Blaine was thus separated from her husband when she fell ill in the fall of 1889, thereby preventing her debut under Frohman. The benefit performance consisted of signed letter. Please read it, and show it, and this letter of mine, to Mr Wheatcroft. He saw me on Monday evening with Miss Cayvan, after I had left Mr Frohman, and I could not possibly speak to him. I did not know what sort of a person Mr Frohman was, or I would not have entered into the affair. I send this to you instead of Miss Cayvan, because I know she would not care to take the trouble to send Mr Frohman's letter back to me, which I will ask you to please be sure and do. Also show it to Mrs Kelcey, if she still feels any interest in us –

Yours very sincerely

Alice Lawrence.

58, West Eleventh St.

My dear Mr Kelcey,

I send this to the Theatre, as I do not know your address now. I want to tell you what has happened, for Mr Frohman has told me so many lies of late, that I do not know how he speaks of us – if he has spoken at all. He asked us to play for the Blaine benefit – we did not seek it in any way. He acknowledges this, both to Papa and myself,

and in his letter. We expected to go with pleasure to the Blaine benefit, and to enjoy seeing it. Not content with that, Mr Frohman led us into it, tricked us into it, and then insulted us in the eyes of the other amateurs. He saw me three times, talked it over most conclusively, let me send for Mr Morrell, arrange with Mr de Cordova, a professional, who was sent me by Miss Otis, also let us engage Mr Bond to coach us – we engaged him on our own account, as no coach, of course, was allowed by the management. I asked Mr Frohman on Saturday if any changes were possible, as I was to see Mr Bond and the others Sunday evening. He assured me it was all right. I made all arrangements, and then on Monday, he sent his secretary to say he did not want us. I did not know such discourtesy was possible. I have never heard of such a thing before. Papa and I went to his office on Monday evening, and he ~~gave us~~ got from him a letter of explanation to show our cast – towards whom I am placed in a most dreadful position. I send you a copy of Mr Frohman's

Alice Lawrence to Herbert Kelcey, [1890]. Alice and Rita Lawrence Papers 1874-1935. Box 1. Columbia University Rare Book and Manuscript Library, New York multiple acts, including performances by Mrs. Kendal, Richard Mansfield, The Lyceum Theatre Company and at least two shows contributed by amateur performers who were friends and sometimes co-stars with the Lawrence sisters in amateur theatricals.[4] Lawrence's letter claims that Frohman had requested their participation but then dropped them from the bill, and a typed statement that Frohman issued to the Lawrences confirms this version of events.[5] That the Lawrences were originally part of the bill is clear from the letter to Kelcey, the statement from Frohman and an early announcement about the benefit that clearly lists the Lawrences as participants.[6] Thus, scholars can piece together a production history, but the interpersonal relationships and character slights at which the letter hints remain hidden from view.

In the case of this letter, the historian's quest to divine the background situation is hampered by a number of difficulties, not the least of which is the relative lack of extant documentation available for amateur theatre performances. Archival practices privilege commercial theatre, and yet the historian of amateur theatricals is provided with significantly more information about the Lawrence performances than most amateur productions through a number of sources: the Lawrence sisters' scrapbooks, housed at Columbia University's Rare Book and Manuscript Library, newspaper coverage of amateur theatricals in New York in the 1880s and 1890s, and Rita's 1936 memoir. The fact that Alice and Rita chose to format their scrapbooks as an archive of information about their amateur theatrical career provides invaluable documentation, but programs, reviews, receipts and correspondence can only hint at the underlying social issues which seem to have driven their production choices and which clearly haunt Alice's letter to Herbert Kelcey. Rita's memoir partially augments the story, but the social issues that might explain Alice's tone and panic in the letter remain largely unspoken in each of these sources. Further, while many of the involved parties are well known to theatre historians, the Lawrences are not, except insofar as they have recorded their amateur theatrical careers in the scrapbooks and memoir.

Even though it is clear that Alice meant to save evidence of this dispute, the letter to Kelcey is one of only two items in the scrapbooks about the conflict or the benefit; the other is a statement from Frohman about the event. None of the scrapbooks contain any other information about the Blaine benefit; however, this is not particularly remarkable, as the scrapbooks are almost entirely a record of *their* theatrical activity. A few other notable scandals punctuate the sisters' theatricals, archived variously: sometimes the documents relating to these affairs were collected together in one envelope that was pasted into the scrapbook; later, archivists removed most loose materials, documents, and photographs for preservation purposes; sometimes the empty envelope remains in the scrapbook. In this case, the envelope labeled "Frohman" is included with the letter in a separate archival folder, and page 65 of Alice's first scrapbook contains materials from late 1889 and early 1890, as well as a section where it appears an envelope might have been removed.[7] This envelope and Alice's request that Kelcey "care to take the trouble to send Mr Frohman's letter back to me"[8] implies that she intended to save a record of the event as a distinct conflict with Frohman. The letter to

Kelcey might be an original or a copy, but the crossed out section where she replaces "gave us" with "got from him"[9] points, perhaps, towards this particular document's status as a draft or a copy maintained, in either case, for posterity.

While this episode is a sufficiently important event for Alice and Rita to intentionally document in their historical materials, a minor dispute with two amateur performers does not appear to factor heavily into the broader historical record.[10] What seems to be an emotionally charged episode for the amateurs was apparently a momentary business hiccup to Frohman. Upset by the decision, Alice and her father went to Frohman to get a written explanation, which enables us to learn why Frohman says that he dropped them from the bill: "I regret that my action in the making up of the programme necessitated my having to omit from the bill the last three attractions secured. . . . in order to make no distinction I was compelled by reason of securing several important professional attractions, to curtail the programme on account of its length, and omit several important features."[11] Why they were cut seems logical from a producer's standpoint, and other materials support Frohman's claim about the length of the program. Initially advertised as a 2 pm start,[12] the start time was pushed back to 1 pm and a series of reminders of the "unusual length" of the event appears in articles leading up to the benefit: "Holders of tickets for the testimonial performance for the benefit of Mrs. James G. Blaine, Jr., at the Broadway Theatre this afternoon are requested by the ladies of the committee to be in their seats early. The unusual length of the programme will compel the raising of the curtain promptly at 1 o'clock."[13] As predicted, the performances "closed just before dinner time,"[14] with the Lyceum Company production of the comedy *Gabrielle* serving as the final piece of the bill.[15]

This apparently simple business decision does not, however, resonate well with Alice's response in her letter to Kelcey, and this is where her letter becomes most problematic for the historian, who has no ability to truly divine what was driving Alice's panic. Potential hints are scattered throughout the letter, but none lead to a conclusive interpretation of the event or her reaction. Envisioning that Alice thought they were dropped because of a perceived slight on her talent makes some sense at first, but little in either letter suggests that as a root cause of her distress. Alice writes that "Mr Frohman . . . insulted us in the eyes of the other amateurs,"[16] while Frohman comments that he needed to make space for "several important professional attractions."[17] This combination of comments could be construed as a suggestion that the other amateurs, many of whom did indeed eventually turn professional,[18] were somehow more talented than the Lawrences. But, so little of Alice's letter addresses talent or the other amateurs that this interpretation remains easy but unsatisfying.

Parallel content in her letter and his statement suggests that her concern might center not on talent but instead on how the sisters came to be part of the original bill. Alice, after calling Frohman a liar, repeatedly protests that she and Rita did not ask to be part of the bill: "He asked us to play for the Blaine benefit—we did not seek it in any way. He acknowledges this, both to Papa and myself and in his letter. . . . Mr Frohman led us into it, tricked us into it."[19] The statement which she and her father "got from" Frohman "to show our cast"[20] echoes this concern: "Last Wednesday I asked the Misses Lawrence to take part in a benefit that is being gotten up for Mrs. Blaine for February 18th. They did not volunteer their services."[21] Were they seen as presumptuous or crossing boundaries by offering their services, or did Alice suspect this might be the case? Such character aspersions, perceived or real, might be sufficient to cause Alice to react so vehemently to Frohman's decision and to feel a need to protect her reputation. If not a critique of their talent, then is there, hidden within the lines of the letter, some condemnation of the Lawrences' aspirations and increasingly elaborate charity theatrical productions?

By 1890, the Lawrences had established reputations as amateur performers who would loan their talents and fundraising abilities to a variety of charitable organizations. They regularly performed theatricals in public theatres, raising thousands of dollars for charities across greater metropolitan New York and in summer resorts. There was, however, a lull in their public performance activity during the fall and winter of 1889–1890; rather than the usual series of fully-staged entertainments at the holidays and in the late winter, they participated in a few parlor events and variety nights. Alice's defensive declarations to Kelcey that they did not seek this performance opportunity, combined with the production lull, might suggest a parental or societal condemnation of their activities; however, there is simply no concrete evidence to suggest why they were not performing as much in the months leading up to the Blaine benefit. Their production habits returned to normal levels shortly after the Blaine benefit as well, so if this lull was related, then it was short-lived. Furthermore, their parents approved their participation in the Blaine benefit.

Another potential source of scandal might have been that the sisters would have performed in public alongside professionals. Alice notes that they "expected to go with pleasure to the Blaine benefit, and to enjoy seeing it,"[22] but perhaps performing in the benefit might have appeared unseemly while attending it would not have been problematic. This notion is quickly undermined by their production history, for they had already performed alongside professionals in charity productions and hired professionals such as Frederick Bond, Nelson Wheatcroft, and David Belasco as coaches and stage managers. In the previous spring, they had even thanked Daniel Frohman for allowing them to perform in the theatre in a program from April 11, 1899.[23] Two of Frohman's Lyceum Company members, Walter Bellows and Mrs. Thomas Whiffen, also appeared in this benefit performance, albeit in the second show on the bill, *A Wild Idea*; Alice and Rita performed in the first show, *The Dead Shot*, but their performance record up until this point reveals that working with professionals apparently had not been problematic.

This relationship with the professional stage seems to be the crux of Alice's concern in the letter, but why? After all, not only had they hired and performed with professionals, they quite clearly had ongoing relationships with multiple members of Frohman's company. The whole final section of the letter is full of pleading to save their reputations with the company members, which seems to contradict the story they told Frohman during their visit. Indeed, Frohman's statement does not mention the professionals Alice hired for this production; instead, he suggests that the Lawrences told him that they were concerned about how he "apparently placed[d] them in a somewhat distressing position with the friends whom they had asked to assist."[24] While Alice does write, briefly, about the cast, "towards whom I am placed in a most dreadful position,"[25] this line seems almost a throwaway when it is followed by a full discussion of how she would like Kelcey to show her letter and Frohman's statement to others in the Lyceum Company. The letter to Kelcey is an attempt to clear her name with the members of the company, revealing a relationship that is further underscored by her very first comment: "I send this to the theatre, as I do not know your address now";[26] clearly she used to know it. Rita's memoir confirms the closeness of their relationship with the Kelceys but without time references.[27] Mrs. Caroline (Hill) Kelcey was to attend a matinee with Rita in early February 1890, but she reportedly fell ill.[28] Does this missed matinee have anything to do with the concurrent Blaine situation, or am I looking for connections that are not there? Was she ill, was she embarrassed by their behavior, or is Alice blowing things out of proportion when she includes as the last line of her letter: "Also show it to Mrs. Kelcey, if she still feels any interest in us."[29] The letter seems to point mostly towards Alice's desire to remain untainted in the eyes of the Lyceum Company, but what had she done to deserve the opprobrium that she so clearly feared? Why attack Frohman and, frankly, why were those choice words not seen as problematic?

As noted above, the Lawrences left more than the usual amount of information about their amateur theatricals, and I had hoped that Rita's memoir might shed some light on the situation. It does not:

> After we had been acting many times at the Lyceum, Mr. Daniel Frohman, who had always been so nice to Alice and to me and whom we liked very much, suddenly became offended at something and withdrew the offer he had made to have us play at a Charity benefit in which Elsie de Wolfe and Miss [Elita] Proctor [Otis] were to have separate plays. He wrote an apology immediately afterwards and a letter to show our company but he did not explain what had angered him or who had made the trouble between us. After that, he continued to give us the Lyceum Theatre whenever we wished it, and everything was done for our comfort as before. We were never sure who had made the trouble between him and ourselves.[30]

Clearly, a memoir published 45 years after the event is an equally troublesome document. Rita's narrative is rarely marked by historical placeholders and is structured in a stream of consciousness fashion. Her tone, throughout, reveals a fascination with the commercial theatre and a frustration with gender dynamics of the period. Despite her gloss on the situation, lingering damage to their relationship with Frohman is implied by the historical record, although it is unclear whether his refusal to include them in the bill or Alice's reaction was the source of their failed relationship. For, while Rita writes in her memoir: "he continued to give us the Lyceum Theatre whenever we wished it, and everything was done for our comfort as before,"[31] there is a distinct reduction in their use of the Lyceum after the Blaine Benefit. While the sisters staged seven events at the Lyceum Theatre between 1887 and the Blaine Benefit in February 1890, they appear to have staged just one more event on 9 May 1890. After this time, the sisters continued to use a variety of theatres, as they had prior to 1890, but a significant number of their shows were staged at the Berkeley Lyceum and the Madison Square Theatre and notably not at the Lyceum Theatre.

Rita's implication that someone spoke ill of the sisters does parallel another odd situation at the Lyceum in the late winter of 1890, though. Operating underneath and concurrently with the Blaine benefit saga was the disintegration of Belasco's relationship with Frohman and the Lyceum over Mrs. Leslie Carter, yet another actress who might have been too close to Alice and Rita's social standing and theatrical desires. Winter suggests that Georgia Cayvan was responsible for Frohman's edict that Belasco no longer rehearse with Carter at the Lyceum; Belasco resigned at the end of March, 1890.[32] The Lawrences, too, had worked with Belasco over the years, and yet historians are left to reach for connections here that cannot be proved, grasping at what may be mere coincidence.

Thus, the only significant differences between the Blaine benefit and the Lawrences' other charity productions were the nature of the charity and the fact that this was a professional bill to which they had been invited rather than vice versa. While the professional setting might be problematic for their reputations, the mixed nature of the bill and the participation of their fellow amateur performers—with whom the Lawrences performed regularly—renders it less likely that society might have condemned their choice.[33] The reviews offer no critique to support this notion either. This particular charity opens up a potential line of inquiry that is also potentially undermined by that very same critique. Thus, I am left wondering whether the letter is an over-reaction by someone that Nelson Wheatcroft reportedly called "too super-sensitive"[34] or if we can read anything into her unspoken fears. Was Marie Nevins Blaine, fallen socialite and ill would-be actress who never embarked on her professional career somehow an inappropriate charity? Or, were the sisters inappropriately attempting to parlay their relationships with the Lyceum into pseudo-professional acting opportunities? For an historian looking for reasons behind the seeming scandal which causes Alice's reaction in the letter, the events at the Lyceum Theatre in late winter of 1890 provide an alluring if unclear layering of society women interacting with the professional stage, despite lingering societal and familial concerns that a professional stage career might have been an inappropriate choice for members of the New York elite, as it certainly was for the Lawrences in the eyes of their parents.[35]

ENDNOTES

[1] Alice Lawrence to Herbert Kelcey, [1890]. Alice and Rita Lawrence Papers 1874–1935. Box 1. Columbia University Rare Book and Manuscript Library, New York. I must extend my grateful thanks to the staff at the Columbia University Rare Book and Manuscript Library for their assistance with this collection over the years. This paper was made possible in part by grants received from Martin Shaffer, Dean of Liberal Arts, and Thomas Wer-

muth, Dean of Faculty, at Marist College. I am also indebted to my research assistants at Marist, Amy Jacaruso, Thomas Lotito and Ashleigh Whitfield, for their assistance corralling traces of the Lawrences from the contemporary press and constructing a performance history.

[2] "Mrs. Blaine Too Ill to Act," *New York Times*, 30 August 1889, 5. See also "Mrs. Blaine an Actress," *The Pittsburg Dispatch*, 29 January 1889, 6; "Theatrical Gossip," *New York Times*, 11 September 1889, 8; "Stage Whispers," *The Pittsburg Dispatch*, 15 September 1889, 12; "Marie Blaine's Wrongs," *New York Times*, 30 September 1889, 1; "Farce at the Lyceum," *New York Times*, 22 October 1889, 5.

[3] For various interpretations of their marital woes and financial situation, see for example: "Marie Blaine's Wrongs," *New York Times*, 30 September 1889, 1; "Young Blaine's Answer," *The Salt Lake Herald*, 7 October 1891, 1; "Mrs. Blaine's Divorce Suit," *The Sun*, 5 December 1891, 3; "Marie Blaine is Firm," *Pittsburg Dispatch*, 24 December 1891, 7.

[4] See, among others, "Young Mrs. Blaine's Benefit," *New York Times*, 19 February 1890, 4.

[5] Daniel Frohman, Statement about Alice M. and Rita Lawrence, [1890]. Alice and Rita Lawrence Papers 1874–1935. Box 1. Columbia University Rare Book and Manuscript Library, New York.

[6] "Theatrical Gossip," *New York Times*, 2 February 1890, 16.

[7] Alice Lawrence, Alice Lawrence book 1, 1874–1890, 65. Alice and Rita Lawrence Papers 1874–1935. Flat Box 281. Columbia University Rare Book and Manuscript Library, New York.

[8] Alice Lawrence to Herbert Kelcey, [1890]. Alice and Rita Lawrence Papers 1874–1935. Box 1. Columbia University Rare Book and Manuscript Library, New York.

[9] Alice Lawrence to Herbert Kelcey, [1890]. Alice and Rita Lawrence Papers 1874–1935. Box 1. Columbia University Rare Book and Manuscript Library, New York.

[10] A brief mention that Frohman asked Belasco to train Blaine in 1888 appears in William Jefferson Winter, *The Life of David Belacso*, vol 1 (New York: Moffat, Yard and Company, 1918), 340. The episode is not mentioned in his memoir, Daniel Frohman, *Memories of a Manager* (New York: Doubleday Page, 1911). The Lawrences are largely absent from searchable archival finding aids, aside from their own, which is logical from an archival standpoint since they are not well-known entities in the theatre of the time.

[11] Daniel Frohman, Statement about Alice M. and Rita Lawrence, [1890]. Alice and Rita Lawrence Papers 1874–1935. Box 1. Columbia University Rare Book and Manuscript Library, New York

[12] "Advertisement," *New York Times*, 5 Feburary 1890, 7.

[13] "Theatrical Gossip," *New York Times*, 18 Feburary 1890, 8.

[14] "Young Mrs. Blaine's Benefit," *New York Times*, 19 February 1890, 4.

[15] "Cavalier Georgia Cayvan," *New York Times*, 17 February 1890, 8.

[16] Alice Lawrence to Herbert Kelcey, [1890]. Alice and Rita Lawrence Papers 1874–1935. Box 1. Columbia University Rare Book and Manuscript Library, New York.

[17] Daniel Frohman, Statement about Alice M. and Rita Lawrence, [1890]. Alice and Rita Lawrence Papers 1874–1935. Box 1. Columbia University Rare Book and Manuscript Library, New York.

[18] In particular, Elita Proctor Otis and Elsie de Wolfe turned professional over the next few years. Edward Fales Coward continued to act as an amateur but wrote professionally about the theatre.

[19] Alice Lawrence to Herbert Kelcey, [1890]. Alice and Rita Lawrence Papers 1874–1935. Box 1. Columbia University Rare Book and Manuscript Library, New York

[20] Alice Lawrence to Herbert Kelcey, [1890]. Alice and Rita Lawrence Papers 1874–1935. Box 1. Columbia University Rare Book and Manuscript Library, New York

[21] Daniel Frohman, Statement about Alice M. and Rita Lawrence, [1890]. Alice and Rita Lawrence Papers 1874–1935. Box 1. Columbia University Rare Book and Manuscript Library, New York.

[22] Alice Lawrence to Herbert Kelcey, [1890]. Alice and Rita Lawrence Papers 1874–1935. Box 1. Columbia University Rare Book and Manuscript Library, New York.

[23] Alice Lawrence, Alice Lawrence book 1, 1874–1890, 63. Alice and Rita Lawrence Papers 1874–1935. Flat Box 281. Columbia University Rare Book and Manuscript Library, New York.

[24] Daniel Frohman, Statement about Alice M. and Rita Lawrence, [1890]. Alice and Rita Lawrence Papers 1874–1935. Box 1. Columbia University Rare Book and Manuscript Library, New York

[25] Alice Lawrence to Herbert Kelcey, [1890]. Alice and Rita Lawrence Papers 1874–1935. Box 1. Columbia University Rare Book and Manuscript Library, New York.

[26] Alice Lawrence to Herbert Kelcey, [1890]. Alice and Rita Lawrence Papers 1874–1935. Box 1. Columbia University Rare Book and Manuscript Library, New York.

[27] Rita Lawrence, *Amateurs and Actors of the 19th-20th Centuries (American, English, Italian).* (Menton, France: Imprimerie Mentonnaise, 1936), 119.

[28] Herbert Kelcey to Alice M. Lawrence, [4 February 1890]. Alice and Rita Lawrence Papers 1874–1935. Box 1. Columbia University Rare Book and Manuscript Library, New York.

[29] Alice Lawrence to Herbert Kelcey, [1890]. Alice and Rita Lawrence Papers 1874–1935. Box 1. Columbia University Rare Book and Manuscript Library, New York.

[30] Rita Lawrence, *Amateurs and Actors of the 19th-20th Centuries (American, English, Italian).* (Menton, France: Imprimerie Mentonnaise, 1936), 159.

[31] Rita Lawrence, *Amateurs and Actors of the 19th-20th Centuries (American, English, Italian).* (Menton, France: Imprimerie Mentonnaise, 1936), 159.

[32] William Jefferson Winter, *The Life of David Belacso*, vol 1 (New York: Moffat, Yard and Company, 1918), 367–369.

[33] However, it is worth remembering that some of those other amateurs did eventually turn professional.

[34] Rita Lawrence, *Amateurs and Actors of the 19th-20th Centuries (American, English, Italian).* (Menton, France: Imprimerie Mentonnaise, 1936), 148

[35] Throughout her memoir, Rita comments upon how their father tolerated their theatricals and enjoyed them, but would never have permitted them to have a professional career. Their mother, on the other hand, reportedly viewed the stage as a viable profession, but only in the event of destitution. See, for example: Rita Lawrence, *Amatuers and Actors of the 19th–20th Centuries (American, English, Italian).* (Menton, France: Imprimerie Mentonnaise, 1936), 147.

Oscar Wilde's Ground Plan for a Production of *Salomé*

JOSEPH DONOHUE

As both theatre historian and textual scholar, I seem to have an odd combination of specialties. And yet, editing a group of Oscar Wilde's plays for the Oxford *Complete Works*[1] has felt like the perfect way to combine the two interests, captured in the familiar phrase "page and stage." I have never felt a conflict between the two, but at times they have led me down strange pathways and even posed considerable obstacles.

No more striking example of this scholarly double jeopardy have I encountered than on a day in July, 1991, when I arrived at the Rosenbach Museum & Library in Philadelphia, planning to transcribe a holograph manuscript of Oscar Wilde's French play *Salomé*—one of the most challenging of the works I had contracted with Oxford to edit. On my list of libraries and archives were institutions in London, Geneva, New York, Los Angeles, Austin, and various other locations, some of which I had already visited; Philadelphia was next. I had encountered numerous fascinating manuscripts by Wilde, but not a single piece of what would be called graphic evidence had to the best of my knowledge survived, except for two small-scale sketches Wilde had embedded in a letter to George Alexander regarding Alexander's staging of *Lady Windermere's Fan*.[2] That negative record was now about to be contraverted: a piece of evidence was about to emerge that would prove a unique survivor of its kind.

That the Rosenbach manuscript was the third surviving manuscript of the one-act play eventually entitled *Salomé: drame en un acte* was highly likely; examination over the next three days would make that a certainty. Of Wilde's manuscripts, all written originally in French, mostly in Paris and finally in England over the autumn and winter of 1891, this one was a unique case: its basic text was in Wilde's hand, but there were four other hands present as well, intertwined with his. They represented the efforts of French or French-speaking friends whom he had asked to critique it.[3] What I had been only vaguely aware of, until this two-volume manuscript was set before me in the Rosenbach reading room and I began to turn the pages, was that it also contained a ground plan for a production of the play, drawn in ink on one of the constituent leaves of the manuscript, on the verso of the list of the dramatis personae ("Personnes") and facing, on the visible recto,

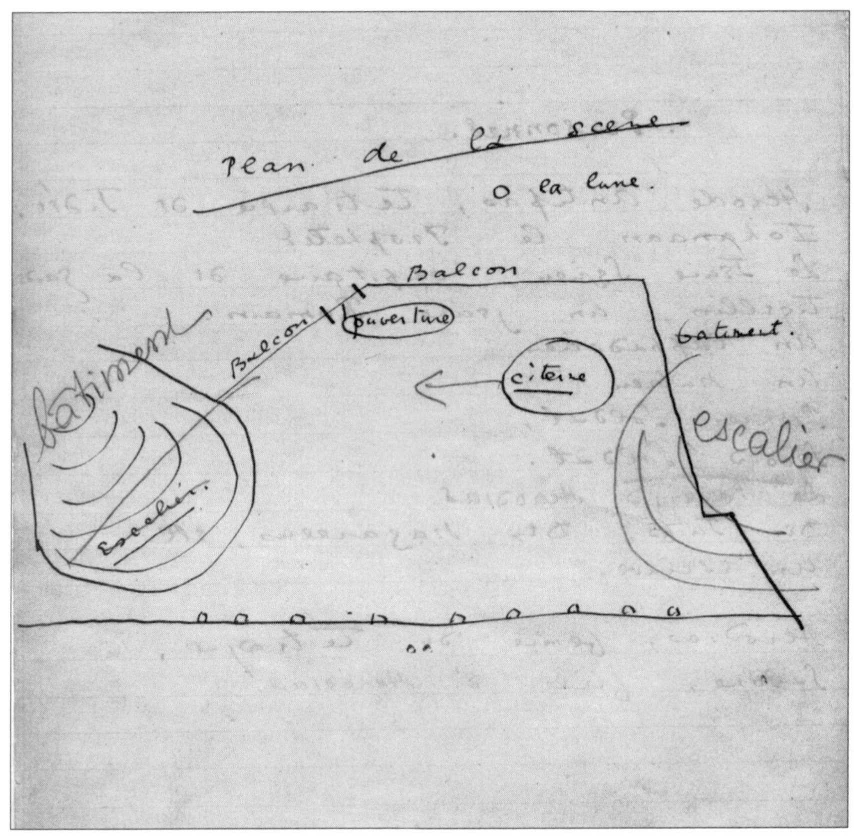

Oscar Wilde's ground plan for *Salomé* (EL3 W672s MS). Courtesy of the Rosenbach Museum & Library, Philadelphia.

the first page of the play proper. From many hours spent in rare book and manuscript rooms on either side of the Atlantic studying and transcribing Wildean holographs, I had become very familiar with his hand. The writing on the ground plan though sparse was unquestionably Wilde's, and the sketch as a whole appeared certainly to be his. And yet, the plan had also been revised by someone else: another hand, clearly not Wilde's, using pencil rather than pen, had moved three of the key features of Wilde's sketch from one part of the stage to another.

I made a quick pencil copy that would do until I could obtain a photograph (see illustration above). I also wrote out a full description of it, which in a later, revised version read as follows:

> Sketch of a ground plan for *Salomé,* in ink, undated, in Wilde's hand, entitled at the top *"Plan de la scene,"* augmented and revised by annotations in pencil in an unknown hand. The sketch features an irregular angular space walled around by a balcony (*"balcon"*) which begins at the upstage limit of the staircase and terminates, at a point upstage left, by

> way of a connection with a building (*"batiment"*) of some kind; the balcony has an opening (*"ouverture"*) in it upstage right, presumably to be used as an entrance; a very large, imposing staircase (*"escalier"*) downstage right, which juts well out onto the stage floor; and a cistern (*"citerne"*) upstage left. The moon (*"la lune"*) is indicated as visible upstage, above the scene. The front edge of the stage is shown with footlights in place. Another hand, in pencil, has altered the position of some of the features of the scene, moving the wall of the building and the staircase to opposite positions and the cistern to the center of the stage.

I read through the opening scene description to see how closely consistent it was with the sketch. Here is the description presented in the first edition of Wilde's play:

> (SCÈNE. *Une grande terrasse dans le palais d'*HÉRODE *donnant sur la salle de festin. Des* SOLDATS *sont accoudés sur le balcon. A droite il y a un énorme escalier. A gauche, au fond, une ancienne citerne entourée d'un mur de bronze vert. Clair de lune*).[4]

The text of the opening stage direction in the Rosenbach manuscript was nearly identical. Moreover, comparison of the verbal scene description with the features that appear on the ground plan served to indicate beyond doubt, not only that it was Wilde's own plan for the setting of his play, but that, by this point in the composition process, Wilde's visual sense of the space where the action of the play would take place was full and clear. The overall plan has few features; it could appropriately be described as "minimalist." As a result, the enormous staircase at right and the old walled cistern upstage left stand out in a bold, unambiguous way. In addition to the indication of the building at the perimeter of the stage (evidently the imagined site of Herod's banqueting hall), these are the features that had been moved by the unknown person who wielded the pencil visible in the sketch.

The provenance of this sketch is seemingly quite clear: Wilde made it either while preparing the manuscript or at some later point, perhaps soon after completion. The blank page that he used for that purpose would have been ready and available, a fact consistent with his normal practice of drafting a play on the recto page of the bound notebook and leaving the facing verso for additions, corrections, or insertions—as in the case of the stage plan here. This sketch together with its penciled alterations nevertheless raises several questions, not all of which can be confidently answered. When did Wilde make this sketch? We don't actually know—though we may speculate that he made it there at the beginning of the manuscript to serve as a ready reference as he prepared this latest revised version of his play. A considerably greater unknown is that of the pencil revisions. Clearly, they are the work of some other, unknown person. Does the fact of their having been made imply that the manuscript passed out of Wilde's hands and so out of his control at some point?[5]

Let us cast our minds back to the time of composition. The two bound volumes together comprising the Rosenbach manuscript each have a paste-on label at the back with the name of a stationer in the Strand, London, whereas the two previous manuscripts have a different but identical label, that of a stationer in the Boulevard des Capucines, Paris, where Wilde stayed during his sojourn there in late 1891, from the end of October to the middle of December, working continually on *Salomé*, before returning home for the Christmas holidays. We also know that by the end of December he was off again, this time to Torquay, Devon, where he borrowed the house of a wealthy patron and stayed until about the middle of January.[6] He probably completed the play there or came very close.

The intriguing question occurs, was Wilde preparing this text for a possible production? Some potentially helpful facts and circumstances suggest that he was. While in Paris he met an enterprising young writer named Pierre Louÿs, who introduced him to a boy genius named Paul Fort. Fort, no more than twenty-one at the time, had already begun to implement grandiose plans for a theatre of ancient and modern classics, plus new plays, including everything from the traditional Indian *Shakuntala* to Maeterlinck, Ibsen, and Strindberg. Fort's enterprise, at first called "Le Théâtre Mixte," was soon renamed "Le Théâtre d'Art."[7] Sensing a promising opportunity, Wilde sent an unfinished but coherent manuscript of *Salomé* to Louÿs to be passed on to Fort. Fort was highly enthusiastic and scheduled it for production early in the coming year. This manuscript turns out to be the second surviving one, in order of composition; it is now in the Harry Ransom Center at the University of Texas, Austin. Fort ran out of funds and the production would never occur, but in mid-January of 1892 Wilde could not have known that. And so we can imagine him generating what he might have hoped would be the final version of his play with a production by the Théâtre d'Art in mind. The ground plan that he had drawn was thus perhaps doing double duty, as a visual mnemonic for the author as he wrote and as a ready indicator of the staging requirements that its producer would need to know about. And the very fact that Wilde had seized this chance for his as yet unfinished play indicates an indisputably clear intention of having the play produced.[8]

So far, there were no direct indications of Wilde's intention to publish the play; that would come later—though not much later. Meanwhile, we need to return to those penciled changes, whose author so far remains unidentified. Do they, or don't they, suggest that the manuscript may have left Wilde's hands? Can they, like the original sketch itself, be related to some production or other of Wilde's play—the first, in Paris, finally, in 1896, or to some even later mounting?

As it happens, Wilde's documentable intentions toward production by Paul Fort fortunately yield a clue to the possible identity of the second hand present in the sketch. The hand may likely be that of Charles Ricketts, Wilde's close friend, an artist and designer in several media and one of the most interesting figures in the literary and theatrical arts of the age. In 1913 Ricketts published an important book, *Pages on Art*, in which he recalled that Wilde had consulted with him early on about a possible production of *Salomé*. At Wilde's request, he recalled, "I sketched out a plan for *Salome*, which at that time had a chance of being given in Paris, that is, before Madame Sarah Bernhardt thought of giving it in London."[9] Can we identify, or at least associate, the ground plan in Wilde's hand with the sketch Ricketts said he made for Wilde? Possibly. Could Wilde have gotten in touch with Ricketts and asked for his advice about a Parisian staging of the play? Could he have made the sketch in advance of their meeting, or have simply had the manuscript with its sketch at hand when he met with his friend to consult him about the theatrical prospects of the play? And might Ricketts have offered advice about moving the staircase, the cistern, and the boundary wall? Of course, other compatible scenarios are possible as well.

In any case, a later analysis of Ricketts's 1906 private London production of the English translation of *Salome* offers intriguing evidence of Ricketts's possible meeting with Wilde. It verifies that the shift of the staircase to the other side of the stage and the movement of the cistern to center stage, as indicated in the penciled revisions on Wilde's plan, are in full accord with Ricketts's design for that production. And so it may be that Ricketts's early advice to Wilde is replicated in the consistency of his later design and staging.[10] Further details provided by Ricketts in *Pages on Art* about that early discussion with Wilde ring true—and are exceedingly interesting to contemplate.

Evidently, Ricketts did know when he was writing in 1913 that Wilde's play had received its world première production in Paris in 1896, while Wilde was in prison,[11] mounted by what was by that time the foremost symbolist theater in existence, Aurélien Lugné-Poe's company the Théâtre de l'Œuvre.[12] Ricketts seems not to have known about Paul Fort's short-lived enterprise, and so he thought, retrospectively, that perhaps Wilde had been negotiating with Lugné-Poe in 1891. Lugné's company, the offspring of Fort's Théâtre d'Art, in fact did not come into existence until two years later, with its wonderful inaugural production of Maeterlinck's *Pelléas et Mélisande*, in May, 1893. Ricketts's memory appears to be more reliable when it comes to the scenic details that he and Wilde discussed. "Here is my scheme," he recalled:

> I proposed a black floor—upon which Salome's white feet would show; this statement was meant to capture Wilde. The sky was to be a rich turquoise blue, cut across by the perpendicular fall of strips of gilt matting, which should not touch the ground, and so form a sort of aerial tent above the terrace. Did Wilde actually suggest the division of the actors into separate masses of colour, to-day the idea seems mine! His was the scheme, however, that the Jews should be in yellow, the Romans were to be in purple, the soldiery in bronze green, and John in white. Over the dress of Salome the discussions were endless: should she be black "like the night"? silver "like the moon"? or—here the suggestion is Wilde's—"green like a curious poisonous lizard"? I desired that the moonlight should fall upon the ground, the source not being seen; Wilde himself hugged the idea of some "strange dim pattern in the sky."[13]

The decor Ricketts devised for his dramatic club's private production in 1906[14] ended up varying considerably from these details—featuring "dim cypress-like curtains against a star-lit sky" and players "clothed in every shade of blue, deepening into dark violet and green, the general harmony of blue on blue being relieved by the red lances of the soldiers." Yet in other ways they bore a close correspondence.[15]

As for Ricketts's reference to a point in time before Sarah Bernhardt had "thought" about producing the play, he evidently had in mind the doomed production of *Salomé* by Bernhardt in June 1892, intended as a kind of epilogue to her highly successful London season at Richard D'Oyly Carte's Royal English Opera House. The play was in rehearsal when the Lord Chamberlain's Examiner of Plays, E. F. Smyth Pigott, banned its performance, officially on the grounds that it presented forbidden biblical characters on the public stage. The full story was much more complex than that.[16] Important here is that Ricketts's reference serves to fix the time when he discussed the production of *Salomé* with Wilde, in the context of a prospective Parisian production, as late 1891 or early 1892—the exact moment when the author of the play was putting its text into final shape. We can therefore add further confirmation to our conclusion that Wilde's pen-and-ink sketch of a ground plan for his one-act tragedy dates from a time beginning when he had recently returned to London from Paris, in mid-December, a revised manuscript of *Salomé* in hand, to spend the Christmas holidays with his family and extending to a period later on in January when he had returned from a post-New Year's retreat to Torquay, Devon, where he had virtually or completely finished his play, and was in London once again.[17] At this time, as we have seen, the prospect of a Théâtre d'Art production was still a real possibility, and Wilde would have been able to sit down with Ricketts and discuss an imminent Parisian production at length. He could have brought along with him his ground plan, previously prepared, or could have sketched it out on the spot as he and Ricketts talked. Ricketts could then have penciled in some alternative solutions to the staging. It is an attractive fantasy, imagining an expansive conversation on how to mount a French production of *Salomé*, between two close, like-minded friends sitting by a cozy fire on a winter afternoon. Unfortunately, there is not a scrap of hard evidence that it was Ricketts who wrote a few words and drew one or two arrows on Wilde's plan.[18] All we have to go on are some tantalizing statements in a memoir composed over twenty years after the recollected meeting, together with some circumstantial information about people Wilde met in Paris and an approximate knowledge of his movements between Paris, London, and Devon around Christmas 1891.

Of course, the advantage of positing a Christmas meeting between the dramatist and Ricketts is that we have the artist annotating Wilde's plan but leaving it in Wilde's possession, while storing up the concept and details in his own mind for later use. Let us return to the manuscript and ponder its acquisition by A. S. W. Rosenbach, the co-founder of the Rosenbach Museum & Library, in hopes of further enlightenment. A typewritten card loosely placed inside the back cover of the first volume reads as follows: "The manuscript, complete even to the stage plan, was given by Wilde to Pierre Louÿs, who arranged for its publication. Tipped in, also, is the receipt for 200 francs which Louÿs gave as a guarantee to the publisher." It is quite true that, when Wilde was seeing the manuscript through the press to publication in 1892–93, Wilde's friend Louÿs forwarded on the author's behalf an additional amount of money to his Paris publisher, Edmond Baillie, to underwrite the expenses of publication, and in due course sent Wilde a receipt for the payment dated June 4, 1892—a receipt now tipped in to the back of the Rosenbach manuscript. No one examining the heavily interlineated state of the manuscript, however, would believe that either Wilde or any dramatist in his right mind would pass on such a manuscript to Baillie as a viable copy-text from which to set type. Wilde must have made a fair copy, perhaps incorporating still further changes, and sent that to his Parisian publisher to pass on to Baillie's printer, Paul Schmidt (or else to Louÿs to pass on to him).[19] That hypothetical fair copy does not survive, but the manuscript now in the Rosenbach collection nonetheless stands, poised and in high profile, bearing in its embrace two excellent pieces of additional evidence confirming its special "page and stage" status: evidence simultaneously of Wilde's intentions to see the play produced and to see it published—whichever might happen first.

We have good reason to believe, then, that the manuscript, with its stage plan and publication receipt enclosed, remained in Wilde's possession after the publication of the French *Salomé* in 1893. In the event, Wilde not only saw his play published, but lived to know of (although not actually to see, languishing as he was in Reading Prison) its stage première, by Lugné's Théâtre de l'Œuvre company, with Lina Munte, a ferociously feminine actress in her mid-forties, in the title role.[20] Information about certain aspects of Lugné's *Salomé* remains unfortunately scant. The reviews have much to say about the leading actress and almost nothing about the staging, nor are Lugné's memoirs much better.[21] Almost surely, the first French edition of the play, published three years before by Baillie, served as the script for Lugné's production, though it was very likely cut. And so what we can say is merely that Lugné presumably followed the indications for the setting printed in the initial stage directions.

In doing so, of course, he would have been unknowingly replicating the ground plan sketched by Wilde, perhaps as an aid toward visualization of the ensuing action, or as a reference for what must have been an exceedingly productive talk with Ricketts—if in fact it did occur! Although Lugné was a talented stage director and a fine, sensitive actor who typically played the heavy—he was the Hérode in his own production of Wilde's play—he would not have had access to the brilliant insights brought to Wilde's stage plan by his good friend Charles Ricketts, whose London production was still ten years in the future. There are, after all, almost always limitations of some kind to theatrical production. There are to scholarship as well.

ENDNOTES

1 Oxford University Press, Oxford English Texts series, general editor Ian Small (University of Birmingham); four volumes published to date.

2 Letter dated approximately mid-February 1892, *The Complete Letters of Oscar Wilde*, ed. Merlin Holland and Rupert Hart-Davis (London: Fourth Estate, 2000), 513. In the letter Wilde explains that he makes rough sketches of staging, presumably as aids to visualizing the action, as he is writing the play. As I later discovered, two other ground plans survive, in manuscripts for the play later entitled *A Woman of No Importance*; see Ian Small, *Oscar Wilde Revalued: An Essay on New Materials & Methods of Research* (Greensboro, NC: ELT Press, 1993), 114–15.

[3] For the record, Wilde's four friends were the expatriate American Stuart Merrill, Adolphe Retté, Pierre Louÿs, and Marcel Schwob, whom the author asked to help him rid his French-language play of any glaring anglicisms or grammatical faults. Protesting that they were hesitant to rob Wilde's play of its idiolectic charm, they still managed to exert such a heavy hand that the author found it necessary to reject a number of their emendations. This information was first unearthed by Rodney Shewan and included in his PhD dissertation, "Oscar Wilde's *Salomé*: A Critical Variorum Edition from Three Extant Manuscripts Proofsheets and Two Early Printed Texts Transcribed in Parallel" (2 vols., University of Reading, 1982).

[4] Oscar Wilde, *Salomé: drame en un acte* (Paris: Librairie de l'art indépendant; London: Elkin Mathews et John Lane, 1893). The scene description in Lord Alfred Douglas's English translation of this first edition, published by Mathews and Lane the following year, reads as follows: "SCENE—*A great terrace in the Palace of Herod, set above the banqueting-hall. Some soldiers are leaning over the balcony. To the right there is a gigantic staircase, to the left, at the back, an old cistern surrounded by a wall of green bronze. The moon is shining very brightly.*"—Oscar Wilde, *Salome: A Tragedy in One Act* (London: Elkin Mathews & John Lane; Boston: Copeland & Day, 1894); the dedication reads "To Lord Alfred Bruce Douglas, the translator of my play." The book includes a now-famous set of illustrations "Pictured by Aubrey Beardsley."

[5] An additional complicating factor is that, sometime in recent years, the page on which Wilde made the plan became detached from the manuscript. The librarian of the Rosenbach Museum & Library, Elizabeth E. Fuller, has assured me that the leaf on which the plan is written is "identical in size to the other leaves and all the same paper, with small irregularities on the inner edge that align exactly with the stitching." Moreover, there is "no adhesive residue or other indication that it was ever tipped into anything" (private communication to the author from Elizabeth E. Fuller, October 4, 2010). So there is no doubt of its authenticity and character, but it remains unclear how it became detached; could this have occurred, as Ms. Fuller speculates, as a result of stress from repeated opening during frequent exhibitions of the manuscript?

[6] The dates and postmarks of surviving letters help us to track his movements; see *The Complete Letters of Oscar Wilde*, ed. Merlin Holland and Rupert Hart-Davis (London: Fourth Estate, 2000).

[7] For an authoritative history of the French symbolist theatre, from Fort to Lugné-Poe, see Jacques Robichez, *Le Symbolisme au Théâtre: Lugné-Poe et les Débuts de l'Œuvre* (Paris: Editions de l'Arche, 1957).

[8] The letter Wilde sent as cover for his manuscript, dated by its editors as "[December 1891]," is included in *Complete Letters*, ed. Holland and Hart-Davis, 506. Wilde's literary executor, Robert Ross, maintained that Wilde had not intended the play primarily for theatrical production, and he cited such reasons as the dance of the seven veils and Herod's verbose attempts to persuade Salome to choose some other reward for it than the head of Iokanaan (Wilde's John the Baptist). Wilde, as the extensive history of the play in production abundantly demonstrates, had a much better sense of theatre than his devoted friend.

[9] Charles Ricketts, *Pages on Art* (London: Constable, 1913), 243.

[10] For a detailed description of Ricketts's two later productions of *Salome*, see Richard Allen Cave, "Stage Design as a Form of Dramatic Criticism," *Irish Literature and Culture*, ed. Michael Kinneally (Savage, MD: Barnes and Noble Books, 1992), 72–89; and Cave, "Power Structuring: The Presentation of Outsider Figures in Wilde's Plays," *Rediscovering Oscar Wilde*, ed. C. George Sandulescu, Princess Grace Irish Library: 8 (Gerrards Cross: Colin Smythe, 1994), 37–51. Cave's analysis of personal space claimed at first by Herod and then usurped by Salomé as she performs her dance supports his argument that the transferring of the staircase to stage left and centralizing of the cistern combine to underscore the importance of recognizing Salomé's expanding personal space in the course of the play.

[11] Wilde had been convicted in the course of three trials in spring 1895 and sentenced to two years of imprisonment with hard labor, the maximum punishment called for by the

Statutes, 48 and 49 Vict. c. lxix, forbidding acts of "gross indecency" between men; see Merlin Holland, *Irish Peacock & Scarlet Marquess: The Real Trial of Oscar Wilde* (London: Fourth Estate, 2003), and the earlier book edited by H. Montgomery Hyde, *The Trials of Oscar Wilde* (London: William Hodge, 1948), published in the United States as *The Three Trials of Oscar Wilde*, ed. H. Montgomery Hyde (New York: University Books, 1956).

[12]For details of the Lugné *Salomé*, see Robichez, *Le Symbolisme au Théâtre*, and William Tydeman and Steven Price, *Wilde: Salome*, Plays in Production (Cambridge: Cambridge University Press, 1996).

[13] Ricketts, *Pages on Art*, 243–44.

[14] The Lord Chamberlain's ban on *Salomé* (see the next paragraph) was still in force, not to be lifted until over two decades later; and so the only way to produce the play was to do so as a private club performing to members. Of course, anyone with the nominal price of "membership" could obtain a ticket.

[15] Ricketts, *Pages on Art*, 244. For details of Ricketts's production at the Kings Hall, Covent Garden, London, 18 June 1906 by the Literary Theatre Society and their close correspondence to the details Ricketts recalls of his suggestions for Wilde's first production, see Tydeman and Price, *Wilde: Salome*, 44–56.

[16] See, for example, Kerry Powell's discussion of the censoring of *Salomé* in *Oscar Wilde and the Theatre of the 1890s* (Cambridge: Cambridge University Press, 1990), 33–54.

[17] These details of Wilde's comings and goings as he put the finishing touches on *Salomé* form part of the Introduction to my edition of the play, to be included in my volume of Wilde's plays for the Oxford English Texts edition of the *Complete Works*. Also explained there is the fact that the "completed" manuscript was then passed on to Wilde's Parisian friends to critique, resulting in a surprising, extraordinarily dense manuscript in which Wilde may be perceived rejecting many of his friends' suggestions. He was then evidently faced with the necessity of making a fair copy of it before sending it to his publisher, Edmond Bailly, in Paris, from which Bailly's printer would set type.

[18] Tracking down examples of Ricketts's handwriting would be the obvious next step.

[19] Louÿs, young though he was, had published a volume of poems with Baillie and so was well known to him. It may have been the case that Louÿs, who became great friends with Wilde almost immediately after their meeting in early November 1891, commended Baillie to Wilde's attention. In any event, the young poet-turned-novelist soon became Wilde's intermediary in the publication process.

[20] See Robichez, *Le Symbolisme au Théâtre*, and (eventually) my Introduction to the edition of the play in the *OET Wilde*.

[21]A lively anecdotal read: Aurélien Lugné-Poe, *Le Sot Du Tremplin: Souvenirs et Impressions de Théâtre, La Parade*, I (Paris: Librairie Gallimard, 1930).

A Queer Victorian Marriage: Henry Blake Fuller's *At Saint Judas's* and the "Tyranny" of the Archival Document

ERIC COLLEARY

"Who wants to be definitely classified and pigeon-holed? Nobody in our age."

—Henry Blake Fuller, 1896[1]

Henry Blake Fuller died on July 29, 1929 at the age of seventy-two. At the height of his career as a novelist in the 1890s, he was considered the most talented writer in the emerging genre of American realism—a gifted man who would surely be remembered for his contributions to literature. However, Fuller died in debt, struggling for over twenty years to find publishers who would take interest in his work. His death went largely unnoticed outside his circle of friends and his native city of Chicago.[2] A self-proclaimed bachelor from a young age, Fuller's estate was left in the hands of his two nieces who sold whatever could fetch a high enough price to pay off their uncle's debts. The large bulk of Fuller's papers were ultimately purchased by Chicago's Newberry Library for preservation and, his nieces hoped, would secure their uncle's place in history.

Yet you will be hard-pressed to find Fuller's name on any syllabus surveying the history of American literature. Within the last decade, however, a modest but growing number of scholars primarily working in LGBT studies have turned their attention to Fuller. In 1896, after a roller coaster of career successes and failures, Fuller published an anthology of twelve play-lets titled *The Puppet Booth,* drawing inspiration from European symbolists like Maurice Maeterlinck and Henrik Ibsen. One of these plays, *At Saint Judas's,* concerns a Bridegroom who, minutes before his wedding, discovers that his Best Man has tried numerous times to sabotage the engagement. The Bridegroom becomes enraged, insisting that the Best Man kill himself. What happens next in the play is a bit of a mystery. Fuller's detailed descriptions give way to sudden brevity—all that can be certainly stated is that the play ends

Manuscript title page of Henry Blake Fuller's "At Saint Judas's" (1896). Photo Courtesy of The Newberry Library, Chicago.

with the Bridegroom exchanging vows with his Bride, while a dead body lies in a pool of blood in the church's sacristy.

Recent scholars have heralded *At Saint Judas's* as the earliest American play to have a central gay theme.[3] In 2000, such proclamations led to Henry Blake Fuller's posthumous induction into the Chicago Gay and Lesbian Hall of Fame, even though Fuller took great pains to guard his personal privacy during his life and never openly discussed his sexuality. The Newberry Library accepted the award on his behalf, and have archived it in his papers alongside the writer's worn Remington portable typewriter.[4]

What evidence is there to justify claims that *At Saint Judas's* is a "gay play," and what, if any, statement is Fuller making about homosexuality at this particular moment? Hoping Fuller's manuscript at the Newberry Library offered some insight, I made my way to Chicago for a week of research. The result, as I will explain, led to more questions than answers but also a greater appreciation for what the 'tyrannical document' can offer to scholars of theatre and sexuality studies.

Before discussing the manuscript itself, however, a more detailed description of the play may be necessary in order to understand the questions that stem from it. In the sacristy of the church of St. Judas, the Bridegroom exalts in the excitement of his impending nuptials, while his Best Man reacts with constrained anxiety. We learn, through the Bridegroom's nostalgic reminiscences, that the two men are close. As soldiers, they fought together in the deserts of Africa where both, at different times, saved each other's life. In the time since, the two men have shared everything from clothes to each other's confidences. Except, we learn, the Bridegroom was, for whatever reason, reluctant to inform the Best Man of his engagement. Indeed, the Best Man discovers the Bridegroom's intentions because the two men share the same bed, and the Bridegroom spoke of the marriage in his sleep.[5]

As the Bridegroom continues to dress, he recounts the difficulties he experienced in the weeks leading up to the ceremony. An unknown person has attempted to sabotage the wedding by spreading false rumors. The Bridegroom has been accused of being a less-than-honorable soldier, an excessive gambler who cheats at his games, and a man who has engaged in undefined premarital promiscuities. "I have indeed lived freely," the Bridegroom mentions, "but who shall say that I have seriously overpassed the bounds?"[6]

Each accusation the Bridegroom describes is punctuated by one of eight stained glass windows whose figures come to life as if performing a non-literal representation of the accusation being described. For example, as the Bridegroom describes being accused of promiscuity, a window depicting "a band of chaste young damsels" comes to life.[7] The damsels, who had been standing tall among a field of lilies, blush and hide their faces among the flowers.

Suddenly, a clock strikes noon and the Sacristan enters to announce that the Bride has not come, and rumors are circulating in the church that she will not arrive at all. With the Sacristan's exit, the Best Man, who has largely been silent through the Bridegroom's remembrances, explains that he too does not expect the Bride to come—that congregants in the church "say that she has sinned, and sinned—with me."[8] Insisting that his Bride will appear, the Bridegroom is directly confronted by his Best Man:

> I am here and she will never be. You may wait, but you shall wait in vain. (*He places his hand upon the other's shoulder.*) If she were to come, I should not let her have you. She shall not have you. Nobody shall have you. . . . Our friendship has been too long, too close, too intimate. It shall not be destroyed; it shall not be broken. No one shall come between us.[9]

With this pronouncement, the Bridegroom realizes it was his Best Man who had been trying to sabotage the wedding. While insisting that he will kill the Best Man with his own hands, a procession of wheels and ringing chimes announce the arrival of the Bride to the church. The Best Man attempts to physically place his body between the Bridegroom and the path to the altar. The Bridegroom, furious, exclaims "Stand aside. I hate you; I detest you; I despise you; I loathe you." The Best Man, incredulous, responds "You loathe me? I, who have done so much. . . ." "You are not fit to live," proclaims the Bridegroom. "You are not fit to die. But die you shall. I shall not kill you. You shall kill yourself. You shall do it now, and I shall see you do it. You have no other road to redemption."[10]

What happens next is a bit of a mystery, and it is worth quoting in full. The final stage directions read as follows:

> *The EIGHTH WINDOW. The Angelic Host trumpeting from the clouds, while Lucifer plunges headlong toward the Pit: the wonder is that he can fall so long, so fast, so far.*
>
> *When the BRIDEGROOM opens the door into the church, the BRIDE is seen coming up the aisle, while the choirboys and the organ unite in a resounding Gloria. Upon the floor of the sacristy lies the body of a man in a pool of blood. As the BRIDE and the BRIDEGROOM meet before the altar rail, the EIGHT WINDOWS, dappling the floor of the sacristy with a thousand varied splotches of color—(but there is one, broader and brighter than them all)—shudder back convulsively to their pristine selves.*[11]

While embodying many traditional markers of a resolved ending, Fuller's text raises several questions. After describing seven previous windows depicting archetypal figures (knights, damsels, acolytes, etc.), why does Fuller choose to specifically reference Lucifer? Is the Best Man meant to be reflected in the figure of Lucifer's fall? Or the Bridegroom? What can we make of the splotches of color—"one broader and brighter than them all"—shuddering back convulsively to their pristine selves? After being so descriptive of events throughout the rest of the play, why doesn't Fuller describe the death that happens here? And is it significant that the Bridegroom and the Bride are named specifically in this last passage, yet the dead body on the floor is not specifically identified as the Best Man's?

Armed with many interpretations of this play,[12] but still no closer to understanding how *At Saint Judas's* could be affirmatively claimed as a "gay play" or what Fuller was trying to accomplish by writing it, I headed to the

Newberry Library of Chicago, home to the largest single collection of Henry Blake Fuller's papers, including the bulk of his original manuscripts.

The crumbling, hand-written manuscript revealed many surprises compared to its published counterpart. The first variation I noticed was the title, which reads "*At Saint Judas's*: A Play for Marionettes." In fact, all twelve of the plays include "A Play for Marionettes" in their title, which was removed in each instance for the published manuscript. Fuller does not suggest how the marionettes are meant to be used. In the case of *At Saint Judas's,* are all of the characters meant to be portrayed with puppets or just the windows? How would the use of marionettes change the way an audience would relate to the play, particularly if they were used to represent the Bridegroom and Best Man? Apart from the title of the anthology—*The Puppet Booth*—why did Fuller remove the reference to puppetry? Though some contemporary scholars have labeled *At Saint Judas's* as a closet drama, meant to be read and not performed, the title at the very least suggests that Fuller considered the play to be performable.[13]

Just under the title, written at an angle in a space off to the side, is a short epigraph from Dante's *Inferno* in the original Italian. The epigraph is included in the published version along with an English language translation by Longfellow: " . . . in the abyss which swallows up Judas with Lucifer." This caught my eye mainly because it was written in darker ink, squeezed in as if an afterthought. The line clearly relates to the depiction of Lucifer falling into the pit described in the last window of the play, when the dead body appears with no explanation.

In this particular scene from the *Inferno,* Dante described the circle of hell reserved for those who betray the ones who care for them. Here, Lucifer, the archangel, turned his back on God and was banished from heaven, Brutus and Cassius whose betrayal led to the assassination of Julius Caesar, and Judas Iscairot, whose kiss betrayed Jesus to the Romans. By including this epigraph, the allusion to Judas in the title of the play, and the depiction of the fall of Lucifer in the final window (which is described in place of whatever murder/suicide happens in the sacristy), Fuller seems to be drawing a parallel with the relationship of the Bridegroom and Best Man. Yet Fuller makes it seem equally plausible that the Best Man could be either the betrayer or the betrayed. The Best Man's perceived death at the end is frequently read as following in the Victorian tradition of killing the sexual/moral deviate, and Fuller seems to be playing into this tradition while also possibly—if not subtly—turning it on its ear by not actually depicting the death, nor identifying the dead body as belonging to the Best Man. Thus, as Christ was betrayed by Judas and then crucified, the Best Man could be seen as a sacrificed man, a Christ-like figure, who, possibly, dies following the Bridegroom's venomous betrayal of love.

I want to stress that Fuller's manuscripts—published and unpublished—do not favor one of these readings over another. What I am arguing is that Fuller seems to be intentionally ambiguous, allowing the reader/audience to find their own hero and villain within the story. This intentional ambiguity is made all the more apparent when reviewing the final scene of Fuller's handwritten manuscript.

Published Edition:

When the BRIDEGROOM opens the door to the church, the BRIDE is seen coming up the aisle, while the choir-boys and the organ unite in a resounding *Gloria*. Upon the floor of the sacristy lies the body of a man in a pool of blood. As the BRIDE and the BRIDEGROOM meet before the altar rail, the Eight Windows, dappling the floor of the sacristy with a thousand varied splotches of color—(but there is one, broader and brighter than them all)—shudder back convulsively to their pristine selves.

Manuscript Edition:

When the Bridegroom opens the door within the church, the bride is seen coming up the aisle, while the choir boys and the organ unite in a resounding Gloria. Upon the floor of the sacristy lies the body of the best man, in a pool of blood. As the bride reaches the alter rail, the Eight Windows, dappling the floor of the sacristy with a thousand splashes of color, shudders back to their proper selves.

There are three major differences between these two versions. First, in the original manuscript, no mention is made that the Bridegroom meets the Bride at the altar. Second, the "splotch" of color "broader and brighter than them all" was added to the published text. Finally, the unnamed body described in the published text is identified specifically as the body of the Best Man in the original manuscript. While the two manuscripts offer significantly different endings, paradoxically, what remains clear is Fuller's lack of clarity in both manuscripts. Indeed, by not identifying the dead body in the published edition, Fuller seems to be intentionally making it difficult for the reader/audience to say "Ah, this is what happened. This is what this play is about." Fuller is consistent with his obfuscation throughout the play—always stopping just short of offering a moral judgment for or against the Best Man's professed love, just short of creating a conclusive villain out of either the Best Man or the Bridegroom, just short of depicting the play's climactic death scene. *At Saint Judas's* seems to offer imagery—through the windows, through the allusions to Judas and Lucifer—which allows the reader/audience to draw their own conclusions, as evidenced by the profusion of contradictory critical and academic studies of the work.

It seems my visit to the archive to see if Fuller's manuscript offered any clarity into a play that has become so important to LGBT performance studies, leads me to the conclusion that the play is intentionally unclear. If it seems like I've led you through an archival mystery only to bring you to a rather anti-climactic ending, then perhaps it is because of the way we think of approaching archival research. Can *At Saint Judas's* be classified as a "gay play" when it seems Fuller is intentionally resisting classification? What is the motivation behind the desire for some scholars to claim this play as gay? Why is it that the relationships depicted in this play are difficult to identify? Because human sexuality, in all of its various constructions, will always push against terms like "gay" and "homosexual" which create the illusion that we know what these terms mean. Ultimately, if the play resists such a classification, it is not because of the tyranny of the document that withholds the necessary details, but rather because of the tyranny of the scholar who insists on such an interpretation.

Failing to find clarity in a document's meaning should be a warning sign for the scholar to stop and ask "what am I implicitly expecting of this document?" Rather than asking how this play fits into a teleological narrative of gay American literature and drama, we can ask, for example, how this play articulates different ways of thinking about love, loyalty and brotherhood in Victorian America. Thus, the ambiguity of *At Saint Judas's* becomes one of its most interesting attributes—a queer play in the truest sense of the word.

ENDNOTES

[1] Quoted in "Books for the Week." *Chicago Evening Post*, May 23, 1896.

[2] One friend—Professor Robert Morss Lovett—wrote after Fuller's death that his passing was no great loss for Chicago literature, as Fuller had failed to contribute to the innovations in writing he had developed in his early novels. See Kenneth Scambray, *A Varied Harvest: The Life and Works of Henry Blake Fuller* (Pittsburgh: University of Pittsburgh, 1987), 160.

[3] See, for example, Michael Bronski, *Culture Clash: The Making of Gay Sensibility* (Boston: South End Press, 1984), 111; Joseph Dimuro, "The Salient Angle: Revising the Queer Case of Henry Blake Fuller's *Bertram Cope's Year*." *Textual Cultures* 2 (Spring 2007): 147; Ken Furtado and Nancy Hellner, *Gay and Lesbian American Plays: an Annotated Bibliography* (Metuchen, NJ: Scarecrow Press, 1993), 57; Terry Helbing, *Gay Theatre Alliance Directory of Gay Plays* (Baltimore: Johns Hopkins Press, 1980), 12; Alan Sinfield, *Out on Stage: Lesbian and Gay Theatre in the Twentieth Century* (New Haven: Yale University Press, 1999), 53; Marc Stein, *LGBT Encyclopedia of Lesbian, Gay, Bisexual, and Transgender History in America* (New York: Charles Scribner's Sons, 2004), "Theatre and Performance," 181.

[4] The responsibility of an archive to carry on the legacy of an individual whose papers they maintain, and how they treat matters such as the individual's sexuality, is the subject of another paper entirely. I mention the Newberry's actions here, however, to stress that extent to which Fuller and his work have been claimed by contemporary LGBT scholars.

[5] "BEST MAN: How did you tell me? In your sleep—your own pillow close to mine." In Henry Blake Fuller, *The Puppet Booth: Twelve Plays* (New York: Century Co, 1896), 89. This line can, and has, been read by some scholars as confirmation that the two men's relationship was sexual. It should be noted, however, that it was not uncommon for bachelors who were friends to share a bed during the Victorian period, without giving the impression that the relationship was necessarily sexual. The line is suggestive, yes—particularly through contemporary eyes—but I wish to stress that Fuller seems to emphasize themes of love and loyalty in this play, rather than sex. For scholarship on same-sex affection in the Victorian period: Axel Nissen, *The Romantic Friendship Reader* (Boston: Northeastern, 2003); and Carolyn Oulton, *Romantic Friendship in Victorian Literature* (Aldershot: Ashgate, 2007).

[6] Fuller, *Puppet Booth*, 92.

[7] Fuller, *Puppet Booth*, 91.

[8] Fuller, *Puppet Booth*, 95.

[9] Fuller, *Puppet Booth*, 96.

[10] Fuller, *Puppet Booth*, 98.

[11] Fuller, *Puppet Booth*, 98–99.

[12] A survey of scholarship on *At Saint Judas's* suggests few scholars allude to the play's ambiguity. Yet, reading these scholars together, there appears to be disagreement about what actually happens in the play. In *Out on Stage*, Alan Sinfield suggests the Best Man is the Judas of the story, and therefore must kill himself; Sinfield, *Out on Stage* 53. Ken Furtado more or less agrees in his brief synopsis in *Gay and Lesbian American Plays*, adding that the Best Man is forced into suicide specifically by the Bridegroom; Furtado and Hellner,

Gay and Lesbian American Plays, 57. Laurence Senelick's *Lovesick*, which includes Fuller's play in its entirety alongside other "modernist plays of same-sex love," acknowledges the ambiguity of the ending only so far that it is unclear who struck the deadly blow that killed the Best Man—not that the dead body is unidentified or the significance of the window is unexplained; Laurence Senelick, *Lovesick: Modernist Plays of Same-sex Love, 1894–1925* (New York: Routledge, 1999), 63. Most bizarrely, Michael Bronski's *Culture Clash* claims the play is "about a groom who discovers, minutes before the wedding, that he is really in love with his best man"; Bronski, *Culture Clash*, 111.

[13] Correspondence held by the Newberry Library between Fuller and *Puppet Booth* publisher Century Co. indicate that Fuller had expressly requested that he maintain the sole right to grant permission for the plays to be performed, and that he would be entitled to 100% of royalties related to its performance. That *At Saint Judas's* was never performed in Fuller's lifetime should not indicate that it wasn't necessarily meant to be.

Fixing the Fix: Medicine Show Trading Cards and the Slipperiness of Souvenirs in the Archive

CHASE BRINGARDNER

As I flip through the glossy sheets of reprinted color illustrations nestled in between numerous pages of dull type on either side, my eye suddenly rests on an image. Three women. No small children or animals in this one. These three women's faces appear almost identical and they each clutch toothpaste (or dentaroma—a derivative of toothpaste) in one hand, toothbrush in another. They wear silk kimonos of different colors. Pastels: periwinkle, pale yellow, rosy pink. Their hair dotted with small paper fans. They crouch forward as if about to bow subserviently to their male counterparts. Their eyebrows arched, their faces convey a certain eagerness to please as if saying "this toothpaste is so great that we will put it on your teeth for you." I think immediately of Gilbert and Sullivan. "Three Little Maids from school are we." They certainly display girlish glee. Yet the text I see conveys something different. The words "we can never be persuaded" gives them a power that the image refuses them. To me, the words paint them as resolute, determined in their stance to support this toothpaste to the end yet their faces and demeanor suggest subservience. They are the exotic, the other conforming to the sanitization of Western culture. If these Asian characters whose eyes perhaps betray a hint of barbarism or perhaps insanity can use toothpaste and display shimmering, white smiles then surely rural Medicine Show audience members can. I see women being doubly colonized. They portray the colonized Asian female, oppressed, passive, and meek while simultaneously existing as white women whose bodies are "colonized" by this advertising medium. Their bodies are being used to fabricate truths. Yet I wonder if these women actually read as Asian for a rural audience of the time period? Would such an audience have the visual vocabulary to distinguish the actor from the character? Did rural America seek to actively compare themselves to the exotic inhabitants of "the Orient"? What is the relationship between toothpaste or toothpowder or dentaroma and Asianness? I feel attacked by these women. Their unrelenting giddy, crazed stares implicate me and compel me to want to free them of the confines of the advertisement. I become the colonizer. By purchasing this dentaroma, I enact

'Ricksecker's Dentaroma,' courtesy of Dr. Harold Kanthor, original held in the Department of Rare Books and Special Collections at the University of Rochester.

the role of privileged white male, bent on colonization and the spread of Western values.

In the first edition of his groundbreaking study of Medicine Shows, *Step Right Up*, Brooks McNamara includes a glossy, colorful collection of reprints of a wide variety of trading cards found in the William Helfand Collection located at the New York Academy of Medicine Library.[1] These trading cards survive as one of a few material remains of Medicine Shows, which traveled throughout the US from about 1870 to 1930 using a variety of entertainments to sell questionable medicinal products across rural America. As a historian of Medicine Shows like McNamara, I am fascinated by the multiple meanings offered by these pieces of ephemera which exist both as advertisement for a given product and as cherished souvenir of a fleeting moment of performance. The Medicine Show trading card sits at a most complicated crossroads. In attempting to make meaning of this artifact, I find myself questioning the very nature of the performance form itself and the complicated layering of transactions taking place between manufacturer, salesperson, performer, and audience. While most cards depict images of nature, children, or animals, this particular card stands out in its use of a rather transparent Orientalist fantasy to hawk toothpaste. Three smiling, ornately costumed white women stare intently at the holder enticing them to buy the product, yet what does this individual card really reveal about the product, the salesperson and the purchaser? Images of cute animals and smiling babies lead me to believe people collected these cards for purely aesthetic reasons, but the presence of this card, in pristine condition, refuses such a simple interpretation. My interaction with this trade card ultimately became emblematic of my larger journey to understand Medicine Show performance: an appealing, colorful, and provocative image that masks a complicated network of layers, meanings and monetary and psychological transactions.

Medicine Shows reached their height of popularity in the late nineteenth and early twentieth century, peaking in number in the nineteen twenties just before the Great Depression. They traveled throughout the United States and brought urban ideas and practices, such as sophisticated advertising campaigns and increased standards of cleanliness, to rural areas, forcing audiences to reassess their identities. Using performance as a means to sell a variety of quasi-medicinal products, medicine shows drew from a variety of popular performance traditions including minstrelsy, vaudeville, and burlesque. Medicine show performers erected small wooden stages in the center of town, often an extension of the carts (or eventually trucks) on which they rode into town, on which they would stage their pitch for products like Kickapoo Indian Remedy, Snake Oil, or Women's Friend. They presented characters that relied on an audience's shared understanding of regional stereotype and theatrical stock characters such as melodrama's Noble Savage, a peaceful Native American in touch with nature, the Tent show's Toby, the "carrot-topped rustic," and various minstrel show characters like Sambo, the happy, mischievous slave. In addition to more formal pitches, medicine shows also offered free evenings of performance as further enticement to purchase their products. Underneath large canvas tents similar to those of the Christian revival or early circus, medicine show performers presented evenings of variety performance comprised of skits, audience contests (like the ever popular female nail driving competition), and local talent competitions. Audiences actively engaged with these performances both through physical (sitting in audiences, performing in talent shows, etc.) and financial (purchasing tickets, buying products, etc.) participation.

A typical medicine show broke down into two primary parts: the pitch and the entertainment. How to integrate these two elements into an enjoyable show was the responsibility of the medicine showman, the equivalent of a theatrical producer. The typical medicine show, according to McNamara in *Step Right Up*, would last up to two hours "and was made up of eight or ten selections, including two or three" pitches.[2] Most shows would begin with "a banjo solo or two designed to settle the audience down or a song and dance number featuring the whole cast" followed by a comedy routine, usually "a rapid-fire exchange of jokes and stock bits between the blackface comedian and the straightman," often the pitch doctor.[3] Then more music came, or a specialty act like "mind-reading, magic, or perhaps a sword swallower or ventriloquist followed by the first pitch and sale of the evening."[4] This first item was usually something rather common, inexpensive, and practical, like soap, in order to get the audience in the mood to consume. Following the first pitch "came another act or two, usually a comic bit and a musical act or specialty number, and the second lecture and sale," after which came another bit or specialty act, then "the prize candy sale," where participants could win prizes if the piece of candy they bought had a special marking on the wrapper.[5] The show would end with the "traditional medicine show afterpiece, [which was] almost invariably" a short, humorous, scripted "blackface act" featuring the characters of "Jake, the straightman, and a ghost" intended for the audience to leave in high spirits, so to speak.[6] Yet McNamara's ordering of events only suggests a possible (if not probable) order. Depending upon the size of the medicine show and the number of troupe members, this bill could drastically change. Moreover it would also necessarily change based upon the specific location and audience present. But no matter what the size or location or audience composition, the basic structural components of pitches intertwined with entertainments remained, as did the presence of advertising or trade cards.

Medicine Shows used trade or advertising cards to extend the performance beyond the traditional stage space. These cards were created by patent medicine companies and handed out during the shows to provide purchasers with a kind of souvenir of their consumer experience, whether they purchased the product or not. They depict a variety of images from young children at play to animals and infants to other more idiosyncratic images like the one I am examining here. These cards were widely collected by those who attended medicine shows and, according to McNamara, "were often pasted into albums, many of which survive today in museums and private collections" illustrating the important role these cards played in their lives.[7] While the cards depicting the more serene, innocent, or innocuous images seem to suggest an easily understood aesthetic or nostalgic desire for their collection, the more eccentric, outlandish ones challenge these assumptions about the motives of the spectator/consumer/collector. McNamara, when discussing the often peculiar nature of some of these print advertisements, states that "essentially guileless but often brutal caricatures appeared almost as a matter of course."[8] These "casual" caricatures ranged from sexist images of olds maids, shrewish mothers-in-law, and cantankerous suffragists to effeminate foreign men, simple-minded country folk, and "absent-minded" professors.[9] Additionally, these images also borrowed heavily from racial and ethnic stereotypes including the Jew, the Irishman, the Italian, the German, as well as a bevy of racist African American and Asian depictions. In this particular card, we can see both the racial stereotyping seen through the Orientalist fantasy created by three white women donning yellow face and Asianesque attire and the sexist caricature seen through the women's submissive, passive posturing.

Yet the nature of the card itself, a piece of imprinted card stock handed out to an audience to promote a product that may or may not actually even appear on the card, speaks to a more complicated relationship. We cannot simply dismiss these cards as racist, sexist, etc and thus deem those who collected them as such. The desire to hold on to such ephemera reveals something more complicated about the medicine show audience that such an approach negates. Perhaps the growing body of scholarship on souvenirs might provide some insight. Susan Stewart, in her book *On Longing: Narrative of the Miniature, the Gigantic, the Souvenir, the Collection*, comments on how the souvenir itself performs:

> The souvenir distinguishes experiences. We do not need or desire souvenirs of events that are repeatable. Rather we need and desire souvenirs

> of events that are reportable, events whose materiality has escaped us, events that thereby exist only through the invention of narrative. Through narrative the souvenir substitutes a context of perpetual consumption for its context of original. It represents not the lived experience of its maker but the 'secondhand' experience of its possessor/owner.[10]

These Medicine Show trade cards then came to stand in for the experience these individuals had at the Medicine Shows long after the performance ended. While the actual product, be it soap, salve, or ointment, may be used up or discarded, the card was preserved. McNamara's description of the scrapbooks of cards he encountered during his research, speaks to the care with which individuals kept these material artifacts and the importance these collections had in their lives. Through the lens of Stewart's work then we can read these cards as reminders for the holder of the embodied experiences they had as both consumer and performer and an attempt to capture the ephemeral, thus temporarily fixing a transient performance form. The owner could look at the card to remind them of a particular act or song they enjoyed. The cards also reminded the individual of their previous role of consumer while continually conditioning them, upon every glance at that card, for their next opportunity to spend. For the medicine company, the cards provided a constant reminder of their product within the consumer's home and familiarized and normalized their audience/customer base with commodification.

Though a focus on the trade card as souvenir emphasizes the economic transaction and the subsequent, lingering psychological impact, such an approach negates the obvious racial implications implicit in this particular image. In much of Medicine Show performance, pitch doctors co-opted Asian identity, creating personas which relied on stereotypes of the exotic and fantastical. Under the guises of characters such as Princess Lotus Blossom, performers spun elaborate tales set in ancient China detailing the origin of products like Tiger Balm. Performers entertained their audiences in full yellow face, decked out in elaborate Asian garments and stage makeup to elongate the eye and literally yellow the face. In many ways, this trade card mirrors the type of performance audiences would see in the actual Medicine Shows themselves. The performance techniques illustrated in the card and on stage further mirror that of late nineteenth, early twentieth century practices of Asian representation. How similar do the ladies on the trade card look to posters for a Gilbert and Sullivan operetta or marketing campaigns for the Chinatown mysteries or yellow peril thrillers of early Hollywood? This trade card thus connects medicine shows to larger practices of Asian representation.

Yet to state simply that the women who collected this card participated in a larger racist project undercuts the complexity of the image. For the three white women contained in this image are shown laboring for a specific product, caught themselves in the act of the sales pitch. Their positioning as both salesperson and product engages with contemporary notions of Orientalism as posited by Edward Said by presenting the viewer with a highly exoticized image of Asian femininity available for consumption alongside the products. Mari Yoshihara, in *Embracing the East: White Women and American Orientalism*

(2003), posits that "the evolution of both U.S.-Asian relations and white women's social roles in America" pre-WWII "meant changes in white women's relationship to Orientalism."[11] White women now played the roles of "consumers, producers, practitioners, critics, and experts."[12] As producers of Orientalism, white women, alongside white men, would have perhaps viewed the women in this image as possessing some level of authenticity, for it was thought that "as gender became an increasingly effective tool with which to understand, negotiate, and represent the complex and intensifying U.S.-Asian relations, white women with material or discursive access to Asia came to play the role of expert authorities in American Orientalism."[13] The Asian personas of these women also read as an attempt to comment on their roles as females in the mostly male dominated form of the medicine show. As Yoshihara asserts, "white women often used Orientalism not only to make their intervention in American ideas about Asia per se but also to assert, address, and/or challenge women's roles in American society."[14] Until the beginnings of WWII and the subsequent changes in U.S.-Asian relations, such images in combination with some female Medicine Show performers who performed Asian characters were able to use these personas to both sell product and assert their presence in the business in print and on stage.

The slipperiness of souvenirs as evidence results from the variety of subject positions contained within the item itself, as illustrated in the example of the dentaroma trade card. Within the one card we must account both for the manufacturer, the off-site corporation that bottled the salve or boxed the powder and produced the card, the performer or pitchman, the physical supplier of the card to the individual, and the audience, the receiver of the card who then decides the future life of the object. This three tiered system complicates the making of meaning for the artifact as each of the three steps offers a plethora of potential meanings that are hard to quantify, most especially that of the individual who comes into possession of the card itself. While we have evidence of how some audience members chose to store, preserve, and display their cards, we have very little way of knowing the actual scope of these trade cards. For every audience member who took great care to collect the advertising cards, many perhaps discarded them immediately or never accepted them in the first place. Furthermore, for those who did collect them that relationship between the individual and the souvenir also proves most complicated. Even though the souvenir stands in as a permanent reminder of an ephemeral experience, the specifics of that meaning are located within the individual's own experience which depends upon many factors, including background, socio-economic status, and geographical region, to name a few. For a performance form like the Medicine Show, where a great deal of information exists on the performance techniques, stage configurations, and content of both pitches and skits, the medicine show trade cards throw a huge wrench into what it is we think we know. They insist upon the inclusion of the audience in any consideration of the form.

This particular trade card contains a bevy of possible interpretations and its function as a souvenir thrust into the hands of many willing (and perhaps unwilling) spectators allows for a multitude of simultaneous meanings. These three white women smiling out at the viewer simultaneously might welcome, beckon, entice, confuse, anger, or even frighten depending upon the circumstance. The act of commodification exists both within the manufacturing and distribution of these cards as well as in the content of the card itself, which in essence is an advertisement wherein white women become commodified objects to sell toothpaste. But the freedom of the holder to determine the meaning of a souvenir forces an even broader understanding of this card. Some viewers may admire the beauty of the image with its striking colors and delicate fans. Others might respond to the direct nature of the women's gazes and feel connected to the image by the way it draws them in. Still others might delight in the allusions to the Gilbert and Sullivan operetta *The Mikado* and might use the trade card as a way of remembering that performance in addition to or even instead of the Medicine Show.

As a historian encountering these magnificent artifacts, I must learn not only to live with the ambiguities, but to revel in them and to embrace the performative nature of the artifact itself. For unlike a memoir or letter that remains disconnected from the actual moment of performance, these cards were in essence commercial props created by the company to advertise a product or lifestyle, distributed by the performers, and activated by the audience. Their presence in the archive forces a wrestling with embodied performance history and challenges notions of audience reception.

ENDNOTES

[1] Although Brooks McNamara locates the medicine show card as part of the William Helfand Collection at the New York Academy of Medicine Library in his book *Step Right Up*, recent inquires show that the card has in fact been relocated to the University of Rochester's archival collection.

[2] Brooks McNamara, *Step Right Up*. Rev. ed. (Jackson: UP Mississippi, 1995), 127.

[3] Brooks McNamara, *Step Right Up*. Rev. ed., 127.

[4] Brooks McNamara, *Step Right Up*. Rev. ed., 127.

[5] Brooks McNamara, *Step Right Up*. Rev. ed., 127–128.

[6] Brooks McNamara, *Step Right Up*. Rev. ed., 128.

[7] Brooks McNamara, *Step Right Up*. (Jackson: UP Mississippi, 1976), 106a.

[8] Brooks McNamara, *Step Right Up*, 137.

[9] Brooks McNamara, *Step Right Up*, 137.

[10] Susan Stewart, *On Longing: Narratives of the Miniature, the Gigantic, the Souvenir, the Collection* (Durham: Duke UP, 1993), 135.

[11] Mari Yoshihara, *Embracing the East: White Women and American Orientalism* (Oxford: Oxford UP, 2003), 7.

[12] Yoshihara, *Embracing the East*, 7.

[13] Yoshihara, *Embracing the East*, 8.

[14] Yoshihara, *Embracing the East*, 8.

The Silent Laugh of *Laughing Ben*

AMMA Y. GHARTEY-TAGOE KOOTIN

Introduction

In the Library of Congress, there exists the only known film footage of a performance featuring the most famous character of the 1901 Pan-American Exposition.[1] For the 8 million people who flocked to the Buffalo, NY world's fair that year, Ben Ellington's "chief claim to fame was that he could laugh . . . better than anyone."[2] The title bears his stage name, *Laughing Ben*, and features him guffawing for the camera.[3] Yet, the format of this archival document contradicts the very performance it should have preserved. It is a silent film that failed to fully capture the most celebrated feature of a man hailed as "the greatest laughing genius known to the country."[4] The document cannot provide answers to some of the most basic questions surrounding Ben's performance: What did his laugh sound like? Was it high pitched or deep and booming? Were there breaths for air? How infectious was it? How annoying could it become? Did it sound fabricated or genuine?

Sound, however, is but one aspect of a laugh. What of the reasons behind the laugh? If a laugh is defined as "an audible expression to an emotion,"[5] what was the emotion Ben felt that provoked and sustained his act? Is sound even necessary to experience the laugh of Laughing Ben? The film, serving as the most experiential piece of evidence of Laughing Ben's popular act, demonstrates the paradox not just of silent laughter, but of the incomprehensibility of Ben's performance. Laughing Ben reportedly was a 96–year-old, former black slave who made his money not only laughing for "never [-] less than 30 seconds" but also by telling stories of his life as a slave.[6] 'I had a good time when I was good,' one newspaper transcribed his monologue, 'and a bad time when I was bad.'[7]

Elsewhere, I have explored the meaning of Laughing Ben's performance in the context of the times in which he lived and used ideas such as trauma theory to understand why a former slave would create a laughing act around his slave past.[8] This article will explore my experiences with a document that perpetually unsettles any conclusions I attempt to make. The tyranny of *Laughing Ben* is in its unique format, what it failed to capture, and the challenges for the historian who must work within and beyond the silences of the historical record.

Tracing a Laughing Career

The genesis of Laughing Ben's career is still a mystery. After being freed, Ben Ellington remained near his old plantation in a town called Dublin, Georgia.[9] Though employed as a mail carrier in 1900, it is possible that Ben became Laughing Ben out of financial necessity.[10] Reportedly, "he was just about in debt all the time"[11] but possessed a peculiar gift of a laugh with not "much music to [it], but [which] was loud and long."[12] That being the case, Ben at some point in time decided to "never ceas[e] to laugh long enough to make a support".[13] He quickly gained "local fame as a laugher," but it was at the 1901 Pan-American Exposition where Laughing Ben would claim "national notice".[14]

Managed by Hardy Smith, Jr., Ben made his way to the Buffalo world's fair to be a part of a concession called the Old Plantation.[15] The recreated antebellum southern plantation, featuring a large mansion and a working cotton field, aimed to "amuse and instruct" the fairgoer in what slave life was like in the "old plantation befo' de wah."[16] Out of the 150 southern blacks who lived in "real" slave log cabins, picking cotton while singing work songs, and performing "camp style" meetings and minstrel shows for the visitor, northern audiences distinguished Ben as the star of Old Plantation almost immediately.[17] "He has a laugh that will coin him money on the Midway," a Buffalo newspaper reported upon his arrival. "All he will have to do is to stand out on the pavement in front of the Old Plantation and roar. The crowd will do the rest."[18] What the crowd did was to pay Ben five cents to laugh on cue. Likening his laughter to a "hysterical donkey," one newspaper said audiences paid Ben another five cents just to stop his "perpetual brays".[19] A genius, a nuisance or an entertaining spectacle, Laughing Ben's manager wrote home to report that he was "the feature of the exposition—'the whole thing'—and that the northern visitors [were] completely carried away with the old man."[20]

Vivid descriptions of Ben's act at the 1901 world's fair confirm that northern audiences found him to be an entertaining and intriguing phenomenon. The sound of his laugh played a key role in that success, but there was also something about the spectacle of Ben laughing that audiences found just as engaging. A reporter who encountered Ben upon his arrival set forth the following:

> Uncle Ben is a little weazened fellow. He isn't over five feet two and weighs less than 100 pounds. He has gray wool on the back of his head and a good deal of the same article is scattered over his face. He always laughs after he makes a remark, and, as his laughs are longer than his remarks, he laughs more than he talks. As soon as he says anything his mouth will open wide enough for the admission of a large orange and then a succession of hearty laughs rends the adjacent air. He never laughs for less than 30 seconds and frequently his manufactured peals last more than a minute. Three lone teeth in his upper jaw and six in his lower one add to the ludicrous expression of his face when his mouth is expanded.[21]

Such a physical description of Ben—the gray wool scattered over his face, the hanging teeth and the mouth that gapes wide enough for "the admission of a large orange"—confirms that seeing Laughing Ben was as important as hearing him. Perhaps this is what Arthur Marvin, a cinematographer from the American Mutoscope & Biograph Company, thought when he filmed Laughing Ben as part of several short clips he made of the world's fair. This is the film that resides in the Library of Congress today.

Finding *Laughing Ben*

In 2004, I had almost given up on finding anything beyond audience descriptions in newspapers of Laughing Ben's performances. As part of a larger project on black performers in the 1901 fair, I had been searching for two years and but for a few newspaper articles and a handful of photographs, I had scant information on Laughing Ben. Just when I thought I couldn't search anymore, a fortuitous viewing of Spike Lee's 2000 film *Bamboozled* led me straight to Ben's performance. In this satirical film about a modern-day televised minstrel show, Lee features a powerful historical montage of demeaning portrayals of African Americans captured in film and cartoons. In a sea of countless footage, Ben's gaping, laughing mouth flickered for about two seconds. I was astounded! I had seen Lee's film at least twice before. *How could I have missed this?* I rewound the DVD, paused it to go look for photographs I had of Ben, and confirmed that the elderly man on the screen was the same man in my hands. I re-watched in captivated shock as the static image I had known for years was now animated and most of all, proof that Ben's performance had been archived somewhere.

The film's credits however did not immediately reveal the location. It would take me almost another year and a random Google search to yield a listing on the Internet Movie Database website for footage of "Laughing Ben" (which was not there a year before). It was then that I discovered that this footage had been housed in the Library of Congress. On a February morning in 2005, I called and spoke to a reference librarian in the Motion Picture & Television Reading Room who confirmed that *Laughing Ben* was a paper print, a document in which Marvin's film had been duplicated frame-by-frame onto a special kind of photographic paper.[22] Intended to be an initial form of copyright and having outlasted the original nitrate footage, paper prints are literal strips of rolled paper, which means that had not these paper prints been re-discovered and converted to 16mm film in the 1950's, Ben's performance would have literally been archived as a strip of paper.[23] Sidestepping that deeper level of tyranny, however, I was granted permission to view the 16mm reference film. Three days later, I journeyed to Washington, D.C. to watch Laughing Ben's performance for myself.

Confronting Laughing Ben

I knew that it was a silent film, but my excitement to finally see this footage eclipsed that obvious detail. It didn't occur to me that I wouldn't be able to fully experience the very thing that defined Laughing Ben, until I was led into the darkened viewing room and sat before a machine reminiscent of a manual microfilm reader, with a hand crank to boot. Having to work with the 16mm reference film provided me an experience of Ben's performance

Figure 1. Still shots captured by the author from the film *Laughing Ben* (1901). Reproduced courtesy of the Library of Congress.

that made it a much more profound case study than I had anticipated. With the film carefully threaded, I gingerly turned the hand crank until the first frame of Ben appeared.

The spectacle of Laughing Ben eclipses the absence of sound. In a collared, light-colored shirt and dark-colored vest, he stands with mouth wide-open facing the camera in broad daylight. The camera frames his head and shoulders aptly fulfilling the library guide's description of the film: "The photographer placed his camera so close to the subject that only his head is visible. The subject is a toothless, white-haired black man who is laughing heartily. He continues laughing for the full length of the film."[24] Moreover, the film confirms what the newspapers had described. The same newspapers I wanted to write off as exaggerated, racist perceptions of Ben's performance had found words to illustrate what I was seeing.

It is an eerie and almost grotesque scene to watch (Figure 1, Still 1).[25] Three teeth from Ben's bottom gums and three more from the top protrude into part of the blackness of his mouth, while his tongue is just as visible in the background. His snow-white hair is even scragglier than the newspaper articles describe and covers his entire head and much of his face. With his head cocked to his right, his nostrils are aimed directly at the camera making them appear large and revealing short, spiky hairs. His eyes are shut with his brow furrowed in a state seemingly bordering between merriment and anger. Veins pop out on either side of his forehead, while his mouth remains open. His body is still and his head slightly bobs (Figure 1, Still 2). His head begins to turn left and right while his mouth remains hung open. He closes his mouth after some time, as if taking in some air or smacking back saliva (Figure 1, Still 3 and Still 4). Just as quickly as he has closed his mouth, it opens again in an even larger burst of laughter punctuated by a gust of air from his gut (Figure 1, Still 5 and Still 6). His torso bends backward and to the right, tugging the collar of his shirt. His head cocks even more to his right (Figure 1, Still 7). His eyes shut even tighter. The explosive force of the laugh tilts him forward before bending his torso back again (Figure 1, Still 8). The scene ends with a semi-smile on his face, a nodding of his head, and a slight opening of his eyes to the camera lens (Figure 1, Still 9, Still 10, Still 11 and Still 12). After finishing his performance in a 1901 newspaper article, Ben reportedly said "I usually gets a dime, gem'n, when I laughs like dat."[26]

Seeing Laughing Ben in this manner struck me more than I anticipated. It confirmed the basic descriptions I'd read in newspaper accounts, but this viewing left me with so many more questions than answers as I began to watch it again frame by frame. There are distinct moments in which Ben opens his eyes and peers back into the camera (Figure 1, Still 4, Still 12). If one were to watch the converted DVD version of the film, these moments would last for fractions of seconds. However, in the frame-by-frame viewing, these instances become obvious if not deliberate breaks, thus foregrounding the multiple stagings and audiences of Ben's performance: his act for general white audiences vs. his act for the cinematographer vs. his act for the future viewer of the film. Is Ben looking back at Arthur Marvin to see if he has obtained the approval of his onlooker? Did he do this in all of his acts? Or, is he looking back at the viewer as if to say "I know something you don't know"?

Furthermore, the absence of sound heightened the oddity of watching someone laugh and not knowing what they are laughing about. Did something cause Ben to break from his sustained laugh level into the laugh that literally bent him over backwards (Figure 1, Still 8)? Or, did he manufacture it? Was it all part of the act? Other explosive moments of laughter from Ben's monologues are recounted in the newspaper articles, when "Uncle Ben then doubled up like a jackknife and laughed a full minute," after saying he had a good time when he was a good slave, and bad time when he was bad.[27] Such monologues suggest that Ben laughed at, about, or because of his slave experience. Which one was it? The film further complicates all of this when we see Ben laughing and looking back at the viewer. For whom was he laughing? For himself? For the audience? Most importantly, why?

Perhaps it was the physical feat of laughing which audiences appreciated about Laughing Ben. Indeed after the Buffalo world's fair, Ben continued to entertain audiences in carnivals near the Georgia coast, Coney Island, and San Francisco before ending up at the 1904 St. Louis world's fair.[28] When he died a year later, his obituary revered him as "the only one in his class."[29]

Recapturing Laughing Ben's Laugh

Silence notwithstanding, the film document compels me to work with the most active feature on screen: the physicality of laughter. A laugh requires the body—a torso to contain it, breath to yield its creation, vocal cords to produce its pitch, facial muscles to expand it, and a mouth to allow for its exit. Depending on the intensity, the arms and legs may get in on the action, the tear ducts may produce water, and in extreme cases, the whole body may crumple forward, collapse in rolls, or lean back in abandon. If we cannot hear Ben's laugh or know what reasons he had for laughing, can we in some way experience what it took for him to laugh, continuously everyday for audiences? Is there something to be learned about performing a laughing act?

Laugh for a minute.

I entreat the reader to try laughing for a minute. Re-enactments are one way in which I have attempted to recapture some aspect of the performance of Ben's laugh. Working with performing artists, I have discovered that it is no small feat to laugh on cue, loudly, for an extended length of time, or for an audience. For 96–year-old lungs to produce such a laugh is astonishing. Most of all, the exercise of laughing confirms that although it is difficult to laugh, the laugh can take on a life of its own. When one reaches that point, the laugh is self-perpetuating and the laugher may find a certain ease and an enjoyment in that state. Laugh too long, however, and it can become painful to the body. This experience of glee, escape, release, and pain may apply to Ben's act. While I may never know Ben's laugh or his reasons for laughing, these experiential exercises have provided a better grasp of what it took for him to perform his act.[30] These exercises confirm that for an individual to be marked as "the greatest laughing genius known to the country," means that his performance must have truly been extraordinary.[31]

Conclusions

The film *Laughing Ben*, being the only film footage of Ben Ellington in action, should offer us the opportunity to understand why this was the case. Instead, I encountered three levels of "tyranny" when working with this document. First, there is the inescapable and puzzling fact that this is a silent film about an auditory experience. Though one can see the physicality of his act, this glaring omission limits the impact of the performance. Even if there had been sound, however, the film still may not have been able to contain the complexity of Ben's laugh (i.e. its production, its history, nor the power it held over its audiences.) Second, it is difficult for me to understand a performance centered on a former slave laughing about a life spent in bondage. Even after countless viewings for the past five years, the film does not help me to understand why this aspect was either ignored or made light of by audiences and, more importantly, whether Ben himself truly made light of the situation. That latter point brings me to the third level: the moments in the film when Ben appears to look into the camera. Part of the tyranny of this document is the need to generate significance out of such moments. Those quick flashes of expression forever leave me with unanswered questions about his motivations and at whom or what he was truly laughing. The silent laugh of *Laughing Ben* perpetually haunts the archive, as if Ben is still laughing, perhaps at the researcher.

ARCHIVAL INSTITUTIONS

Buffalo & Erie County Public Library—Special Collections and Rare Books (B&ECPL), Buffalo, New York Newspaper clippings, Pan American Scrapbooks, vols. 1–24

Library Of Congress (LOC), Washington, DC Paper Print Collection, Motion Picture, Broadcasting, and Recorded Sound Division

Oconee Regional Library (ORL), Dublin, Georgia

ENDNOTES

[1] "Old Uncle Ben," *Commercial Advertiser* (Buffalo), July 27, 1901, clipping, Buffalo & Erie County Public Library, "Pan-American Exposition, Buffalo, New York, Newspaper Clipping Scrapbook," microfilm, (cited hereafter as B&ECPL PAX Scrapbook), vol. 15.

[2] "Pan-Am Trivia" in *A Guide to the Pan-Am Grounds* [Pamphlet] (n.p.: Buffalo and Erie County Historical Society, n.d.); "Death Gets the Laugh on a Famous Laugher," *Atlanta Constitution (1881–2001)*, April 30, 1905, http://www.proquest.com/ (accessed August 22, 2005).

[3] *Laughing Ben*, produced and directed by Arthur Marvin, American Mutoscope and Biograph Co., 1903 (?), 16mm, LOC, Motion Picture, Broadcasting, and Recorded Sound Division.

[4] "Death Gets the Laugh on a Famous Laugher."

[5] Laugh, n. *Webster's Third New International Dictionary, Unabridged*. (accessed September 20, 2010).

[6] "Midway Negroes Here," *Express* (Buffalo), May 12, 1901, clipping, B&ECPL PAX Scrapbook, vol. 10. Although Ben said he was 96 years old, most newspaper articles seemed to question his claim.

[7] Ibid.

[8] Amma Ghartey-Tagoe, "Chapter Four: 'Amused Pity': Re-enacting Trauma: Old Plantation's Happy Southern Darkeys," in "The Battle Before *The Souls of Black Folk*: Black Performance in the 1901 Pan-American Exposition," (PhD diss: New York University, 2009), 168–213.

[9] Dublin is located between Macon and Savannah in the southeastern section of the state.

[10] "'Laughing Ben' Died Tuesday," *Courier-Dispatch* (Dublin, GA), May 28, 1905, pg. 6. Oconee Regional Library, Dublin, Georgia.

[11] Ibid.; "Death Gets the Laugh on a Famous Laugher."

[12] "Death Gets the Laugh on a Famous Laugher."

[13] Ibid.

[14] "'Laughing Ben' Died Tuesday."

[15] "Georgia Negro in Buffalo."

[16] *Official Catalogue and Guidebook to the Pan-American Exposition, Buffalo, N.Y., U.S.A., May 1st to Nov. 1st, 1901*, (Buffalo: Charles Ahrhart, 1901), 42. "Old Plantation Befo' De Wah," *News* (Buffalo), May 6, 1900, clipping, B&ECPL PAX Scrapbook, vol. 5.

[17] For more information on Old Plantation, see: Ghartey-Tagoe, "Chapter Four: 'Amused Pity': Re-enacting Trauma: Old Plantation's Happy Southern Darkeys."

[18] "Ibid.

[19] "Midway in Full Swing," *Express* (Buffalo), May 14(?), 1901, clipping, B&ECPL PAX Scrapbook, vol. 11.

[20] [Unknown Article title]. *Courier-Dispatch* (Dublin, GA), May 23, 1901. ORL.

[21] "Midway Negroes Here."

[22] See "Early Motion Pictures Free of Copyright Restrictions in the Library of Congress," *Motion Picture and Television Reading Room-Library of Congress*. http://www.loc.gov/rr/mopic/earlymps.html (accessed December 14, 2010). Thank you again to Library of Congress staff for the assistance: Rosemary Haynes, Josie Walters-Johnson, and Jerry Hatfield.

[23] Ibid. I am indebted to discussions with the editor of this journal, Stephen Johnson, regarding this deeper level of tyranny in *Laughing Ben*.

[24] Kemp Pr. Niver, *The Early Motion Pictures: The Paper Print Collection in the Library of Congress*, ed. By Bebe Bergsten with an introduction by Erik Barnouw. (Washington, D.C.: Library of Congress, 1985), 179.

[25] The following description is a revision from: Ghartey-Tagoe, "Chapter Four: 'Amused Pity': Re-enacting Trauma: Old Plantation's Happy Southern Darkeys."

[26] "Midway Negroes Here."

[27] Ibid.

[28] "Death Gets the Laugh on a Famous Laugher."

[29] Ibid.

[30] Finding period surrogates may also be helpful as Laura Wexler has done in equating Laughing Ben's performance with that of the "Laughing Song," a musical recording by another African American who sings and laughs melodically in the choruses. See: Laura Wexler, "'Laughing Ben' on the 'Old Plantation'," *English Language Notes*, 44.2 Fall/Winter 2006: 181–187.

[31] "Death Gets the Laugh on a Famous Laugher."

Special Acknowledgements: Abenaa F. Ghartey-Tagoe, Esi B. Ghartey-Tagoe, and Stephen Johnson

With Houdini in the Margins of Theatre History: On the Trail of the Mysterious Browning

MATTHEW SOLOMON

> Browning. We do not know the present address of "Milwaukee Rapp." If you mean Augustavus Rapp, his permanent address is Hesperia, Mich.

The author of these two sentences, which were published in the November 15, 1906, issue of the *Conjurers' Monthly Magazine* as part of an unsigned column simply titled, "Answers to Various Questions," is easy enough to determine. They were doubtless written by the magazine's publisher, Harry Houdini, who ran the magic monthly out of the Harlem brownstone where he lived after returning to the United States following a successful tour of European theatres. It is also fairly straightforward to ascertain who is mentioned in Houdini's reply: magician Augustus Rapp, the turn-of-the-century "small town showman" who made his home in Michigan and Wisconsin at various points, and left behind a colorful memoir in which he mentions his long friendship with Houdini; "My old friend Harry Houdini," Rapp recalls, "referred to me as Augustavious."[1] But, who is the "Browning" to whom the reply is addressed? Could Houdini's response have been written to Tod Browning? After all, Tod Browning had been a sometime magician's assistant before becoming an accomplished Hollywood director who made several films set in the world of stage magic during the 1920s.[2] Houdini was in Hollywood as an actor between 1919 and 1920 fulfilling a contract with Famous Players-Lasky at the very time when Browning's career as a filmmaker was gaining momentum at Universal.

Tod Browning was one of a number of magicians involved in various areas of filmmaking during the silent period, and I wondered if my discovery of this quotation revealed the then-unknown Browning's correspondence with the most famous magician of the early twentieth century. For a film historian interested in documenting the magic careers of as many filmmakers as I could find, this small item seemed like an intriguing lead. Browning's biographers conclude that in 1907, he lived in Louisville and may have gone on the road as a "vaudevillian and blackface comedian."[3] Might he also have done some work in magic theatre? Was this the same Browning who wrote to Houdini through the pages of the *Conjurers' Monthly Magazine*?

Could I make this connection? Could I prove an affiliation between the two, even if it only amounted to this one single fragment of correspondence? Where would I look for evidence, and how reliable would it be? If I did locate such evidence, or demonstrate a biographical connection between Houdini and Browning, would it prove significant? And, perhaps most pertinent of all, why was I so interested in proving this connection? Here, I revisit the line of research that brought me to this small item in the *Conjurers' Monthly Magazine* in order to reflect upon these and other historiographic questions. Convinced that crucial evidence can sometimes be found in the most obscure recesses of the archive, I consider some of the methods I struggled with in researching and writing about magic history—methods that can and have been brought to bear, for better or for worse, on other popular forms.

Houdini was not only a world-renowned magician, but also a prolific writer who left an indelible mark on the periodical literature of the early twentieth century through scores of articles published in magazines, running the gamut from *Ladies' Home Journal* to *Scientific American*, as well as countless newspapers. From the beginning of his career, Houdini was keenly aware of the power of the press, and used the print media both as a means of publicity and as a powerful mouthpiece for shaping public opinion—the latter perhaps most especially in his tireless anti-spiritualist crusade of the mid-1920s. Houdini enjoyed being authoritative in print and he used the *Conjurers' Monthly Magazine* to make his first forays into writing magic history—it was here that Houdini's attacks on his namesake Robert-Houdin were originally printed[4]—as well as to chronicle events in the contemporary world of show business, to correct the perceived errors of others, to belittle his rivals, and to publicize himself. The magazine was sold by yearly subscription, but single issues could be purchased from magic shops and at Houdini's performances. He boasted that the *Conjurers' Monthly Magazine* was "THE biggest circulated conjurors' paper in the world," with "more paid for subscribers and readers than all the other Magician's periodicals of the world combined!"[5]

In addition to writing many items and articles for different magic magazines (including his own, which ceased publication after only two years in the summer of 1908), Houdini was also a frequent contributor to entertainment industry newspapers. Although many of his contributions are characteristically self-promotional and/or self-congratulatory—and thus of putative research value mainly to the would-be biographer—Houdini was also an inveterate chronicler of contemporaneous show business whose extensive, if sometimes idiosyncratic, comments about his fellow entertainers and their acts provide fascinating glimpses into otherwise unknown corners of entertainment history. For example, Houdini's "irregular contributions" to the *New York Dramatic Mirror* just after the turn of the twentieth century, as a biography of fellow vaudevillian W. C. Fields notes, are "pithy, humorous and very informative."[6] In Houdini's dispatches, one finds discussion of the protective associations French and German vaudeville artists formed along the lines of the White Rats of America;[7] tidbits on European "freak" exhibition;[8] and countless commentaries on the individual magicians and other variety performers who were then plying their trades in continental circuses and music halls.

Beside this public correspondence, Houdini also carried on an extensive private correspondence that included such twentieth-century luminaries as Theodore Roosevelt, Sir Arthur Conan Doyle, and Upton Sinclair (to name but a few notables). It is in these letters, composed largely without recourse to secretaries, ghost-writers, or editors, that one can read—through all the misspellings and poor grammar—Houdini's most direct voice as a writer, not to mention his un-redacted opinions about people and issues that concerned him. Much of Houdini's correspondence survives, but it is scattered between private collections and public archives and only selectively accessible to the researcher.[9]

A sort of blogger *avant la lettre*, the better part of Houdini's published output consists of very specialized and highly topical short pieces (in most cases, one hesitates to term them articles)—like his contributions to the *New York Dramatic Mirror* and the *Conjurers' Monthly Magazine* (and later to *Variety*, *M-U-M*, and other show business periodicals and magic magazines)—which were written on a week-to-week or a month-to-month basis. Houdini generated innumerable handwritten and typed written fragments, which were only transformed into publishable manuscripts through considerable work of assembly and editing.[10] A voracious collector throughout his entire adult life, Houdini's preferred form was the scrapbook, and thus the books attributed to him as an author are chockablock with long quotations from, and reproductions of, rare documents in his personal collection.[11] Through newspaper clipping services and private secretaries, Houdini compiled more than one hundred scrapbooks concerned less with his own exploits than with documenting aspects of the entertainment landscape that are well beyond the ken of most traditional theatre histories. The idiosyncratic contents of these scrapbooks, which are only loosely organized by theme, comprise an invaluable resource for the historian of late-nineteenth- and early-twentieth-century popular entertainment.[12] Such written fragments, like the reply with which I began, convey the texture of popular entertainment in a vivid way while mapping constellations of entertainers who worked, associated, and corresponded with one another.

Although stage magic falls within the history of theatre, most histories of magic—up until recently—have been written not by theatre historians but rather by amateur or professional magicians interested in documenting past masters of their specialized art.[13] In addition to magicians' memoirs and surviving documents of magic performance, the magicians' journals that began publication at the turn-of-the-century as magic began to professionalize are an essential resource for historians of twentieth-century magic.[14] The *Conjurers' Monthly Magazine* was one of these journals, coming slightly after *Mahatma* and *The Sphinx* among magic magazines published in the United States. These journals are not without interest for researchers in adjacent fields, for here one finds sustained attention not only to performances of professional magicians, but also a dense record of their activities, controversies, and writings. As chronicles of the cultural milieu of magic, magic journals point to the historical relationships between stage magic and other forms of cultural practice—a topic that has already proven to be of interest to art historians as well as cultural historians.[15] Issues of both *Mahatma* (1895–1904) and the *Conjurers' Monthly Magazine* (1906–1908) are reproduced in the microfilm compilation *American Theatre Periodicals of the Nineteenth and Early Twentieth Centuries*.[16]

In his pioneering monograph on magicians and the early cinema, *The Magician and the Cinema*, media historian Erik Barnouw makes good use of the evidence of magic history, noting in the preface, "Much of it derives from the literature of magic, a source most film historians have neglected," and elsewhere adding, "Much of the story has lain buried in the annals of magic."[17] Part of the "annals of magic" to which Barnouw alludes here are magic journals. Indeed, several pages from the magic journals *Mahatma* and *The Magician* are reproduced as illustrations in Barnouw's book and the bibliography also includes several more—though the *Conjurers' Monthly Magazine* is never referenced.[18] As a Dutch immigrant to New York during the 1920s, the young Barnouw had found work helping catalog the library of the magician and magic collector John Mulholland (who would later serve as the editor of the magic journal *The Sphinx*, the official organ of the Society of American Magicians, for some 23 years). In his memoirs, Barnouw writes, "Half a century later, when I . . . ran into John Mulholland . . . I mentioned that in exploring early film history I had often run across names I had first met in his collection. It had me wonder whether magicians had played a larger role in the genesis of the motion picture than had generally been realized."[19] Barnouw confirmed this hunch during the 1970s while heading the Motion Picture, Broadcasting and Recorded Sound division at the Library of Congress, where he made extensive use of the Houdini Collection, which includes runs of a number of early-twentieth-century magic magazines (including, of course, Houdini's own *Conjurers' Monthly Magazine*)—research that resulted in the book *The Magician and the Cinema*.

I became curious about what else might be buried in the annals of magic as I was researching my dissertation.[20] I was surprised to come across the name Browning while scrutinizing issues of the *Conjurers' Monthly Magazine* on microfilm. I was, however, not surprised to find a potentially valuable piece of information among letters to the editor. In his book *Silent Cinema: An Introduction*, an indispensable resource for the study of silent film, Paolo Cherchi Usai writes, "Historical documents on silent cinema should be consulted analytically rather than selectively."[21] For Cherchi Usai, this is one of ten "rules" for the researcher (rule #4, as it were). He explains:

> In other words, if we are searching through a silent film periodical to find information about our subject, we should (ideally) go through the whole thing. It seems madness, but we must accept the idea that a piece of essential information could be in a tiny recess of the most insignificant article. Many years ago, American specialists used to ask Italian film historian, Davide Turconi, where he found the cast and credits of films about which little or nothing is known in the United States. Turconi candidly replied that the columns of answers to readers' questions in American magazines include fragments of evidence which are virtu-

> ally impossible to find elsewhere, and that the names of performers are among them.[22]

The professional marginalia contained in trade journals can be revealing, but the method needed to locate potentially useful pieces of information within them typically involves a great deal of tedium, especially when one is reading text from the screen of a microfilm reader or computer monitor rather than from the pages of a hard copy of the journal itself. Even for those few specialized journals from the period that have been fully digitized—and for this period of theatre and film history, the number remains truly few, at least at this time, although this may one day change[23]—and processed with character-recognition software, a page-by-page examination is often the most fruitful approach since one does not always know exactly know what key words will yield answers to a research question.

Apart from inherent thoroughness, the "analytical" approach to historical journals has other benefits. As Cherchi Usai explains, "Working with old magazines is never as simple as consulting a book neatly divided into chapters and with an index, or even as consulting a modern specialised journal. Leafing through an old periodical is both a pleasure and an adventure for the eyes: it is like travelling in a time machine, and reliving—with no filters of any kind—the enthusiasms and tensions of a project in process. But it is an adventure that requires patience, precision and a certain amount of unrelenting stubbornness."[24] This is more or less the way I found a trace of a letter from Browning to Houdini—and with it, a possible link between Houdini and *Tod* Browning.

Tod Browning's biographers suggest that he may have worked as an assistant to the magician Leon Herrmann in 1905.[25] At this time, Herrmann's act was a large one that involved a total of fifteen people and some thirty-two trunks traveling with the show.[26] While appearing on the Orpheum circuit in 1905, Herrmann featured four large stage illusions and required the assistance of six different onstage assistants.[27] Late in his life, Browning told William S. Hart, Jr., that he worked with Herrmann, but did not specify what role or roles he played in the Herrmann show.[28] The physical skills Browning later showcased as a slapstick comedian in burlesque, vaudeville, and a series of films for the Komic Company would have served him well onstage as a magician's assistant, perhaps one who used comedy to both entertain and misdirect the audience.[29] I also came across the name Browning (again without mention of a given name) while examining vaudeville manager's reports from the Keith/Albee circuit. On May 11, 1903, for example, a Mr. and Mrs. Browning performed late on the bill in New York in a "rather coarse turn" in which, "The man is made up as a genteel tramp and the woman acts as a feeder."[30] Two years later, on May 29, 1905, a Browning is reported as the male member of a comedy trio performing early on the bill in Boston (a few acts before, I was careful to note, the magician Lafayette): "Two women and a man, in a supposed comedy sketch with singing and dancing specialties."[31] Could one—or both—of these Brownings be Tod Browning? How many different Brownings were working in show business at this time? Were any of them the Browning who would later work as a film actor and director? As Browning's biographers point out, "most of the 'record' of Tod Browning's early career cannot be confirmed by documentary evidence, and is likely an uneasy amalgam of truth, half-truth, embellishment, and, in some cases, outright fabrication."[32] Perhaps more importantly, how important is it to establish such facts? Why the urge to put these two individuals on opposite ends of a letter?

I leave my earlier questions about the identity of these Brownings (whether single or multiple) to subsequent researchers should they be of interest to any one other than me. But, the latter questions raise larger issues that perhaps have methodological consequence beyond this specific set of examples, especially for those of us whose research involves—to some extent—documenting the historical milieus in which performers, filmmakers, and other kinds of artists worked and interacted. Although in many cases we may never know just who met and corresponded with whom in such milieus, particular connections such as these are far less important for the historian than the biographer. Indeed, for the historian, the characteristics of the milieu, its relation to other social-cultural formations, and the ways it changed over time, are more significant than its exact composition at any specific point in time. In other words, whether or not *Tod* Browning ever wrote a letter to Houdini, both of these individuals worked in the realm of early-twentieth century magic, experiences that appear to have had profound effects on their subsequent work. Thus, for the historian, this fragment of possible correspondence between Houdini and Browning is ultimately less important than the surrounding pages of the *Conjurers' Monthly Magazine* in which it is embedded. By consulting this journal, along with others like it, analytically (as Cherchi Usai puts it)—or exhaustively, as I would have it—rather than selectively (as is typical with full-text digitized resources), one gains access to an indispensible record of the historical milieu under investigation, complete with its particular alignments, biases, controversies, details, and, yes, mysteries—some of which we may never solve nor indeed need to in order to nevertheless make productive use of these periodicals.

ENDNOTES

Thank you to Stephen Johnson for his helpful comments and suggestions on this essay.

1 Augustus Rapp, *The Life and Times of Augustus Rapp: The Small Town Showman* (1959; Glenwood, Ill.: David Meyer Magic Books, 1991), 166.

2 See my "Staging Deception: Theatrical Illusionism in Browning's Films of the 1920s," in *The Films of Tod Browning*, ed. Bernd Herzogenrath (London: Black Dog Publishing, 2006), 49–67. See also my "Reframing a Biographical Legend: Style, European Filmmakers, and the Sideshow Cinema of Tod Browning," in *Authorship and Film*, ed. David A. Gerstner and Janet Staiger (New York: Routledge, 2003), 235–246.

3 David J. Skal and Elias Savada, *Dark Carnival: The Secret World of Tod Browning, Hollywood's Master of the Macabre* (New York: Anchor Books, 1995), 31.

4 See my *Disappearing Tricks: Silent Film, Houdini, and the New Magic of the Twentieth Century* (Urbana: University of Illinois Press, 2010), 54.

5 The Editor, "Editorial," *Conjurers' Monthly Magazine* 1, no. 2 (October 15, 1906): 36; "Editorial," *Conjurers' Monthly Magazine* 1, no. 3 (November 15, 1906): 68.

[6] Simon Louvish, *Man on the Flying Trapeze: The Life and Times of W. C. Fields* (New York: W. W. Norton and Co., 1999), 96.

[7] "Vaudeville in Germany," *New York Dramatic Mirror*, June 22, 1901, 16; "Vaudeville in Germany," *New York Dramatic Mirror*, July 27, 1901, 18; "Vaudeville on the Continent," *New York Dramatic Mirror*, September 21, 1901, 18; "Houdini's Entertaining Chat," *New York Dramatic Mirror*, November 8, 1902, 18. On the White Rats, see George Fuller Golden, *My Lady Vaudeville and Her White Rats* (New York: Broadway Publishing, 1909).

[8] "Harry Houdini in Bavaria," *New York Dramatic Mirror*, October 25, 1902, 20; "Houdini's Entertaining Chat," *New York Dramatic Mirror*, November 8, 1902, 18; "Houdini's Interesting Letters," *New York Dramatic Mirror*, April 11, 1903): 22. On the comparatively well-documented history of American "freak shows," see Robert Bogdan, *Freak Show: Presenting Human Oddities for Amusement and Profit* (Chicago: University of Chicago Press, 1988).

[9] Only Houdini's correspondence with Conan Doyle has been partially published, in Bernard M. L. Ernst and Hereward Carrington, *Houdini and Conan Doyle: The Story of a Strange Friendship* (New York: Albert and Charles Boni, 1933).

[10] Kenneth Silverman, *Houdini!!! The Career of Ehrich Weiss* (New York: Harper Collins, 1996), 228. See also Harry Houdini, *A Magician among the Spirits: The Original Manuscript*, ed. Maurine Christopher (Washington: Kaufman and Greenberg, 1996). Some of these fragments have been preserved in the Houdini collections at the Library of Congress and the Harry Ransom Humanities Research Center.

[11] Solomon, *Disappearing Tricks*, 120.

[12] *Harry Houdini Scrapbooks* (1858–1926), 110 vols., microfilm, 21 reels, Library of Congress, Washington.

[13] See, for example, Milbourne Christopher, *The Illustrated History of Magic* (New York: Thomas Y. Crowell, 1973) and James Randi, *Conjuring: Being a Definitive History of the Venerable Arts of Sorcery, Prestidigitation, Wizardry, Deception, & Chicanery and of the Mountebanks & Scoundrels Who Have Perpetrated these Subterfuges on a Bewildered Public, in short, MAGIC!* (New York: St. Martin's Press, 1992).

[14] See my *Disappearing Tricks*, 137n9.

[15] See, respectively, Michael Leja, *Looking Askance: Skepticism and American Art from Eakins to Duchamp* (Berkeley: University of California Press, 2004), esp. 153–183; and James W. Cook, *The Arts of Deception: Playing with Fraud in the Age of Barnum* (Cambridge, MA: Harvard University Press, 2001), esp. 163–213.

[16] *American Theatre Periodicals of the Nineteenth and Early Twentieth Centuries* (Woodbridge, CT: Research Publications, 1989), microfilm, reels 6, 11.

[17] Erik Barnouw, *The Magician and the Cinema* (New York: Oxford University Press, 1981), 6.

[18] Barnouw, *The Magician and the Cinema*, 52, 76, 110, 111, 122.

[19] Erik Barnouw, *Media Marathon: A Twentieth-Century Memoir* (Durham, NC: Duke University Press, 1996), 9.

[20] "Stage Magic and the Silent Cinema: Méliès, Houdini, Browning" (Ph.D. dissertation, University of California, Los Angeles, 2001).

[21] Paolo Cherchi Usai, *Silent Cinema: An Introduction* (London: British Film Institute, 2000), 94. I read Cherchi Usai's rules for the silent film researcher as they appeared in the earlier, significantly different, English version of this book. Compare Cherchi Usai, *Burning Passions: An Introduction to the Study of Silent Cinema*, trans. Emma Sansone Rittle (London: British Film Institute, 1994), 36–37. Here it is rule #2. Originally published in Italian as *Una passione infiammabile: Guido allo studio del cinema muto* (Turin: UTET Libreria, 1991).

[22] Cherchi Usai, *Silent Cinema*, 94.

[23] The situation is a bit different for magic history due to the efforts of Bill Kalush, who has digitized a large number of magic periodicals and made them available online to subscribers of the "Ask Alexander" resource of the Conjuring Arts Research Center. See http://conjuringarts.org.

[24] Cherchi Usai, *Silent Cinema*, 94.

[25] Skal and Savada, *Dark Carnival*, 27–28.

[26] "Les Prestidigitateurs Célèbres: Léon Herrmann," *L'Illusionniste*, no. 16 (April 1903): 125.

[27] Letter from Leon Herrman [*sic*] to Jean Caroly, February 20, 1905, *L'Illusionniste*, no. 41 (May 1905): 46.

[28] William S. Hart, Jr., unpublished interview by Elias Savada, April 8, 1972, Elias Savada Collection. I am grateful to Elias Savada for sharing the full text of this interview with me. On Browning's relationship with the Hart family, see William S. Hart, Jr., interview by Alan Buster, August 10, 1980, Tod Browning biography file, microfiche, Margaret Herrick Library, Academy of Motion Picture Arts and Sciences, Beverly Hills, CA.

[29] On traces of slapstick in Browning's later films, see Boris Henry, "Tod Browning and the Slapstick Genre," trans. Catherine Gamonnet and Helen Bouvÿ, with Jennifer Panara, in *The Films of Tod Browning*, 41–47.

[30] S. K. Hodgdon, "New York Show, May 11th," unpublished *Managers' Report Books*, vol. 0, 263, Keith/Albee Collection, Special Collections, University of Iowa Libraries, Iowa City.

[31] F. J. O'Connor, "Boston Show, Week of May 29, 1905," unpublished *Managers' Report Books*, vol 3, 185, Keith/Albee Collection.

[32] Skal and Savada, *Dark Carnival*, 29.

Four Exhibitions and a Data Base: Reading a White Studio Photograph of Aida Overton Walker

BARBARA COHEN-STRATYNER

There is a White Studio portrait of Aida Overton Walker that inspires and aggravates me. It is, first and foremost, a photograph of an extraordinarily beautiful woman that, in *noir* tradition, haunts me. Since I use my doctoral training with Brooks McNamara now as a museum curator and exhibition developer, I express my obsession by considering the artifact in the context of as many exhibitions as possible. In the eighteen year span of this search, there have been two revolutions in the scholarly community. First, the combination of feminist and Africanist performance studies has made Walker into a recognized icon of the early 20th century. It is always good to share a crush, especially with revisionist scholars.[1] But also, technological advances have brought us the gift of on-line access to indexed periodicals, especially the African American newspapers of her time. These new sources have made me re-evaluate what I do and do not know about the artifact/text.[2]

The artifact is a photographic portrait by the White Studio of New York, showing an African American woman against a white background. The print that belongs to the Billy Rose Theatre Division, The New York Public Library for the Performing Arts, is currently faded to sepia. She seems to be sitting on a chair—a finial and ladder back can be seen by her right arm. Her torso is facing slightly to her left, while her face looks to the right. She is wearing a sequined, low-cut bodice, with one inch wide shoulder straps. There are two crystal arm bands on her left arm and a matching headband, as well as a structured necklace in a symmetrical arabesque pattern with crystals. There are chandelier earrings of white or crystal beads, which have been inked in on the print. There is black ink on the print darkening her eyebrows and eyelashes. Her dark hair is tousled. The glass negatives for this period do not exist and we have been unable to find a key sheet for the image, so we do not know whether the earrings were added, or existed but were retouched for clarity.[3]

White Studio was using a phosphorescent, flash pan lighting in the early 1900s, which reflected and enhanced metallic surfaces, so the photograph shows the bodice in exquisite detail. The surface reveals that it was a cloth

Aida Overton Walker. Photograph circa 1910 by White Studio, NY, in the Billy Rose Theatre Division, New York Public Library for the Performing Arts.

covered with a pattern of diagonal lines of sequins, with 6 repeats across her torso. One can, literally, count the sequins and determine that the pattern is: an overlapping single-sequin line, a denser 1″ area, a strip with short 3–sequin lines repeating on a shallower diagonal, and an uncovered strip.

The original inscription on the reverse of the photograph is "Aida Overton Walker/with Smart Set/ at Lyceum/ latter part of next week/Dec 18, 1910." It bears a pre-Lincoln Center Library stamp ("New York Public Library Reference Department Theatre Collection") and that of the Robinson Locke Collection, which means that it was acquired with the thousands of scrapbooks and newspaper clipping files collected by the publisher of the *Toledo Blade*. It is currently housed in the B-file for Aida Overton Walker, Billy Rose Theatre Division, The New York Public Library for the Performing Arts.

Aida Overton Walker was one of the great stars of early African American musical theater, beginning as an adolescent with Sisserietta Jones and as a Cakewalking soubrette in the Williams & Walker troupe shows. She received a dance direction credit for their *In Dahomey* (February 18, 1903), thus vying with Gertrude Hoffmann for first female choreographer on Broadway.[4] After [George] Walker's illness dissolved the troupe in 1910, she appeared in *The Red Moon*, the S. H. Dudley's Smart Set company in *His Honor the Barb*er, and her own vaudeville act, before her death in 1914.

A range of questions immediate arise. Was the portrait unique or are there other extant photographs from this session? How does this image fit in with the other Walker portraits by White, Apeda, and other studios? Why was the photograph re-touched? Why was the re-touch paint used to add eyelashes and earrings? Why was it re-touched in a way that did not in any way obscure her dark skin and features? Although the inscription on the back specifies the future Walker appearance that is being promoted, it does not clarify which production is represented by the photograph. Did the inscription mean that the promoted performances took place at the Lyceum Theater in Toledo?[5] Was S. H. Dudley's Smart Set company there in December 1910? If so, did the photograph represent Walker in that production? Did it illustrate Walker in a previous appearance in *The Red Moon* (May 1909)? Was the costume from an interim vaudeville appearance? Was it, as is usually stated, her costume as Salome, a popular specialty dance in 1908–1909 interpolated into that or other productions? My additional research interests add a level of complication to the search. Not knowing which costume Walker is wearing means that I cannot determine who designed and made it. I surmise and would like to prove that it was Pauline Reed, who is credited as designer of women's clothes for *In Dahomey*, *Bandana Land* and *The Red Moon*, which would make her one of the earliest credited woman designers on Broadway.

It is with these questions in mind that that I have returned, repeatedly, to this artifact in the course of preparing a number of exhibitions at the New York Public Library.

Jazz in New York (Summer 1993)

We developed a building-wide set of 6 exhibitions, public programs and teacher symposia on Jazz for the summer of 1993. *Jazz in New York* was in the Amsterdam Gallery. In order to reinforce my belief that the African American professional song writing community should be considered an integral part of Jazz history, the exhibit began with two photo-enlargements and a group of illustrated sheet music covers from the first decade of the century. The enlargement of the Aida Overton Walker portrait was paired with one of a White Studio performance photograph of Abbie Mitchell in *The Red Moon* (1909), one of the few shows in which these famous singers appeared together. That image, designed to imply that the African American musical theater was similar in many ways to the white shows, features a conventional stage picture with painted scenery, and Mitchell in the center of a semi-circle of male dancers, all in fashionable modern dress clothes. Although uncertain whether the Walker portrait was also from *The Red Moon*, I felt justified in displaying it since all of the possible Williams & Walker musicals and the *Smart Set* shows had songs by the featured songwriters, Bob Cole and J. Rosamond Johnson.

The Founders of Times Square (Winter 1993–4)

This exhibition in the Amsterdam Gallery was developed in conjunction with the Times Square Centennial, a season-long project of the League of American Theatres. We were given no official history or restrictions, so we posited some alternative scenarios, emphasizing the roles of women and the African American theater/popular music community over that of the theater owners. The *Red Moon* photograph and both published and recorded music represented the presence of the Williams & Walker and Bob Cole & J. Rosamond Johnson musicals on Broadway, as well as the popular songs that they wrote for interpolation into other shows.

A section of the exhibition was organized around the many rivalries and performance wars waged by the founders of Times Square. It focused on the Syndicate Wars (of theater owners and booking agents), but also included the *Merry Widow* and *Salome* "Wars," of presentations, imitations, burlesques, and plagiarisms. The Walker photograph had by this time acquired a cataloguing annotation identifying it as "Salome." Willy and Oscar Hammerstein maintained a very high-visibility feud between their Manhattan Opera House and the Metropolitan Opera House at their Paradise Garden Roof shows from 1907 to 1909.[6] Following the first salvos of Gertrude Hoffmann's imitation of Maud Allan's specialties, Walker had been one of the many scheduled theatrical and concert dancers to perform as Salome, the first African American to be so honored. She danced it to music by Joe Jordan, as well as his "That Teasin' Rag." I could not resist the opportunity to feature my favorite un-appreciated dance figures, so we inserted photo-enlargements of both Hoffmann and Walker into the exhibition.

On Stage: African American Designers (Spring 1995)

Shortly after the Times Square exhibition, we were approached by Kathy A. Perkins, a lighting designer and professor at the University of Illinois, who had created an oral history and research project on African American scenery, costume and lighting designers. We had the great pleasure of working with her over 18 months to develop her research into a major exhibition and public programming project. During this period, I focused my research on the African America dressmakers/designers who had been identified by Lois Alexander to see if they could be linked to specific shows or performers.[7] At the turn of the century, the few costume design credits appear in small print after the cast lists and musical numbers. Even when there is an extant program for a show, that section is often missing. We could, however, identify two designers for the African American musicals that reached Broadway in the first decade of the century—gowns in Williams & Walker's *In Dahomey* (1903), *Abyssinia* (1906), and *Bandana Land* (1908), and Cole & Johnson's *The Red Moon* (1909) were credited to Pauline Reed. Those in Cole & Johnson's *Shoo-Fly Regiment* (1907) were credited to Siren Navarro, who was also a dancer in the cast.[8] This research resulted in an essay on "Crediting the Uncredited" but did not verify Reed or Nevarro as actively committed to performance design to the extent of the other focuses of Perkins' research.

These discoveries did lead me to compare the design and dressmaking details visible in the White portrait with other photographs of Walker in Reed shows (small gallery of these photographs can be found on the www.nypl.org/vaudeville site; go to tab shows and related images). The portrait from *The Red Moon* (by Apeda) provides the greatest number of elements in common. The costume is dominated by a huge shawl with knotted fringe wrapped over the bodice. But there is beading detail on the collar, necklace and headband that compares to the quality of the sequined bodice. Although we cannot determine color schemes, the beading patterns of the collar and headband could be called African-inspired. Her left arm is out of focus, but seems to show crystal arm bands.

I came closer to including Reed in a 2008 exhibition, *Curtain Call: Celebrating a Century of Women Designing for Live Performance*. My curatorial responsibility, 1900 to 1960, was set as 50 costume, scenery and lighting designers. To keep down to the number, we had to limit ourselves to artists for whom there were drawings or garments, as well as photographs.

Vaudeville Nation (Winter/Spring 2005–6)

The exhibition provided more opportunities for alternative histories of popular entertainment. Aida Overton Walker showed up in four places. She was featured in sections on child imitators (see image in the vaudeville on-line exhibition) and on gender impersonation, for her performances of Ford T. Dabney and Cecil Mack's "That's why They call Me Shine" from *His Honor the Barber* (1910).[9] She was also included in cases on the various comic-led troupes of Williams & Walker, Ernest Hogan and S. H. Dudley.

During the research for this exhibition, I developed severe doubts that the White portrait showed the Salome costume. All of the costumes worn by other Hammerstein Salomes and their imitators follow a similar pattern of draping and beading that is missing in Walker's bodice. The bust covering has concentric beading or sequins (think bulls-eye rashes or burlesque tassels), with strings of pearls or beads hanging down the sides and looped up over the midriff (see, for example, the image of Trixie Friganza in the *Passing Show of 1912* on the *Vaudeville Nation* on-line exhibition).

The African American Newspapers Database

Since the 1990s, The New York Public Library and research centers around the country had participated in an NEH-funded project to document urban African American newspapers. With the computer era, these efforts paid off in access to searchable issues of the historical newspaper morgues that could document these theater artists. Although most of these newspapers were founded after her career, this resource has allowed me the extraordinary opportunity to re-open my searches for information that could answer my questions.

My first project was to clarify the performance tours for the years around the portrait's publication date. Luckily, the *Chicago Defender*'s theater critic was as obsessed by her as I was. This was a period of traumatic change for the African American theater and songwriting communities. The illnesses and deaths of Bob Cole (1911), Ernest Hogan (1909) and George Walker (January 13, 1911) led to conglomerations and re-casting for the troupes. With Williams & Walker on what became a permanent hiatus, Overton Walker had joined S. H. Dudley's Smart Set company of *His Honor the Barber* as a featured performer in fall 1910. The *Chicago Defender* announced that he was "surrounded this season by the very best company he has ever installed," naming Aida Overton Walker "the greatest female comedy performer her race ever produced . . . " and noting that she was "America's best known singing and dancing comedienne . . . "[10]

The tour of this show included her "That is Why they Call me Shine" in men's clothing. The *Defender*'s Sylvester Russell wrote in his December 10th column that she also appeared as a child (without specifying the song). Rejecting the Salome solution, there are two possible dance specialties in *His Honor the Barber* that suggest more appropriate sources for the sequined costume. "Panama," by William Henry Tyers, was offered by Walker "and her Panama Girls" in the show during the 1910–1911 tour, according to the sheet music cover, but it is not mentioned in the reviews. Russell's column suggested an alternative: "Her second number was "Porto Rico," in which Mr. Dudley added very skillful and intelligent bits of comedy . . . Mrs. Walker's Spanish costume was a dream of perfection that dazzled with splendor and no living woman was ever handsomer to look upon."[11] She remained in the show for at least a season, using the White image for publicity. We agree that it dazzled with splendor, but still can not determine if it was designed to be Spanish, rather than Panamanian or Puerto Rican.

In Fall, 1913, she was headlining her own All Star Concert Company, appearing at Chicago's Pekin Theater for a special engagement. The advertisement in the *Defender* stated: "A very pleasant week is promised. There will be pretty girls, pretty costumes, special scenery, tuneful music—in fact, every effort will be made to entertain you. Watch for further particulars regarding this engagement. Don't forget the time—week of November 3rd, the place—Pekin Theater, the girl—Aida Overton Walker."[12] She was held over at least through mid-November. In this period, her name became associated with a make-up firm. Advertisements by the Overton-Hygine Manufacturing Company, Chicago, mentioned "Ro-Zol Face Bleach, Aida Overton Walker Pomade and other Toilet Articles."[13]

My pleasant stroll through Russell's paeans of praise in *the Defender* online came to a halt with her death in October 1914. The editorial page paid homage to her on October 24, 1914:

> The death of Aida Overton Walker last week passes in review the men and women of color who made the last decade notable in the histrionic world. Mrs. Walker was the foremost exponent of terpsichorean art the race has produced and almost the last of the old guard. The others save one or two, have been called to the Great Beyond. Like her lamented predecessors, she died young before her star had reached its zenith, yet she leaves behind a fragrance and memory of lavender and old lace which our children's children will read of in history and folk-lore. What a child she was in mimicry and pantomime, graceful as the lily and with supreme art making our hearts laugh and be glad . . . .[14]

With the obituary article above, the *Defender* ran a variant of the White photograph, facing front with her torso facing more to the left. A colorized, all gold version of this can be found on flickr.com and other on-line sources. A third version, with frontal face and torso, ran with a 1916 article citing the deaths of George Walker, Aida Overton Walker, Hogan, and Cole in an appreciation of Sam Lucas,[15] so the newspaper must have owned prints of at least two of the images. The newsprint half-tones do not show enough detail to determine whether these poses also feature re-touching. I wish even more that we could locate the key sheet in The New York Public Library for the Performing Arts' huge White Studio Collection.

My search of the ProQuest Historical African American Newspapers turned up many more posthumous references to Walker, including multiple comparisons to Florence Mills[16] and Ethel Waters.[17] As late as 1933, the *Amsterdam News* cited her as a model for performers. The article cites her talent, but it is aimed at the producers who demanded light skinned performers: "Our Girls of Darker Hue Need a Chance . . . We have had individual artists of dark hue who have set not only New York but the whole world ablaze. Aida Overton Walker was dark, not deep black, but dark enough to scare any Negro producer from engaging 12, 15, or 20 girls of her hue to grace a chorus, and she went further than any woman of color on the stage."[18] This specific citation relates to my still un-answered question: Why was the photograph re-touched? Why was it re-touched in a way that did not in any way obscure her dark skin and features?

Over the years, I have learned so much more about Aida Overton Walker, and her colleagues in performance and popular music, and theatrical portraits, and White Studio. It will not surprise any PAR reader that my searches have answered some questions, only to raise others. I will keep trying to interpret this visual document, and teaser.

ENDNOTES

[1] Among many new studies, please see Daphne A. Brook's *Bodies in Dissent* and Marlis Schweitzer's *When Broadway was the Runway* (2009), as well as articles by Camille Forbes and Thomas DeFrantz. The pioneering research on African American popular theater at the turn of the century can be found in Henry T. Sampson's *Blacks in Blackface* (1980) and *The Ghost Walks* (1988), both published by The Scarecrow Press, as well as Edward Mapp's 1990 edition of *Directory of Blacks in the Performing Arts.* For equivalent studies of the African American songwriting community, please see the writings of John Graziano and Wayne D. Stanley.

[2] As Brooks McNamara preached, any artifact can be a text.

[3] The Billy Rose Theatre Division holds the vast White Studio Collection of key (contact) sheets and post-1918 negatives. There are also thousands of White Studio prints in show and personality files which were received from performers, press agents, producers and publications.

[4] Full disclosure—Brooks dissuaded me from writing my dissertation on Walker and Hoffmann since there was no primary documentation and remarkably little description of their choreography.

[5] I have since verified that Toledo had a Lyceum Theater which did accommodate African American performers and audiences, and that S. H. Dudley did perform there.

[6] See my "The Borrowed Art of Gertrude Hoffmann" (*Dance Data* 2, 1977), 4– 6.

[7] Lois Alexander. *Blacks in the History of Fashion* (1982).

[8] Navarro, who also received a partial dance direction credit for that show, was later an instructor at the Delsarte Dancing Academy in Chicago (display ad in the *Chicago Defender,* February 22, 1919). She is a dance history thesis waiting to happen.

[9] Like so many of these songs, it is now considered a jazz standard and is performed without lyrics.

[10] *The Chicago Defender* (December 3, 1910), p.3 and p. 1. This and subsequent citations were found on ProQuest on www.nypl.org.

[11] *The Chicago Defender* (December 19, 1910), p.1

[12] *The Chicago Defender* (October 18, 1913)

[13] These advertisements ran in the *Defender* from March through October 1915, and appeared as late as May 1919.

[14] p. 8.

[15] *Chicago Defender* (October 7, 1916), p.4

[16] *New York Amsterdam News* (July 22, 1925), p.6

[17] W. Rollo Wilson, *Pittsburgh Courier* (September 17, 1927), p. A2

[18] Romeo L. Dougherty, *New York Amsterdam News* (September 13, 1933), p. 7

White Lies and Stony Silence: Reconstruction in the Personal Narrative of America's Most Popular Female Impersonator on the Minstrel Stage

HEATHER MAY

In August 2006, I visited Mount Carmel, a prominent Catholic cemetery in Chicago, Illinois, to look for the gravesite of "The Only Leon," at one time the highest-paid performer in American minstrelsy. An elusive four-line obituary in the *Chicago Daily Tribune* on August 22, 1922 led me to the cemetery;[1] I was unable to obtain the exact location of his grave without going to the main office, which was closed when I arrived. I decided to drive around the grounds, hopeful I could find him in an older section, since he had died in 1922 and the tombstones I passed looked shiny and new. My optimism quickly diminished, however, when I discovered that the gravesites were simply well-maintained, and the whole cemetery was filled with tombstones from his era. Given that Mount Carmel houses 232,296 gravesites, the chances of blindly finding Francis Leon's was as likely as procuring a needle in a haystack.[2] Leaving the Italian section of the cemetery, I drove to where I was surrounded by Irish names, parked the car, and gave myself one hour to see what I could find before postponing my search for a trip when I had time to check in with the main office and uncover the precise location of his grave. After parking the car near section B, I got out and began covering ground on foot. Yet I was unsure of what I should look for—would he be buried under his given name (Patrick Francis Glassey) or his stage name (Francis Leon)? Would he be buried alone, or amongst family? His obituary was in his stage name, but it gave more details about his nieces than the career that spawned the name. I scanned for both and by some strange happenstance, after fifteen minutes a tombstone marked "Leon" caught my eye. I ran over to find that he was buried under his stage name, with only this inscription: "Leon 'The Only' of Kelly & Leon's Minstrels." There was nothing more, and no allusion to his life (or death) outside of the stage.

My excursion that day parallels most of my interactions with this enigmatic figure, the pristine white marble stone marking Leon's grave both a

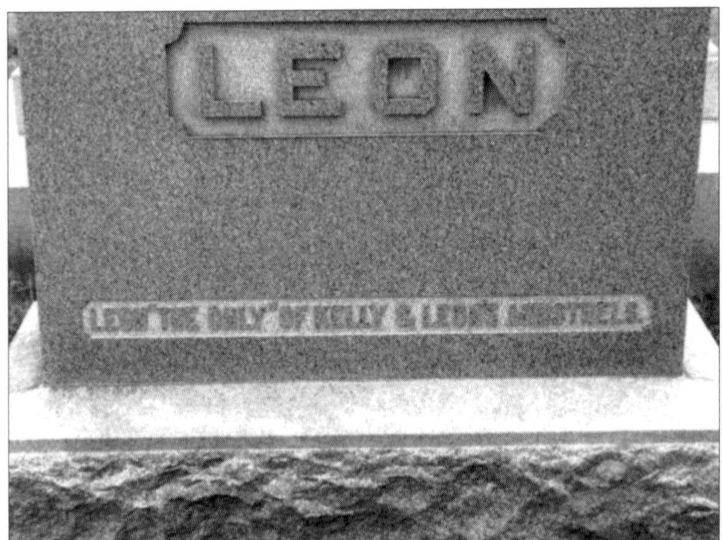

Tombstone in Mount Carmel Cemetery for "The Only Leon." Author's photo taken in August 2006.

fitting and frustrating symbol of his life and career—the details of the former carefully hidden behind his whitewashed public persona, and the details of the latter lost to the ravages of time and a desire to erase the shame of minstrelsy from our past. A performer who obsessively obscured himself behind the characters he impersonated, painting over his whiteness with burnt cork and burying his masculinity behind layers of petticoats and lace, Francis Leon built his reputation upon his ability to perform the Other by obliterating himself. Leon's obstruction was not limited to the stage. As with his enigmatic tombstone, the few clues that Leon left behind about his personal life contradict at every turn.

As a performer who made his fortune off of his ability to transform himself into his characters, Leon's continued star power depended on the maintenance of a personal life that was boring enough not to attract attention to the real man. The publication of detailed personal information about Leon's private life could focus too much attention on the real man behind the women he created onstage. On the one hand, Leon's reputation as a consummate female impersonator depended upon his audience's knowledge that there was in fact a man performing women's roles so brilliantly. In an age obsessed with virtuosity, cross-dressed performances served to highlight actors' talents because they put on display the ways in which actors could impersonate qualities that they were not expected to have naturally and therefore had to studiously acquire. An actor like Leon, who could successfully make audiences wonder about his true sex, showed himself to be highly skilled. As one reviewer marveled, "It is difficult to believe that the smiling, simpering person is a man. His dresses are marvels of the modiste's art, and his figure is so cunningly shaped and arranged that any but a student of anatomy would be deceived by the sex of Mr. Leon."[3] Although the author of this review claimed that no one could know the true sex of Leon without seeing him naked, Leon's performance clearly relied on an audience knowledgeable about his offstage gender and therefore able to judge the completeness of his transformation.

On the other hand, Leon ensured that awareness of his true sex remained limited, protecting the power of his performances. If Leon's offstage life, in which he lived exclusively as a man, dominated public discourse to the extent that audience members associated him with traditionally masculine behaviors, the believability of his performances of femininity onstage would have been jeopardized. Leon depended upon his audiences' ability to willingly suspend disbelief and accept him as a woman, an impossibility if their immediate and lasting associations with him were as a man. In order to protect his ability to convincingly portray minstrel women, therefore, Francis Leon cultivated an evolving and ambiguous personality.

My early web searches and scans of forty years of *New York Times* microfilm for evidence of Francis Leon uncovered performance reviews and advertisements, but the man behind the "Only Leon" remained completely obscured. Two newspaper accounts revealed Francis Leon's family name.[4] A rather odd three-line space-filler in the June 3, 1869 *Decatur Republican* announced that "'The only Leon,' of Kelly & Leon's Minstrels, was born an Irishman, and christened Patrick Glassey." An 1886 article about his destitute sister Mary's decision to check in to Bellevue Hospital recorded that Mary responded to questions about relatives by saying that "Everybody knows my brother, Patrick Francis Glassy [sic]." When no one recognized his name, she retorted:

> "You don't know 'the only Leon,' the female impersonator of Haverly's Minstrels? . . . Where have you lived all of your life? 'The only Leon,' when he's at home, is Patrick Francis Glassy [sic], and if any trouble comes to me he'll probably take care of his poor sister, for he's worth a great many thousand dollars, but won't give me any money unless he thinks I am dying[?] If he thought that, he'd probably act like a brother."[5]

This article, and the contentious sibling relationship it depicted, led me to wonder about Leon's upbringing.

I began by investigating United States Census records in an attempt to uncover the "true" private man who existed underneath the women he performed in public. I searched for variations on Patrick Glassey, both with an "e" and without, and discovered one Census record, most likely the closest we will ever get to an unedited account of the man. The 1860 Census revealed that Edward and Ellen Glassey, both Irish immigrants, brought a son named Patrick Francis into the world in 1842. Patrick grew up in New York City with two younger sisters, Mary and Ellen, as well as an Irish servant. His parents owned their home, valued at $7,000, and had an additional $1,300 in Edward's personal estate.[6] Because his father was a successful merchant who traded in goods and not his own persona, and therefore did not stand to benefit from lying to census takers, this account of Patrick's upbringing is likely the most accurate out of the myriad of options published during his lifetime.

Patrick Francis Glassey reportedly left his parents' home in New York City to embark upon a career on the minstrel stage in 1860, and seemingly never looked back. He retained only his middle name, Francis, after leaving his family, choosing Leon as his surname instead of Glassey. The origins of Leon's name remain unclear, though it certainly hid his Irish identity behind something more ethnically and sexually ambiguous. It was the only name he used after leaving his family, and appears on all documents, both personal and professional, including advertisements, legal transcripts, bills of sale, newspaper interviews, United State Census records, and reviews. Even those documents meant to summarize the totality of the person referenced therein, his tombstone and obituary, identify Patrick Francis Glassey by his stage name, Francis Leon.

Early searches for "Francis Leon" in the United States Census turned up only one probable entry between 1840 and 1920. The 1870 Census showed a Francis Leon living with an Edwin Kelly in a New York City apartment.[7] Although Francis Leon incorrectly reported his birthplace as California at this time, the record is clearly of the two performers—noting Kelly's profession as a musician as well as his English nationality. Leon shared twenty years of his career with Edwin Kelly, beginning with Christy and Wood's Minstrels in the late 1850s/early 1860s. By 1863, the two men formed their own minstrel company, and although they frequently disbanded their company, Kelly and Leon's Minstrels, to seek better fortunes with other companies when times were hard, the two men performed together continuously for the next sixteen years. Though Edwin Kelly was a widower with two children who left England to immigrate to the United States and begin a career in minstrelsy, the extremely close nature of his onstage performances with Francis Leon, typically playing lovers, raises questions about the men's sexuality.[8]

These questions intensified for me when I discovered a newspaper article reporting a legal dispute surrounding an 88–acre farm in New Jersey the two men purchased together in 1871.[9] The rhetoric of the court case revealed that the performers were concerned with maintaining their image as family men and business partners. The defendant in the case, Walter Mitchell, claimed that Leon said that "he wanted wild land, the more acres and the wilder the better; that he wanted some place where, in vacation, he could go and rest in the enjoyment of hunting and fishing; that as to houses, his stage carpenters could go out and put up what they wanted." Kelly and Leon, on the other hand, claimed they desired the farm so that it could serve as a home for their extended families. Leon said he wanted to bring his sister to the farm, and Kelly had "prepared to remove his family there." This argument appears disingenuous. Although Edwin Kelly's son, Edwin Lester, moved to the United States to perform with Kelly and Leon's Minstrels, he did not join the company until 1874.[10] No evidence exists that Kelly ever brought other members of his family to the United States. For his part, although Leon became the caretaker of his nieces late in his life, he was largely estranged from his sister, as evidenced by the previously referenced

New York Times article about Mary's insanity. Given the extreme physical distance between Kelly and his children and the emotional distance between Leon and his sister, a secluded New Jersey farm was an unlikely home for the two men's extended families, though arguably well suited for the privacy of a romantic relationship.

If Kelly and Leon were involved in an intimate relationship offstage, nineteenth century attitudes about homosexuality certainly would have encouraged the men to hide this relationship from the public in order to survive and thrive as popular entertainers. Although close male friendships were the norm of the period, men, unlike single women, did not often live together, but were expected to marry and have children.[11] Men who openly challenged standards of masculinity and heterosexuality ran the risk of imprisonment.[12] In this case, no additional documentation exists to support the possibility that Edwin Kelly and Francis Leon cohabited for a substantial period of their lives, much less that they were lovers. By the time of the 1880 Census, the two men moved to Australia, where they re-formed Kelly and Leon's Minstrels. Their living arrangements went undocumented in Australia, though they did spend the bulk of their time in Sydney, where they built a 1500–seat opera house.[13] Though Sydney was known as the "Sodom of the South Seas" at this time, the driving force behind Kelly and Leon's move was much more likely professional than personal.[14] Kelly and Leon took their company to Australia in 1878 after struggling through a year's worth of sporadic touring productions in small cities across the United States. While they struggled to find an audience in the U.S. due to growing fatigue with the art form, they were an instant success in Australia. Although not the first minstrel company to head to the continent, the art form was still novel enough to captivate audiences.[15]

For reasons unknown, but likely related to Edwin Kelly's extreme expenditures for the construction of the Kelly and Leon's Opera House, the two men parted company at the end of 1880, approximately twenty years after their first performances together. Kelly remained in Australia, where he performed in comic opera for a lengthy and successful second career, and Leon returned to the United States, where he alternated between star engagements with other minstrel and variety companies, and attempts to form his own minstrel organizations.

For many years the last Census record I could find for Leon was 1870. He was still in Australia in 1880, but he reignited his fame as a female impersonator in American minstrelsy with his return to the U.S. in 1881, although he never again received the same notoriety he earned working with Edwin Kelly. Francis Leon effectively terminated his career on the American stage when he toured Australia from 1885–1886 with his new partner, Frank Cushman. Upon his return to the United States, his name occasionally appeared in the papers during short-lived associations with other minstrel or variety organizations, but after a disastrous attempt to revive Kelly and Leon's Minstrels in Chicago in 1900, performing entirely "in black face, with no vaudeville," Leon disappeared from the stage without a trace.[16]

Popular entertainment underwent drastic changes in the latter part of the nineteenth century, almost none of which worked in Leon's favor. Minstrelsy, which lost popularity throughout much of the post-war period, was increasingly replaced by variety entertainment and vaudeville, art forms that were less expensive to produce and for which there was no constant demand for a female impersonator. Throughout the 1880s, electric lighting began to catch on in American theatres, shining light on the distances between performers and the characters they performed, and increasing the difficulty for audiences to willingly suspend disbelief for an older man's cross-dressed impersonations of pretty young opera divas. Likewise, increasing interest in realistic staging practices and acting techniques made it more difficult for Leon to bridge the gap between himself and the women he attempted to portray convincingly onstage. Perhaps as a response to an entertainment world in which he found himself (and the skills he spent a lifetime developing) increasingly irrelevant, Francis Leon cultivated an ever-changing biography throughout the rest of his life.

A *Chicago Tribune* interview with Leon from 1902 provided a retrospective look at his life and revealed information that led me to Census records I had long overlooked in my quest to find details about his personal life. In this interview, Leon claimed he was "absolutely satisfied" with his life, even though he had lost "three good-sized fortunes" over the span of his career, and "it was doubtful if a dozen [of his old admirers] could tell" where he could be found. In fact, Leon told the *Tribune* that he no longer cared to be found, preferring to relax quietly in his summer garden on the roof of a four-story flat that he built with "his last earnings on the stage" in order to realize "his ambition to live quietly and in close communication with the creations of nature." The paper gave the address for Leon's retreat as West Lake and Kedzie, which prompted me to re-examine the Census for a Francis Leon living on Kedzie Avenue.[17]

The 1900 Census revealed just such a person, along with his housekeeper Anna Barth, but his given age was forty-four (my Leon would have been fifty-eight at the time), his birthplace was listed as New York, and he claimed a French father and New York mother.[18] Ten years later, the Census recorded a fifty-year-old Francis Leon living at 144 N. Kedzie Avenue with his housekeeper Anna Barth and his niece, Eugenia Oberist. This time, Leon claimed New York as the birthplace of both his parents as well as himself.[19] And in 1920, the last Census for which Leon was alive, Leon managed to stop aging altogether, giving his age as fifty, though he still lived in the same location with his nieces Eugenia and May.[20] Francis Leon's determination to freeze his age at fifty over the last thirty years of his life is perplexing given his apparent withdrawal from the public stage for a secluded private life with family and a select group of friends. Although he depended upon his audience's ability to accept his impersonations of beautiful divas throughout most of his career, he stood to gain nothing from the acceptance of government officials. In fact, it is difficult to imagine how he could have convinced someone standing a few feet away from him that he was fifty-years-old just two years before he died at the age of eighty.

This final act of willful fiction suggests to me just how deeply intertwined Leon's self-perception was with the onstage fiction he mastered of youth, beauty, and desirability. Though he may have been "perfectly satisfied" with his final years out of the limelight, he never truly appears to have accepted himself as Patrick Francis Glassey, a son of Irish immigrants and a family man. A walk to his simple and unadorned, yet still perfectly maintained grave, in a cemetery famous for housing Al Capone and other members of the mafia elite, paints the final picture of his complete submersion into life as a performer. The stone shows no record of his birth or death dates, nor of his given name. He survives in death as he created himself in life, as "Leon," of "Kelly and Leon's Minstrels."

ENDNOTES

[1] His death came surprisingly late given that his forty-year career ended in 1900. The full text of his sole published obituary reads: LEON—Francis Leon of Kelly and Leon Minstrels, beloved uncle of Miss May Leon and Eugene [sic] Oberest [sic]. Funeral from his late residence, 144 N. Kedzie-av., Monday, Aug. 21, 9:30 a.m. Interment at Mount Carmel cemetery. "Obituary 2," *Chicago Daily Tribune*, August 20, 1922, 9.

[2] Mount Carmel staff provided the number of graves in a phone conversation on August 28, 2006.

[3] As reprinted on a Nugget Theatre Playbill in the Minstrels-Playbills folder from the Harvard Theatre Collection.

[4] Scholars like Annemarie Bean, Laurence Senelick, and Edward LeRoy Rice also made mention of Leon's real name in works that I read when embarking upon my own research into the performer, but those two newspaper accounts are the only newspaper articles in which Leon is referenced by his given name, Patrick Francis Glassey.

[5] Untitled, *Decatur Republican*, June 3, 1869 and "Wandering into a Hospital: A Sister of the 'Only Leon' Insane at Bellevue," *New York Times*, March 20, 1886, 2.

[6] U.S. Department of Commerce, Bureau of the Census. *1860 United States Federal Census*. New York Ward 16 District 1, New York, NY. Roll: M653_806. Washington, DC: National Archives and Records Administration: 496. Accessed through *Heritage Quest Online* on November 7, 2006.

[7] U.S. Department of Commerce, Bureau of the Census. *1870 United States Federal Census*. New York Ward 15 District 9, New York, NY. Roll 593_994. Washington, DC: National Archives and Records Administration: 8. Accessed through *Heritage Quest Online* on November 7, 2006.

[8] Contemporary scholars, including Annemarie Bean and Laurence Senelick, note the possibility of a homosexual relationship between the two men, though as Senelick notes, "no breath of homosexual scandal touched Leon" at the time. Laurence Senelick, *The Changing Room: Sex, Drag and Theatre* (New York, NY: Routledge, 2000), 302.

[9] The legal dispute revolved around the fact that the property the two men believed they had purchased based upon an advertisement in the *New York Herald* was not the same property as the one in the sales agreement that they signed with Walter Mitchell. "Marine Court Trial Term Part II," *New York Times*, April 27, 1871, 2.

[10] Although tangential to this paper, Edwin Lester's different last name from his father, Edwin Kelly, caused me to overlook the addition of Kelly's son to the company, with which he performed for nearly ten years, until a recent quest for Edwin Kelly's obituary led me to the link between the father and son. "The Late Mr. Edwin J. Kelly," *Advertiser*, January 2, 1899, 6.

[11] Marilyn Coleman, Lawrence H. Ganong and Kelly Warzinik, *Family Life in Twentieth-Century America*, Family Life through History (Westport, CT: Greenwood Press, 2007), 291.

[12] Although illegal in the United States, gay culture was "spotlighted by the press and frequented by out-of-town businessmen and uptown slummers alike. . . . Gay men . . . socialized extensively and overtly with 'normal' workingmen as well." Still, acknowledgement

of a gay counterculture in New York City, and the subsequent stimulation of a sort of exotic and voyeuristic tourism, was a far cry from political, cultural, and personal power. In order to be certain to avoid arrest and imprisonment for their sexuality, gay men and women were required to keep their private lives completely private. George Chauncey, *Gay New York: Gender, Urban Culture, and the Making of the Gay Male World, 1890–1940* (New York, NY: BasicBooks, 1994), 2.

[13] Leon spent 15 months in Sydney and 11 months in Melbourne out of the total 37 months he was in Australia. The rest of his time was spent touring. Kelly and Leon's Opera House opened on Boxing Day 1880 and was located at the corner of King and York Streets. "Amusements in Australia," *Era*, February 22, 1880, Issue 2161 and "Amusements in Australia," *Era*, March 21, 1880, Issue 2165.

[14] Definition of Sydney as the "Sodom of the South Seas" comes from Robert Aldrich, "Homosexuality and the City: An Historical Overview," *Urban Studies* 41.9 (August 2004): 1720, *Academic Search Premier, EBSCOhost*, http://bert.lib.indiana.edu:2048/login?url=http://Search.ebscohost.com/login.aspx?direct=true&db=aph&AN=14010908&site=ehost-live.

[15] Edwin Kelly and Francis Leon also had the benefit of being newcomers to Australian audiences, which meant that they were able to experiment with their performances in ways that American audiences were unwilling to accept. As a result, Kelly and Leon opened a production of Gilbert and Sullivan's *H. M. S. Pinafore* without burlesque or blackface to great success.

[16] "Music and the Drama: Leon Announces Membership," *Chicago Daily Tribune*, September 20, 1900, 7.

[17] "Chicago Man Satisfied on a Roof," *Chicago Daily Tribune*, June 22, 1902, 51.

[18] U.S. Department of Commerce, Bureau of the Census. *1900 United States Federal Census*. Chicago Ward 12. Roll 259_T623. Washington, DC: National Archives and Records Administration: 34. Accessed through *Heritage Quest Online* on November 7, 2006.

[19] U.S. Department of Commerce, Bureau of the Census. *1910 United States Federal Census*. Chicago Ward 14. Roll 256_T624. Washington, DC: National Archives and Records Administration: 305. Accessed through *Heritage Quest Online* on November 7, 2006.

[20] His nieces were by his sister, Mary, and an unknown man. Mary married John Oberist in 1868, but she was widowed by the time she checked herself into Bellevue in 1886. If their Census records are to be believed (admittedly a bit of a challenge given Leon's history), both nieces were born after 1888. John Oberist performed with Kelly and Leon's Minstrels from 1867 to 1869. I often wonder whether or not there was bad blood between Oberist and Leon given Mary's later claims that Leon had no contact with her, and the relatively short period of time that Oberist performed with the company following his nuptials.

The Performance Historian as Cold Case Detective: Reopening Nikolai L'vov's Investigation of the Blue Blouse Movement[1]

ROBERT CRANE

The CBS television serial *Cold Case* followed a simple formula for the duration of its seven seasons: a long forgotten and inadequately resolved investigation would attract the attention of Detective Lilly Rush and her team, who would then reexamine the case, reevaluating details in the file, finding overlooked clues, and turning up new leads until they succeeded where the previous investigators had not. If, as this volume of *Performing Arts Resources* suggests, historians are detectives, we sometimes have the opportunity to reopen cold cases, following in the tracks of our predecessors in the hope that a reevaluation of their evidence will bring new insights into the problems that they were trying to solve. This can be a highly rewarding exercise, or a highly frustrating one. While the television show ended every episode with wrongs righted and justice served, the performance historian's documents, unfortunately, sometimes don't lend themselves to such an easy resolution.

Moscow: 1929

The Blue Blouse movement was the largest and most important organizer of do-it-yourself living newspapers in the Soviet Union.[2] Founded in Moscow in 1923 as a class project at the Communist Institute of Journalism, The Blue Blouse developed a massive following, eventually garnering nearly 600 registered affiliates spread across the country in addition to thousands of unregistered followers. Their bi-weekly periodical, *Blue Blouse* (1924–1928), published scripts, staging instructions, song lyrics and theoretical pronouncements, enabling provincial workers to emulate the movement's professional Moscow troupes by producing constructivist-inspired agit-prop theatre in workers' clubs and factory halls. At their peak, the Blue Blouse were, as Frantisek Deak notes, "The largest movement in the history of theatre in which the avant-garde participated."[3]

The scale of the Blue Blouse movement is its main source of significance.

The first page of the tables generated by Nikolai L'vov, compiling the results of his survey of registered affiliates of the Blue Blouse (1929). Manuscript collection, Bakhrushkin State Central Theatre Museum (GTsTM f.150 op.1 d.47 ed. khr.6 l.1)

Without the thousands of ordinary people who used their material to become theatrical activists themselves, the Blue Blouse would have remained a fairly unremarkable variety theatre performing in Moscow's bars and cafeterias. However, the size of the movement has always been a difficult topic to discuss well. This was true even for the editors of *Blue Blouse*, who alternately printed bombastic pronouncements of the movement's size and delved into the minutiae of individual troupes. I am aware of only one published attempt to deal with the movement as a whole in a coherent and detailed manner: a 1929 article by director, critic and theatre historian Nikolai L'vov (1893–1981) titled "On the Blue Blouse Front." This article examines the decline of the Blue Blouse movement following the discontinuation of *Blue Blouse* via a survey of responses to a questionnaire sent by the author to all of the groups that had been registered with the Blue Blouse as of the final issue of their magazine.

L'vov's article, however, cannot be taken at face value. Published in the short-lived magazine *Small Forms of Club Entertainment* (1929–1931) (which was founded by Boris Iuzhanin, formerly the founder and editor of *Blue Blouse*), the article is at least as much a polemic in the debates and struggles of the Cultural Revolution following Stalin's consolidation of power as it is a work of scholarship. The Blue Blouse organization and the theatrical forms that it advocated had come under attack from proletarianist groups like the Revolutionary Association of Proletarian Writers, who argued that working class audiences had outgrown the infantile variety theatre and deserved to see full-length plays, done in a realist style on the stages of their clubs.[4] L'vov, who had been an ally and occasional employee of the Blue Blouse, concluded that there was a crisis in the living newspaper movement. This crisis had been brought on, however, not by natural causes like "the outdatedness of living newspapers or a turning away of the Masses from variety theatre," as the proletarianists argued, but by artificial "pressure from the centre against living newspapers."[5] The major manifestation of this pressure was the closing of *Blue Blouse* by opponents of the living newspaper movement and his suggested remedy was the reestablishment of *Blue Blouse*'s editorial board as the organizational center of the movement.

L'vov's conclusions were, in other words, probably the only ones he would have published (certainly the only ones that would have been published in *Small Forms of Club Entertainment*), regardless of the results of his research. This is nowhere more obvious than in his interpretation of one of the most striking pieces of evidence generated by his investigation: the fact that only 54 of the 551 recipients of L'vov's questionnaire—less than 10%—responded to his request for information. This terrible rate was due, he concluded, not to a loss of prestige by the Blue Blouse, or a lack of interest in living newspapers, but to the disintegration of the non-responding groups, despite their own wishes. The low response rate was an indication of the severity of the crisis. The point of this critique is not to fret over L'vov's scholarly ethics (the stakes for him were considerably different than they are for most of us: Iuzhanin, for example, was arrested in connection with his activities with the Blue Blouse only one year after the article was published), but to highlight the deficiencies of his article for contemporary scholars.[6] This unique attempt to discuss the scale of the Blue Blouse movement renders itself (and the pieces of evidence selected to support its argument) suspect due to its bias.

Moscow: 2009

80 years after the article was published, I was conducting research on the Blue Blouse movement in the manuscript collection of the Bakhrushkin State Central Theatre Museum. After a discussion of the work I was doing, the reading room attendants directed me to a collection of L'vov's personal papers in their holdings. In addition to a vast amount of information on L'vov's personal involvement in the Moscow theatre scene in the 1920s, the collection held a file containing the evidence he used in his analysis of the living newspaper movement.[7]

The file contained a typed copy of the project proposal L'vov submitted to Glavpolitprosvet (the Chief Committee on Political Enlightenment), a copy of the request for information he circulated to the registered affiliates of the Blue Blouse, a single example of a letter received in response, a list of the groups that responded, a table charting their responses, and a draft of the article (which was shortened significantly for publication). Because only a single letter from the living newspaper troupes was preserved, the tables (fig. 1–3) provide the most complete record of the information gathered by L'vov during his investigation, and the starting point for a re-opening of his case.

The tables gather a wide range of information from the respondents. The columns chart the material the groups used to construct their repertoire; their opinions about and relationships with local and nation-wide organizations; details related to leadership within the groups; and assessments of their material existence, their contemporary situation, the evolution of their activities, and their feelings towards living newspapers in general.[8] This information provided a valuable and reasonably detailed snapshot of the individual collectives at the time of their response. I learned, for example, that the collective at the Karl Marx club in the Siberian city of Khaitinsk (number 54) drew their texts from *Blue Blouse* (the return of which they called for) and *Club Stage* in addition to their own compositions (which were created with difficulty). They called for some sort of organizational order, and had received training at an instructional gathering.[9] The resources available to them were sufficient, and their productions were cheerfully received by their audiences. They continued to produce living newspapers using "the old methods" while striving towards greater beauty and artistic quality, the lack of which they cite as the major deficiency of the living newspaper form.

The table showed some interesting trends across the respondents as well. Most of the collectives, for example, were still using material from old issues of *Blue Blouse* in their performances. Almost all of the groups claimed to write a portion of the material themselves, a fact which fascinatingly complicates the relationships between center and periphery and professional and amateur that existed within the movement. The overwhelming majority of the groups were still performing living newspapers and expressed an interest in continuing to perform them. The report shows significant variety among the clubs as well. Some had paid group leaders (one boasted a director from the local State Theatre), while others divided the responsibilities among themselves or relied upon an "inexperienced Komsomol member."

However, the table was also plagued by major deficiencies. Some of the columns were too sparsely populated to provide very much information. Fewer than 1/3 of the respondents, for example, provided any information about their material existence, rendering impossible any generalizations about the resources available to collectives within the Blue Blouse movement. The major failing of the document, however, was its size. With only 10% of the Blue Blouse's registered member groups responding, any generalization based on this data seems dangerous. Were these groups the only producers of living newspapers remaining, as L'vov supposed? This seems unlikely, as the living newspaper movement survived in the Soviet Union until the early 1930s. Could the geographic locations of the respondents hide important regional trends? The Blue Blouse had registered members dispersed throughout the Soviet Union, with a significant presence in most of the national republics. L'vov's survey respondents, however, were overwhelmingly from the Russian heartland, with only one response coming from east of the Urals, none from Central Asia, and only two from Ukraine. The Blue Blouse's diversity was one of its major selling points at a time when Moscow was renegotiating its relationship with the periphery of the former Tsarist Empire. Indeed, registered collectives performed in nearly a dozen languages. However, this diversity was not reflected in L'vov's results.

These evidentiary shortcomings made it nearly impossible to reassess L'vov's conclusions. The only way to pursue the case—to find out what was really happening in the Blue Blouse movement in 1929—was to do what L'vov had not done at the time. In order to fill in the glaring holes left by the low response to the survey and the relative geographic homogeneity of the respondents, I had to leave Moscow and search for more evidence in the periphery. In order to take L'vov's investigation to its conclusion, I had to expand my pursuit of the newly reopened case.

Kharkiv: 2010

Limited resources (and my committee chair's insistence that the scope of my dissertation should not expand so far as to endanger its completion) led to a significant reduction in the scale of my search for new evidence. I was to spend five weeks in Ukraine: two in Kharkiv, which had been the capital of the Ukraine in the 1920s, and three in Kiev, where the national archives are kept. Kharkiv had had two registered Blue Blouse troupes. The first performed at the Polish worker's club, about which I was unable to find any records other than a registration book listing the work histories of sixteen club members.[10] The second was organized by the club of the Kharkiv regional committee of the metalworkers' trade union, "Metallist," whose considerable records are held in the State Archive of the Kharkiv Region[11]. The annex in which these records were kept, however, was only open on Tuesdays and Thursdays, which, because of the archive's firm policy of delivering only 10 files a day, meant that it would take the full five weeks to make it through all of the records of the cultural division of the Union, even with the archivists generously rushing my requests. By necessity, the scope of the renewed investigation was narrowing rapidly.

My work with the Metallist archive provided most of the information required to fill in an additional row of L'vov's table: the club had two living newspaper troupes, with a paid organizer. The living newspaper had an "editorial board," which met to determine its repertoire.[12] The performances on the club's thrust stage were well attended, although the collective seems to have had a meager budget.[13] The living newspaper collective existed until at least 1928. I also turned up important details that might not have made it into the tables. The collective performed in Russian (the first language of most club members—Kharkiv remains a predominately Russian-speaking city), but the club was coming under increasing pressure in the late 1920s to conduct activities in Ukrainian, in accordance with the then-ongoing Ukrainianization drive.[14] Additionally, while the club itself continued to function, the All-Union Central Council of Trade Unions dissolved the Regional Committee of the Trade Union in 1931 during a consolidation of its power.[15] If the living newspaper collective did cease to exist around this time, it seems likely that it had to do with these pressures (which had nothing to do with theatrical form, but a lot to do with the first five-year plan), rather than the discontinuation of *Blue Blouse*.

I spent the days that the archive was closed at the city's research library (the second largest in the country) pouring over local periodicals. This work led to the revelation that the two registered Blue Blouse groups were only a tiny portion of the living newspapers in the city. There were notices for performances by more than a dozen groups attached to various clubs throughout the city. Kharkiv even had a professional living newspaper group called At the Workbenches [*U Stankakh*], organized by the Kharkiv Regional Council of Trade Unions.[16] While At the Workbenches freely acknowledged their debt to *Blue Blouse* and were probably the most important member of the Blue Blouse movement in Kharkiv, they never registered with the group, and would not, therefore, have received L'vov's request for information.

Pittsburgh: 2010

Considering the results of my trip to Kharkiv, it seems less and less likely that this cold case can be closed. The evidence at the Metallist club suggests that regional and local factors played as much of a role as artistic considerations, the maturation of the working class, or the closing of a Moscow magazine in the continued existence of living newspaper collectives. But the localized nature of these conditions makes them a poor basis for generalizations. What local conditions were at play in the other 495 registered but unaccounted-for groups? A combination of time constraints, economic constraints and the difficulties of working in underfunded archives will probably prevent any sort of thorough exploration. At the same time that I was discovering just how important these specific conditions were to the investigation, the realization that important living newspaper collectives were unregistered suggests that the already-unmanageable scale of the investigation had just expanded exponentially.

Without unlimited time and resources, it seemed that the case I had begun to investigate would not be brought to any final conclusion. At the rate of two and a half weeks per collective, which I maintained in Kharkiv, it would take about 24 years of continuous archival work to investigate the rest of the registered collectives—significantly longer than the one-hour primetime slot allotted to Detective Rush and her *Cold Case* team. While my investigations did indeed turn up useful new evidence that provided insight into the scope of the Blue Blouse movement, the clues that I uncovered pointed in too many directions for a single detective—or performance historian—to pursue. For now, the case of L'vov's survey of the Blue Blouse will have to remain on the cold case shelf, waiting for other investigators to pick up the file.

ENDNOTES

[1] The Author would like to thank Olga Klimova for her help deciphering Nikolai L'vov's handwriting as well as the incredibly helpful staffs at the Bakhrushkin State Central Theatre Museum, the State Archive of the Kharkiv Region and the Korolenko Kharkiv State Scientific Library.

[2] For further discussion of the Blue Blouse, see Deak, Frantisek. "The Blue Blouse." *TDR* 17.1 (March 1973). 35–36. Dmitriev, Iurii A. *Teatral'naia Moskva 1920–e gody*. Moscow: Iskusstvo, 2000. Mally, Lynn. *Revolutionary Acts: Amateur Theater and the Soviet State*. Ithaca, NY: Cornell UP, 2000. Stourac, Richard and Kathleen McCreery. *Theatre as a Weapon: Workers' Theatre in the Soviet Union, Germany and Britain 1917–1934*. London: Routledge, 1986. Uvarova, Elizaveta. *Estradnyi Teatr: Miniatiury, obozreniia, miuzik-kholly (1917–1945)*. Moscow: Iskusstvo, 1983.

[3] Deak, p.46.

[4] This struggle led to the creation of the periodical, *Club Stage* [*Klubnaia stsena*] (1927–1932), which was published by the All-Union Central Council of Trade Unions (VTsSPS). *Club Stage* published full length plays and instructions on staging plays within the aesthetic framework of realism (plans demonstrating the layout of a box set were printed in the first issue, for example). 1928 *Blue Blouse*, Published by the Moscow Regional Council of Trade Unions (MGSPS), a subsidiary of the VTsSPS was dissolved with the understanding that there would a section of that periodical devoted to living newspapers. Such a section never appeared, however, and *Club Stage* remained committed to its aesthetic, while the MGSPS began publication of *Small Forms of Club Entertainment* [*Malye formy klubnogo zrelishcha*] the following year.

[5] L'vov, Nikolai. "Na sinebluzom fronte."*Malye formy klubnogo zrelishcha* 8 (1929):59–63. p. 63.

[6] On Iuzhanin's arrest, see Dimitriev, p. 62.

[7] Gosudarstvennyi Tsentralnyi Teatral'nyi Musei im. Bakhrushkina (GTsTM) f.150 op.1. d.47 ed. khr.1–7.

[8] The Columns of the table do not correspond exactly to the information requested by L'vov in his initial letter, which asks collectives to inform him "Whether this collective exists at the present tome or the living newspaper at your club has ceased to exist. If the living newspaper exists, please tell: 1) What changes in the work of the collective have occurred in the last year? 2) What textual material does the living newspaper use . . . ? 3)Is the work of the living newspaper acceptable for your auditorium? If the living newspaper has ceased to exist, please tell: 1)When and why did the liquidation of the living newspa-

per occur? 2) Did the collective turn to other forms of work or dissolve completely? What kinds of spectacle are desired in the auditorium of your club?" GTsTM f.150 op. 1. d. 47 ed. khr.2.

[9] The Blue Blouse organized annual congresses beginning in 1925 and the Moscow troupes provided instructional sessions while on their tours, which were frequent.

[10] Derzhavnyi Arkhiv Kharkiv'skogo Oblast' (DAKhO) f. f.820. op.1 d.909, l.1–13.

[11] DAKhO f.1010

[12] Unfortunately no records of their meetings exist in the archive.

[13] A request to buy a pair of boxing gloves for a sketch met with refusal.

[14] See, for example, DAKhO f.1010 op.1 d.1814 l.8.

[15] DAKhO f.1010. op.1 Opis'. p.1.

[16] See, for example Fonarev, A. "Zhivaia Gazeta 'U Stanka'." *Rabochii klub* 1 (1925). p. 83.

The Multiple Editions of Ellen Terry's Autobiography

THOMAS POSTLEWAIT

In 1908 the actress Ellen Terry (1847–1928) published her autobiography, *The Story of My Life*. Initial installments of the early chapters, under the title of *Memories of my Childhood*, had first enticed readers in *McClure's Magazine* (New York 1907) and *Mainly about People* (London 1907).[1] Terry's autobiography, hereafter referred to as *Story*, appeared in several distinct editions in 1908 in London and New York. Page numbers in the London and New York editions do not agree, and no two editions have the same number of illustrations.[2] *Story* was published five years after Terry's partnership with Henry Irving had dissolved (with a final performance of *The Merchant of Venice* on 14 July 1903), three years after Irving's death (9 October 1905), two years after the "Jubilee" at Drury Lane in celebration of Terry's professional career (12 June 1906), and one year after her third marriage (to the young American James Carew).

Terry died in 1928. Four years later her daughter Edith 'Edy' Craig (1869–1947) and Edy's partner Christopher St. John (Christabel Marshall, 1879?-1960) published a new edition of the autobiography, entitled *Ellen Terry's Memoirs, with a Preface, Notes and Additional Biographical Chapters*.[3] Craig initiated the project; St John did the editing and writing. Part I presents a revised edition of *Story* (276 pages); Part II offers a biography of Terry's life from 1906 to 1928 (83 pages). The expanded *Memoirs*, with its detailed notes for each chapter and a biographical supplement, would appear to be the definitive edition of one of the famous theatre autobiographies. In the "Preface" to the *Memoirs*, the two editors define their aims and methods:

> In this new edition of Ellen Terry's autobiography . . . very few alternations have been made in the original text, beyond some cuts necessitated by the addition of the biographical chapters which complete the narrative. Corrections of slips, and other revisions calculated to increase the value of the book as an authoritative record, have been included in the editorial notes. We felt that if we began tinkering with Ellen Terry's work we might deprive it of its spontaneity, and decided to let well alone.[4]

This reassuring statement invites us to trust the editing of Craig and St John, but what was their mission? Were they inspired to produce an authoritative edition of Terry's autobiography? If so, did they achieve this aim? If not, what other factors contributed to the publication of the *Memoirs*?

These questions, though fairly standard queries for this kind of editorial project, have been ignored or set aside by most biographers and theatre scholars who write on not only Ellen Terry but also Henry Irving, Edward Gordon Craig, Edy Craig, and Bernard Shaw (to say nothing about other figures and topics in Victorian and Edwardian theatre history). The *Memoirs* has served as the preferred—and usually the exclusive—source for biographers, including Laurence Irving (1952), Marguerite Steen (1962), Roger Manvell (1968), Edward Craig (1968), Tom Prideaux (1975), Nina Auerbach (1987), Moira Shearer (1998), Joy Melville, (1987 and 2006), and Michael Holroyd (2008).[5] Prideaux expresses a widespread assumption that the text of *Story* "was republished twenty-five years later in a more useful book call *Ellen Terry's Memoirs*."[6] In the assessment of Roger Manvell, the *Memoirs* is the "principal published source" for Terry's autobiography.[7] Nina Auerbach concurs: "This is a later, annotated edition of Terry's *The Story of My Life*."[8] Basically, they all agree: why bother with *Story* when the *Memoirs* is available?

Yet over the years a few biographers, such as St. John Ervine (1956), Madeleine Bingham (1978), A. M. Gibbs (2005), and Jeffrey Richards (2005), have continued to use *Story* instead of the *Memoirs*.[9] They have not, however, explained their decision. Other scholars have used both texts. For instance, Margot Peters (1980), W. D. King (1993), and Russ McDonald (2005) tacked back and forth, sometimes using *Story*, sometimes the *Memoirs*.[10] They too have failed to explain or justify their practice, so readers are left in the dark about the alternating choices.

Only a few scholars have recognized that there are significant differences between the *Memoirs* and *Story*, as David Cheshire commented in 1989. In his "Note on Sources" Cheshire points out that Terry's *Story* "was extensively revised (with some curious excisions) and re-issued as Ellen Terry's *Memoirs*."[11] Cheshire quotes from *Story*, but he says nothing more on this issue. Even when a scholar, such as W. D. King, notices that statements in *Story* failed to appear in the *Memoirs*, the potential problem is not addressed. Despite his discovery, King continued to use the *Memoirs* as a primary source for Terry's quoted statements in his book *Irving's Waterloo* (1993). By contrast, Michael Booth favored *Story* as his primary source for his study of Terry's acting. Yet inexplicably he used the *Memoirs* for one quotation, even though the statement appears in *Story*.[12]

The first scholar to offer a critique of the editing of the *Memoirs*, as far as I can tell, was Gail Marshall in 1998. In the conclusion to *Actresses on the Victorian Stage* (1998), she points out that St John's "interference with Terry's own words is extensive and not a little distorting." Marshall complains, for example, that the two editors "distort Terry's record of her relations with her male partners, notably increasing Godwin's share in Terry's narrative, and almost eradicating her affectionate account of her second husband, Charles Kelly." The *Memoirs* also omits "many of the humorous passages which give the autobiography its charm, and which woo the reader into a sense of intimacy through the actress's rueful confessions." From Marshall's perspective, the *Memoirs* "represents a substantial rewriting of Terry's story, and as such implicitly offers a new interpretation, a re-building of the 'monument' Terry left behind."[13]

Marshall's brief but pointed critique invites a much needed—and long delayed—assessment of the mission and procedures that guided the revisionist publication of the autobiography. But from the perspective of Michael Holroyd, the changes do not really matter. In *A Strange Eventful History: The Dramatic Lives of Ellen Terry, Henry Irving, and Their Remarkable Families* (2008), Holroyd acknowledges but dismisses Marshall's complaint. In an appeal to authority, which of course is a familiar type of appeal in rhetoric, Holroyd notes that Harley Granville Barker, in a letter to John Gielgud, proclaimed that the *Memoirs* was "the best of its sort I know." Holroyd also contends that St John's stylistic and organizational changes made Terry's writing "more grammatically stable and chronologically coherent," thereby improving what A. W. Pinero called Terry's "thoughtless passages." Holroyd, who used the *Memoirs* in his study, praises St John's "diplomatic revisions."[14]

How should we judge St John's revisions: distortion or diplomacy? Some revisions seem to be warranted, and indeed St John herself provides the justification.[15] Between 1904 and 1906, when Terry wrote much of the autobiography, St John "was collaborating" with her.[16] We do not know the details of this collaboration, yet St John insists that Terry wrote the autobiography, while St John served editorially as a "literary henchman." But what exactly is a "literary henchman"? St John's explanation focuses on Chapter XIV, which covers the "Last Days at the Lyceum" and the period from 1903 to 1907. According to St John, this chapter, which is quite disorganized, did not get finished until 1907—after Terry had returned from a tour of America, where she had married for the third time. Soon after her return to England, she set out on a provincial tour with her new husband, James Carew, performing a small repertoire, including Bernard Shaw's *Captain Brassbound's Conversion*. St John blames the marriage for Terry's loss of "interest in things past."[17] At that point, according to St John, Terry "left the task of finishing the book almost entirely to her collaborator." St John explains that she was forced to make do with Terry's letters and notebooks, hence the "scrappiness of the last chapters."[18]

St John cobbled together Terry's miscellaneous descriptions of people and anecdotes, and, as instructed by Terry, inserted a few letters to her from Shaw, Nellie Melba, James Barrie, Will Rothenstein, Lewis Carroll, and Edward Burne-Jones. It is still easy to recognize Terry's familiar voice in parts of the final chapter, especially her description of her last meeting with Irving just before he died. But this long chapter of *Story*, which rambles from topic to topic, lacks a developmental order. Her 1906 Jubilee, which might well have concluded the narrative, is inserted awkwardly halfway through the chapter (as is her "Apologia"—a lament for things said and unsaid). And the last pages, which offer "bits from my Diary" for the years of 1887, 1890, 1892, and 1897, are a very poor substitute for a conclusion that should cover the post-Irving years.

Not surprisingly, St John takes the opportunity in the *Memoirs* to reorganize the last section, but she assures readers that the changes "are not in the text itself, but in its arrangement." The revised chapter, now entitled "The End of the Lyceum (1892–1902)," covers the final days of Ellen Terry's partnership with Irving, her short-termed venture into management in 1903, and Irving's illness and death. Other matters, such as Terry's reflections on Madame Melba, E. Burne-Jones, Frank Benson, Alfred Tennyson, and Lewis Carroll, are redistributed to earlier chapters in which these people were first discussed. St John relocated various sections, short and long, and then offered a new, final chapter of two pages called "Jubilee (1906)"—derived from two short sections in the middle of *Story*'s last chapter.

Overall, this reorganization delivered a sequential chronology for the last chapter. A narrative order was imposed. Yet we may wonder: is it possible to make major changes in narrative order without also modifying character and voice? Did the new arrangement sacrifice some of the "spontaneity" of Terry's memories? Part of the charm of the autobiography resides in Terry's quicksilver mind and appealing voice. In *Story*, as in Terry's letters, one recollection often triggers another, and then another. On those occasions she bounds through time, unrestrained by chronology. St John tamed that voice and its intellectual energy, but at what price?

Perhaps, if St John's revision of the text proved to be merely a case of "arrangement," we would be beholden to her and Edy Craig for their editorial task (and tack). We would praise their accomplishment because, as they proclaimed in the Preface, "very few alternations have been made in the original text." We might even be willing to believe St John when she asserts that "tinkering with Ellen Terry's work" did not "deprive it of its spontaneity." We might then believe that the integrity of the text was honored. Yet in a note to Chapter XIV, St John reveals a second agenda that should trigger alarms: "I might have hesitated to revise the last pages so drastically if I had not known that Ellen Terry, after their publication, was dissatisfied with them. They are annotated in her copy with many unflattering remarks. The passages she disliked most have been omitted altogether."[19]

This justification may seem reasonable to some readers, for it implies that St John and Craig honored the wishes of Terry. Under cover of Terry's second thoughts and reservations, they removed some statements—a matter of self-censorship. But a full comparison of the *Memoirs* to *Story* reveals that St John and Craig also followed their own agenda with many of the revisions and cuts—a matter of censorship.[20] A widespread pattern of rewriting occurs throughout the autobiography. For example, in Chapter XIV Terry's statements about Irving becoming a "changed man" by 1902 were distorted by revisions and cuts (*Story* p. 317; *Memoirs* p. 250). Terry wrote: "He became more republican and less despotic as a producer," but this was revised to read, "He became less autocratic both as a producer and manager." Then, in the same paragraph, two stanzas of a poem by W. E. Henley that Terry featured were eliminated, despite her stated admiration for the poem. She applied its "stoical lines" (e.g., "My head is bloody but unbowed") to Irving in his late years. In the next paragraph the second half of the following sentence was removed: "In this last phase Henry was reproached more than ever for neglecting modern English dramatists, and of course the reproach included me to a certain extent."[21] Why does St John remove a self-reproach? These changes—typical of a revisionist agenda throughout the *Memoirs*—reformulate Terry's voice and identity. St John, in partnership with Edy Craig, repeatedly softens, refines, and whitewashes aspects of Terry. She is contained within a smaller, less complex world.

Besides a pervasive pattern of changing and cutting words, phrases, clauses, and sentences, St John regularly modified or eliminated whole paragraphs. For instance, in Chapter XIV two paragraphs on Shaw were cut, which St John tried to justify (*Memoirs*, notes 1 & 3, pp. 265–66). But missing as well is Shaw's critique of Terry's acting in *Much Ado about Nothing* in 1903. Also missing are eight paragraphs of the "Apologia," two pages on Frank Benson and her acting at Stratford, and a paragraph on playing Hermione in *The Winter's Tale*. Terry's caustic commentary on being praised by critics as "a womanly woman" was rewritten and condensed into a bland phrase about being a "graceful and charming" actress. Statements about Irving's injury and subsequent illnesses in 1896 were cut, as were key clauses and sentences from her description of the last visit to Irving. And St John also eliminated a paragraph on Gordon Craig's acting. Hundreds of changes occur without justification or even acknowledgement.

In short, St John did much more than rearrange *Story*; she rewrote it. As illustration, here is a quick catalogue of representative sentences and paragraphs that were removed. St John cut some of Terry's statements on acting, including comments on playing heroines in Shakespeare's comedies, acting Desdemona, and portraying Katherine in *Henry VIII*. Also missing are Terry's judgments on the "harmonies" in acting and the loudness of her voice. Removed, as well, are select statements by Terry on the marriage to G. F. Watts, the six years in the country with E. W. Godwin, and the initial happiness of the third marriage to Charles Kelly. Gone too is her assessment of Kelly's acting. The *Memoirs* also lacks key reflections on Robert Browning, R. L. Stevenson, and the novels of Disraeli. And we are denied miscellaneous comments on the actors George Alexander, Walter Montgomery, Tom Mead, J. Forbes-Robertson, and 'Daddy' Howe. The cuts on actresses are perhaps more severe, for St John removes statements on May Irwin, Kate Rorke, Lillie Langtry, Lena Ashwell, Mary Anderson, Helena Modjeska, and Fanny Janausche. Also missing are Terry's reflections on Helen Faucit in *Iolanthe* and *As You Like It*. Various other statements disappeared, including anecdotes on Adelaide Neilson, Edmond Rostand, E. Burne-Jones, V. Sardou, Jack Robertson, and W. G. Wills. Apparently readers do not need Terry's reflections on high culture (Michaelangelo) or low culture (American slang); nor do we need to know of her sympathy for labor strikes or her thoughts on the French Revolution. And for some inexplicable reason, St John removed Terry's praise for the immortal artistic 'soul' of Oscar Wilde. Also cut is the three-page self-parody that Terry featured in *Story*. Collectively, these various cuts not only distort Terry's autobiography but also falsify and diminish her character. Terry's cultural and social world becomes a constricted domain in which a much lesser person lived her life. The *Memoirs* is thus a willful distortion of *Story*.

Moreover, in addition to the hundreds of textual revisions and cuts, we are faced with a drastic reduction of illustrations in the *Memoirs*, which provides only twelve, whereas the three 1908 editions of *Story* (in London and New York) provided 56, 81, or 101 illustrations, depending upon which edition we examine.[22] Basic pictorial evidence is thus eliminated in the *Memoirs*, which offers only two stage images of Terry—one from *Romeo and Juliet*, a partial image of a young Terry reclining as the drugged Juliet, and the other a posed headshot in 1919 as the Nurse, her last role. St John offers no explanation for the drastic cut in visual evidence. Yet for anyone who is attuned to Michael Booth's analysis of Terry as a pictorial actress, the elimination of these many images of Terry, including many in various roles and costumes, is a major loss. Her gestures, her facial features, and her body postures all offer clues to her great appeal as an actress. Though few of the illustrations are taken directly from performances, they still provide suggestive images of Terry the actress. In a cumulative way, the many illustrations contribute to our appreciation of the qualities of Terry's unique beauty and great stage presence.

Most, if not all, of these changes are indefensible. St John's statement about honoring Terry's text and identity is not merely misleading. It is a calculated falsehood that disguises the actual procedures and agendas that guided the writing and publication of the *Memoirs*. The revisionist *Memoirs* reformulates, trims, and eliminates events, people, and reflections from *Story* so that Terry's life is less about the many people she interacted with and more about her dependence upon Edy and her community. The key agenda becomes apparent in Part II, which delivers the new biography by St John of Terry's life from 1906 to 1928. The added narrative serves to illustrate—and to insist upon—the roles of Edy Craig and St John in her life. In two interlocking ways, therefore, Part Two completes and reinterprets Part One. As revised, Terry's autobiography achieves its fulfillment in not only St John's rewritten narrative, which supposedly improves her style and organization, but also St John's insistent descriptions in Part II of Edy's love and care of her mother. In this reformulation of Terry's career, character, and voice, the *Memoirs* takes control of Terry's life and its meanings.

By placing Terry within the Smallhythe community of women, the *Memoirs* establishes Edy as the central figure in her mother's life. This insistence in the *Memoirs* upon her centrality contrasts with the narrative in *Story*. Although the 1908 edition of *Story* is dedicated to Edy, she remains a minor figure in that narrative. But in the *Memoirs* she becomes the caring—though also controlling—figure of Part II. Of course, Edy's dedicated care for her mother in her last years is praiseworthy, but the narrative of the *Memoirs*, as shaped by St John, has an agenda quite distinct from Terry's narrative in *Story*.

Primarily, Part II focuses on Terry's last years of failing health. These events highlight Edy's care for her mother. With rare exceptions, only those people who served as members of the Smallhythe community now appear in a positive light. Also, St John makes only a limited attempt to provide a record of Terry's theatrical activities subsequent to the Jubilee in 1906. A number of them are ignored or barely mentioned. St John does cover some aspects of Terry's international tours and performances for the 'lectures' on

Shakespeare's characters (1910–1915), but here too the theatrical details are briefly described. Much of Part II charts the events at Smallhythe, the farm that Terry had purchased. Here Edy, St John, and others lived with and cared for her until her death in 1928.[23]

The *Memoirs* concludes with a description of the funeral and memorial services in 1928, followed by a final chapter—"In Memoriam (1928–1932)"—that charts Edy's attempts to turn the Terry estate at Smallhythe into a national monument. St John closes out the book with a justification for another "monument": Edy Craig's publication in 1931 of the correspondence between Terry and Shaw, with a preface by Shaw.[24]

The publication of the Terry-Shaw letters angered Edward Gordon Craig, who rapidly wrote and published *Ellen Terry and Her Secret Self* (1932). Countering the versions of Terry that Shaw, Edy Craig, and St John had put forward in support of the publication of the correspondence, Gordon Craig insisted that "Nelly," his dear mother, had "a secret self—the life of her heart's spirit" that he alone knew and "adored."[25] His book, along with its "Annex" or appendix entitled "A Plea for G.B.S" (inserted in a back pocket), attempted to recover the Nelly Terry that his sister, St John, and Shaw had co-opted improperly in their endeavors to possess her. But in this narrative 'Nelly' belonged to 'Teddy'. Thus, before the *Memoirs* appeared, brother and sister were already involved in what Gail Marshall calls "the wrangling over the 'ownership' of Terry's memory."[26]

Marshall suggests that the struggle between brother and sister began with the publication of the Terry-Shaw letters in 1931.[27] But we need to recognize that the battle for ownership was in fact being fought on several fronts, across many years. For Edy and Gordon the struggle began in childhood, and carried forward. For St John, the process began at the turn of the century, when she first sent letters to Ellen Terry and began showing up at the theatre, determined to attach herself to Terry. Her friendship with Edy dates from that period. Then in 1907 St John placed her own claim on Ellen Terry, not only by serving as the "literary henchman" for *Story* but also by publishing her own book called *Ellen Terry,* a short biography that anticipated the publication of *Story* by a year.

We thus need to see the agenda of the *Memoirs* in terms of the three decades over which Edy and St John established their control of—and their narratives about—Ellen Terry. The *Memoirs* became part of a daughter's campaign to build a 'monument' for her mother, a monument composed of several parts: the memorial services of 1928, the Terry-Shaw letters (1931), the *Four Lectures on Shakespeare* (1931),[28] and the *Memoirs* (1932). St John edited all three publications, in partnership with Edy. The revisionist autobiography, realigned to fit the narrative of Part II, is the justification for these several activities. And since Terry's death, the Smallhythe farm, with its archive of her papers and its annual Shakespeare event that Edy organized in the 1930s, has become the shrine or monument for honoring both Ellen Terry and Edy Craig.

In conclusion, the *Memoirs* needs to be read and evaluated in terms of these events and the complex mission of Edy Craig and Christopher St John. One thing seems obvious now: the *Memoirs,* whatever its value, should not be mistaken as the definitive edition of Terry's autobiography. Perhaps some day such an annotated edition of *Story* will be produced, in accord with Terry's own words and agenda. Yet even then, in order to understand Terry's life and family, we will need to read both *Story* and the *Memoirs*, along with the other books that Edy Craig, Christopher St John, and Gordon Craig published. As biographers and theatre historians, we will need to make clear how and why we are quoting from these texts. We fail as researchers and historians if we ignore or dismiss the issues and problems before us.

ENDNOTES

[1] Years earlier in 1891 Terry published "Stray Memories" in *The New Review*. This was the only other autobiographical publication during her lifetime.

[2] *The Story of My Life*. London: Hutchinson & Co., 1908 (xvi plus 381 pages with index; 81 illustrations). *The Story of My Life*. Extra Illustrated Edition. London: Hutchinson, & Co., 1908 (xvi + 381 pages with index; 101 illustrations). *The Story of My Life*. New York: McClure Co., 1908 (xvi unnumbered + 407 pages with index; 56 illustrations). *The Story of My Life*. New York: Doubleday, Page & Co., 1908; 1909. (xvi + 407 pages with index; 55 plates.) In 1982 a reprint appeared: Woodbridge, Suffolk: The Boydell Press, 1982; New York: Shocken Books, 1982 (viii + 240 pages; hardback and paperback; no illustrations; no editor identified).

[3] Ellen Terry. *Ellen Terry's Memoirs. With preface, notes, and additional biographical chapters by Edith Craig and Christopher St. John*. Eds. Edith Craig and Christopher St. John. London: Victor Gollancz, 1932; reprinted 1933 (xvi + 367 pages with index; 12 illustrations). Also, a New York edition was published by G. P. Putnam's Sons, 1932; reprinted 1932 (xvi + 367 pages with index; 12 illustrations). The brief index of 5 pages fails to list any plays or roles; instead, the roles are tabulated at the close of each chapter but without page references. Two reprints have appeared: New York: Benjamin Blom, 1969; Westport, CT: Greenwood Press, 1970. Both have the same number of pages as the 1932 edition and the same twelve illustrations.

[4] Christopher St John and Edith Craig, "Preface," *Ellen Terry's Memoirs*. New York: G. P. Putnam's Sons, 1932: p. v. All quotations are derived from the New York edition, hereafter identified as *Memoirs*.

[5] Laurence Irving. *Henry Irving: The Actor and His World*. New York: Macmillan Co., 1952; Marguerite Steen. *A Pride of Terrys: Family Saga*. London: Longmans, 1962; Roger Manvell. *Ellen Terry*. New York: G. P. Putnam's Sons, 1968; Edward Craig. *Gordon Craig: The Story of His Life*. New York: Alfred A. Knopf, 1968; Tom Prideaux. *Love or Nothing: The Life and Times of Ellen Terry*. New York: Charles Scribner's Sons, 1975; Nina Auerbach. *Ellen Terry: Player in Her Time*. New York: W. W. Norton, 1987; Joy Melville. *Ellen and Edy: A Biography of Ellen Terry and Her Daughter, Edith Craig, 1847–1947*. London: Pandora, 1987; Moira Shearer. *Ellen Terry*. Glouchestershire: Sutton Publishing Ltd., 1998; Joy Melville. *Ellen Terry*. London: Haus Books, 2006; and Michael Holroyd. *A Strange Eventful History, The Dramatic Lives of Ellen Terry, Henry Irving, and Their Remarkable Families*. London: Chatto & Windus, 2008; New York: Farrar, Straus and Giroux, 2009.

[6] Prideaux (1975: 275).

[7] Manvell (1968: 331).

[8] Auerbach (1987: 488).

[9] St. John Ervine. *Bernard Shaw: His Life, Work, and Friends*. New York: William Morrow & Co., 1956; Madeleine Bingham. *Henry Irving: The Greatest Victorian Actor*. New York: Stein and Day, 1978; A. M. Gibbs. *Bernard Shaw: A Life*. Gainesville, FL: University Press of Florida, 2005; Jeffry Richards. *Sir Henry Irving: A Victorian Actor and His World*. London: Hambledon and London, 2005. Bingham quotes from *Story* on several occasions and lists it

instead of the *Memoirs* in her bibliography, though typical of many theatre biographers, she does not provide notes for her sources. She also confusingly credits Terry's *Four Lectures on Shakespeare* with having "biographical notes and additional biographical chapters" (p. 304). This collapsing together of the *Lectures* and the *Memoirs* suggests, at best, a sloppy attention to detail. By contrast, Jeffrey Richards seems to be in full control of his research sources and methods. He consistently cites *Story* (London, 1908) in his notes, but he does not provide any explanation for why he stays clear of the *Memoirs*. One clue, however, is his reference to Gail Marshall's *Actresses on the Victorian Stage: Feminine Performance and the Galatea Myth* (Cambridge: Cambridge University Press, 1998). Marshall offers a critique of the *Memoirs*, a critique which I will take up presently. Although Richards does not discuss her commentary, it may well have influenced his decision to use *Story* exclusively in his study of Terry.

[10] Margot Peters. *Bernard Shaw and the Actresses: A Biography*. Garden City, NY: Doubleday & Co., 1980; W. D. King. *Henry Irving's Waterloo: Theatrical Engagements with Arthur Conan Doyle, George Bernard Shaw, Ellen Terry, Edward Gordon Craig, Late Victorian Culture, Assorted Ghosts, Old Men, War, and History*. Berkeley: University of California Press, 1993; Russ McDonald. *Look to the Lady: Sarah Siddons, Ellen Terry, and Judi Dench on the Shakespearean Stage*. Athens: University of Georgia Press, 2005.

[11] David F. Cheshire. *Portrait of Ellen Terry*. London: Amber Lane Press, 1989, p. 109.

[12] Michael R. Booth. "Ellen Terry." In *Bernhardt, Terry, Duse: The Actress in Her Time*. Written by John Stokes, Michael R. Booth, and Susan Bassnett. Cambridge: Cambridge University Press, 1988, pp. 65–118. In endnote #19 Booth quotes from the *Memoirs*, but he does not note that St John mistakenly credits the passage to Terry's notebook; in *Story* it is part of a letter from Terry to Edy. Booth also quotes from the *Memoirs* on two other occasions: a selection from Part II of the *Memoirs* and one of St John's notes (#118). Otherwise, he depends upon *Story*.

[13] Gail Marshall. *Actresses on the Victorian Stage: Feminine Performance and the Galatea Myth*. Cambridge: Cambridge University Press, 1998. All quotations are from pp. 182–85.

[14] All quotations are from the New York edition: Farrar, Straus and Giroux, 2009: p. 528. The Granville Barker statement derives from a letter to John Gielgud, but Holroyd provides no date; nor does he identify any source for the Pinero statement. This same cavalier attitude toward documentation appeared in Holroyd's four-volume biography of Bernard Shaw. He published the first three volumes (1988; 1989; 1991) without any notes for quotations and sources, as if readers don't need or desire such information. In volume four (1992) he finally presented his sources, but he and the publisher arranged to print two versions of volume four: one lengthy edition with sources and a cumulative index for all four volumes and one short, cheaper edition without the 301 pages of notes; its index applied only to volume four.

[15] See the "Preface" (pp. v-xi) and notes 1 & 6 to Chapter XIII (pp. 265, 268). To their credit, the editors decided to add an "appendix" to Chapter XIII, a collection of Terry's private comments on Henry Irving (pp. 268–74). The editors state that they found "a shabby little account book" in which Terry had recorded her "frank and honest" comments between 1894 and 1900 (the same period that she and Shaw had carried out much of their correspondence). These reflections, including some decisive judgments on Irving's merits and faults as a person and a performer, are often insightful on both the character of Irving and Terry's relationship with him. One statement, for instance, puts in doubt that they had a love affair at any time: "I think he has always cared for me a little, very little, and has had passing fancies, but he really cares for scarcely any one" (31 August 1895, p. 270).

[16] Christopher St John, "Preface" to *Memoirs*, 1933: p. viii. In 1907 St John published a biography of Ellen Terry (London: The Bodley Head). In terms of writing skill, St John lacks Terry's lively style. This difference in verbal style and voice is also apparent if we compare *Story* to Part II of the *Memoirs*, which is often wordy and turgid. St John was a journeyman writer.

[17] Ibid.

[18] Ibid. Note that St John refers to 'chapters,' not just a single chapter here.

[19] St John, p. 265.

[20] When carrying out research at the Terry Memorial Museum at Smallhythe, Kent, which holds Terry's notebooks, letters, and other materials, Gail Marshall discovered that Terry had annotated her own copy of *Story* with intended revisions. Marshall thus posits that "the editors seem not to have used these annotations as a basis for their revisions" (184). But this is incorrect, for St John mentions these annotations in the 'Preface' to *Memoirs,* and claims in a note to Chapter XIV that she was guided by at least some of them. But which ones? A close comparison is needed to reveal how St John used and misused Terry's annotations.

[21] *Story*: p. 318; *Memoirs*: p. 250.

[22] For instance, the 'extra illustrations' edition of *Story* (London, Hutchinson) has 101 plates, including over 50 images of Terry; she is featured in most of her roles. As far as I can determine, no biographer or theatre historian has examined each of the 1908 editions.

[23] Terry's performances and touring between 1907 and 1918 paid for the farm and its maintenance. Besides cataloguing and celebrating Edy's good deeds, St John tells the story in Part II of Terry's short-lived marriage to James Carew (1907–09), a marriage Edy opposed and fought against. Terry's separation from Carew after two years of living together at Smallhythe was a victory for Edy.

[24]*Ellen Terry and Bernard Shaw: A Correspondence*. Ed. Christopher St John. London: Constable, 1931; New York: G. P. Putnam's Sons, 1931.

[25] Edward Gordon Craig. *Ellen Terry and Her Secret Self.* London: Sampson, Low, Marston, & Co., 1932: p. 15.

[26] Gail Marshall, p. 184. The 'ownership' issue concerned many people during Terry's career and lifetime, including three husbands, Irving, Shaw, Stephen Coleridge, various theatre reviewers, and the public that also adorned her. But the most important 'ownership' claim is that of history itself. In this matter, the establishment of a 'correct' version of the autobiography is part of our historical agenda and responsibility as scholars, but one that we have not fulfilled so far.

[27] Marshall sees the *Memoirs* as a response to *Ellen Terry and Her Secret Self.* But because both books were published in 1932, we should be careful about reading the *Memoirs* as a response to Gordon Craig's angry yet defensive book. It was already in the works when his book appeared. Even if he had not published his version of his mother, the *Memoirs* would have put forward its ownership agenda and its criticism of him.

[28] Ellen Terry. *Four Lectures on Shakespeare*. Ed. Christopher St. John. London: Martin Hopkinson, 1931. With some help from St John, Terry wrote these lectures, which she developed into costumed recitals. The first lecture, "The Triumphant Heroines," was the most popular on the lecture tours.

Page 48: Vaudeville of a Historian

ANN FOLINO WHITE

SENIOR SCHOLAR. Where's your research?

VERY JUNIOR SCHOLAR. In a Rubbermaid tub.

Like many good (well, at least standard) vaudeville bits, in the above joke the auditors' expectations are thwarted through the felicitous coming together of a word's denotation, the power dynamic between character types, and commonly-held truths. In fact, I said those words to a prominent theatre scholar in an effort to both endear myself and divert attention from discussion of my research, which, at that very moment, was indeed housed in a Rubbermaid container on the floor of my office.

Hundreds of documents—photographs, newspapers, official reports, oral histories, private letters—from ten different archives neatly enclosed, opening the container embodied the transformation from dissertation (and graduate student) to book (and scholar). All sorts of things existed in there that I had yet to make satisfactory meaning of. . . .

One of the documents I had literally tucked away, but failed to contain intellectually, is embedded in the manuscript of the Federal Theatre Project's living newspaper *Triple-A Plowed Under*. The night that *Triple-A* premiered at New York City's Biltmore Theatre, March 14, 1936, police removed an audience member for singing the national anthem in protest of Communist Party-USA leader Earl Browder's (played by an actor) appearance on the stage. The rest of the performance played without incident, but the following week *Triple-A* was one scene shorter. Browder remained in the production and in headlines of reviews. Director Joseph Losey had cut the scene "Cotton Patch." Page 48 contains his explanation of why.

Paginated and in identical typescript with the rest of the manuscript, page 48 niggles and captivates me because it is out-of-place and a contradiction in terms. I imagine Thomas Postlewait chiding me, "If we find [. . .] beliefs, statements, and actions unreasonable, we fail to comprehend a key aspect of the rationality that we confront in the documents."[1] In what follows, I attempt to order page 48, to make sense of all that seems illogical in the document according to its immediate, historical, and aesthetic contexts. I fail.

COTTON PATCH

CHARACTERS

Sam, a Negro Farmer

The Sheriff

Note:

"We are not using this scene as it was impossible to get actors to play it with the necessary simplicity. The scene is conceived to be played entirely without props, with vaudeville technique, but not to be played up or plugged. If this scene is to be used, it should be played in front of a cyclorama framed with blacks, and the subsequent Sharecropper Scene, should be played in front of Blacks."

J.L.

-48-

Page 48. *Triple-A Plowed Under*. 1936. Editorial Staff of the Living Newspaper, Federal Theatre Project for New York City. Publication No. 35, Reissued March 1938, National Service Bureau. Production Records, NYC, Production Title File, 1934–39, Production Records, 1934–43, Federal Theatre Collection, Library of Congress, Washington D.C., and Federal Theatre Project Collection, Fenwick Library, Special Collections and Archives Department, George Mason University, Fairfax, VA.

Textual Materiality: Why is a Director's Note About Bad Acting Included in a Script?

Page 48 features a scene title—"Cotton Patch"—a dramatis personae—"Sam, a Negro Farmer" and "The Sheriff"—and brief note punctuated as a direct quotation of Joe Losey ("J.L."). The note's tense suggests that Losey composed it during the show's run, but for the benefit of others, as it suggests what to do if "Cotton Patch" is staged.[2] Notes by living newspaper production staff are not uncommon in FTP manuscripts; some are handwritten, but much marginalia, as well as production notes, are typed. Production materials were mimeographed by the WPA National Service Bureau for distribution to FTP regional units and other interested parties. Filed with NYC production records, this manuscript's cover-page confirms that it is a March 1938 "reissue" of *Triple-A Plowed Under* and thus likely a straightforward reprinting of the (lost or undiscovered) 1936 script used in rehearsals. The bureau distributed 600 copies of a *Triple-A* manuscript to colleges, little theatre groups, libraries, and individuals by January 21, 1938, the same year that Random House published *Triple-A Plowed Under* in *Federal Theatre Plays.*[3] While "Cotton Patch" appears in this version, Losey's note is absent, inappropriate to a published play.

If the archived edition is the one that circulated among regional units for ease of mounting another production of *Triple-A,* it is still odd that a director's note concerning actors' failure to get a scene right is included. Each regional unit producing the play was required to employ local actors. On the other hand, by way of insult / proscription the note stipulates the manner in which the scene should be played, functioning like typical stage directions. Yet Losey's instructions are incongruous, perhaps even counterintuitive for an actor used to "playing up" in vaudeville.

Dramaturgy: What is "Cotton Patch" Doing in *This* Vaudeville?

Loren Kruger names Joseph Losey and "satiric vaudeville" as exemplars of the artists and the workers' theatre aesthetics absorbed by the Federal Theatre Project.[4] Both FTP personnel and theatre critics referred to *Triple-A* and other living newspapers as "revue." Vaudeville technique permeates *Triple-A.* Structurally, it is a collection of self-contained short scenes that concern normal situations turned upside-down. Its dialogue features inversions of words' meanings, puns, and repetitions of words and phrases. Here, these techniques are aimed toward a sardonic, not a comedic, tone. For example, in scene fourteen, a bowl of oatmeal that cost two cents yesterday is three cents today, and now out of the hungry customer's price range. In scene twenty-one, Dorothy Sherwood cries that she drowned her child because he was "Hungry, hungry, hungry, hungry, *hungry*"; her plea is met with a dozen voices calling out a "Guilty" verdict. In scene two, a Banker explains his need to foreclose on a farm, "You see my situation, Fred"; Fred responds, "I don't see a damn thing."[5] These formal aspects of vaudeville effectively represent the domino effects of the New Deal agriculture program (i.e. the

Agricultural Adjustment Act, called "triple A") on citizens nationwide. The pacing that this style enables also facilitates a panoramic portrait of the contemporaneous situation, realizing the scope and temporal qualities of a newspaper. It is a drama that nearly forecloses the possibility of "plugging."

As for "Cotton Patch," it adheres to the vaudeville style used throughout *Triple-A*, and the plot itself is not funny. Sam becomes a farmer through federal loan programs, buying himself a bit of land and a mule. The Sheriff comes to collect Sam's mule in order to reconcile overdue taxes. Sam is exasperated because this is the second mule the Sheriff has taken, leaving Sam, again, without a means to work his land. In terms of Sam's characterization, however, "Cotton Patch" falls squarely in the realm of light minstrel comedy, the type that graced big time and small time vaudeville stages, and film. Sam sings and admires his (pantomimed) mule, which he has named "Guv'ment" in honor of his new benefactor. Sam's dialogue is written in stereotypic dialect that abounds in "sho'nuffs" and syntactical disorder:

> (singing) Sho'nuff got a mule. /Sho'nuff have. / Sho' 'nuff goin' raise a crop/ Sho' 'nuff am. (He stops singing and begins to admire his mule.) (Continuing and talking) Boy! Yo! Sho' is a purty mule. Ol' Guv'ment goin' to be mighty pleased with yo'! Yeah, man! Yo' sho' look like you goin' pull dis ol' patch back.[6]

Professor and poet Sterling A. Browne, in his 1933 enumeration of white authors' representations of African American characters, describes the stock "Comic Negro" as possessing a "[nature] of sunshine and song, whose wretchedness becomes nothing since [his] in (sic) a simple philosophy of mirth!"[7] Indeed, Sam's good-humored nature is rendered in his blazon of Guv'ment, while the character's simple-minded "alarm" in his question, "Mr. Sheriff, yo' ain't goin' take my mule, is you?" registers his crisis as pitiable, rather than tragic. That is to say, Sam's fall is not so great because he lacks the natural capacity to understand the workings of the world, to ever really have become a farmer.

Not until the scene's final moment—structured like a vaudeville punch line—does the tenor shift to doleful satire:

> SHERIFF. Come on, mule, we gotta get goin'. (To Sam) What you call this mule to make him go?
>
> SAM. (Woefully) I calls him Guv'ment.
>
> SHERIFF. Giddap, Guv'ment.[8]

By naming his mule, "Guv'ment," Sam inadvertently characterizes the Roosevelt Administration a jackass. Both humorous and politically biting, the joke (a parody of the Democratic donkey) suggests the short-sightedness of government programs that give with one hand and take with the other. Yet, satire or not, to land the punch line the actor must sustain Sam's character as a sympathetic minstrel.

John O'Connor counts "Cotton Patch" one of the original scenes composed the weekend following director of the New York City FTP unit Elmer Rice's resignation over the censorship of *Ethiopia* and just before the announcement that agriculture would be the subject of the next living newspaper. *Ethiopia's* subject was Mussolini's invasion of that African country. The U.S. State Department, for fear of offending Mussolini, shut down this production and prohibited the depiction of foreign officials in future living newspapers "on the grounds that the impersonation of foreign statesmen might lead to diplomatic embarrassment."[9] O'Connor accounts for Losey's intentions for "Cotton Patch" as indicative of the political critiques staged by living newspapers:

> The absurdity of the situation was to be emphasized by the staging, but [. . .] Losey could not find an actor to play Sam [. . .] to his satisfaction so the scene was cut in production. [. . .] Although it seems likely that Losey was attempting to comment on the subject through the staging, there is an uneasy quality about this scene, especially when it is compared with the Colonel Julian Scene in *Ethiopia*. Someone in the Living Newspaper Unit apparently considered blacks as comic relief.[10]

I want to agree with O'Connor's interpretation of Losey's goal for the scene. First, *Triple-A*, including "Cotton Patch," represents the national situation as inane. Photographs may magnify how *Triple-A* embodied the chaos and absurdity of the Great Depression through seminal, singular gestures. Nonetheless, actor Norman Lloyd compared the performance style more to Meyerhold and Eisenstein than to American vaudeville (for example, a farmer in the scene "Dust," who stands full-front to the audience as dirt pours out of his fist like sand, creates a concentrated, stark expression of a wasted landscape and life's work—decidedly not a vaudeville sketch).[11] O'Connor substantiates his claim about Losey's intentions in "Cotton Patch" by collapsing what he perceives as racist comedic writing with Losey's explicit displeasure with the acting. Arthur Arent, Philip Barber, and Morris Watson—the FTP personnel O'Connor credits with writing the scene—or the unnamed authors on the Editorial Staff of the Living Newspaper may have considered African Americans comic relief. The note implies that Losey didn't and yet Losey also did not suggest that the script is problematic.

Second, O'Connor cites black actors' refusal to play Colonel Julian. Julian, an American pilot known as the "Black Eagle of Harlem," had renounced his U.S. citizenship to serve Ethiopian Emperor Haile Selassie.[12] Upon his return to the U.S., following a failed performance, Julian had publicly demeaned Ethiopians as "savages." The script of *Ethiopia* retained this degrading language. And so a white actor, who would wear blackface, was cast in the role.[13] That black actors in *Ethiopia* took a political stance is comparable to the instance of actors in *Triple-A Plowed Under*, who protested the inclusion of Earl Browder in the show. These actors, also members of the Federal Theatre Veterans League, threatened to strike unless the scene featuring Browder was cut because "as loyal Americans, [they] regard[ed] as an insult the placing of Earle [sic] Browder on a level with our patriotic forefathers, Thomas Jefferson and Abraham Lincoln, and our distinguished fellow citizen [former New York Governor] Alfred E. Smith."[14] Both of these situations are very unlike that of "Cotton Patch." One of the only things that is clear from Losey's note is that Losey, *not* the actor playing Sam, had problems with the portrayal.

In the playbills, Clifford Green is named only in the role of Sam. This is unusual; the greater than 100 roles required most actors to play at least two parts. However, single casting is common to the character Sam. This was true even in Milwaukee, where the very limited number of actors (37 total) required some actors to play six parts. Los Angeles is a bit of an exception; Earl Smith played the waiter in both restaurant scenes, and Sam.[15] Here, the class status of a waiter may have allowed for a black actor to perform this role as well as Sam. On the one hand, single casting might mean that black actors portrayed Sam. Alternately, *Triple-A* took only between forty and fifty minutes to perform twenty-five scenes and sub-scenes, perhaps not adequate time needed for a white actor to remove or apply blackface makeup in order to play another (white) role.

A photograph of the NYC production's finale features two African American actors among the ensemble.[16] One of these men could very well be Clifford Green. These men also could have played the additional sharecroppers (the actors in these roles are not named in the program) or they could be Jack Denver and Raoul Henry, who played the second sharecropper and the fourth sharecropper, respectively. These characters appear in the scene "Sharecroppers."[17] The anomaly of Sam's casting along with the presence of black actors on the NYC stage suggests that Clifford Green (about whom I have not to date been able to find any information) may have been an African American actor. I, however, cannot exclude the possibility that Green may have been a white actor in blackface. From a contemporary perspective, casting black actors to play the sharecroppers, while using a white actor in blackface to play Sam in NYC would present an obvious contradiction, but this was not the case for early-twentieth-century staging.

In the 1930s, use of blackface makeup did not necessitate a comedic portrayal of African Americans or an all white cast. Likewise, "minstrelsy," "comedy" and "blackface" were not entirely synonymous or inextricable. *Ethiopia* offers a case in point. While, as mentioned above, Colonel Julian was to be played by a white actor in blackface due to the absence of willing black actors; this makeup signified only that the audience should "see" the white actor as "black." In fact, the Colonel Julian scene is decidedly serious and depicts Julian through quotation of his public speeches: "I left [Ethiopia] because the Ethiopians are savages, just plain savages, that's all. It is an act of God that Italy should go in there and take over the land."[18]

Losey's dissatisfaction with Green's playing of the scene may demonstrate his perception that no generic confusion exists in the script; that the only scene featuring singing and dancing "fits" in an otherwise abstract, stylized documentary of the nation's current events. From this angle, I could fault the power of racial performativity to conclude that Losey believed Sam represented "authentic blackness," and lacked theatricality. The scene "Sharecroppers," which immediately follows "Cotton Patch," suggests that this theory is untenable. Based on activities of the Southern Tenant Farmers' Union, known for being a radical mixed-race union, the scene's southern dialect is spoken by both the white farmer and the black and white sharecroppers.[19] And if, as Paul Nadler suspects, Losey helped Elmer Rice plan and write the unfinished living newspaper play *The South*, the writing in "Cotton

Patch" would seem highly artificial to Losey.[20] *The South* was an anti-lynching play about black sharecroppers that exhibits the same episodic structure and reliance upon public documents as *Triple-A*. Finally, Losey's theatrical career—his history in workers' theatre, his blacklisting by HUAC and his entire filmography—suggests that it would have been out of his character to hold such a perspective on matters of race. Even if Nadler is wrong, if Losey's biography is misleading, and if performativity is at play, it is paradoxical for Losey to have perceived Sam's scripting as "natural," but not Green's performance as such.

Performance Records: What Did Clifford Green Do Wrong?

In the Federal Theatre Collection at the Library of Congress, hundreds of newspaper reviews—most often, typed excerpts of sections deemed relevant by WPA staff—are catalogued for each play and production. In addition to this, scrapbooks and clippings archived at George Mason University and in the Records of the Federal Theatre at the National Archives offer a near-comprehensive set of press reviews. In all of these, I have found only one mention of "Cotton Patch," in a *Brooklyn Eagle* review: "The authors erred, I believe, in bothering to burlesque Mr. Smith and his derby and in characterizing a Negro planter in minstrel show terms." The reviewer's criticism comes by way of his comparison of these scenes with the "exciting" staging of current events "sans exaggeration" in the Sherwood scene and the fast-paced, choreographed movements of stockbrokers in the Wheat Pit scene.[21]

In the case of the portrayal of conservative democrat and anti-New Dealer Alfred E. Smith, all the evidence (negative press reviews and the play's actual quoting of Smith) points to Rickey White's subpar portrayal.[22] "Cotton Patch" is another story. The reviewer blames the writers, perhaps implying that the text over-determined the performance. However, I have found no other records of this scene to help clarify what the achievement of "sans exaggeration" in the reviewer's terms (or "simplicity" in Losey's) may have looked like on stage. No extant records answer why Losey found Green's performance discordant *within* the scene, but evidently felt White's performance passable. Unlike the twenty-four other scenes, there is no trace of "Cotton Patch" in the NYC production records—records that include scene-by-scene music and lighting cues, costume and properties notes, staging diagrams, and many photographs. The crew may have "erased" notes once "Cotton Patch" was cut in order to keep cues clear, and it is possible that production photos were taken after March 16, 1936, the latest date on the first and only NYC playbill that lists "Cotton Patch."

In fact, though the 1936 productions in Cleveland, Milwaukee, Los Angeles and Chicago all included "Cotton Patch," no photographs of this scene appear in the collections. Only Charles Gardner's conductor cuts from the Chicago production exist, in which "Dixie" is played "till (sic) colored man on stage."[23] Directed by H. Gordon Graham, the Chicago production's use of perhaps the U.S.'s most famous minstrel song to open "Cotton Patch" is important because Graham assisted Losey as the NYC production's Associate

Director. George Kondolf, in his report on the Chicago production to Hallie Flanagan, boasted of Graham's success (to his own credit): "I told [Graham] when he arrived that I felt the only way to do TRIPLE A was to do it exactly as it was produced in New York. Both he and I felt [. . .] if any changes were to be made in the production, they should be improvements based on Graham's past experience; we should add only what we were SURE were improvements, etc."[24] It is impossible to know if Graham's rendition of "Cotton Patch" represented his idea of an improvement upon Losey's or a faithful realization of Losey's vision for the scene. Ironically, either option presents a paradox.

I want to know how Losey understood the place of "Cotton Patch" in the progressive aesthetics and politics of the living newspaper form. I want to understand what Losey saw when he watched Clifford Green perform Sam. It makes sense to believe that the politics surrounding *Ethiopia's* cancelation and the FTP as a whole made it difficult for Losey to openly criticize *Triple-A*, the first living newspaper allowed to be performed for the public. But to make such a speculation is to create another contradiction: a story in which Losey throws Clifford Green under the bus, an actor who is on relief and possibly marginalized because of his race. I can't tell that story because of page 48, all that it evokes and all that it evades.

ENDNOTES

1 *The Cambridge Introduction to Theatre Historiography* (Cambridge: Cambridge University Press, 2009), 230.

2 Editorial Staff of the Living Newspaper, Federal Theatre Project for New York City, *Triple-A Plowed Under*, Publication No. 35, Reissued March 1938, National Service Bureau, Production Records, NYC, Production Title File, 1934–39, Production Records, 1934–43, Federal Theatre Collection, Library of Congress, Washington D.C., 48.

3 "Report on Federal Theatre Living Newspaper Scripts, January 21, 1938," Correspondence of the Living Newspaper Project Re: Accumulation of Information, 1936–1939, Work Projects Administration Records of the Federal Theatre Project, Record Group 69, National Archives and Records Administration, College Park, MD.

4 *The National Stage: Theatre and Cultural Legitimation in England, France and America* (Chicago: University of Chicago Press, 1992), 139–40.

5 Editorial Staff, *Triple-A Plowed Under*, 38, 57, and 7.

6 Ibid., 49.

7 "Negro Character as Seen by White Authors," *The Journal of Negro Education*, 2.2 (April 1933), 188.

8 Editorial Staff, *Triple-A Plowed Under*, 50.

9 Qtd. in "Uncle Sam is Producer Now," *New Jersey Press*, May 15, 1936, Triple A Plowed Under Publicity, Production Title File, 1934–39, Production Records, 1934–43, Federal Theatre Collection, Library of Congress, Washington D.C.

10 "The Drama of Farming: The Federal Theatre Living Newspapers on Agriculture," *Prospects: An Annual of American Cultural Studies*, 15 (1990), 338–9.

11 Norman Lloyd, interview with John O'Connor, Hollywood, CA, January 5, 1976, transcribed by Rhoda Durkan Nov 1977, Oral History New Deal Culture, Federal Theatre Project Collection, Fenwick Library, Special Collections and Archives Department, George Mason University, Fairfax, VA. Norman Lloyd was a very successful actor throughout the twentieth century. He played multiple roles in *Triple-A Plowed Under*. Lloyd then played the

famous everyman character Angus Buttonkooper, a staple character in subsequent living newspapers.

[12] David R. Griffiths, "John C. Robinson," *African American Lives*, Eds. Henry Louis Gates, Jr. and Evelyn Brooks Higginbotham (Oxford University Press, 2004).

[13] O'Connor, endnote 23, 358.

[14] "Actors Resent Red in Scene," *New York Sun*, March 14, 1936, Triple A Plowed Under Publicity, Production Title File, 1934–39, Production Records, 1934–43, Federal Theatre Collection, Library of Congress, Washington D.C.

[15] Triple-A Plowed Under Playbills, Production Title File, 1934–39, Production Records, 1934–43, Federal Theatre Collection, Library of Congress, Washington D.C.

[16] Photograph no. 18, Work Projects Administration Records of the Federal Theatre Project, Record Group 69, National Archives and Records Administration, College Park, MD.

[17] I have been unable to locate substantive information on these actors. Raoul Henry performed the "Voice" in Scene Eleven, "Birth of Triple-A." This role is not the "Voice of the Living Newspaper." Henry also performed in the 1940 production of *The Fifth Column*. Paul Williams, who played Sam in Chicago, was also in the chorus of *The Swing Mikado*, indicating that Williams is African American. Internet Broadway Database, www.ibdb.com, accessed September 1, 2010.

[18] Arthur Arent, "*Ethiopia*: The First Living Newspaper," Intro. Dan Issac, *Educational Theatre Journal* 20.1 (March 1968), 27. Such uses of dark makeup to suggest a character's "blackness" was a common convention in America to the mid-twentieth century. Some famous examples include Edwin Forrest's and Orson Welles's depictions of the tragic character Othello in the 1860s and 1952, respectively. Perhaps more pertinent, the 1920s production of *The Emperor Jones* demonstrates how combining white actors in blackface and black actors on stage did not seem contradictory; Charles Gilpin played the title role, and white actors in blackface played the natives.

[19] J.H. Pollack described the scene as one in which "colored sharecroppers united with white" in "Two Significant Plays," *Pennsylvanian*, April 6, 1936, Triple A Plowed Under Publicity, Production Title File, 1934–39, Production Records, 1934–43, Federal Theatre Collection, Library of Congress, Washington D.C.

[20] "Liberty Censored: Black Living Newspapers of the Federal Theatre Project," *African American Review*, 29.4 (Winter 1995), 615.

[21] "Average Intelligence." *Brooklyn Eagle*, March 22, 1936, Triple A Plowed Under Publicity, Production Title File, 1934–39, Production Records, 1934–43, Federal Theatre Collection, Library of Congress, Washington D.C.

[22] The reviewer for *Variety* wrote, "Al Smith is badly burlesqued," March 18, 1936. Other reviewers, without making a value judgment, described how White as Smith wore Smith's signature derby hat and used Smith's signature prop—a cigar—in a very theatrical manner. Numerous reviews cite that audiences booed the characters Alfred E. Smith and Earl Browder because of these men's politics. Triple A Plowed Under Publicity, Production Title File, 1934–39, Production Records, 1934–43, Federal Theatre Collection, Library of Congress, Washington D.C.

[23] July 24, 1936, Triple A Plowed Under Orchestration, Production Title File, 1934–39, Production Records, 1934–43, Federal Theatre Collection, Library of Congress, Washington D.C. Walter Monfried, in his review of the Milwaukee production, tells us only what went wrong with the scene, "a few pardonable errors in stage technic (sic). A backdrop of a Detroit meat shop for a plantation episode." "Players Show Farm Plight," *Milwaukee Journal*, June 17, 1936, Federal Theatre Project Scrapbooks Complied by the Department of Information, NYC Office, Feb–June 1936, Work Projects Administration Records of the Federal Theatre Project, Record Group 69, National Archives and Records Administration, College Park, MD.

[24] July 10, 1936, Correspondence of the National Office with the Regional Offices, 1935–39, Work Projects Administration Records of the Federal Theatre Project, Record Group 69, National Archives and Records Adminstration, College Park, MD.

Mistaken Identities, Miscegenation, & Missing Origins: The Curious Case of *Haiti*[1]

SHANNON ROSE RILEY

As an archive gumshoe, I've never seen another case like the 1938 Federal Theatre Project (FTP) play, *Haiti*. Researching the play had all the suspense of film noir, including unverifiable clues, phantom origins, and mistaken identities. My investigations revealed that although *Haiti* was written by white *New York Times* journalist, William DuBois, it has been misattributed to W.E.B. Du Bois in several archives including the Library of Congress (LC), the Schomburg Center for Research in Black Culture, the British Library, and WorldCat.[2] I also found that the work had been misattributed to W.E.B. in a French translation and that both the translation and library catalogs have become sources for a phantom body of scholarship on the play, *Haiti*, by W.E.B. Du Bois—a play that never existed. Regarding the script by William DuBois, there were several versions to track: the published version and production scripts based on the collaboration between the white playwright and black FTP director Maurice Clark—and the white playwright's "original," which has gone missing from the archive. In its day, the play was part of a federal court drama: investigated by the FBI and used by the Dies Committee, or House Committee on Un-American Activities (HUAC),[3] to argue for closing the FTP. The play's life has all the elements of noir down to its racy and dangerous reputation . . . indeed, *Haiti* resisted most of my inquiries—many of its mysteries have never been revealed. I've gone on the record about part of the case, but there's more to the story.[4] In what follows, I will trace some of my footsteps.

Voiceover: "It was a curious case of mistaken identity . . . "

I had been looking for plays about the Haitian Revolution (1791–1803) that were written or produced in the U.S. during its military occupation of Haiti[5] when I found four citations for a play called *Haiti* in the LC database.[6] Two referred to graphic materials from a 1938 FTP production: the first attributed to William DuBois; the second to both William and W.E.B. The other two citations referred to works of dramatic literature attributed to W.E.B. Du Bois—one published in French (1983), the other in a Random House collection of FTP plays (1938).

I had heard of the play by the white DuBois and retraced my sources. Most scholars of the play reference the author's race, including Glenda E. Gill, Mary Renda, Errol Hill and James V. Hatch.[7] FTP scholars Lorraine Brown and John O'Connor also discuss the once-famous Negro Unit play written by the white journalist.[8] Not one mentions a play of the same title and date by W.E.B. Du Bois.

I determined the W.E.B. citations were incorrect or referred to another play of the same title. What were the odds? Given the similar names and the fact that W.E.B. frequently wrote about Haiti, perhaps confusion was inevitable. I began looking for historical reviews and soon found several that named the white DuBois as author.[9]

Who could be trusted? The LC? FTP scholars? Historical reviewers? I compared the 1938 and 1983 publications. A first edition copy of the 1938 Random House publication did not attribute the work to W.E.B. Du Bois as the LC catalog indicated, but to William DuBois on both the title and contents pages.[10] The 1983 French publication was attributed inconsistently to "W.B. [sic] Du Bois" on the cover, "William Du Bois" on the title page, and "William Burghardt Du Bois" in the introduction, even as it confirmed the translation source was the FTP play.[11] A scene-by-scene comparison confirmed they were indeed the same.

I proved beyond a shadow of doubt that *Haiti* had been misattributed in both the French translation and the LC catalog, even though the play's contemporaries knew its author. I argued that the source of confusion was not a mere similarity in names, but a racialized logic at work in the archive, which assumes that a play staging the revolution of the "Black Republic" and produced by a black theatrical unit *must* be written by a black author. At the very least, this logic erases the play's interracial collaboration.[12]

I sent a copy of my findings to the LC and soon received a reply. The librarian handling the case confirmed the play was attributed correctly when catalogued with the 1938 Random House collection. The authority card specifically contains the following handwritten note: "Letter rec'd Sept. 1938 from William Edward Burghardt Du Bois=not the same person as above." She stated that the LC "acknowledged that the misattribution occurred during the creation of the online catalog entry."[13]

I was concerned with this last statement, partly because I theorized the item had been changed intentionally. I acknowledged cataloging procedures could be partly responsible, but I was suspicious of the claim that it alone was at fault. A few days later, I received another email confirming the catalog records were being corrected, although it was unclear whether they would track the misattribution in the permanent record, as I suggested.[14] And despite restating concerns over the cataloging process itself (especially replacement processes and digitizing), the LC finally confirmed my suspicions: someone had "touched" the record by hand.[15]

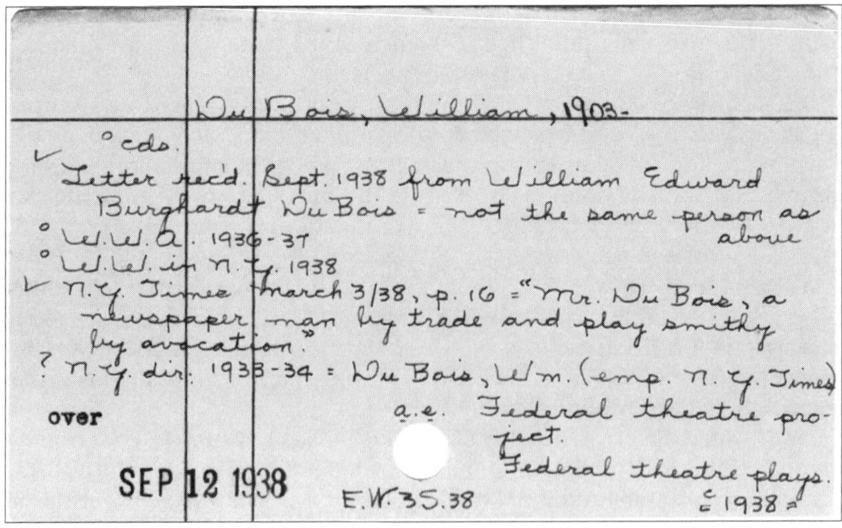

Du Bois, William, 1903-

° cds.

Letter rec'd. Sept. 1938 from William Edward Burghardt Du Bois = not the same person as above

° W.W.A. 1936-37

° W.W. in N.Y. 1938

N.Y. Times March 3/38, p. 16 = "Mr. Du Bois, a newspaper man by trade and play smithy by avocation."

? N.Y. dir. 1933-34 = Du Bois, Wm. (emp. N.Y. Times)

a.e. Federal theatre project.

Federal theatre plays. c1938

over

SEP 12 1938

E.W. 3.5.38

LC Authority Card for the author William DuBois. Note that W.E.B. Du Bois sent a letter to the LC clarifying he was "not the same person as above."

Voiceover: "Harlem, 1938. Black and white. Angular shots of cityscape in shadows. Disorienting perspectives. No one can be trusted. Told as a flashback or sequence of flashbacks."

In the spring of '38, *Haiti* was hot in Harlem.[16] The Lafayette Theatre saw 74,000 audience members in less than three months—77,000 before the play moved on to Boston and Hartford.[17] The press was taken with the extravagant play—even the Shuberts wanted to buy the production.[18] In April, two men claimed authorship of *Haiti* and sued DuBois, Clark, and the producer for $25,000 damages and "an accounting of profits."[19] They even tried to stop performances at the Lafayette. By July, I got wind that the FBI was keeping tabs on the cast and crew.

The play was threatening for many reasons. For one, it depicted the Haitian Revolution—the only successful slave revolt in the Americas. By the early 20th century, the "Black Republic" was "the symbolic center of Pan-Africanist discourse"[20] and a persistent symbol of challenge to white political and cultural power. Certainly Haiti and its revolution had long been a source of racial anxiety in the U.S.[21] Moreover, the play was staged soon after the lengthy U.S. occupation of Haiti and debates on the country's capacity for "self-determination," the rhetoric of which was also crucial to black radical political thought.[22] Finally, it was one of the first plays to stage black on white violence and was performed by a racially integrated cast for racially integrated audiences. For these reasons as well as witness allegations, the play was ultimately targeted in the successful argument for closing the federally funded FTP.

In a *New York Times* article dated July 27, 1938, Republican Congressman J. Parnell Thomas of New Jersey, Dies Committee member, declared that *Haiti* was "un-American" due to "communistic leanings."[23] The Committee, formed in May 1938, aimed primarily to discredit the New Deal and its "socialist" programs—but even before it could begin its formal hearings, Thomas had targeted the FTP. As O'Connor and Brown note, "any [play] where blacks and whites worked together to overcome oppression automatically signaled Communist propaganda."[24]

The play also caused panic through its interracial collaboration, audience desegregation, and providing equal pay regardless of race. The success of the Negro Unit and the integration of casts and audiences were seen as signs of communist influence.[25] The goal of the HUAC witch-hunt was not only rooting out communism, but equally—and with no great subtlety—policing black resistance and interracial relationships. "Un-American" activities included the interracial collaboration the FTP exemplified. More than any other Federal One project, HUAC targeted the FTP because it saw the possibilities for using theatre "as a weapon."[26]

One undercover FBI agent remarked that the "immoral degenerate practices" indulged in by both blacks and whites during FTP rehearsals aroused tremendous bitterness during HUAC hearings.[27] One Department of Investigation (DOI) informant specifically mentioned *Haiti* in his lurid description of interracial mixing; he testified that the white woman who played the part of the mixed-race Odette lived with one of the black actors, visited various nightclubs and bars in his company, and was arrested for disorderly conduct. He claimed *Haiti* was closed for these reasons.[28]

Voiceover: "Oh—wait—I was going to tell you about the white origin . . . "

Like the misattribution, most scholarship on *Haiti* obscures the play's racial complexities. Confusion begins in 1978 when O'Connor and Brown publish Maurice Clark's account.[29]

> [. . .] So I called the playwright up to my apartment. I said, "Look, this play should be done in Harlem, but if it is done in Harlem, I can tell you one thing. They will come right over the footlights and tear us to pieces."
>
> "But," I said, "we can make a play out of this that they will love." And so we went to work, and we rewrote this play from top to bottom. It was about the victorious Haitian republic over the greatest army that had ever been in existence.
>
> DuBois was a southerner, a real southern Cracker, and his play was about miscegenation, which excited him terribly. So finally, when the play was all finished and I was ready to go ahead with it, he said, "Listen now, Clark, listen. I've given in to you on every single thing but I want to tell you one thing right here and now that I demand, and that is that on that stage no white hands and no black hands shall touch." And I said, "Well, now, that's fair enough."
>
> So, during the play the white and black actors didn't touch, but the encore was mine. When the curtain came up for the encore, the whites were among the blacks, holding hands, and that's how they took their bows. (Clark)[30]

Clark highlights the blackness of his dramatic revision by marking its political opposite in the figure of the racist Cracker who is excited (read both aroused and made anxious) by miscegenation. Clark also claims power at the end of the play—and the end of his narrative—by denying the playwright's one wish and offering in its place an image of miscegenation . . . of interracial collaboration. What Clark ultimately foregrounds in his conclusion isn't revolution or the play's black on white violence—but the racially integrated cast coming defiantly together at curtain call. Further, Clark states "so *we* went to work, and *we* rewrote this play from top to bottom" [my italics].[31] He even elaborates on bringing the white man into his personal space. As noted above, interracial relationships of all kinds mattered in the play's historical context.[32] It certainly caught the popular imagination; one *Time* reviewer used similar rhetoric in describing how the "half-white, half-Negro cast" took their first bows while holding hands before a wildly enthusiastic, "half-white, half-Negro audience."[33]

However, in the pages surrounding the director's words, O'Connor and Brown effectively erase Clark's "we" by amplifying the racially polemical aspects of Clark's stance:

> Actually, southerner DuBois' original script focused on the evils of miscegenation, but New York director Maurice Clark was able to rewrite enough of it to bring forth the underlying dramatic story of the struggle for racial identity and self-determination for black Haiti. (O'Connor and Brown)[34]

With this, O'Connor and Brown reduce the critical power of the interracial collaboration that took place in Clark's apartment—an all the more powerful collaboration if indeed DuBois was a racist who feared interracial mixing. To this black/white polarization, O'Connor and Brown add the rhetoric of "evil," fanning the flames around DuBois's position as a white racist.

Since then, most scholarship on the play reduces Clark's commentary to the equivalent of a historiographical one-liner by amplifying the story of the script's epic revision.[35] Significant difference is reproduced between the "white" original and the "black" revision—even as the image of the mixed cast taking its bow on opening night is repeated. The original script becomes "a *morality play* about the *grave dangers* of miscegenation" and "a *tirade against* miscegenation" [my italics].[36] One scholar notes, "By the time *Haiti* hit the stage [. . .] it had been *utterly transformed*. No longer a play about the *tragic demise of the French*, it was *now a dramatization of the black struggle for freedom* [my italics]."[37] The most recent version goes as far as to claim that DuBois stipulated "no white person should touch a black person in performance" before "granting rights" to stage "his plays" in general.[38]

Yet I located a *NYT* article dated March 20 1938, in which DuBois describes the play's production—and there is none of the rhetoric one might expect from a racist.[30] DuBois describes a positive experience with the Negro Unit and shows clear respect for the FTP, which he describes as "what may some day be a representative national theatre."[40] DuBois relates in detail how Ullman had contacted him saying he had a perfect venue at the Negro Unit's Lafayette Theatre, although the same producer had rejected the script the year before. Nowhere does DuBois sound upset that the play was selected for black Harlem. A *Daily News* article dated March 11, 1938—just a week after opening night and over a week before DuBois wrote the *NYT* article—described how the Shubert brothers, then-dominant theatre producers in the U.S., had made an offer to take *Haiti* to Broadway and were turned down by DuBois who felt "extremely reluctant" and doubted whether a "commercial producer could or would do as well by it."[41] DuBois stated that the FTP "did well indeed" by his play and it "never would have seen the light of day without the Federal Theatre,"[42] noting that the play had been rejected by thirty-three [white] Broadway producers.[43] You'd think a racist, anti-miscegenist playwright would sell to the Shuberts right away—get the work in the hands of a white producer and director so the "original" tale could be told and the bodies kept separate onstage. But that was not the case.

Given all of the mistaken identities, false leads, and whitewashing thus far, I wondered to what degree the story about the play's revision was obscuring the complexities of interracial collaboration and the risks of staging race revolution in the context of 1938 America. One would need to do a close comparative reading of DuBois's original script with the 1938 Random House publication in order to find out just how "utterly transformed" from one racialist perspective to another the play had been . . . I went in search of this white origin.

According to Renda, the Billy Rose Theatre Collection (BRTC) houses the "Production Files," and a "Complete Working Script" (CWS), which I hoped was the original—or would reveal some anti-miscegenist rhetoric.[44] Unfortunately for this story, a close reading of the CWS revealed it was one of the already collaborative performance texts.[45] I hoped to have better luck with the "Production Files," but they were missing. A senior archivist verified that in 1996, several years after Renda completed research, the FTP archives in the BRTC had been unboxed, unbound, and reorganized with a new call number system. Most went into a new section called the Hallie Flanagan Papers and the rest was kept in the general collection. Another archivist confirmed some files had been lost.[46] I contacted Renda to find out what she remembered of the original. But she hadn't found it either; instead, she pieced her narrative together from secondary sources, especially Clark's account in O'Connor and Brown.

I continued looking for the original script and any traces of this "white" *Haiti* at Princeton, George Mason, and the LC. None had manuscripts other than the Random House publication and a 1938 National Service Bureau copy, which resembles the CWS.[47] Not even the William DuBois Collection at Boston University has an original manuscript.[48] The rumored white, anti-miscegenist original has simply disappeared.

There are parts of the two working scripts that didn't make the Random House publication—and these may reveal a white, racist perspective. My investigation shows that both the CWS and the Service Bureau copy describe a moment when the French General LeClerc rubs Jacques's head "for luck"[49] however this was omitted from the Random House version. Yet they also share an extremely graphic image of the white Boucher hanging by the neck[50]—and it too was removed from the Random House version. This image hardly depicts a white racist position, but is a figure both of white anxiety and black justice.

Analyzing the play as an interracially collaborative, or miscegenated, text—as the product of DuBois *and* Clark, as well as the mixed cast, crew, and audience—poses more than mere methodological problems as soon as one attempts to trace bloodlines, parse out authorship. Hunting for bits by the white or black author may reinscribe overly simplistic racialized stereotypes. It may seem logical to attribute certain moments to the white author, such as Odette's horror when she discovers she is part black—and other moments to the black director, such as the Odette's ultimate action at the end of the play where she embraces her blackness and joins the revolution. Then again, this may be the kind of logic that permitted the misattribution in the first place.

The lack of this white origin—its dramatic and somewhat comedic disappearance from the archive—frustrates any desire to trace bloodlines. The very performance of the archive denies the status of an original, forces us to read the racial constructions/performances as they exist in various textual formations, misfires, and uptakes rather than fantasizing a neat comparison of a "white" *Haiti* with a "black" one.

Voiceover: "it always seems to be night, and the atmosphere is charged and angst ridden . . . "[51]

The complexities and frustrations encountered in researching *Haiti* were particularly instructive and point to the "not to be trusted" aspects of the knowledge we inherit. In this case, it was not so much a tyranny of documents as a tyranny of inherited interpretations—the momentum of scholarship that provides "'preferred readings' of texts, in that they structure possible telling and impose interpretation, producing the object of which they speak."[52] Once the ball was rolling, in the case of *Haiti*, all interpretations moved along a particular pathway with consistent momentum. Only one scholar seems to have actually read any of the play's scripts—the rest replicating increasingly exaggerated, overly simplistic versions of Clark's narrative. This is not to dismiss the historical or political value of Clark's comments, but to ask what was at stake in Clark's rhetorical flourish as well as in each amplification of the play's origin myth. Given everything at stake in interracial contact in the 1930s, and the sheer complexity of this play's history, scholars have an obligation to question "preferred readings" and provide more than simple "black" or "white" interpretations of the work. Being a paranoid, noir, theatre historian means triple-checking, second-guessing, and not (only or entirely) trusting the interpretations we inherit. The paranoid noir detective knows she cannot trust any source—everything is under suspicion and the worst might be assumed.

ENDNOTES

[1] I offer my gratitude to all the librarians who have helped me work this case. Special thanks goes to Lynette Hunter, Sarah Juliet Lauro, Julia Medina, Jeremy Vaughan, my colleagues at San José State University, and above all, my dear friend and mentor, the late Marc E. Blanchard.

[2] The spelling of the last name (DuBois or Du Bois) is inconsistent in reference to both men. For the sake of clarity, I will use the latter to refer to W.E.B.

[3] HUAC was initially chaired by Martin Dies Jr., and until the termination of his involvement in 1945, was most commonly referred to as the Dies Committee.

[4] For thorough documentation of the misattribution and the way it reveals a logic of racialization in the archive (and for details on the "phantom body of work" on the nonexistent play by W.E.B.), *see*, Shannon Rose Riley, "Racing the Archive: Will the Real William DuBois Please Stand Up?," *English Language Notes (ELN)* 45, no. 1 (2007).

[5] The occupation generally dates from 1915 to 1934, but Mary Renda marks the termination as 1940 due to continued U.S. economic control after military evacuation. *See* Mary Renda, *Taking Haiti: Military Occupation and the Culture of U.S. Imperialism, 1915–1940* (Chapel Hill: University of North Carolina Press, 2001).

[6] *Library of Congress Online Catalog,* United States Library of Congress, 10 Dec. 2006 <http://catalog.loc.gov/>.

[7] The few scholars that have worked on William DuBois's *Haiti* are (chronologically): Loften Mitchell, *Black Drama: The Story of the American Negro in Theatre* (New York: Hawthorn Books, Inc., 1967); John O'Connor and Lorraine Brown, *Free, Adult, Uncensored: The Living History of the Federal Theatre Project* (Washington D.C.: New Republic Books, 1978); Glenda Eloise Gill, *White Grease Paint on Black Performers: A Study of the Federal Theatre, 1935–39* (New York: Peter Lang, 1988); VèVè A. Clark, "Haiti's Tragic Overture: (Mis)Representations of the Haitian Revolution in World Drama (1796–1975)," in *Representing the French Revolution: Literature, Historiography and Art,* ed. James Heffernan (Hanover: University Press of New England, 1992); Renda, *Taking Haiti: Military Occupation and the Culture of U.S. Imperialism, 1915–1940*; Errol G. Hill and James V. Hatch, *A History of African American Theatre* (Cambridge: Cambridge University Press, 2003). I analyze the play, its politics, and its reception at length in my current book project, *Performing Race and Erasure: Cuba and Haiti in U.S. Culture, 1898–1940.*

[8] Along with LC librarian John Cole, O'Connor and Brown helped organize FTP materials at George Mason University and interviewed numerous FTP artists including Maurice Clark. The story of the FTP documents is also the stuff of noir detective work—many cubic feet of documents had been lost and/or buried under "red scare" rhetoric. *See* O'Connor and Brown, *Free, Adult, Uncensored: The Living History of the Federal Theatre Project,* vii-viii.

[9] I was able to locate numerous reviews of the play, all attributing the work to the white *NYT* journalist William DuBois. *See* "A Climactic Scene of a Big Battle Gave Him a Fight: The Playwright Provided a Little Dialogue; the Rest Was up to the Director," *New York Herald Tribune,* March 27 1938; John Anderson, "'Haiti' a Vivid, Exciting Picture of Rebellion," *Journal American,* March 4 1938; Brooks Atkinson, "The Play: William Du Bois's 'Haiti' Opens in Harlem—'There's Always a Breeze' Opens Downtown," *New York Times,* March 3 1938; Howard Barnes, "'Haiti' Play by William Du Bois [sic] Produced in Harlem," *Herald Tribune,* March 3 1938; "'Haiti' Viewed by 74,000," *Daily Mirror,* May 22 1938; "Hit at Lafayette," *The Daily Worker,* May 2 1938; Arthur Pollock, "The Theatre: Rex Ingram and the Federal Theater Make a Picturesque and Exciting Show out of 'Haiti' at Harlem's Lafayette," *Brooklyn Eagle,* March 3 1938; ———, "Haiti, a Play and a Lorelei for Liars: Apparently It Is Full of Voodoo Drums and Breath-Taking Black Nudes," *Brooklyn Daily Eagle,* July 11 1939; "Review of 'Haiti'," *Time* 31, no. 10 (1938); Louis Sobol, "The Voice of New York by Louis Sobol," *Journal American,* March 10 1938; Robert Sylvester, "WPA's 'Haiti' Exciting and Well Staged," *Daily News,* March 3 1938; Stark Young, "To Keep the Wind

Away," *The New Republic* 94, no. March 23 (1938). *See also* William Du Bois [sic], "Thanks to the Federal Theatre," *New York Times*, March 20 1938.

[10] William DuBois, "Haiti," in *Federal Theatre Plays*, ed. U.S. Federal Theatre Project and Pierre de Rohan (New York: Random House, 1938).

[11] The translator notes: "Origine du texte sur lequel a été faite la traduction: Federal Theatre Project Records, George Mason University, Fairfax, Virginia." *See* W. B. Du Bois, *Haïti*, trans. Nicole Vincileoni, CEDA Theatre (Abidjan: Editions CEDA, 1983), 8.

[12] For a full analysis of racialized logics in the archive, see Riley, "Racing the Archive: Will the Real William Dubois Please Stand Up?."

[13] Evelyn M. Timberlake, email, January 15 2008.

[14] *See* Riley, "Racing the Archive: Will the Real William DuBois Please Stand Up?," 107–8. David Beard references my analysis in his work on documents in the archive in "From Work to Text to Document," *Archival Science* 8, no. 3 (2008).

[15] Evelyn M. Timberlake, email, January 24 2008.

[16] The play opened at Harlem's Lafayette Theatre on March 2, 1938; the original cast included Louis Sharp as Toussaint L'Ouverture, Alvin Childress as his adjutant Jacques, Elena Karam as Jacques's long lost and secretly mixed race daughter, Odette, and Rex Ingram starring as the Haitian General Henri Christophe. The play, set in 1802, tells the story of the final turning point in the twelve-year-long Haitian Revolution—Napoleon has sent more troops to reclaim the former French colony from the rebelling slaves and mulattos, but is soon to be defeated. However, the play turns on Odette's awakening to political consciousness. At the end she chooses to remain in Haiti and claim her newly-discovered black roots.

[17]"'Haiti' Viewed by 74,000." Clipping available in the Hallie Flanagan Papers, (New York: NYPL Library for the Performing Arts, Billy Rose Theatre Collection). Library of Congress, "Federal Theatre Project Collection: A Register of the Library of Congress Collection of U.S. Work Progress Administration Records [Finding Aid]," (2005), http://hdl.loc.gov/loc.music/eadmus.mu995001. Total audience figures for Harlem are from O'Connor and Brown, *Free, Adult, Uncensored: The Living History of the Federal Theatre Project*, 117.

[18] The Shubert brothers built the most prominent theatre empire in the early 20th century United States. "By the eve of the Depression, the Shuberts owned, operated, managed or booked close to a thousand houses across the United States." Shubert Foundation, 11 Dec. 2010 http://www.shubertfoundation.org/about/brothers.asp

[19] "3 Sued for $25,000 in 'Theft' of 'Haiti'," *Variety*, August 10 1938.

[20] Matthew Pratt Guterl, "The New Race Consciousness: Race, Nation, and Empire in American Culture, 1910–1925," *Journal of World History* 2005, no. June 3 (1999): 345.

[21] *See*, for example, Alfred N. Hunt, *Haiti's Influence on Antebellum America: Slumbering Volcano in the Caribbean* (Baton Rouge: Louisiana State University Press, 1988).

[22] James Weldon Johnson wrote a four-part series called "Self-Determining Haiti," that criticized the U.S. occupation. James Weldon Johnson, "Self-Determining Haiti," *Nation* 111, August 28–September 25 (1920). W.E.B. Du Bois also published widely against the occupation.

[23] "Theatre Project Faces an Inquiry," *New York Times*, July 27 1938. *See also* Renda, *Taking Haiti: Military Occupation and the Culture of U.S. Imperialism, 1915–1940*, 287; Gill, *White Grease Paint on Black Performers: A Study of the Federal Theatre, 1935–39*, 31.

[24] O'Connor and Brown, *Free, Adult, Uncensored: The Living History of the Federal Theatre Project*, 20.

[25] Susan Quinn, *Furious Improvisation: How the WPA and a Cast of Thousands Made High Art out of Desperate Times* (New York: Walker & Company, 2008), 247.

[26] During Hallie Flanagan's testimony, she was repeatedly asked if art, especially theatre, was a weapon for social change and for communist and socialist propaganda. *See* "Statement of Mrs. Hallie Flanagan, National Director, Federal Theater Project," in *Investigation of Un-American Propaganda Activities in the United States: Hearings before a Special Committee on Un-American Activities House of Representatives* . . . (Washington D.C.: Government Printing Office, 1938).

[27] From the 1939 FBI Report, qtd. in Judith Ellen Brussell, "Government Investigations of Federal Theatre Project Personnel in the Works Progress Administration, 1935–1939 (the Show Must Not Go On!)" (City University of New York, 1993), 283–4.

[28] From the 1939 FBI Report on Federal Project One. Conspiracy to Defraud the United States, File 46–72 (1–30–39) in 117–11, DOJ, RG 60, NNFJ-J, National Archives. *See* Ibid., 274–305.

[29] O'Connor and Brown do not state the source of Clark's quote, but they produced an oral history as part of their FTP archiving strategies in the mid 1970s. Presumably, Clark's statements are from that work.

[30] Maurice Clark qtd. in John O'Connor and Lorraine Brown, "Haiti and Black Empire," in *Free, Adult, Uncensored: The Living History of the Federal Theatre Project,* ed. John O'Connor and Lorraine Brown (Washington D.C.: New Republic Books, 1978), 119.

[31] Ibid.

[32] According to Matthew Guterl, a "new race consciousness" was emerging in the U.S. in the early 20th century—as notions of racial purity were negotiated in the shifting public sphere, the topic of "miscegenation" was at the fore. Every major black or white racialist at the time addressed the topic, including W.E.B. Du Bois, Hubert Henry Harrison, Marcus Garvey, Lothrop Stoddard, and Earnest Cox. *See* Guterl, "The New Race Consciousness: Race, Nation, and Empire in American Culture, 1910–1925."

[33] *See* "Review of 'Haiti'," 34.

[34] O'Connor and Brown, "Haiti and Black Empire," 117.

[35] The only two scholars that don't reproduce this narrative are Loften Mitchell and Glenda E. Gill. Loften Mitchell writes on *Haiti* over a decade before O'Connor and Brown publish Maurice Clark's account of the play. Mitchell's rhetoric foregrounds black power and resistance: he describes a play on the "black nation's uprising" and notes that it was "the first time Harlemites sat in a theatre and saw Negroes beating up whites and getting away with it." *See* Mitchell, *Black Drama: The Story of the American Negro in Theatre,* 102–3. Like Mitchell, Gill foregrounds the theme of the Haitian Revolution as an articulation of the play's blackness and describes HUAC concern over the play.

[36] Renda, *Taking Haiti: Military Occupation and the Culture of U.S. Imperialism, 1915–1940,* 286; Hill and Hatch, *A History of African American Theatre,* 318.

[37] Renda, *Taking Haiti: Military Occupation and the Culture of U.S. Imperialism, 1915–1940,* 286.

[38] Hill and Hatch, *A History of African American Theatre,* 318–9.

[39] Du Bois [sic], "Thanks to the Federal Theatre."

[40] Ibid.

[41] From an unidentified newspaper clipping. Hallie Flanagan Papers. *See also* Anonymous, "Shuberts Want 'Haiti'," *New York Times,* March 10 1938.

[42] Du Bois [sic], "Thanks to the Federal Theatre."

[43] Ibid., 150.

[44] Renda, *Taking Haiti: Military Occupation and the Culture of U.S. Imperialism, 1915–1940,* 362. n. 142; n. 144

[45] William Du Bois [sic], "Complete Working Script of 'Haiti' by William Du Bois [sic]," (New York: Billy Rose Theatre Collection, New York Public Library for the Performing Arts (unpub.), 1938).

[46] Renda cites two items in the BRTC: the "Complete Working Script of 'Haiti'"—which I was able to locate in the card catalog (Call #s 9–NCOF; NCOF+), and "Production Files," however nothing could be found under the latter name in the larger Theatre collection. (Besides the CWS, I also found many clippings, etc. in 2 folders called "Programme" and several photographs in files "A", "B" and "C".) I searched for the item called "Production Files" in the newly organized Hallie Flanagan Papers: I found three boxes titled "Production Files" (Call #s T-MSS 1964–002 Boxes 10 - 12) which were sorted alphabetically by play, however several alphabetical files were missing, including the letter "H." In the card catalog, I found a reference to something called "Haiti Scrapbook" (1938) that had the call #'s MWEZ X n.c. 20,

308–20, 309. However, these old call #s, when converted, refer back to the three boxes I had already searched in the Flanagan collection. (I also looked at Box 46 of the Flanagan collection because it contains miscellaneous production files—but nothing was there on "Haiti" either.) The Collection issued a library-wide search to locate the missing items, with as yet no success.

47 William Du Bois [sic], *Haiti*, Federal Theatre Project Records, George Mason University ed. (National Service Bureau, 1938).

48 William DuBois Papers, (Boston University: Howard Gotlieb Archival Research Center).

49 *See* Du Bois [sic], "Complete Working Script of 'Haiti' by William Du Bois [sic]." *See also* ———, *Haiti*, 2–1–6.

50 *See* Du Bois [sic], "Complete Working Script of 'Haiti' by William Du Bois [sic]." *See also* ———, *Haiti*, 2–1–35.

51 Mark T. Conard, ed. *The Philosophy of Film Noir* (Lexington: The University Press of Kentucky, 2006), 1. I would also point to the fruits of considering racialization, noir, and Haiti—both the play and the place—together. To summarize: Eric Lott has analyzed "the racial unconscious of noir"—its production of whiteness—and what he describes as the genre's "strategies of artistic othering." Charles Scruggs has also taken up a useful racialized reading of noir to consider African American literature. More recently, however, Edwidge Danticat challenges simple black/white readings of noir and to some degree, the genre's historical development, by situating the term within the Haitian context—and this is a very useful maneuver. She notes that *nwa* (Kreyol), refers to any Haitian citizen, "regardless of race." She also mentions the many "dark tales" of zombies and cannibals that were produced by white US Marines during the first US occupation of Haiti as a kind of antecedent to 1940s noir. Think of the 1932 film, *White Zombie*, for example. *See* Eric Lott. "The Whiteness of Film Noir." *American Literary History* 9, no. 3 (1997): 542–66; Charles Scruggs. "'The Power of Blackness': Film Noir and Its Critics." *American Literary History* 16, no. 4 (2004): 675–87; Edwidge Danticat, ed. *Haiti Noir*. New York: Akashic, 2011, 12.

52 Ron Eyerman, "The Past in the Present: Culture and the Transmission of Memory," *Acta Sociologica* 47, no 2 (2004): 162.

Good Stories and Closed Subjects: Ida Van Cortland and the Great Chicago Fire

PAULA SPERDAKOS

At around 9 PM on Sunday evening, 8 October 1871, the most infamous cow in history kicked over a carelessly positioned kerosene lantern in the barn of a poor family named O'Leary, and started the Great Chicago Fire. Or so goes one version—the most proverbial ("The cow acted alone")—of the story about how and where the fire originated, even though Michael Ahern, the *Chicago Republican* reporter whose scoop the cow-and-lantern story allegedly was, admitted many years later that he had made the whole thing up.[1] There are other versions of the story, exonerating the cow but incriminating a wide array of suspects: Mrs. Catherine O'Leary herself; a pipe-smoking neighbour; Biela's Comet; a friend of one of the O'Leary sons, playing craps with him in the barn; spontaneous combustion; an "incendiary Communard"; and so on.[2] Regardless of the actual cause of the fire, the fact remains that after it had burned itself out by Tuesday morning, more than two thousand acres of the city had been destroyed; a third of the city's 300,000 inhabitants had been left homeless; and 200–300 people were dead.

In 1944, Corolyn Cox[3], an American free-lance journalist who was living in Canada at the time and writing a regular column—"Name in the News"—for Toronto's *Saturday Night* magazine, profiled the man who had played a major role in making Canada an internationally respected centre of ornithological research, Percy A. Taverner. It is one paragraph of this "tyrannical document," entitled "Famous Canadian Ornithologist Gave Up Back-Stage for Birds,"[4] which is the focus of my gumshoe investigation for this volume. Carrying the heading "Peripatetic Youth," it reads:

> Taverner's is the tale of a lad who didn't have either breaks or chances, finding them for himself, making himself into something. He was born in Guelph, sixty-nine years ago, the son of two school teachers. *His mother had been a child in school in Chicago at the time of the fire, lost her home and entire family in the disaster but had stayed on at her school and eventually taught there.* [Emphasis mine]

Percy Taverner's mother was the now-forgotten but once well-known late 19th century Canada/ US cross-border touring star, Ida Van Cortland (1854–1924), one of the seven actresses whose careers I have been researching for some time now, in anticipation of telling their remarkable stories in a book.[5] Corolyn Cox's assertion that Taverner's mother had survived the Chicago fire is the earliest extant reference to this most intriguing biographical detail; furthermore, hers is the *only* extant account that mentions the loss of Ida's home and entire family. Soon after Taverner's death in 1947, W. L. McAtee, a longtime friend, memorialized him for *The Auk*[6] ; McAtee's notice affirmed only that Percy's mother was a survivor of the fire.[7]

Early in the 1980s, John L. Cranmer-Byng, a University of Toronto professor of history with a "long standing fascination with birds" was disappointed to discover that, other than McAtee's memorial notice in *The Auk*, no biography had been written about Percy Taverner, in whom Cranmer-Byng had taken an interest; the result was a 1996 special issue of *The Canadian Field-Naturalist*, "A Life with Birds: Percy A. Taverner, Canadian Ornithologist, 1875–1947."[8] At about the same time that Cranmer-Byng embarked on his research, Kathleen Fraser was conducting doctoral work at the University of Western Ontario; her dissertation was entitled "Theatrical Touring in Late Nineteenth-Century Canada: Ida Van Cortland and the Tavernier[9] Company, 1877–1896."[10] These two researchers communicated several times to compare notes about Ida Van Cortland and her somewhat mysterious past, including, of course, the tantalizing references to her experience as a survivor of the legendary Chicago Fire.[11] As the source for her statement in the dissertation that "In October of 1871, [Ida] became [her] family's sole survivor as a result of the Great Chicago Fire," Fraser cited Corolyn Cox's article, but pointed out that "Prof. Cranmer-Byng has found no other proof of this. . . ."[12] Indeed, in "A Life with Birds," published more than ten years after Fraser's dissertation, Cranmer-Byng was at pains to demonstrate that he had made every effort to verify Cox's assertion, attempting to track down Taverner's mother's family in Chicago, "but without any success. Chicago's records of this period are incomplete and difficult to trace. Some were destroyed in the fire of 1871; thus there are no documents to corroborate the statement that Percy's mother was orphaned during the Chicago fire, and no evidence to show that her family lived in Chicago."[13]

Where then did Corolyn Cox, writing her article in 1944, get the idea that Percy Taverner's mother "lost her home and entire family in the disaster" of the Chicago Fire, and why subsequently has no one been able to confirm—or categorically refute—Cox's declaration? Unlike Michael Ahern, with his cow-and-lantern tall tale, Cox can't be suspected of having invented the story. Although there is no evidence that she ever spoke to Taverner directly, it seems likely that if this were merely Cox's embellishment, Percy Taverner would have challenged it and discredited her. So where did the story originate, and what—or who—was Cox's source?

The lives and careers of all my actress subjects abound with such intriguing mysteries and puzzles. In trying to solve these, I have made it a mission in each case to re-examine, replicate and interrogate all the evidence that, due to the dedicated sleuthing of my scholarly predecessors, is available to me, and periodically to re-visit the beginning of the sequence of that evidence in order to see if I can arrive at some conclusion independently of them.[14]

To begin at the beginning, then . . . .

Ida Van Cortland started life in 1854 as Emily Ellen Buckley on the outskirts of Manchester, England.[15] Her father, George Buckley (b. about 1827 in Lancashire, England) was identified as a Commercial Traveller in the 1861 England Census; her mother, Mary Heyward (née Hind) Buckley, had been born about 1826 in Ireland. Emily had an older sister, Mary B[ridget?] (b. about 1852), and a younger brother, John W. (b. 1859). At some point during the 1860s, the Buckley family immigrated to the United States, and Emily and her sister Mary were enumerated twice as part of the 1870 US Federal Census. As of 23 June, Emily (then 16) and Mary (18) were attending Dyhrenfurth College in Chicago, boarding at the College with its President, Julius Dyhrenfurth and his family. Two months later, when Emily and Mary were presumably on summer vacation, they were enumerated again with the rest of the Buckley family—father George, identifying himself as a "Short hand writer"; mother Mary; and brother John—at their home . . . in Princeton, Bureau County, Illinois.

In one of my very first efforts to place Emily and her family in Chicago at the time of the Great Fire, I examined the Chicago directories of the period—as Cranmer-Byng had done before me—but it was clear to me that none of the Buckleys listed were the ones I was looking for. I also pored over the lists of names of some of the victims printed in the *Chicago Tribune* in the days immediately following the fire,[16] but found no Buckleys at all. Not that these lacunae were conclusive of anything, but they did at least faintly argue against the presence of the whole Buckley family in Chicago on the fateful day. However, it was my discovery—through Ancestry.com[17]—that the Buckleys lived in Princeton, Illinois, *115 miles south-west of Chicago*, which allowed me to conclude—as Cranmer-Byng had been unable to do—that it was *highly unlikely* (indeed, virtually impossible) Emily Ellen Buckley actually did lose "her home and entire family in the disaster."

Notwithstanding the laws of simple improbability which seem to be operating in this case, Corolyn Cox's statement in her *Saturday Night* article continues to tyrannize me as Ida Van Cortland's would-be biographer. If it's unlikely that Emily was actually orphaned and left homeless after the events of 8 October 1871, then why is the story a matter of record? And if the story, or at least that part of the story, is not true, but a fabrication, then who invented the story, *and why*?

There is documentary evidence, then, proving that Emily Buckley *was* at school in Chicago at the time of the fire, although at 16 years of age, she was not quite the "child" that Cox made her out to be.[18] Dyhrenfurth College was located at 160 North Carpenter Street, which fell outside (to the west) of the area almost completely destroyed by the fire. There is no record of what Julius Dyhrenfurth, his family, and the boarders at his school—including Emily and her sister—did on that Sunday night in October; whether they evacuated the school and took refuge somewhere until the fire was over, or if they stayed where they were and watched the progress of the fire as it consumed so much of the city. There is also documentary evidence that almost six years later, when Toronto's Grand Opera House opened its season, the resident company[19]included a young woman with a two-year-old child who had just recently turned to the theatre and adopted the glamorous stage name of Ida Van Cortland. What happened to Emily between the night of the Chicago Fire and her theatrical debut (as Amiens in *As You Like It*[20]) in September of 1877 goes to the heart of this—and her—mystery.

The newly minted actress Ida Van Cortland's two year-old-child was her son Percy Algernon, who had been born in Guelph, Ontario, on 10 June 1875, and baptised at St. George's Anglican Church, Guelph, on 7 July 1875. Both Percy's birth and baptism certificates identified his mother as Emily E. Buckley and his father as Edwin Fowler. Fowler's occupation was recorded as "principal" on the birth certificate, and as "school teacher" on the certificate of baptism.

Who was Edwin Fowler, when and where had he and Emily met, and under what circumstances had Emily come to be in Guelph? According to the 1870 US Federal Census, Edwin Fowler, age 29, was enumerated on 15 June in Chicago, Illinois. Living with him was his wife, Mary, age 21. Both had been born in England, and Edwin identified himself as a teacher.[21] In his search for information about Percy Taverner's parents, his biographer John Cranmer-Byng made the following discovery:

> In the Chicago *Street Directory* for 1871 [Edwin Fowler] was shown as a teacher at Dyhrenfurth College, a business school. In the 1873 *Directory* he was listed as superintendent of the college, and as boarding at 160 North Carpenter. The last mention of Edwin Fowler in the Chicago records was in the 1874 *Directory*, where he was shown as residing with the president of the college, Julius Dyhrenfurth, at 160 North Carpenter.[22]

Subsequently, Cranmer-Byng determined that "According to an account of some of the private schools in Guelph in the nineteenth century, a boarding school known as the Guelph Academy was sold to Edwin Fowler, B.A. [in 1874]." In the Guelph city directory for 1875–76, Fowler is listed as the Principal of Guelph Academy, 175 Woolwich Street. The Woolwich Street address is also his home, which he shares with the Guelph Academy "directress ladies department," Mrs. E. Fowler.[23] Further, "this account [stated that Fowler] had attended Oxford University." However, upon inquiry to the Registrar of Oxford University, Cranmer-Byng received " . . . a negative reply. 'I have searched our records for the nineteenth century but regret that I am unable to find that he was ever a member of, or obtained any degree from Oxford University.'"[24]

There are no records, either in Chicago or in Guelph, to prove that Edwin Fowler and Emily Buckley were married. Cranmer-Byng, who clearly would rather believe that Percy's parents were legally married, is scrupulous in pointing out that "this means little. They might have been married in Chicago without any record of the marriage surviving. They could also have been married in Guelph without any record being preserved." Cranmer-Byng is also at pains to explain that "a new marriage act came into effect on 1 July 1874."

> Instead of a marriage licence, which required the publishing of the banns of marriage, a certificate could be obtained by one of the parties swearing an affidavit that there was no legal cause to prevent the solemnization of the marriage. Since Emily Buckley was under twenty-one years of age *she had to swear an affidavit that her father and mother were dead* and that there was no one with authority to give consent to the marriage [Emphasis mine].[25]

Of course, the difficulty with all this is that speculation is rife and uncertainties and unknowns abound. Certain questions do need to be asked, though.

Firstly, what happened to Mary Fowler, Edwin Fowler's wife—or so she was enumerated in 1870? To echo Cranmer-Byng, they—Edwin and Mary—might have been divorced in Chicago without any record of the divorce surviving. However, *if* this were the case, and *if* Fowler and underage Emily had to avail themselves of the new marriage act's affidavit option, then it would appear that in swearing her father and mother were dead (in the Chicago fire, of course), she was committing perjury, with Edwin Fowler as her abettor. These 'ifs' and 'what-ifs' are compounded by subsequent events for which certain documents do exist.

On 11 June 1881, Ida Van Cortland married Albert Tavernier, whom she had met in 1879, in New York. I am unable to find a marriage certificate for the couple, either under variations on their real names or under their stage names, but the wedding was reported in the *Dramatic Mirror* of 25 June 1881.[26] On the birth certificate of their daughter, Ida Clare, who was born in Markham, Ontario in 1887, Albert gave his last name as Taverner, and Emily was listed as Ida Fowler. It seems likely that, for the sake of respectability, they decided to continue the fiction [?] that Ida (as Ellen, of course) had been married to her son Percy's father, Edwin Fowler.[27] *If* she had been married to Fowler, though, her certificate of divorce from him is yet another important but non-surviving document.

In "A Life with Birds," Cranmer-Byng comments on several occasions that Percy Taverner's earliest years, including or even especially information about his biological father, "seemed to have been a closed subject to his mother, his half sister and his wife (Martha Hohly Wiest, whom he married in 1930)."[28] In 1927, after Ida Van Cortland had died, Percy Taverner seems to have made contact with a Mrs. Fowler, living in California; he and his sister Ida Clare made a visit to California, and met with her. Unable—or unwilling?—to say categorically who she was, however, Cranmer-Byng could only comment—obliquely—that "At last Percy was able to ask someone who had been married to his father . . . all the questions that had been puzzling him . . . ". However, frustratingly, Percy left nothing in writing about Mrs. Fowler or anything else to do with his father.

Kathleen Fraser writes in her dissertation that "It would appear that Percy Taverner had an older half-brother named Sidney Herbert Fowler. Percy and Sidney met in Los Angeles in the summer of 1927. This information is courtesy of Prof. Cranmer-Byng and comes from research done in the Los Angeles area."[29] Intriguingly, Cranmer-Byng does not mention Sidney Herbert Fowler at all in "A Life with Birds." Nevertheless, the 1900 US Federal Census includes the record of a Sidney Herbert Fowler, born on 23 October 1870 in Chicago, Illinois, to English-born parents; newly married and presently living in San Francisco, California. The 1920 and 1930 federal censuses also located Sidney Herbert Fowler in San Francisco. So was this Mrs. Fowler whom Percy and Ida Clare met in 1927 Sidney Herbert's mother Mary? Or yet another "Mrs. Edwin Fowler"?

What happened to Edwin Fowler after the domestic arrangement between him and Emily dissolved is unknown, but apparently Guelph local gossip for many years held that Mrs. Fowler deserted her husband, went to New York, and became a well-known actress on the Broadway stage.[30] There's no evidence of any subsequent contact between Emily and Edwin, and it's certain that Percy never saw his biological father again.

From the time I first began to research and write about the life of the remarkable woman who became Ida Van Cortland, I made the assumption that Ida (Emily) herself had claimed—to her children if to no one else—that as a Chicago schoolgirl she was the only member of her family to survive the Great Fire of 1871, and I deemed this an intriguing example of self-mythologizing in order to erase an unwanted—and possibly quite scandalous—past. I still believe this to be true, but after chasing down and teasing out every clue available to me, I can't actually prove it.

Nevertheless, the clues suggest to me that when she was teenager going to school in Chicago, Emily had witnessed the Great Fire, which spared her family who lived well away from the city, but which unforgettably swallowed up the lives of many other families. At around the same time, or shortly thereafter, Emily fell in love with one of her teachers (or possibly a fellow teacher), Edwin Fowler, a charming married man with a new-born son. They began an affair, and upon discovering that she was pregnant, the couple left Chicago and the United States and moved to Guelph in Canada. Perhaps her family disowned her when they learned of the affair and its consequences; in any case, there's no evidence to suggest that she ever saw any of them again.[31] She and Fowler represented themselves as a married couple in their new town; their son, Percy Algernon Fowler, was born; and they made their living by running a school. However, as a former pupil of the school wrote to a friend of Percy's after his death in 1947, her twelve-year-old girl's memory of Emily and Edwin was " . . . of charming people who were unsuited to each other."[32] Perhaps, too, Edwin Fowler's propensity for representing himself as that which he was not—for example, as an Oxford University graduate—began to take its toll on the relationship. In any case, and for whatever reasons, when her son was two years old Emily decided to divest herself of her former life, and to fundamentally reinvent herself. Her story about losing everything to the Great Chicago Fire is a template for how to bury one's (scandalous?) life.

As many gifted raconteurs maintain, what matters about a story is not whether it's true but whether it's good. Early in 2010, I made contact with a great-great nephew of Albert Taverner's, Clyde Taverner, who has reiterated the information on his Ancestry.com family tree page that Ida Van Cortland's family all perished in the Chicago Fire. I asked him if he has any proof for his assertion, and he replied that this account had been told to the author of "Theatrical Touring in Late Nineteenth-Century Canada" by "a family member." (This is not the case, in fact.) He is also persuaded that this is the truth because he has "researched her family and cannot find her parents or sister after the fire occurred." My disclosure to him that the Buckley family lived 115 miles away from Chicago elicited the response that " . . . they may have been in town visiting their daughters. You certainly didn't have to live there to die there." Finally, though, until he can "find evidence otherwise" Clyde Taverner is "going to take *her* word for it." No amount of telling him that we don't actually have anyone's direct word for it, much less Ida Van Cortland's, can convince him of the simple improbability of the record.

After all, it's such a good story.

ENDNOTES

[1] See Richard F. Bales, *The Great Chicago Fire and the Myth of Mrs. O'Leary's Cow*. Jefferson, NC: McFarland, 2005, 56. There's evidence that Ahern may have lied about being the author of the cow-and-lantern story in the first place.

[2] See Karen Sawislak, *Smoldering City: Chicagoans and the Great Fire, 1871–1874*, Chicago: U of Chicago P, 1995; The Great Chicago Fire and the Web of Memory, http://www.chicagohs.org/fire/; retrieved 29 September 2010 and Did the Great Chicago Fire Really Start with Mrs. O'Leary's Cow? http://www.howstuffworks.com/chicago-fire-cow.htm; retrieved 29 September 2010.

[3] For information about Corolyn Cox (c. 1892–1967), see "Corolyn Cox, Journalist, Free Lancer," *The* (Phoenix) *Arizona Republic*, 31 March 1967, 70; and "Mrs. Corolyn Cox Dies: Former Syracusan," *The Syracuse* (New York) *Post-Standard*, 13 April 1967, 11.

[4] Corolyn Cox, "Name in the News: Famous Canadian Ornithologist Gave Up Back-Stage for Birds," *Saturday Night*, 4 November 1944, 2.

[5] The other six actresses who are the subjects of my book—tentatively entitled *A Trail through a Jungle: The Way of the Canadian Actress, 1846–1993*—are Elizabeth Jane Phillips (1830–1904); Charlotte Nickinson Morrison (1832–1910); Catherine Proctor (1878–1967); Margaret Bannerman (1895–1976); Judith Evelyn (1909–1967); and Kate Reid (1930–1993).

[6] *The Auk* is a quarterly journal of ornithology, published by the American Ornithologists' Union.

[7] See W. L. McAtee, "Percy Algernon Taverner, 1875–1947," *The Auk*, 65:1 (January 1948), 85–106: "After about two or three years of this phase of the Port Huron life [1900–1902], Taverner joined his mother and sister in Chicago. The mother (who was a survivor of the great Chicago fire of 1871) had retired from the stage about 1898 or 1899, and was engaged in organizational work for a fraternal insurance company." (95) http://elibrary.unm.edu/sora/Auk/v065n01/p0085–p0106.pdf

[8] John L. Cranmer-Byng, "A Life with Birds: Percy A. Taverner, Canadian Ornithologist, 1875–1947," *The Canadian Field-Naturalist* 110: 1 (January-March 1996; Special Issue), 2.

[9] Ida Van Cortland's husband and stage partner was Albert Tavernier, whose real name was Taverner. Albert was not Percy's biological father. When Ida married Albert in 1881, Percy was six years old. Albert informally adopted Percy, and he was known thereafter by Albert's real family surname, Taverner.

[10] Kathleen D. J. Fraser, "Theatrical Touring in Late Nineteenth-Century Canada: Ida Van Cortland and the Tavernier Company, 1877–1896." Unpublished PhD dissertation, U of Western Ontario, 1985.

[11] Both Kathleen Fraser and John Cranmer-Byng had occasion to consult Dr. Murray Edwards' book *A Stage in Our Past*, which includes the earliest research in any depth on the careers of Ida Van Cortland and her husband Albert Tavernier; unfortunately, the book has many inaccuracies. Edwards does not concern himself with Ida's life before she began her acting career, however, so he does not mention the Chicago fire story at all. See Murray D.

Edwards, *A Stage in Our Past: English-Language Theatre in Eastern Canada from the 1790s to 1914*, Toronto: U of Toronto P, 1968. Fraser was also allowed access to Edwards' collection of Tavernier material, consisting of photographs, family correspondence and interviews with the Taverniers' daughter, Ida C. Taverner McLeish. Another—earlier—researcher to make use of *A Stage in Our Past* and of Dr. Edwards' private collection was Ann Stuart, who was a Research Assistant of the Canadian Theatre History Research Programme in 1975–76, and who wrote a paper entitled "The Taverniers: A Preliminary Study," at the behest of Heather McCallum, the Programme's Research Associate and Head of the Theatre Department of the Metropolitan Toronto Library. (We have the redoubtable Heather McCallum to thank for much of that library's extraordinary theatre collection.) It is to the Metropolitan Toronto Library (now known as the Toronto Reference Library) that Percy Taverner and Ida C. Taverner McLeish donated a large collection of primary material in 1938: this is known as the Taverner Collection, and Ann Stuart's paper is to be found in Box 8 (Miscellaneous), Envelope #15. Stuart does not mention the Chicago Fire story either.

[12] Fraser, 9; 34. Corolyn Cox herself had returned to the US in 1947, the same year that Percy Taverner died; she died in 1967, well before either Fraser or Cranmer-Byng had begun their work.

[13] Cranmer-Byng, 4.

[14] See Paula Sperdakos, "Untold Stories: [Re]Searching for Canadian Actresses' Lives," in *Theatre and AutoBiography: Writing and Performing Lives in Theory and Practice*, Sherrill Grace and Jerry Wasserman, eds. Talonbooks, 2006, 202–224.

[15] "Emily Ellen Buckley's birth certificate is #327 in 1854. The registration district is Rochdale, the sub-district is Wardleworth, and the county is Lancashire. The residence of her family and her birthplace is Holyrood Terrace, Prestwich, a suburb of Manchester. Her father's profession is listed as bookkeeper." Fraser, 9; 34

[16] See "Who Died in the Chicago Fire?" (The Newberry Library Genealogy News) at http://www.newberry.org/genealogy/news/default.asp?id=47&action=single; and "The Chicago Fire, October 8–10, 1871 at http://web.archive.org/web/20030209195700/http://users.anet.com/~flannery/fire.html; retrieved 29 September 2010.

[17] Ancestry.com, based in Provo, Utah, is a subscription-based genealogy website - "the world's largest family history website"—with billions of records online and more being added daily; it is a great boon to historians and researchers.

[18] Ida Van Cortland's children seem to have believed her to be a year younger than she actually was: on her headstone in Ottawa's Beechwood Cemetery are carved the words, "IDA VAN CORTLAND TAVERNIER MOTHER 1855–1924." (An inset plaque reads "THE PLAY IS DONE/ THE PLAY-HOUSE DARK/ THE PLAYER IS . . . AT REST").

[19] The Grand Opera House was managed by Charlotte Nickinson Morrison, Canada's first actress-manager (1874–78).

[20] "Miss Ida Van Courtland's (sic) Amiens was the best that we have seen at the Grand Opera House; her singing showed expression and good voice." (Toronto *Globe*, 17 September 1877)

[21] Source Citation: Year: *1870*; Census Place: *Chicago Ward 12, Cook, Illinois*; Roll *M593_206*; Page: *227B*; Image: *457*; Family History Library Film: *545705*.

[22] Cranmer-Byng, 4.

[23] See Cranmer-Byng, 204.

[24] Cranmer-Byng, 4; 204. Hugh Douglass, "An Account of Some of the Private Schools of Guelph, 1827–1900." Unpublished ms. 1960, Public Library, Guelph. Letter from Registrar's Office, University of Oxford, 9 July 1984.

[25] Province of Ontario, C. 6, An Act Respecting the Solemnization of Marriages, 1874. The Guelph *Daily Herald* published an official notice about the new marriage certificates issued by authority at the Guelph Divisional Office. It stated that no bondsmen were required. Cranmer-Byng, 4; 204.

[26] Notice in the *Dramatic Mirror*, 25 June 1881: "Albert Tavernier, of the Madison Square Theatre Company, and Ida Van Cortland, of W.H. Powers' Galley Slave Company were united in marriage by the Rev. Henry Wosse, at his residence . . . on the evening of June 11." See Cranmer-Byng, 204–205.

[27] "The registration number of Ida Clare Tavernier's birth certificate is 1887–05–040130. She was born 23 June 1887 in Markham Village. Her father is listed as Albert Taverner, a salesman. Her mother is listed as Ida Fowler. No address is recorded." Fraser, 35.

[28] Cranmer-Byng, 5; 140.

[29] Fraser, 34.

[30] Douglass, 10.

[31] Certainly Percy—and Ida Clare—never knew any of them, but whether they thought this was because the Buckleys had all died in the fire is not clear.

[32] See Cranmer-Byng, 5 and 204, note 18.

Doing *Tennessee Justice* in Oregon[1]

ANDREW RYDER

Prologue

Sometime in 1943, Reverend John Marshall, an African-American pacifist, visited his local draft board in Jackson, Tennessee seeking copies of Form 47, the "Special Form for Conscientious Objectors," for several of his drafted parishioners. He was reportedly "cursed and chased out of the draft board office."[2] They eventually obtained the forms by appealing to Selective Service's Memphis headquarters, where they were assured the draftees would be classified as conscientious objectors (hereafter COs). On approval, they were assigned to Civilian Public Service (hereafter CPS) to do "work of national importance under civilian direction."[3] Either because they did not understand what CPS was, or because they insisted that even this option required them to contradict their conscience, they "refused assignment to CPS," effectively rejecting the draft, and were arrested. These nine members were tried for their failure to participate in the government's alternative service, and Reverend Marshall was tried for "violating the Selective Service Act" by helping them avoid the draft. All ten were convicted and sentenced to three years in prison, with an additional $1000 fine for Marshall.[4]

This story was summarized in the local Jackson paper, according to the May 1944 issue of *Fellowship*, the journal of the Fellowship of Reconciliation.[5] *Fellowship*'s writer pointed out that there was more to the story. Based on eyewitness courtroom accounts, *Fellowship* printed a two-page "transcript" of the key exchanges and speeches from the trial, which "reveals vividly the sincerity of the defendants and the prejudice of the prosecution."[6] Martin Ponch, a trained theatre artist who was a CO at Camp Waldport in Oregon, read this summary. He felt passionately that the story of these African-American COs needed to be told and decided to create a play based on these events. That play, which Ponch called *Tennessee Justice*, was produced at Waldport early in 1945 under his direction. In describing the camp's response to the production, CO Adrian Wilson wrote, "the Barbary Coast [the huntin'-fishin'-shootin' men] thought it was the best thing ever done here, the Holy Joes said, 'Maybe the Fine Arts has got some good in it after all,' but the Fine Arts thought it stunk . . . "[7]

Wilson's assessment was the centerpiece for my understanding of the play and the larger fine arts group at that point. I wanted to know what made the production so objectionable to the artists, yet so successful with the rest of the camp. Wilson's language evoked three groups: the Jehovah's Witnesses, whom he called "the Barbary Coast;" the very religious COs, or "Holy Joes"; and the artists. Here we had an experience with the potential to bring campers together, but the artists stuck to what seems to have been an elitist attitude, in this case toward the work of some of their own. The other key issue was the racial context of the play. The story of the trial includes at least 11 African-Americans: ten defendants and one of the defense attorneys. There were African-American COs at Waldport, and racial equality was a significant issue for COs generally as part of their progressive agenda. However, none of my sources said anything beyond the fact that the play addressed what Charles Cooley, who played the prosecutor, called "a racial problem."[8] I knew the names of some of the African-Americans at Waldport, but did not know which, if any of them, participated in the production, though I assumed some must have. I also assumed that the script had streamlined the defendants, since the group could not have cast eleven African-Americans. These two "facts" provided the most significant challenges to my understanding and interpretation of this production.

Background

As part of my study of the theatre work of the Oregon collective of CPS artists called "The Fine Arts at Waldport," I was intrigued by this original play. My work draws primarily on the rich repository of information on the Oregon CPS camps maintained in the Special Collections of Aubrey Watzek Library at Lewis and Clark College in Portland, Oregon, particularly the papers of CO Kermit Sheets.[9] *Tennessee Justice* was tangential to my initial study of the better-known plays put on by the group: Millay's *Aria da Capo*, Ibsen's *Ghosts*, Shaw's *Candida*, and Chekhov's *Seagull*. And while there were multiple letters, audience comments, and even sets of production photos for these plays, I knew relatively little about *Tennessee Justice*. I knew when and where it had been produced, had an idea what some of the groups of people in the camp thought of it, and possessed a few second-hand descriptions of the play. But I didn't have access to a script, or even a program, with the exception of an image of the program cover, reproduced in the memoir of the CO who designed it, Adrian Wilson.[10] My most complete resources came from Wilson, who also designed the set and ran the lights. Additional information came from the following individuals, each a Waldport CO and at least loosely connected to the production: William Eshelman, a leader of the Fine Arts Group; Warren Downs, a cellist who was involved in musical activites at Waldport, but didn't participate in *Tennessee Justice*; and two COs who briefly described the play in 2003 oral history interviews. In the paragraphs which follow, I will discuss each of these resources, and analyze the information gleaned from and the questions raised by each. First these two COs: Francis Barr and Charles Cooley.

In 2002 and 2003, oral historians in the Portland area, led by Portland State University's Katrine Barber, conducted a series of interviews with surviving members of the Waldport camp. The results of these interviews of 66 men and/or their wives were published in a collection of transcriptions entitled, *Camp 56: An Oral History Project.*[11] Among those interviewees were several COs with connections to the arts at Waldport, and even to *Tennessee Justice*, including Martin Ponch. However, Ponch's interview does not mention that play. Three interviewees did: William Eshelman, whom I will discuss in more detail below, Francis Barr, and Charles Cooley. Both Mr. Barr and Mr. Cooley participated in the production, though neither mentioned that in his interview. Mr. Cooley told the interviewers, "We had a very good play called *Tennessee Justice*. It was a combination of a racial problem connected with a conscientious objector deal."[12] While he referred to himself as part of the group, he did not indicate his particular involvement. Francis Barr acknowledged working with the Fine Arts, but did not recall participating in *Tennessee Justice*. An interviewer told him, "We have a copy of a play that was put on which you were in. It's called *Tennessee Justice*"[13] (if only they had said the same to Martin Ponch!). Mr. Barr replied with a lengthy description of his work making "light dimmers out of salt water and tin cans," claiming, "I never acted in any of those plays."[14]

William Eshelman, on the other hand, offered useful (or at least intriguing) information about *Tennessee Justice* in his interview, as well as in his own memoir and in an article about Fine Arts Group director William Everson. In his oral history interview, he said, "Marty Ponch . . . wrote a play called *Tennessee Justice* and it was an obviously political play. He wrote it just from excerpts from the trial . . . .That play he took to Elkton and put it on there and he took it to Eugene and put it on there."[15] This adds the information that the play was performed beyond Waldport, and that Eshelman perceived it as political. In 1992, in an appreciation essay about Everson, Eshelman wrote:

> The first dramatic production of the Fine Arts group in 1945 was a "play" written by [Martin] Ponch based on true incidents, called *Tennessee Justice*. The only one of our plays to have an overt message. . . . Only a few of the Fine Arts members liked the play, most finding it to be too melodramatic.[16]

Eshelman wrote similarly about the play in his 1997 memoir, *NO SILENCE!: A Library Life*, where he called the play a "docudrama," and pointed out that it "was successful with the campers at large but judged too political by many fine arts members."[17] As the assistant director of the group, Eshelman is a very important source for suggesting the conflict between the artists and the other campers over their response to *Tennessee Justice*, though it's not entirely clear what he meant by "too melodramatic" or "too political." A "Chronology," assembled by Eshelman, perhaps with the assistance of Kermit Sheets, further suggested the arts group's perspective. This document cites a letter dated February 16, 1945, in which Eshelman called *Tennessee Justice* an "inferior production," and wrote, "It is my belief that until we get rid of Ponch, the group hasn't got a chance."[18] While it is not clear what made the play "inferior," and even less clear whether Ponch's work on *Tennessee Justice* had anything to do with Eshelman's desire to get him out, these clues reinforce the arts group's resistance to the play.

Warren Downs summarized the experience of *Tennessee Justice* in a brief unpublished memoir of theatre in CPS called "The Spoken Word—From Pulpit To The Stage." Many of the facts, as well as the response, are drawn from Adrian Wilson, whom I will discuss below. But unlike Wilson, Downs called the performance of CO Joseph Gistirak "especially effective," writing that "his arrival had been a real stimulus to the theater contingent of Fine Arts."[19] He highlighted Gistirak's experience with Hedgerow Theatre, and said when it came to his personality, "Joe was also not shy about probing others' psyches, asserting views and generally taking charge on and off stage."[20] The description of Gistirak's success, combined with the basic description of the play as a courtroom drama, led me to assume that Gistirak must have played the prosecutor, as he would not have played the African-American pastor.

The most complete description of the response to the play comes from Adrian Wilson's memoir *Two Against the Tide*. In a diary entry from January 14, 1945, he called *Tennessee Justice* "a discouragingly bad play," though he hoped the stage effects, "the transformation of the church into court and vice-versa," might "save it."[21] On January 28 he described the first performance, in which he ran "three [salt water-jug] dimmers"[22] like those Francis Barr had made, suggesting they were built for that production. He went on to offer the above-cited comments about the camp response which reinforced Eshelman's statements about the artists' distaste for the show.[23]

In summary, these sources suggested the following limited set of information. Ponch's play was reported to be "based on a *Fellowship* magazine account of an actual courtroom drama."[24] *Tennessee Justice* was a "docudrama," based on real events. As such, I compared it in my mind to the "Living Newspapers" of the previous decade, assuming an attempt to show the audience "real life" with a political purpose. Actor Joseph Gistirak, one of two Waldport artists who had worked at Pennsylvania's Hedgerow Theatre prior to the war, was in the production and his work was considered notable or even exemplary, at least by some. And some African-American COs presumably participated, though I didn't know who they were or what the experience was like for them.

Research Process

In the late summer of 2008, I began to try to track down the original magazine article on which Ponch's script was based. I searched for libraries with complete runs of *Fellowship*, which began publishing in the 1930s. I did not know when the account had been published, but knew it had to have been after the Selective Service Act of 1940, and before Ponch's work with the play in mid-1944. Then, in September 2008, I received word from the archivist at Lewis and Clark College that Mr. Cooley had sent him a copy of the script.[25] He put me in contact with Mr. Cooley, who is quite committed to keeping the memory of CPS alive, having self-published his own memoir of his time in the Oregon camps. Mr. Cooley forwarded me a copy of the program,[26] along with his answers to some of my questions about casting.[27] At the same time, I had located back issues of *Fellowship* at George Fox Uni-

THE PEOPLE	PORTRAYED BY
Reverend Marshall	James Williams
District Attorney Mooney	Charles Cooley
Defendent Reaves	Glenn Evans
Defense Attorney Harden	Joseph Gistirak
Witness	Tom Polk Miller
Judge Boyd	Mark Rouch
Clerk	Linwood Flowers
Foreman of the Jury	Arthur Snell
Jury-Choir	Francis Barr John Bechtelheimer Lloyd Brandt Wesley DeCoursey Russell Eisenbise Don Fillmore Warren Kessler Louis Kolenda Victor McLane Carroll McMillan
SCENE DESIGN AND CONSTRUCTION	U. Adrian Wilson
CHOIR DIRECTED BY	Arthur Snell
ELECTRICIANS	Francis Barr Floyd Minear Warren Kessler Rudolph Cinco
AUDIENCE RELATIONS	Isabel Mount
PROGRAM	U. Adrian Wilson William Shank

Tennessee Justice was lived, not written. If anyone were credited with its authorship, it should be one to whom could also be attributed the ordering, or disordering, of human destinies. For its incidents are straight out of the disordered life of these times. Its people resemble, in essence, those who partook in them on the scene. Its words, almost *verbatim*, are from the following sources: (*a*) notes published in *Fellowship* magazine and taken by a Fellowship of Reconciliation member during the trial in Jackson, Tennessee, of nine Negroes and their peace church pastor for "draft evasion"; (*b*) a peace sermon preached by another Negro minister years before World War II as recorded in Benjamin May's *The Negro and His Church;* (*c*) the *Bible*.

The social message of this "play" was, of course, considered of utmost importance by the pacifists who participated in its production.

> These words apply as well to ourselves and our times as they did to the people of ancient Jerusalem,

says the Reverend Marshall. As for the future, we are of the conviction that what this dramatized court record has to say, must be heard if mankind is to have a future.

But as a group primarily dedicated to expressing our experience of, and convictions about life through artistic media, we are moved and fascinated not so much by pacifist convictions *per se* as by their statement in terms of people. Not merely people as "characters" that make good subjects for portrayal but simply, people. In placing these events upon the stage, we therefore worked from the faith that if our art were couched in terms of human reality and our techniques chosen with no other purpose but to penetrate and thereby heighten that reality, our audience would take whatever of truth we had to give.

No, it was not alone the forceful words of Lawyer Harden's address to the Jury that motivated our production:

> Turn 'm loose or not . . . men will listen to these boys . . . Even if you send 'm to the pen they'll get a hearing there . . . They've got somethin' you can't put down! . . .

It was as much and more the warmth, geniality and human awareness that shines through the man as vividly as the sun which bronzed and browned and blackened the skins of his African ancestors.

Program, *Tennessee Justice*, directed by Martin Ponch, Camp Waldport, Oregon, February 1945. Image courtesy of the Lewis & Clark College Special Collections, Kermit Sheets Collection, item 7.2.

versity in Oregon, and found the original article which described the trial in the May 1944 issue.[28]

So I went from speculation about the character and quality of the script to having the opportunity to evaluate it for myself, and to consider the physical arrangement of the space, based on a drawing on the script cover,[29] Adrian Wilson's vague descriptions, the script's demands, and Mr. Cooley's memories. I also was able to consider more accurately the potential impact on the camp of the production's preparation and performance, as I knew the specific members who participated in *Tennessee Justice*, as well as their connections (or not) to the Fine Arts and to other groups at Waldport. I also was able to track down (some) statistics on race from Katrine Barber based on her extensive oral history work and other writing about CPS in Oregon. While incomplete, Barber's notes clarified who was at Waldport when and collected in one place the comments about race from her oral history.[30]

The Challenging Fact

As exciting as all of these details were, and as far as they pushed my analysis of the production, there was one fact which exerted its "tyranny" over my prior conclusions. I continued to assume that Joseph Gistirak played the prosecutor as I read the script and trial transcript, as both set up a primary conflict between the prosecutor and the pastor. However, on receiving the program and Mr. Cooley's answers, I was quite surprised to see that Mr. Cooley himself portrayed the prosecutor, and Gistirak played Defense Attorney Harden, who is clearly identified in both the trial transcript and Ponch's script as an African-American.[31] First, I wondered if I had been hasty to assume that Gistirak was NOT African-American, but I quickly confirmed that he was not. This left me with a mystery to some extent greater, or at least more disconcerting, than I had before receiving the script.

Wrestling with the "Fact"

Here are the possible conclusions this information has led me to, none decisive. First, it is possible that Gistirak performed the role in blackface, delivering the lines in the "dialect" in which they are written. This is a very uncomfortable conclusion for a group which advocated for the equal treatment of their fellow COs of all races, though it may tell us more about how attitudes toward race have changed in America since the 1940s. And in a play which calls attention to the negative treatment of a group of COs because of their race, it seems incongruous (to me) to have had an actor perform in blackface, particularly when that actor was a former (and future) member of the company at Jasper Deeter's Hedgerow Theatre. Deeter, playing Smithers for the Provincetown Players, may have insisted to Eugene O'Neill that he cast an African-American as the title character in *The Emperor Jones*, rather than a white actor in blackface.[32] Finally, it seems that at least *someone* would have commented on the fact that Gistirak was performing in blackface. Mr. Cooley, who participated, does not remember any such issue, but also is hazy on many details at the distance of 65 years.[33]

These potential factors lead to other conclusions. Perhaps Gistirak suggested the "dialect" of the script, but without makeup. Or—and this is the conclusion I most want to reach for the sake of the "story" as it makes sense to me from the perspective of 2010—the script as published for the purpose of rehearsals was adapted in performance to the existing cast. But having been encouraged more than once in historical research to begin my struggle with the past by trying to understand the fact that seems completely impossible, I am forced to concede that it is possible that Gistirak performed in blackface, and that it meant something different to his audience than it might to us. After all, onstage descendants of *Uncle Tom's Cabin* and other minstrel shows persisted well into the twentieth century. And even within CPS, African-Americans faced prejudice: one CO from Waldport, as one example, was turned back from a North Carolina medical experiment because the study leaders wanted only white candidates.[34] So it is necessary, due to the presence of this combination of documents—the program, the script, and the *Fellowship* article—to conclude that it is possible that this group, even in the midst of presenting a play which called attention to the particular plight of African-American pacifists, engaged in an activity which most would consider despicable today.

But, should it be the case that they did this, would it have been considered despicable then? It is of course impossible to say given the shortage of evidence. There are no statements about any aspect of it from the African-Americans who acted in the play. There are no statements from anyone else about the specific racial issues within the script. But it is possible that, even for a group of progressives in 1945, it would have been considered progressive just to raise the issues, and if there were no other African-Americans who auditioned for the play, the producers considered it more important to do the play than to try to find other African-Americans to perform.

In conclusion, I remain intrigued and fascinated by this play: for what it might say about the interaction between pacifism and race relations during World War II; for the ways it points out how bound we are in our own historical moments and perspectives toward such powerful issues as race and performance; and for the possibility that this play really did bring about a kind of unity in the camp for most of the campers, excepting the artists. I am hopeful that additional sources or recollections will come to light which will clarify additional questions, from how Joseph Gistirak played Defense Attorney Harden to just what the artists found "inferior" about the play. And I hope to learn more about how the apparent "success" of this production compared with the responses to the more "traditional" plays put on by Waldport's theatre group. Finally, however, I am forced to accept that, with the distances of time and cultural change, it is incredibly challenging either to capture all the details of a previous event or to exclude our own cultural presuppositions on the elements of the past we examine. Both freed and frustrated, I continue to make the attempt, collaborating with the past to make meaning.

ENDNOTES

1 Special thanks are due to a number of people who have been instrumental in this research, chief among them Mr. Charles Cooley, who retained and generously shared copies of the program and script of *Tennessee Justice* with me. My connection with Mr. Cooley, and my access to the stories and experiences of the Waldport theatre artists, are both due to the generosity of the staff in the Lewis and Clark College Aubrey Watzek Library Archives & Special Collections, Portland, Oregon: Paul Merchant, Doug Erickson, and Jeremy Skinner. Thanks also to Professor Katrine Barber of Portland State University for sharing her notes and observations about African-Americans at Waldport. Portions of the basic descriptions of the production appear, in slightly different form, in a forthcoming article in the online journal *Platform*.

2 "Trial in Tennessee," *Fellowship* 10.5 (May 1944): 92.

3 Franklin Delano Roosevelt, Executive Order 8675, February 6, 1941, http://www.archives.gov/federal-register/executive-orders/1941.html.

4 "Trial," 92.

5 *Ibid.*, 92, 97.

6 *Ibid.*, 92.

7 Adrian Wilson, *Two Against the Tide: A Conscientious Objector in World War II* (Austin, TX: W. Thomas Taylor, 1990), 119.

8 Charles Cooley, Interview, in *Camp 56: An Oral History Project*, ed. Katrine Barber, Jo Ogden, and Eliza Jones (Portland, OR: Siuslaw National Forest and History Department, Portland State University, 2003), 24.

9 The Kermit Sheets Collections, OLPb006SHE, Lewis and Clark College Aubrey Watzek Library Archives & Special Collections, Portland, Oregon, hereafter identified as *LC Sheets*.

[10] Wilson, figure 17. Figures appear between pages 96 and 97.

[11] Katrine Barber, Jo Ogden, and Eliza Jones, eds., *Camp 56: An Oral History Project* (Portland, OR: Siuslaw National Forest and History Department, Portland State University, 2003). http://www.ccrh.org/oral/co.pdf. The original transcripts and recordings are available in the Lewis and Clark College Aubrey Watzek Library Archives and Special Collections, collection OLPb045USF. For a finding aid, see http://nwda-db.wsulibs.wsu.edu/print/ark:/80444/xv16964.

[12] Cooley, 24.

[13] Francis H. Barr, Interview, in *Camp 56: An Oral History Project*, ed. Katrine Barber, Jo Ogden, and Eliza Jones (Portland, OR: Siuslaw National Forest and History Department, Portland State University, 2003), 19. On reading this interview, I inquired of Professor Barber whether they had a copy of *Tennessee Justice*; to her knowledge they did not, so apparently the interviewer was mistaken.

[14] *Ibid.*

[15] William Eshelman, Interview, in *Camp 56: An Oral History Project*, ed. Katrine Barber, Jo Ogden, and Eliza Jones (Portland, OR: Siuslaw National Forest and History Department, Portland State University, 2003), 56.

[16] William Eshelman, "Everson and the Fine Arts at Waldport," in *Perspectives on William Everson*, ed. James B. Hall, Bill Hotchkiss, and Judith Shears (Grants Pass, OR: Castle Peak Editions, 1992), 18.

[17] William Eshelman, *NO SILENCE!: A Library Life* (Lanham, MD: Scarecrow, 1997), 31.

[18] Eshelman, William, "Fine Arts at Waldport: Chronology" (*LC Sheets*, Box 6, Folder 13), 14.

[19] Warren Downs, "The Spoken Word: From Pulpit To The Stage," (*LC Sheets*, Box 1, Folder 3), 13.

[20] *Ibid.*, 14.

[21] Wilson, 119.

[22] *Ibid.*, 121.

[23] *Ibid.*

[24] Downs, "Spoken Word," 13.

[25] Martin Ponch, *Tennessee Justice: A Play in One Act, LC Sheets.*

[26] Martin Ponch, *Tennessee Justice* program, *LC Sheets*. See Figure One.

[27] Charles Cooley, personal correspondence with the author, September 2008.

[28] "Trial," 92, 97.

[29] See Figure Two.

[30] Katrine Barber, "African Americans at Camp 56" (unpublished manuscript), collection of author.

[31] Ponch, Program. See also Figure One.

[32] Joanna Rotté, "Jasper Deeter," in American National Biography V. 6, 335–337 (NY: Oxford University Press, 1999) 336. Other sources suggest that others might have first proposed this idea to O'Neill. Deeter himself always claimed that he was the first.

[33] In spite of 65 years, it still is rather surprising to me that Mr. Cooley does not remember the solution to this problem, given that he was the prosecutor in the production. That fact encourages me to conclude that nothing so dramatic as blackface was used, but again, witjout concrete evidence.

[34] Barr, 20.

Minstrelsy as White Americana: Kurt Weill's "Notes on the Minstrel Show"

DAN VENNING

In 2008, as the final paper for Professor David Savran's course "Critical Perspectives on American Musical Theatre" at the City University of New York, I wanted to write on Kurt Weill's short student opera *Down in the Valley,* which had originally been conceived as a radio opera in 1945, but was rejected by NBC, and finally opened on July 15, 1948 in a production of the Opera Department at Indiana University School of Music.[1] *Down in the Valley* was composed using popular traditional American songs and Weill wrote this work with the relatively unknown librettist Arnold Sundgaard. I had performed in a concert version of *Down in the Valley* as a freshman in college, and was still drawn to the show. When I went to the Weill-Lenya Research Center (only a few short blocks from the CUNY Graduate Center, at 7 East 20th Street), to do some preliminary research, the archivist Dave Stein suggested I also look at Weill's lesser-known Broadway musical *Love Life,* which appeared on stage in the same year as *Down in the Valley*. I had never heard of this show.

In contrast to *Down in the Valley,* which Weill and Sundgaard intended to be produced by students and amateurs, *Love Life* was written with lyricist Alan Jay Lerner, whose *Brigadoon* with Frederick Loewe had been a popular success.[2] *Love Life* was produced by Cheryl Crawford, directed by Elia Kazan, and had a cast consisting of Nannette Fabray, Ray Middleton, as well as other stars of Broadway and the vaudeville circuit.[3] It was filled with spectacle, featuring a large cast, vaudeville acts and magic tricks, and eighteen original musical numbers for which Weill had written 738 pages of orchestration.[4] This musical is definitely not simple; Terry Miller calls it "expressionist"[5] and Charles Willard argues that it is "a vastly important artifact of the American musical theater, indeed *the* 'missing link' in the evolution of the modern concept musical."[6]

Weill's work is fascinating not only because of how it influenced the development of musical theatre, but also in the way that Weill's later works reflect American folk culture. Born in 1900, Kurt Weill emigrated from Germany in 1933 to escape the Nazis, and arrived in New York in 1935. He

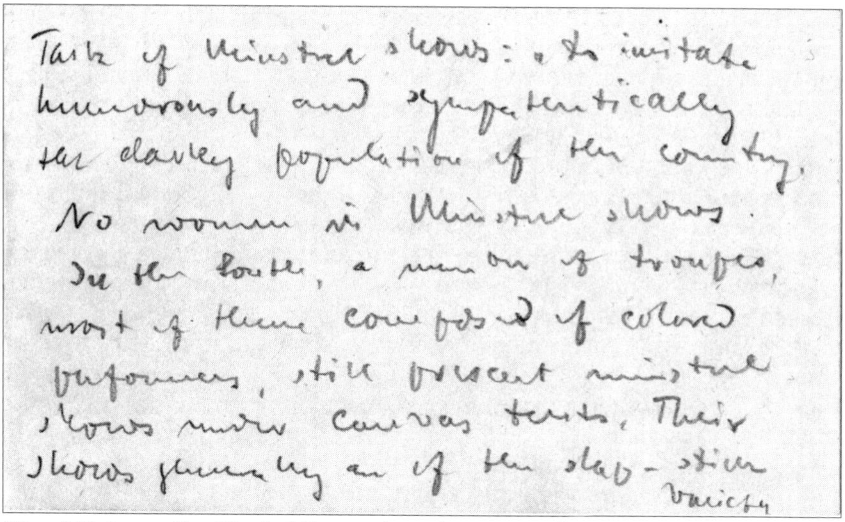
Task of Minstrel shows: to imitate humorously and sympathetically the darkey population of the country.
No women in Minstrel shows.
In the South, a number of troupes, most of them composed of colored performers, still present minstrel shows under canvas tents. Their shows generally are of the slap-stick variety

"Pencil Notes on the Minstrel Show," from the Papers of Kurt Weill and Lotte Lenya, Irving S. Gilmore Music Library, Yale University (MSS 30). Reprinted with the permission of the Kurt Weill Foundation for Music, New York.

began the process of applying for American citizenship in 1937, and finally became naturalized in 1943. He lived only seven more years, dying suddenly in 1950.[7] In 1947, *Life* magazine referred to Weill as a German composer, a description he protested intensely: "I am an American citizen."[8] Yet despite his protests and his becoming a naturalized American, there has often been critical discussion of "two Kurt Weills": the German composer who worked with Brecht and created brilliant artistic and political music, and the self-styled "American" who emulated American forms in order to make money and please a bourgeois audience without discerning musical taste.[9] However, recent critics and Weill scholars combat the tendency to argue for two Kurt Weills; J. Bradford Robinson powerfully argues in Grove Music Online that *all* of Weill's works "addressed different audiences" while he "basically used the same working methods at all stages of his career."[10]

Stein suggested that since I wanted to examine Weill's relationship with American culture, in addition to working at the Weill-Lenya center, I consult some materials held in a collection at the Irving S. Gilmore Music Library at Yale University in New Haven.[11] This collection—MSS 30, "The Papers of Kurt Weill and Lotte Lenya"—consists of 107 boxes of music, correspondence, journals, theatrical programs, notes, and photographs. It was while exploring this archive and its materials related to *Love Life* that I came across a problematic document: Weill's "Pencil Notes on the Minstrel Show" (n.d., Yale MSS 30, Box 68, Folder 18). These notes on the minstrel show are troubling because when juxtaposed with an article Weill published in the *New York Times* just before *Love Life* opened, it seems that Weill posits that minstrel shows are a part of American folk culture specifically because the shows usually originate not from African American folk traditions, but from mainstream (white) America. Weill, who was so devoted to being American, despite being foreign-born, seems—from this one document and in spite of his other liberal writings and works for the stage—to exclude authentic black traditions from "American" folk. Instead, this document suggests he privileges black*face*—white imitations of blackness—as Americana. In this essay, I explore the implications of Kurt Weill's "Notes on the Minstrel Show" on his work for the theatre, especially *Love Life*, and discuss how they complicated my own examination of this musical and Weill's career.

In order to fully examine the significance of the pencil notes, it is worthwhile to begin with a brief overview of *Love Life*, since the plot and themes explain why Weill was interested in minstrelsy. *Love Life*, subtitled *"A Vaudeville,"* examines the institution of American marriage from 1791 to 1947 through the figures of Samuel and Susan Cooper. The central conceit of the musical is that the Coopers never age. Sam and Susan remember the entire history of their marriage—in the opening scene, set at a magic show in 1947, Susan asks her husband, "Sam, don't you remember what we had together . . . a hundred and fifty years ago[?]"[12] Although Sam and Susan develop emotionally and deal with changing American society, they never deal with the fact that they're unusual by virtue of their immortality.

Despite their mutual love, Sam and Susan's marriage slowly breaks down in the face of the specter of "Progress" until they divorce, although at the end of the show they try to get back together. Weill describes the piece as "tell[ing] the saga of 150 years of American home life but also the love life of two people and the gradual changing of their personalities as life becomes more complex."[13] The couple is happy when they move to Mayville, CT., in 1791, where Sam works as a carpenter and Susan is a housewife. As industry develops in America, Sam is forced to work at a factory, and then with the railroads; these advances in technology disrupt the couple's love (and sex) life. Susan joins the suffrage movement while Sam remains oblivious. By the 1940s, they sleep in separate bedrooms. Sam moves out and the couple divorces. Yet when they meet again at the "Illusion Minstrel Show," they decide to try to make a second go of their marriage.

Narrative scenes are separated by vaudeville numbers. Before Sam begins working at the factory, eight vaudevillians in black and white costumes sing "Progress," a number about how economic progress can harm individuals at the same time as it advances society. Prior to the scene in which the couple's sex life is literally interrupted by railway schedules, a "Negro Quartette" sings "Economics," about how what's "good economics" can be "awful bad for love."[14] In the second act, vaudeville singers in the style of a glee club sing the madrigal "Ho, Billy O," about how men and women are neurotic and unable to emotionally connect in the modern world, immediately before the scene with Susan and Sam's frigid home life. Before the couple divorces, there is "An All American Puppet Ballet" entitled "Punch and Judy Get a Divorce." The vaudeville and narrative scenes come together in the opening and closing scenes of the musical: in the first scene, Sam and Susan are in a magic show, where Susan has been cut in half and Sam is levitated; the two are unable to connect with each other or escape. In the final scene, the "Illusion Minstrel Show," the couple rejects the illusionary pleasures of the minstrelsy and vaudeville acts in order to attempt to reconnect by walking across a tightrope towards one another as the curtain falls.

Love Life ran for 252 performances, a modestly successful run, then fell into obscurity because of union strikes that prevented the music from being recorded or played on the radio, and Lerner's unwillingness to allow the piece to be revived during his lifetime.[15] It was first revived at the University of Michigan by students in 1987; the first professional revival was at the American Music Theater Festival in Philadelphia in 1990, and since then it has been performed in a staged reading at the Victoria and Albert Museum in 1991 and at Opera North in Leeds in 1995. No audio recording yet exists, only a video of the Michigan student production.[16] Part of the reason that *Love Life* didn't have a longer lifespan is that it received a relatively negative review in the *New York Times*. In his review of *Love Life*, in which he expresses "a feeling of general disappointment" at a "cute, complex and joyless" work that he calls "a general gripe masquerading as vaudeville," Brooks Atkinson nevertheless praises Kurt Weill's "versatile" and "glorious" music, as well as the acting, directing, and design of the musical.[17]

Perhaps another reason the musical did not gain lasting renown was its reliance on the minstrel show tradition. In the final scene, the "Illusion Minstrel Show," Sam and Susan become the end men in a routine with an Interlocutor, a pair of magicians known as the Madame Zuzus, and a comic figure named Mr. Cynic—probably intended to be performed in blackface—who sings a song about the futility of marriage. All of these figures speak in a stereotypical minstrel dialect; for example, at one point Susan says, "sure 'nough!" and Sam says "My! My! My!"[18] Although this dialect is present and Sam and Susan seem to be portraying the end men, it is not entirely clear who, if anyone, was in blackface. The publicity photographs from the Broadway production, which are also held at the Yale Music Library, do not show this scene, and there is no mention of blackface (or its absence from a minstrel show) in newspaper reviews I read.[19]

Less than a week before the musical opened, Lerner and Weill published a "scene" in the *New York Times* as an advertisement. In this "scene," Weill and Lerner make the point that vaudeville and minstrelsy are forms of performance particularly suited to comment on American society. Weill and Lerner—characters in the "scene" but also its authors—convince a random man they meet on the street to come see the show. When the man expresses surprise at the use of vaudeville, Weill says, "Why not? If you want to tell an American story, isn't that the most typical form of American theatre?" The man responds, "I suppose so," and Lerner says, "After the minstrel show, it certainly is the most native form."[20]

It is this assertion of the American folk spirit of minstrelsy that becomes so troubling when juxtaposed with Weill's pencil notes at Yale. This document is a tiny part of the Weill archive. The pencil notes consist of seventeen unlined thin three-by-five inch index cards. Weill has written on both sides of a few of the cards, but most have writing on one side only. Weill writes in English, although occasionally adding minor German grammatical quirks, such as commas where they would appear in German, or abbreviations such as "usw" ("und so weiter," or "and so on," basically the same as "etc"). The cards are not numbered, and seem to be independent meditations on the minstrel show, so their order in the archive may be arbitrary. This theory is supported by the fact that sequential cards sometimes look quite different in terms of handwriting and paper quality.

Some of the notes deal with the organization and structure of the minstrel show, famous performers and troupes, or its reception and popularity. A few of the notes have bibliographic entries for sources. The front of the twelfth card, for example, consists entirely of three lines: "Lawrence [sic] Hutton / The Negro on the Stage / Harpers Magazine LXXIX," which obviously refer to Laurence Hutton's 1889 article,[21] a fascinating and beautifully illustrated—although also uncritical and entirely racist—overview of blackness on the stage from *Othello* and *Oroonoko* through black roles played by Lewis Hallam the Younger, Edwin Forrest, Joseph Jefferson, T. D. Rice, and minstrel stars of the end of the nineteenth century. On the reverse of this same card, Weill has written the words "Tambo and Bones," perhaps referring to Carl Wittke's book.[22] Other bibliographic entries Weill has written include "White, American Negro Folksongs (Harvard University Press)" (published in 1928), "William A. Fischer, Seventy Negro Spirituals" (published in 1926), "James Weldon Jonson, The Book of American Negro Poetry" (published in 1931), and "Brander Matthew [sic]. The rise [sic] and Fall of Negro Minstrelsy. Scribners. LVII" (published in 1915).[23]

However, the most fascinating cards deal with the relation between minstrelsy and white Americana. On the first card, Weill has written: "Only slight relation between Minstrel songs and Negro folkmusic [sic]. Most minstrel men northern born or foreigners. Only early songs based on Negro music." The third card has: "Task of Minstrel Shows: to imitate, humorously and sympathetically the [darky???] population of the country. No women in Minstrel shows." On the fifth card, Weill has written, "Music minstrelsy by white composer [sic] who has never seen the [South???]. (Foster was a few days in Kentucky after most of his songs had appeared). Less than 10% of minstrel songs were genuinely Negro. The Principal minstrel performers were white men."[24] As far as I could tell from my readings of some of his sources, Weill is not simply copying material, but instead synthesizing these works and developing his own opinions about the history of minstrelsy and African-American music. Even if some of this material was directly copied, what Weill chose to note is quite telling.

Weill's notes on the minstrel show are not bad history; Eric Lott summarizes the origins of minstrelsy by noting that "in the decades before the Civil War, northern white men 'blacked up' and imitated what they supposed was black dialect, music, and dance,"[25] and begins his book *Love and Theft* by noting that "minstrelsy was an established nineteenth-century theatrical practice, principally of the urban North."[26] It is worthwhile to note that Weill certainly does not follow the overtly racist agenda of authors such as Carl Wittke, who situates the origins of blackface minstrelsy with "the singing and dancing of the slaves in Southern plantations,"[27] nor does Weill display Wittke's blatant nostalgia for minstrelsy and apologism for slavery.[28] Nevertheless, Weill's notes on minstrel history are deeply troubling when combined with his project in *Love Life*. If, as I have argued elsewhere, *Love Life* is about what it means to be an American and if, as Weill argued in the scene he and Lerner published in the *New York Times*, minstrelsy is the most original American theatrical form, these pencil notes suggest that Weill sees the American spirit as solely the property of white Americans, even—or especially—when those white Americans ridicule and imitate blacks. Weill thus does not allow black Americans the archetypal American subjectivity granted to whites like *Love Life*'s Sam and Susan. This implied assertion is a far cry from George Gershwin's inclusive comments, made over two decades earlier, that "the American soul . . . is black and white. It is all colors and all souls unified in the great melting pot of the world."[29]

Weill, researching the minstrel show to prepare for *Love Life*, and focusing on the form as particularly American, seems to have missed most of the ways in which the form serves as racist domination and excludes many American men and women from the spirit of American folk culture. Only once in the notes does Weill seem to consider this issue, when he writes the short question, "What happened when real Negros saw Minstrel shows?"[30] Weill was no stranger to such alienation; he himself had struggled to become an American; it was only a year before *Love Life* came to Broadway that *Life* magazine had called Weill a German and the composer had responded so strongly. One could build upon this to the rather sinister hypothesis that Weill, in his own attempts to identify as an American—like Jewish entertainers such as Al Jolson or Eddie Cantor, who employed blackface in the 1920s and 1930s—needed to identify and exclude that which was un-American. On the other hand, I am inclined to be generous and conclude that Weill, in displaying this slight—and almost certainly unconscious and unintended—racist impulse, was a product of his time. In the 1940s, actors could still perform blackface routines in film or on Broadway, which would have been perceived (by most white audiences) not as racist but old-fashioned, nostalgic, or quaint.[31]

Michael Rogin notes that most of these later blackface works fell into "two subcategories . . . either backstage musicals about putting on a show or biographies of the central figures in the history of American popular music."[32] In some sense, *Love Life* qualifies as an example of the first of Rogin's subcategories: there is the metatheatrical vaudeville show, and *Love Life* could be seen as displaying American theatrical forms (vaudeville and minstrelsy) as a stand-in for American culture. This also fits into Rogin's general theory of blackface: that "imaginary blackness" served to "Americanize," or solidify the identity of a (white) immigrant population, who previously had been diverse and separately identified, whether as Russian, Polish, Irish, or, like Weill, Jewish.[33] This is part and parcel of what is most troubling about Weill's pencil notes on the minstrel show: Weill appears to be dismissing all of African-American cultural experience and its influence on American culture on the whole. To be fair, the show itself is not at first clearly the work of a leftist. The overall tone of the libretto of *Love Life* is obviously anti-progressive; some might even call it reactionary.

Weill was certainly interested in American pastoral and folk culture (as is also illustrated by *Down in the Valley*, which led me to *Love Life*), but most of his musicals—which he wrote with intensely leftist authors such as Brecht,

Maxwell Anderson, Langston Hughes, and Elmer Rice—clearly demonstrate not only his aesthetic and musical talent but also a strong liberal political sensibility. *Knickerbocker Holiday* (1938), which Weill wrote with Anderson, was an allegory decrying fascism; *Street Scene* (1947), which Weill wrote with Rice and Hughes, showed how people of varying ethnicities and classes can all fit into American society; *Lost in the Stars* (1949), written with Anderson, is an adaptation of Alon Paton's *Cry, The Beloved Country*, and examines racial tension in South Africa. Weill was certainly a forward-looking humanitarian artist, and thus what is most tyrannical about his notes on the minstrel show is that they demonstrate that Weill's racism there and in *Love Life* was not purely a mistake: he conducted research, made notes, and thought a great deal about blackface, consciously enacting a racist agenda, not "merely" enacting it as a part of normative culture.

ENDNOTES

For comments, suggestions, and help at the Yale Music Library archives, I wish to thank Emily Ferrigno and Richard Boursy. Very special thanks are due to Dave Stein, the archivist at the Weill-Lenya Research Foundation. Stein's guidance and assistance were invaluable: he first suggested I examine *Love Life* and also made suggestions regarding what I should look for during my trip to Yale. I am grateful to Kevin Byrne for comments on the popular reception of blackface minstrelsy in the mid-twentieth century, and for sharing his dissertation. Thanks also to Leo Cabranes-Grant and Emma Halpern, who read earlier drafts of this article and offered useful comments and suggestions for revision, David Savran for his engaging course, and Stephen Johnson for many helpful comments and suggestions for revision.

[1] Arnold Sundgaard, "Writing Folk Opera with Kurt Weill: Portrait of the Librettist as a Silenced Composer," *Dramatists Guild Quarterly* xvi, no. 4 (1980), 30.

[2] Lerner and Loewe would go on to write *My Fair Lady*, the most successful musical of its time.

[3] Foster Hirsch, *Kurt Weill on Stage: From Berlin to Broadway* (New York: Limelight Editions, 2003), 277–99.

[4] In a letter to Mr. Irving Lazar on June 28, 1948, Weill claims he has to write 500 pages of orchestration before rehearsals begin—in other words, within two months. Yale MSS 30, Box 47, Folder 9.

[5] Terry Miller, "*Love Life* Begins at Forty," *Kurt Weill Newsletter* 5, no. 2 (Fall 1987), 8.

[6] Charles Willard, "Life's 'Progress': *Love Life* Revisitied," *Kurt Weill Newsletter* 2, no. 2 (Fall 1984), 5. Emphasis in original.

[7] For a good biography, see Jürgen Schebera, *Kurt Weill: An Illustrated Life*. Trans. Caroline Murphy (New Haven and London: Yale University Press, 1995), 258–9. Hirsch's book is also a good biographical source, although its primary focus is not Weill's work, not his life.

[8] Quoted in Hirsch, 274.

[9] For example, the composer and critic Alec Wilder, who freely admits that he "happen[s] not to be a Kurt Weill fan" makes the suggestion that "one" is always aware that Weill's music is "not rooted in this culture." See Alec Wilder, *American Popular Song: The Great Innovators, 1900–1950*, Ed. James T. Maher (New York and Oxford: Oxford University Press, 1990), 511, 357. These are two of the only three times Wilder mentions Weill in his book: in the third, Wilder suggests Weill is a master of "astute imitation" (133) of American music, but has no personal involvement whatsoever. Arnold Sundgaard, who worked with Wilder on several occasions, suggests that Wilder's distaste for Weill might have been motivated by some degree of professional envy. See Sundgaard, "Alec Wilder: Curt about

Weill." *Kurt Weill Newsletter* 10, no. 2 (Fall 1992), 10–11. In addition to Wilder, Theodor Adorno who had lauded Weill in Germany as the creator of "the only music of genuine social-polemic impact," later accused Weill of vapidity and opportunism in his compositions for the American stage, suggesting Weill had "sacrificed" his earlier greatness "in the conscious search for accessibility." In a scathing obituary published on April 15, 1950, Adorno argues that Weill "could barely be called a composer," and that when he began writing for Broadway "talked as if concession to the commercial field were no concession." See Theodor W. Adorno, "On the Social Situation of Music" and "Farewell to Jazz," *Essays on Music*, trans. Susan H. Gillespie (Berkeley, Los Angeles, and London: University of California Press, 2002), 409, 499 and Adorno, "Kurt Weill," *Frankfurter Rundschau*, 15 April 1950, quoted and translated in David Drew, "*Der Kuhhandel* as a Key Work," in Kim Kowalke, ed. *A New Orpheus: Essays on Kurt Weill* (New Haven and London: Yale University Press, 1986), 218–9.

[10] J. Bradford Robinson, "Posthumous Reputation," in "Weill, Kurt," Grove Music Online, www.oxfordmusiconline.com/subscriber/article/grove/music/3032. Accessed 13 August 2010.

[11] This article focuses on my findings during my research and materials in this archive. For this reason, I do not have space to fully explore the argument I laid out in my paper in Savran's course. In that paper—from which several sections of this essay are drawn—I noted that while *Down in the Valley* and *Love Life* seem, at first glance, to be polar opposites, they are thematically similar. They certainly differ: one is a full-length Broadway musical with original music and an intricate plot, requiring complex staging and a large professional cast, the other a brief school opera, designed for simple production, with music adapted from existing pieces. In terms of reception, *Down in the Valley* proved to be a massive commercial and popular success, while *Love Life* has languished in relative obscurity since its first production. In my paper for Savran's course, I argued that *Down in the Valley* and *Love Life* came from a similar impulse: Weill's desire to explore through musical theatre the idea of the American spirit. In *Down in the Valley*, the American spirit is manifested as Pastoral folk, deceptively simple. In *Love Life*, the spirit of the American folk struggles within a society fueled by the Dionysian revue of vaudeville and minstrelsy.

[12] Kurt Weill, *Love Life* (Libretto), Book and Lyrics by Alan Jay Lerner, Weill-Lenya Foundation LRC Series 20/L8/1948C, I.i.3–4.

[13] Kurt Weill and Alan Jay Lerner, "Collaborators Stage a Scene Aimed at Explaining Their Musical Play," *New York Times*, 3 October 1948. Reprinted *Kurt Weill Newsletter* 2, no. 2 (Fall 1984), 8.

[14] *Love Life* (Libretto), I.v.33.

[15] Hirsch, 297.

[16] *Love Life: A Vaudeville* (1/4 inch tape converted to DVD), Dir. Brent Wagner, University of Michigan Department of Theater, April 18, 1987, with Sharon Rosin as Susan and Doug LaBrecque as Sam.

[17] Brooks Atkinson, "At the Theatre," *New York Times*, 8 October 1948, 31.

[18] *Love Life* (Libretto), II.vi.29, 30.

[19] There was certainly no blackface used in the 1987 University of Michigan revival production, which I watched on tape at the Kurt Weill Foundation archive in New York.

[20] Weill and Lerner, "Collaborators Stage a Scene . . . ."

[21] Laurence Hutton, "The Negro on the Stage," *Harper's Magazine* 79 (1889): 131–45; available online at http://books.google.com/books?id=T_gvAAAAMAAJ&printsec=frontcover. Accessed 15 December 2010.

[22] Carl Wittke, *Tambo and Bones: A History of the American Minstrel Stage* (Durham, NC: Duke University Press, 1930; reprinted Westport, CT: Greenwood Press, 1968).

[23] Full citations for these works are: Newman Ivey White, *American Negro Folk-Songs* (Cambridge: Harvard University Press, 1928); William A. Fischer, ed., *Seventy Negro Spirituals* (Boston: Oliver Ditson Company, etc., 1926); James Weldon Jonson, ed., *The Book of*

American Negro Poetry (New York: Harcourt Brace, 1931); Brander Matthews, "The Rise and Fall of Negro Minstrelsy," *Scribner's Magazine* LVII (January-June, 1915). The first of these is on the reverse of card five, and the other three entries are on the reverse of card thirteen.

[24] Kurt Weill, "Pencil Notes on the Minstrel Show," n.d., Yale MSS 30, Box 68, Folder 18. A few of Weill's words are difficult to read. Where I am unsure as to whether I transcribed the correct word, I indicate with a bracket and question marks. Quotations reprinted with the permission of the Kurt Weill Foundation for Music New York. All rights reserved.

[25] Eric Lott, "Blackface and Blackness: The Minstrel Show in American Culture," in Annemarie Bean, James V. Hatch, and Brooks McNamara, eds., *Inside the Minstrel Mask: Readings in Nineteenth-Century Blackface Minstrelsy* (Hanover and London: Wesleyan University Press, 1996), 4–5.

[26] Eric Lott, *Love and Theft: Blackface Minstrelsy and the American Working Class* (New York and Oxford: Oxford University Press, 1993), 3. A similar assessment can be found in Kevin Byrne's recent dissertation on blackface minstrelsy and its pervasive presence from its creation into the twentieth century, in which Byrne introduces the form by noting that "the minstrel show proper developed out of the performances of white racial impersonation that were part of the cultural landscape from the beginning of the nineteenth century" and that blackface makeup, which "supplied the necessary racial impersonation" was "the most crucial element to the minstrel show." See Kevin Byrne, "The Circulation of Blackface: Nostalgia and Tradition in US Minstrel Performance of the Early 1920s" (Ph.D. diss., CUNY Graduate Center, 2010), 3–6.

[27] Wittke, 6.

[28] Most troubling are Wittke's apologist assertion that "without negro slavery, the United States would have been deprived of perhaps the only . . . body of song sprung from the soil . . . [and] the only distinctively American contribution to the theatre—the Negro minstrel show" (3) and his blatant nostalgia when he describes his interest as "more than professional" and based in "happy memories of the burnt-cork semi-circle, gathered during barnstorming student day . . . and a real love for the old-time minstrel show" (vii).

[29] George Gershwin, "Jazz Is the Voice of the American Soul," *Theatre*, March 1927, 52B, quoted in David Savran, *Highbrow/Lowdown: theater, Jazz, and the Making of the New Middle Class* (Ann Arbor: The University of Michigan Press, 2009), 68.

[30] Weill, "Pencil notes."

[31] Lott notes that well into the twentieth century, minstrelsy was "enveloped in a reactionary nostalgia." *Love and Theft*, 7.

[32] Michael Rogin, *Blackface, White Noise: Jewish Immigrants in the Hollywood Melting Pot* (Berkley: University of California Press, 1996), 167.

[33] Ibid., 80.

"Me Tondalayo": The Burlesque Politics of Mammy Palaver

JULIE VOGT

In March 1962, veteran burlesque dancer Ann Corio debuted her satiric recreation of early-twentieth century burlesque in the East Village. Although the critical reception for *This Was Burlesque* was lukewarm, audiences came by the busload to see the legendary Corio back on stage at the age of 53.[1] Corio served primarily as curator and host; her performances were limited to the recreation of her signature striptease, which closed the show, and speaking roles in a few comic scenes. One of the mainstays of the *This Was Burlesque* (*TWB)* repertoire was the classic sketch "White Cargo," a parody of a dramatic play by the same name that toured America in the 1920s and 1940s.[2] In the scene, Corio played Tondalayo, a half-caste woman who seduces the overseer of a British plantation in West Africa. As Tondalayo, Corio would slink across the stage wearing a batik halter top and sarong tied thigh-high, her hips bumping to the orchestra drum as she seduced her mark, the company "top banana," Steve Mills. With gigantic clusters of fake flowers embellishing her hair and wrist she would purr at overseer "Helo, Helo. Me Tondalayo."[3]

If I never had to face Ann Corio's niece this skit was easy to explain: it was a vestige of minstrelsy. "White Cargo" was evidence of a seemingly indelible cultural stain—colonialist fantasies in which racial impersonations are grafted onto eroticized female bodies. But Carole, Corio's niece, had never read and wouldn't care about postcolonial theory. She wouldn't be persuaded by the thick volumes of academic writing that pointed me toward the conclusion that her beloved aunt peddled a diluted form of minstrelsy. When you know and respect someone, it's hard to look that person in the eye and blithely label her spiritual mother an opportunistic racist. If I'd never met Carole, I could have complacently yielded to the explanation tyrannically demanded by corroborating evidence and secondary criticism: by performing a half-caste, south-seas islander woman who was defined by her aggressively "savage" sexuality, Ann Corio sustained the nineteenth-century minstrel influence on burlesque entertainment.

Rather than hedging away from an unpleasant truth, or veiling my true meaning in pedantic technical language, my relationship with Carole forced me to seek in the "White Cargo" script fragments and photographs a more

Ann Corio and Steve Mills in "White Cargo." Photographed by Bob Gomel for *Life Magazine* (September 16,1966), 133. Used with the permission of Mr. Gomel.

complex answer for Corio's performances as Tondalayo. The reflexive critique could have offended the guardian of Corio's private archive—a vast cache of burlesque scripts, scrapbooks and costumes—and a woman who was fast becoming a personal friend. Unlike my other research sources Carole, the accidental archivist, remembered to send cards on my birthday and Mother's day. The genealogy of burlesque, the provenance of the sketch and Corio's performing career endorsed a simplistic reading which classified "White Cargo" as revived minstrelsy. But, as I found when forced by friendship to look deeper, these data streams couldn't fully explain the humor or enduring popularity of the sketch; why did *White Cargo* endure long after burlesque comics abandoned their thick accents, putty noses and burnt cork? Important clues lay in the script fragments, but this minutiae might have been ignored if not for the personal connection to the guardian of Ann Corio's intellectual property and familial memory.

The genealogy of burlesque entertainment has a direct lineage to minstrelsy. As Robert Allen documents in *Horrible Prettiness,* following the box-office triumphs of Lydia Thompson and her British Blondes several producers in the 1870s simultaneously hit upon a profitable muddling of the "gendered nature of burlesque entertainment with the tripartite structure of the blackface minstrel show."[4] Minstrelsy and theatrical burlesque blended easily because both functioned as carnivalesque parodies of "high" culture and, as Allen notes, women were regarded by evolutionary scientists as situated "between the primitive savage and civilized white male."[5] Defined by their quasi-primitive nature, women were absorbed easily into the animalistic representations of former slaves in minstrel entertainment. Racial caricatures endured into twentieth-century burlesque because both comic techniques relied on improvisation around established stock archetypes. The structured improvisation of the burlesque repertoire freed comics to interject more racy (or demure) material and expand dialogue that sparked an audience to laugh. But this technique also limited the development of new routines and reinforced a limited roster of stereotypes; consequently broad racial caricatures were the base ingredients of American burlesque.[6]

Carole was well aware that her aunt's comic performances were racially insensitive but acceptable in the milieu of American culture at the time. Although I believed that racial hostility could not be absolved by social conformity, it's not possible to demand reparations or apologies from a deceased artist and faulting Corio for a lack of social progressivism might have insulted Carole. It was some consolation to Carole and myself that Ann Corio did not invent Tondalayo; she was an established character. Tondalayo arose from the dual minstrel-burlesque traditions of low parodies of literary drama and eroticized, semi-savage women. *White Cargo,* the play, by Leon Gordon, opened in New York City in 1923. The drama was critically dismissed as lurid, yet it ran for 702 performances on Broadway and toured extensively for the next decade.[7] The potboiler concerns the travails of Langford, an overseer at a West African plantation, who becomes enamored of Tondalayo. Seeking to uphold his civilized morality, Langford marries Tondalayo rather than engage in an informal sexual relationship (as his predecessors had done). But Tondalayo quickly becomes bored with the arrangement and attempts to poison Langford; her assassination attempt is thwarted and she is forced to drink the poison by other plantation executives. Variations of "White Cargo," the skit, circulated around burlesque houses when the play was popular (Gypsy Rose Lee claimed she performed the role of the "native girl in 'Black and Blue Cargo'").[8] Ann Corio first performed the burlesque version of Tondalayo while employed by the Minskys—a family of theatrical entrepreneurs who owned several stock burlesque houses in the 1930s. The premise was not original when *White Cargo* was a touring success; "Teddy in the Jungle" scenes were common on the popular stage during Theodore Roosevelt's expeditions to Panama, Africa and Central America.[9] *White Cargo* variants are also structurally similar to sailor-on-the-island sketches popular from the turn of the century.[10]

The sketch was common in burlesque houses, but Corio was especially entwined with the dramatic and comic figure Tondalayo. Corio's first role on the legitimate stage was Tondalayo in a 1941 touring production of *White Cargo;* she also performed the role in New York City and in summer stock theatres on the East Coast in the mid-1940s. *White Cargo* marked Corio's only known foray into makeup-enhanced racial impersonation—when she performed Tondalayo in Cambridge, MA, she wore a heavy brown makeup on her body.[11] In 1963, Ann Corio's audiences were probably more familiar with her movies, which were distributed nationally, than arcane variations on a play about British colonialism. The "White Cargo" sketch performed in *This Was Burlesque* would have simultaneously recalled for those who knew her Corio's ill-fated film career because her cinematic characters were extensions of the Tondalayo prototype.

The titles of Corio's films evoke the untamed eroticism that was ascribed to indigenous, non-white women in *White Cargo*: *Swamp Woman* (1941), *Jungle Siren* (1942), *Sarong Girl* (1943), *Sultan's Daughter* (1944), and *Call of the Jungle* (1944).[12] Some of the films are now available on DVD and Carole confessed that she found them difficult to watch because the quality of the films was so poor and her aunt's performances were weak. Corio found herself typecast as an attractive native (or half-caste) help-mate in jungle adventures alongside athletic male co-stars. In the hour-long, black and white movies Corio's dark hair and olive skin are metonymic for the indigenous "darkness" and primitive sexuality that the white, American hero encounters on his foreign travels. The archetype presents women who were not beholden to "civilized" western traditions such as courtship and marriage. What perplexed both Carole and I was the enduring popularity of the character. Some graphic novels and fan letters in the vast archive connected Corio's films to comic-book heroines such as Vooda, the jungle princess. But I couldn't explain why the archetype migrated so easily into other mediums.

Corio's public image was a palimpsest of her demure strip tease persona and her roles in B-movies. It is hard to imagine that she revived the "White Cargo" sketch in *This Was Burlesque* (*TWB*) for any purpose other than facile racial humor. The freedom from the evidential tyranny—was a scribble on a partial script, one of many notations hastily inscribed by burlesque comics playing variations on the scene. In one fragment, the geography of the scene was specific: the margin note read "Hawaii." Hawaii was the location of the iconic attack on Pearl Harbor and it continues to host a strategic naval base. It occurred to me that for Corio's mid-century audiences, the "jungle" of the sketch was not an English colony, but the territories occupied during *American* imperialist expansion, and two world wars.

Classic burlesque sketches were politically cautious; burlesque comedy centered on the shared, quotidian experiences of working-class men and functioned as an alternate form of sexual education. Sketches did not criticize or endorse politicians, to avoid alienating members of the audience with varying political affiliations. But the "White Cargo" skit is exemplary of political references that percolated under the surface of broad physical comedy. The "Teddy in the Jungle" burlesque sketches were precipitated by the United States' armed annexation of Hawaii (1887–1893) and the Philippines (1899–1902). The play *White Cargo* was first popular during the 1920s when American economic imperialism expanded into Central America. The tropical setting of the "White Cargo" sketch was a cipher for occupied territories that stretched from the Caribbean to the South Pacific.[13] Military veterans in the audience could project the settings of their tours of duty onto the generic island of the sketch.

Enlisted men were loyal patrons of burlesque theatres, which were often proximate to a naval port or a military recruiting office. Corio's archive contained fan letters from servicemen who saw her perform at the Old Howard theatre in Boston and pictures of her rallying for war bonds. When *This Was Burlesque* played in New York City servicemen and veterans were invited to attend through the USO.[14] This archival evidence gave clarity to the scribble in the script. "White Cargo" was not simply some phantom of nineteenth-century minstrel afterpieces, but a veiled gag about conscription and Tondalayo was an allusion to the sexual experiences of men serving abroad, liaisons which disrupted domestic segregation and military policy.

"White Cargo" was a preferred sketch in the *This Was Burlesque* repertoire because it alluded to the discreet sexual experiences of the large population of men who participated in military deployments. But what made this dramatization comic and not melodramatic? Was it Corio's exaggerated performance of a dangerously lascivious woman or Mills' inability to resist a non-white "native"? It is possible that Corio's company regularly played the skit *because* it was so flexible. In the civil-rights era the show toured to audiences that would have had varying sympathies concerning integration. Burlesque technique allowed comedians to be adaptive, deploying a straight face or mugging a line based on audience response. Tondalayo could be a predatory wench or a sexually-curious everywoman as provoked by audience laughter. Returning to the centrality of race in earlier burlesque humor, did Corio subvert the "native maiden" stereotype, or did she reinforce it? This question presents one of the most significant challenges in the historiography and analysis of humor, because the query is riddled with variables: burlesque technique is rooted in improvisation, so the representation changed with every location and showtime; the static imagery of the archive does not adequately convey indicators of irony. More dynamic evidence may lie in the approximately 75 reel-to-reel sound recordings of *TWB* and other burlesque performances made by Harry Conley, the comedian employed by Corio who collected the hundreds of burlesque scripts also housed in Carole's archive. But I knew that to play the tapes without preservation could destroy the fragile media, so this resource could not be utilized.

Dramatic irony and camp cannot be recovered from a three page script. It is possible, however, to present possible interpretations of Corio's "White Cargo" and identify the comic triggers by mapping the departures from the play and evaluating what the sketch could have symbolized to the servicemen and veterans in the audience. The "White Cargo" sketch introduced themes and ideas that were contrary to the dramatic conflicts in the original play it burlesqued. In Gordon's potboiler, Langford's boss Wetzel rejects his attempts to validate miscegenation through marriage: "Trick it out with your ceremony, but it's mammy-palaver; sanctify it with the church if you like, but it's mammy-palaver."[15] In *This Was Burlesque* the term "mammy-palaver" is a punchline, an eccentric euphemism for sexual activity. In one script, the phrase is defined by the straight man, "some call it love, some call it emotion, some call it passion." In this text, inter-racial sexual activity is provoked by common human impulses that are shared across cultural boundaries. The union of Tondalayo and the overseer is one of willing consent in *TWB*. Some part of the humor arises from Mills' brief and insincere attempts to resist

Corio's advances. In Gordon's play, Langford resists Tondalayo's advances because he does not want to pollute his whiteness by fraternizing with a woman whose "blood and instincts are all nigger."[16] (The "White Cargo" sketch contains no racial epithets). Langford's failure to uphold his whiteness is the cause of his near-poisoning (metaphoric and literal) and serious debilitation that causes him to be sent back to England as white cargo; the title phrase suggests a fallen superiority which places him dangerously close to the category of black cargo, or slavery. In the "White Cargo" sketch, Mills is cautioned against "going native" but his indulgences in local music and whiskey make him content—his sexual and social tourism is felicitous and there are no pretensions of marriage in the sketch,

The "White Cargo" sketch potentially subverts cultural resistance to miscegenation by emphasizing sexual desire as a universal aspect of the human experience. But the sketch is not without the residues of imperialist hierarchies. The very fear of "going native" and the guttural, grunting dialect of Tondalayo's native lover, Unga, affirms the notion that indigenous islanders do not have the capacity for civilization or sophisticated speech. (While the Yiddish-language inspiration for Unga's dialect simultaneously creates a parallel to Jewish identities subsumed in assimilationist American culture). The hierarchies of colonialism that frame the dramatic play are carried over into the satire.

The most subversive aspect of the "White Cargo" sketch is the emphasis on mutually-consenting sexual activity without racial anxiety. But placed in the context of the material conditions to which the skit subtly refers—the sexual life of enlisted men serving in foreign territories—the subversive potential is deflated. Consent, when language is not shared, is far from concrete. In men's magazines of the era, tropical native women are the locus of narrative fantasies.[17] Retail sexual commerce surrounded American military bases. (Hawaii did not become a U.S. state until 1959; during World War II prostitution was not illegal). As Cynthia Enloe details in *Bananas, Beaches, and Bases* the United States military tacitly permitted brothels and allowed servicemen to patronize them. The sexual outlets provided by prostitution were considered ameliorative to more serious threats to company morale—such as homesickness and homosexual contact. United States military further acknowledged the sexual commerce around bases when it distributed condoms and provided educational materials about venereal diseases during World War II. The specter of non-consent haunts the women of colonized countries who performed sexual labor around military bases, but during periods of military draft there is a spectrum of consent, enthusiasm, and commitment to ideology among servicemen.

Conscripted men are rarely written of as a forced diaspora, taken from the normative "ideal" of being domestic providers, contributing to a national economy. The sketch was a nostalgic glimpse back at an era in which men quietly fulfilled their commitment to the selective service, in contrast to the public draft-resistance waged by conscripts to the Vietnam war and Nixon's draft lottery, implemented in 1971. The retention of the sketch into the Vietnam war era acknowledged that more young men were being forcibly sent into new "jungles" and that the map of occupied territories continued to expand. Although burlesque entertainment is notorious for objectifying women, in "White Cargo" the narrative center is the comedian, Steve Mills. The woman-as-object is not the exclusive focus of the audience's attention; the alleged male gaze has a plasticity in which the erotic and political form a binocular vision of the scene.[18]

The "White Cargo" skit discreetly recognized the pains of conscription by creating a scenario in which the pleasure of sexual activity takes priority over nationalism and military objectives. Understanding Tondalayo as a metaphor for deployment liaisons was consistent with burlesque's function as a sphere for expression of working-class sexual and material experiences, conditions that diverged from the putative middle-class ideals of domestic harmony and prosperity. This reading of "White Cargo" didn't absolve Corio for reifying racial stereotypes but it did add a layer of complexity, supported by evidence from the same sequestered archive, that I hoped would explain the enduring appeal of the embarrassing Tondalayo performances to Carole. I believe that Corio retained the sketch for several decades because it anchored her authority as a preservationist of the genre: she was a veteran who valued other veterans—of both the stage and American military.

There are no formalized ethics for research in dead subjects and documents; institutional research boards are only concerned with the consent of living humans. But should the ethical requirements of the Belmont report—the 1979 basis for the regulation of human subjects research by the U.S. Department of Health and Human Services—be taken into consideration when a diary is opened or a letter is transcribed? Having to face a real person (a woman who fed me lunch while we organized her aunt's personal effects in a tidy Del Web home) pushed me to read the margins more closely, to write about Ann Corio as if she was a living subject instead of an abstract research topic. Historians dig and sift through archives, discovering hidden sexualities, suppressed desires and lost dreams, imagining that we are absolved from ethical contracts by the passage of time, the evaporation of old codes and social strictures that mandated silence and secrets. But what if we, as scholars and historians, had to treat the long dead with the same tender diplomacy as we address the living?

ENDNOTES

[1] Audiences and the press liked to speculate about Corio's true age and birthdate (1909) but she never disclosed this information while she was alive.

[2] I use *White Cargo* to refer to Gordon's published play and the typesetting "White Cargo" to refer to unpublished sketch parodies, of which there are many variants.

[3] Recreations of the sketch were taken from: Ann Corio's private archive in the possession of Carole Nelson; "Castanet Clicks and the New Bumper Crop in Burlesque," *Cavalier*, November 1962; Marshall Smith, "It's Ladies' Day at the Burleyque," *Life*, September 16, 1966. Variant spellings of Tondalayo from burlesque scripts and *White Cargo* programs include: Tondeleyo, Tondelayo and Tondalaya.

[4] Robert C. Allen, *Horrible Prettiness: Burlesque and American Culture* (Chapel Hill, NC: University of North Carolina Press, 1991), 163.

[5] Ibid., 228.

[6] Minstrel elements were still evident in revival burlesque well after the civil rights era; the 1979 Broadway musical *Sugar Babies* was so faithful to a nineteenth-century sensibility

that it included an adapted minstrel routine. In the number "Down at the Gaiety Burlesque" the lyrics referenced the 1870s burlesque troupe Madame Rentz as Ann Miller led her chorines "sister bones" and "sister tambourine" in a ladies minstrel show. The routine did not use blackface, instead Miller wore a sparkling-white tap outfit covered in sequins, as if to cleanse burlesque of any association with the use of burnt cork. *Sugar Babies,* recorded 1980, Theatre on Film and Tape (NCOV 139), New York Public Library.

[7] *White Cargo* became a movie in 1929 and again in 1942 staring Heddy Lamar.

[8] *Gypsy Rose Lee Remembers Burlesque,* 33-1/3 rpm LP (Fort Lauderdale, FL: Fletcher Smith Studios, 1962). Lee tells a different variation of her induction into speaking roles in her biography; in the book, she plays Tondalayo in a hula skirt. Gypsy Rose Lee, *Gypsy: A Memoir* (New York: Harper & Brothers 1957), 192.

[9] Patricia Sandberg Conner, "Steve Mills and the Twentieth Century American Burlesque Show: A Backstage History and a Perspective" (Dissertation, University of Illinois at Urbana-Champaign, 1979), 260–61.

[10] Andrew Harvey Davis, "Baggy Pants Comedy: Burlesque and the Oral Tradition" (dissertation, New York University, 2000), 66–68.

[11] Corio quipped in her pictorial history book that when local censors faulted her for being scantily clad, she wore a pound and a half of brown body powder. Ann Corio and Joseph DiMona, *This Was Burlesque* (New York: Grosset & Dunlap/Madison Square Press, 1968), 176.

[12] Despite the critical reception, Corio's movies acquired cult status. In December 1983 the non-profit Cooperative Film Society hosted an Ann Corio film festival, which was attended by Corio. Advertisement from the folder: Clippings, Corio, Ann, the Billy Rose Theatre Collection, New York Public Library.

[13] Cynthia Enloe reports, "Between 1880 and 1930 the United States colonized or invaded Hawaii, the Philippines, Puerto Rico, the Dominican Republic, Cuba and Nicaragua. Each was strategically valuable for its plantation crops." Cynthia Enloe, *Bananas, Beaches and Bases: Making Feminist Sense of International Politics* (Berkeley: University of California Press 2000), 124.

[14] John G. Rodgers, "Something for the Girls: Burlesque " *New York Herald Tribune,* May 5, 1963

[15] Leon Gordon, *White Cargo* (Boston, MA: Four Seas Press, 1925), 90.

[16] Ibid., 30. Langford tells Wetzel, "I'm white and I'm going to stay white. I'm going to keep myself clean if I have to take the last drop of water out of your damn river." Ibid, 41.

[17] These range from ethnographic-styled studies of island culture nearly free of conventional moralizing, to disturbing rape scenarios, such as the short story "Girl on the Beach" from *Sir Magazine*. In the World War II tale, eighty-five sailors encounter an woman alone on an island, "she blurted out a few words of broken English. Her words meant only one thing, and with a terrific shout the men mobbed her." Jay L. Fowler, "Girl on the Beach" *Sir* Vol. 15 No. 7, 1958, reprinted by Java's Bachelor Pad, http://javasbachelorpad.com, accessed January 17, 2010.

[18] I am grateful to my committee member Andrea Harris for highlighting this disruption of the supposedly rigid male gaze.

Aura and the Archive: Confronting the Incendiary Fliers of Kommune 1

MICHAEL SHANE BOYLE

"The more one loses oneself in a document, the denser the subject matter grows."

—Walter Benjamin, "One-Way Street"[1]

On May 22, 1967, a fire in a large Brussels department store claimed the lives of over 300 shoppers. The next day the entire front and last pages of West Germany's most popular newspaper, the *Bild-Zeitung*, featured graphic details and photographs of the blaze. In their coverage, the paper dubiously connected the fire to a series of recent anti-Vietnam War protests in the Belgian capital. Since at that time the New Left across Europe had so far refrained from employing destructive tactics, many activists in West Germany took the reporting to be another blatant example of the conservative West German media's strategy of defaming the emerging New Left.[2] Yet within days of the fire, a series of incendiary fliers produced and circulated in West Berlin by the anti-authoritarian activist collective Kommune 1 seemed to confirm the paper's speculations.[3]

The most provocative of the four fliers, labeled simply "#8," read like a manifesto issued by a militant West Berlin Maoist group. It opened with a question that quickly became infamous throughout West Germany: "When will the department stores in Berlin burn?"[4] In addition to corroborating the *Bild-Zeitung*'s coverage that the fire was in fact set by Belgian activists, the flier called on West German students to repeat the action in West Berlin as a protest against the Vietnam War. "Our Belgian friends have gotten the knack of letting the public take part in the humorous hustle and bustle in Vietnam," the flier declared:

> No one needs to shed any more tears for the poor Vietnamese people while reading the morning paper. From now on, a person can go into the clothing department of KaDeWe, Hertie, Woolworth, Bilka, or Neckermann and casually light a cigarette in the dressing room. [. . .] Don't be surprised if sometime soon a fire erupts, if somewhere a barracks blows up, if somewhere the grandstands in a stadium collapse. No more so than when the Americans marched over the demarcation line, when Hanoi's city center was bombed, or when the marines invaded China.[5]

Wann brennen die Berliner Kaufhäuser ?

Bisher krepierten die Amis in Vietnam für Berlin. Uns gefiel es nicht, daß diese armen Schweine ihr Cocacolablut im vietnamesischen Dschungel verspritzen mußten. Deshalb trottelten wir anfangs mit Schildern durch leere Straßen, warfen ab und zu Eier ans Amerikahaus und zuletzt hätten wir gern HHH in Pudding sterben sehen. Den Schah pissen wir vielleicht an oder, wenn wir das Hilton stürmen, erfährt er auch einmal, wie ohltuend eine Kastration ist, falls überhaupt nocht was dranhängt... es gibt das so böse Gerüchte.

Ob leere Fassaden beworfen, Repräsentanten lächerlich gemacht - die Bevölkerung konnte immer nur Stellung nehmen durch die spannenden Presseberichte. Unsere belgischen Freunde haben endlich den Dreh heraus, die Bevölkerung am lustigen Treiben XXXXXX in Vietnam wirklich zu beteiligen:sie zünden ein Kaufhaus an, zweihundert saturierte Bürger beenden ihr aufregendes Leben und Brüssel wird Hanoi. Keiner von uns braucht mehr Tränen über das arme vietnamesische Volk bei der Frühstückszeitung vergießen. Ab heute geht er in die Konfektionsabteilung vom DaDeWe, Hertie, Woolworth, Bilka oder Neckermann und zündet sich diskret eine Zigarette in der Ankleidekabine an. Dabei ist nicht unbedingt erforderlich, daß das betreffende Kaufhaus eine Werbekampagne für amerikanische Produkte gestartet hat, denn wer glaubt noch an das "made in Germany" ?

Wenn es irgendwo brennt in der nächsten Zeit, wenn irgendwo eine Kaserne in die Luft geht, wenn irgendwo in einem Stadion die Tribüne einstürzt, seid bitte nicht überrascht. Genauso wenig wie beim Überschreiten der Demarkationslinie durch die Amis, der Bombardierung des Stadtzentrums von Hanoi, dem Einmarsch der marines nach China.

Brüssel hat uns die einzige Antwort darauf gegeben:

burn, ware-house, burn !

KOMMUNE I (24.5.67)

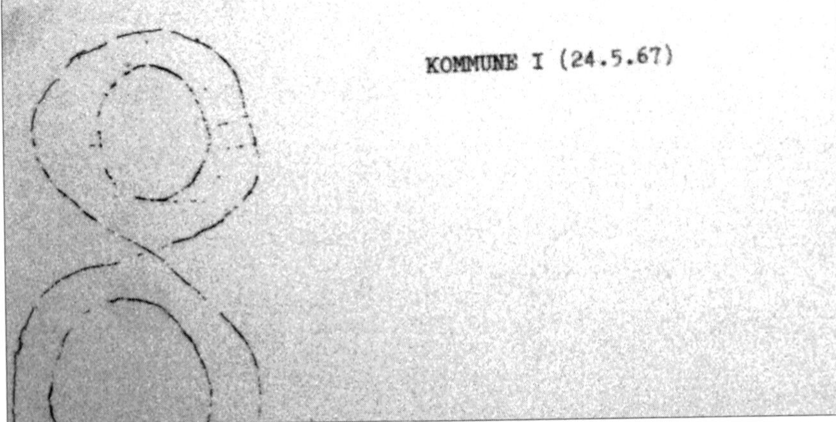

Kommune 1, Flier #8, from the Archive "APO und soziale Bewegungen," Free University of Berlin.

It only took a matter of days for the courts to bring charges against two of those behind the provocative texts. For writing the fliers, Fritz Teufel and Rainer Langhans—both university students at the time—were indicted under "suspicion to incite life-threatening violence" and faced stiff penalties of nine months in jail.[6] The charges might have been justified were it not that the fliers were in fact meant to be ironic; their militant rhetoric merely an attempt at satirizing the *Bild-Zeitung*'s groundless insinuations about the Brussels fire. Teufel and Langhans had created the fliers together with other members of Kommune 1 the morning the *Bild-Zeitung*'s story appeared. Yet the joke obviously failed to land with judicial authorities.[7]

The trial that ensued repeatedly made headlines throughout West Germany, due in large part to the defiant and often humorous behavior of the defendants in court.[8] The actual judgment hinged on the meaning attributed to and the intention behind the fliers. Against the prosecution's claim that the fliers were an incitement to violence, the Kommunards' defense attorney Horst Mahler argued for the fliers to be understood as satiric works of art, and thus of no threat to public safety. To this end, Mahler submitted the testimony of no less than 16 notable professors, artists, writers, and filmmakers including prominent figures like Günter Grass, Peter Szondi, and Alexander Kluge. This panel of experts disputed the prosecution's accusations by describing the literary merit and avant-garde character of the fliers. Although the Kommunards were eventually acquitted of all charges, the hermeneutic struggle over the fliers flared back up just 11 days after the close of the trial when two close acquaintances of of Kommune 1, Andreas Baader and Gudrun Ensslin, set fire to a pair of department stores in Frankfurt am Main. Soon after the arson attacks, Baader and Ensslin founded the Red Army Faction, marking the start of a two and a half-decade campaign of left-wing political violence in West Germany.

For historians of the German New Left, the contentious history of Kommune 1's arson fliers prompts numerous questions. Were the fliers works of art or crass incitements to violence? Can such static categories even adequately contain the fliers? What might the fliers reveal about the line between artistic forms of political engagement and violent provocation? Did the Kommune 1 fliers influence the actions of Baader and Ensslin? Needless to say, many scholars and journalists have weighed in with wildly different answers to these and other questions over the past forty years.[9] While I am certainly interested in the ongoing debates around Kommune 1, in the essay that follows I take an altogether different approach to discussing the fliers, one which eschews attempts at analyzing the fliers themselves.

As someone who has spent considerable time working in archives examining posters, letters, magazines, and manifestos produced by New Left activists in 1960s West Germany, I find myself increasingly curious about the actual experience of conducting archival work. In particular, I am intrigued by how encounters with the materiality of historical documents impact the very historiographic analysis one brings to bear upon such documents. What follows is a brief reflection on how historiographic analysis is shaped by the oft-ignored relationship between a scholar's knowledge of a document's history and reception, and the experience of being in the material presence of a document. I am specifically interested in how the knowledge one brings into an archive—among the other baggage (both literal and figurative) researchers carry with them—might shape the very experience of archival research, and how the experience of archival research in turn shapes one's knowledge of the document being studied. To explore these questions, I take my first archival encounter with the Kommune 1 arson fliers as an opportunity to examine the aura that surrounds archival documents. In addition to discussing under what conditions an archival document might be said to possess aura, I pay special attention to how auratic experience affects historiographic analysis. By taking seriously the advice of Performance Studies scholar Shannon Jackson who recommends a "performative understanding of historical documents," I argue that the interpretation one brings to bear on a particular archival document often reveals more about the proclivities and experiences—including the experience of archival research—of the researcher than anything intrinsic to the document itself.[10]

I open the brown box labeled "Kommune 1" and the first thing I look for are the fliers. The Kommunards made so many and they all seem to be here—multiple copies of each. But as I begin to dig, I realize the contents are barely organized, undoubtedly a consequence of the box's frequent perusal by researchers, artists, and (as I note by glancing at the visitor's list) even former Kommunards themselves. It takes me some time to sort through the hundreds of documents before I finally find the four I am after. I lay them out on the table and turn on the fluorescent desk lamp. Through the window in front of me I see that outside the afternoon sky is a dark gray. A cold wind is whipping through a copse of trees. As I waited on the platform for the train that would take me to the Extra-Parliamentary Opposition Archive of Berlin's Freie Universität this morning, snow began to fall. It is only October.

The four fliers are not in order so I take a moment to arrange them numerically: fliers #6, #7, #8, and #9. They look hardly any different than they do in the books I have seen them reproduced in. Typewritten. A large number corresponding to the flier scrawled by hand serves as a background for each. A plain and straightforward design, save for flier #6, of course, whose words are arranged in a dwindling spiral. In short, they are exactly as I expected—except for their odor. I didn't anticipate that. The forty-two year-old documents have been kept in a box for at least two decades, I remind myself, of course they smell musty. And the texture of the paper is like nothing I had imagined, if I even had had any expectations of such a thing at all. I am bemused that these fliers which caused such a stir are so delicate. I first recognize their fragility when I clumsily remove flier #8 from the box using significantly less care than I admit later to my fiancée, who is studying to be a rare-books librarian. My right hand hits the paper's already creased bottom right corner. A small piece of the most controversial of the fliers which notoriously asks "When will Berlin's Department Stores Burn?" simply falls away.

Although I am finally close enough to touch and smell the fliers—an encounter I find remarkable after having studied reproductions of the "originals" in books and catalogues for so long—the absent history that their presence before me signifies remains permanently distant. In my long-awaited encounter with the most controversial of the Kommune 1 fliers, I am reminded of Walter Benjamin's discussion of aura as the "here and now of the work of art—its unique existence in a particular place."[11] To think of the fliers in this way is of course ironic, not only because Benjamin himself made the careful distinction that, "No document is as such a work of art," but because Kommune 1 would never have given a thought to their fliers as possessing "aura."[12] Nor did they consider them works of art that served the ritual function Benjamin describes as emblematic of auratic bourgeois art. In fact, Rainer Langhans even criticized the experts commissioned by his lawyer to attest to the literary quality of the fliers for trying "to explain our actions as art." These experts, Langhans declared, "believed in art—we didn't. That is a business which works to make life more tolerable." Echoing the German New Left's iconoclastic view that art was an unequivocal "instrument of domination" whose "affirmative character" leaves it empty of any utopian vision of how society could be, only to affirm it as it is, Langhans continues:

> What we wanted with Kommune 1, what we lived and what we believed was: All art must disappear. And be disappeared. Why? Art is always only the tasteless Utopia for the actual dead. For this dead bourgeois world with its wars that are always so beautifully hidden in the background. Artists make it possible for people to feel human. All in order to make them better able to continue with their inhuman life. Since this was clear to us, we tried to make all of life into art, therefore to really live. The artists and intellectuals knew exactly that with this we called into question their entire existence.[13]

It is surely ironic then that Kommune 1's Situationist-inspired actions and sardonic fliers have increasingly become of interest to art historians and even curators. By coincidence, I am carrying in my bag that day a catalogue for a 1991 gallery exhibit in Berlin where Kommune 1's arson fliers were displayed alongside work by now canonized groups like the French Surrealists, CoBrA, and the Situationist International.[14]

While I remain wary to categorize the fliers as art, their aura for me that day remained unmistakable:

> What is aura actually? A strange web of space and time: the unique appearance of a distance, no matter how close it may be. While at rest on a summer's noon, to trace a range of mountains on the horizon, or a branch that throws its shadow on the observer, until the moment or the hour becomes part of their appearance—this is what it means to breathe the aura of those mountains, that branch.[15]

No doubt, Benjamin's enigmatic description of aura is elusive, its phenomenological dimension difficult to rationally comprehend to say the least. As Eugene Lunn explains, aura for Benjamin consists of the "traces left upon art through its successive historical functions as part of magic and ritual, religious worship, and of the secular cult of beauty since the Renaissance."[16] Moreover, Benjamin's metaphysical insistence on the authenticity, authority, and uniqueness of a work whose "presence" bears the traces of its history raises red flags for a student of performance schooled in deconstructionist suspicions of such things.

Despite these concerns, the aura of the fliers was nonetheless striking. But from where did this aura emerge, and of what consequence should it be to the researcher? Certainly the auratic quality of archival documents should be distinguished from the aura Benjamin describes. The auratic works of which Benjamin speaks remain immutably distant, literally both out of reach and untouchable for the viewer, a necessary condition of their staying sacred. They are, in short, a sight to behold but not to be held. While the preservation methods used to protect some archival documents endows these documents with a similar sense of inviolableness, most archival documents must be handled, and thus demand to be dealt with sensually.

Although the "here and now" of the fliers carried an unmistakable aura for me sitting alone in the archive that frigid Fall morning, was this aura intrinsic to the fliers? Or did it emerge from a disjuncture between my encounter with the fliers in the archive and my previously mediated experiences of them? Among the millions of people who have read these fliers, very few have actually touched or smelled the originals. Most often, the Kommune 1 fliers meet "recipients halfway" via their reproduction in newspapers and books.[17] Before entering the archive that morning, I too had only encountered the fliers in mediated fashion. These previous meetings undoubtedly shaped my experience in the archive and my sense of the fliers' auratic character. Like Philip Auslander's oft-debated critique of the liveness ontology of performance as being dependent on "recording technologies that made it possible to perceive existing representations as 'live',"[18] or Jacques Derrida's argument that the very value of presence in spoken exchanges only comes into being with and against the written word, my auratic experience in the archive depended on my other encounters of the fliers as technologically reproduced and circulated. In saying this, I do not mean to posit my encounter as somehow exemplary, but am only looking to account for the specificity of my experience. A crucial aspect of this experience was, of course, the very material presence of the fliers before me. While I learned nothing new about the history or content of the fliers after having already previously studied reproductions of them, something about touching them, inadvertently smelling them, and even hearing the shuffling sound they made as I moved them around on the desk was striking.

In his famous discussion of aura, Benjamin does not limit aesthetics to Hegelian "beautiful semblance." Particularly in "The Work of Art" essay, he foregoes all notions of aesthetics that conflate aesthetics with art. Instead Benjamin refers explicitly to a notion of aesthetics that predates Enlightenment era conceptions of aesthetics as having to do with truth, beauty, or even the work of art. He turns to the term's etymological roots in the Greek word Aisthitikos, which Susan Buck-Morss notes roughly means "perceptive by feeling." Buck-Morss explains: "The original field of aesthetics is not art but reality-corporeal, material nature. [. . .] It is a form of cognition, achieved through taste, touch, hearing, seeing, smell-the whole corporeal sensorium."[19] The notion of aesthetics Buck-Morss describes is of course a far cry from the Hegelian or Kantian conception of aesthetics as being "robbed of its sense."[20] Yet even Kant in his "Third Critique" does not narrow the aesthetic to any distinct sphere of art; the reflective judgement of aesthetic experience hardly need be sparked by a masterful painting.

While there is nothing intrinsic to the fliers that would lead one to categorize them as art, this hardly means my experience of them in the archive did not entail an aesthetic dimension in the sense to which Benjamin refers. And the aesthetic dimension of researching in an archive—the sensory cognition that accompanies archival work—is not without significance. If anything, the auratic experience of a historical document makes evident this oft-ignored aesthetic aspect of archival work. It stands as a stark reminder of the specificity of one's encounter with a historical document. Research and analysis never occurs in a vacuum. There are always conditions of possibility—both institutional and otherwise—for archival research. What brings one into the archive undoubtedly bears upon the ideas one brings out of the archive—no matter whether one critically reflects on or fully senses this fact.

ENDNOTES

[1] Walter Benjamin, "One-Way Street," in One-Way Street and Other Writings, trans. Edmund Jephcott and Kingsley Shorter, (London: NLB, 1979), 66. Special thanks to Morgan Wadsworth and Dennis Johannßen for their valuable suggestions for this essay. Ulrike Groß of the Archive-APO at the Freie Universität Berlin was very helpful in the course of my archival research.

[2] Historians and journalists have long noted how maligning the Left had become a hallmark journalistic practice by 1967. This was particularly the case for those newspapers and magazines owned by the powerful publishing empire owned by Axel Springer, the most powerful media mogul in postwar Western Europe. Throughout the 1960s, Springer-owned newspapers regularly attacked New Left groups in West Germany. See for example Hans-Dieter Müller Press Power: A Study of Axel Springer, J.A. Cole trans. (London: MacDonald & Co, 1969); Peter Humpheys, Media and Media Policy in Germany: The Press and Broadcasting since 1945 (Oxford: Berg, 1994).

[3] Founded in early 1967, Kommune 1 was a West Berlin commune originally made up of nine students, artists, and antiauthoritarian activists. If not the most influential group of the German New Left, Kommune 1 certainly remains the most (in)famous. From 1967 to 1969, the group regularly made headlines for the unconventional communal lifestyle of its members as well as the group's creative approach to activism which drew inspiration from the Situationist International, the Dutch Provos, and the Civil Rights Movement in the United States. For the most comprehensive history of Kommune 1, see Ulrich Enzensberger, Die Jahre der Kommune 1 (Munich: Wilhelm Goldmann Verlag, 2006).

[4] Unless otherwise noted, all translations originally in German are my own.

[5] The four fliers were distributed by Kommune 1 on May 24, 1967 on the campus of the Free University, Berlin where many of them were enrolled as students. The fliers have since been reproduced in numerous books, journals, and gallery catalogues. See for example Wolfgang Dreßen and Eckhard Siepmann, Nipferd des Höllischen Urwalds: Situationisten, Gruppe SPUR, Kommune 1. Originals of the fliers can be found at the "Archiv 'APO und soziale Bewegungen" located at the Freie Universität, Berlin, Fachbereich Politik- und Sozialwissenschaften, Otto-Suhr-Institut für Politikwissenschaft (APO-Archiv), folder Kommune 1 (last accessed 9 December, 2009). For other discussions of the fliers in English, see for example Charity Scribner, "Buildings on Fire: The Situationist International and the Red Army Faction," Grey Room 26 (Winter 2007), 30–55; Simon Teune. "Humour as a

Guerrilla Tactic: The West German Student Movement's Mockery of the Establishment," in International Review of Social History (52: 2007), 115–132.

[6] Teufel and Langhaans were charged under section 111, paragraphs 2 and 306 of West Germany's Basic Law. See the reproduction of the "Anklageschrift" [Bill of Indictment] dated June 9, 1967 and published in Kommune 1's pamphlet Gesammelte Werke Gegen Uns (Collected Works Against Us), 15, located in the International Institute for Social History, Amsterdam, The Netherlands, Kommune 1 Archive, File 2.

[7]It did not take long for the Bild-Zeitung to weigh in on the fliers: "Whoever glorifies this catastrophe which was likely started by radical leftist arsonists, and recommends copying it should be put behind bars! Police and the district attorney should prosecute the creators of these fliers to the fullest extent of the law." Just a day later the paper continued its coverage, this time running another article which claimed Kommune 1 had "direct connections to the Brussels terrorists" responsible for the arson. Their evidence, however, consisted only of an excerpt from flier "#6" in which Kommune 1 quotes an entirely fictional member of the entirely fictional Maoist group "Action for Peace and Friendship of the People" blithely describing the protest action as a "happening." Both of these articles were reprinted together by Kommune 1 as flier "#10" which was distributed at the Free University on May 28, 1967.

[8] For a discussion of the trial in English, see for example, Martin Klimke, "'We are not Going to Defend Ourselves Before Such a Justice System!'—1968 and the Courts," in German Law Journal (10:3, 2009), 261–274. For a full transcript of the trial including commentary by Kommune 1, see Fritz Teufel and Rainer Langhans, Klau Mich (Frankfurt am Main: Edition Voltaire, 1968).

[9] Recently the Kommune 1 fliers have again become a topic of debate in Germany, being invoked in the increasing public discourse around the provocative text The Coming Insurrection by the Invisible Committee. See for example, Cord Riechelmann, "Ein Feuer auf die Erde zu bringen," Jungle World 49 (December 9, 2010).

[10] Shannon Jackson, "Performance at Hull-House: Museum, Micro-fiche, Historiography," in Exceptional Spaces: Essays in Performance and History, ed. Della Pollock. (Chapel Hill: U of North Carolina Press, 1998), 261.

[11] Walter Benjamin, "The Work of Art in the Age of Its Technological Reproducibility," in The Work of Art in the Age of Its Technological Reproducibility and Other Writings on Media, ed. Michael W. Jennings et al, trans. Edmund Jephcott and Harry Zohn (Cambridge: Harvard University Press, 2008), 21.

[12] Walter Benjamin, "One-Way Street," 66.

[13]Rainer Langhans, Ich bin's: Die Ersten 68 Jahre (Frankfurt am Main: Blumenbar Verlag, 2009), 67. For an influential articulation of the German New Left view of art as an "instrument of domination," see Culture and Revolution, "Art as Commodity of the Consciousness Industry," in Die Zeit (November 29, 1968), 22.

[14] Wolfgang Dressen, Ed., Nilpferd des höllischen Urwalds : Spuren in eine unbekannte Stadt: Situationisten, Gruppe SPUR, Kommune 1, (Giessen: Anabas-Verlag, 1991).

[15] Walter Benjamin, "Little History of Photography," in The Work of Art in the Age of Its Technological Reproducibility and Other Writings on Media, ed. Michael W. Jennings et al, trans. Edmund Jephcott and Harry Zohn, (Cambridge: Harvard University Press, 2008), 285.

[16] Eugene Lunn, Marxism and Modernism: An Historical Study of Lukacs, Brecht, Benjamin, and Adorno (Berkeley: University of California Press, 1982), 151.

[17] Walter Benjamin, "The Work of Art in the Age of Its Technological Reproducibility," 21.

[18] Philip Auslander, Liveness: Performance in a Mediatized Culture (London: Routledge, 2008), 55.

[19] Susan Buck-Morss, "Aesthetics and Anaesthetics: Walter Benjamin's Artwork Essay Reconsidered," October (62, Autumn, 1992), 6.

[20] Ibid, 9.

A Skull with Wings: Meaning and Mourning in a Theatre Lobby

REBECCA HARRIES

A new theatre is built for a small University in Canada and named for its principal benefactor. There is a flurry of excitement before the opening. The walls of its lobby display artwork—a collection of European (mostly Polish) theatre posters[1]—and all is in place in time for the opening. The event is well attended; the next year, the number of students in the Department rises. However, in ten years, maybe less than that, there are difficulties. The equipment is old, the chairs are broken, and nobody connected with the theatre seems to understand why those strange posters are hanging in the lobby. This is a lobby story—a story of a place that is in the theatre but not the theatre and of one of the posters on the wall, which was stolen and never found.

The University is Bishop's, where I teach, a small self-described Liberal Arts-centered institution, the smallest in Canada. The theatre was first named the Consolidated Bathurst Studio Theatre and it officially opened in March 1989.[2] An article in the March 16 edition of the *Campus* celebrates this fact and a photo shows a crowded theatre lobby with the dedication plaque the focus of attention. Behind the heads of the small crowd, one can only partially discern framed posters. I was not present at this opening ceremony, but at the time of this writing I have spent certainly well over a thousand hours there. Until recently, however, I knew relatively little about its history. I had a sense of the space suspended somewhere between gratitude towards the place (visitors too are often impressed) and a feeling of dissatisfaction—that the space and especially its artwork do not represent 'what we are all about', a notion in itself fraught with interpretive differences and ambivalence.[3]

A theatre lobby is, in an important sense, a space that contextualizes the activity of performance. Especially in the case of the contemporary Studio space, the theatre itself is largely defined as a space of potential, of transformation, signifying the ephemeral nature of performance itself; the lobby, in contrast, suggests a kind of permanence or meaning peripheral to the activity of performance. Theatre lobbies used as galleries for local or international art encourage spectators to read the theatre as a related field of artistic endeavor and cultural value.[4] Other theatre lobbies use the space to communicate the theatre's history and its mandate, including evidence of past

From an article in the Bishop's Univeristy newspaper *Campus*, March 16, 1989 "Gala Opening." It shows the Turner Studio Theatre lobby before the posters were stolen, and gives an idea of the original appearance of the space with some of the posters clearly visible.

productions, especially if these are widely recognized. In such cases, the lobby is a relatively formal site of collective memory.[5] The practice of its decoration can be seen as a collective version of what Paul Connerton describes as 'official memoir writing': "These writers of memoirs see their life as worth remembering because they are, in their own eyes, someone who has taken decisions which exerted, or can be represented as having exerted, a more or less wide influence and which have visibly changed part of their social world" (Connerton19). A theatre lobby often is a chance to reflect both the past-related notion of "legitimating origins" (and here it is perhaps worth noting that the opening ceremonies of the theatre in question were in the lobby) and the future-related reflection of accumulation of "power or money or influence." Both are reflected in the importance of the commemorative plaque, which actively focuses the site as one of official history.[6] This "official history" overlaps but often contrasts with the informal histories of memory. If you were to ask many of the students about the donation that built the theatre or even the year it was built, they would not be able to answer. A lobby provides a specific spatial framework for the collective memory of the theatre (Connerton 37). The physical objects in it with which theatre workers and less frequently spectators are in regular contact form an image of permanence and stability. On the one hand, the lobby is an official space that signifies the institution and both its past and future continuance. On the other, it is a site of accumulated and often contradictory narratives, of events that are officially unrecorded and remembered anecdotally or forgotten.

The Turner Studio lobby is a conflicted space, the mediated version of the composite, and often contradictory things my colleagues and I feel about the theatre and our own practice. As a place of official memory, it is where one would expect commemorative displays of achievement and success, but even defining what these should be is contentious. What is, for example, a successful performance? After the display of European posters was removed (the unanimous decision by the Department) no new display took its place. Certainly, the walls remain bare in part because the process is time-consuming, but the absence of such display can be seen as a collective displacement or forgetting, as evidence of a suppressed or unsuitable history that is nevertheless powerful enough that seemingly resists being overwritten. I speak here of the collective, but the suspicion of isolation lurks in this notion—the idea that I am after all the only one who perceives this, that sometimes a wall is just a wall.

Considered collectively, our shared understanding of the situation of the Studio theatre as belonging to a small English-speaking community in a francophone province brings with it a sense of special community and intimacy, but also the suspicion of irrelevance. Colleagues have made comparisons to the dying aristocratic world of landowning Russians in Chekhov and to the closed society of moneyed theatergoers in Restoration England. My impression of the theatre culture here is one that combines a sense of good fortune and abundance with a sort-of remoteness and lack of recognition—the Moscow that the Prozorov sisters long for replaced with Toronto. Justifiable pride in accomplishment is mixed with a sort of philosophical resignation.[7]

I know that there is a belief that the construction of the theatre was the 'making' of the Bishop's drama program. After 1989, the number of drama majors doubled. The theatre itself, a studio black-box space with a rehearsal room over the lobby and a student-friendly mesh lighting grid, was described in glowing terms in the *Alumni Magazine* article of that year.[8] In brief, the smaller space, more flexible in terms of design than the 650–seat fan-shaped auditorium Centennial Theatre that preceded it, would be conducive to theatrical experimentation and smaller-scale productions. With a maximum capacity of 150, the theatre provided an intimate relationship between the house and actor. Although the space is more or less conventionally set up, the space has been adapted for theatre in the round and more recently for a labyrinth, which also doubled as audience seating.[9] This use of space mirrors the belief that an academic theatre program should support and allow for current experiments in staging and for the production of challenging texts, texts that are likely not to fill the auditorium of Centennial theatre but may get enough of a crowd for the Studio. In this sense, the form of the theatre already presupposes certain beliefs about the agenda of a University Theatre.[10]

But there is also a negative story, a tale of frustration. For years, faculty and students alike seemed confused and frustrated by the identity of a collection of theatre posters in the Studio. Why were not the walls adorned with posters and images from our own productions? What was 'the deal' with the *3Penny Opera* from the Netherlands or all of those posters from Poland with their unreadable titles? Secretly, I felt an affinity towards some of the posters, although I kept this sentiment to myself. There were favorites:

one of monstrous faces that seemed to be melting into one another and a vivid green Hamlet figure, seen from the back against a fuchsia background.[11] The associations with Polish theatre of the 1970s spoke to a glamorous and dynamic theatre history: Grotowski, ascetism, Richard Cieslak in those impossible postures, Peter Brook talking about 'a black mass'[12]—the importance of that theatre, its commitment and dissidence, seemed to haunt the place, which saw A. R. Gurney, two productions of *Our Town*, one of *Picnic*, as well as the occasional Greek or Early Modern European production. So I felt a kind of awe toward the posters and their world, yet I had to agree that it didn't really represent what kind of theatre performances took place here.

In 2008, I was asked by the curator of the Foreman Gallery, Vicky Chainey-Gagnon to write a piece about a personal relationship to one of the artworks in the BU Art Collection as part of their *Connections* series. I thought of the posters, which were a regular feature of my working day and my ambivalence towards them. A trip to the BU Art Collection Archive led to a surprising discovery. I had never seen two of the posters before. Both were listed as stolen. The reproduced images were small, of poor quality and incomplete, but these posters seemed to me the most compelling and most beautiful of the collection. One in particular impressed—a dark background out of which loomed a skull peeking behind a Renaissance-style ruffled collar. The title was *Don Carlos,* but I couldn't discern any other identifying markers on the reproduction.[13] The secrecy of the image and its stolen identity combined to create a feeling of mystery and loss. Here at last was my subject, my lost artwork and here is part of what I wrote in a mood of intense and to me inexplicable romance:

> Who will speak for this lost object? . . .
>
> The skull cannot speak; its mouth is concealed, muffled in the folds of its garment, which looks to me like wings. Death has no jaws, just eyes: a cross instead of a mouth. The cross on its forehead is redemption, a symbol of undying life, or is it one of judgment? One side of the ruff is suffused with light. The glowing fabric (or is it bone? A fabric of bone?) takes all available light and the background is left the deep black of space, a black of air and not of earth. Air that the winged skull transverses, for I sense that it hovers in this image, that it alone has motion in the still black world. . . .
>
> If it speaks what would it say?
>
> But what could the image say when the object is gone, when I am addressing not a death's head, but a skull that has flown away, addressing an absence, even an absence of death.
>
> What would I ask it?
>
> Where are you? What happened to you?
>
> "I was stolen."[14]

The image from the archive was displayed in the fall of 2008 with my reflection. Few commented on it, and I left the issue of lobby posters alone. Maybe part of me didn't want answers to the questions. Sure, this was no

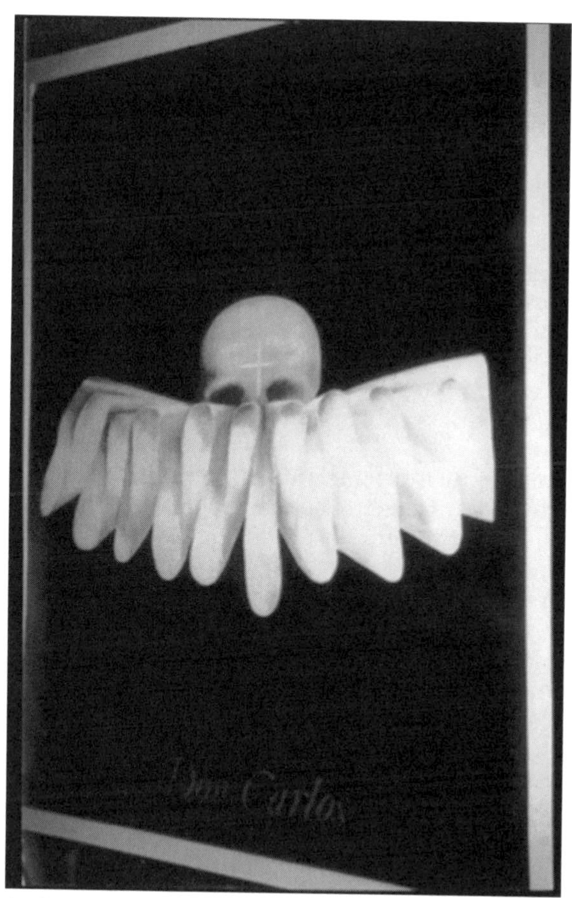

A photograph documenting Bishop's University Art Collection Accession #1993196, *Don Carlos* by Maciej Urbaniec, later stolen from the lobby of the Turner Studio Theatre.

Raymond Chandler novel where someone was warning me off the case. I was surrounded by collective amnesia and indifference as to the identity and whereabouts of 'my' *Don Carlos*—I had become proprietary. There were no thugs waiting outside my office, not at least because of my writing. But sometimes it is better not to know. Is not this the Oedipal narrative at the heart of the noir?[15] The mystery returns to find its origins or identity and finds broken taboos, incest, unspeakable corruption and often an irredeemable feminine evil. The quest for what is absent exposes the corruption of its enveloping world, as in *Don Carlos*, a kind of Schiller noir—no, best to leave it alone. It seemed impossible, too personal, too close-to-home, the place where I worked each day after all.

In 2010, a combination of seemingly chance events re-ignited my interest. Also, now Chair of the Department, I felt guilt over the empty walls of the lobby. Our program deserved an official history, and the lobby seemed a space of unfulfilled potential. I knew I wanted students involved in the decision-making process, but also, why did I know so little about the place in which I worked? Why was I so reluctant to write over these bare walls? It is dangerous for academics or anyone to make a decision based on magical thinking, but when I read the call for submission for a volume on missing documents, *Don Carlos* resurfaced and would not be suppressed.

But what did I actually know about the poster? The artist was Maciej Urbaniej and it was executed in 1971 for a 1972 performance of Schiller's play at the illustrious Teatrum Athenaeum in Warsaw, directed by Maciej Prus and starring Jan Swiderski. It was one of a collection of the fourteen posters, donated to BU by esteemed Canadian theatre critic and artist Herbert Whittaker in 1987. Polish poster art from this time period is enjoying a cultural moment, and among the collection are well-known figures, including three by Jan Lenica.[16]

While a number of persons interviewed remembered the theft, few could remember details.[17] A notable exception to this was Michael Medland. The technical director of the theatre since 1988, he had a vivid recollection of the night of the theft, because he was, in fact, there. According to him, the evening was in the spring—he was uncertain of the year but guessed around 1992—and the theatre was holding a party in the Studio. This was a now-abandoned tradition, often started with a cabaret in the rehearsal room, and later turning into a general gathering in the Studio. They typically went late, as this one did, and became very rowdy. For this particular party, Michael remembered coming downstairs from the rehearsal space above the lobby (where most of the action was) to the Studio Lobby only to discover that three (to his recollection) of the posters were missing. He was furious as this meant that the theft had taken place while he was still in the building. He reported the thefts to security at the University and to Jonathan Rittenhouse, the then Chair of the Department, who remembers the events hazily.[18]

According to Michael Medland, security found two of the posters in a utility closet in Norton Hall, a residence about a week later. He distinctly remembers the recovery and telephoning Jonathan Rittenhouse the same day with the good news. Therefore, some mystery remains over the number of posters stolen and recovered; one of a number of problems in the investigation that was never satisfactorily resolved.

Interestingly, a letter from the Metro Police of Ascot-Lennoxville, written to Bertrand Noel, the then-head of security on June 16 1995, shows that someone did file a report of the theft to the police, although when I spoke with Michael Medland he had no knowledge of it and it appears that two reports had been independently filed without the knowledge of anyone working in the theatre.[19] The date of the letter also suggests that either the remembered year is wrong or that the report was filed well after the date of the actual theft. Whatever the circumstances, the correspondence and the fact that it was unknown to the theatre suggest that no investigation took place, which is not surprising.

And what does this unofficial and semi-obscure history signify, fifteen years later? Is the only significance my obsession with an out-of-focus image of the lost? Or perhaps because it helped to spell the end of parties held in the theatre (an incident with a broken toilet was the coup-de-grace)?

I do not know who stole my *Don Carlos*. I can guess that the theft was spontaneous and along the lines of what is called here a prank and elsewhere often a crime. The culprits would have been easy enough to discover at the time—it seems likely that they were in someone's dorm room for a while and the posters were large enough. The number and size of the portraits and the circumstance of the party certainly suggest more than one thief. Did *Don Carlos* end up in someone's house, as seems likely? Maybe it is still there now. Perhaps the individual is even fond of it in some way. They both have a certain gothic charm, and the image could conceivably work in a kind of 'heavy-metal' album way.

The walls of the lobby stand empty now, waiting to be inscribed with a kind of image-history of the Department—an 'image-mandate' to be more precise. What is it we believe ourselves to be and what do we imagine as our heritage? I do not know what it will look like but it will be homegrown and more literal and, as is the case with histories, a memory of triumphs, of the famous who have visited us, of alumni who have had success, of productions that have positive memories . . . 'remember when?'

So, I somewhat obsessively choose to remember and search. It is partly a postmodern Canadian romance for Polish theatre forty years past, for an imagined passionate belief in an art form, which is here often seen itself as a kind of quaint artifact of bygone days. But it is closer than that: it is the nameless thing, which is at the periphery of articulation; it is tragedy, detaching itself from history . . .

The skull drifts in the empty black air, behind or maybe within its clownish ruff. It is the dead bones of European theatre in the crisp confusion of Canadian drama, the photo not on the website, the distant memory of the not quite right, the failed production, the dropped lecture and the unsolved mystery of a student who left after the first term. It is against such specters that we bolster an image of success and continuance. A lobby promises that theatre will signify and that it has both its own identity and that of a larger community and so it speaks an official language. The memory of dissidence that happened somewhere else, the memory of crime called something else—this too is part of the history of the place and the pictures that once hung on its walls.

ENDNOTES

[1] Fourteen theatre posters were donated to the Bishop's University Art Collection in 1987. They were a gift from esteemed Canadian theatre critic Herbert Whittaker. In Whittaker's letter to then-chairperson of the Art Committee, Gary Retzleff (Feb. 4, 1987), he writes "I prefer to think of my gift as something that may catch the eye of future students and even subtity [sic] educating them in the diversity of theatre beyond Lennoxville, even beyond Canada." I would like to thank the following for their help in locating documents or agreeing to interviews: Ruth Sheeran, Head Librarian of Bishop's University and Chair of the Bishop's University Art Committee; Michael Medland, Technical Director of Bishop's University; Anna Grant, Bishop's University Archives and Special Collections; Kevin Donelle, Bishop's University student and photographer; Vicky Chainey-Gagnon, Curator of

the Foreman Art Gallery; and to Stephen Johnson for his inspired and very welcome editorial suggestions.

[2] See the article "Gala Opening" in the March 16 *Campus* (1989).

[3] This is based on years of observation. When we were finally successful in having the posters removed in 2008, it was a cause for celebration. Their removal and the re-painting of the lobby was led by a grassroots student movement with the full support of the faculty, although the yellow and orange colour scheme would prove to be controversial.

[4] Theatre Lac Brome in Knowlton displays posters from previous productions, as does the Centaur Theatre, which also has an attached gallery space. The Stratford Festival theatre features numerous archival images and sometimes costumes and props from past productions. The National Arts Centre features special exhibitions as well as a gallery space. The Stanley Theatre in Vancouver features work by artists—to give a few among many examples.

[5] For collective memory see especially Paul Connerton, *How Societies Remember* (Cambridge: Cambridge University Press, 1989), Maurice Halbwachs, *La mémoire collective* (Paris: Les presses universitaires de France,1950) and E. Hobsbawn and T. Ranger (eds.) *The Invention of Tradition.* (Cambridge: Cambridge University Press, 1983).

[6] In 2004, the Studio Theatre was re-named and officially dedicated to William Turner, who was Chancellor at Bishop's University from 1987–1995. See *Bishop's University News*, Winter 2004. The photograph shows the plaque, which is currently the only object displayed on the walls of the lobby.

[7] Obviously, here I am speaking from personal observation, and it is more than a little presumptuous to speak of a collective *geist*. However, anecdotally every member of my Department has agreed that the Chekhov comparison is apt. Retired English professor and Dean of Humanities Gary Retzleff was fond of making the Restoration theatre comparison—small audience, in-jokes, plenty of leisure time and a fervid interest in gossip. The reference, of course, is to Anton Chekhov's *Three Sisters* (1900).

[8] *Bishop's University Alumni Magazine* Spring 1989

[9] The Labyrinth in question was designed for the March 2009 production of Sally Clark's *Lost Souls and Missing Persons* I directed; Michel Charbonneau was responsible for lighting and set design. The theatre has also been configured for an in-the-round staging of *Lysistrata*, directed by Margot Dionne (March 2007).

[10] According to the article in the *Campus* "Architects and actors alike were consulted in deciding upon the design and the result is a facility that has many possible stage-audience configurations. Due to its small size, it also allows more intimate productions.

[11] The *Hamlet* is a 1970 poster by Andrzej Krauze. It is currently displayed in my office. At the time of writing, most of the posters are in the Foreman Art Gallery subspace, which is used as a community art lab, one is in the gallery office and one is in Michael Medland's office. According to the BU Art Collection records only two were stolen.

[12] Jerzy Grotowki is the famed Polish director, who developed his 'poor theatre' approach with the Polish Laboratory Theatre. I can remember studying *Towards a Poor Theatre* (New York, 1968) as an undergraduate and attempting some of the exercises on my own—with predictable minor injuries resulting. As well as reading about the director's work in Peter Brook's *The Empty Space* (1968). Bishop's University Library also possesses a video recording of *Akropolis* (1962), prefaced by an interview with Peter Brook who compares the experience to a 'black mass.'

[13] I guessed, correctly as it turns out, that the poster was for a performance of Friedrich Schiller's 1787 tragedy and not the opera by Verdi. The image seems strikingly apt for the tragedy. I wrote at the time: "Schiller's *Don Carlos* is an impossibly romanticized version of historical rumors of an incestuous love triangle between Phillip II, his wife Elizabeth and his disturbed and mentally disabled son Don Carlos, this latter being transformed into a romantic hero, fighting corruption, the father, the death-in-life—only to embrace it. Caught in its folds. The play is one of prisons: the prison of marriage, the name and royal blood—

true escape is unimaginable, a dream of flight. Reality is the tower, favoured prison of nobility, inescapable. To languish. To pine. To endure."

[14] The Connections series was the idea of Foreman Art Gallery curator Vicky Chainey-Gagnon. Mine was one of four pieces, which were displayed in the hallway between the Foreman Art Gallery and Centennial Theatre in November 2008. For the display, the image was enlarged as much as possible without compromising its already imperfect image.

[15] Following Julia Kristeva's discussion of melancholy in *Black Sun*: does the melancholic mourn an actual object or a 'Thing': is it the "intolerable other that I crave to destroy so as to better possess it alive?" Or is it rather something that cannot be named. "Knowingly disinherited of the Thing, the depressed person wanders in pursuit of continuously disappointing adventures and loves; or else retreats, disconsolate and aphasic, alone with the unnamed Thing". *Black Sun: Depression and Melancholia*. Trans. Leon S. Roudiez (New York: Columbia University Press, 1989). Freudian, Lacanian and post-Lacanian psychoanalytic theories have a strong tradition in the study of film noir. See E. Ann Kaplan and Slavoj Žižek.

[16] Documents include the recorded minutes of the Art Collection Committee of February 3, 1989 and September 26, 1990, an invoice for 14 frames at a cost of $1383.21 from the 7 Feb, 1989, a letter to the then-chairman of the Art Collection Committee of April 10, 1989, positively mentioning the theatre posters, which "serve in a very handsome manner" and a letter thanking Herbert Wittaker [sic]. The letter evidently accompanies a copy of the Art Collection catalogue, *University Art Collection: An Art Compendium* and it mentions that the posters are a "relevant display in an otherwise Spartan environment of ciment [sic] block architecture."

[17] All of my current colleagues—Jo Jo and George Rideout, Greg Tuck and Michael Medland—were members of the Department at that time.

[18] As per email correspondence in July.

[19] My interview with Mike Medland was on the 1 September of this year, 2010. Relevant police reports were made far apart from the now-no-longer-existing Metro Police of Ascot-Lennoxville: one on 16 June 1995 to M. Bertrand Noel and one to Mme. Francine Godbout on the 29 April 1996. The wording is formulaic and says that they consider the investigation unsuccessful, but will re-open it in light of further information.

"They Might Not Go Blind": Cherub's *Kinsmen* and the Drama Officer's Report

BRIAN COOK

In 1928, during what is known as the "Golden Age" of crime fiction, writer S. S. Van Dine composed a set of twenty rules to govern the writing of detective stories. "The detective story," he began, "is a kind of intellectual game. . . . And for the writing of detective stories there are very definite laws—unwritten, perhaps, but none the less binding; and every respectable and self-respecting concocter of literary mysteries lives up to them."[1] He dismissed the attempts of some writers to over-complicate and therefore trick the reader; according to Van Dine, the best detective stories are those with a detective who, when confronted with a crime, goes in search of clues which lead clearly and unambiguously to the culprit. In spite of Van Dine and others' attempts to formalize a simpler detective story, however, the complexity of real crime was far too tempting for many writers. Agatha Christie, the certainly respectable *grande dame* of mystery herself, probably broke every single one of Van Dine's 20 rules in one story or other.

As researchers in the archive, we often attempt to compose a list of rules as clear as Van Dine's which will govern our attempts to make sense of the miscellany and chaos found within. We often enter the archive hoping to prove a hypothesis, and we look for a smoking gun: a document or documents which will conclusively prove our theories. But, in tandem with Agatha Christie, the archive often refuses to respect our rules, and our plans to simplify often backfire. As Miss Marple and Hercule Poirot have repeatedly demonstrated, the most obvious solution is often not the correct one when you are unraveling a mystery: sometimes the "smoking gun" turns out not to be the only murder weapon. The gun's involvement does prompt all sorts of questions about why it's there and how it was used, and it often provides the first glimpse at a deeper and more complicated mystery.

The Company

I began investigating and documenting the work of The Cherub Company, London, in 2004. Cherub was started in 1978 by Polish actor/director Andrew Visnevski with British actor Simon Chandler. Seeking to counter what he considered largely uninteresting productions on the West End and at the national theatres, Visnevski produced more than 30 productions of rarely-performed European and English classical plays before he left the company in 2003. In that 25–year span, Visnevski made multiple attempts to receive subsidy for his company from the government-financed Arts Council of Great Britain (ACGB) but was never successful.[2] Reviewers praised the company's productions, and the company often received warm responses from its audiences, but Cherub never somehow caught the positive attention of the funding agency that could best secure its survival.

Forced to live hand-to-mouth for 25 years, Cherub's productions usually were performed at small London fringe venues or on short tours of the provinces, though some of their shows lived on for longer national tours or were sponsored for international tours by the British Council. I continue to be fascinated by a company that managed to survive for so long without either reliable government subsidy or corporate sponsorship, the budget mainstays of most British theatre companies. Much of my research continues to focus on the reasons why ACGB consistently refused funding to a company that managed to sustain a regular schedule of productions with positive notices from newspaper reviewers and consistent audience attendance, and whose mission was to produce theatre "at comparatively low production costs."[3]

The Production

The company successfully produced Pedro Calderon de la Barca's *Life is a Dream* in 1978 as their inaugural production, after which Chandler opted to leave and Cherub became a co-operative company. Visnevski decided to continue the company's foray into classical works, and choose for his next production Shakespeare's collaboration with John Fletcher, *The Two Noble Kinsmen* (1979). The production had a successful run at the Edinburgh Festival Fringe in the summer of 1979, followed by a run in the Young Vic Studio later the same year. The play is a re-telling of Chaucer's "Knight's Tale,"[4] with the two kinsmen declaring a solidarity which immediately disappears when both fall in love with the same woman. With very little money, Visnevski had no choice but to work within his means for the production, continuing to establish what would become Cherub's hallmark spare but visually-arresting style. Quoted in an *Evening Standard* article on the production, Visnevski explained his vision: "Feliks [Topolski[5]] and I looked through the play and were immediately struck by the modern, punkish theme. So the leather and chains, the spiky hair and violent colours seemed appropriate. The codpieces lay great stress on the virility of the men."[6]

The design featured a very simple set, and Visnevski's costumes (created with input by Topolski) outfitted the shirtless all-male cast in black leather trousers. The Amazon women characters (played by barely-disguised men) were indicated by body paint over their left breasts, and the male characters by the addition of false codpieces. As they had for *Life is a Dream*, the company received positive reviews for *Kinsmen* from the newspaper critics. Bonnie Lee in *The Scotsman* wrote of the production at the Edinburgh Festival Fringe:

> Black leather and chains. Actors' shadows against white walls. Short-haired, bare-chested men with painted red and white circles around their nipples, playing Emilia and Hippolyta. Cod-pieces hand-made by the director. Spasms of fighting and kissing. Gay group therapy through the medium of Shakespeare and Fletcher? Not at all. Cherub Company's startling all-male production [. . .] is a revelation, through visual art, of the work's essential bitter brutality. [7]

Upon the production's premiere in London at the Young Vic Studio, B.A. Young wrote in the *Financial Times:*

> [The] company are all male and all young and all dressed in black "leather" trousers with only a suitable decoration to indicate their status. The women have a circle painted round the left breast; the men wear protuberant codpieces. The difference between the sexes is thus shown to be merely a stage convention, the love between the several pairs a dramatic machinery [. . .] Charles Grant as Emilia and Martin Ransley as Hippolyta do not pretend to be anything but men in women's makeup, and there is no hint of embarrassment about their endearments with [the two kinsmen] Anthony Rothe (Arcite) and Daniel Foley (Palamon). Even the more intimate scenes between Anthony Best as the jailer's daughter and Tom Hunsinger as the warder are free from awkwardness[8].

The Document: The "Smoking Gun"?

The more I researched Cherub and its relationship with ACGB, the more a potential narrative became clear to me. The plot I began to sketch out for myself pitted the heroic Cherub company and its stalwart leader Andrew Visnevski against the forces of the ACGB, a willing and complicit agent of the policies of Thatcherism toward the arts. The Arts Council began in 1946 as an extension of a wartime effort to maintain the arts during the war to buoy the spirit of the citizenry. As the Council evolved after the war, its mission changed from supporting myriad artists, including amateurs, to one which supported a select few of the best theatres, a policy that Sandy Craig reports was known as "few but roses".[9] As they developed, the Royal Shakespeare Company and the Royal National Theatre became (and remain) two of the largest recipients of government subsidy for theatre in Britain. The emergence of alternative theatre in the late 1960s and 70s was funded, in limited ways, by the ACGB and other local arts funding bodies.[10] Under Margaret Thatcher, the funding for the Arts Council was reduced, and an expectation for theatres to demonstrate results (i.e. box office returns) became paramount.[11]

During my archival work, I came across a drama officer's show report on Cherub's production of *Kinsmen* housed along with thousands of other records from the ACGB at Blythe House, the Victoria and Albert Museum's depository in West Kensington, London. The report is in a file with 13 other show reports dated between 1979 and 1981 from productions by the Cherub Company:

ARTS COUNCIL OF GREAT BRITAIN — DRAMA OFFICER'S REPORT

TO: JM / JF / DA / JAB / PM / JL / HG / CD / SE / File JL

FROM: PJP — DATE: 26th March 1980

~~REVIEW~~ NAPS ~~CHILDREN'S THEATRE~~ (delete as applicable)

COMPANY: CHERUB THEATRE CO

SHOW: TWO NOBLE KINSMEN

WHERE: EDINBURGH FESTIVAL 1979

WHEN: -----

REMARKS:

Written far too long after the event for anything but an overall impression. That impression is of gross self-indulgence on the part of the actors and the director. The play is not a good one, at least by Shakespeare's standards, but that surely does not excuse the very bad speaking of the text and the contortions of the verse which happened here. Neither does it account for the interpretation forced on it here in much the same way as the all-male cast forced themselves into PVC trousers with huge false codpieces for the male and painted nipples for the female characters. This might have been diverting if the bodies on display had been better or their ability to act commensurate. Not the case. Add to that no clear reason for treating the play in this way beyond a visual one and I think one might put it in a new category along Brookian lines marked jerk-off theatre. Should not be encouraged in front of a paying public - they might not go blind!

The Drama Officer's Report on Cherub Theatre Company's *Two Noble Kinsmen*, dated March 26, 1980. Reproduced with the permission of the Arts Council of Great Britain, courtesy of the Victoria and Albert Museum, London (ACGB/96/145 Cherub Company).

Written far too long after the event for anything but an overall impression. That impression is of gross self-indulgence on the part of the actors and the director. The play is not a good one, at least by Shakespeare's standards, but that surely does not excuse the very bad speaking of the text and the contortions of the verse which happened here. Neither does it account for the interpretation forced on it here in much the same way as the all-male cast forced themselves into PVC trousers with huge false codpieces for the male and painted nipples for the female characters. This might have been diverting if the bodies on display had been better or their ability to act commensurate. Not the case. Add to that no clear reason for treating the play in this way beyond a visual one and I think one might put it in a new category along Brookian lines marked jerk-off theatre. Should not be encouraged in front of a paying public—they might not go blind![12]

On the surface, the review appears to be a rather harsh critique of Cherub's *Kinsmen* at the Edinburgh Fringe. Criticizing not only Cherub's selection of a text, the reviewer also criticizes the direction, design, speaking of the text and the appeal of the actors' bodies, all of it a "gross self-indulgence."

As in a good detective story, the drama officer's report seemed to be the "smoking gun" I was seeking in the archive. It seemed to validate my theory of a profoundly conservative ACGB which was unprepared for the adventurous spirit of Visnevski's productions, and the drama officer even calls his own report into question, admitting it was written "far too long" after the show to be reliable. But something about it set my "little grey cells" churning, and like Poirot I stepped back and began to review the things I knew about Cherub's *Kinsmen*. Thus far, my knowledge of the production was filtered through production reviews and photographs and the recollections of members of the company. The officer's report was the first thing I had encountered which opposed the positive memories of the production that I had been able to access. I began to notice that my initial impulse was to sanctify Cherub: I admired Visnevski and his work and felt that they had been unjustly overlooked not just by ACGB but also by history. I found myself to be bound and determined to recover the company and its works, though I was concerned by my temptation to summarily dismiss the criticism in the officer's report. As a result of the report, I began to see Cherub's production (and its work in general) in a more complicated way.

Kinsmen was only Cherub's second production, and to my knowledge, only the second play that Visnevski had ever directed. He had trained at Central as an actor, not as a director, though he did serve as Frank Dunlop's assistant director for a time at the Young Vic.[13] Certainly the company had very little money, and perhaps rehearsals were somewhat chaotic and haphazard as they did not have a permanent home and there was very little money to pay the actors. Yet despite these shortcomings, the newspaper reviews had proclaimed the production "a revelation." This single document raised all manner of questions for me, not the least of which is how can a production both be so "good" and also so "bad?"

I looked more closely at the main points of contention in the drama officer's critique. Cherub's publicity material advertised *Kinsmen* as "Shakespeare's last play," and he[14] rejects right away the selection of *Two Noble Kinsmen* itself, notably basing his criticism of the play text on the "usual" quality of Shakespeare's writing ("not a good one, at least by Shakespeare's standards"). After dismissing the actors' verse-speaking abilities, he begins to focus his attention on the "interpretation of the text." Even though this might be a bad play, he writes, that does not excuse the number of poor choices the company made in its production. The primary flaw he sees is the half-clad, all-male cast sporting black leather trousers. Indeed, the latter half of the very short[15] report deals almost exclusively with the bodies of the male actors and, implicitly, on the activities of those bodies. While the drama officer regards the actors' bodies as poor, and his comment that they had to "force themselves" into leather pants implies that the actors were out of shape or even fat, production photographs reveal fairly svelte actors, in no way heavier than the average adult male. They are not all Adonises with clearly defined musculature, but neither are they unattractive or unsightly.

The drama officer's more implicit objections to the activities that these male bodies were performing are more interesting. The various couplings between male and female characters were each enacted by two clearly male actors. The photographs show that while the men playing women did wear some makeup, they were not actually in drag. All of the actors wore the same black leather trousers and went shirtless, a constant reminder that the "women" in the play were actually men. While Young describes these couplings as "free from awkwardness," the drama officer's discomfort with the largely obvious display of homosexuality is clear. He even calls the play "jerk-off theatre," indicating his preoccupation with the fairly blatant sexuality in the production.

While the sexuality seems to dominate the report, the final line of the report provides an additional clue to the drama officer's objection to the "interpretation" in the production: he invokes the name of Peter Brook while castigating the production for its "visual" excesses. While clearly the drama officer disagreed with many of Visnevski's choices, the mention of Brook in this review is significant. Brook is now (and was then) seen as one of the foremost British theatre practitioners of the 20th century. In the years after he departed England for France in 1970, Brook's work in France not only precipitated questions about why he couldn't undertake his experiments in Britain (as Peter Hall wished him to do),[16] but also about the exact nature of the experiments themselves. Springing from both his study of Artaud and the subsequent Theatre of Cruelty Season (1964) as well as his friendship with Jerzy Grotowski, Brook's new project involved experimenting with theatre outside the need for box office success. Though Brook's need to leave Britain may have been largely due to his needing to find a new perspective, I believe that he also knew that the sort of experiments he was planning would have been a hard sell with the funding agencies in Britain. Brook had been at the Royal Shakespeare Company long enough to have lived through the vicissitudes of the government's funding of the arts and had a good understanding of what type of work the Arts Council would fund and what it would not.

Brook's productions were always noted for their visual (code for non-text-based) components, and the rejection of a strictly textual approach to theatre was what, in some circles, made Brook into a traitor to British drama. The visceral responses to his *King Lear* (especially the scene where Gloucester is blinded) and *Midsummer Night's Dream* were coupled with the revelation that he was willing to fiddle with the text of a production, something always frowned upon in British theatre (especially with Shakespeare's plays). Visnevski also viewed text as something subject to the director's interpretation of the production. This is similar to the work of other European artists, including Vsevelod Meyerhold in Russia and Jerzy Grotowski in Poland.

The "European" desire to work with classic texts but not to treat the text as sacred marks the real problem with Cherub's productions, as it runs counter to the importance placed on the dramatic text in British theatre. What's more,

Cherub's choice to perform classic (if under-produced) texts also ran counter to the received expectation for an alternative company. A sizable percentage of alternative theatre companies in Britain through the 1970s and 80s were left-wing political companies. And, as Sandy Craig points out, these companies' desire to be alternative was a deliberate and political decision.[17] While Cherub similarly rejected mainstream theatre and some of its goals, the plays the company produced were classic texts, not blatantly political plays. As a draft of a publicity document in Cherub's own archive notes, the company was "determined to prove against all current odds that great plays can be made accessible and exciting to a wide audience at comparatively low production costs."[18] Cherub's all-male casting was at least partly a political decision. Perhaps the melding of the two (Shakespeare and political/alternative theatre) was the true basis of the drama officer's critique. The affront of a young, upstart company at producing Shakespeare and other classic plays in a manner quite different from the standard interpretation—in other words, the "Brookian-ness" of the production—was too much, warping Shakespeare in a manner beyond what the drama officer was able to endure.

This particular drama officer's report is certainly revealing about why ACGB never gave Cherub funding, but it is far from conclusive. It may be a smoking gun, but the wound it caused is by no means the only mark on Cherub's metaphorical body. The report has raised many questions about the complexity of producing theatre as an alternative company in Britain in the 1980s, especially as competing agendas both within and without the ACGB and limited funding continued to affect what the ACGB wanted a company to produce. As the Thatcher government continued to cut funding for the arts, subsidy became increasingly difficult to acquire for any company by the mid-1980s. Cherub and other companies attempted to secure funding by adapting their production models to become more "mainstream." In Cherub's case, this meant producing "known" Shakespeare plays like *Twelfth Night*[19]. With these productions, Visnevski perhaps hoped that the Arts Council would see Cherub's merits and would relent.[20] However, Cherub's *Twelfth Night* was hardly the conventional production of that play[21], and even with a change in material, the drama officers from ACGB saw that Visnevski hadn't altered his aesthetic vision. Visnevski was trying to walk the line between his own artistic principles and the ones that he perceived the Arts Council was placing on his productions. This report, while certainly problematic, opens up a window into larger issues at stake for the Cherub Company and its history.

ENDNOTES

1 S. S. Van Dine. "Twenty Rules for Writing Detective Stories", *American Magazine*, Sept. 1928. Accessed June 20, 2010, http://gaslight.mtroyal.ab.ca/vandine.htm.

2 Cherub received only one production grant in its 25 years, a £5000 grant for the tour of *A Chaste Maid in Cheapside* in 1981.

3 Unknown author, Draft of Publicity Letter for The Cherub Company, undated.

4 Stanley Wells and Gary Taylor, "Introduction to *The Two Noble Kinsmen*," *The Oxford Shakespeare*, Oxford, UK: Clarendon Press, 1988, 1225.

[5] Topolski was a noted artist who had emigrated to London from Poland, and following his work on *Kinsmen*, continued his association with Cherub by creating poster designs and sketching rehearsals and performances for the next several years.

[6] Martin Bailey, "A punk fight for the Bard", *Evening Standard*, November 21, 1979. (All newspaper reviews are from clippings found in the Cherub Company archive, temporarily housed at the University of Oregon. The clippings have dates written on them, but no page numbers. The library at the University of Oregon does not have microfilm of any of the newspapers cited here, and online archives do not go back as far as 1979.)

[7] Bonnie Lee, 'The Two Noble Kinsmen', *The Scotsman*, 3 September 1979.

[8] B.A. Young, 'The Two Noble Kinsmen', *Financial Times*, 26 November 1979.

[9] Sandy Craig. "The Bitten Hand: Patronage and Public Theatre," *Dreams and Deconstructions: Alternative Theatre in Britain*, Ambergate, UK: Amber Lane Press, 1980, 178.

[10] For more information on the history of the Arts Council of Great Britain and British arts subsidy, please see Sandy Craig (above) and Rebellato, Dan, *1956 and All That: The Making of Modern British Drama*, London: Routledge, 1999.

[11] Indeed, as Michael Billington notes in his book *State of the Nation*, Thatcher lauded the theatrical achievements of Andrew Lloyd Webber, presumably for his ability to bring in audiences in large numbers for his musical spectaculars (London: Faber and Faber, 2003, 284).

[12] Arts Council Great Britain (ACGB) Drama Officer's Report, *The Two Noble Kinsmen* (Edinburgh 1979), March 26, 1980.

[13] Visnevski, interview, August 5, 2005.

[14] I should note at this point, however, that while I refer to the drama officer as a male, I do not have proof that this is the case. In my initial research in 2005, the reports in the Arts Council files had not yet passed the 30–year threshold of the British Freedom of Information laws, and the reviewer's name was blacked out on all of the documents in the file. I have chosen to use the male pronoun here for clarity, and while I do indeed suspect that the drama officer was male, the objections as noted in the report would not be any less fascinating if they were written by a woman.

[15] The report is 172 words long, by far the shortest of the reports on Cherub in the ACGB archive.

[16] Michael Kustow, *Peter Brook: A Biography*, New York: St. Martin's Press, 2005, 201.

[17] Craig, "Reflexes of the Future," *Dreams and Deconstructions*, 10.

[18] Unknown author, Draft of Publicity Letter for The Cherub Company, undated.

[19] A huge success for the company, their production of *Twelfth Night* remained in their repertoire for many years, and was sponsored for a number of international tours by the British Council.

[20] Visnevski did not know, however, how the Arts Council viewed his company. The Arts Council officer reports were not available to the artists. All Visnevski and the company was told was that the ACGB needed to see more work from them.

[21] Cherub's *Twelfth Night* was directed by Visnevski and designed by Danusia Schebal. The production featured only 6 actors performing Shakespeare's text uncut. Elaborate but meaningful doubling of all the roles in the show, including Viola and Sebastian—the twins—being played by the same actress, was a key feature, as was the music by Peter Fincham.

The Tyranny of Absence: One Account of Archival Practice at the Fringe of the State

MARK DAVID TURNER

The Case

On January 5, 2010, I began work as a Program Coordinator at the Labrador Institute of Memorial University at Happy Valley-Goose Bay, Labrador, Canada. While my job title was intentionally vague, my more immediate purpose at this small academic outpost was to digitize and archive the 500 or so video items in the Institute's possession. This opportunity arose out of a longer standing connection I had cultivated with the Institute. I made my first visit in 2008 to assess its archival holdings for my doctoral thesis on film production in Newfoundland and Labrador. Since that point, I maintained a semi-regular working relationship with the Institute, researching and digitizing their film collection, a relationship that has become more formal with my present full-time engagement. At the time of this writing, I have digitized and described approximately three quarters of the Institute's collection—the remaining work will be finished within this calendar year.

My desire to work on and with this collection was wholly tempered by my introduction to it. Suffice it to say, a photograph of its original state would be the more appropriate visual counterpoint to this prose; however, no photograph was ever taken. On a typical sub-arctic February day with temperatures dipping to –40°C, I was led to the basement of a semi-abandoned building in Happy Valley-Goose Bay—the building was once occupied by the Institute. There, on a large wooden pallet were stacked approximately two-dozen boxes, none of which were labelled. Skimming through the contents of the outer-lying boxes I discovered a range of audio-visual media: 8mm film, 16mm film, betamax, VHS, and what appeared to be an endless stream of 3/4-inch u-matic tape. As both a student and researcher of theatre and film in the province of Newfoundland and Labrador, titles such as *Newfoundland and Labrador Heritage Stories*, *Solomon Curl—Fox Harbour* and *The Mummers Troupe—Gros Mourn*[1] immediately jumped out at me. But with no equipment readily available with which to view these items, my introduction to this collection only afforded me the opportunity to make the most preliminary attempt at an inventory, for indeed, none existed. Here lay a pallet of films that had absolutely no accompanying textual record whatsoever—a little like receiving the crates containing Walter Benjamin's library without a Benjamin to unpack them.

Adding to the mystery was the geographical location of this pallet of texts. How was it that this volume of audio-visual material came to rest here in central Labrador? Certainly, uncovering collections of this sort was not uncommon in the Canadian North—the 1978 discovery of the Dawson City Collection of early film stands as the most obvious example. But these films were unlike the Dawson City Collection in that (1) the earliest known item in the collection was produced in 1967; (2) the bulk of this material was produced in Labrador; (3) these materials *seemed* to have been produced for a local audience; and (4) the known network of distribution did not extend beyond the region. This was a relatively new collection of audio-visual documents that, given their comparative youth, appeared to be bafflingly lacking in context.

As I now know, the motivations that led to the creation of these films were relatively straightforward, if otherwise unaccounted for. The majority of these items were in fact produced by either the Labrador Institute of Northern Studies (known as such until 1997) or by the Media Unit of the organization from which it originated: the Memorial University of Newfoundland Extension Service. Those familiar with Canadian film history will likely know the latter of these two organizations. In 1967, Colin Low, filmmaker with the National Film Board of Canada partnered with then Extension director Don Snowden to pioneer the "Fogo Process," a form of participatory community-based filmmaking. The advent of this technique vaulted audio-visual media to a place of significance in the work of Extension Services, which, at that time, was embarking upon community development projects in coastal Labrador. Arising out of Extension Services' work in the region, the Labrador Institute of Northern Studies inherited Extension's predilection toward the use of audio-visual media both in the execution of its programs and as a means by which to engage with the region—a predilection that seems to have been more or less sustained until the early 1990s.

But this institutional history still provided me no clues for the larger anti-archival imperative that seemed to be at work here. Indeed, given the newness of the media and its apparent institutional significance, why had the act of archiving not been ongoing? The Institute had maintained its own library since its inception; however, these films were never subject to the same level of description and organization as those texts that contained the written word. The question remained: *how* did these texts come to rest *here*?

I do not rehearse these questions to beleaguer a line of inquiry that is no doubt central to the work of all archivists—such questions must necessarily be posed in order to arrange and describe archival materials. Rather I want to suggest that there is a unique relationship between the *how* and *here* of this collection of texts in this location—of film and video in Labrador—in order to interrogate some of the issues that arise out of archival practice in a region that is otherwise physically, psychically and ethnographically remote to the rest of Canada. The mystery of this *how* and *here* reveals much about the mutability of, to use Derrida's phrase, the *archontic* principle; that theory of institutionalization that authorizes the archives' right *as* archive.

The Background

Archival practice is rooted in an ontological imperative; that is, its practice provides textual and thereby organizational legitimacy to its co-ordinating objects.[2] But the shape of this imperative in Canada, a nation that is still functionally addressing and imagining itself as "post-colonial," is unequivocally statist or a sub-manifestation thereof.[3] The comparatively recent flowering of the local or theme-based archives in this country has been functionally authorized by the existence of the state archive: the scope and volume of the local archive provides the necessary significatory and contextual basis for the state archive to exist. A number of these "sub-state" archives are centrally linked via the Archives Canada-maintained Canadian Archival Information Network, suggesting the centripetal nature of this specific process of archival signification. Their linkage to a centralized and federally authorized archive furthers the statist imperative embedded within our national archival project. But the ability of these archives to function in this manner is entirely dependent upon a more or less uniform education-technical infrastructure that provides the citizenry with both the analytical tools and physical access necessary for this process of archival interpretation; an infrastructure that is only now beginning to extend into Labrador.

Tempered as it is by the degree to which education-technical infrastructure has been developed, archival practice and use takes on a markedly different aspect in Labrador, a region that has functionally existed adjacent to rather than within a model of federal governance.[4] Even with its formal inclusion in the Canadian Confederation in 1949, infrastructure development in this region has been sporadic, focussed and generally localised within central and western Labrador. Confederation did not bring with it the opportunity to access a centrally mediated national identity as it did for much of the remainder of the country; instead it sparked a desire to articulate, explore and assert a regional Labrador identity whose poetics owe something to the larger trend of Canadian regionalism that rose to prominence in the 1960s. Unlike many regionalist movements from the period, however, Labrador's was decisively not spearheaded by an ethnically and economically uniform educated class. Rather, it was instigated and maintained by ethnically and geographically diverse (albeit economically uniform)[5] groups that were mobilised in part by the activities of the Memorial University of Newfoundland Extension Service. Their efforts toward articulating a common Labrador identity were focussed on the shared experiences of material existence—what we would now refer to as intangible cultural heritage—rather than through the assemblage and interpretation of documents that would *traditionally* authorize claims of regional identity.

Historically, archival practice and use in Labrador has been guided by the defining aspect of its regionalism—through an insistence on articulating a common identity through the shared experience of material existence. This organizing principle is best evidenced in the region's only functionally pan-Labrador archive—*Them Days* Labrador Archives (TDLA)—which itself arose out of a perceived need to document a mode of existence that was believed to be passing.[6] Established in 1984, TDLA is the archival wing of *Them Days* Magazine—the latter was established in 1975, squarely in the middle of the most active period of Labrador's regionalist movement. Favouring, as the subtitle of the magazine attests, "Stories of Early Labrador," a good deal of the TDLA's holdings is of first person accounts of lived experience—the raw material used in the composition of many of the magazine's articles. In this region, access to *a* narrative of events takes precedence over the quality and type of document that narrates those events—content always dominates form. This specific type of archival practice and use has been instrumental in the negotiation, maintenance, and (re)invention of a Labrador regional identity.

The Client

The mystery deepens. If, as we have already established, this pallet of film and video in the basement of a semi-abandoned building in central Labrador contained a specific set of tools used for the purpose of community development in the region, and if this set of tools was deployed during this epoch of the more or less formal manufacture of regional identity, why were these films not bestowed the status as items worthy of archiving? Certainly, they would have functioned in a similar fashion as the content of *Them Days* Magazine with the obvious exception that these films and videos were documents of a contemporary Labrador, not of its emerging cultural-historical narrative. I would suggest two reasons for this neglect. First, similar to any area engaged in minority nationalism, there is a relative antipathy toward the present (albeit, for our purposes, the present we are discussing occurred thirty years ago). In the construction of regional identity, the events of the present do not afford the same authority as the events of an emerging past. Second, and this is more specific to the region itself, the implementation and manufacture of this media during the moment of a developing regionalism did not prove to be unequivocally successful along its original lines: the scope and range of expectations embedded in this regionalism gradually affected the direction and momentum of the movement.

This shift is both documented by and mirrored within the media that compose this collection. Early period films produced directly by the Extension Service of Memorial University of Newfoundland are interventionist texts whose value lay in the act of their production rather than in the events they recorded. Films such as *Time for Change, Cape St. Charles* (1970), and *Introduction to Labrador* (1970), for instance, were catalysts for social-political change on the south coast of the region as their production literally brought residents of the area face-to-face and asked them to address and posit solutions to issues they perceived as being detrimental to the region. A similar strategy was employed in the NFB Challenge for Change-Societé Nouvelle co-production *Labrador North* (1973); in this instance the focus was on the northern communities of Labrador. Interestingly, with the formal establishment of the Labrador Institute of Northern Studies in 1979, the manner of film and video production began to change. Rather than engaging in interventionist film and video-making for the purpose of community change, the Institute began to employ media in a more passive manner; i.e. using it to *document* both internal and external initiatives rather than approaching the creation of the media as an event in and of itself. Series such as *The Fisheries Co-Operative Education Project* (LINS, c.1984, incomplete), *Labradorians at Work* (LINS, 1988) and the *Labrador Creative Arts Festival* (LCAF, c.1980–c.1996) were never conceived of as video projects *per se*. Instead they were attempts to document projects, both internally and externally generated, which had their beginnings in the moment of acute regionalist activity.

It is precisely within this procedural shift that we can locate the origin of *archontic* indifference—the non-archival imperative that relegated this collection to its subterranean dwelling for what seems to have been no less than a decade. For unlike the material of the TDLA that supplied the narrative historical material that would serve as the basis for a perpetually emerging regional identity, these films and videos were documents of a present that was in stasis—of events and programs so focussed and specific that they would resist being pressed into the service of an historical narrative that was and still is being negotiated and narrated. Their inability to function as polysemetic historical signifiers resulted in their perceived lack of utility—these documents had no place in the unique process of historical signification occurring in Labrador. Ultimately, this begs the question: according to the logic of the region, can this collection rightly be called an archive?

Regardless of the imperatives that led this collection to its state of dormancy, it is, in fact, in the process of becoming an archival collection (in the most technical sense of the word). Indeed, I would not be able to offer this account here if it were not for this very fact. It is, however, important to note that this drive to organize these texts as archive is *institutionally* motivated. The Labrador Institute's desire to interpret these texts as archive arises out of a related but oppositional signifying imperative: to authorize its claim *as* institution. But unlike the region itself, which is able to assemble the archive through the collection of intangible cultural heritage, the stuff of an institutional archive is highly circumscribed and regulated—determined by the larger education-institution apparatus. Documents generated by the institution itself stand as the most appropriate candidates to create "legitimate" archives in that they provide an historical record of the institution's operations thereby offering historical legitimacy. For a comparatively young institution such as the Labrador Institute, this legitimacy is paramount in order to sustain its existence both within the region and as part of the larger conglomeration of Memorial University of Newfoundland. The archiving of these documents provides it with the opportunity to authorize these claims.

Case Closed?

How then are we to proceed with archiving a group of texts that is, on the one hand, without utility in the context of the archival imperative at work in Labrador, yet extremely rich in the context of the institution that was responsible for their creation? The archival process and end product must necessarily pay deference to these conflicting imperatives—they must archive these imperatives as well.

The immediate issue that arises is that digitization—the process that must

Masking historical utility—the arranged and described analogue originals that constitute the bulk of the Labrador Institute Film and Video Collection. Photograph by Mark David Turner, December 2010.

occur in order to make these documents accessible to patrons—ultimately inflicts violence upon these items as historical documents. Divorcing them from their historical form (8mm film, 16mm film, betamax, and 3/4-inch u-matic. all become digital versions of their analogue originals), the public-access archive is itself a distant reproduction of the original texts. The most significant problem this poses is that the public access archive cannot offer patrons the opportunity to see the facades of the texts—the location where the narrative of their indifference is best evidenced. Neither does it allow the patron to see the aggregation of that indifference, nor the opportunity to witness the organizational logic that governed its dormant state. These markings are perhaps the best evidence of the regional archival imperative at work.

It seems then that the only way forward is, however digitally, to attempt to provide some degree of synchronous context—to support these documents with material that will be able to, at the very least, contextualize their production. Otherwise, there is a very real risk that these digital reproductions will become hollow signifiers, disembodied images catalogued and described in an electronic database that bears no trace of the historical utility of its contents. The vitality of this archive would necessarily need to be achieved by embracing the very imperative that resulted in its neglect: the archiving of its own intangible cultural heritage; that is, its original use by the people that used it. This record, however subjective and personal, is necessary for the archive to historically account for itself. It must pay deference to regional models of archival practice. To that end, we are conceiving of this archival project as having a supplementary oral history project that will document, where possible, people's involvement with these materials as both producers and audience. Transcripts of these testimonies will be linked to each of the individual items via a searchable database. In light of our inability to achieve archival fidelity (at least with regard to the texts themselves), fidelity to archival process will have to serve in its stead.

But this process is itself merely hypothetical—a postulation of a way for these archives to address and embody regional particularity while standing as a discrete collection. Our ability to proceed in this manner will be affected by the motivations that underwrite both archival imperatives—it remains to be seen whether or not they can be mobilised in an attempt to solidify this collection as archive. It seems that it is equally as likely that this essay will itself be a document of one stage of conflicting imperatives that will continue to deny and celebrate these films as an archive. The representation of Labrador's regionalist awakening that these texts offer is another case altogether, much more complex than the reasons that informed their decade-long sleep.

ENDNOTES

1 I offer these titles as representative examples here as I have not discovered copies of these films in any other collection. *Newfoundland and Labrador Heritage Stories* is a collection of short animated films produced by the Newfoundland and Labrador Department of Education during the 1970s or 80s in which a quintessential Newfoundland old-timer narrates events from the province's history. *Solomon Curl—Fox Harbour* is a Memorial University of Newfoundland Extension Services film produced in 1970 depicts and addresses living conditions on Labrador's south coast, while *The Mummers Troupe—Gros Mourn* is an undated MUN Extension production containing some of the only known film footage of the Newfoundland theatre-collective, The Mummers Troupe.

2 For Derrida, the genealogy of this ontological imperative can be traced back to the coordinating principles of its root, *arkhē* (*archē*): commandment and commencement. Jacques Derrida, *Archive Fever: A Freudian Impression*. Trans. Eric Prenowitz (Chicago: Chicago UP, 1995) p1.

3 One need look no further than the opening message on the Archives Canada website to confirm this imperative: "In homes, schools and libraries across Canada, people are looking for evidence of what it means to be a Canadian. Archives Canada is a gateway to archival resources found in over 800 repositories across Canada—it's your gateway to Canada's collective memory!" Canadian Archival Information Network. "Index," Canadian Council of Archives, http://www.archivescanada.ca/english/index.html (accessed October 1, 2010).

4 The trajectory of this governance is most richly and succinctly described by Bill Rompkey in *The Story of Labrador* (Montreal: McGill-Queens University Press, 2003), x: "Although both the Innu and the Inuit had their own forms of governance, for some time after the coming of the Europeans there was really no government at all. Then there was government by non-governmental organizations. Finally, the government governed. But how and for who?"

5 Despite their economic uniformity, there is no uniform internal attitude toward their own economic position.

6 From the opening message on the *Them Days* website: "Them Days Incorporated is dedicated to keeping the history of Labrador alive by documenting and preserving the "old ways and early days" of Labrador." *Them Days: Stories of Early Labrador*. "Index," Them Days Incorporated, http://www.themdays.com/index.shtml (accessed December 4, 2010).

A Queer Memory: Guilt, Disappearance, and the YouTube "Archive"

ANDREW BROWN

We met in cyberspace, a serendipitous Youtube encounter that left me reeling with joy and pain, as any good cyber relationship should. The Youtube clip was of a South African performer named Pieter-Dirk Uys, who explicitly uses his most famous drag persona, Evita Bezuidenhout, in touring his solo HIV/AIDS awareness cabaret to middle schoolers across his country. The editor of the Youtube video is named "WarontheHorizon."[1] He has taken a clip of a preexisting documentary that praises Pieter's activist work, titled *Darling! The Pieter-Dirk Uys Story*, and has interspersed black slides that threaten in large, white, block letters: "Pieter-Dirk Uys effeminizes black African youth," "Homosexuality is unAfrican," and "Fags go home or die." Initially, and perhaps surprisingly, I met this clip with unexpected amusement, a mocking gasp and some shadowy laughter. It was outrageous, over the top. My laughter was somewhat covert, a result of shame and anxiety. I wouldn't realize until later that my initial reaction was thanks to the privilege and safe distance of academia.

The ignorant diatribe of the clip, along with its surrounding comments, were of course painful to read, but they also made me giddy with the anticipation of academic critique. I had witnessed the 'original' *Darling!* documentary a few times and could appropriately situate this Youtube clip in its wildly erroneous reading of Uys's work. In fact, it was so far from what I understood the documentary's intentions to be that it became a source of humor to me. It was also so drastically contradictory to my own experience of Pieter's work in person that I could completely separate WarontheHorizon's reading of the performance from the live performance event itself. These variant documents jockeyed parodically for authority in a way that I found humorous because I knew which document had to 'win': the 'real', the 'original', the 'authentic'.

As I began to extract the clip from its ideological home through my critique and from its material home on the Internet to place in a conference presentation, a mounting sense of dread struck me. I couldn't understand how the clip accumulated such weight when I knew full well how excessive it was. It was only in daydream, as I imagined my conference presentation playing out, that I realized how, in addressing the clip as a self-contained object, I was unmooring it from my knowledge of its quite contradictory antecedent. In using Youtube as my archive, the clip became dehistoricized from its original, evacuated of context. Though I could tell my audience about the footage's prior context and though they were watching segments of the very same 'original' footage, as compiled and edited on the Internet WarontheHorizon's clip came to stand on its own as a new autonomous original. Inevitably, the immateriality and immediacy of the Internet, especially sites like Youtube, where public and private archives so violently reciprocate, notions of originality, ownership, and personal knowledge become highly contested and competitive. I was soon catapulted into even deeper distress when I realized that for the tens of thousands of viewers and subscribers, this clip *was* the original, with no conference presentation to filter and recontextualize its message, no intimate fieldwork through which to personalize and empathize.

I was quite literally out of control. Paranoia led to obsession. I was watching the video daily, multiple times a day, watching all of WarontheHorizon's posted videos, and then all of his subscribers' posted videos. I even subscribed to his Youtube channel myself. As the video's watch-count increased I became nauseated by my own complicity, constantly reassuring myself that *my* contribution was for the sake of research. About seven subscribers in total have commented on the Pieter-Dirk Uys video, all (in agreement with WarontheHorizon) expressing their horror and disdain for what they see as Uys's abhorrently explicit homosexuality in an African context. All but one of the commentators are in their mid-thirties and forties and are located in the United States (one woman is located in Japan). All are committed to fighting what they see as the 'good fight' on behalf of the South African students shown in this film, against invasive homosexuality.

I can't stop thinking about how WarontheHorizon creates a transnational dialogue with the original documentary footage, using the process of video editing to create a new 'original' that becomes the foundation upon which a community is built, as evidenced by the accumulation of responses. The trans- and inter-national community created around this new original (which does not, interestingly enough, include anyone from the African continent itself) establishes its own discourse, ideology, and politics mobilized by this recontextualized film footage, which thanks to digital technology requires no physical congregation or shared temporal interaction with the document. To an extent the community is imagined and yet their ramifications are affective and effective, emotive and material—they make me laugh and worry, and they hunch my back over a keyboard in protest. Eventually, at a conference, they make me stand up in rebuttal.

And then, days before the conference, when I went to insert the clip into my presentation . . . nothing. It's gone. Nowhere to be found. I feel betrayed. I begin to question my memory: Who was the editor? What did I search? What was the title of the video? Did it even exist in the first place? Was it taken down? Down from what? Or has its intricate layering of 0's and 1's dissipated into some electronic ether, its binary code fractured, scattering in all directions? Or perhaps in no direction at all, but the same 0's and 1's palimpsestually recycled to write another image with another meaning for another audience. I do not know how binary code works, except through opposition. The failure of my archive's permanence indicates the fragility of binaries, collapsing so readily in the face of the multiplicity of imagination—sparked both by internet and performance technologies. WarontheHorizon's subscribers imagined themselves familiar—calling each other "brother," feeling connected, until their entire conversation, their traces, their shared material disappeared. I too imagined myself a part of the community, even in resistance. I also imagined I had a research home—an archive, a project, a presentation. My memory has failed me and continues to fail me not only as this story slips immeasurably away, but as the very site of my memory: so concrete, so effective, so moving, so *real* to me reveals its transience. It is a site-less memory. My memory spaces happen this way. And perhaps, as I hope to gesture towards, queer memory spaces happen this way too.

As any good Performance Studies scholar would (and considering the imminent time pressure), I quickly decided to incorporate my personal journey and relationship with the material into my presentation. I would not only embody my rebuttal to the material itself, now I would perform in defiance of the failure of the archive. Performance shares the promise of multiplicity with the Internet but distinguishes itself most obviously through materialization. The lush multidirectionality of this Youtube video is possible largely because of the disembodied nature of digital technology. But performance, as live embodiment, assembles that multiplicity in space and time, combusting fragmentation around and through shared experience and concrete material.

The contradictory increase in individualism and possibility for expansive communities, characteristic of what some might call our "global condition," is nowhere more apparent than on Internet sites like Youtube. This contradiction results in multiple, contradictory archives, with their inherent misunderstandings. It is the very immateriality of this archival document that allows it to circulate so diversely. Perhaps my anxiety marks a postmodern archivist's anxiety toward unruly fragmentation, uncontrollable multiplicity, degrading the authority of any single archive and indeed archival and memory practices themselves. My turn to performance also indicates a worry for the state of memory practices in the face of disembodiment through digital technology: where the internet promises a permanent, limitless, disembodied memory bank, performance acknowledges its ephemeral, fleeting nature while simultaneously reprivileging embodied and emotional memory, created in the affective space opened through collective presence, witness, and liveness.

I can see myself standing in front of the conference, alone, my sophisticated technology failing behind me. So I decide to fill in the absence or rewrite the empty space with performance. I will invoke and present the video and its community through performance. The archive becomes a performance task. But do I remember the lines, the gestures? And how do I best invoke the multiple characters? Suddenly performance reveals the loss of memory, the constant minute shifts inherent in repetition. Another unstable archive. And once again I find that through performance I am perpetuating the video, its community, and their sentiments.

What I thought was certain is no longer so. I am disoriented, as Sarah Ahmed would say: "disorientation diminishes capacities for action . . . if we inherit the failure of things to be habitual, then we might also acquire a tendency to look behind us."[2] I am certainly turned around, looking behind, suddenly catapulted in many directions, excavating the traces and labors that edited the film and brought it to Youtube in the first place: who, why, when, how? Disappearance reinscribes the archival anxiety for preservation and permanence just as disorientation questions my ability to faithfully reproduce the document. I even create a Youtube account just to email WarontheHorizon, saying, "I'm interested in your stuff . . . especially about that Pieter-Dirk Uys guy from South Africa. I can't find your video about him anymore. Where did you find it and do you happen to have a copy you could send me?" I should probably just let it go. But I am obsessed. The video does not exist anymore, at least not publicly, and shouldn't I be relieved? But I am haunted by its residues, its vibrations in the airwaves; it burns just here on the inside of my skull and here near my heart. It continues to emanate not from the screen, but from my memories, my emotions, and my critique. My body recreates, sustains the document. The performance controls and writes me.

The footage from WarontheHorizon's video is taken from a documentary called *Darling! The Pieter-Dirk Uys Story* that follows Uys' activist performances in schools throughout South Africa. In one particularly important moment, Uys's spiel about what size condom to use is interrupted by the appearance and advice of his most famous drag persona, Evita Bezuidenhout. We watch him transform into her, explaining each step as he goes along. He puts on lipstick, pouting at the audience, shows the audience how he (how to) put on earrings and a shawl, and finally asks, "What have I forgotten?" while prompting the audience to respond by pointing to his head. The young audience explodes with "Hair!" and upon arrival of the wig, bursts out in raucous laughter. He is teaching his audience about safe sex, HIV/AIDS prevention, as well as how to dress like a woman and, on a less explicit level, that gender deviance can be funny, fun, smart, and important. His audience laughs. From discomfort? From joy? With? At? Probably the laughter is saturated with all of these readings.

The unabashed uproar of laughter marks the joyous and uncomfortable combination of humor with the serious. The productive tension of discomfort and the disarming conjunction of humor and seriousness allow Uys's audiences to witness queer possibilities, and as embodied performance, queer practices. Even if his audiences, predominantly young teenagers, don't directly identify the work of Uys's drag performance and camp education style as queering the content of the presentation and their own selves as well, his physical presence queers the space through embodied, affective modes of meaning-making and the transmission of knowledge. But here, he educates, politicizing bodies and minds in the present and suggesting a political potential for the multivalence of queer membership, imaginaries, and bodies. He embodies a performative queering that signifies, enacts change, has residue, but is ultimately transient. Gone before we know it. Just passing by. Was it ever really there in the first place?

The transnational migration of Pieter's queer practices, over the Internet foregrounds and privileges the sexuality in the videotaped performance (*Darling!*). Pieter is seen as unAfrican because of his homosexuality vis-à-vis WarontheHorizon's specifically U.S. reading of camp drag performance, but perhaps also because Pieter is a white Afrikaner.[3] Though he has lived in South Africa his entire life, he is also the product of a cultural immigration responsible for apartheid. WarontheHorizon reads an invasive, perhaps colonial homosexuality onto the situation, "Whites are on a world tour to force sexual backwardness on Black people. South Afrika [sic] and amerikkka [sic] are no different. They have us laughing at sexually confused freaks while they mentally and psychologically molest our children's minds."[4] I would argue that this situation actually nuances the way camp aesthetics and queer politics are performed and form transient communities at the interstices of the global and local, much like WarontheHorizon's video itself.

My hyper anxiety, and the eventual collapse of any resolute archive made me realize that I am involved in a competition over the cultural high ground of Youtube, establishing myself in a resistant relationship to the pre-established community as a means of comforting my attraction to and perpetuation of the material's circulation. I have, unwittingly, positioned myself within yet another binary code with the archive, which upon disappearance collapses my meaning-making capacities. Technological failure fractures into multidirectionality, which I can only account for through performance. Performance fills, embraces, and responds to the failed archive.

As with many binary systems, the establishment of a public sphere or discourse is often accompanied by the appearance or development of a counterpublic. Counterpublics circulate an alternative discourse, but as Michael Rothberg points out in his book *Multidirectional Memory*, though they recognize the exclusionary potential of the discursive space, counterpublics also frequently participate in practices of "exclusion and domination."[5] Using the notion of multidirectionality, Rothberg complicates preexisting constructs of how publics and counterpublics relate to one another, suggesting instead a rhizomatic fragmentation without disregarding the categories altogether. For instance, if Uys's performance might be seen as producing a counterpublic to the HIV-phobic policies of South African government, then WarontheHorizon's video produces a second counterpublic by delimiting the performance. This secondary counterpublic is different from the original public (governmental policy) while still remaining oppositional.

Publics and counterpublics are symbiotic and reproduce one another. Publics enact and sustain memory practices, reliant on the repetition of particular knowledges and behaviors in order to codify membership and create group coherence, allegiance, and solidarity. Archives, as a territorial marker over the past, follow suit insofar as publics seek authorship over knowledge and control over constructions of history. In response to the competitive nature of binaries, Rothberg offers multidirectionality as an alternative system—one that looks at how various divergent memories intersect around events and locations in non-possessive ways. The fragmentation, multiplicity, and unpredictability of all this reminds me of qualities often attached to queer theory. The difference between queer and multidirectional is that queerness continually points us towards gender and sexuality as embodied practices, forced to concretize and materialize an archive on bodies in action while maintaining an openness and fluidity through performance. What queerness offers, then, that multidirectionality conceived of alone might not, is the constant redirection back to performative embodiment.

The conversation into which the Youtube clip is edited tells Pieter-Dirk Uys, the "beastly transvestite," and presumably any viewers who identify with him or as "fags", to "go home or die." I wonder where WarontheHorizon expects Uys to go. Or the rest of us, for that matter. Would he be happier if all the gays came to join him in the States? The homelessness of the queer community that WarontheHorizon inadvertently identifies speaks to the complications that globalizing queer politics experience in identity, community, and cultural formation. Homelessness may also offer a useful metaphor for thinking about and imagining the contextual politics of place and the transgressive, multidirectional circulation of archival documents as they shape ideological, political, emotional, and physical space.

What I wonder, then, is if queerness might work in tandem with multidirectionality, attaching it to the body and the way bodies lay claim to memory, opening it up to notions of performativity to diffuse oppositional tension and dissolve the cyclical stagnation of binaries. What I desire is a queer memory practice(s) that might bring about a transportable, homeless, embodied, covert, contradictory, disoriented archive. A queer archive.

WarontheHorizon eventually emailed me back, lamenting that the clip had been pulled by Youtube due to offensive material. I certainly wasn't the one to complain, but I wonder who did. I still return, searching every now and then just to see if the clip might happen to reappear. I wonder what it might look like now and what my reaction might be if I ever do see it again. WarontheHorizon would almost certainly be opposed to participating in the circulation of a queer archive. But, it is the very self-perpetuating power of embodiment to exceed simplistic opposition and reinvigorate complex, multidirectional, queer resistances that this essay advocates.

The pain of absence.

The twinge of finding myself site-less.

The shock of disappearance, the blur of misrecognition,
of looking back to locate oneself in a memory,
to validate and stabilize myself, my critique, my experiences
only to find myself oriented around nothing—an empty site.

A moment, an experience, a memory vacant, vacated, evacuated.

My incessant return to the document is also about futurity—the way hauntings bleed past into future. Performance does this too. My return is about the potential of my encounter with someone I disagree with. Someone who injures me. The productive possibilities, pleasure even, of discomfort. Repeated discomfort. My interaction with WarontheHorizon is just as temporary, immaterial, homeless, as the artifacts and performances, politics and economics, histories and trajectories that brought us together in the first place. I look back in order to move forward. My memory spaces happen this way. And, perhaps, queer memory spaces happen this way too.

ENDNOTES

[1] http://www.youtube.com/user/WarontheHorizonWOH

[2] Sara Ahmed, *Queer Phenomenology: Orientations, Objects, Others* (Durham: Duke University Press, 2006),

[3] South Africa became the first country in the world with a constitutional that protected against abuses due to sexual orientation. The strategies employed to ensure inclusion, however, were highly contested in their privileging of gay, white, middle-class priorities. This has led to a fragmented, ambivalent relationship between LGBTI communities, especially towards political activism. For a more in depth conversation around these matters, see Carl Stychin's article "Constituting Sexuality: The Struggle for Sexual Orientation in the South African Bill of Rights" and Jacklyn Cock's "Engendering Gay and Lesbian Rights: The Equality Clause in the South African Constitution."

[4] http://waronthehorizon.com/site/?m=200903&cat=1

[5] Michael Rothberg, *Multidirectional Memory: Remembering the Holocaust in the Age of Decolonization* (Stanford: StanfordUP, 2009) 202.

Afterword—Scarred Texts: Etudes on Absence

ODAI JOHNSON

I: Oblivion and Archives

In 451 CE the Bishops of the Eastern Roman empire gathered for the Council of Chalcedon to continue the debate on ecclesiastic issues that would, in essence, define the articles of the Catholic faith. They had last convened two years earlier in Ephesus, and the first order of business this day was to approve the minutes of the last meeting, as we would say. It was at that early point the first dispute arose over a deliberate erasure of the official records of the last council. It was not unusual for contests of memory to erupt—indeed, so frequent had they become that the bishops began each to bring with them their own clerks for verbatim recording (*tachygraphia*), a sort of transcription short-hand. The minutes, as they were read aloud, officially recorded that the august body at Ephesus had unanimously endorsed several resolutions, including one that prohibited any further debate: "if anyone reverses [a doctrine], let him be anathema! If anyone over-elaborates, let him be anathema! Let us preserve the faith of the Fathers!" The objections to the tampered minutes were immediate: "While this was being read out, the Anatolikoi (Easterners) and the most pious bishops with them shouted out 'We did not say these things! Who said these things?'"

In the investigation that followed it was revealed that Dioscorus, Bishop of Alexandria, had ordered his notary to interdict the transcriptions of the other bishops. The deposition reads:

> "Stephanus, the most pious bishop of Ephesus said, 'My notarii, Iulianus, the present bishop of Lebedus, and Crispinus, deacon, were taking a record, and there came the notarii of the most pious bishop Dioscorus and wiped out their tablets and all but broke their fingers in their desire to take their pens. Neither did they take copies of the records, nor do I know what happened."[1]

Tablets at the ecumenical councils are wiped clean, and the memory, rebelling at the injustice of the erasure, finds a record of its own rebellion. It was the resistance to erasure that made the story. The historiographical challenge is to catch the vandals in the act of erasure, in the act of defacing the text, that is, in transit from archive to oblivion, and arresting them before the disappearance is complete. The damaged text preserves the traces of its own erasure.

Such accounts remind us that memory is a subversive act against the natural status of oblivion. Monuments (memorials, history, wax tablets), howsoever enduring, throw but brief redoubts against erasure ("look on my work, ye mighty, and despair!" boasted Ozymandias of his great works now under the "lone and level sands").[2] Oblivion is the natural order against which all monuments face off. Viewed in this light, archives are unnatural places. They arrest deterioration, they arrest the slide into the oblivion that all memory and matter (wax, vitriol ink, vellum, parchment, or temple architecture) must eventually rest. Good archives stave off oblivion for centuries, they keep their monuments above the sand for a while more, and that is the best we can hope for. But memory sanctions, vitiated records, such as those undertaken by the 'most pious Dioscorus,' acts of mnemocide, (the willful destruction of memory) these are perversities of a more brutal nature. They are the opposite of the archive-impulse: they vandalize memory. Mnemocide defaces the past and seeks to lock its records into a memorial contract that outlives their authenticity. I want to evoke the Bishops' outrage at the council's act of mnemocide, in attempting to archive what never occurred, because that is where the poignancy is deepest, being a crime against memory itself. For that, I turn to a small case study, very small, that nonetheless began with a similar archival abuse, motivated less by malice than a kind of drunken neglect, but nonetheless a scarring excision whose violation was recorded but whose records remained unrestored, flagging still its own absence. I evoke it not in the attempt to offer a systematic reconstruction of what has not been preserved, or to replace the vitiated record, but to puzzle out the problems that such scarred texts present, problems of reading absence, the hegemony of memory, and ultimately, to trace the marks of absence, the scars that such erasures leave behind.

Like the Council at Chalcedon, some of the most basic and accessible archives are clerical: church records, parish records, census records, preserving the most vital of facts employed by scholars and genealogists alike: the births, christenings, marriages, occupations, and deaths within the parish. Many parishes have astonishingly complete records well back into the early seventeenth century and beyond. Some have gaps that betray the damage of fire, war, and weather, or occasionally bad archivists, who have not just neglected their capacity as memory-keeper of the Parish, but have scarred the text in quietly violent ways. One such is St. Cuthbert's Parish, Edinburgh, where, some years ago, I encountered the following problem while working on a biography on David Douglass, actor-manager of the American Company, (the proverbial 'founding father' of the American stage), and have been thinking about absence ever since.

II: The Carelessness of Mr. Wilson

> "There is Missing in the Register fifty four Baptisms for any of which Mr. Wilson does not so much as pretend to account for."
>
> —*Minutes of the Kirk, St. Cuthberts,* 1743–1745, 2.[3]

When the West Kirk session of the Scottish Presbyterian church of St. Cuthberts Parish was called to assemble on 10 November 1743, the subject was not the usual refractory parishioner, but their own archivist: Mr. Wilson, the long-standing parish clerk, and the grievances against him were legion and serious. For more than two decades Mr. Wilson had been derelict in his clerical functions, and when, one night, he took a stick to a parishioner, the Kirk finally had enough. In preparing their case for his dismissal, the full extent of his dereliction was revealed. Sampling a third of the parish, the Heritors of the church (what we might call a board) found fifty four Baptisms unrecorded in the last four years alone, and in the absence of a legal repository—like Birth Certificates lodged in City Hall—being unregistered at the local parish severely diminished one's legal identity. Wilson, it seems, had often been "absent" on such days "when Parents come to Register their children, for which he has been often complained of." Later in the session we would discover "absent" was a polite phrase for drunk beyond function. Even in those rare fits of duty when sobriety interfered and the Baptisms were recorded, Wilson frequently still confused the gender of the children, "males being put for females & *e contra.*" Particularly egregious were the marriage records, so "irregularly" registered that they invited no end of legal confusion, or worse, left open to suspicious minds the charges of "ante-nuptial fornication" between the parties. Without reputable or consistent census records, it had become impossible to prove or disprove the numerous instances of infidelity and adultery carried on openly in the parish, impossible to prove which children were born in or out of wedlock, consequently, who had rights to property, inheritance, social legitimacy, and who didn't: legal identity was thrown over in a parish of bastards and shack-ups. Upon close inspection, the Kirk concluded that the Register of Marriages and Baptisms was found to be "so vitiated, that it cannot bear faith in the proper courts" (4). Equally vitiated were the financial records, in which donations and distributions to the poor of the Parish ended up in the pub cash box instead, with no credible account of who received what or what was disbursed to whom in any given year. The investigation concluded that Mr. Wilson had egregiously failed in his post "from the very beginning" and upon review found the records of the Parish during his tenure as clerk "so untrue, and in several instances so ridiculous and absurd, that it was necessary to order it to be wrote over again" (3). Of these derelictions, "Mr. Wilson makes no defence [sic] for it." At the close of the inquest, Mr. Wilson was not only dismissed, but locked out of the church.[4] The census records, however, were not 'wrote over again', and remain still a scarred text for the extent of that clerk's long tenure at the parish, and marked as such in a hand-written note on the pages of the parish register.

Historiographically, the carelessness of the parish clerk reminds us that it was the church that held the lion's share of official memory in the community, and that memory was occasionally severely flawed. And so for one generation born into the largest parish in the capital of the Scottish Enlightenment (that remarkable generation who shared Edinburgh with David Hume, Adam Smith, and John Millar), their early lives were without official record. One such born into St. Cuthbert's parish during the long tenure of Mr. Wilson was David Douglass, the founder of the American theatre, sometime in the 1720s. Of his exact birth and parentage, his early life, of his family home, his father's vocation, his parent's death and burial records, as well as those of his siblings (if he had them), any discipline at the hands of the Kirk, or his own early marriage, all remain an absence in the "vitiated" records of a drunken clerk. The biographer of the life of William Smellie, a minor writer of the Scottish Enlightenment (first editor of *The Encyclopedia Britanncia*), and a contemporary of Douglass, born into the same parish, corroborated the problem when he wrote of young Smellie: "The precise date of his birth cannot now be ascertained either from the Parish Records of the time having been incorrectly kept . . ."[5]

Consequently, the early life of Douglass is utterly unknown (his parents were married in the parish, and there certainty ends and Wilson's tenure begins). The opening chapters of any biography that establishes the early life of its subject—is an irrecoverable gap.[6] David Douglass remains to this day, a subject without a biography.

III: In the Presence of Absence

Still, it is nature that abhoreth a vacuum, not scholars. Scholarship adores them. We rush to fill in the lost years in the early life of Shakespeare, the murder of Christopher Marlowe, the missing elbow of the Loacoön, that cavernous hole that is nearly the entirety of ancient Greek theatre. Scholars, like dentists, fill cavities by habit. Or perhaps more like cautious knife-throwers, we exercise our acumen by precisely tracing the outline of a subject that is safely not present. When it is done well, even the measurement of the absence can be enormously moving—I'm thinking here of the archeologist Giuseppe Fiorelli who excavated Pompeii, and when he encountered holes in the stratigraphy he poured in a mixture of plaster of Paris to recover the size of the holes. When the plaster dried, the reconstituted holes proved to be bodies, the asphyxiated victims of Vesuvius, preserved in their most poignant final moment when the ash covered them. Vivifying absence is something of a poet's calling. More prosaically, most biographers, like the biographer of William Smelle, confronted with the absence of his subject, embraced a different solution, one later and more famously deployed by Stephen Greenblatt in his treatment of the missing years of Shakespeare: both backfilled experiences from the culture at large to stand in for the individual and unrecoverable life.[7] In the hands of clever writers, inventive thinkers, availing themselves of the rich social context that did leave records—literary journals, newspapers, Club minutes—the undocumented life can be somewhat approximated by the culture they inhabited, if one is content with somewhat approximations, and the now famous opening line: 'let us imagine'.

But I am less interested here in imagining, in a speculative reconstruction of absent records, or the daunting task to attempt to recontextualize the vexing and incomplete document that by rights should contain the basic vital records of its community, or even to measure the size of the hole, evocative as it is, but rather to use it to explore the problem of absence itself, which is not as empty, straightforward, or illegible as it may seem. Absence, for example, is seldom synonymous with oblivion—that is, where nothing is recorded—but rather absence often marks its own erasure, and the scars where the text was removed, leaves traces that remain legible. That distinction of absence and oblivion is one of prior presence. Absence is not what is not there, but rather it is the place (the marking) where something once was and is no more, flagged to be no more, where something is palpably missed on the landscape. Like the haunting silence of Rachel Carson's *Silent Spring*, or the hole in the skyline where the eye lingers on the once-was, absence is poignant, a present longing for what is no longer present. Above all, absence leaves placeholders.

IV: Amnesty

There was once a very precise word for this formation of marking absence as the missed item in the landscape of a culture's memory. The Greeks called it amnesty: it was the public promise to remember to forget. This is quite different from its cognate, amnesia. Amnesia is a return to oblivion. Amnesty is a memorial contract (complete with anniversaries) to publicly remember to forget. It happened in the wake of the Athenian defeat at the close of the Peloponnesian war, in 403 BCE, after the brutal Tyranny of Thirty was overthrown and democracy restored, one by one the citizens of Athens publicly took an oath not to pursue vengeance against the tyrants. "me mnesikakein" ('I will not recall the misfortunes") they recited, one after another. The public oath binding the citizens to set aside their recent memory was itself marked and remembered. Those who broke their oath, Aristotle tells us, were publicly put to death, to preserve the Democracy. They were condemned because they refused to forget, but their deaths remind us that not forgetting was not to be forgotten. Amnesty makes monuments of forgetting, and this is a most useful formation. If one becomes accustomed to looking into holes for the marks of memory left behind, sometimes even the holes become texts; sometimes, even the absence becomes legible.

Rome employed the same feature when it disappeared the revolted. It was called 'damnatio memoriae', and it too left public monuments of its erasing, leaving the traces of its own operation as a public record, testifying to the endurance of the erased.[9] In the center of the Arch of the Argentarii in Rome, for example, two figures of the imperial family have been chiseled out. Everybody knew the identity of the defaced figures, they had stood there for many years. But the emperor Caracalla standing against the left frame is all that remains of an imperial family portrait. The erased who formerly occupied the voided center and right of the panel, belonged to Plautilla,

Caracalla's young wife, and her father Plautianus, but have been razed clean—"blotted out" in the imperial language—and the void of their excision is the most compelling aspect of the panel of memory, mutilation, and memory. Plautianus was accused by Caracalla of plotting a murder against himself and his father Septimius Severus, for which he was executed and his daughter was exiled. Their removal from the imperial family was symbolically registered in their excision from public statuary. In the text of official Roman memory, they had become *lacunae*, amputated, blank holes in the text. Like the Greek notion of amnesty, what the monuments remember most is the public promise to forget.

In the case of both amnesty and *damnatio memoriae*, absence is itself a text, and as such, useful models for reading other scarred texts in which preservations and erasures cohabit. In these classical cases, absence remained an active verb; it occurred in the historical present and the ideology behind the absenting remains perfectly legible: like the de-facing of the post-iconoclasm mosaics in which human forms were chipped out, but only partially, leaving the subject and the erasure equally visible: the preservation preserves the destruction and the destruction preserves the ideology of memory.

Because, in the end, even memory is finite, and in its finite capacity, carries its own cultural criteria, its own hegemony, preserving some things, discarding others according to cultural values and those values might themselves be read as a legible absence. (If little is known of an aspiring young actor from Stratford, a great deal is recorded about the young life of his contemporary, William Cecil, Lord Burleigh, his genealogy, schooling, instructors, even curriculum, marriages, appointments, on his way up to the highest positions of state under Elizabeth). If certain subjects are historically more available (statesmen over actors), less visible is operation of the hegemony of memory whose very preservations may also carry with it an excision of what did not survive.

The values of any present moment may be a curatorial given of any museum or archive, but if we accustom ourselves to the notion that each preservation may also represent a disappearance ghosting behind it, (that something survived because something else did not), what remains must also flag the stumpage of what was cut away, and in that scar lies the great attraction of reading absence. Artifacts become *damnatios*, sharing panels with the disappeared.

V: Probate: St. Catherine's Parish

Through most of the history of the profession, the lives of most actors, David Douglass included, were and remain historically unavailable. The rare impulse to celebrity occasionally thrust a figure like Siddons or Garrick into public memory via print, but for the most part, the profession itself was immemorial for centuries, and the long 18th century was no different. Perhaps to leave it so is to honor the culture of the century, to honor its own hegemony of memory, one that frankly preferred actors below the threshold of visibility, one that acknowledges a nodding acquaintance to the great, but content in the back pews, and out of civic office, out of courts, present on the playbills, but in the drawing room of history, better seen than heard. That indeed, their very absence may represent its own kind of record, equally authentic, perhaps even legible(?) as subjects largely unworthy of attention, if one could but catch the vandals in the act of disappearance (the denotation moment, if you will, in which the invisibility is articulated: the elopement to the actor, because the marriage could not happen, the disowned daughter scratched from the will, the disinherited son, the moment that consigns the subject out of the record-status). And occasionally we do find exactly such moments and they open up the century in ways more direct evidence cannot. There is a wonderful such ellipsis in the letters of Josiah Wedgwood, the English ceramicist, whose nephew, young Thomas Byerley, ran away from the pottery shop to become an actor. When Byerley took to the stage he utterly dropped from the family correspondence until that ambition failed, and with its failure, he returned to textual visibility. This is Uncle Josiah writing to his business partner of his wayward nephew:

> I have just now received a letter from my nephew Tom Byerley acquainting me that he had quitted the stage from 'a conviction of his inability to succeed in any tolerable degree.' He is gone to London & desires we will get him a writer's place, or some such birth in the service of the East India Co. I do not know what we shall do with him, to keep him out of mischief, & put him into a way of being of some use in the World.[10]

But young Tom was not to be in a useful way, not to his uncle nor much of his culture, and returned again and again to the stage, always in provincial companies, and for years became the not-to-be-spoken-of in the family correspondence. His longest stint: when young Tom was hired by David Douglass in Philadelphia, and in whose company he remained for many (nearly invisible) years. During that time, the first half of the 1770s, not a word passed between Thomas Byerley and Josiah Wedgwood of his progress in a profession that his rising middle-class artisan uncle could not even name: "I am sorry for poor Tom Byerley," wrote Wedgwood, "but much more so for his Mother & dare not acquaint her with this last instance of his incurable madness. Nothing more can be done for him & he must take the consequences of his own misconduct."[11] Byerley is written off, but more to the point, he is written out of the family, conscripted into archival silence as a subject no longer to be spoken of, but a subject that left a blot behind. These kinds of evasions, ellipses, remind us of the politely unspeakable nature of the profession itself, but such elisions, when you catch them, can also become in themselves a legible record of their own absence: an amnesty of memory, a preserved contract on the part of the century to remember to forget, a *damnatio memoriae*.

It doesn't in any way compensate for the want of solid descriptions. Far preferable would still be the autobiography, Byerley's memoir account of his five years with the American Company. But it does speak in a very authentic way to a cultural position of what is speakable and what is not, of what is worthy of memory, of what has earned presence, and what has been disowned, un-presented, and why it is not present is a ghost that refuses to lay quiet.

The long sustained metaphor of the profession from Colley Cibber's *Apology* (1740) is that of the bastard child left at the steps of the parish church, or the house of the great man.[12] In this light, it is tempting to read the carelessness of Mr. Wilson—to return to the Kirk—as a fitting archivist for the early life of a subject below his culture's memory. For most actors of the eighteenth century to command public memory meant to change professions, like Tom Byerley who ultimately did, and re-entered the records of the Wedgwood family as a business manager in the pottery. David Douglass, in the end, was also one of these. At the outbreak of the American Revolution, Byerley returned to his uncle's household, and Douglass carried his company to Jamaica and there he too left the stage, bought into a printing house, secured several lucrative government contracts, and with his transition from the stage to the state, he also transitioned into a subject worthy of the state's memory. He archived himself. His civic appointments—and they were numerous—all found records, as did his final marriage, to Mary Peters, daughter of Dr. Peters, the birth and baptism of their two children, Mary and David Douglass (his previous marriage to the former Mrs. Hallam, actress, left no record). Douglass' appointments as Master of the Revels (1777), His Majesty's Printer (1779), Officer of the Militia (1783), Lieutenant in the Battery (1783), Master-in-Ordinary (1785), Justice of the Quorum (1785), Member of Council (1784), all found official memory, as did, finally, his death, probate, and inventory.[13] If his birth was obscured by Mr. Wilson, his death in Spanish Town, Jamaica was in many ways over-remembered. News of it was carried as far as 'Mr. Urban's column' in the *Gentleman's Magazine* of London. His wife maintained his appointment after his passing. His entire estate was inventoried at the time of his death, and this list (as well as his partner's holdings) runs to seven pages: every material item in his house and shop, every debt and asset found an archive. How many spoons and chairs he owned, what books were on his shelves, how many horses, carriages, slaves, every viol of red ink, every map, book and quill pen in his shop and print-house, every contract, debt, sale and i.o.u, meticulously recorded, in contrast to a thirty year career on the stage that left not a rack behind. Probate became the final repository of the material holdings of a most invisible man.

And there in the probate inventory is the tantalizing note of an absence behind an absence, a slave in the Douglass printing house, a pressman named Bacchus, who, by his given name, suggests an association with Douglass's prior business of the stage, and if one is truly considering a history of absence, one can only wonder if a biography of his life—Bacchus, the invisible subject of an invisible subject—might also be undertaken. Such a vivifying might be as poignant as Fiorelli's plaster-casts.

ENDNOTES

[1] *Verbatim Reports of the Proceedings from the Reign of Theodosius II*, Fergus Miller, A Greek Roman Empire, Berkeley, University of California Press, 2007, appendix B, 252–253.

[2] 'Ozymandias' Percy Bysshe Shelley

[3] National Archives of Scotland, CH2 718/19, 2.

[4] The whole account of the trial and termination of Wilson is found in the *West Kirk Minute Books,* National Archives of Scotland, CH2 718/19, 2–11, from which the above account is summarized. Page numbers in parentheses.

[5] Robert Kerr, *The Memoirs of the Life of William Smellie,* Edinburgh, 1811, 11–12.

[6] Of his first marriage, the only clue is the imprecise line in John Bernard's memoir's of his father's life, Bayle Bernard, related to him from Owen Morris, an elderly actor in the American Company. According to that account, the actor John Moody had been playing successfully in Jamaica, returned to London to secure more actors, and there "[A]n offer was made him by Mr. Garrick to enlist at Drury Lane; and whether he was content with the harvest he had reaped already, or had some secret misgivings as to the chance of renewing it, he closed with the manager, and transferred his expedition to more adventurous hands—to the company in fact, which he had already collected, the chief members of which were Messrs. Douglas[s] and Kershaw, Smith, Daniels, and Morris, with their wives, and a Miss Hamilton, who was their principal actress." - John Bernard, *Early Days of the American Stage* ran as a two part serial in *Tallis' Dramatic Magazine,* January and February 1851.

[7] Stephen Greenblatt, *Will in the World: how Shakespeare became Shakespeare,* New York, Norton and Co. 2004.

[9] As Peter Stewart has reminded us, the term was first employed by Scheiter-Gerlack as a dissertation title in 1689. The ancient term, *memoria damnata,* has found less circulation. Peter Stewart, 'The Destruction of Statues in Late Antiquity,' in Richard Miles, ed.., *Constructing Identities in Late Antiquity,* London, Routledge, 1999, 159–189, 161. Tacitus, Ann. XI. 38: "the Senate assisted his [Claudius'] forgetfulness by decreeing that her [Messalina] name and her statues should be removed from all places, public or private." Harriot Flower, *The Art of Forgetting, Disgrace and Oblivion in Roman Political Culture,* (Chapel Hill, University of North Carolina Press, 2006) traces more epigraphical and inscriptional evidence of damnatio, pps. 10–12.

[10] Katherine Euphemia Farrer, *Letters of Josiah Wedgwood,* Manchester, Trustees of the Wedgwood Museum, 1973, Josiah Wedgwood to Thomas Bentley, 2 March 1767. Vol i: 121.

[11] *Letters,* JW - TB, 18 June 1769. Vol i: 263

[12] Colley Cibber, *An Apology for the Life of Mr. Colley Cibber,* London, 1740, (re-print AMS press, New York, 1966), Dedication 'To a Certain Gentleman'.

[13] Inventory List, Liber 76 folio 8; Liber 69, folio 9–22; St. Catherine's Parish Minute Books, Baptisms, Marriages, Burials.

CONTRIBUTORS

Justin A. Blum is a playwright and performance historian who will shortly complete his PhD thesis, a history of late-19th and early-20th century popular entertainment and the "Jack the Ripper" murders, at the Graduate Centre for Study of Drama, University of Toronto. He has taught undergraduate courses at Washington University in St. Louis, where he earned an MA in Drama, and most recently at the Cinema Studies Institute, University of Toronto.

Jeanne Bovet is Associate Professor in French literature at University of Montreal, where she teaches the history and aesthetics of theater. A founding member of the international CNRS/CRI research program on Theatre Sound, she mainly researches the aesthetics of voice, both on stage and within the dramatic text, and has published several essays and book chapters on the topic. Thanks to funding from the Social Sciences and Humanities Research Council of Canada (SSHRC) and the Fonds québécois de recherche sur la société et la culture (FQRSC), she has recently completed a book on the oratorical inscription of declamation in 17th Century French drama (to be published in 2011), and is currently investigating the relations between voice, text and media in 20th Century theater.

Michael Shane Boyle is a doctoral candidate in performance studies at the University of California, Berkeley. His dissertation examines the role of performance, violence, and Western Marxism in shaping the activist practices of the German New Left. He is currently spending the year at the Freie Universität Berlin on a Fulbright Research Grant and a research fellowship from the Social Sciences Research Council. His work can be found in edited collections and forthcoming issues of *TDR: The Drama Review, Theatre Journal, Theatre Survey,* and *South Atlantic Quarterly.*

Chase Bringardner is an Assistant Professor in the Department of Theatre at Auburn University who specializes in the study of popular entertainments such as medicine shows and musical theatre, regional identity construction, and intersections of race, gender, and class in popular performance forms. He graduated from the University of Texas at Austin in 2007 with a PhD after defending his dissertation entitled "Popular Entertainments and Constructions of Southern Identity: How Burlesques, Medicine Shows, and Musical Theatre Made Meaning and Money in the South, 1854–1980." He has a chapter forthcoming in the new *Oxford Companion to the Musical* on Region, Politics, and Identity in musical theatre. His current book length project details the socio-cultural history of the Fabulous Fox Theatre in Atlanta. He is an active member of the Association of Theatre in Higher Education (ATHE) and the American Society for Theatre Research (ASTR).

Andrew Brown is currently a graduate student in the Department of Performance Studies at Northwestern University. He received his BA in Theatre and English from Muhlenberg College in 2009. His solo performances *Fat Camp, Mother May I?* and *Row, Row, Row* explore the intersections of memory, technology, gender, and sexuality. They have been presented in London, Cape Town, New York, Providence, and Chicago. This piece was originally presented as a conference paper for the 16th meeting of Performance Studies International.

Mark Evans Bryan is an historian of the theatre of the long nineteenth century in the United States. His work has appeared in the *Journal of American Drama and Theatre, William and Mary Quarterly,* and *Blackwell's Companion to Twentieth-Century American Drama,* and is forthcoming in the *Journal of Popular Culture* and *"To Have or Have Not": New Essays on Commerce and Capital in Modernist Theatre.* His dramatic writing has been produced in the United States and abroad and published in the *Kenyon Review.* Currently at work on a book on the Bradford family and popular culture in Philadelphia, Bryan is an associate professor at Denison University.

Barbara Cohen-Stratyner serves as Judy R. and Alfred A. Rosenberg Curator of Exhibitions, The New York Public Library for the Performing Arts, for which she has developed over 70 exhibitions. She is the author of *Ned Wayburn and the Dance Routine, Popular Music 1900–1919,* and *Touring West,* as well as numerous articles, catalogues and exhibition web sites. She holds a Ph. D. in Performance Studies and degrees in Theater Design and Museum Education Administration.

Eric Colleary is a doctoral candidate in Theatre Historiography at the University of Minnesota and an Interdisciplinary Doctoral Fellow at the university's Institute for Advanced Study. His dissertation project, "Beyond the Closet: Identities and Histories in LGBT Archives in the United States," explores the role of archives in forming complex structures of belonging and exclusion from the ONE Institute in 1956 through the present.

Brian Cook is a PhD candidate in Theatre Arts at the University of Oregon. He received his MA in Text and Performance from the Royal Academy of Dramatic Art and King's College, University of London, in 2005. At present, he is working on a full-length study of the history of the Cherub Company, London, and specializes in the study of alternative British theatre artists. He has presented papers at various theatre conferences on British theatre, indigenous performance, playwriting, and stage management. He is the current Associate Editor for Media for ASTR Online.

Nena Couch is curator of the Jerome Lawrence and Robert E. Lee Theatre Research Institute, The Ohio State University, and professor, OSU Libraries and Department of Theatre. Her publications and creative works include *Documenting: Lighting Design* (co-edited with Susan Brady), *Sidney Kingsley: Five Prize-Winning Plays,* numerous publications on performing arts librarianship and historical dance, exhibitions, and dance performances. Her current research focus is eighteenth-century Spanish dance, and late nineteenth- and early twentieth-century American expression. She serves on the board of the Dance Heritage Coalition and the council of the International Association of Libraries and Museums of the Performing Arts (SIBMAS).

Robert Crane is a doctoral candidate in the Department of Theatre Arts at the University of Pittsburgh. He is presently writing his dissertation on the Blue Blouse movement and spatial practices in the early Soviet Union.

Eileen Curley is an Assistant Professor of English and Theatre at Marist College in Poughkeepsie, NY. Her publications include articles in *Theatre Symposium* and *The Journal of American Drama and Theatre,* and she is writing a manuscript based on the Lawrence sisters and their theatricals. Her research interests include nineteenth-century British and American theatre, the performance of gender and nation, and the role of theatre in the British Empire. She received her MA and PhD in Theatre History, Theory and Literature from Indiana University, and a BA in Theatre from Grinnell College.

Heather Davis-Fisch is currently a SSHRC post-doctoral fellow in the theatre department at the University of British Columbia and has accepted a permanent faculty position in the English and Theatre departments at the University of the Fraser Valley beginning in August 2011. She received her PhD in theatre studies from the University of Guelph in 2009.

Joseph Donohue, a theatre historian and textual scholar, is Professor Emeritus of English at the University of Massachusetts Amherst, where he taught for thirty-four years. Author and editor of books and articles on post-Shakespearean British theatre and drama, he is currently preparing a group of Oscar Wilde's plays, including the French and English *Salomé* and the four-act and three-act *Importance of Being Earnest,* for the Oxford University Press collected works of Wilde. His translation of Wilde's French *Salomé* into contemporary American English, with illustrations by Barry Moser, will be published in late 2011 by the University of Virginia Press.

Annette Fern (now retired) is a Reference Librarian specializing in the humanities and performing arts. She held positions at the University of Chicago, the Art Institute of Chicago, and the University of Illinois at Chicago, and from 1996 to 2003 was Research and Reference Librarian at the Harvard Theatre Collection. In 2004 she received a Distinguished Service Award from the Theatre Library Association. Her articles and reviews have appeared in *Theatre Survey* (for which she was, briefly, editor of the Re-Sources section), the *Harvard Library Bulletin, Performing Arts Resources, Theatre Design and Technology,* and various encyclopedias and newsletters.

Tim Fitzpatrick's academic career has been substantially in the Department of Performance Studies, University of Sydney, and his research field is late 16th and early 17th century European popular theatre. He has published on the oral/popular origins and processes of the *Commedia dell'Arte,* and has subsequently focussed on Elizabethan and Jacobean staging at the public playhouses in London. In that regard he has published articles in *Theatre Research International* and in *Theatre Notebook* on the spatial implications of Elizabethan playtexts, and articles in *Early Modern Literary Studies* and *Shakespeare Bulletin* re-assessing the iconographic evidence for the Globe playhouses and its implications for historical reconstructions. He has just completed a book, *Playwright, Space and Place in Early Modern Performance: Shakespeare and Company*, on the evocation of fictional place in Elizabethan and Jacobean staging, to be published by Ashgate early in 2012. He is involved in a large-scale research project with John Golder, Laura Ginters and Tiffany Stern on historical European rehearsal practices.

John Frick is Professor of Theatre and American Studies at the University of Virginia. He is the author of *Theatre, Culture and Temperance Reform in Nineteenth-Century America* and *New York's First Theatrical Center: The Rialto at Union Square*; co-editor of *The Directory of Historic American Theatres and Theatrical Directors: A Biographical Dictionary*. Dr. Frick is Past Editor of *Theatre Symposium*; a former Stanley J. Kahrl Fellow at Harvard University; is the Immediate Past-President of the American Theatre and Drama Society; and is the 2010 recipient of the Betty Jean Jones Award as the Outstanding Teacher of American Theatre and Drama.

Amma Y. Ghartey-Tagoe Kootin is a Mellon Postdoctoral Fellow in the Department of Theater, Dance and Performance Studies at UC-Berkeley. With an A.B. in Afro-American Studies from Harvard University and the M.A./Ph.D. from New York University's Performance Studies program, her work is to create performance-centered methodologies of studying the past. This essay and research is part of a larger project, "The Battle Before *The Souls of Black Folk*: Black Performance in the 1901 Pan-American Exposition," which is currently being adapted into a book and a musical production.

Rebecca Harries is Associate Professor of Drama and Department Chair at Bishop's University in Sherbrooke, Québec. She completed her doctorate at the University of Toronto, Graduate Centre for Study of Drama, where she and fellow graduate student Marlene Moser co-founded F.O.O.T., a combination of theatre festival and academic conference, which thrives today. Current research interests include early-twentieth century German film and theatre (the topic of her dissertation), the phenomenology of theatre and theatrical space. Recent work includes the direction of Canadian playwright Sally Clark's *Lost Souls and Missing Persons*, staged in a labyrinth, and writing on mediated sound in contemporary performance.

Andrea Harris, Assistant Professor at the University of Wisconsin-Madison, is the author of essays in *Interrogating America through Theatre and Performance*, *Discourses in Dance*, and the forthcoming *Avant-Garde Performance and Material Exchange: Vectors of the Radical*. She is also the editor of *Before, Between, Beyond: Three Decades of Dance Writing*. Previously on the faculties at Texas Christian University, the University of Oklahoma, and the Universidad de las Américas Puebla, Harris's performance credits include the Martha Graham Dance

Company and Li Chiao-Ping Dance. Her current research examines the Americanization of ballet during the Cold War.

John Wesley Hill has a Master of Theater Arts degree from the Russian Academy of Theater Arts (GITIS) in Moscow where he studied opera directing under Professor Boris Pokrovsky. His PhD in Theater Studies is from the University of Michigan. His dissertation, "The Russian Pre-Theatrical Actor and the Stanislavsky System," explores convergences and continuities in performer training and socialization between the Russian folk performance tradition and the emergence of the System at the First Studio of the Moscow Art Theater under Leopold Sulerzhitsky.

Amy E. Hughes is Assistant Professor of Theater History & Criticism and Deputy Chair for Graduate Studies in the Department of Theater at Brooklyn College (CUNY). Her articles and reviews have appeared in *Journal of American Drama and Theatre, New England Theatre Journal, Theatre Journal, Theatre Research International,* and *Theatre Topics*; and one of her essays is featured in *Interrogating America through Theatre and Performance* (Palgrave Macmillan, 2007), edited by William Demastes and Iris Smith Fischer. She is developing a book manuscript, *Sensation Seen: Spectacle and Reform in Nineteenth-Century America,* which explores the cultural histories of theatrical images in U.S. reform culture.

Odai Johnson is a Donald Peterson Endowed Fellow at the University of Washington's School of Drama. He directs the PhD program and the Center for Performance Studies. He has published widely in the field. He is currently finishing a study of classical theatre titled *Ruins*.

Stephen Johnson is Director of the Graduate Centre for Study of Drama at the University of Toronto. He has taught theatre, film and performance studies at the University of Guelph, McMaster University, and at the University of Toronto Mississauga, as well as at the Drama Centre. His publications include *The Roof Gardens of Broadway Theatres,* numerous book chapters, and articles in *The Drama Review, Canadian Theatre Review, Theatre Topics* and *Nineteenth Century Theatre,* as well as *Theatre Research in Canada,* which he (co)edited for ten years. In addition to this volume of *Performing Arts Resources,* he is currently editing *Burnt Cork: Traditions and Legacies of Blackface Minstrelsy* for the University of Massachusetts Press. His recently completed research project on blackface minstrelsy resulted in a database and website, available at link.library.utoronto.ca/minstrels. He is currently developing a web-based project focusing on performance in Southern Ontario during the 19th and early 20th centuries, available as it develops at link.library.utoronto.ca/ontheroad/canadawest.

Heather May is an Assistant Professor at Auburn University where she teaches courses ranging from theatre history to stage management and directing. Her Ph.D. in Theatre History, Theory and Literature is from Indiana University, with a minor in Gender Studies and a specialization in nineteenth century American theatre, particularly minstrelsy. She is currently completing a biography of Francis Leon, and has previously published and presented papers on female impersonation on the minstrel stage.

David Mayer, Emeritus Professor of Drama and Research Professor at the University of Manchester, UK publishes extensively on British and American popular entertainment of the Nineteenth and early Twentieth centuries. His books include *Harlequin in his Element: English Pantomime, 1806–1836* (1969), *Henry Irving and "The Bells"* (1980), and *Four Bars of "Agit", Music for Victorian and Edwardian Melodrama* (1983). His recent books, *Playing Out the Empire: Ben-Hur and Other Toga Plays and Films* (1994) and *Stagestruck Filmmaker: D.W. Griffith and the American Theatre* (2009), explore the interstices between the late-Victorian stage and early motion pictures.

Amy Muse is an associate professor of English at the University of St. Thomas in Minnesota whose research is focused on Romantic-era drama, theatre culture, and performance studies. This essay is part of a book project on female Hamlets' influence on the transformation of Hamlet as a literary character; another article, "Actresses and the Making of the Modern Hamlet," appears in *Text & Presentation* (2007). She has also taught Shakespeare seminars as a visiting lecturer at the University of Glasgow and as a Fulbright Scholar at the University of Athens.

Thomas Postlewait teaches in the doctoral program of the School of Drama, University of Washington. His early publications include *William Archer on Ibsen: The Major Essays, 1889–1919* (1984), *Prophet of the New Drama: William Archer and the Ibsen Campaign* (1986), and the co-edited *Interpreting the Theatrical Past: Essays in the Historiography of Performance* (1989). Since 1991 he has served as editor of the award-winning series, "Studies in Theatre History and Culture," at the University of Iowa Press. Over forty books, by scholars from a dozen countries, have been published in the series. In recent years he co-edited *Theatricality* (2003), and *Representing the Past: Essays in Performance Historiography* (2010), and published *The Cambridge Introduction to Theatre Historiography* (2009).

Shannon Rose Riley is Assistant Professor of Humanities at San José State University. She is co-editor, with Lynette Hunter, of *Mapping Landscapes for Performance as Research: Scholarly Acts and Creative Cartographies* (2009). Her work has been published in *Theatre Topics, English Language Notes, Baylor Journal of Theatre and Performance,* and the edited collection, *Kathy Acker and Transnationalism* (2009); she is currently working on a manuscript titled *Performing Race and Erasure: Cuba, Haiti, and US Culture, 1898–1940*. Riley has an MFA in Studio Art from Tufts University and the School of the Museum of Fine Arts and a PhD in Performance Studies and Critical Theory from UC Davis.

Andrew Ryder is Associate Professor of Theatre at Seattle Pacific University, where he teaches courses in Theatre History, Dramatic Literature, Play Analysis, Directing, and Acting. Andrew is also a director, with credits ranging from a medieval passion play to contemporary musicals. His research on performance in Oregon's Civilian Public Service camps has been published in *The Western States Theatre Review* and *Theatre Annual*, and presented at the American Society for Theatre Research Annual Conference. In addition to twentieth-century American theatre, his research interests include community-based theatre, theatre education, and medieval English theatre.

Marlis Schweitzer is Assistant Professor in Theatre Studies at York University where she teaches courses on nineteenth- and twentieth-century American theatre with a focus on popular performance genres. She is the author of *When Broadway Was the Runway: Theater, Fashion, and American Culture* (Penn Press) and has published articles in *Theatre Journal, Theatre Survey, Theatre Research in Canada,* and the *Journal of American Drama and Theatre.*

Virginia Scott is Professor Emerita of Theater, University of Massachusetts at Amherst. Her most recent book (Cambridge 2010) is *Women on the Stage in Early Modern France.* Her other books on the French theatre of the ancien regime include *Molière: A Theatrical Life* (Cambridge, 2000) and *The Commedia dell'Arte in Paris* (Virginia 1990). She is also a playwright and translator.

Daniel Smith received his PhD from the Interdisciplinary Program in Theatre and Drama at Northwestern University in 2010 and currently teaches in The Theatre School at DePaul University. His dissertation is entitled "Libertine Dramaturgy: Reading Obscene Closet Drama in Eighteenth-Century France." His article on Pierre de Ronsard's Biblical metaphors of female beauty appeared in *Dalhousie French Studies* (Fall 2008). From 2009–2011, Dan has served as Chair of the Theatre History Focus Group in the Association for Theatre in Higher Education (ATHE).

Matthew Solomon is Associate Professor of Cinema Studies at the College of Staten Island, City University of New York. He is author of *Disappearing Tricks: Silent Film, Houdini, and the New Magic of the Twentieth Century* (University of Illinois Press, 2010) and editor of *Fantastic Voyages of the Cinematic Imagination: Georges Méliès's* Trip to the Moon (SUNY Press, 2011, in press).

Paula Sperdakos is Associate Professor and Program Director of Theatre and Performance Studies at the University of Toronto Scarborough, where she teaches courses in the history, theory and practice of acting and directing, and directs student productions. Her area of scholarly interest is Canadian actresses; she has published in *Theatre Research in Canada, Canadian Theatre Review, Essays in Theatre, Modern Drama,* and *Queen's Quarterly*; and she is the author of the Ann Saddlemyer Award-winning *Dora Mavor Moore: Pioneer of the Canadian Theatre.* She was a contributor to *Theatre and AutoBiography: Writing and Performing Lives in Theory and Practice*, and her current book project-in-progress is entitled *A Trail through a Jungle: The Way of the Canadian Actress.*

Paul J. Stoesser is Technical Director responsible for production and scenography at the Graduate Centre for Study of Drama, University of Toronto. In addition to the Commedia dell'arte, Dr. Stoesser's research interests include the radical developments in early modernism at the turn of the last century, especially as it is dramaturgically expressed in the profound alterations to scenographic interpretation and artistic direction. His latest article, "Fortunato Depero's Scenographic Reception in New York" is pending publication while most recently he has edited *Futurist Dramaturgy and Performance* (2011), a centenary collection of essays celebrating the continuing influence of Futurism.

Mark David Turner is a Program Coordinator at the Labrador Institute of Memorial University, Happy Valley-Goose Bay and is responsible for the arrangement, description and expansion of the Labrador Institute Film and Video Archive. He is completing a PhD at the Graduate Centre for Study of Drama, University of Toronto on Newfoundland and Labrador cinema. Selected publications include articles in *The Northern Review* and *Canadian Theatre Review*. His film and video work has been exhibited in Canada, and will be used in a Parks Canada application to UNESCO to create a world heritage site at Red Bay, Labrador. He is also a professional musician.

Dan Venning is a doctoral candidate in Theatre at the CUNY Graduate Center. His dissertation examines the popular reception of Shakespeare in Germany 1817–67. He has a BA from Yale University and an M.Litt. in Shakespeare Studies from the University of St Andrews. Dan has presented papers at a variety of graduate student, national, and international conferences, and has published book and theatre reviews in *Theatre Journal, Theatre Survey,* and *Western European Stages*. He has published articles (on Shakespeare in Central Park and the Merchant Ivory film *Shakespeare Wallah*) in *Forum for Modern Language Studies* and *Asian Theatre Journal.*

Julie Vogt is an Assistant Professor for Theatre and Integrated Arts at Colby-Sawyer College in New London, NH. She earned a B.A. and M.A. from the University of Colorado-Boulder and a Ph.D. in theatre and drama at the University of Wisconsin, Madison. At CU-Boulder she worked as dramaturg and assistant director at the Colorado Shakespeare Festival. She serves as co-Regional Contact for the Burning Man organization in NH and VT while continuing to expand her research in burlesque. Her work is available on scribd.com

Ann Folino White holds an Interdisciplinary Ph.D. in Theatre and Drama from Northwestern University. She is an Assistant Professor jointly appointed in the Residential College in the Arts and Humanities and the Department of Theatre at Michigan State University, where she teaches performance theory, stage direction and theatre history, literature, and criticism. Her current research concerns how theatrical uses of food in protests against New Deal agricultural legislation materialized citizens' struggles to reconcile capitalism and morality. Dr. Folino White's scholarship on early-twentieth-century U.S. theatre and performance has appeared in *Text and Performance Quarterly* and *American Drama.*

Don B. Wilmeth, an Emeritus Professor (2003) at Brown University, is the author, editor, coeditor, or series editor of over four dozen books, including the award-winning three-volume *Cambridge History of American Theatre*. In 2007 he completed a new edition of the *Cambridge Guide to American Theatre*, a standard in the field. In 2004 he received the distinguished service award from TLA. Don is a former president of the American Society for Theatre Research and dean emeritus of the College of Fellows of the American Theatre. In 2008 Brown bestowed upon him the William Williams Award, the most prestigious honor given by the Brown University Library.